BARRON'S

6 SAT* PRACTICE TESTS

3RD EDITION

Philip Geer, Ed.M.

Stephen A. Reiss, M.B.A.

*SAT is a registered trademark of the College Board, which was not involved in the production of, and does not endorse, this book.

Dedication

To my teaching colleagues in the United States, Singapore, Hong Kong, and Australia, particularly Dr. Peter Saunders and Dr. Robert Wilks, with whom I enjoyed many interesting discussions about the English language and other subjects over the years.

And, as always, to my wife Susan for all her help and support.

—Philip Geer

To Iris Lowe-Reiss, my in-home editor and wife-for-life. And thanks to my parents, Elinor and Oscar Reiss, who supported me in all of my endeavors.

—Steve Reiss

About the Authors

Philip Geer has taught English language and literature for many years in the United States and abroad. He is the author of a number of textbooks and test preparation books, including the *GRE Verbal Workbook* and *Essential Words for the GRE,* and is the director of Mentaurs Educational Consultants.

Steve Reiss is the founder and owner of the Math Magician and the Reiss SAT Seminars, test preparation centers in San Diego. Jokingly referred to as "San Diego's most boring author," he has authored, co-authored, and edited more than forty books for the test preparation industry. Reiss is also a member of Mensa, the high IQ society.

Published by Kaplan, Inc., d/b/a Barron's Educational Series
750 Third Avenue
New York, NY 10017
www.barronseduc.com

Library of Congress Catalog Card Number: 2017937081

ISBN: 978-1-4380-0996-4

9 8 7 6 5 4

Kaplan, Inc., d/b/a Barron's Educational Series print books are available at special quantity discounts to use for sales promotions, employee premiums, or educational purposes. For more information or to purchase books, please call the Simon & Schuster special sales department at 866-506-1949.

Contents

SAT Format and Test Dates

SAT Format	
Section 1: Reading **52 Questions** *Time—65 minutes*	5 Reading Passages, including 1 paired passage 1 Literature Passage 2 Social Studies Passages (one will be a "Founding Document" or "Great Global Conversation" passage) 2 Science Passages 32 "Analysis" Questions 10 "Command of Evidence" Questions 10 "Words in Context" Questions
Section 2: Writing and Language **44 Questions** *Time—35 minutes*	4 Passages 24 "Expression of Ideas" Questions 20 "Standard English Conventions" Questions
Section 3: Math, No Calculator **20 Questions** *Time—25 minutes*	15 Multiple Choice, 5 Grid-in 8 "Heart of Algebra" Questions 9 "Passport to Advanced Math" Questions 3 "Additional Topics in Math" Questions
Section 4: Math, Calculator **38 Questions** *Time—55 minutes*	30 Multiple Choice, 8 Grid-in 11 "Heart of Algebra" Questions 17 "Problem Solving and Data Analysis" Questions 7 "Passport to Advanced Math" Questions 3 "Additional Topics in Math" Questions
Essay (Optional) **1 Question** *Time—50 minutes*	Write an essay analyzing how the author of a given passage has made his or her argument. Evaluated on reading, analysis, and writing.

You can register for the SAT at *sat.collegeboard.org.*

Note that the SAT will no longer offer a January test administration. An August test date is now available. You can register for the SAT at *sat.collegeboard.org*.

SAT Test Dates		
	Registration Deadlines	
Test Dates	Regular	Late
2017–2018 School Year*		
October 7, 2017		
November 4, 2017		
December 2, 2017		
March 10, 2018		
May 5, 2018		
June 2, 2018		
2018–2019 School Year*		
August 25, 2018		
October 6, 2018		
November 3, 2018		
December 1, 2018		
March 9, 2019		
May 4, 2019		
June 1, 2019		

*As of press time, exam dates for the 2017–2018 and 2018–2019 school years are approximate. Check *collegeboard.org* periodically to confirm the anticipated test dates and the registration and late registration deadlines.

Countdown to the SAT

The day before you take the test, don't do practice tests. Do look over all the tactics listed below so they will be fresh in your mind.

BEFORE THE TEST

If the test location is unfamiliar to you, drive there before the test day so that you will know exactly where you're going on the day you take the test.

Set out your test kit the night before. You will need your admission ticket, a photo ID (a driver's license or a non-driver picture ID, a passport, or a school ID), your calculator, four or five sharpened No. 2 pencils (with erasers), plus a map or directions showing how to get to the test center.

Get a good night's sleep so you are well rested and alert.

Wear comfortable clothes. Dress in layers. Bring a sweater in case the room is cold.

Bring an accurate watch—not one that beeps and not your cell phone—in case the room has no clock. You'll want to use the same watch or small clock that you've been using during your practice sessions.

Bring a small snack for quick energy.

Don't be late. Allow plenty of time for getting to the test site. You want to be in your seat, relaxed, before the test begins.

Pick your favorite letter from among A, B, C, and D. This is the letter you will always use when you have to make a quick guess.

DURING THE TEST

Pace yourself. Don't work so fast that you start making careless errors. On the other hand, don't get bogged down on any one question.

Feel free to skip back and forth between questions within a section.

Play the percentages: always eliminate as many of the answer choices as possible and then make an educated guess, not a random one.

If you have no idea, quickly guess your favorite letter and move on.

If you are running out of time in a section, use your last 20 seconds to fill in your favorite letter on every question you didn't get to.

Watch out for eye-catchers, answer choices that are designed to tempt you into guessing wrong.

Change answers only if you have a reason for doing so; don't change them on a last-minute hunch or whim.

Check your assumptions. Make sure you are answering the question asked and not the one you *thought* was going to be asked.

Remember that you are allowed to write anything you want in your test booklet. Make full use of it.

- Do math calculations and draw diagrams.
- Underline key words in reading passages and sentence completions.
- Cross out answer choices you are *sure* are wrong.
- Circle questions you want to come back to, but first make a guess.

Be careful not to make any stray marks on your answer sheet. The test is graded by a machine, and a machine cannot always tell the difference between an accidental mark and an intentionally filled-in answer.

Check frequently to make sure you are answering the questions in the right spots.

Remember that you don't have to attempt every question to do well. Just be sure to fill in answers for every question you don't attempt.

TIPS FOR THE EVIDENCE-BASED READING QUESTIONS

Read all the answer choices before you decide which is best.

Think of a context for an unfamiliar word; the context may help you come up with the word's meaning.

Break down unfamiliar words into recognizable parts—prefixes, suffixes, roots.

Consider secondary meanings of words. If none of the answer choices seems right to you, take another look. A word may have more than one meaning. When you have a choice, tackle reading passages with familiar subjects before passages with unfamiliar ones.

Make use of the introductions to acquaint yourself with the text.

Read as rapidly as you can with understanding, but do not force yourself.

As you read the opening sentence, try to predict what the passage is about.

When you tackle the questions, use any line references given to help in the passage.

Base your answer only on what is written in the passage, not on what you know from other books or courses.

In answering questions on the paired reading passages, first read one passage and answer the questions based on it; then read the second passage and tackle the remaining questions.

On graph analysis questions, take time to evaluate the graph labels and axes. Be mindful that you will often need to integrate information from the reading passage with what is presented in the graph.

The vocabulary in context questions typically involve unusual meanings of words you know—be sure you read enough of the text in which the word appears so that you'll be able to figure exactly how the word is being used in the passage.

If you notice that a question is immediately followed by a second question that asks which lines in the passage provide evidence supporting your answer to the first question, don't waste time going over the second question's answer choices. Instead, as you answer the first question, note where you found the evidence supporting your answer choice. Mark the lines with an asterisk, or set them in brackets. Then answer the second question.

Do not hesitate to come back to questions if you are unsure; a question that initially seems confusing will often be far easier when you consider it a second time.

TIPS FOR THE MATHEMATICS QUESTIONS

Whenever you know how to answer a question directly, just do it. The tactics that are reviewed below should be used only when you need them.

Memorize all the formulas you need to know. Even though some of them are printed on the first page of each math section, during the test you do not want to waste any time referring to that reference material.

Be sure to bring a calculator for use on the long math section, but use it only when you need it. Don't use it for simple arithmetic that you can easily do in your head.

Remember that no problem requires lengthy or difficult computations. If you find yourself doing a lot of arithmetic, stop and reread the question. You are probably not answering the question asked.

Answer every question you attempt. Even if you can't solve it, you can almost always eliminate two or more choices. Often you know that an answer must be negative, but two or three of the choices are positive, or an answer must be even, and some of the choices are odd.

Unless a diagram is labeled "Note: Figure not drawn to scale," it is perfectly accurate, and you can trust it in making an estimate.

When a diagram has not been provided, draw one, especially on a geometry problem.

If a diagram has been provided, feel free to label it, and mark it up in any way, including adding line segments, if necessary.

Answer any question for which you can estimate the answer, even if you are not sure you are correct.

Don't panic if you see a strange symbol in a question; it will always be defined. Getting the correct answer just involves using the information given in the definition.

When a question involves two equations, the most useful thing to do is to add them or subtract them. If there are three or more, just add them.

Never make unwarranted assumptions. Do not assume numbers are positive or integers. If a question refers to two numbers, do not assume that they have to be different. If you know a figure has four sides, do not assume that it is a rectangle.

Be sure to work in consistent units. If the width and length of a rectangle are 8 inches and 2 feet, respectively, either convert the 2 feet to 24 inches or the 8 inches to two-thirds of a foot before calculating the area or perimeter.

Standard Multiple-Choice Questions

Whenever you answer a question by backsolving, start with choice (C).

When you replace variables with numbers, choose easy-to-use numbers, whether or not they are realistic.

Choose appropriate numbers. The best number to use in percent problems is 100. In problems involving fractions, the best number to use is the least common denominator.

When you have no idea how to solve a problem, eliminate all of the absurd choices before you guess. Remember, you should provide an answer to each and every question. Guess if you have to. *Bubble in an answer to every question.*

Student-Produced Response (Grid-in) Questions

Write your answer in the four spaces at the top of the grid, and *carefully* grid in your answer below. No credit is given for a correct answer if it has been gridded improperly.

Remember that the answer to a grid-in question can never be negative.

You can never grid in a mixed number—you must convert it to an improper fraction or a decimal.

Never round off your answers. If a fraction can fit in the four spaces of the grid, enter it. If not, use your calculator to convert it to a decimal (by dividing) and enter a decimal point followed by the first three decimal digits.

When gridding a decimal, do not write a zero before the decimal point.

If a question has more than one possible answer, grid in only one of them.

There is no penalty for wrong answers on grid-in questions, so you should grid in anything that seems reasonable, rather than omit a question.

TIPS FOR THE EVIDENCE-BASED WRITING AND LANGUAGE QUESTIONS

This section is all about your essay-editing skills. To edit well, you must take your time. Fortunately, this section is generally easy to finish. So use the full amount of time allowed, taking about 9 minutes per passage.

Silently *mouth out* the wording to pick up on errors. Even though you may not know the "official" grammar rule, hearing what *sounds best* can help you figure out the correct option.

Grammar "pet peeves" will not be tested, but grammar rules will. Be on the lookout for some of the most common issues (punctuation, wordiness, verb tense, parallelism, subject–verb agreement, misplaced modifiers, logical comparisons, and diction/proper word usage).

Jumping to an answer without considering enough context will not work—the incorrect answers will be very tempting. If, however, you are having trouble determining what concept the question is testing, narrow down the likely issue by reviewing the answer choices to see what is different among them. "No Change" has just as much of a chance of being correct as does any other option.

On graph interpretation questions, use only the evidence in the graph and the passage. No background knowledge will be required. Carefully review the graph labels and axes to avoid making careless mistakes.

Many questions go beyond simple grammar to assess broader writing topics, like paragraph transitions, essay introductions, and argumentative evidence. As you work through the questions, be ready to shift gears between focused proofreading and general editing. Sometimes you will need only a sentence to answer the question, while other times you will need a paragraph or more. *When in doubt, check it out.*

TIPS FOR THE ESSAY

The essay prompt will not change from test to test—you will always be asked to explain how the author of a source text has made an argument.

The source text will change from test to test, but it will always be a broad argument for a general audience.

Do NOT insert your personal opinions on the topic into your response. Your job is to examine the author's argument, not to give your views on the subject.

Do NOT waste time writing about supposed flaws in the source text. These are very well-written arguments. Your job is to analyze them, not to rip them apart.

Start by taking several minutes (no more than 10) to read and take notes on the source text. Ask yourself *what* the author is arguing and *why* he or she has chosen to make that argument.

Take time to prewrite (no more than 5 minutes). Plan to show how the author makes use of *evidence, reasoning,* and *style* to make his or her case.

Start with a solid thesis, and use clear transitions and excellent organization throughout. Have variety in your sentence structure; use precise vocabulary and specific descriptions.

Write for the full 50 minutes. The essay comes last in the test—finish strong, drawing on your last reserves of energy. A longer essay (as long as it has well-written, focused material) will score better.

Write legibly—the graders are human. They can grade only what they can understand.

Watch out for spelling and grammar issues. However, don't spend so much time proofreading that you fail to develop your essay fully.

Pace yourself so that you can make all of your points and have a strong conclusion. This essay is very different from many you likely have written—don't let test day be the first time you try writing an SAT essay within the time constraints.

Introduction: Let's Look at the SAT

- → WHAT IS THE SAT?
- → THE READING TEST
- → THE WRITING AND LANGUAGE TEST
- → THE MATH TEST
- → CALCULATOR TIPS
- → THE OPTIONAL ESSAY
- → WINNING TACTICS FOR THE NEW SAT

WHAT IS THE SAT?

The SAT is a standardized exam that most high school students take before applying to college. Generally, students take the SAT for the first time as high school juniors. If they are happy with their scores, they are through. If they want to try to improve their scores, they can take the test a second or even a third time.

The SAT has two areas: English and Math. The English sections are further divided into two areas: Evidence-Based Reading as well as Writing and Language. In addition, there is an optional essay. Each time you take the SAT, you receive several scores and subscores. On each of the two main areas, English and Math, you receive a score between 200 and 800. You also receive a composite score, a number between 400 and 1600, which is the sum of your two area scores. If you write the optional essay, two readers will evaluate it. Each reader will award a score between 1 and 4 on each of three criteria. Those scores will be added together, so you will receive essay scores between 2 and 8.

> **HOW DO I SIGN UP TO TAKE THE SAT?**
>
> Online: Go to *www.collegeboard.org*
>
> Have available your social security number and/or date of birth.
>
> Pay with a major credit card.
>
> **Note:** If you are signing up for Sunday testing, or if you have a visual, hearing, or learning disability and plan to sign up for the Services for Students with Disabilities Program, you *cannot* register online. You must register by mail well in advance.
>
> By mail: Get a copy of the SAT Program Registration Bulletin from your high school guidance office or from the College Board. (Write to College Board SAT, P.O. Box 6200, Princeton, NJ 08541-6200, or phone the College Board office in Princeton at 866-756-7346.)
>
> Pay by check, money order, fee waiver, or credit card.

WHAT IS SCORE CHOICE?

Score Choice is the College Board's policy that enables students who take the SAT more than once to choose which scores to send to the colleges to which they are applying. Each time you take the SAT, you will receive a score report. When you are a senior and are actually applying to college, you can decide which of your score reports you want the College Board to send out.

> **CAUTION**
>
> Most colleges allow you to use Score Choice; some do not. Some want to see all of your scores. Be sure to go to *http://sat.collegeboard.org/register/sat-score-choice* to check the score-use policy of the colleges to which you hope to apply.

Here's How Score Choice Works

Suppose you take the SAT in May of your junior year and again in October of your senior year, and your October scores are higher than your May scores. Through Score Choice you can send the colleges only your October scores; not only will the colleges not see your May scores, they won't even know that you took the test in May. The importance of the Score Choice policy is that it can significantly lessen your anxiety anytime you take the SAT. If you have a bad day when you take the SAT for the first time, and your scores aren't as high as you had hoped, relax: you can retake it at a later date, and if your scores improve, you will never have to report the lower scores. Even if you do very well the first time you take the SAT, you can still retake it in an attempt to earn even higher scores. If your scores do improve, terrific—those are the scores you will report. If your scores happen to go down, don't worry—you can send only your original scores to the colleges and they will never even know that you retook the test. However, if you get your best Math score on one administration of the test, say in May, and your best English score on another administration of the test, say in October, you should submit your scores from both months. Admissions officers always give you credit for your best English score and your best Math score. Just because Score Choice is available does not mean you have to use it. No matter how many times you take the SAT, because of Score Choice, you can send in only the scores that you want the colleges to see.

WHAT IS THE FORMAT OF THE SAT?

The SAT consists of four sections that take a total of exactly 3 hours, not counting a short break between sections 2 and 3. The English part of the SAT consists of two sections: a 65-minute Reading Test and a 35-minute Writing and Language Test, for a total of 100 minutes. Note that both sections consist entirely of multiple-choice questions; there is nothing to actually write on the SAT unless you stay for the optional essay. The Math part of the SAT also consists of two sections: a 55-minute section on which you are permitted to use a calculator and a 25-minute section on which calculators are not permitted, for a total of 80 minutes.

When the English and Math parts are over, students who are not writing the optional essay will hand in their test materials and leave the building. Once they leave, the students who choose to write the essay will have 50 minutes to complete that task. So for those students, the total time spent working on the SAT will be 3 hours and 50 minutes.

Of course, whether you write the essay or not, you will be in the exam room for much longer than the time required to take the test. Time is needed for you to fill out your bubble sheet and for the proctors to take attendance, pass out the exam materials, read the instructions, collect the test materials, and give you a short break in the middle of the test. So you should expect to be at the exam site for about 4 hours if you are not writing the essay and for about 5 hours if you are writing the essay.

THE READING TEST

There are 52 questions on the Reading Test of the SAT.

Below is one typical reading test format for the SAT. You should expect to see something like the following on your test, although not necessarily in this exact order:

52-Question Reading Test (65 minutes)

Questions 1–10	U.S./world literature passage
Questions 11–21	social studies passage (with graphic)
Questions 22–31	science paired-passages
Questions 32–42	social studies passage (U.S. founding document/global conversation)
Questions 43–52	science passage (with graphic)

Two passages on your test will be accompanied by infographics—one or two tables, charts, flow maps, graphs, time lines, etc. The graphics will accompany one of the history/social studies passages and one of the science passages.

Of the 52 questions on your test, 10 will be vocabulary questions, testing relevant words and phrases whose meaning depends on the context in which they appear (2 per passage). An additional 10 will be "command of evidence" questions in which you have to decide which part of a passage supports a specific conclusion or backs up the answer choice to a previous question (2 per passage).

All of the reading questions on the SAT directly test your skill at comprehending what you read, based on the evidence you find in the selected passages.

The questions are not necessarily arranged in order of difficulty. Instead, they generally follow the organization of the passage on which they are based. Questions about material found early in the passage precede questions about material found later. Main idea questions are likely to appear early in the question set. Questions about accompanying information graphics or questions contrasting passage pairs are likely to appear toward the end of the set. This information can help you pace yourself during the test.

Here are examples of some specific types of evidence-based reading questions you can expect.

Evidence-Based Reading

Evidence-based reading questions ask about a passage's main idea or specific details, the author's attitude about the subject, the author's logic and techniques, the implications of the discussion, or the meaning of specific words.

(The following passage is far shorter than the usual 500–750 word passages you will find on the test. It is here only to give you a quick idea of the sorts of questions you will face.)

Directions: Each passage or passage pair below is followed by questions based on its content.

Answer the questions on the basis of what is *stated* or *implied* in that passage or passage pair and in any associated information graphics (tables, graphs, flow charts, time lines, etc.).

Certain qualities common to the sonnet should be noted. Its definite restrictions make it a challenge to the artistry of the poet and call for all the technical skills at the poet's command. The more or less set rhyme patterns occurring regularly within the short space of fourteen lines afford a pleasant effect on the ear of the reader and can create truly musical effects. The rigidity of the form precludes too great economy or too great prodigality of words. Emphasis is placed on exactness and perfection of expression. The brevity of the form favors concentrated expression of ideas or passion.

1. The author's primary purpose is to

(A) contrast different types of sonnets
(B) criticize the limitations of the sonnet
(C) identify the characteristics of the sonnet
(D) explain the sonnet's loss of popularity as a literary form

The first question asks you to find the author's main idea. In the opening sentence, the author says certain qualities of the sonnet should be noted. In other words, he intends to call attention to certain of its characteristics, identifying them. The correct answer is choice (C). You can eliminate the other answers with ease. The author is upbeat about the sonnet: he doesn't say that the sonnet has limitations or that it has become less popular. You can eliminate choices (B) and (D).

Similarly, the author doesn't mention any different types of sonnets; therefore, he cannot be contrasting them. You can eliminate choice (A).

2. As used in line 4, "afford" most nearly means

(A) spare
(B) exaggerate
(C) pay for
(D) provide

The second question asks you to figure out a word's meaning from its context. Substitute each of the answer choices in the original sentence and see which word or phrase makes most sense. Some make no sense at all: the rhyme patterns that the reader hears certainly do not *pay for* any pleasant effect. You can definitely eliminate choice (C). What is it exactly that these rhyme patterns do? The rhyme patterns have a pleasant effect on the ear of the listener; indeed, they *provide* (furnish or supply) this effect. The correct answer is choice (D).

3. The author's attitude toward the sonnet form can best be described as one of

   (A) amused toleration
   (B) grudging admiration
   (C) strong disapprobation
   (D) scholarly appreciation

The third question asks you to figure out how the author feels about his subject. All of the author's comments about the sonnet are positive: he approves of this poetic form. You can immediately eliminate choice (C), *strong disapprobation* or disapproval. You can also eliminate choice (A), *amused toleration* or forbearance. The author is not simply putting up with the sonnet form in a good-humored, somewhat patronizing way; he thinks well of it.

Choice (B) is somewhat harder to eliminate. The author does seem to admire the sonnet form. However, his admiration is unforced: it is not *grudging* or reluctant. You can eliminate choice (B).

The only answer that properly reflects the author's attitude is choice (D), *scholarly appreciation.*

THE WRITING AND LANGUAGE TEST

There are 44 questions on the Writing and Language Test of the SAT.

Below is one typical writing and language test format for the SAT. You should expect to see something similar to this on test day, although likely in a different order:

44-Question Writing and Language Test (35 minutes)

Questions 1–11	career-related topic
Questions 12–22	humanities
Questions 23–33	social studies
Questions 34–44	science

One or two of these will be informative/explanatory texts, one or two of these will be arguments, and one will be a narrative.

One or two passages on your test will be accompanied by an infographic—a table, chart, graph, map, or some combination of graphics.

Of the 44 questions on your test, 24 will be about expression of ideas (improving the quality of the author's message) and 20 will be about standard English conventions (grammar, usage, and mechanics). Eight questions will test your command of evidence (some with the infographics and some based on the text), and 8 questions will test words in context (e.g., determining the correct "fit" given the rhetorical goal). The writing and language questions are in a random order of difficulty.

Here are examples of particular types of writing and language questions you will find. (This is only intended to give you a brief sample of some questions—typical passages have 11 questions accompanying them.)

Directions: The passages below are accompanied by several questions, some of which refer to an underlined portion in the passage and some of which refer to the passage as a whole. Some questions ask you to determine how the expression of ideas can be improved. Other questions ask you to determine the best sentence structure, usage, or punctuation given the context. A passage or question may have an accompanying graphic that you will need to consider as you choose the best answer.

Choose the best answer to each question, considering what will optimize the writing quality and make the writing follow the conventions of standard written English. Some questions have a "NO CHANGE" option that you can pick if you believe the best choice is to leave the underlined portion as it is.

Properties of Water

We hear about water every day. More than 70 percent of **1** our planets surface is covered with water. Water is a requirement for terrestrial life. Water makes up the majority of our bodies. Drink your eight glasses of water **2** during every 24 hour period. But what makes water so special, so ubiquitous? It's a rather simple compound: **3** 2 hydrogen atoms covalently bonded to 1 oxygen atom. However, it has several unique chemical properties that make it rather suitable for life.

1. (A) NO CHANGE
   (B) their planets
   (C) our planet's
   (D) their planets'

The first question concerns the proper use of possessive words and apostrophes. In order to be consistent with the use of "we" in the previous sentence, you should use "our." You can therefore eliminate choices (B) and (D) since they use "their." You can also eliminate choice (A). It fails to show that the "planet" possesses the "surface" because it lacks an apostrophe followed by an "s." That leaves you with choice (C) as the correct answer. It properly uses "our" to be consistent with the previous sentence and "planet's" to demonstrate that the singular planet possesses the surface.

2. (A) NO CHANGE
   (B) each day when you are awake.
   (C) throughout the daytime.
   (D) daily.

The second question is about wordiness and description. You should consider which choice gives a clear idea without unnecessary wording. Choice (D) is correct because "daily" provides the same amount of information as choices (A), (B), and (C) but does so far more concisely. Economy in writing is preferable as long as the language is clear and specific.

3. Which choice provides the most specific and relevant conclusion to the sentence?

(A) NO CHANGE
(B) water has many properties that distinguish it from most substances.
(C) in its frozen form, water is called "ice," while in its gaseous form, it is called "steam."
(D) it is composed of a unique combination of material.

The third question asks you to choose what will be most *specific* (precise and detailed) and *relevant* (on topic) at this point in the sentence. You can eliminate choices (B) and (D) because they are far too vague. Choice (B) gives no clarification of the "properties" that distinguish water, and choice (D) provides no elaboration on the "unique combination of material" that water is. Although choice (C) is specific, you can eliminate it because it is not relevant—it fails to describe what makes water a "simple compound" as described earlier in the sentence. Choice (A) is correct since it gives both a specific scientific description and a relevant elaboration on what makes this compound relatively simple, i.e., its structure.

THE MATH TEST

The math part of the SAT has a total of 58 questions divided into two sections, each of which has its own format.

- The 25-minute section, during which calculators may not be used, has 20 questions: 15 multiple-choice questions and 5 grid-in questions.
- The 55-minute section, during which calculators may be used, has 38 questions: 30 multiple-choice questions and 8 grid-in questions.

Multiple-Choice Questions

On the math portion of the SAT, 45 of the 58 questions are multiple-choice questions. Although you have certainly taken multiple-choice tests before, the SAT uses a few different types of questions, and you must become familiar with all of them. By far, the most common type of question is one in which you are asked to solve a problem. The straightforward way to answer such a question is to do the necessary work, get the solution, look at the four choices, and choose the one that corresponds to your answer.

➡ Example 1

What is the average (arithmetic mean) of all the even integers between –5 and 7?

(A) 0
(B) $\frac{5}{6}$
(C) 1
(D) $\frac{6}{5}$

Solving this problem requires only that you know how to find the average of a set of numbers. Ignore the fact that this is a multiple-choice question. *Don't even look at the choices.*

- List the even integers whose average you need: –4, –2, 0, 2, 4, 6. (Be careful not to leave out 0, which *is* an even integer.)
- Calculate the average by adding the six integers and dividing by 6.

$$\frac{(-4)+(-2)+0+2+4+6}{6}=\frac{6}{6}=\mathbf{1}.$$

- Having found the average to be 1, look at the four choices, see that 1 is choice (C), and blacken **C** on your answer sheet.

Example 2

A necklace is formed by stringing 133 colored beads on a thin wire in the following order: red, orange, yellow, green, blue, indigo, violet; red, orange, yellow, green, blue, indigo, violet. If this pattern continues, what will be the color of the 101st bead on the string?

(A) orange
(B) yellow
(C) green
(D) blue

Again, you are not helped by the fact that the question, which is less a test of your arithmetic skills than of your ability to reason, is a multiple-choice question. You need to determine the color of the 101st bead, and then select the choice that matches your answer.

The seven colors keep repeating in exactly the same order.

Color:	red	orange	yellow	green	blue	indigo	violet	
Bead number:	1	2	3	4	5	6	7	
	8	9	10	11	12	13	14	etc.

- The violet beads are in positions 7, 14, 21, . . . , 70, . . . , that is, the multiples of 7.
- If 101 were a multiple of 7, the 101st bead would be violet.
- But when 101 is divided by 7, the quotient is 14 and the remainder is 3.
- Since $14 \times 7 = 98$, the 98th bead completes the 14th cycle, and hence is violet.
- The 99th bead starts the next cycle; it is red. The 100th bead is orange, and the 101st bead is yellow.
- The answer is **B**.

In contrast to Examples 1 and 2, some questions *require* you to look at all four choices in order to find the answer. Consider Example 3.

NOTE

Did you notice that the solution didn't use the fact that the necklace consisted of 133 beads? This is unusual; occasionally, but not often, a problem contains information you don't need.

➡ Example 3

If a and b are both odd integers, which of the following could be an odd integer?

(A) $a + b$
(B) $a^2 + b^2$
(C) $(a + 1)(b - 1)$
(D) $\frac{a+1}{b-1}$

- The sum of two odd integers is always even. Eliminate choice (A).
- The square of an odd integer is odd; so a^2 and b^2 are each odd, and their sum is even. Eliminate choice (B).
- The product of two even integers is even. Eliminate choice (C).
- Having eliminated choices (A), (B), and (C), you know that *the answer must be* choice (D).

Check to be sure: $\frac{a+1}{b-1}$ need not even be an integer (e.g., if $a = 1$ and $b = 5$), but it *could be*. For example, if $a = 3$ and $b = 5$, then

$$\frac{a+1}{b-1} = \frac{3+1}{5-1} = \frac{4}{4} = 1,$$

which *is* an odd integer. The answer is (D).

Another kind of multiple-choice question that appears on the SAT is the Roman numeral-type question. These questions actually consist of three statements labeled I, II, and III. The four answer choices give various possibilities for which statement or statements are true. Here is a typical example.

➡ Example 4

If x is negative, which of the following *must* be true?

I. $x^3 < x^2$

II. $x + \frac{1}{x} < 0$

III. $x = \sqrt{x^2}$

(A) I only
(B) II only
(C) I and II only
(D) II and III only

- To answer this question, examine each statement independently to determine if it is true or false.

  I. If x is negative, then x^3 is negative and so must be less than x^2, which is positive. (I is true.)

  II. If x is negative, so is $\frac{1}{x}$, and the sum of two negative numbers is negative. (II is true.)

  III. The square root of a number is never negative, and so $\sqrt{x^2}$ could not possibly equal x. (III is false.)
- Only I and II are true. The answer is (C).

> **NOTE**
>
> **You should almost always attempt a Roman numeral-type question. Even if you can't solve the problem completely, there should be *at least one* of the three Roman numeral statements that you *know* to be true or false. On the basis of that information, you should be able to eliminate at least one or two of the answer choices. For instance, in Example 4, if all you know for sure is that statement I is true, you can eliminate choices (B) and (D). Similarly, if all you know is that statement III is false, you can eliminate choice (D). Then, you simply guess among the remaining choices.**

Grid-in Questions

On the math portion of the SAT, 13 of the 58 questions are what the College Board calls student-produced response questions. Since the answers to these questions are entered on a special grid, they are usually referred to as *grid-in* questions. Except for the method of entering your answer, this type of question is probably the one with which you are most familiar. In your math class, most of your homework problems and test questions require you to determine an answer and write it down, and this is what you will do on the grid-in problems. The only difference is that, once you have figured out an answer, it must be recorded on a special grid, such as the one shown at the right, so that it can be read by a computer. Here is a typical grid-in question.

	/	/	
.	.	.	.
	0	0	0
1	1	1	1
2	2	2	2
3	3	3	3
4	4	4	4
5	5	5	5
6	6	6	6
7	7	7	7
8	8	8	8
9	9	9	9

Example 5

At the diner, John ordered a sandwich for \$3.95 and a soda for 85¢. A sales tax of 5% was added to his bill, and he left the waitress a \$1 tip. What was the total cost, in dollars, of John's lunch?

- Calculate the cost of the food: \$3.95 + \$0.85 = \$4.80
- Calculate the tax (5% of \$4.80): .05 × \$4.80 = \$0.24
- Add the cost of the food, tax, and tip: \$4.80 + \$0.24 + \$1.00 = \$6.04

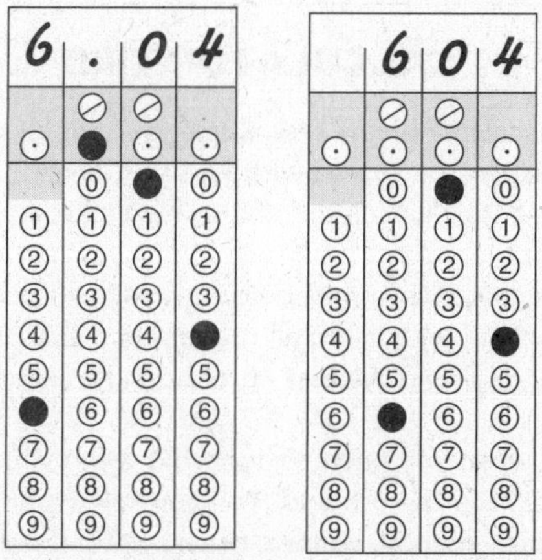

To enter this answer, you write 6.04 (*without* the dollar sign) in the four spaces at the top of the grid, and blacken the appropriate circle under each space. In the first column, under the 6, you blacken the circle marked 6; in the second column, under the decimal point, you blacken the circle with the decimal point; in the third column, under the 0, you blacken the circle marked 0; and, finally, in the fourth column, under the 4, you blacken the circle marked 4.

Always read each grid-in question very carefully. Example 5 might have asked for the total cost of John's lunch *in cents.* In that case, the correct answer would have been 604, which would be gridded in, without a decimal point, using only three of the four columns (see above).

Note that the only symbols that appear in the grid are the digits from 0 to 9, a decimal point, and a fraction bar (/). The grid does not have a minus sign, so *answers to grid-in problems can never be negative.* When you take the diagnostic test, just enter your answers to the grid-in questions exactly as was done in Example 5.

NOTE

Any multiple-choice question whose answer is a positive number less than 10,000 could be a grid-in question. If Example 1 had been a grid-in question, you would have solved it in exactly the same way: you would have determined that the average of the six numbers is 1; but then, instead of looking for 1 among the four choices, you would have entered the number 1 on a grid. The mathematics is no harder on grid-in questions than on multiple-choice questions. However, if you don't know how to solve a problem correctly, it is harder to guess at the right answer, since there are no choices to eliminate.

CALCULATOR TIPS

- You must bring a calculator to the test. Some, but not all, of the questions in the 55-minute section cannot be solved without using one.
- You should use a scientific calculator. A graphing calculator is acceptable but offers no real advantage.
- *Don't* buy a new calculator the night before the SAT. If you need one, *buy one now* and become familiar with it. Do all the practice exams in this book with the calculator you plan to take to the test—probably the same calculator you use in school.
- Use your calculator when you *need* to; ignore it when you don't. Most students use calculators more than they should. You can solve many problems without doing *any* calculations—mental, written, or calculator-assisted.
- The College Board's position is that a "calculator is a tool" and that knowing when to use one and when not to use one is an important skill. Therefore, they intentionally include some questions in the calculator section on which it is better not to use your calculator.
- No SAT problem ever requires a lot of tedious calculation. However, if you don't see how to avoid calculating, just do it—*don't spend a lot of time looking for a shortcut that will save you a little time!*

THE OPTIONAL ESSAY

The optional SAT essay asks you to *analyze an argument.* This section comes at the end of the test. The argument will be on a general topic and written for a broad audience—you will not need any background knowledge on the subject to formulate your response. You will have *50 minutes* to respond to a source text and question like the following:

Sample Essay Prompt

Directions: You will be given 50 minutes to complete the assignment, including reading the source text and writing your response.

Read the following passage, and think about how the author uses:

- Evidence, such as applicable examples, to justify the argument.
- Reasoning to show logical connections among thoughts and facts.
- Rhetoric, like sensory language and emotional appeals, to give weight to the argument.

Beauty Is in the Eye of the Beholder

1 It's entirely possible that I am a dolt. It's not out of the question that I am uncultured, uncivilized, ignorant, and misinformed. It could be that I do not understand true talent—that my personal mediocrity prevents me from the recognition of unparalleled brilliance in another. So if what I'm about to say to you reeks of blasphemy, please forgive me for my tastelessness. But, is the "Mona Lisa" really that great?

2 I love the concept of the "Western Canon." If you are unfamiliar with it, this is a de facto collection of art, music, and literature that scholars generally accept as masterpieces. The theory is that, if the world's self-proclaimed "experts" view a subjective issue with near unanimity, then the debate ceases to be subjective; it becomes a matter of certainty, a perspective that can be criticized only by the intellectual heretic.

3 Now this is where I begin to laugh. When did the people of the world become so wishy-washy as to require the assistance of the opinions of others on what is bad or good or indeterminable in its quality? Though far from Emersonian in my insistence on self-reliance, I do believe that I am more than capable of formulating opinions on my own. Truly, of the seven billion people in the world, I'd go so far as to say that I'm the best in the world at deciding what is pleasing to me.

4 Here is another qualm with the validity of the canonical process: what of those who gain fame of the least satisfying sort, which is to say, posthumously? Vincent van Gogh lived his entire life in unacknowledged anonymity. Similarly, F. Scott Fitzgerald was not enshrined by the masses until well after his death. Is this to say that the caliber of their works increased after their deaths—that they are far more adroit from the crypt? Are today's experts more expert than those of yesteryear? Of what purpose does popular opinion serve if it is a fickle, dynamic, wavering thing? Masterpieces should transcend generational trends, wouldn't you agree?

5 However, I do not question that the "Mona Lisa" resonates in its profundity with many critics. And, if somebody values da Vinci's piece at 200 million dollars, well, I am in no position to dispute this appraisal. But, to me, the "French Madame" is of minor consequence. See, she rouses nothing in my breast; she incites nothing of passion or empathy or intrigue. I see a woman—a regular woman, and nothing more.

6 I cannot help but wonder if the "Mona Lisa's" renown comes from its inherent aesthetic appeal, or more from the unusual historical incidents associated with it—it hung in Napoleon's bedroom for a time, and it was famously stolen and missing for a time. Do seemingly limitless museum-goers line up to see the "Mona Lisa" because of its artistic depth? Or, are they drawn to it because of the novelty of seeing a single painting in a room all to itself, behind bullet-proof glass?

7 Ultimately, this is the intrinsic value of art and literature and music: how it personally makes you feel. To defer to the judgments of others on the topic is to miss the entire purpose of the venture. For, if a painting leads one man to weep and another to

swoon, of what value is it to me if I feel nothing stirring inside? I am but an intruder into the trysts of others. I am crashing a soirée to which I was uninvited.

8 So go forth today and define your own canon. If your professor tells you that Ernest Hemingway revolutionized American literature, refuse to accept this at face value. Rather, read "Old Man and the Sea" and decide for yourself; see if Santiago's tribulations ignite something poignant and lasting within you. If not, cast the thing aside, for it is of no value to you. Conversely, refuse to be belittled for your interests. If a certain musician inspires you to chase your dreams, or bestows upon you an unbreakable peacefulness, or makes cloudy January days feel like warm June nights, this is your masterpiece, no matter what anybody else says. For this is how you build your very own canon, by eschewing the measuring sticks of others and gauging instead with your very own soul. Take comfort in your aptitude for the task. None is better suited than you, especially when the alternative is accepting the "because I said so" of another.

Write a response that demonstrates how the author makes an argument to persuade his audience that artistic merit should derive from subjective preference. In your response, analyze how the author uses at least one of the features from the essay directions (or features of your own choosing) to develop a logical and persuasive argument. Be certain that your response cites relevant aspects of the source text.

Your response should not give your personal opinion on the merit of the source text but, instead, show how the author crafts an argument to persuade readers.

Your essay will be evaluated by two graders who will consider these three factors:

- **READING:** Did you properly comprehend the source? Did you show clear evidence of your understanding?
- **ANALYSIS:** Did you show how the author used *evidence*, *reasoning*, and *style* to make his or her argument?
- **WRITING:** Did you write a clear, organized response with appropriate word choice and proper grammar?

Each grader will evaluate your reading, analysis, and writing on a 1–4 scale; the graders' individual scores will be combined so that each of these categories will have a score from 2–8. Your score on the essay will be reported separately and will not affect your overall 400–1600 composite score.

HOW TO USE THE PRACTICE ESSAYS

The practice tests in this book contain essay prompts for you to practice your writing, and suggested essays written in response to these essay prompts. You can use the suggested essays to see how you can improve your own essays. Note that the suggested essays are longer than you would have time to write on the test. This is so that they can cover many features of the essay prompts and thus be more useful to students.

Ideally, you should have your practice essays evaluated by a qualified person, such as a high school or college English teacher. If this is not possible, you can e-mail *info@mentaurs.com* to learn about having your essay assessed by teacher and author Philip Geer.

To assess your essay yourself use the following criteria:

SAT Essay Scoring

SAT Essay Scoring Rubric

	Score: 4
Reading	Excellent: The essay shows excellent understanding of the source. The essay shows an understanding of the source's main argument and key details and a firm grasp of how they are interconnected, demonstrating clear comprehension of the source. The essay does not misinterpret or misrepresent the source. The essay skillfully uses source evidence, such as direct quotations and rephrasing, representing a thorough comprehension of the source.
Analysis	Excellent: The essay gives excellent analysis of the source and shows clear understanding of what the assignment requires. The essay gives a complete, highly thoughtful analysis of the author's use of reasoning, evidence, rhetoric, and/or other argumentative elements the student has chosen to highlight. The essay has appropriate, adequate, and skillfully chosen support for its analysis. The essay focuses on the most important parts of the source in responding to the prompt.
Writing	Excellent: The essay is focused and shows an excellent grasp of the English language. The essay has a clear thesis. The essay has a well-executed introduction and conclusion. The essay shows a clear and well-crafted progression of thoughts both within paragraphs and in the essay as a whole. The essay has a wide range of sentence structures. The essay consistently shows precise choice of words. The essay is formal and objective in its style and tone. The essay demonstrates a firm grasp of the rules of standard English and has very few to no errors.
	Score: 3
Reading	Skillful: The essay shows effective understanding of the source. The essay shows an understanding of the source's main argument and key details. The essay is free of major misinterpretations and/or misrepresentations of the source. The essay uses appropriate source evidence, such as direct quotations and rephrasing, representing comprehension of the source.
Analysis	Skillful: The essay gives effective analysis of the source and shows an understanding of what the assignment requires. The essay decently analyzes the author's use of reasoning, evidence, rhetoric, and/or other argumentative elements the student has chosen to highlight. The essay has appropriate and adequate support for its analysis. The essay focuses primarily on the most important parts of the source in responding to the prompt.
Writing	Skillful: The essay is mostly focused and shows an effective grasp of the English language. The essay has a thesis, either explicit or implicit. The essay has an effective introduction and conclusion. The essay has a clear progression of thoughts both within paragraphs and in the essay as a whole. The essay has an assortment of sentence structures. The essay shows some precise choice of words. The essay is formal and objective in its style and tone. The essay demonstrates a grasp of the rules of standard English and has very few significant errors that interfere with the writer's argument.

Score: 2	
Reading	Limited: The essay shows some understanding of the source. The essay shows an understanding of the source's main argument, but not of key details. The essay may have some misinterpretations and/or misrepresentations of the source. The essay gives only partial evidence from the source, showing limited comprehension of the source.
Analysis	Limited: The essay gives partial analysis of the source and shows only limited understanding of what the assignment requires. The essay tries to show how the author uses reasoning, evidence, rhetoric, and/or other argumentative elements the student has chosen to highlight, but only states rather than analyzes their importance, or at least one part of the essay's analysis is unsupported by the source. The essay has little or no justification for its argument. The essay may lack attention to those elements of the source that are most pertinent to responding to the prompt.
Writing	Limited: The essay is mostly not cohesive and shows an ineffective grasp of the English language. The essay may not have a thesis, or may diverge from the thesis at some point in the essay's development. The essay may have an unsuccessful introduction and/or conclusion. The essay may show progression of thoughts within the paragraphs, but not in the essay as a whole. The essay is relatively uniform in its sentence structures. The essay shows imprecise and possibly repetitive choice of words. The essay may be more casual and subjective in style and tone. The essay demonstrates a weaker grasp of the rules of standard English and does have errors that interfere with the writer's argument.
Score: 1	
Reading	Insufficient: The essay shows virtually no understanding of the source. The essay is unsuccessful in showing an understanding of the source's main argument. It may refer to some details from the text, but it does so without tying them to the source's main argument. The essay has many misinterpretations and/or misrepresentations of the source. The essay gives virtually no evidence from the source, showing very poor comprehension of the source.
Analysis	Insufficient: The essay gives little to no accurate analysis of the source and shows poor understanding of what the assignment requires. The essay may show how the author uses reasoning, evidence, rhetoric, and/or other argumentative elements that the student has chosen to highlight but does so without analysis. Or many parts of the essay's analysis are unsupported by the source. The support given for points in the essay's argument are largely unsupported or off topic. The essay may not attend to the elements of the source that are pertinent to responding to the prompt. Or the essay gives no explicit analysis, perhaps only resorting to summary statements.
Writing	Insufficient: The essay is not cohesive and does not demonstrate skill in the English language. The essay may not have a thesis. The essay does not have a clear introduction and conclusion. The essay does not have a clear progression of thoughts. The essay is quite uniform and even repetitive in sentence structure. The essay shows poor and possibly inaccurate word choice. The essay is likely casual and subjective in style and tone. The essay shows a poor grasp of the rules of standard English and may have many errors that interfere with the writer's argument.

If your essay is, like that of most students, strong in some areas but weak in others, read through the passage prompt again and think about how you can improve your essay. For example, you may have correctly stated that the author uses an anecdote but did not adequately explain how this adds to the effectiveness of the argument. Or perhaps your sentences were not varied enough in structure to make interesting reading. After you have identified a number of such weak areas, you may wish to rewrite your essay, incorporating these improvements.

TACKLING THE ESSAY

Reading the Passage

Read carefully and critically, always keeping in mind the central argument of the passage. You may want to highlight important words or sentences, but do not overdo it.

Your task is to analyze the **argument** and the **language strategies** used to support that argument.

ARGUMENT

Every passage for the SAT essay prompt will feature an argument that you must identify, understand, and analyze. Everything else, including language used, is subordinate to this argument. After you have identified the argument, note down some of its key features. You may wish to state its central point in the form of a brief *proposition.* Remember that your task is to analyze how effective the argument is, not to agree or disagree with it. The following questions will help you do this (definitions of key *argument* terms—in italics below—are given in the box on page 26). Focus on the questions most relevant to the passage you are analyzing.

You will not have time to consider all of them in depth.

1. What is the central *proposition* of the *argument*?
2. What are the *premises* of the argument? Are they valid?
3. Are there any *assumptions* made? Stated? Implied? Examined? Are they valid?
4. Are *assertions* supported adequately by logic and *evidence*?
5. Are any *generalizations* made? Are they valid? (For example, are they too sweeping?)
6. Is the conclusion (or conclusions) reached warranted by the argument presented?
7. Does the conclusion reached need to be *qualified* to make it valid?
8. What counter-arguments, if any, are given and *rebutted*?
9. What *implications* might the conclusion have that are not discussed in the passage?

KEY TERMS IN ANALYZING AN ARGUMENT

PROPOSITION: something proposed or offered for consideration or acceptance

ARGUMENT: a connected series of statements intended to establish (or subvert) a conclusion

PREMISE: a proposition assumed as a basis for argument or inference

ASSUMPTION: a fact or statement taken for granted

ASSERTION: something declared or stated positively

EVIDENCE: something that furnishes proof

GENERALIZATION: a general statement, law, principle, or proposition

QUALIFICATION: something that qualifies (i.e., limits) meaning

REBUT: to refute, especially by offering opposing evidence for arguments

IMPLICATION: something implied (i.e., included as a natural or necessary though not expressly stated part or effect)

LANGUAGE STRATEGIES

Only after you have analyzed the argument should you examine how language is used to support the argument. Below are listed the most important language strategies to look for:

1. Active and Passive Voice
2. Adjectives
3. Alliteration and Assonance
4. Appeals (e.g., to authority, emotional, or targeting particular interests)
5. Attack
6. Bias
7. Cliché
8. Colorful Language
9. Connotation
10. Formal/Informal Language
11. Humor
12. Hyperbole/Exaggeration
13. Figurative Language
14. Inclusive and Exclusive Language (using personal pronouns)
15. Irony
16. Repetition
17. Rhetorical question
18. Sarcasm
19. Satire
20. Sensationalism
21. Vocabulary Choice

It is not enough to merely identify language features. To get a high score you need to *explain* how language strategies *support* the argument at a particular point in the passage. After identifying notable language strategies used, write them down. Among these select several that you find most effective and interesting to focus on in your essay.

Some Important Argument and Rhetoric Terms

Following is a list of 50 important terms used in argument and rhetoric (rhetoric is the art of effective expression and the persuasive use of language).

Familiarity with these terms will help you to evaluate the passage's argument and language, and using them in your essay will help you express your ideas accurately and concisely.

AMBIGUITY: uncertainty regarding interpretation

ANALOGY: a comparison between two things. For example, "The free market is like a jungle."

ANECDOTE: a short account of an interesting incident

COGENT: convincing; logically compelling

COLLOQUIAL: typical of informal speech

CONCLUSION: a judgment reached by reasoning

CONJECTURE: inference or judgment based on incomplete evidence

CONSENSUS: general agreement

CONTENTION: an assertion

COROLLARY: a proposition that follows logically from one already proven; a natural consequence

CORROBORATE: to support the correctness of; make more certain

CRITERION: a standard used in judging

CRITIQUE: a critical commentary

DEDUCTION: reaching a conclusion through reasoning

DEFINITIVE: conclusive; authoritative and complete

DIGRESSION: act of straying from the main point

DISINTERESTED: unprejudiced; objective

DOGMATIC: stating opinions without proof

EMOTIVE: appealing to or expressing emotion

EXPLICIT: very clear; definite

EXTRAPOLATION: the act of estimation by projecting known information

FALLACY: a mistaken belief, especially one based on an argument that is not logical or well supported by evidence: "It is a fallacy that the Moon is made of cheese." Fallacy can also refer to faulty reasoning: "The debater used an illustration to show the fallacy of the argument."

GLOSS OVER: to make attractive or acceptable by deception or superficial treatment

IMPLICIT: implied; understood but not stated

INDUCTION: reasoning that moves from specific cases to established general principles. For example, a scientist studying 300 species of mammals, observing that each has two eyes, and concluding from this that all species of mammals have two eyes.

INFERENCE: conclusion based on reasoning and evidence

NUANCE: shade of meaning; subtle distinction

OBJECTIVE: (adj.) not influenced by emotions; fair; unbiased

PARADOX: a statement or situation exhibiting contradictory aspects. A famous example of a paradoxical statement is the liar's paradox: "This statement is false."

PERSPECTIVE: a point of view; the relationship of aspects of a subject to each other and to a whole

PLATITUDE: stale, overused expression

PREDICATE: to found or base on

PROPONENT: person who argues for something; advocate

RATIONALE: fundamental reason

RECONCILE: to make compatible or consistent

RED HERRING: something that is or is intended to be misleading or distracting

REFUTATION: disproof of opponent's argument

RHETORIC: the study of the effective use of language to persuade; the use of effective language. The term *rhetoric* can also be used to refer to the use of techniques to persuade with little concern for the truth and to language that is pretentious and relatively lacking in intellectual content.

SKEPTICISM: adopting a doubting attitude toward accepted opinions

SPECIOUS: seeming to be logical and sound, but not really so

SPECULATION: taking something as true based on insufficient evidence

STIPULATION: specifying as an essential condition

SUBJECTIVE: taking place within a person; particular to a person

SUCCINCT: terse, brief, concise

SYNTHESIS: blend, combination

TENABLE: defensible, reasonable

THESIS: a theory put forward as a premise to be proved. For example: "The book's central thesis is that humanity originated in Africa."

TRUISM: a statement that is obviously true and that says nothing new

UNDERSTATEMENT: a restrained statement

VALID: well grounded; correctly inferred or deduced from a premise

WRITING THE ESSAY

Using your notes on argument and language strategies, write an essay evaluating the effectiveness of the argument. Remember that you do not have to explore every feature. Focus on several that you find most relevant and effective, and explain these in some depth. Your essay should make what the College Board describes as "a precise central claim." As you write, keep referring to the passage; use paraphrases or short quotations from it to support your analysis. Your first paragraph should be a brief introduction. Each of the following paragraphs should focus on a major feature of the argument and one or more language strategies used to persuade. The final paragraph should sum up your analysis.

Keep in mind that your writing will be assessed, so make sure to follow the conventions of standard written English. This means that:

1. Your essay and the paragraphs within it should be well-organized and cohesive, with a clear and logical progression of ideas.
2. Your style should be formal.
3. Your tone should be objective.
4. Your word choice should be precise, appropriate, and varied.
5. Your sentences should vary considerably in structure.

WINNING TACTICS FOR THE SAT

You now know the basic framework of the SAT. It's time for the big question: How can you become a winner on the SAT?

- First, you have to decide just what winning is for you. For one student, winning means breaking 1000; for another, only a total score of 1400 will do. Therefore, the first thing you have to do is set *your* goal.
- Second, you must learn to pace yourself during the test. You need to know how many questions you are going to attempt to answer.
- Third, you need to understand the rewards of guessing—how *random guesses* can improve your score and how *educated guesses* can boost your scores dramatically. Educated guessing is a key strategy in helping you to reach your goal.

Here are your winning tactics for the SAT.

1 Set your goal.

Before you begin studying for the SAT, you should set a realistic goal for yourself. Here's what to do.

1. Establish your **baseline score**. You need to know your math, reading, and writing scores on one actual PSAT or SAT to use as your starting point.

   - If you have already taken an SAT, use your actual scores from that test.
   - If you have already taken the PSAT but have not yet taken the SAT, use your most recent actual PSAT scores.
   - If you have not yet taken an actual PSAT or SAT, do the following:

     ☐ Print out a practice test from the College Board's website.

     OR

     ☐ Get a copy of the College Board's SAT preparation booklet from your school guidance office, which will have a practice test in it.

     ☐ Find a quiet place where you can work for 3 hours without interruptions.
     ☐ Take the SAT under true exam conditions:

     Time yourself on each section.
     Take no more than a 2-minute break between sections 1 and 2 and between sections 3 and 4.
     Take a 10-minute break between sections 2 and 3.

     ☐ Follow the instructions to grade the test and convert your total raw scores on each part to a scaled score.
     ☐ Use these scores as your baseline.

2. Look up the average SAT scores for the most recent freshman class at each of the colleges to which you're thinking of applying. This information can be found online on the colleges' websites or in a college guide, such as Barron's *Profiles of American Colleges.* You want to beat that average, if you can.

3. Now **set your goals**. Challenge yourself, but be realistic. If you earned 470 on the English portion of the PSAT, for example, you might like to get 700 on the SAT, but that's unrealistic. On the other hand, don't wimp out. Aim for 550, not 500.

General Guidelines for Setting Your Initial Goals on the English and Math Parts of the SAT

Current Score	Goal (change in score)	Current Score	Goal (change in score)
Less than 400	+100	550–590	+60
400–440	+90	600–640	+50
450–490	+80	650–690	+40
500–540	+70	700 or more	+30

2 Know how many questions you should attempt.

Why is it so important to set a goal? Why not just try to get the highest score you can by correctly answering as many questions as possible? The answer is that *your goal tells you how many questions you should attempt.* The most common tactical error that students make is trying to answer too many questions. Therefore, surprising as it may be, the following statement is true for almost all students:

THE BEST WAY TO INCREASE YOUR SCORE
ON THE SAT IS TO ATTEMPT FEWER QUESTIONS.

Why is slowing down and attempting fewer questions the best way to increase your score on the SAT? To understand that, you first need to know how the SAT is scored. There are two types of scores associated with the SAT: raw scores and scaled scores. First, raw scores are calculated—one for each part of the test. Each raw score is then converted to a scaled score between 200 and 800. On the SAT, every question is worth exactly the same amount: 1 raw score point. You get no more credit for a correct answer to the hardest math question than you do for the easiest. For each question that you answer correctly, you receive 1 raw score point.

# of correct answers = Raw Score

So let's see how this strategy of slowing down works in your favor.

Suppose you rush through the Reading Test, answering all 52 questions in the 65 minutes allotted, and you get 35 right and 17 wrong. Then your raw score would be 35 (one point for each correct answer) and your scaled score would be about 600. That's actually not so bad for answering only two-thirds of the questions correctly. Now suppose that you slow down and use all your time to work on just 44 questions. And suppose that as a result of slowing down, being more careful, and avoiding most careless errors, you answer 38 of the 44 questions correctly and miss only 6. So far your raw score is 38. Of course when you have 10 or 15 seconds left, you should quickly guess at the 8 questions you didn't have time for. On average, you would get 2 right and 6 wrong. So you would have 2 more raw score points, for a total of 40. Now your scaled score is about 650. WOW! You just earned an extra 50 points by attempting fewer questions and making fewer careless mistakes. So it is worth repeating: For most students:

THE BEST WAY TO INCREASE YOUR SCORE ON THE SAT IS TO ATTEMPT FEWER QUESTIONS.

Many students prefer to think about the statement above paraphrased as follows:

THE BIGGEST MISTAKE MOST STUDENTS MAKE ON THE SAT IS TRYING TO ANSWER TOO MANY QUESTIONS.

3 Know how to pace yourself.

On every section, work slowly but steadily. Always keep moving. Never get bogged down on any one question. If you get stuck, guess and move on.

4 Always guess.

The rule is this: if you have worked on a problem, you should be able to eliminate at least one of the choices. This is what is called an *educated* guess. You are not guessing wildly, marking answers at random. You are working on the problem, ruling out answers that make no sense. The more choices you can rule out, the better your chance is of picking the right answer and earning one more point.

You should almost always be able to rule out some answer choices. Most math questions contain at least one or two answer choices that are absurd (for example, negative choices when you know the answer must be positive). In the reading section, once you have read a passage, you can always eliminate some of the answer choices. Cross out any choices that you *know* are incorrect, and go for that educated guess.

Of course, if you truly have no idea, make a wild guess. Whenever you are about to run out of time, quickly guess at all of the remaining questions.

5 Keep careful track of your time.

Bring a watch. Even if there is a clock in the room, it is better for you to have a watch on your desk. Before you start each section, set your watch to 12:00. It is easier to know that a section will be over when your watch reads 12:25 than to have a section start at 9:37 and have to remember that it will be over at 10:02. Your job will be even easier if you have a digital stopwatch that you start at the beginning of each section; either let it count down to zero, or start it at zero and know that your time will be up after the allotted number of minutes.

6 Don't read the directions or look at the sample questions.

For each section of the SAT, the directions given in this book are identical to the directions you will see on your actual exam. Learn them now. Do not waste even a few seconds of your valuable test time reading them.

7 Remember, each question, easy or hard, is worth just 1 point.

Concentrate on questions that don't take you tons of time to answer. If interpreting graphs is easy for you but algebra is hard, do the data questions first.

8 Feel free to skip back and forth between questions within a section or group.

Remember that you're in charge. You don't have to answer everything in order. You can temporarily skip a question that's taking you too long and come back to it if you have time. But first make a guess and bubble it in. If you have time to come back, you can always change your answer.

9 In the Reading Test, read each choice before choosing your answer.

In comparison to math questions, which always have exactly one correct answer, reading questions are more subjective. You are looking for the *best* choice. Even if A or B looks good, check out the others; C or D may be better.

10 Make sure that you answer the question asked.

Sometimes a math question requires you to solve an equation, but instead of asking for the value of x, the question asks for the value of x^2 or $x - 5$. Similarly, sometimes a reading question requires you to determine the LEAST likely outcome of an action; still another may ask you to find the exception to something, as in "The author uses all of the following EXCEPT." To avoid answering the wrong question, circle or underline what you have been asked for.

11 Base your answers only on the information provided—never on what you think you already know.

On passage-based reading questions, base your answers only on the material in the passage, not on what you think you know about the subject matter. On data interpretation questions, base your answers only on the information given in the chart or table.

12 Remember that you are allowed to write anything you want in your test booklet.

Circle questions you skip, and put big question marks next to questions you answer but are unsure about. If you have time left at the end, you want to be able to locate those questions quickly to go over them. In reading passages, underline or put a mark in the margin next to any important point. On math questions, mark up diagrams, adding lines when necessary. And, of course, use all the space provided to solve the problem. In every section, math, reading, and writing and language, cross out every choice that you *know* is wrong. In short, write anything that will help you, using whatever symbols you like. But remember: the only thing that counts is what you enter on your answer sheet. No one but you will ever see anything that you write in your booklet.

13 Be careful not to make any stray pencil marks on your answer sheet.

The SAT is scored by a computer that cannot distinguish between an accidental mark and a filled-in answer. If the computer registers two answers where there should be only one, it will mark that question wrong.

14 Don't change answers capriciously.

If you have time to return to a question and realize that you made a mistake, by all means correct it, making sure you *completely* erase the first mark you made. However, don't change answers on a last-minute hunch or whim, or for fear you have chosen too many A's and not enough B's. In such cases, more often than not, students change right answers to wrong ones.

15 Use your calculator only when you need to.

Many students actually waste time using their calculators on questions that do not require them. Use your calculator whenever you feel it will help, but don't overuse it. Remember, just because the longer math section is labeled "calculator" does not mean you need to use your calculator for each question.

16 When you use your calculator, don't go too quickly.

Your calculator leaves no trail. If you accidentally hit the wrong button and get a wrong answer, you have no way to look at your work and find your mistake. You just have to do it all over.

17 Remember that you don't have to attempt every question to do well.

You have learned about setting goals and pacing. You know you don't have to attempt all the questions to do well. It is possible to work on only half of the questions and still be in the top half of all students taking the test. Of course, you should fill in an answer for every question. After you set your final goal, pace yourself to reach it.

18 Don't be nervous: if your scores aren't as high as you would like, you can always take the SAT again.

Relax. The biggest reason that some students do worse on the actual SAT than they did on their practice tests is that they are nervous. You can't do your best if your hands are shaking and you're worried that your whole future is riding on this one test. First of all, your SAT scores are only one of many factors that influence the admissions process, and many students are accepted at their first-choice colleges even if their SAT scores are lower than they had expected. But more important, because of Score Choice, you can always retake the SAT if you don't do well enough the first or second time. So, give yourself the best chance for success: prepare conscientiously and then stay calm while actually taking the test.

ADVICE ON TAKING THE 6 PRACTICE SAT TESTS IN THIS BOOK

This book contains six practice SAT tests, each of which resembles an actual SAT in format, in difficulty, and in content.

For optimal results, you should use this book in conjunction with the latest edition of Barron's *SAT*, the leading test-prep book for over 50 years. Of course, this book of practice tests provides complete solutions and answer explanations for all of the questions on each of the exams. But, whenever you miss a question or leave one out and you want more information than is provided in the explanation, you can find it in Barron's *SAT*—whether it's a more complete analysis of a grammar rule or a fuller review of a particular math concept. Barron's *SAT* also includes dozens of test-taking tactics that can help you earn higher scores on the tests in this book, as well as on the actual SAT that you eventually take.

If you have not yet taken any practice SATs, you should take the first test in this book without timing yourself, just to get used to the types of questions that are on the test. During this first test you can carefully read the directions for each section and look at the sample questions. Later, when you take the other tests in this book, and especially when you take your actual SAT, you should *never* spend even one second reading directions. When the proctor says, for example, "Open your booklets to Section 2 and begin work," the first word you should read is the first word of Question 1—you shouldn't look at the directions, because you will already know them.

As mentioned above, if, after taking the first test and reading the solutions for all of the questions you missed or left out, you find that there are math topics that you don't understand and/or grammar rules that aren't clear, you should try to learn them by reading the relevant sections of Barron's *SAT* before tackling the other tests in this book.

Finally, it is very important to set a realistic goal for yourself, based on the information on pages 29–33 in this book. If you haven't yet done that, do it now. Once you have done that, you should then start taking the other tests in this book at a rate of about one per week.

Before the date of your actual SAT, you should take at least two or three of the exams in this book under true exam conditions. *You should take the entire test in a single sitting adhering to the following suggestions:*

- **TAKE THE TEST IN A QUIET SPOT.** Try to complete the entire test in a place where you won't be distracted or interrupted.
- **TIME YOURSELF ON EACH SECTION.** The SAT consists of four sections that take a total of exactly 3 hours. The English part of the SAT consists of two sections: a 65-minute Reading Test and a 35-minute Writing and Language Test, for a total of 100 minutes. Both sections consist entirely of multiple-choice questions; there is nothing to actually write on the SAT unless you stay for the optional essay. The Math part of the SAT also consists of two sections: a 55-minute section on which you are permitted to use a calculator and a 25-minute section on which calculators are not permitted, for a total of 80 minutes.
- **TAKE BREAKS.** Take one break between sections 2 and 3. Your break should last 10 minutes. During this time, you may go to the bathroom, walk around, or eat a snack. Between all the other sections, take a one minute break to relax and take a few deep breaths.

- **PACE YOURSELF.** Concentrate and work carefully, without going too fast. Remember, it is better to answer fewer questions and avoid making careless mistakes than to race through trying to answer all the questions.
- **TAKE EDUCATED GUESSES.** If you read a question and don't know the correct answer, always try to eliminate some choices and guess. *Never omit a question if you can eliminate any of the choices.*
- **SCORING ANALYSIS.** After you have completed each practice test, you can calculate your final score by referring to the scoring analysis information that appears after the answer key pages for each test.

If you use the guidelines listed above, you will be making the best use of the time you devote to preparing for the SAT. When you finally take the SAT for real, you will know exactly what to expect. GOOD LUCK!

Practice Tests

ANSWER SHEET
Practice Test 1

Section 1: Reading

1. Ⓐ Ⓑ Ⓒ Ⓓ	14. Ⓐ Ⓑ Ⓒ Ⓓ	27. Ⓐ Ⓑ Ⓒ Ⓓ	40. Ⓐ Ⓑ Ⓒ Ⓓ
2. Ⓐ Ⓑ Ⓒ Ⓓ	15. Ⓐ Ⓑ Ⓒ Ⓓ	28. Ⓐ Ⓑ Ⓒ Ⓓ	41. Ⓐ Ⓑ Ⓒ Ⓓ
3. Ⓐ Ⓑ Ⓒ Ⓓ	16. Ⓐ Ⓑ Ⓒ Ⓓ	29. Ⓐ Ⓑ Ⓒ Ⓓ	42. Ⓐ Ⓑ Ⓒ Ⓓ
4. Ⓐ Ⓑ Ⓒ Ⓓ	17. Ⓐ Ⓑ Ⓒ Ⓓ	30. Ⓐ Ⓑ Ⓒ Ⓓ	43. Ⓐ Ⓑ Ⓒ Ⓓ
5. Ⓐ Ⓑ Ⓒ Ⓓ	18. Ⓐ Ⓑ Ⓒ Ⓓ	31. Ⓐ Ⓑ Ⓒ Ⓓ	44. Ⓐ Ⓑ Ⓒ Ⓓ
6. Ⓐ Ⓑ Ⓒ Ⓓ	19. Ⓐ Ⓑ Ⓒ Ⓓ	32. Ⓐ Ⓑ Ⓒ Ⓓ	45. Ⓐ Ⓑ Ⓒ Ⓓ
7. Ⓐ Ⓑ Ⓒ Ⓓ	20. Ⓐ Ⓑ Ⓒ Ⓓ	33. Ⓐ Ⓑ Ⓒ Ⓓ	46. Ⓐ Ⓑ Ⓒ Ⓓ
8. Ⓐ Ⓑ Ⓒ Ⓓ	21. Ⓐ Ⓑ Ⓒ Ⓓ	34. Ⓐ Ⓑ Ⓒ Ⓓ	47. Ⓐ Ⓑ Ⓒ Ⓓ
9. Ⓐ Ⓑ Ⓒ Ⓓ	22. Ⓐ Ⓑ Ⓒ Ⓓ	35. Ⓐ Ⓑ Ⓒ Ⓓ	48. Ⓐ Ⓑ Ⓒ Ⓓ
10. Ⓐ Ⓑ Ⓒ Ⓓ	23. Ⓐ Ⓑ Ⓒ Ⓓ	36. Ⓐ Ⓑ Ⓒ Ⓓ	49. Ⓐ Ⓑ Ⓒ Ⓓ
11. Ⓐ Ⓑ Ⓒ Ⓓ	24. Ⓐ Ⓑ Ⓒ Ⓓ	37. Ⓐ Ⓑ Ⓒ Ⓓ	50. Ⓐ Ⓑ Ⓒ Ⓓ
12. Ⓐ Ⓑ Ⓒ Ⓓ	25. Ⓐ Ⓑ Ⓒ Ⓓ	38. Ⓐ Ⓑ Ⓒ Ⓓ	51. Ⓐ Ⓑ Ⓒ Ⓓ
13. Ⓐ Ⓑ Ⓒ Ⓓ	26. Ⓐ Ⓑ Ⓒ Ⓓ	39. Ⓐ Ⓑ Ⓒ Ⓓ	52. Ⓐ Ⓑ Ⓒ Ⓓ

Section 2: Writing and Language

1. Ⓐ Ⓑ Ⓒ Ⓓ	12. Ⓐ Ⓑ Ⓒ Ⓓ	23. Ⓐ Ⓑ Ⓒ Ⓓ	34. Ⓐ Ⓑ Ⓒ Ⓓ
2. Ⓐ Ⓑ Ⓒ Ⓓ	13. Ⓐ Ⓑ Ⓒ Ⓓ	24. Ⓐ Ⓑ Ⓒ Ⓓ	35. Ⓐ Ⓑ Ⓒ Ⓓ
3. Ⓐ Ⓑ Ⓒ Ⓓ	14. Ⓐ Ⓑ Ⓒ Ⓓ	25. Ⓐ Ⓑ Ⓒ Ⓓ	36. Ⓐ Ⓑ Ⓒ Ⓓ
4. Ⓐ Ⓑ Ⓒ Ⓓ	15. Ⓐ Ⓑ Ⓒ Ⓓ	26. Ⓐ Ⓑ Ⓒ Ⓓ	37. Ⓐ Ⓑ Ⓒ Ⓓ
5. Ⓐ Ⓑ Ⓒ Ⓓ	16. Ⓐ Ⓑ Ⓒ Ⓓ	27. Ⓐ Ⓑ Ⓒ Ⓓ	38. Ⓐ Ⓑ Ⓒ Ⓓ
6. Ⓐ Ⓑ Ⓒ Ⓓ	17. Ⓐ Ⓑ Ⓒ Ⓓ	28. Ⓐ Ⓑ Ⓒ Ⓓ	39. Ⓐ Ⓑ Ⓒ Ⓓ
7. Ⓐ Ⓑ Ⓒ Ⓓ	18. Ⓐ Ⓑ Ⓒ Ⓓ	29. Ⓐ Ⓑ Ⓒ Ⓓ	40. Ⓐ Ⓑ Ⓒ Ⓓ
8. Ⓐ Ⓑ Ⓒ Ⓓ	19. Ⓐ Ⓑ Ⓒ Ⓓ	30. Ⓐ Ⓑ Ⓒ Ⓓ	41. Ⓐ Ⓑ Ⓒ Ⓓ
9. Ⓐ Ⓑ Ⓒ Ⓓ	20. Ⓐ Ⓑ Ⓒ Ⓓ	31. Ⓐ Ⓑ Ⓒ Ⓓ	42. Ⓐ Ⓑ Ⓒ Ⓓ
10. Ⓐ Ⓑ Ⓒ Ⓓ	21. Ⓐ Ⓑ Ⓒ Ⓓ	32. Ⓐ Ⓑ Ⓒ Ⓓ	43. Ⓐ Ⓑ Ⓒ Ⓓ
11. Ⓐ Ⓑ Ⓒ Ⓓ	22. Ⓐ Ⓑ Ⓒ Ⓓ	33. Ⓐ Ⓑ Ⓒ Ⓓ	44. Ⓐ Ⓑ Ⓒ Ⓓ

ANSWER SHEET
Practice Test 1

Section 3: Math (No Calculator)

1. Ⓐ Ⓑ Ⓒ Ⓓ
2. Ⓐ Ⓑ Ⓒ Ⓓ
3. Ⓐ Ⓑ Ⓒ Ⓓ
4. Ⓐ Ⓑ Ⓒ Ⓓ
5. Ⓐ Ⓑ Ⓒ Ⓓ
6. Ⓐ Ⓑ Ⓒ Ⓓ
7. Ⓐ Ⓑ Ⓒ Ⓓ
8. Ⓐ Ⓑ Ⓒ Ⓓ
9. Ⓐ Ⓑ Ⓒ Ⓓ
10. Ⓐ Ⓑ Ⓒ Ⓓ
11. Ⓐ Ⓑ Ⓒ Ⓓ
12. Ⓐ Ⓑ Ⓒ Ⓓ
13. Ⓐ Ⓑ Ⓒ Ⓓ
14. Ⓐ Ⓑ Ⓒ Ⓓ
15. Ⓐ Ⓑ Ⓒ Ⓓ

16.

	⊘	⊘	
⊙	⊙	⊙	⊙
	⓪	⓪	⓪
①	①	①	①
②	②	②	②
③	③	③	③
④	④	④	④
⑤	⑤	⑤	⑤
⑥	⑥	⑥	⑥
⑦	⑦	⑦	⑦
⑧	⑧	⑧	⑧
⑨	⑨	⑨	⑨

17.

	⊘	⊘	
⊙	⊙	⊙	⊙
	⓪	⓪	⓪
①	①	①	①
②	②	②	②
③	③	③	③
④	④	④	④
⑤	⑤	⑤	⑤
⑥	⑥	⑥	⑥
⑦	⑦	⑦	⑦
⑧	⑧	⑧	⑧
⑨	⑨	⑨	⑨

18.

	⊘	⊘	
⊙	⊙	⊙	⊙
	⓪	⓪	⓪
①	①	①	①
②	②	②	②
③	③	③	③
④	④	④	④
⑤	⑤	⑤	⑤
⑥	⑥	⑥	⑥
⑦	⑦	⑦	⑦
⑧	⑧	⑧	⑧
⑨	⑨	⑨	⑨

19.

	⊘	⊘	
⊙	⊙	⊙	⊙
	⓪	⓪	⓪
①	①	①	①
②	②	②	②
③	③	③	③
④	④	④	④
⑤	⑤	⑤	⑤
⑥	⑥	⑥	⑥
⑦	⑦	⑦	⑦
⑧	⑧	⑧	⑧
⑨	⑨	⑨	⑨

20.

	⊘	⊘	
⊙	⊙	⊙	⊙
	⓪	⓪	⓪
①	①	①	①
②	②	②	②
③	③	③	③
④	④	④	④
⑤	⑤	⑤	⑤
⑥	⑥	⑥	⑥
⑦	⑦	⑦	⑦
⑧	⑧	⑧	⑧
⑨	⑨	⑨	⑨

ANSWER SHEET
Practice Test 1

Section 4: Math (Calculator)

1. Ⓐ Ⓑ Ⓒ Ⓓ
2. Ⓐ Ⓑ Ⓒ Ⓓ
3. Ⓐ Ⓑ Ⓒ Ⓓ
4. Ⓐ Ⓑ Ⓒ Ⓓ
5. Ⓐ Ⓑ Ⓒ Ⓓ
6. Ⓐ Ⓑ Ⓒ Ⓓ
7. Ⓐ Ⓑ Ⓒ Ⓓ
8. Ⓐ Ⓑ Ⓒ Ⓓ
9. Ⓐ Ⓑ Ⓒ Ⓓ
10. Ⓐ Ⓑ Ⓒ Ⓓ
11. Ⓐ Ⓑ Ⓒ Ⓓ
12. Ⓐ Ⓑ Ⓒ Ⓓ
13. Ⓐ Ⓑ Ⓒ Ⓓ
14. Ⓐ Ⓑ Ⓒ Ⓓ
15. Ⓐ Ⓑ Ⓒ Ⓓ
16. Ⓐ Ⓑ Ⓒ Ⓓ
17. Ⓐ Ⓑ Ⓒ Ⓓ
18. Ⓐ Ⓑ Ⓒ Ⓓ
19. Ⓐ Ⓑ Ⓒ Ⓓ
20. Ⓐ Ⓑ Ⓒ Ⓓ
21. Ⓐ Ⓑ Ⓒ Ⓓ
22. Ⓐ Ⓑ Ⓒ Ⓓ
23. Ⓐ Ⓑ Ⓒ Ⓓ
24. Ⓐ Ⓑ Ⓒ Ⓓ
25. Ⓐ Ⓑ Ⓒ Ⓓ
26. Ⓐ Ⓑ Ⓒ Ⓓ
27. Ⓐ Ⓑ Ⓒ Ⓓ
28. Ⓐ Ⓑ Ⓒ Ⓓ
29. Ⓐ Ⓑ Ⓒ Ⓓ
30. Ⓐ Ⓑ Ⓒ Ⓓ

31.

32.

33.

34.

35.

36.

37.

38.

ANSWER SHEET
Practice Test 1

Essay

PLANNING PAGE

START YOUR ESSAY HERE

READING TEST

65 MINUTES, 52 QUESTIONS

Turn to Section 1 of your answer sheet to answer the questions in this section.

Directions: Following each of the passages (or pairs of passages) below are questions about the passage (or passages). Read each passage carefully. Then, select the best answer for each question based on what is stated in the passage (or passages) and in any graphics that may accompany the passage.

Questions 1–10 are based on the following passage.

This passage is from Peter Matthiessen, *Indian Country,* © 1984 by Peter Matthiessen.

The traditionals have always been wary of the white man's consumer mentality, and now they were worried about what could happen when the Black Mesa mine was dead, when a dependent and poverty stricken people, having been left with waste and desecration where a sacred mountain had once stood, found themselves forced to accept more leases and more desolation. This threat was increased by the prospect of legal "termination," or dissolution of a people as a cultural unit, with which Indians are threatened every other year. Termination legislation, which had already wiped out a number of small tribes, not only withdraws all federal aid, but turns the Indians over to the mercies of state jurisdiction and property taxation, forcing a people with no other recourse to put their last resource—land—upon the market. ("That is all we have. When the land is gone, we will walk away from our homes with our beds upon our backs.") By eliminating an Indian nation, termination quiets Indian claims to tribal lands that were never ceded to the U.S. government by treaty, which happens to describe almost all the "federal" land in the Far West; instead, the people must accept whatever monetary settlement has been bestowed upon them by the Court of Claims, which was set up not to administer justice but to expedite adjudication of land titles and head off any future claims that Indians might make on lands already coveted by the white economy.

The Hopi chairman's brother, Wayne, a prosperous Mormon, proprietor of a thriving Hopi craft shop, with holdings in the family ranch and a construction company, complains in his progressive newspaper, *Qua Toqti,* of the poor attitude of the traditionals toward "their fellow tribesmen in business," and criticizes white supporters of the traditionals for "wanting to keep us in our 'primitive' state." He has declared, "We will never go back to our cornfields and orchards unless we are forced to." In another column in the newspaper, Wayne Sekaquaptewa inquires, "When will someone come along to convince us that we are squabbling like untrained children over everything in the name of our useless religion?" (Sekaquaptewa believes that the true story of the Hopi may be found in the Book of Mormon.) Not surprisingly, *Qua Toqti* vociferously supports the eviction of the "enemy Navajo" from Hopi land.

The progressives feel that there is no place for old, slow Hopi ways in a world

GO ON TO THE NEXT PAGE

that is going on without them; they look down on the traditionals, with their wood stoves and kerosene lamps and outhouses, their "useless religion." (I notice, however, that outhouses in Oraibi and Hotevilla are not locked to keep out witches, as are the Christian outhouses of Walpi.) The traditionals know that those who follow the lead of the progressives will be assimilated—that is, swept away into a competitive economy for which they have no training. So long as the Hopi hold their land, those still able to make corn grow in the slow, patient techniques of dry farming will survive even when all help has been taken away, proceeding as best as they can according to their sacred instructions until the Day of Purification restores harmony and balance to all land and life, until the bad road taken by the white man comes to its inevitable end, as foretold in the stark etching on the Life Plan Rock.

1. According to the author, the Court of Claims referred to in line 30
   (A) adjudicates cases fairly
   (B) almost always favors Indian claims to land over white claims to land
   (C) has little real effect on Indian affairs
   (D) is biased toward white people in its judgments

2. The word *quiets* as it is used in line 24 most nearly means
   (A) reduces in volume
   (B) softens
   (C) lessens
   (D) eliminates

3. The author most likely put quotation marks around the word "federal" in line 27 to
   (A) show that he understands that the term is an informal, unofficial one
   (B) remind the reader the notion of a federal government is a controversial one
   (C) emphasize that most of the land in the Far West is owned not by the states but by the U.S. government
   (D) indicate that ownership of most of the land claimed by the U.S. government in the Far West is open to dispute

4. Which of the following words, as it is used in the passage, can most accurately be described as sarcastic?
   (A) "forced" (line 8)
   (B) "mercies" (line 17)
   (C) "vociferously" (line 55)
   (D) "stark" (line 79)

5. What does the author aim to imply in lines 62–65: "I notice, however, that outhouses in Oraibi and Hotevilla are not locked to keep out witches, as are the Christian outhouses of Walpi."
   (A) Traditional Hopi religion has not developed even to the point at which it believes in witches.
   (B) Followers of traditional Hopi religion are careless in the practice of their religion compared to the progressives, who scrupulously follow the teachings of Christianity.
   (C) Followers of traditional Hopi religion might be less superstitious than the Hopi followers of the white man's predominant religion, Christianity.
   (D) Progressive Indians are, sensibly, aware of the danger presented by witches.

GO ON TO THE NEXT PAGE

6. The traditionals believe that

(A) the only way in which the Hopi can survive as a distinct culture is to follow the lead of the progressives and adapt to the white man's ways
(B) Hopi religion is based on a misplaced faith that balance will eventually be restored in the world
(C) it is very possible that the truth about the origin and destiny of the Hopi is to be found in the Book of Mormon
(D) the only chance that the Hopi have to survive as a cultural unit is to cling to their traditional ways

7. The author's main purpose in citing the views of Wayne Sekaquaptewa is to help

(A) present the views of the progressives in the Hopi nation
(B) show that progressive Hopis are more realistic than traditional Hopis
(C) illustrate the influence of Mormonism on Hopi society
(D) show that Indians, if given the opportunity, can be as successful in business as whites

8. Which of the following statements best describes the author's view of the "Day of Purification" referred to in lines 75–76?

(A) He believes it will come as long as enough Hopis abandon their traditional culture and adopt the ways of the white man.
(B) He is certain that it will come one day, precisely as predicted in Hopi teaching.
(C) He thinks that it is a myth believed by a primitive culture that contains no truth, even on a symbolic level.
(D) He respects it as an important Hopi belief and sees it as symbolic of a future time that may very possibly come to pass.

9. Which word or phrase would traditional Hopi be most likely to use to describe the white man?

(A) trustworthy
(B) altruistic
(C) materialistic
(D) respectful of nature

10. Which choice provides the best evidence for the answer to the previous question?

(A) "The . . . desolation." (lines 1–9)
(B) "Termination . . . market." (lines 13–20)
(C) "The . . . state.'" (lines 35–44)
(D) "The . . . religion.'" (lines 57–62)

GO ON TO THE NEXT PAGE

Questions 11–20 are based on the following passages.

Each of the following passages is from the beginning of short stories by F. Scott Fitzgerald in *Flappers and Philosophers*, originally published in 1920.

PASSAGE 1

This unlikely story begins on a sea that was a blue dream, as colorful as blue-silk stockings, and beneath a sky as blue as the irises of children's eyes. From the western half of the sky the sun was shying little golden disks at the sea—if you gazed intently enough you could see them skip from wave tip to wave tip until they joined a broad collar of golden coin that was collecting half a mile out and would eventually be a dazzling sunset. About half-way between the Florida shore and the golden collar a white steam-yacht, very young and graceful, was riding at anchor and under a blue-and-white awning aft a yellow-haired girl reclined in a wicker settee reading *The Revolt of the Angels*, by Anatole France. She was about nineteen, slender and supple, with a spoiled alluring mouth and quick gray eyes full of a radiant curiosity. Her feet, stockingless, and adorned rather than clad in blue-satin slippers which swung nonchalantly from her toes, were perched on the arm of a settee adjoining the one she occupied. And as she read she intermittently regaled herself by a faint application to her tongue of a half-lemon that she held in her hand. The other half, sucked dry, lay on the deck at her feet and rocked very gently to and fro at the almost imperceptible motion of the tide.

The second half-lemon was well-nigh pulpless and the golden collar had grown astonishing in width, when suddenly the drowsy silence which enveloped the yacht was broken by the sound of heavy footsteps and an elderly man topped with orderly gray hair and clad in a white-flannel suit appeared at the head of the companionway. There he paused for a moment until his eyes became accustomed to the sun, and then seeing the girl under the awning he uttered a long even grunt of disapproval. If he had intended thereby to obtain a rise of any sort he was doomed to disappointment. The girl calmly turned over two pages, turned back one, raised the lemon mechanically to tasting distance, and then very faintly but quite unmistakably yawned.

PASSAGE 2

The sunlight dripped over the house like golden paint over an art jar, and the freckling shadows here and there only intensified the rigor of the bath of light. The Butterworth and Larkin houses flanking were entrenched behind great stodgy trees; only the Happer house took the full sun, and all day long faced the dusty road-street with a tolerant kindly patience. This was the city of Tarleton in southernmost Georgia, September afternoon.

Up in her bedroom window Sally Carrol Happer rested her nineteen-year-old chin on a fifty-two-year-old sill and watched Clark Darrow's ancient Ford turn the corner. The car was hot—being partly metallic it retained all the heat it absorbed or evolved— and Clark Darrow sitting bolt upright at the wheel wore a pained, strained expression as though he considered himself a spare part, and rather likely to break. He laboriously crossed two dust ruts, the wheels squeaking indignantly at the encounter, and then with a terrifying expression he gave the steering-gear a final wrench and deposited self and

GO ON TO THE NEXT PAGE

car approximately in front of the Happer steps. There was a heaving sound, a death-rattle, followed by a short silence; and then the air was rent by a startling whistle. Sally Carrol gazed down sleepily. She started to yawn, but finding this quite impossible unless she raised her chin from the window-sill, changed her mind and continued silently to regard the car, whose owner sat brilliantly if perfunctorily at attention as he waited for an answer to his signal. After a moment the whistle once more split the dusty air.

11. The phrase "quick gray eyes" (line 19) is most likely used to suggest that the girl portrayed in Passage 1 is

(A) alert
(B) nervous
(C) shifty
(D) distracted

12. The phrase "adorned rather than clad" (lines 20–21) suggests that the girl described in Passage 1

(A) is indifferent to how her feet look
(B) likes to make herself attractive
(C) is wearing slippers because they are the most practical footwear for a passenger on a yacht
(D) does not know much about fashion

13. The word closest in meaning to the word *rise* as it is used in line 43 in Passage 1 is

(A) increase
(B) greeting
(C) reaction
(D) wave

14. What can most reasonably be inferred about the man portrayed in Passage 1?

(A) He is the girl's grandfather.
(B) He does not enjoy being on a yacht.
(C) He does not often come on deck because his illness confines him to bed below deck.
(D) He does not approve of the girl spending so much of her time reading.

15. In Passage 2 the author uses the words and phrases "tolerant kindly patience" (lines 56–57), "indignantly" (line 70), and "death-rattle" (lines 74–75) mainly to

(A) satirize the way of life in Tarleton
(B) help the reader imagine what is being described
(C) exaggerate and distort reality to give the reader a fresh perspective
(D) encourage the reader to sympathize with the people described in the scene

16. The whistle mentioned in line 76 of Passage 2 was most likely produced by

(A) a passerby
(B) Clark Darrow's car
(C) Clark Darrow
(D) a policeman

GO ON TO THE NEXT PAGE

17. One can reasonably infer that the words "sat brilliantly if perfunctorily at attention" in Passage 2 (lines 81–82) suggest that Clark Darrow regards his visit to the Happer house largely as
    (A) a dramatic way to demonstrate his romantic interest in Sally Happer
    (B) a great honor
    (C) an uninteresting routine duty to be performed, albeit in a somewhat showy manner
    (D) an exciting change from his regular activities

18. The word *evolved* as it is used in line 64 means
    (A) gave off
    (B) developed gradually
    (C) devised
    (D) retained

19. Which of the following words best describes both of the girls as they are portrayed in Passage 1 and Passage 2?
    (A) pretty
    (B) relaxed
    (C) intelligent
    (D) indolent

20. In both Passage 1 and Passage 2 the arrival of a male character
    (A) primarily helps to create humor
    (B) is followed by a condemnation of self-indulgence
    (C) interrupts a tranquil mood
    (D) establishes a serious atmosphere

GO ON TO THE NEXT PAGE

Questions 21–31 are based on the following passage.

This passage is from Paul Fussell, "Hiroshima: A Soldier's View," © 1981 by The New Republic.

In an exchange of views not long ago in *The New York Review of Books*, Joseph Alsop and David Joravky set forth the by now familiar argument on both sides of the debate about the "ethics" of the bomb. It's not hard to guess which side each chose once you know that Alsop experienced capture by the Japanese at Hong Kong early in 1942, while Joravsky came into no deadly contact with the Japanese: a young, combat-innocent soldier, he was on his way to the Pacific when the war ended. The editors of *The New York Review* gave the debate the tendentious title "Was the Hiroshima Bomb Necessary?" surely an unanswerable question (unlike "Was It Effective?") and one precisely indicating the intellectual difficulties involved in imposing **ex post facto* a rational and even a genteel ethics on this event. In arguing the acceptability of the bomb, Alsop focuses on the power and fanaticism of War Minister Anami, who insisted that Japan fight to the bitter end, defending the main islands with the same techniques and tenacity employed at Iwo Jima and Okinawa. Alsop concludes: "Japanese surrender could never have been obtained, at any rate without the honor-satisfying bloodbath envisioned by . . . Anami, if the hideous destruction of Hiroshima and Nagasaki had not finally galvanized the peace advocates into tearing up the entire Japanese book of rules." The Japanese plan to deploy the undefeated bulk of their ground forces, over two million men, plus 10,000 kamikaze planes, plus the elderly and all the women and children with sharpened spears they could muster in a suicidal defense makes it absurd, says Alsop, to "hold the common view, by now hardly challenged by anyone, that the decision to drop the two bombs on Japan was wicked in itself, and that President Truman and all others who joined in making or who [like Robert Oppenheimer] assented to this decision shared in the wickedness." And in explanation of "the two bombs," Alsop adds: "The true, climactic, and successful effort of the Japanese peace advocates . . . did not begin in deadly earnest until *after* the second bomb had destroyed Nagasaki. The Nagasaki bomb was thus the trigger to all the developments that led to peace." At this time the army was so unready for surrender that most looked forward to the forthcoming invasion as an indispensable opportunity to show their mettle, enthusiastically agreeing with the army spokesman who reasoned early in 1945, "Since the retreat from Guadalcanal, the Army has had little opportunity to engage the enemy in land battles. But when we meet in Japan proper, our Army will demonstrate its invincible superiority." This possibility foreclosed by the Emperor's post-A-bomb surrender broadcast, the shocked, disappointed officers of one infantry battalion, anticipating a professionally impressive defense of the beaches, killed themselves in the following numbers: one major, three captains, ten first lieutenants, and twelve second lieutenants.

David Joravsky, now a professor of history at Northwestern, argued on the other hand that those who decided to use the A-bombs on cities betray defects of "reason and self-restraint." It all needn't have happened, he says, "if the U.S. government had been willing to take a few more days and to be

GO ON TO THE NEXT PAGE

a bit more thoughtful in opening up the age of nuclear warfare." I've already noted what "a few more days" would mean to the luckless troops and sailors on the spot, and as to being thoughtful when "opening up the age of nuclear warfare," of course no one was focusing on anything as portentous as that, which reflects a historian's tidy hindsight. The U.S. government was engaged not in that sort of momentous thing but in ending the war conclusively, as well as irrationally remembering Pearl Harbor with a vengeance. It didn't know then what everyone knows now about leukemia and various kinds of carcinoma and birth defects. Truman was not being sly or coy when he insisted that the bomb was "only another weapon." History, as Eliot's "Gerontion" notes,

> . . . has many cunning passages, contrived corridors
> And issues, deceives with whispering ambitions,
> Guides us by vanities . . .
> Think
> Neither fear not courage saves us.
> Unnatural vices
> Are fathered by our heroism. Virtues
> Are forced upon us by our impudent crimes.

Understanding the past requires pretending that you don't know the present. It requires feeling its own pressure on your pulses without any *ex post facto* illumination. That's a harder thing to do than Joravsky seems to think.

**Ex post facto* means "after the fact."

21. In the opening part of the passage, "In an exchange . . . the war ended" (lines 1–12), what assumption does the author appear to be making?

    (A) A soldier who is captured by the enemy will always feel hatred toward the enemy that will distort that person's judgment about the enemy.
    (B) A person's opinions are determined to a large extent by his or her experiences.
    (C) The views of a soldier who has not experienced combat about the enemy cannot be taken seriously.
    (D) It is not possible for anyone to reach an objective judgment about an emotional topic like the ethics of the dropping of A-bombs on Hiroshima.

22. Why does the author say that the question "Was the Hiroshima Bomb Necessary?" is unanswerable?

    (A) Americans are still so deeply divided about this event that no definitive answer can yet be given.
    (B) The word "necessary" in the question requires that the answer to the question be "no," because the Japanese could have been defeated without the use of the atomic bomb, albeit at the cost of great loss of life.
    (C) Ethical issues can never be conclusively decided.
    (D) Questions about the past are meaningless because the past remains the past no matter what is decided about it in retrospect.

GO ON TO THE NEXT PAGE

23. What does the "Japanese book of rules" mentioned in line 33 refer to?

(A) The guidelines Japanese peace advocates had been following before the destruction of Hiroshima and Nagasaki.
(B) The deeply held values governing Japanese conduct, especially in regard to national pride, individual honor, and conduct in war.
(C) The plan devised at the highest levels of Japanese government to defend the homeland against invasion at all costs.
(D) The code of conduct of Japanese soldiers.

24. What information, if it came to light, would support Joseph Alsop's contention, cited by the author in lines 20–29, that the only way Japan could have been induced to surrender other than by the dropping of the atomic bomb would have been an "honor-satisfying bloodbath"?

(A) Sociological studies suggesting that Japanese people place less value on honor than is generally thought.
(B) Evidence that the case being made by peace advocates in Japan was being received with increasing interest by the Japanese populace.
(C) Surveys of public opinion in Japan near the end of the war suggesting that the vast majority of the population would fight to the death to defend Japan.
(D) Documents showing that the civilian population was poorly organized and unmotivated to fight trained Allied soldiers to defend Japan.

25. Which of the following statements would the author be most likely to agree with?

(A) There is little chance that Kamikaze planes would have been used by the Japanese military against a U.S.-led invasion.
(B) In considering the morality of the atomic bombing of Japan, Americans tend to ignore the fact that Japanese culture places great stress on honor, even if it requires great sacrifice.
(C) There is little reason to think that Japanese civilians would defend their country as ferociously as Japanese soldiers.
(D) The ferocity of the fighting at Iwo Jima and Okinawa has been greatly exaggerated by Hollywood movies.

26. What phrase best expresses what the author means by "a genteel ethics" in line 19?

(A) middle class values
(B) religious morals
(C) generally accepted social norms
(D) the morality of polite society

PRACTICE TEST 1

GO ON TO THE NEXT PAGE

27. What information, if discovered, would support the argument made by Joseph Alsop, cited in lines 48–53 ("The true, climactic . . . led to peace") that the dropping of an atomic bomb on Nagasaki was morally justifiable?

(A) Evidence that a secret offer of unconditional surrender by the Japanese emperor had been received one day after the atom bomb was dropped on Hiroshima.
(B) Studies by the U.S. military arguing persuasively that Japanese civilians would not make an effective fighting force.
(C) Information showing that the Japanese military had nearly run out of fuel at the time the A-bomb was dropped on Nagasaki.
(D) Documents showing that the Japanese leaders possessed secret information that led them to believe (incorrectly) after the atomic bomb was dropped on Hiroshima that the Americans did not possess another atomic bomb that was ready for use, and it would be several months before another one would be ready.

28. Which of the following words or phrases is closest in meaning to the word *tidy* as it is used in line 86?

(A) clean
(B) orderly
(C) substantial
(D) satisfactory

29. The phrase, "as well as irrationally remembering Pearl Harbor with a vengeance" (lines 89–91), suggests that the author believes that

(A) in deciding to drop atomic bombs on Hiroshima and Nagasaki, officials in the U.S. government were partly motivated by a desire for revenge against the Japanese
(B) U.S. government officials were not acting at all rationally in deciding to drop atomic bombs on Japanese cities
(C) in their desire to drop atomic bombs on Japanese cities, the U.S. government was motivated entirely by the memory of the surprise Japanese attack on Pearl Harbor
(D) the U.S. government allowed itself to be distracted from the main business of decisively and expeditiously ending the war by a desire for vengeance for Japan's surprise attack on Pearl Harbor

30. The word *illumination* as it is used in line 112 most nearly means

(A) exaggeration
(B) intellectual enlightenment
(C) pretension to knowledge
(D) spiritual enlightenment

GO ON TO THE NEXT PAGE

31. The lines from T.S. Eliot's poem "Gerontion" serve mainly to

(A) remind historians that to understand an event in the past they must imagine that they are ignorant of what the consequences of the event were
(B) make the point that a heroic action might result in evil, and a cowardly action might result in good
(C) encourage the reader to investigate what great poets have written about both the heroism war inspires and the horrors it entails
(D) reinforce the point that the consequences of an action (for good or ill) are not known by those who decide to take the action at the time of their decision

Questions 32–42 are based on the following passage.

This passage is from David Alpaugh, "The Professionalization of Poetry" in *Heavy Lifting*, © 2007 by Alehouse Press.

As colleges and universities increasingly make the education, publication, sustenance, and honoring of American poets their business, writing program professionals have assumed a number of nonpoetic responsibilities. It has become part of their business to attract students and sponsor an ever-growing body of work produced by graduates and colleagues. Such practical concerns have led professionals to tolerate aesthetic trends designed not so much to make poetry better as to make it easier to produce and publish.

Most obvious is the "prosification" of poetry— the publication of flat, pedestrian prose with the assurance, explicit or implied, that it is the real thing. The notion that lineation is a magic wand that can turn prose into poetry has been uncritically accepted by too many literary editors. So many poets publish lineated prose today that it would be unfair to single out one or two. In "On the Prosing of Poetry," poet Joan Houlihan makes a similar argument, providing poems by writers such as Donald Hall, John Balaban, John Brehm, and Robert Creeley as examples. She writes, "We have reached the point [where] we are being asked to believe that a text block, chopped randomly into flat, declarative lines, is a poem."

If the profusion of prose made to look like poetry is disconcerting, it is equally annoying when similar fare is dished up under the faddish moniker "prose poem," a form in which text is set like prose in

GO ON TO THE NEXT PAGE

ragged or justified type, line breaks thereby losing significance. The "poem" part of the equation promises greater density and compression than we normally expect from prose, achieved through poetic devices such as rhythm, imagery, metaphor, simile, and figures of speech.

William Blake and Christopher Smart wrote prose poems long before the term was invented. Poe and Baudelaire more consciously a century later. In our own time Russell Edson has written brilliantly in this genre, producing a body of original work that can hold its own with the best poetry of our time.

The current popularity of the genre is attested to by Peter Johnson, editor of *The Best of the Prose Poem: An International Journal.* "I have read so many prose poems," he complains, "that I feel as if a large gray eraser is squatting in the hollow of my head. I am not even sure what my criteria are, anymore." At least one prestigious graduate writing program understands the genre well enough to offer students an entire course in "The Prose Poem."

The jury is still out on definitions. Some critics deny that the term has any meaning at all. Others concede that the term is muddied, since it is difficult to define the genre without opening the door to the heightened prose of many a novelist and short story writer. Still, the term leads us to expect a combination of and tension between prose and poetic elements. Unfortunately, these expectations aren't always met.

Examples abound. Here are two excerpts from "Doubt," by Fanny Howe, which appeared in *The Best American Poetry: 2001*, edited by David Lehman and Robert Hass, both long associated with writing programs:

> Virginia Woolf committed suicide in 1941 when the German bombing campaign against England was at its peak and when she was reading Freud whom she had staved off until then.

> Edith Stein, recently and controversially beatified by the Pope, who had successfully worked to transform an existential vocabulary into a theological one, was taken to Auschwitz in August 1942.

These excerpts are part of a "prose poem" that goes on for four pages. Howe offers interesting insights in a style appropriate for a scholarly or critical journal. But it's hard to find any definition from Aristotle to the present that would admit such writing as poetry, certainly not under the term free verse or open form; for it has been the concern of responsible poets in those movements to find non-traditional, personalized strategies for making poetry musical. "Poetry atrophies, when it gets too far from music," Ezra Pound observes in his *ABC of Reading.* Howe's piece lacks the rhythmical, metaphorical texture needed to fulfill the poetry part of the prose-poem equation. In her author's note Howe explains that she "can no longer make distinctions" between poetry and prose. It is unfortunate that the editors of an anthology entitled *The Best American Poetry* are equally unable to make a distinction that readers who buy a book with that title have a right to expect.

The ever-increasing prosification of poetry assures prospective students that they needn't employ meter or rhyme or cadence or figurative language, or any of the devices, for that matter, in a standard poet's dictionary; that the drabbest encyclopedia prose, even

GO ON TO THE NEXT PAGE

technical jargon, can be hailed as "poetry" of the highest order. It's the profession's way of redefining the art downward to accommodate its talent pool.

32. The phrase "aesthetic trends" in line 11 most nearly means

    (A) movements in the arts designed to challenge conventional notions of artistic beauty
    (B) literary theories about what makes one text "better" than another
    (C) fashions in what is regarded as worthwhile in the arts and literature
    (D) the increasing tendency of poetry to be like prose

33. In line 15, *pedestrian* most nearly means

    (A) pedantic
    (B) undistinguished
    (C) popular
    (D) static

34. Based on what he says in the first paragraph of the passage the author would probably agree that

    (A) quite a few people involved in teaching the writing of poetry at American colleges and universities care more about furthering their careers than encouraging the writing and publication of good poetry
    (B) most of the people involved in teaching the writing of poetry in American colleges and universities care more about maintaining a high standard of poetry than they do about encouraging the production of poetry, regardless of its quality
    (C) many of those who teach the writing of poetry in American colleges and universities do so because they are unable to write good poetry themselves
    (D) most teachers of the writing of poetry in American colleges and universities are, as a rule, unable to distinguish good poetry from bad poetry

35. The "real thing" in line 17 refers to

    (A) prose poems
    (B) good prose
    (C) poetry
    (D) original writing of any type

GO ON TO THE NEXT PAGE

36. It is most likely that the author used the phrase "dished up" rather than the word "published" in line 33 in order to

(A) suggest that prose poetry is, in many ways, like fast food
(B) colorfully emphasize his dislike for currently fashionable prose poetry
(C) create the impression in the reader's mind that he is not above using colloquial language
(D) demonstrate that he is capable of poetic expression as well as critical analysis

37. In line 38, "equation" most nearly means

(A) the combination of poetic elements with elements from prose to create prose poetry
(B) the use of poetic devices in prose to create poetic prose
(C) the poetic elements in prose poetry that can be quantified
(D) the widespread but incorrect belief that the production of good poetry (of any sort) is, like everything, governed by precise, definable laws

38. According to the author, William Blake and Christopher Smart

(A) were not aware that some of their work was prose
(B) worked primarily in the genre of prose poetry
(C) did not consciously set out to write work that would later come to be called prose poetry
(D) were largely responsible for the creation of the literary genre now known as prose poetry

39. The author's tone in lines 58–61 ("At least one . . . 'The Prose Poem.'") is most accurately described as

(A) ironic
(B) sarcastic
(C) self-deprecating
(D) ambivalent

40. The phrase "heightened prose" in line 66 refers to

(A) poetic prose
(B) the prose of poets
(C) pretentious writing
(D) profoundly meaningful prose

41. Which of the following statements would the author of this passage be likely to agree with?

(A) Prose poetry never succeeds as poetry.
(B) Writing free verse frees a poet from having to follow the conventions of poetry as a genre.
(C) Any distinction between poetic prose and prose poetry is meaningless.
(D) To be considered poetry a piece of writing must make significant use of rhythm and metaphor.

42. The author includes the two excerpts from "Doubt" (lines 77–86) primarily to

(A) provide examples to support his contention that many prose poems being written do not successfully combine prose elements and poetic elements
(B) provide support for the view that prose poetry is a legitimate genre
(C) demonstrate that prose poems can make effective use of traditional poetic devices
(D) show that prose poems are uniquely suited for literary criticism because they combine the analytic precision of prose with the intuitive insight of poetry

GO ON TO THE NEXT PAGE

Questions 43–52 are based on the following passage.

This passage is from S. Jeffress Williams, Kurt Dodd, Kathleen Krafft Gohn, 1990, Coasts in Crisis, Coastal Change: U.S. Geological Survey Circular 1075.

Diverse and complex natural processes continually change coasts physically, chemically, and biologically, at scales that range from microscopic (grains of sand) to global (changes in sea level). Regional and local characteristics of coasts control the differing interactions and relative importance of these natural processes.

Coastal lands and sediments are constantly in motion. Breaking waves move sand along the coast, eroding sand in one area and depositing it on an adjacent beach. Tidal cycles bring sand onto the beach and carry it back into the surf. Rivers carry sediment to the coast and build deltas into the open water. Storms cause deep erosion in one area and leave thick overwash deposits in another. Plants retain sediment in wetlands and impede movement of coastal dunes. Natural processes that change the water level also affect coastal dynamics. Taken individually, each natural process of coastal transport is complex; taken collectively, they create an intricate system that attempts to achieve a dynamic balance.

Winds create waves that ripple across the surface of lakes and seas until they break on the shallowing bottom and crash into the shore. In many areas, prevailing winds produce waves that consistently approach the coast at oblique angles. Even the slightest angle between the land and the waves will create currents that transport sediment along the shore. These longshore currents are a primary agent of coastal movement; they are a major cause of sand migration along barrier and mainland beaches.

Tides ebb and flood in response to the gravitational attraction of the moon and sun; exceptional high and low tides occur each month when the sun and moon are aligned. Tides help determine where the waves break—low on the beach at low tide, high on the beach at high tide—and, therefore, where sand is deposited and removed. Rip tides, or undertow, occur along most beaches and can move significant amounts of sand offshore.

Storm systems along coasts contain high winds, create large waves, and cause storm surges that raise water levels as much as 7 meters above normal. Although storms are sporadic, they are the primary cause of beach erosion along many coasts. Storms carry sand seaward, forming offshore bars; much of this sand migrates landward during calm weather. Some areas are more storm prone than others. Storms often are concentrated in specific seasons; along the eastern seaboard, for example, hurricanes occur in the late summer and early fall, and storms are especially frequent during the winter months. These seasonal trends result in a general difference between the winter "eroding" beach and the summer "building" beach that is most common along parts of the west coast.

In addition to the daily cycles of tides, many other forces lead to significant changes in water level. Predominantly closed bodies of water such as lakes experience dramatic water-level changes in response to precipitation, spring snowmelt, and evaporation.

Other local changes in water level occur when the land either rises or falls relative to

GO ON TO THE NEXT PAGE

the water. Along tectonically active coasts, such as the coast of earthquake-prone southern California, land may rise as much as 4 centimeters per century. The Earth's crust in parts of Alaska and the Great Lakes area, which was pressed down by the weight of the massive ice sheets that blanketed the north during the last great ice age, is now rising due to the retreat of the glaciers.

Global changes in sea level result from tectonic processes, such as the down- or up-warping of the ocean basins, or from changes in the total volume of water in the oceans. During the last great ice age, which began 36,000 years ago, huge amounts of ocean water were transformed into glaciers, resulting in a 100-meter drop in the global sea level. We are still emerging from that ice age, and sea level has been rising continuously over the last 20,000 years; during the past century, the rate of sea level rise has averaged 10–15 centimeters per century worldwide.

The slope of a coast is critical to determining how water-level changes will affect it. Steeply sloping coasts experience small shifts in their coastlines as the water level changes; however, because wave action along steep coasts is concentrated within a narrow zone, small water-level increases can result in significant erosion of bluffs or dunes. On a gently sloping coast, like the U.S. east coast or around the Gulf of Mexico, small changes in water level cause the coastline to shift dramatically; however, the gentle slope absorbs and dissipates the waves' energy along a broad front.

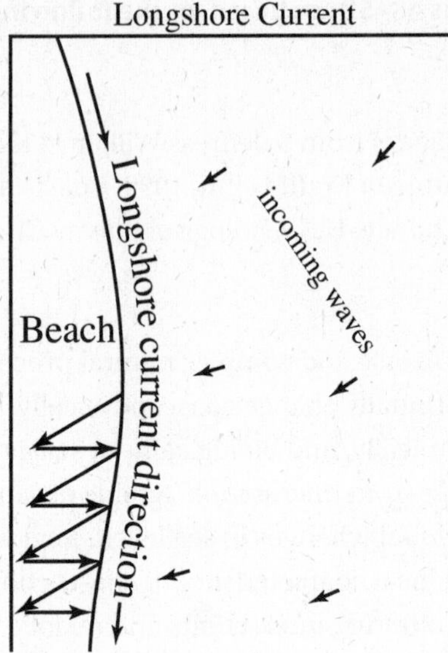

43. The most appropriate title for the passage would be

(A) Ocean Coasts
(B) The Ocean and the Land
(C) Coastal Slope and Sea-level Change
(D) Coastal Change

44. The word *continually* as it is used in line 2 most nearly means

(A) continuously
(B) regularly occurring
(C) gradually
(D) eternally

45. The word *shallowing* as it is used in line 28 most nearly means

(A) becoming more shallow
(B) shallow
(C) varying
(D) becoming less shallow

GO ON TO THE NEXT PAGE

46. Which of the following, mentioned in the second paragraph, are not elaborated on in the rest of the passage?
    (A) waves
    (B) tides
    (C) storms
    (D) plants

47. If waves hit a shore so that there is no angle between the land and the waves
    (A) an undertow will be created
    (B) sediment will be deposited along the shore as a result
    (C) sediment will not be moved along the shore as a result
    (D) currents will be created along the shore

48. Which of the following provides evidence for the answer to the previous question?
    (A) "Breaking . . . beach." (lines 10–12)
    (B) "Winds . . . shore." (lines 26–29)
    (C) "Even . . . shore." (lines 31–34)
    (D) "These . . . beaches." (lines 34–37)

49. In the diagram the arrows in the section marked "Beach" probably represent
    (A) waves coming onto the beach and then back into the ocean, carrying sand along the shore
    (B) areas of the beach that are not affected by waves
    (C) areas of the beach most affected by a longshore current
    (D) waves that have no effect on the shore

50. According to the passage, which of the following does not affect sea level?
    (A) tides
    (B) glaciers melting
    (C) storms
    (D) the slope of coasts

51. Large water-level changes in the ocean off the U.S. east coast would most likely
    (A) cause a great deal of erosion on beaches there
    (B) increase rainfall along the U.S. east coast
    (C) shift the location of coastlines there significantly
    (D) cause beaches to disappear in many places on the U.S. east coast

52. If the Earth's climate became warmer ocean levels would be likely to
    (A) fall
    (B) rise
    (C) remain the same
    (D) rise briefly, then fall dramatically

STOP

If there is still time remaining, you may review your answers.

WRITING AND LANGUAGE TEST

35 MINUTES, 44 QUESTIONS

Turn to Section 2 of your answer sheet to answer the questions in this section.

Directions: Questions follow each of the passages below. Some questions ask you how the passage might be changed to improve the expression of ideas. Other questions ask you how the passage might be altered to correct errors in grammar, usage, and punctuation. One or more graphics accompany some passages. You will be required to consider these graphics as you answer questions about editing the passage.

There are three types of questions. In the first type, a part of the passage is underlined. The second type is based on a certain part of the passage. The third type is based on the entire passage.

Read each passage. Then, choose the answer to each question that changes the passage so that it is consistent with the conventions of standard written English. One of the answer choices for many questions is "NO CHANGE." Choosing this answer means that you believe the best answer is to make no change in the passage.

Questions 1–11 are based on the following passage and supplementary material.

Highlights of Women's Earnings

In 2011, women who were full-time wage and salary workers had median usual weekly earnings of $684, about 82 percent of median earnings for male full-time wage and salary workers ($832). In 1979, the first year for which **1** comparing earnings data are available, women earned 62 percent of what men earned.

2 Women working full time in management, business, and financial operations jobs had median weekly earnings of $977 in 2011, which is more than women earned in any other major

1. (A) NO CHANGE
   (B) comparison
   (C) comparable
   (D) comparability

2. (A) NO CHANGE
   (B) Women worked
   (C) Women have worked
   (D) Women, those working

GO ON TO THE NEXT PAGE

occupational category. 3 The second highest paying job group for women was professional and related occupations, in which their median weekly earnings were $919. Within professional and related occupations, women who were lawyers ($1,631), pharmacists ($1,898), and physicians ($1,527) had the highest earnings.

The occupational distributions of female and male full-time workers differ 4 significantly compared with men. Relatively few women work in construction, production, or transportation occupations, and women are far

3. At this point, the writer is considering adding the following sentence:

Within management, business, and financial operations occupations, women who were chief executives and computer and information systems managers had the highest median weekly earnings ($1,464 and $1,543, respectively).

Should the writer make this addition here?

(A) Yes, because the information in this sentence provides a contrast with the information in the previous sentence.
(B) Yes, because it provides more information about the earnings of women in a sub-category of workers mentioned in the previous sentence.
(C) No, because the information in this sentence is too specific for a report of this kind.
(D) No, because no supporting evidence is given for the information in this sentence.

4. (A) NO CHANGE
(B) significantly. Compared with men relatively few
(C) significantly. It is relative that few
(D) significantly compared with men, relatively. Few

GO ON TO THE NEXT PAGE

Distribution of full-time wage and salary employment, by sex and major occupation group, 2011 annual averages

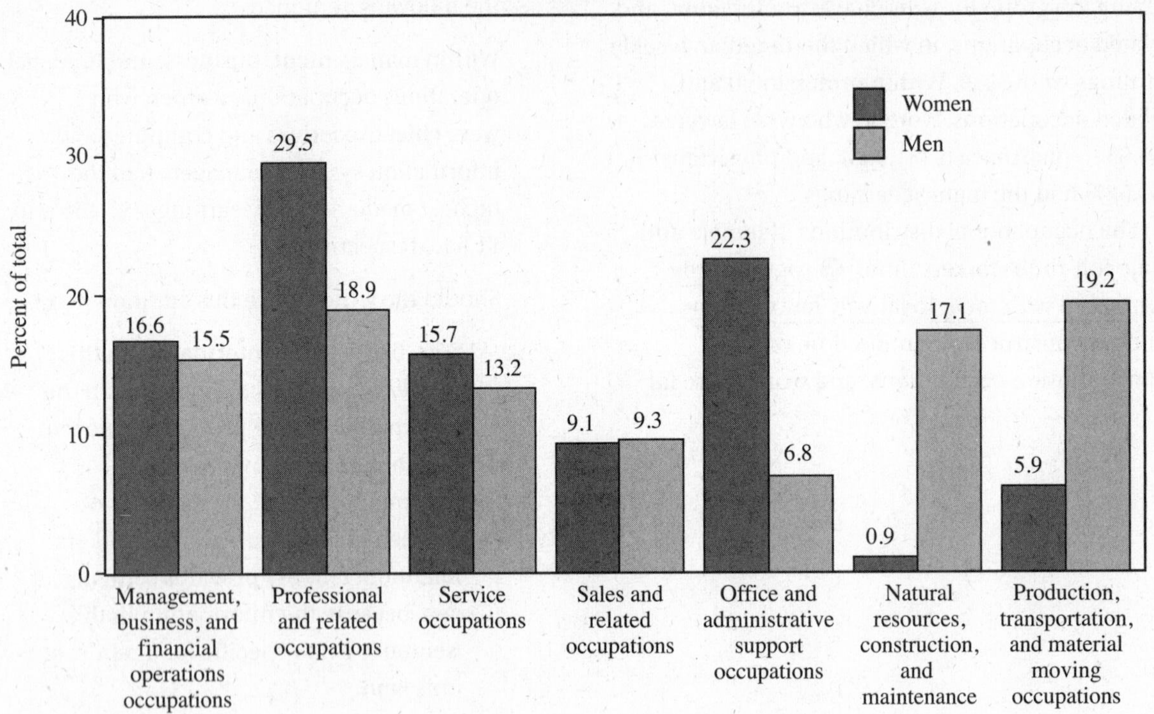

more concentrated in ❺ <u>natural resources occupations.</u>

Women are more likely than men to work in professional and related ❻ <u>occupations. Being within this category, though,</u> the proportion of women employed in the higher paying job groups is much smaller than the proportion of men employed in them. In 2011, 8 percent of female

5. Which choice most accurately and effectively represents the information in the graph?
   (A) NO CHANGE
   (B) sales and related occupations
   (C) office and administrative support occupations
   (D) management, business and financial operations occupations

6. (A) NO CHANGE
   (B) occupations. Within this occupational category, though,
   (C) occupations. Looking at those which are within this category, though,
   (D) occupations which are within this category. Though

GO ON TO THE NEXT PAGE

professionals were employed in (7) the relative high-paying computer and engineering fields, compared with 44 percent of male professionals. Professional women were more likely to work in education and healthcare occupations, in which the pay is generally lower (8) than computer and engineering jobs. (9) Sixty-nine percent of female professionals worked in the education and healthcare fields in 2011, compared with 30 percent of male professionals.

Women are more likely than men to work part time—that is, less than 35 hours per week on a sole, or principal, job. Women who worked part time made up 26 percent of all female wage and salary workers in 2011. (10) Similarly, 13 percent of men in wage and salary jobs worked part time. Unlike full-time workers, women and men who worked part time had similar median earnings. Median weekly earnings for female part-timers were $235 in 2011, (11) a little different than the $226 median for their male counterparts.

7. (A) NO CHANGE
   (B) relating to
   (C) relation to the high-paying
   (D) the relatively high-paying

8. (A) NO CHANGE
   (B) than that which would be earned in
   (C) than that in
   (D) than what employees get paid in

9. The writer is considering deleting the underlined sentence. Should he keep it or delete it?
   (A) Keep it, because it provides a detail that supports the main topic of the paragraph.
   (B) Keep it, because it helps link the paragraph it is in to the following paragraph.
   (C) Delete it, because it contradicts information provided earlier in the passage.
   (D) Delete it, because the information it provides is not relevant to what is described in the paragraph it is in.

10. (A) NO CHANGE
    (B) In contrast,
    (C) Consequently,
    (D) Notwithstanding this,

11. (A) NO CHANGE
    (B) with little difference than
    (C) little different from
    (D) and this is a little different than

GO ON TO THE NEXT PAGE

Questions 12–22 are based on the following passage.

Arctic Science

The Arctic is a gigantic "natural laboratory" of surprising **12** divergence that offers exciting research possibilities in almost every branch of science.

13 The field lines of the magnetic field surrounding the Earth converge in the polar regions. This means that charged particles from the sun enter the Earth's atmosphere in these regions, producing **14** ostentatious effects such as the aurora, magnetic storms, and ionospheric disturbances, which may black out radio communication.

Lower in the atmosphere, the high-velocity westerly jet stream is affected by processes of energy exchange at the Earth's surface in the Arctic—by sea ice distribution and ocean and land temperatures—and **15** in turn effects the weather and climate of the entire hemisphere or even the whole Earth.

Nowhere else is ice and snow in all its forms—sea ice, glaciers, permafrost, river and lake ice—as widespread and diverse as in the Arctic. Alaska is an ideal laboratory for studying these ice **16** forms. It is from individual ice crystals under a microscope to the millions of square kilometers of sea ice as seen by a satellite. The solution of practical problems associated with avalanches, building roads and houses on permafrost, extracting petroleum from ice-covered waters, and numerous others, **17** depending on fundamental research that can be conducted in the Alaska setting.

12. (A) NO CHANGE
    (B) diversity
    (C) discrepancy
    (D) incongruity

13. Which choice is the best transition from the previous paragraph to this one?
    (A) Scientists from several nations have worked for many years in this "laboratory."
    (B) Recent studies show that climate change in the Arctic predicts climate change elsewhere on Earth.
    (C) When one examines this large-scale natural laboratory, starting in outer space above the Arctic, a number of fascinating features become apparent.
    (D) This article will concentrate on the magnetic field in the polar regions.

14. (A) NO CHANGE
    (B) glaring
    (C) conspicuous
    (D) protrusive

15. (A) NO CHANGE
    (B) in turn affects
    (C) in turn effect
    (D) in turn affect

16. Which choice most effectively combines the sentences at the underlined portion?
    (A) forms from individuals, ice
    (B) forming from individual ice
    (C) which form from individual ice
    (D) forms, from individual ice

17. (A) NO CHANGE
    (B) depend on
    (C) depends on
    (D) depended on

GO ON TO THE NEXT PAGE

[1] A major ocean covers a large area around the pole in the Northern Hemisphere. [2] This ocean is largely ice covered and exhibits a wide range of dynamic behavior of its ice and water masses. [3] Since from 5 to 7% of the world's potentially most devastating earthquakes occur in Alaska, this is an ideal location for the study of the Earth's structure and its often violent surface movements. [4] Alaska is also part of the Pacific "Rim of **18** Fire," this is where tectonic activity has created a unique and dangerous environment. [5] Within its boundary, Alaska encloses **19** a long island, the arc associated with a deep ocean trench, 40 active volcanoes, and heavy earthquake activity. **20**

These brief examples illustrate the uniqueness and diversity in structure, dynamics, and behavior of the arctic regions as an important part of the whole Earth. Other nations are expending great efforts in the study of the Arctic because they understand that the keys to many of our planet's present and future problems may lie in this **21** region if the United States is to participate in this process in any meaningful way. It must begin **22** involving in arctic research now.

18. (A) NO CHANGE
    (B) Fire," being
    (C) Fire," where
    (D) Fire." It is where

19. (A) NO CHANGE
    (B) a long island of arc
    (C) a long island arc
    (D) a long island for an arc

20. For the sake of the logic and cohesion of this paragraph, sentence 3 should be placed:
    (A) where it is
    (B) after sentence 1
    (C) after sentence 4
    (D) after sentence 5

21. For the sake of clarity of expression and meaning, the underlined portion of the sentences should be written as follows:
    (A) as they are now
    (B) region if the United States is to participate in this process. In any meaningful way, it
    (C) region. If the United States is to participate in this process in any meaningful way, it
    (D) region, if the United States is to participate in this process, in any meaningful way. It

22. (A) NO CHANGE
    (B) to involve itself
    (C) to involve it
    (D) to involve

GO ON TO THE NEXT PAGE

Questions 23–33 are based on the following passage.

Dining Roman Style

23 The prodigality of the Romans in matters of eating is well-known, 24 extensive to all matters connected with the pleasures of the table. In their rooms, their couches, and all the furniture of their entertainments, 25 this was where magnificence and extravagance were carried to their highest point. The rich had several of these apartments, to be used at different seasons, or on various

23. The writer is considering adding the following sentence to the beginning of this paragraph:

    One of the most important apartments in the whole house was the triclinium, or dining room, named for the three beds which encompassed the table on three sides, leaving the fourth open to the attendants.

    Should the writer make this addition here?

    (A) Yes, because the focus of this paragraph is the triclinium. This sentence thus serves as an appropriate topic sentence.
    (B) Yes, because this sentence introduces the topic of Roman sleeping arrangements, which is discussed further in the rest of the paragraph.
    (C) No, because the focus of the paragraph is on Roman extravagance in dining.
    (D) No, because the information given in the sentence is repeated elsewhere in the paragraph.

24. (A) NO CHANGE
    (B) and it extended
    (C) it extended
    (D) extends

25. (A) NO CHANGE
    (B) it was magnificence and extravagance that were carried
    (C) this was where they carried magnificence and extravagance
    (D) magnificence and extravagance were carried

GO ON TO THE NEXT PAGE

occasions. (26) Lucullus celebrated, for his wealth and profuse expenditure, had a certain standard of expenditure for each (27) triclinium. Telling his servants which hall he was to sup in, they knew exactly the style of entertainment to be prepared. There is a well-known story of the way in which he deceived Pompeii and Cicero, when they insisted on going home with him to see his family supper, by merely sending word home that he would sup in the Apollo, one of the most splendid of his halls, in which he never gave an entertainment for less than 50,000 denarii. Sometimes the (28) ceiling was contriving to open and let down a second course of meats, with showers of flowers and perfumed waters, while rope-dancers performed over the heads of the company.

The triclinium was (29) twice as long, for it was broad, and divided, as it were, into two parts—the upper (30) occupied the table and the couches, the lower left empty for the convenience of the attendants and spectators. Around the former the walls, up to a certain height, were ornamented with valuable hangings. The decorations of the rest of the room were noble, and yet (31) owing to the destination; garlands, entwined with ivy and vine-branches, divided the walls into compartments bordered with fanciful ornaments; in the center of each of which were painted with admirable elegance young Fauns,

26. (A) NO CHANGE
(B) Lucullus, celebrated for his wealth and profuse expenditure,
(C) Lucullus was celebrating his wealth and profuse expenditure, they
(D) Lucullus celebrating his wealth and profuse expenditure, and he

27. Which choice most effectively combines the sentences at the underlined portion?
(A) triclinium, in telling his servants
(B) triclinium, when he told his servants
(C) triclinium, so that when his servants were told
(D) triclinium, being that he told his servants

28. (A) NO CHANGE
(B) ceiling was contrived
(C) ceiling contrived
(D) ceiling had contrived

29. (A) NO CHANGE
(B) in length twice what it was in breadth,
(C) twice as long if it was broad,
(D) twice as long as it was broad,

30. (A) NO CHANGE
(B) occupied by
(C) occupying
(D) occupied with

31. (A) NO CHANGE
(B) appropriate to
(C) surprising for
(D) foreign to

GO ON TO THE NEXT PAGE

or half-naked Bacchantes, carrying vases and all the furniture of festive meetings. Above the columns was a large frieze, divided into twelve compartments; each of these was surmounted by one of the signs of the **32** Zodiac, contained in it paintings of the meats which were in highest season in each month; so that under Sagittary (December) **33** there were shrimps, shellfish, and birds of passage; under Capricorn (January), lobsters, sea fish, wild boar and game; under Aquarius (February), ducks, plovers, pigeons, and water rails.

32. (A) NO CHANGE
(B) Zodiac, wherein contained were
(C) Zodiac, contained within were
(D) Zodiac and contained

33. (A) NO CHANGE
(B) there was
(C) was
(D) being

GO ON TO THE NEXT PAGE

Questions 34–44 are based on the following passage.

Causes of Woman's Subjection
(originally published in 1887)

Writers on the question of the origin of woman's subjection to man differ as to the cause of the universal **34** corruption of woman in all periods and nations.

One of the greatest minds of the century **35** thrown a ray of light on this gloomy picture by tracing the origin of woman's slavery to the same principle of selfishness and love of power in man that has thus far dominated all weaker nations and classes. **36** The slavish instinct of an oppressed class has led it to toil

34. (A) NO CHANGE
    (B) criticism
    (C) knowledge
    (D) fear

35. (A) NO CHANGE
    (B) throwing
    (C) has thrown
    (D) being thrown

36. At this point, the writer is considering adding the following sentence:

    This brings hope of final emancipation, for as all nations and classes are gradually, one after another, asserting and maintaining their independence, the path is clear for woman to follow.

    Should the writer make this addition here?

    (A) Yes, because this sentence provides clear examples of the male domination of nations and classes described in the preceding sentence. These examples serve as a link to the description of female subservience described in the following sentence.
    (B) Yes, because this sentence explains what the "ray of light" mentioned in the preceding sentence is. This sentence says that women's freedom will come about as a result of women asserting their independence just as other oppressed groups did to attain independence.
    (C) No, because the issue of national and class emancipation is not related to the issue of women's emancipation.
    (D) No, because there is nothing stated in the preceding sentence that suggests that women will achieve "final emancipation." On the contrary, it suggests that male domination of nations, classes, and women will continue forever.

GO ON TO THE NEXT PAGE

patiently through the ages, 37 given all and asking little, cheerfully sharing with man all perils and privations by land and sea, that husband and sons might attain 38 honor and success, while justice and freedom for herself is her latest and highest demand.

Another writer asserts that the tyranny of man over woman has its roots, after all, in his nobler 39 feelings; his love, his chivalry, and his desire to protect woman in the barbarous periods of pillage, lust, and war. 40 But anywhere that the roots are traced to, the results at this hour are equally disastrous to woman. Her best interests and happiness do not seem to have been consulted in the arrangements made for her 41 protection, as being bought and sold, caressed and crucified at the will and pleasure of her master. But if a chivalrous desire to protect woman has always been the mainspring of man's dominion over her, it should have prompted him to place in her hands the same weapons of defense he has found to be most effective against wrong and oppression.

It is often asserted that as woman has always been man's slave—subject—inferior—dependent, under all forms of government and religion, slavery must be her normal condition. This might have some weight 42 if not the vast majority of men also been enslaved for centuries to kings and popes, and orders of nobility, who, in the progress of civilization, have reached complete equality. And did we not also see the great changes in

37. (A) NO CHANGE
(B) give
(C) giving
(D) gave

38. For the sake of clarity of meaning and effectiveness of expression, the underlined portion of the sentence should be written as follows:

(A) as it is now
(B) honor and success, justice and freedom for herself have been
(C) honor and success, justice and freedom
(D) honor and success. Justice and freedom

39. (A) NO CHANGE
(B) feelings his love
(C) feelings: his love
(D) feelings and they are his love

40. For the sake of clarity of expression and meaning, the underlined portion of the sentence should be written as follows:

(A) as it is now
(B) wherever the roots may be traced,
(C) the roots may be traced anywhere,
(D) anywhere one traces the roots, it will be found that

41. Write the underlined portion of the sentence to form two distinct sentences that make sense.

(A) protection. Being she was bought
(B) protection. She, as bought
(C) protection. She has been bought
(D) protection. She, bought

42. (A) NO CHANGE
(B) were it not
(C) was it not
(D) had not

GO ON TO THE NEXT PAGE

woman's condition, the marvelous transformation in her character, from a toy in the Turkish harem, or a drudge in the German fields, **43** or a leader of thought in the literary circles of France, England, and America!

In an age when the wrongs of society are adjusted in the courts and at the ballot-box, material force yields to reason and majorities. Woman's steady march onward, and her growing desire for a broader outlook, prove that she has not reached her normal condition, and that society has not yet **44** acquiesced all that is necessary for its attainment.

43. (A) NO CHANGE
    (B) to a leader
    (C) but a leader
    (D) for a leader

44. (A) NO CHANGE
    (B) conceded
    (C) assented
    (D) complied

STOP

If there is still time remaining, you may review your answers.

3

MATH TEST (NO CALCULATOR)

25 MINUTES, 20 QUESTIONS

Turn to Section 3 of your answer sheet to answer the questions in this section.

Directions: For questions 1–15, solve each problem and choose the best answer from the given options. Fill in the corresponding circle on your answer document. For questions 16–20, solve the problem and fill in the answer on the answer sheet grid. Please use scrap paper to work out your answers.

Notes:

- You **CANNOT** use a calculator on this section.
- All variables and expressions represent real numbers unless indicated otherwise.
- All figures are drawn to scale unless indicated otherwise.
- All figures are in a plane unless indicated otherwise.
- Unless indicated otherwise, the domain of a given function is the set of all real numbers x for which the function has real values.

REFERENCE INFORMATION

Area Facts

$A = \ell w$

$A = \frac{1}{2} bh$

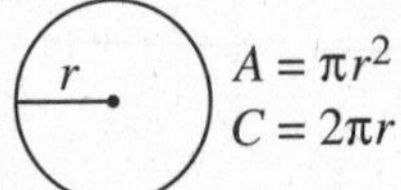

Volume Facts

$V = \ell wh$

$V = \frac{4}{3}\pi r^3$

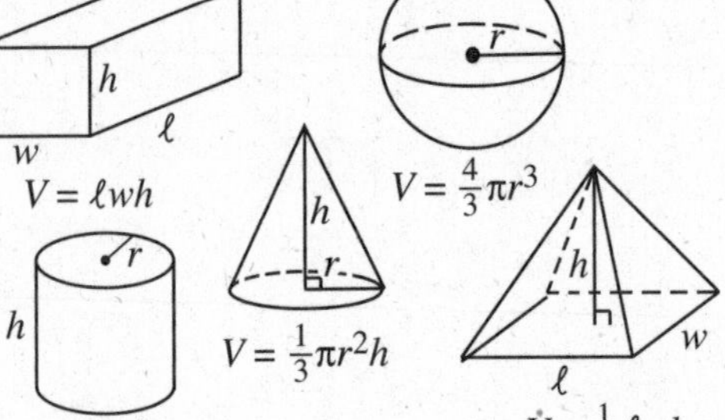

Triangle Facts

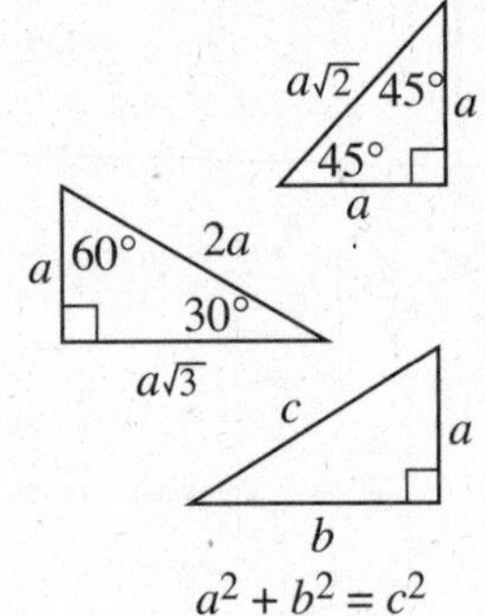

The arc of a circle contains 360°.
The arc of a circle contains 2π radians.
The sum of the measures of the angles in a triangle is 180°.

1. Which of the following is equal to –2 for some value of m?

(A) $|m-2|-2$
(B) $|m-2|+2$
(C) $|2-m|+2$
(D) $|2+m|+2$

2. If $f(x) = x^2 + 2$ and $g(x) = 2x + 3$, what is the value of $g(3) - f(-2)$?

(A) 15
(B) 9
(C) 3
(D) 4

GO ON TO THE NEXT PAGE

3. $2x - 3y = 24$
   $x + 4.5y = -12$

   In the system of equations above, what is the value of the product of x and y?

   (A) 12
   (B) 18
   (C) –24
   (D) –36

4. A shoe manufacturer wants to come up with a general rule to correlate the number of holes with the length of their shoelaces. The following table shows the number of holes in a shoe and the length, in inches, of its shoelace.

Holes	Length
4	12
6	18
8	24

   If the table above represents a linear function, a hiking boot that has 18 holes should have shoelaces that are how long?

   (A) 45 inches
   (B) 48 inches
   (C) 54 inches
   (D) 63 inches

5. If $m = 2x^3 + 3x - 11$ and $n = 4x^2 + 5x - 7$, what is $3n - m$ in terms of x?

   (A) $-2x^3 - 4x^2 - 2x - 18$
   (B) $-(2x^3 + 3x^2 - 5x - 6)$
   (C) $2x^3 - 12x^2 - 12x + 10$
   (D) $-2x^3 + 12x^2 + 12x - 10$

6. If $\frac{1}{3x-1} = \frac{2}{x}$ then $x = ?$

   (A) $\frac{2}{5}$
   (B) 2
   (C) $\frac{5}{2}$
   (D) 3

7. Jenna needs to take a taxicab ride in Chicago to go to an important job interview. The taxi service she has selected provides the following fee schedule:

   First $\frac{1}{4}$ mile: \$2.00

   Each $\frac{1}{4}$ mile after: \$1.25

   Excluding a tip, Jenna's fare was \$15.75. How many miles did she travel?

   (A) 2
   (B) 2.5
   (C) 2.75
   (D) 3

8. $\frac{2}{3}x - \frac{5}{9}y = -7$
   $bx - \frac{10}{3}y = 17$

   In the system of equations above, b is a constant. If the system has no solution, what is the value of b?

   (A) –3.75
   (B) 3.75
   (C) 4
   (D) 4.4

9. $\sqrt{n-b} = n - 2$

   If $b = -4$, what is the solution set to the equation above?

   (A) {–5}
   (B) {0}
   (C) {5}
   (D) {0, 5}

GO ON TO THE NEXT PAGE

10. In a homecoming game, a girls' basketball team scored $\frac{1}{3}$ of its points during the first quarter, $\frac{1}{4}$ of its points during the second quarter, $\frac{1}{3}$ of its points in the third quarter, and 8 points in the fourth quarter. How many points did the team score in the game?

    (A) 84
    (B) 90
    (C) 96
    (D) 102

11. If $x^2 + y^2 = 12$ and $xy = -13$, what is the value of $2(x - y)^2$?

    (A) −26
    (B) 1
    (C) 38
    (D) 76

12. The number of bacteria in petri dish #1 is A. Petri dish #2 contains twice as many as dish #1 and is represented by the value B. Petri dish #3 has 17 more bacteria than the quantity in dish #2 and is represented by C. Which of the following expressions shows C in terms of A?

    (A) C = 3A − 17
    (B) C = 2A + 17
    (C) C = 2A
    (D) C = A + 17

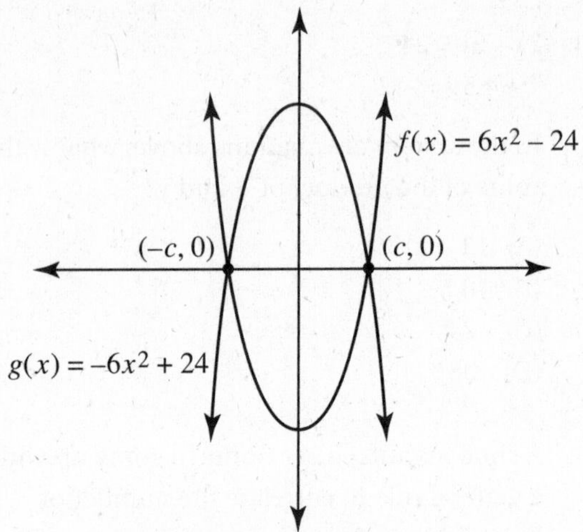

Figure Not Drawn to Scale

13. The functions f and g, defined by $f(x) = 6x^2 - 24$ and $g(x) = -6x^2 + 24$, are graphed in the xy-plane above. The graphs above intersect at the points $(c, 0)$ and $(-c, 0)$. What is the value of c?

    (A) −2
    (B) 0
    (C) 2
    (D) 4

14. Which of the following is an equivalent form of $\frac{7}{2-3i}$ (Note: $i = \sqrt{-1}$)?

    (A) $3.5 + 4i$
    (B) $\frac{14+21i}{13}$
    (C) $1 + 3i$
    (D) $-\frac{14+21i}{5}$

15. What are the solutions to $6x^2 + 12x - 15 = 0$?

    (A) $2 \pm \sqrt{14}$
    (B) $\frac{2 \pm \sqrt{14}}{2}$
    (C) $\frac{-2 \pm \sqrt{14}}{2}$
    (D) $-2 \pm 4\sqrt{2}$

GO ON TO THE NEXT PAGE

Grid-in Response Directions

In questions 16–20, first solve the problem, and then enter your answer on the grid provided on the answer sheet. The instructions for entering your answers follow.

- First, write your answer in the boxes at the top of the grid.
- Second, grid your answer in the columns below the boxes.
- Use the fraction bar in the first row or the decimal point in the second row to enter fractions and decimals.

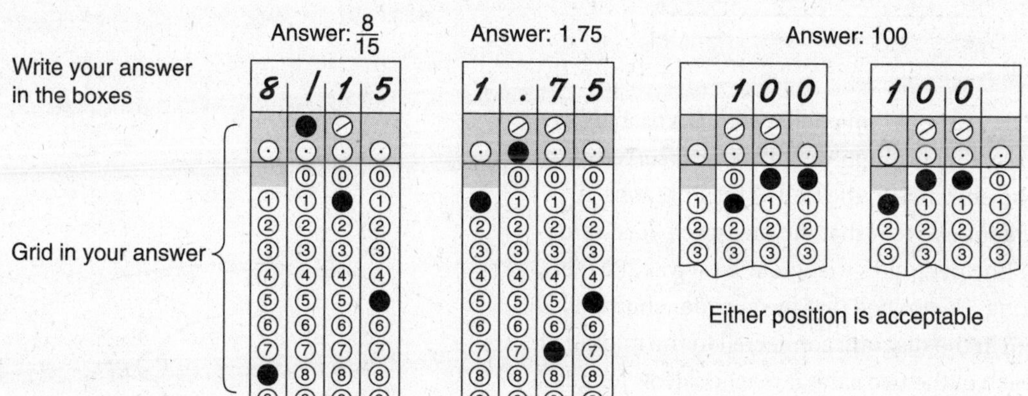

- Grid only one space in each column.
- Entering the answer in the boxes is recommended as an aid in gridding but is not required.
- The machine scoring your exam can read only what you grid, so you **must grid-in your answers correctly to get credit**.
- If a question has more than one correct answer, grid-in only one of them.
- The grid does not have a minus sign; so no answer can be negative.
- A mixed number *must* be converted to an improper fraction or a decimal before it is gridded. Enter $1\frac{1}{4}$ as $\frac{5}{4}$ or 1.25; the machine will interpret 11/4 as $\frac{11}{4}$ and mark it wrong.
- **All decimals must be entered as accurately as possible.** Here are three acceptable ways of gridding

$$\frac{3}{11} = 0.272727\ldots$$

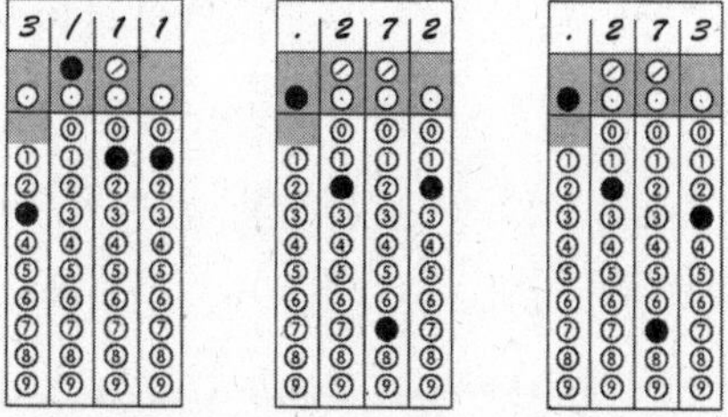

- Note that rounding to .273 is acceptable because you are using the full grid, but you would receive **no credit** for .3 or .27, because they are less accurate.

3

3

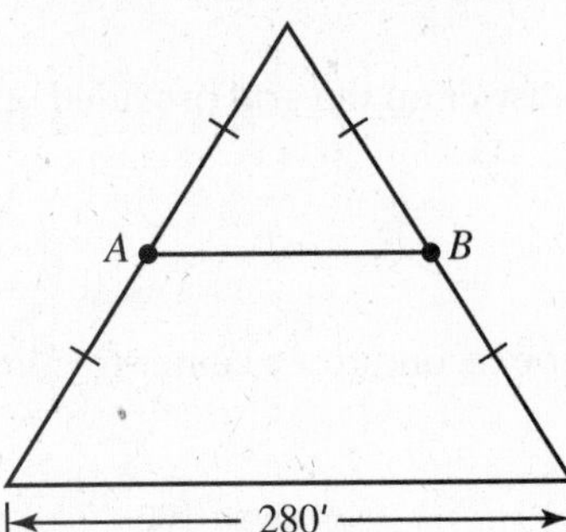

16. The Luxor pyramid in Egypt has a triangular base that is roughly equilateral; it served as the entrance to the Hall of the Pharaohs. A visitor was told that the measure of each side of the pyramid's triangular base was 280 feet long. He noticed that the corridor shown as $\overline{AB}$ in the diagram connected to the middle of each of the two sides it reached. How long is corridor $\overline{AB}$ (units are in feet)?

17. A farmer has 200 feet of fencing to surround a small plot of land. He wants to maximize the amount of space possible using a rectangular formation. The enclosed area will be against the side of a barn so he only needs one of the lengths of the rectangular area to be enclosed by fencing. What is the maximum area that can be enclosed by the fence (ignore the square unit label)?

18. $x^3 - 6x^2 + 2x - 12 = 0$

For what real value of x is the equation above true?

19. If $r = 3\sqrt{3}$ and $2r = \sqrt{3x}$ what is the value of x?

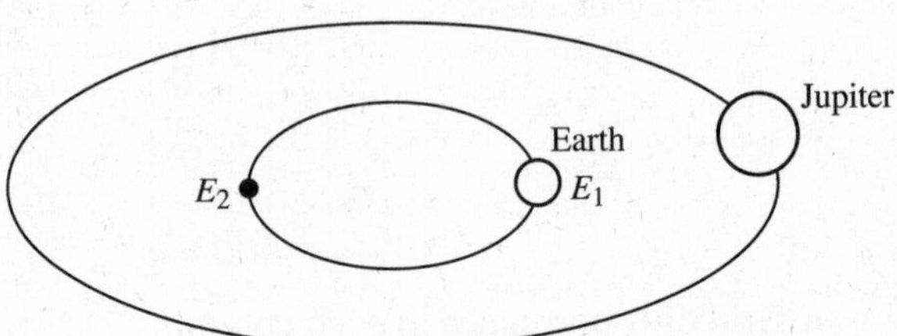

20. In the seventeenth century, the Danish astronomer Ole Roemer concluded that light takes longer to reach Earth from Jupiter when Earth is at E_2 than when Earth is at E_1. The modern figure for this time difference is 1,000 seconds. Modern estimates have the distance from Earth to Jupiter as 600 Gm and 900 Gm for E_1 and E_2, respectively. How long, in seconds, does it take light from Jupiter to reach the Earth at E_1? Give your answer in seconds. (Gm means gigameter, which is equal to 1,000,000,000 meters.)

STOP

If there is still time remaining, you may review your answers.

MATH TEST (CALCULATOR)

55 MINUTES, 38 QUESTIONS

Turn to Section 4 of your answer sheet to answer the questions in this section.

Directions: For questions 1–30, solve each problem and choose the best answer from the given options. Fill in the corresponding circle on your answer document. For questions 31–38, solve the problem and fill in the answer on the answer sheet grid. Please use scrap paper to work out your answers.

Notes:

- The use of a calculator on this section IS permitted.
- All variables and expressions represent real numbers unless indicated otherwise.
- All figures are drawn to scale unless indicated otherwise.
- All figures are in a plane unless indicated otherwise.
- Unless indicated otherwise, the domain of a given function is the set of all real numbers x for which the function has real values.

REFERENCE INFORMATION

Area Facts

$A = \ell w$

$A = \frac{1}{2}bh$

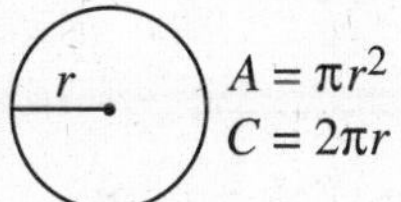

Volume Facts

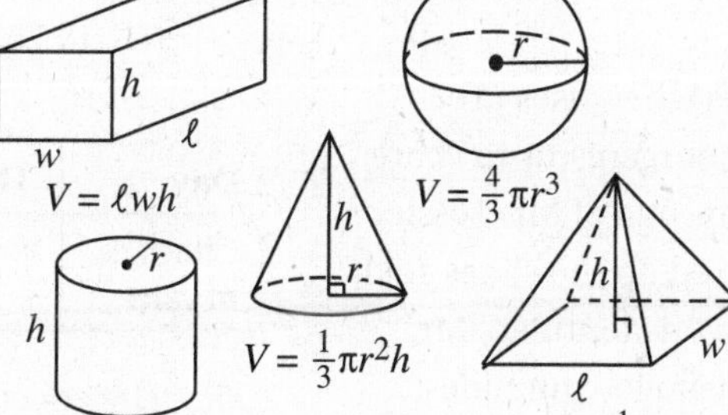

$V = \pi r^2 h$

$V = \frac{1}{3}\ell wh$

Triangle Facts

$a\sqrt{2}$, 45°, a, 45°, a

a, 60°, $2a$, 30°, $a\sqrt{3}$

c, a, b

$a^2 + b^2 = c^2$

The arc of a circle contains 360°.

The arc of a circle contains 2π radians.

The sum of the measures of the angles in a triangle is 180°.

1. If $\frac{m-4}{3} = \frac{x}{9}$, what is x in terms of m?

   (A) $x = 3m + 6$

   (B) $x = \frac{1}{3}m - \frac{4}{3}$

   (C) $x = 3(m - 4)$

   (D) $x = 3m - 4$

GO ON TO THE NEXT PAGE

2. After researching the future cost of a four year college education, Sergio and Maria began saving for their daughter's tuition. After two years, they had accrued \$2,870 for their college fund. After five years, the account balance was \$7,150. If Sergio and Maria continue to save at the same rate as they have for the past five years, approximately what will the savings be after 78 months?

(A) \$7,846.33
(B) \$8,413.17
(C) \$9,290.02
(D) \$9,4107.63

3. The cube less the square of a number is twice the number. If x is a positive integer, what is its value?

(A) 1
(B) 2
(C) 4
(D) 8

4. Mr. Tessler, a biology teacher, uses pre-prepared slides of microorganisms to share with his class. Yesterday, one of Mr. Tessler's aides inadvertently mixed up the slides such that they no longer can be identified. Mr. Tessler knew he had the following slides:

Slides of paramecia: 2
Slides of amoebae: 5
Slides of microbacteria: 3

If Mr. Tessler selects two slides at random, what is the probability that he will select a slide of paramecia followed by a slide of amoebae?

(A) $\frac{34}{45}$
(B) $\frac{16}{45}$
(C) $\frac{1}{9}$
(D) $\frac{1}{10}$

5. A light year, the distance that light travels in one year, is 5.87×10^{12} miles. The Andromeda Galaxy is 1.3×10^{19} miles distant from Earth. How many light years distant is the Earth from the Andromeda Galaxy?

(A) 2.2×10^5
(B) 2.2×10^6
(C) 3.4×10^8
(D) 3.4×10^9

6. Conner needs to plan a production budget for a computer firm. In order to maximize profit, he needs to buy m computer frames at \$18.75 and r keyboards at \$13.25 each. If the cost of this transaction must be less than \$139.00, which of the following inequalities represents Conner's model for profit maximization?

(A) $18.75m + 13.25r < 139$
(B) $18.75m + 13.25r \leq 139$
(C) $18.75r + 13.25m < 139$
(D) $18.75r + 13.25m \leq 139$

Day	Thursday	Friday	Saturday
Chance of rain	65%	74%	31%

7. The coach of the Denver High School baseball team will have to cancel an upcoming tournament if the weather conditions forecast rain. The table presents the probability of rain for the next three days. If it doesn't rain on Friday or Saturday, the coach can plan on holding the tournament at his high school. What is the probability that it will rain on Thursday but not Friday or Saturday?

(A) 18.7%
(B) 16.3%
(C) 14.9%
(D) 11.7%

GO ON TO THE NEXT PAGE

8. For what value of m does the system of equations have an infinite number of solutions?

$7x - 4y = 13$
$mx - 10y = 32.5$

(A) 14
(B) 17.5
(C) 21
(D) 32.5

9. Californians are very concerned about the continued drought conditions in their state. They are therefore curious about the price and quality of different water plans. A certain popular water plan charges a service fee of \$31.50 per month. Each gallon of water used costs \$.17 per gallon plus a local tax of 7.3% (the monthly service charge is tax exempt). Which of the following functions models the monthly cost of the plan?

(A) $f(x) = (.17x + .073)(31.5)$
(B) $f(x) = 31.5 + (.073x)(.17)$
(C) $f(x) = 31.5 + (1.073)(.17 + x)$
(D) $f(x) = 31.5 + (1.073)(.17x)$

Questions 10 and 11 refer to the table below.

The Environmental Protection Agency (EPA) has demonstrated that newer automobile emission standards have had a strong positive correlation with cleaner air in large metropolitan areas. Thus, it is the EPA's responsibility to get older cars off the road.

Cars in Operation in 1997

Age of Car	Millions of Cars
<3 years old	21.5
3 – 5 years old	29.9
6 – 8 years old	22.2
9 – 11 years old	16.7
≥12 years old	14.4

10. What percent of cars in operation in 1997 were between 6 and 11 years old?

(A) 37.2
(B) 41.3
(C) 48.1
(D) 53.2

11. 1.3% of all cars were 20 years old and older. What percent of the 12 years and older category does this number represent?

(A) 8.3
(B) 9.4
(C) 11.3
(D) 14.8

GO ON TO THE NEXT PAGE

Questions 12 and 13 refer to the graph below.

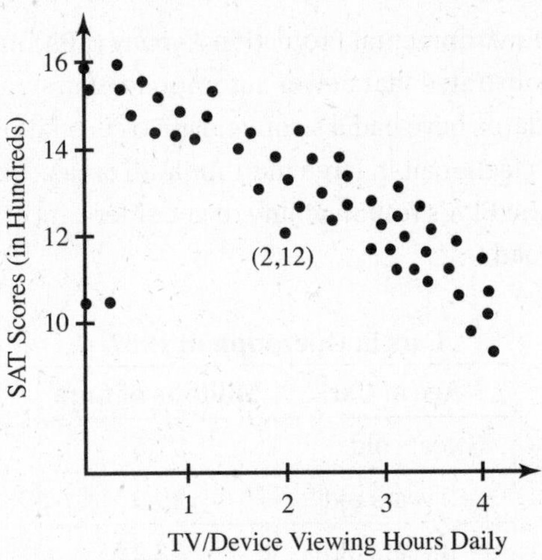

The advent of television, iPhones, and tablets is vying for students' study time. Experts are concerned that the prolonged use of electronic devices adversely affects SAT scores. The graph demonstrates the correlation between hours spent viewing daily and their effect on SAT scores.

12. Which of the following can be inferred from the graph?

 (A) The impact of viewing 3 versus 4 hours resulted in the same SAT score.
 (B) All students who watched one hour or less of television/devices daily scored 1200 or higher on the SAT.
 (C) SAT scores varied inversely with daily television/device viewing.
 (D) SAT scores varied directly with daily television/device viewing.

13. Given the data in the graph, which equation could be the line of best fit?

 (A) $y = 2.3x - 4.8$
 (B) $y = .86x + .23$
 (C) $y = -6.2x - 5.9$
 (D) $y = -2.04x + 15.8$

Questions 14 and 15 refer to the information below.

Home values in America have increased since the 2008 slump in housing prices. Over the past six years, home prices have increased at an annual rate of 3.72%.

14. Which of the following functions models the increase in home values?

 A = accumulated value of the home over time
 P = the purchase price of the home
 t = time in years
 r = rate expressed as a decimal

 (A) $A = P(.0372)^t$
 (B) $A = P(.9628)^t$
 (C) $A = P(1.0372)^t$
 (D) $A = P(3.72)^t$

15. A home costing $187,650 purchased in 2010 would be worth how much in 2013?

 (A) $194,455
 (B) $205,996
 (C) $209,380
 (D) $217,357

16. A data set of five integers features a mean that is 5.5 times as large as the median. Why do these two measures of central tendency differ in size by such a large amount?

 (A) The sample size is large.
 (B) The mode of the data skews the data downward.
 (C) There is an outlier that skews the mean higher.
 (D) There is an outlier that skews the mean lower.

GO ON TO THE NEXT PAGE

17. A sixth-grade class conducted a contest to see who could collect the most cans of food for a local charity. The top five students and the number of cans each collected are listed below.

Student	# of cans collected
Fay	113
George	119
Virginia	X
Anthony	116
Mariah	108

If the median number of cans collected is 113, and no two students collected the same number of cans, what is the greatest value for x?

(A) 113
(B) 112
(C) 109
(D) 107

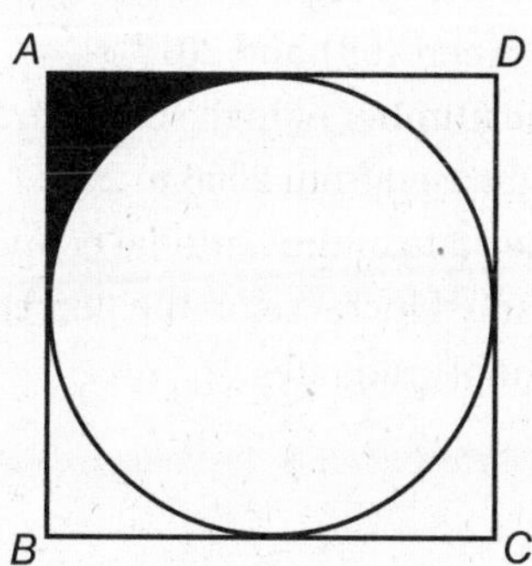

18. A coin toss board is shown above. If square $ABCD$ has perimeter 64, what is the probability of a coin landing on the shaded portion of the board?

(A) .363
(B) .182
(C) .098
(D) .053

19. Given the equation in the xy-plane, $-5x + 6y = -7$, which of the following equations is perpendicular to the graph of the equation above?

(A) $-6x + 10y = 7$
(B) $6x + 5y = 15$
(C) $6x - 20y = 15$
(D) $5x + 6y = -18$

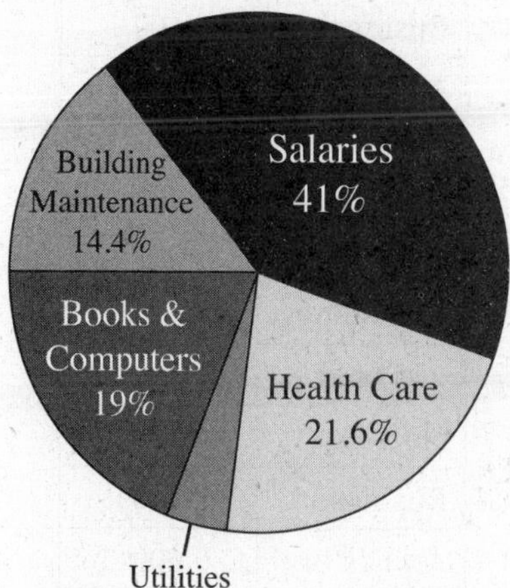

Operating Costs Deerfield HS

20. The above pie chart represents the operating costs for Deerfield High School in 2014.

The cost for health care benefits in 2014 is \$4,100,000. What is the cost for utilities?

(A) \$586,113
(B) \$637,431
(C) \$759,259
(D) \$817,437

GO ON TO THE NEXT PAGE

21. The tables below provide the distributions of majors of students at College A and College B.

College A

Major	Frequency
Psychology	300
Pre-Med	1,400
Nursing	200
Business	100
Art History	100

College B

Major	Frequency
Psychology	600
Pre-Med	300
Nursing	200
Business	400
Art History	600

Which of the following is true about the data shown for these two colleges?

(A) The standard deviation of majors at College A is larger.
(B) The standard deviation of majors at College B is larger.
(C) The standard deviation of majors at College A is the same as the standard deviation of College B.
(D) The standard deviation of both data sets cannot be calculated.

Question 22 refers to the graph below.

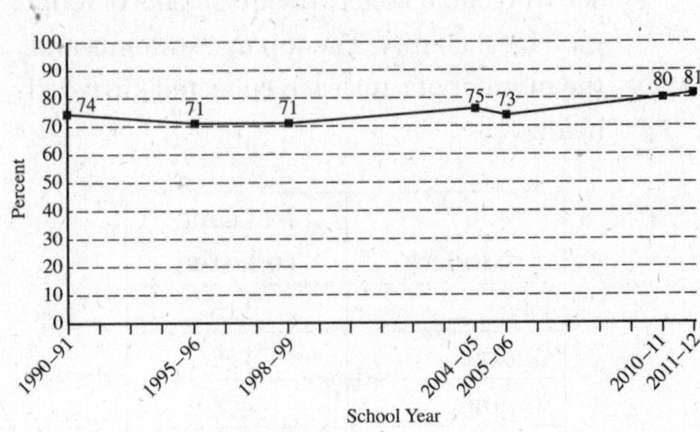

The graph above reflects the average percent of freshman high school students in America who graduate from high school within four years.

22. Which of the following can be inferred from the graph above?

(A) From 2006 to 2012 there was approximately an 11% increase in the percent of high school graduates.
(B) There was a steady increase in the number of high school graduates between 1991 and 2012.
(C) The number of high school graduates decreased from 2006 to 2012.
(D) The state of the national economy had a marked increase on the percent of high school graduates.

GO ON TO THE NEXT PAGE

23. $2{,}500\left[1+\dfrac{r}{1{,}200}\right]^{12}$

The expression shown above provides the sum of money, in dollars, that is earned in a year by an initial deposit of \$2,500 in a savings institution that pays an annual rate r% compounded monthly. Which of the following expressions shows how much additional money is earned at an interest rate of 6% than at an interest rate of 3.2%?

(A) $2{,}500\left[1+\dfrac{6-3.2}{1{,}200}\right]^{12}$

(B) $2{,}500\left[1+\dfrac{\frac{6}{3.2}}{1{,}200}\right]^{12}$

(C) $\dfrac{2{,}500\left[1+\dfrac{6}{1{,}200}\right]^{12}}{2{,}500\left[1+\dfrac{3.2}{1{,}200}\right]^{12}}$

(D) $2{,}500\left[1+\dfrac{6}{1{,}200}\right]^{12}-2{,}500\left[1+\dfrac{3.2}{1{,}200}\right]^{12}$

24. The square root of x varies inversely with y. When $x = 196$, $y = -\dfrac{1}{2}$.

Find the value of x when $y = -3$.

(A) 3

(B) $\dfrac{49}{9}$

(C) $\dfrac{49}{3}$

(D) 49

Questions 25–27 refer to the graph below.

A girls' softball coach was recruiting for Behrens High School's spring softball team. The coach wanted to see if age was a determining factor in gauging the distance each girl could throw a softball.

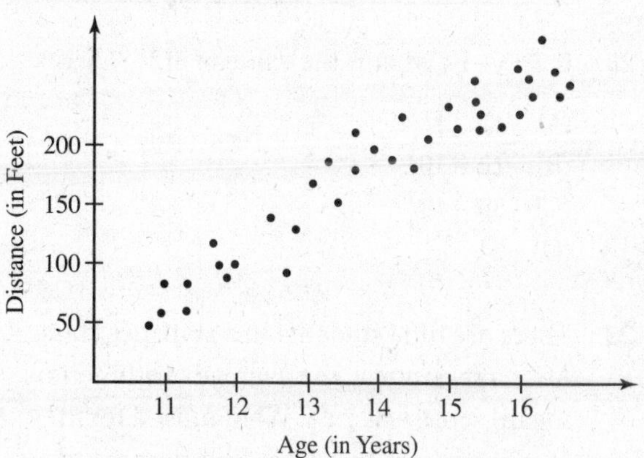

Softball Throws by Age and Distance

25. Which of the following statements can be concluded from the graph?

(A) There is a weak negative correlation between age and the distance thrown.
(B) There is a strong positive correlation between age and the distance thrown.
(C) There is no correlation between age and distance thrown.
(D) There is an inverse relationship between age and distance thrown.

26. Which of the following functions is a line of best fit for the graph?

(A) $y = 5.14x - 123.5$
(B) $y = -43.27x - 231.3$
(C) $y = 33.33x - 299.6$
(D) $y = 14.2 - 2.01x$

GO ON TO THE NEXT PAGE

27. Given the data in the graph, what would be the predicted distance of a throw from a person who is 18-years old?

(A) 247 feet
(B) 277 feet
(C) 300 feet
(D) 319 feet

---

28. If $i = \sqrt{-1}$, what is the value of $3(2 - 4i)^2$?

(A) $-12 - 4i$
(B) $-12 - 16i$
(C) $-36 - 48i$
(D) -84

29. There are nine students in a statistics class. After a recent test, the average (arithmetic mean) score was 79%. What must a tenth student's score be to raise the class average to 81%?

(A) 87
(B) 89
(C) 94
(D) 99

30. The number of students in an elementary class, s, decided to spend D dollars for a present for their favorite teacher, Mrs. Konopka. Each student was to contribute an equal amount. Because 15 students refused to contribute, each of those remaining agreed to contribute an additional, equal amount. What was the additional amount each had to contribute, in dollars?

(A) $(s - 15) \div D$
(B) $(s^2 - 15) \div D$
(C) $\dfrac{15D}{s^2 - 15s}$
(D) $\dfrac{s^2 - 15s}{15D}$

GO ON TO THE NEXT PAGE

Grid-in Response Directions

In questions 31–38, first solve the problem, and then enter your answer on the grid provided on the answer sheet. The instructions for entering your answers follow.

- First, write your answer in the boxes at the top of the grid.
- Second, grid your answer in the columns below the boxes.
- Use the fraction bar in the first row or the decimal point in the second row to enter fractions and decimals.

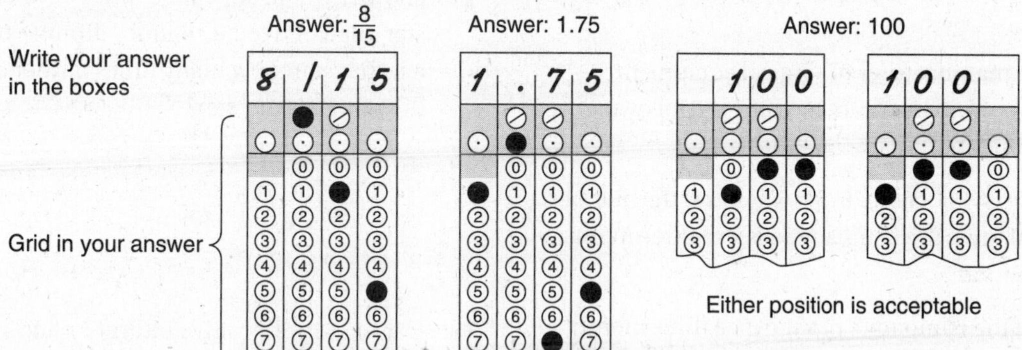

- Grid only one space in each column.
- Entering the answer in the boxes is recommended as an aid in gridding but is not required.
- The machine scoring your exam can read only what you grid, so you **must grid-in your answers correctly to get credit**.
- If a question has more than one correct answer, grid-in only one of them.
- The grid does not have a minus sign; so no answer can be negative.
- A mixed number *must* be converted to an improper fraction or a decimal before it is gridded. Enter $1\frac{1}{4}$ as $\frac{5}{4}$ or 1.25; the machine will interpret 11/4 as $\frac{11}{4}$ and mark it wrong.
- **All decimals must be entered as accurately as possible.** Here are three acceptable ways of gridding

$$\frac{3}{11} = 0.272727\ldots$$

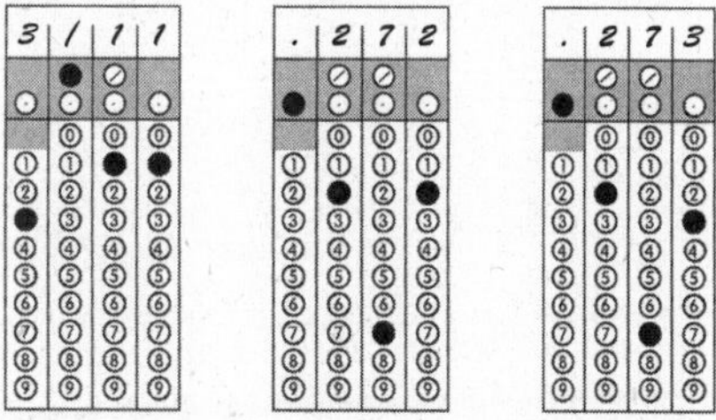

- Note that rounding to .273 is acceptable because you are using the full grid, but you would receive **no credit** for .3 or .27, because they are less accurate.

31. Steve and Iris drive exactly 5 miles from point A to point B. If Iris' average speed is 50 miles per hour and Steve's average speed is 60 miles per hour, how much longer, in seconds, will it take Iris than Steve to drive five miles?

32. A manufacturer of surgical equipment measures its profit by using the following function:

    $P(x) = 11{,}000x - 6750$, where x is the number of units the company sells in a three month period.

    If the company's profit over a three month period was $9,321,250, how many units did it sell?

33. Kari wants to buy a new service plan for a data and internet bundle. One plan offers a monthly fee of $24.00 and $.007 for each minute of use. Another plan offers a flat monthly fee of $36.50. After how many minutes of use will the two plans charge the same monthly cost (round your answer to the nearest minute)?

34. A "standard candle" is a way for astronomers to calculate the distance to an object in space. The apparent brightness of an object varies indirectly with the square of the distance. For example a galaxy that is 1,000,000 times farther than another would appear to be 1,000 times dimmer. Similarly, a nebula that is 900 times more distant than another would appear 30 times as dim. If a star appeared to be 16 times dimmer than another star, how many times farther away is the more distant star?

35. If $x^{\frac{y}{4}} = 81$ for positive integers x and y, what is one possible value of y?

GO ON TO THE NEXT PAGE

36. A central angle in a circle has a measure of 34.4° and the measure of its sector is 139.6 square units. To the nearest tenth of a unit, what is the measure of the circle's radius (use $\pi = 3.14$)?

Questions 37 and 38 refer to the information provided below.

Because of refraction, an object 5 meters below the surface of a lake appears to be 4 meters below the surface.

37. If the apparent depth under water varies directly with the actual depth, what is the actual depth of a rock that appears to be 6 meters below the surface of a small lake?

38. A diver inadvertently left his keys in his shorts when he was swimming. The keys fell out of his shorts and went to the bottom of his swimming pool. The keys appeared to be 9 feet below the surface. What is the difference between the actual depth of the keys and the apparent depth?

STOP

If there is still time remaining, you may review your answers.

ESSAY (OPTIONAL)

Directions: This is your opportunity to show that you can read and understand a passage and write an analysis of that passage. Be sure your essay demonstrates a clear and logical analysis of the passage, using precise language.

On the actual test, you will write your essay on the lines provided in your answer booklet; for now, write your essay on lined paper. Remember to write or print legibly so that others can read what you've written.

You have 50 minutes to read the essay and write a response to the prompt provided.

Carefully read the passage below. As you read, think about how Marie Winn makes use of

- *reasoning* to develop an argument
- *evidence* to support assertions made
- *language* to persuade the reader

From Marie Winn, *The Plug-in Drug*, Penguin Books, 2002.

1 Concern about the effects of television on children has centered exclusively upon the contents of the programs which children watch. Social scientists and researchers invent complex and ingenious experiments to find out whether watching violent programs makes children behave aggressively. But it is easy to overlook the simple fact that one is always just watching television when sitting in front of the screen rather than having any other experience.

2 Parents who are deeply troubled about the effects of television upon their children have centered their concern on the subject matter of the programs. A group called Action For Children's Television (ACT) was formed in the USA not only to reduce the amount of violence in programs but also to protest against incessant commercial breaks which encouraged children to crave fashionable toys and unhealthy foods. One of its founders described its aims: ". . . parents have the right to ask that programs aimed at the young should meet the specific needs of children . . . ." But is it the needs of children which are at stake when parents demand better programs? Surely the fact that young children watch so much television reflects the needs of parents to find a convenient source of amusement for their offspring and a period of quiet for themselves. Their anxieties about the possible ill effects of those hours of passive, quiet viewing are lessened if the time spent at least seems to be educational.

3 The real needs of young children are quite different. They need opportunities to work out basic family relationships, thereby coming to understand themselves; television only reduces these opportunities. They need to develop initiative, and to find out things for themselves: television provides answers too easily. Children need to acquire fundamental skills of communication; television retards verbal development because the child is silent while watching it. Television discourages the sort of games that enable the young to discover their strengths and weaknesses with the result that as adults they will be less fulfilled. Their need for fantasy is gratified far better by their own make-believe activities than by the adult-made fantasies offered on television.

Intellectual stimulation is provided more completely by manipulating, touching and doing than by passively watching and listening.

4 Oddly enough, the television industry, though often cynical and self-serving in its exploitation of children, sometimes unknowingly serves their best interests. Because television offers cheap junk programs, conscientious parents do in fact limit their children's viewing when such undesirable programs are the only ones available. Unfortunately, if organizations like ACT succeed in improving the quality of programs significantly, the effects on young children will be more harmful because their permitted viewing time will increase, and, no matter how good their content, TV programs are always a poor substitute for other activities.

5 There are a number of fallacies that have misled parents into thinking that the problem of television will be solved by improving its quality. It is suggested, for example, that a youngster unfamiliar with TV programs will find making friends difficult and will be labeled as an outsider. On the contrary, other children will usually respect their independence and recognize—even envy—the richness of their alternative activities. More subtle is the mistaken belief that the experience that children gain from watching television is the same as the adult's. This is emphatically not so. As adults watch television, their own past and present experiences come into play, so that they can test the view of the world presented on the small screen against their knowledge of real life. But young children have very few real-life experiences to set against their viewing, so that for them TV is a primary source of experience; their formative years are spent largely in an unreal, unnatural, second-hand world.

6 It is also universally assumed that TV is an important source of learning. Like an animated picture book it presents in an easily digested and entertaining way a great deal of information about the natural world, history, current affairs, other countries and so on. But the "knowledge" of today's television-educated children, spouting words and ideas they do not fully understand and "facts" whose accuracy they cannot judge from their limited experience, cannot compare with the knowledge acquired by reading or activity. It is then that children use their minds and their bodies, their imaginative and reasoning powers, to enrich their lives.

7 Only when parents begin to question the nature of television itself and its effects on their children and on themselves as parents will they begin to realize that it is not the programs but television itself—and *especially* the good programs—which poses the greater threat to their children's well-being.

Write an essay explaining how Marie Winn constructs an argument to convince the reader that watching television—even "good" programs—is harmful to children. Describe and analyze how Winn uses one or more of the elements of persuasive writing listed in the box on page 92 to strengthen her argument. You may also discuss other writing techniques used by the author.

Your essay should not state your opinion on the topic discussed in the passage, but rather analyze how Winn constructs an argument to persuade the reader.

ANSWER KEY
Practice Test 1

Section 1: Reading

1. **D**	14. **D**	27. **D**	40. **A**
2. **C**	15. **B**	28. **B**	41. **D**
3. **D**	16. **C**	29. **A**	42. **A**
4. **B**	17. **C**	30. **B**	43. **D**
5. **C**	18. **A**	31. **D**	44. **B**
6. **D**	19. **B**	32. **C**	45. **A**
7. **A**	20. **C**	33. **B**	46. **D**
8. **D**	21. **B**	34. **A**	47. **C**
9. **C**	22. **B**	35. **C**	48. **C**
10. **A**	23. **B**	36. **B**	49. **A**
11. **A**	24. **C**	37. **A**	50. **D**
12. **B**	25. **B**	38. **C**	51. **C**
13. **C**	26. **D**	39. **B**	52. **B**

Number Correct ______

Number Incorrect ______

Section 2: Writing and Language

1. **C**	12. **B**	23. **A**	34. **A**
2. **A**	13. **C**	24. **B**	35. **C**
3. **B**	14. **C**	25. **D**	36. **B**
4. **B**	15. **B**	26. **B**	37. **C**
5. **C**	16. **D**	27. **C**	38. **D**
6. **B**	17. **C**	28. **B**	39. **C**
7. **D**	18. **C**	29. **D**	40. **B**
8. **C**	19. **C**	30. **B**	41. **C**
9. **A**	20. **D**	31. **B**	42. **D**
10. **B**	21. **C**	32. **D**	43. **B**
11. **C**	22. **B**	33. **A**	44. **B**

Number Correct ______

Number Incorrect ______

ANSWER KEY
Practice Test 1

Section 3: Math (No Calculator)

1. **A**
2. **C**
3. **C**
4. **C**
5. **D**
6. **A**
7. **D**
8. **C**
9. **C**
10. **C**
11. **D**
12. **B**
13. **C**
14. **B**
15. **C**

16. **140**

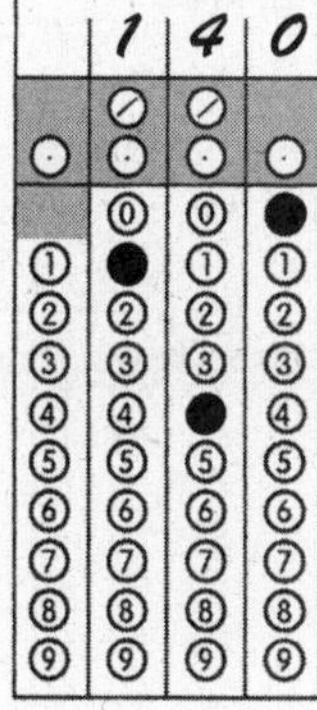

17. **5,000**

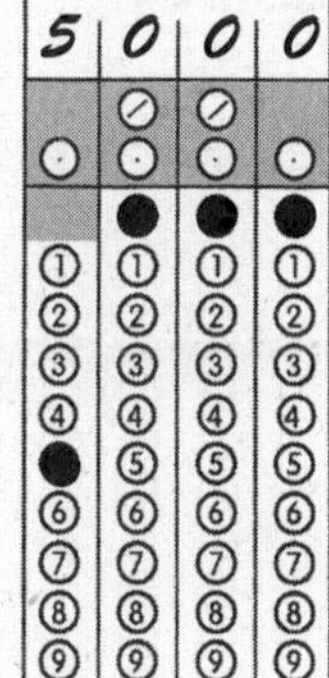

18. **6**

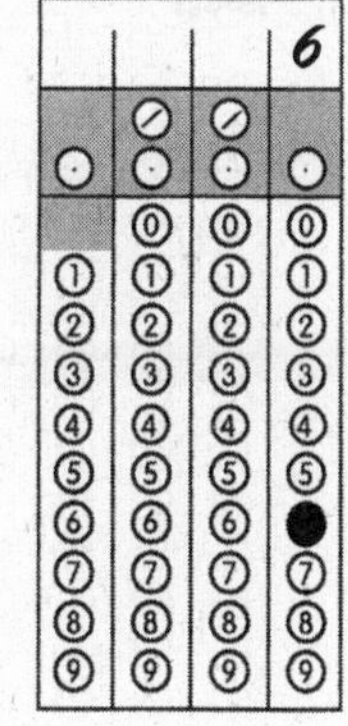

19. **36**

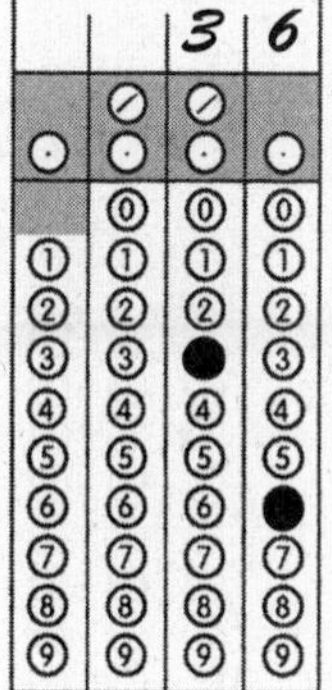

20. **2,000**

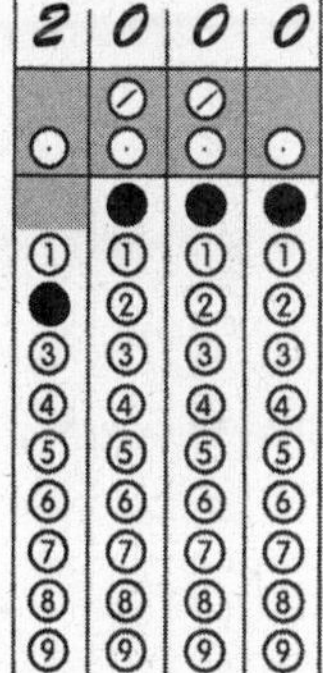

Number Correct ______

Number Incorrect ______

ANSWER KEY
Practice Test 1

Section 4: Math (Calculator)

1. **C**	7. **D**	13. **D**	19. **B**	25. **B**
2. **C**	8. **B**	14. **C**	20. **C**	26. **C**
3. **B**	9. **D**	15. **C**	21. **A**	27. **C**
4. **C**	10. **A**	16. **C**	22. **A**	28. **C**
5. **B**	11. **B**	17. **B**	23. **D**	29. **D**
6. **A**	12. **C**	18. **D**	24. **B**	30. **C**

31. **60**

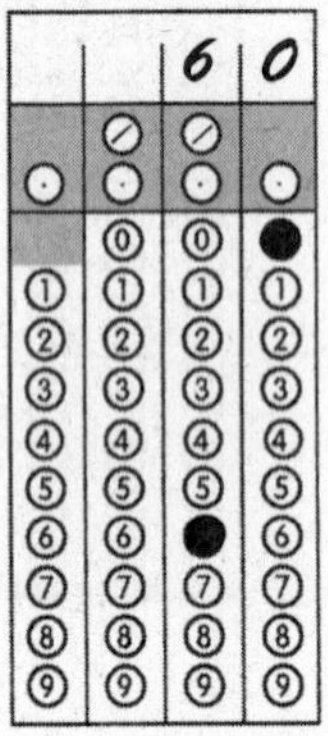

32. **848**

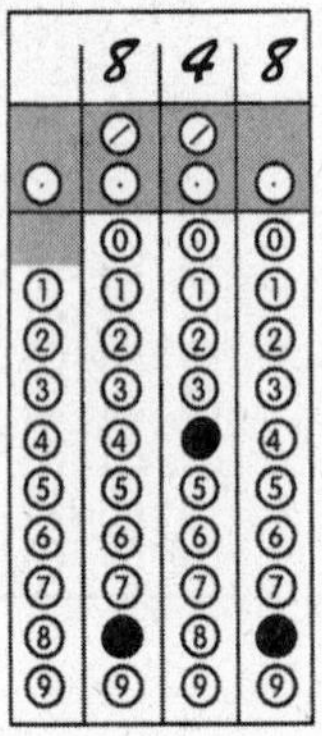

33. **1,786**

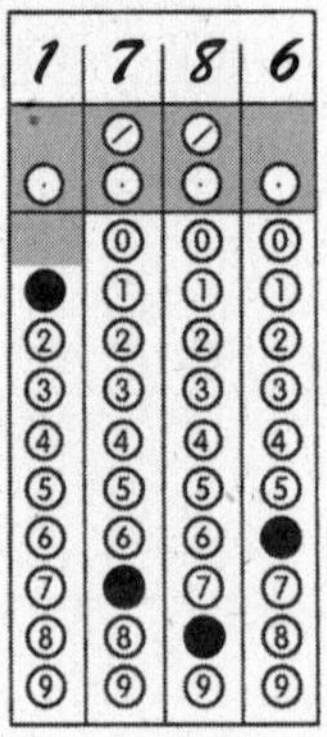

34. **256**

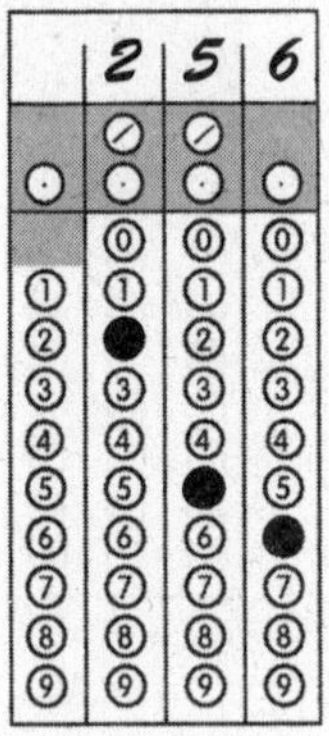

35. **1, 2, 4, 8, or 16**

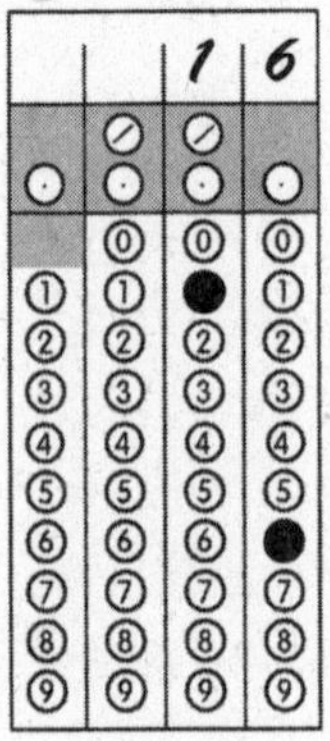

36. **21.6**

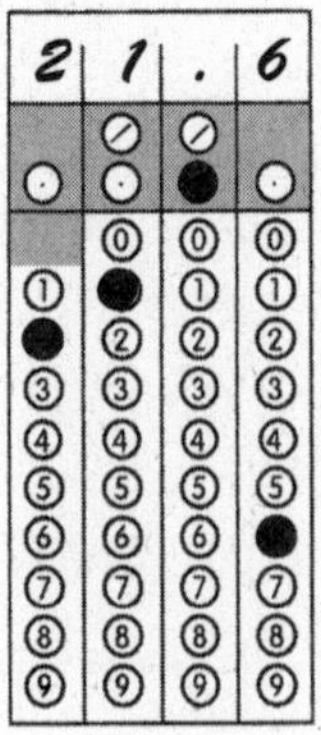

37. **7.5 or 15/2**

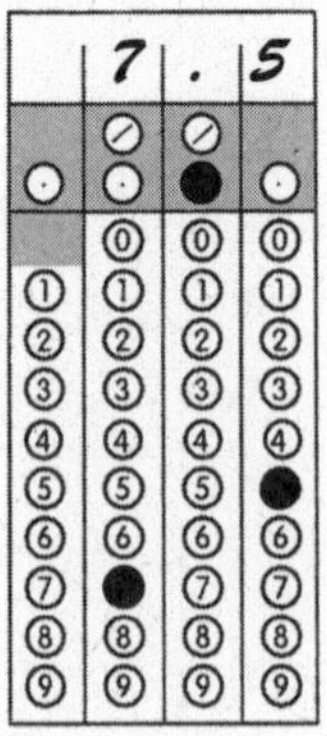

38. **2.25**

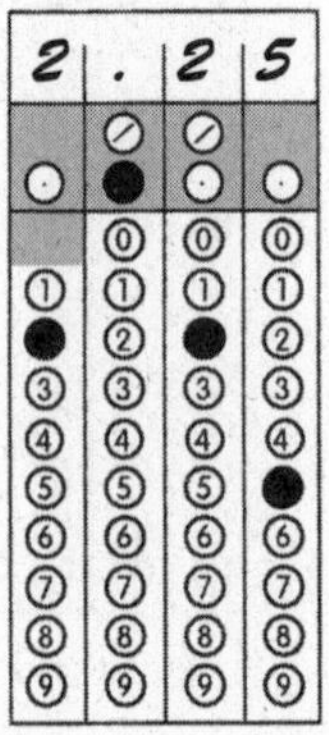

Number Correct ______

Number Incorrect ______

SCORE ANALYSIS

Reading and Writing Test

Section 1: Reading ________ = ________ (A)
correct raw score

Section 2: Writing ________ = ________ (B)
correct raw score

To find your Reading and Writing test scores, consult the chart below: find the ranges in which your raw scores lie and read across to find the ranges of your test scores.

________ + ________ = ________ (C)
range of reading test scores | range of writing test scores | range of reading + writing test scores

To find the range of your Reading and Writing Scaled Score, multiply (C) by 10.

Test Scores for the Reading and Writing Sections

Reading Raw Score	Writing Raw Score	Test Score
44-52	39-44	35-40
36-43	33-38	31-34
30-35	28-32	28-30
24-29	22-27	24-27
19-23	17-21	21-23
14-18	13-16	19-20
9-13	9-12	16-18
5-8	5-8	13-15
less than 5	less than 5	10-12

Math Test

Section 3: ________ = ________ (D)
correct raw score

Section 4: ________ = ________ (E)
correct raw score

Total Math raw score: (D) + (E) = ________

To find your Math Scaled Score, consult the chart below: find the range in which your raw score lies and read across to find the range for your scaled score.

Scaled Scores for the Math Test

Raw Score	Scaled Score	Raw Score	Scaled Score
50-58	700-800	20-25	450-490
44-49	650-690	15-19	400-440
38-43	600-640	11-14	350-390
32-37	550-590	7-10	300-340
26-31	500-540	less than 7	200-290

ANSWER EXPLANATIONS

Section 1: Reading Test

1. **(D)** The author says, "the Court of Claims . . . was set up not to administer justice but to expedite adjudication of land titles and head off any future claims that Indians might make on lands already coveted by the white economy" (lines 30–34).

2. **(C)** In lines 13–20 ("Termination . . . market") the author explains the effect of termination legislation on Indian nations and their land. One of these effects is to *lessen* Indian claims on land because some Indian nations are eliminated by termination and so cannot claim land not previously ceded to the U.S. by treaty.

3. **(D)** Quotation marks are sometimes used, as in this case, to indicate that an assertion made by one party is open to dispute by another party. The U.S. government regards most of the land not ceded to it by treaty with Indian nations as its own, but others—notably many Indian nations—do not agree.

4. **(B)** The author used the word *mercies* in the course of his description of termination legislation that "had already wiped out a number of small tribes" (lines 14–15) and "turns the Indians over to the mercies of state jurisdiction and property taxation" (lines 16–18). It is clear from this context he is using it sarcastically because the Indians are very unlikely to be shown mercy—in fact, they will almost certainly be treated without mercy, in the author's view.

5. **(C)** In the sentence preceding the one cited in the question, the author describes the attitude of the progressives toward the traditionals and their "useless religion" (line 62) as one of scorn for outdated beliefs and practices. The observation that it is the progressives rather than the traditionals who feel it necessary to keep witches out of outhouses suggests that the author believes that it is the progressives rather than the traditionals who are superstitious.

6. **(D)** This is the only statement about the traditionals supported by the passage: "The traditionals know . . . been taken away" (lines 65–73).

7. **(A)** The first paragraph of the passage describes the bleak future the Hopi face, focusing on the views of the traditionals. The second paragraph describes what Wayne Sekaquaptewa, a leading progressive, thinks about the views of the traditionals.

8. **(D)** Although the author does not say that he agrees with the traditionals, he takes a sympathetic view of them and their beliefs throughout the passage. Also, he shows respect for Hopi beliefs in general. In lines 65–80 ("The traditionals know . . . Life Plan Rock") he describes the views of the traditionals very sympathetically, suggesting strongly that he agrees with them that their only chance of survival as a distinct culture is to cling to their traditional beliefs and practices. We can infer, however, that because he is not a Hopi he does not agree with the literal meaning of the Day of Purification, but rather that he sees it as symbolic of a future that may come to pass in which the Hopi survive amid the ruins of the white man's world.

9. **(C)** The author says, "The traditionals have always been wary of the white man's consumer mentality" (lines 1–2).

10. **(A)** This line provides the best evidence because it describes the white men as having, in the view of the Hopis, a "consumer mentality." Having such a mentality (outlook) entails being materialistic.

11. **(A)** The girl's eyes are also described as "full of a radiant curiosity" (lines 19–20), so it makes sense that the phrase "quick gray eyes" is used to suggest that the girl is alert.

12. **(B)** The word "clad" means *clothed*, whereas the word "adorned" means *made attractive*, suggesting the girl likes to make herself attractive.

13. **(C)** Immediately before the word "rise" is used, the old man is described as grunting: "There he paused . . . grunt of disapproval" (lines 39–42), suggesting that he intended to communicate something to the girl. Thus, in context, *rise* means *reaction.*

14. **(D)** The elderly man is described as "utter[ing] a long even grunt of disapproval" (lines 41–42) when he sees the girl sitting and reading a book. It cannot be conclusively inferred that he is disapproving of her reading a novel, but the fact that the grunt is described as one of "disapproval" means that he does not approve of something. There is some evidence for (A), (B), and (C), but none of it is as strong as the evidence for (D). Thus, (D) is the best choice.

15. **(B)** The author is mainly concerned with vividly describing the scene. He uses these words and phrases to *personify* (portray inanimate objects as having human emotions) the house and car in Passage 2 to help the reader imagine the scene.

16. **(C)** It is not stated who or what produced the whistle mentioned in line 76, but it is reasonable to infer that the "signal" referred to in line 83 was the whistle mentioned in line 76. Choices (A) and (D) are possible, but there is no evidence for them. Choice (B) makes some sense because sounds are described as coming from the car, but it is more reasonable to infer that the whistle was a signal.

17. **(C)** Choice (C) is the best answer because "perfunctorily" means *done routinely and with little interest.* The fact that Clark Darrow is sitting in this way suggests that visiting the Happer house is probably part of his routine. "Sat brilliantly . . . at attention" suggests that he regards the visit as something to be done in a somewhat showy manner. (A) Although "sat brilliantly . . . at attention" suggests that Clark Darrow regards the visit as something to be done dramatically, the word *perfunctorily* suggests that he regards the visit as something done as a duty, and which he has little interest in. If Clark Darrow were visiting the Happer house to show his romantic interest in Sally he would probably not be sitting *perfunctorily.* (B) Although the words "sat brilliantly . . . at attention" suggest that he could regard his visit as an honor, one would not normally respond to a great honor by sitting *perfunctorily* (in a manner suggesting that one regards it as a duty). (D) The fact that Clark Darrow sits *perfunctorily* shows that he regards the visit as a routine duty, not as an exciting change from his regular activities.

18. **(A)** In this context, *evolved* means *gave off.* The author says "The car was hot [and] retained all the heat it absorbed or evolved" (lines 62–64). We can infer that the car's engine produced heat that it gave off.

19. **(B)** Both of the girls are depicted as being *relaxed.* The girl in Passage 1 is sitting in a wicker settee, very relaxed, reading a book, and Sally Happer in Passage 2 is resting her chin on a window sill, gazing down sleepily at the car. (A) *Pretty* is not the correct choice

because, although there is some suggestion that the girl in Passage 1 is pretty ("slender and supple . . . alluring mouth," lines 18–19), nothing is suggested about Sally Happer's appearance. (C) There is a suggestion that the girl in Passage 1 is *intelligent* ("quick gray eyes full of a radiant curiosity," lines 19–20), but there is nothing to suggest that Sally is intelligent. (D) Neither girl can be described as *indolent* (habitually lazy) because not enough information is provided to show whether they are frequently lazy.

20. **(C)** In Passage 1 "the drowsy silence" (line 34) is broken by the "heavy footsteps" of the elderly man. In Passage 2 Sally Happer looks down "sleepily" (line 77) at Clark Darrow's noisy arrival in his old Ford. (A) In Passage 1 the arrival of the elderly man does not mainly create humor. In Passage 2 there is a stronger suggestion than there is in Passage 1 that the arrival of the male character is intended, at least in part, to be humorous. However, in neither passage does the male character's arrival mainly serve to create humor. (B) It is possible that the elderly man grunts because he condemns the girl's self-indulgence, but there is nothing to suggest a condemnation of self-indulgence in Passage 2. (D) In Passage 1 the elderly man interrupts the mood briefly but this does not really change the atmosphere; the girl ignores him and continues reading and eating a lemon. In Passage 2 Clark Darrow's arrival does not create a serious atmosphere. On the contrary, it creates a somewhat comical atmosphere.

21. **(B)** The author says in the first few lines of the passage, "It's not hard to guess which side [of the debate about the ethics of using the atomic bomb] each chose once you know that Alsop experienced capture by the Japanese at Hong Kong early in 1942, while Joravsky came into no deadly contact with the Japanese" (lines 5–10). This statement makes the assumption that Alsop's and Joravsky's opinions about whether the use of the atomic bomb was ethical are determined by their experience in the war.

22. **(B)** The author's point is that the question does not fairly and objectively present the crucial issue for debate because it can only be answered "no." A person, such as the author, who on balance favored the use of the atomic bomb, is forced to answer "no" because, strictly speaking, dropping the atomic bomb was not really necessary because the war could have been ended by other means.

23. **(B)** From the context it can be inferred that the atomic bombing of Hiroshima and Nagasaki prompted peace advocates in Japan to call into serious question deeply held Japanese values about national pride and individual honor because the atomic bombing radically changed their significance. A short-hand term for these values is "the Japanese book of rules."

24. **(C)** Such opinion surveys would support Joseph Alsop's contention that a bloodbath would have been inevitable without the use of the atomic bomb because they show that most Japanese would have joined the fight against the invaders and fought fiercely.

25. **(B)** The author quotes Joseph Alsop: "It [is] absurd . . . to hold the common view . . . that the decision to drop the two bombs on Japan was wicked in itself" (lines 39–43). We can see from this that the author agrees with Mr. Alsop's view that most Americans mistakenly condemn the dropping of the atomic bombs on Japan. It is reasonable to infer that one of the reasons the author believes that they make this mistake is that they tend to ignore the great stress placed on honor in Japanese culture, leading them to believe that the Japanese would not have fought an invasion fiercely. The author quotes

Joseph Alsop's conclusion: "Japanese surrender could never have been obtained, at any rate without the honor-satisfying bloodbath envisioned by . . . Anami" (lines 27–30) without the dropping of the atomic bombs on Japan.

26. **(D)** The word *genteel* means "belonging to polite society," so "genteel ethics" are the ethics, or moral values, of polite society. The term suggests that such morality is removed from the harsh realities of life, and is able to stand apart and make fine moral judgments free of involvement in the events that are judged.

27. **(D)** The discovery of documents showing that the Japanese leadership possessed information leading them to (incorrectly) believe that the Americans would not have a second atomic bomb ready for use for several months would suggest Joseph Alsop's argument that dropping an atomic bomb on Nagasaki was morally justifiable because it would strengthen the likelihood that the Japanese would have fought to the death to defend their country, even if it meant a "bloodbath" (line 29).

28. **(B)** In context, the word *tidy* means "orderly." The author is saying that the historian can use hindsight to analyze events of the past in an orderly manner. An example of this is that they know the implications (such as "opening up the age of nuclear warfare") of events, whereas the people involved in them could not know such implications. Thus, the historian, using hindsight, can fit everything into an orderly view of what happened.

29. **(A)** The words "as well as" signal that in dropping atomic bombs on Japan, U.S. government officials were motivated not only by a desire to end the war but also by a desire for revenge against the Japanese for attacking Pearl Harbor and starting the war in the Pacific.

30. **(B)** In context, the word *illumination* means "intellectual enlightenment." The author is saying that to understand the past one must put aside one's knowledge of subsequent events and not consider any intellectual enlightenment that comes with considering these later events.

31. **(D)** The lines from the poem "Gerontion" suggest that when a person acts it is difficult for the person to know the consequences of those actions, and that neither acting from fear nor from courage ensures that history will judge the person's acts as being virtuous. In the context of the passage, these lines are appropriate because the author is arguing that the people who decided to drop atomic bombs on Japan could not know the full implications of their decision. Perhaps "unnatural vices" (the consequences of the atomic bombings) were "fathered by [their] heroism" (lines 105–106) in their deciding to drop the bombs, or perhaps their "impudent crimes" (dropping the bombs) resulted in their being considered virtuous.

32. **(C)** The word *aesthetic* in this context means "relating to aesthetics, theories of what is beautiful." Thus, "aesthetic trends" are fashions in what is considered beautiful and thus worthwhile in the arts and literature.

33. **(B)** In context, *pedestrian* means "undistinguished, ordinary." The author is contrasting ordinary prose made to appear somewhat like poetry with "the real thing" (line 17), which is poetry. It thus makes sense that he describes it rather negatively.

34. **(A)** The author says that writing professionals have made it their business to attract students to their poetry writing programs, and that in so doing having assessed the

value of poetry more on the basis of "practical concerns" (lines 9–10) than on its aesthetic merit. It is reasonable to infer from this that quite a few of these writing program professionals care more about their careers than they do about encouraging the production of good poetry.

35. **(C)** In lines 14–17 ("Most obvious is . . . the real thing") the author discusses the phenomenon of poetry becoming more like prose. The "real thing" refers to writing that has not lost the essential character of poetry—that is, *poetry.*

36. **(B)** In lines 31–37 ("If the profusion . . . thereby losing significance") the author expresses his dislike for prose poetry. Using the informal expression "dished up" helps him to express this dislike colorfully.

37. **(A)** In lines 37–38 the author refers to the "'poem' part of the equation." From this we can infer that in order to create a prose poem it is necessary to add poetic elements to prose elements. (Prose elements + poetic elements = prose poem)

38. **(C)** In lines 45–46 ("Poe and Baudelaire . . . a century later") the author says that Poe and Baudelaire wrote prose poems "more consciously" than Blake and Smart before them. This suggests that the author is saying that Blake and Smart did not consciously decide to write work that would come to be called prose poetry; rather, they wrote in this style because it was one of a number of forms they used in the course of composing their poems.

39. **(B)** The author makes the comment in lines 58–61 immediately after citing Peter Johnson, who says, "I am not even sure what my criteria [for deciding what a prose poem is] are, anymore" (lines 57–58). Thus, we can infer that the author is being sarcastic in saying that one graduate writing program understands the genre well enough to offer an entire course in it. Also, in the paragraph after this comment, the author says that the definition of the genre of prose poetry is still very controversial.

40. **(A)** In lines 64–67 ("Others concede that . . . short story writer") the author says that some critics believe that it is difficult to exclude "the heightened prose of many a novelist and short story writer" from the genre of prose poetry. Since the definition of prose poetry is being discussed, it can be inferred that "heightened prose" refers to prose that has characteristics of poetry.

41. **(D)** Throughout the passage the author describes distinctions between poetry and prose. In lines 37–42 ("The 'poem' part . . . figures of speech") he says that a prose poem is made poetic by the use of poetic devices such as rhythm and metaphor. In lines 94–98 ("for it has . . . making poetry musical") he mentions the importance of music in even free and open verse. In lines 100–103 ("Howe's piece lacks . . . prose-poem equation") he stresses that rhythm and metaphor are essential to poetry.

42. **(A)** In the paragraph immediately preceding the one in which he cites the two excerpts from "Doubt," the author says that the term prose poem leads one to expect a work designated as such to be comprised of "a combination of and tension between prose and poetic elements" (lines 68–70), but that "these expectations aren't always met" (lines 70–71). The sentence "Examples abound" (line 72) signals that the two excerpts from "Doubt" are examples in which prose poetry does not meet these expectations.

43. **(D)** The passage describes various processes that change coasts.

44. **(B)** In context, *continually* means "regularly occurring." The processes affecting coasts the passage describes are not continuous (uninterrupted) but rather occur quite often.

45. **(A)** Waves are described as traveling across the surface of lakes and seas and then breaking as they near the shore. From this we can infer that *shallowing* means "becoming more shallow."

46. **(D)** In lines 18–20 ("Plants . . . dunes") the author describes the effects plants have on wetlands and coastal dunes. He does not elaborate on this in the rest of the passage as he does on waves, tides, and storms.

47. **(C)** In lines 31–34 ("Even . . . shore") the author says even a slight angle between the land and waves "will create currents that transport sediment along the shore." From this we can infer that if there is no angle sediment will not be moved along the shore.

48. **(C)** This provides the best evidence for the previous question because, as described in the explanation of that question, it allows us to infer the correct answer.

49. **(A)** This can be inferred from what the passage says about how currents in the ocean can transport sediment along the shore: "Even . . . shore" (lines 31–34).

50. **(D)** The passage does not say that the slope of coasts affects sea level. In the last paragraph he describes how "the slope of a coast is critical to determining how water-level changes will affect it" (lines 100–102). All of the others are described as affecting sea level.

51. **(C)** The author says, "On a gently sloping coast, like the U.S. east coast . . . small changes in water level cause the coastline to shift dramatically" (lines 108–111).

52. **(B)** In lines 86–99 ("Global . . . worldwide") the author describes how during the last great ice age "huge amounts of water were transformed into glaciers, resulting in a 100-meter drop in the global sea level." Because a colder climate caused sea levels to fall we can deduce that a warmer climate would cause glaciers to melt and thus sea levels to rise.

Section 2: Writing and Language Test

1. **(C)** The adjective *comparable* (admitting of comparison) is the best choice. Comparable data would be needed to allow an accurate comparison of women's earnings in different years.

2. **(A)** This is the best choice. The participial phrase beginning with the word "working" modifies the noun "women," which is the subject of the sentence.

3. **(B)** The previous sentence gave the earnings of women working full-time in management, business, and financial occupations. Choice (B) provides more detailed information about the earnings of chief executives and computer and information systems managers, which is a sub-category of the larger category mentioned in the previous sentence.

4. **(B)** Choice (A) makes no sense. This choice creates two new grammatical sentences that make good sense.

5. **(C)** Of the choices given, the chart shows that women are far more concentrated in this category than the others mentioned.

6. **(B)** Choice (A) makes no sense. This choice creates two new sentences that make good sense.

7. **(D)** The adjective "relative" makes little sense in context. The adverb "relatively" makes good sense because it is saying that these fields are high-paying in comparison to other fields.

8. **(C)** The given sentence has an error in parallelism because it compares "pay" and "jobs," which are not comparable. This choice corrects the error so that pay in two occupational categories is compared.

9. **(A)** This information provides important support for the main point of the paragraph.

10. **(B)** This is the best choice because it makes a *contrast* between the wages of men and women in working part-time.

11. **(C)** Although the given choice is grammatically correct, standard usage is "little different from." Choice (A) would be correct if it read "which is little different than."

12. **(B)** This choice makes good sense in context. A clue is "offers exciting research possibilities in almost every branch of science." A diverse "laboratory" would allow many types of research.

13. **(C)** This sentence provides an effective transition from the first paragraph, which introduces the idea of the Arctic as a "natural laboratory" offering "research possibilities in almost every branch of science," to the second paragraph, which discusses one of these areas of research.

14. **(C)** *Conspicuous* (attracting attention) makes good sense because the atmospheric effects described would attract attention.

15. **(B)** This choice makes good sense. The jet stream is "affected by" (influenced by) processes of heat exchange and then ("in turn") affects Earth's weather and climate. Note that the verb *affects* (influences) is correct in context. Choice (A) *in turn effects* is incorrect because the verb effect means "to bring about."

16. **(D)** This is the best choice. The adjective prepositional phrase beginning with the word "from" and ending with the word "satellite" describes the noun "forms," telling more about them.

17. **(C)** This is the correct choice because it is grammatically correct and makes good sense. The verb "depend" must agree in number with the subject "solution."

18. **(C)** This is the only choice that makes sense and is grammatical and concise. Choice (D) is grammatically correct; however, it is not as good of a choice as choice (C) because it unnecessarily creates two short sentences.

19. **(C)** This is the only choice that is grammatical. The adjectives "long" and "island" modify the noun "arc," which is the direct object of the verb "encloses."

20. **(D)** Choice (A) is incorrect because sentence 3 does not belong in its present position in the paragraph. Sentence 4 and sentence 5 describe "Alaska's relation to" the "Rim of

Fire," which has a lot of earthquakes. Sentence 3 draws a conclusion based on these two sentences.

21. **(C)** This is the only choice that is grammatical and makes sense. Choice (A) is grammatical but doesn't make sense. It creates a new sentence that follows logically from the preceding sentence.

22. **(B)** This choice is correct because the reflexive pronoun *itself* refers back to its antecedent, the pronoun *it,* which here is used in place of "the United States."

23. **(A)** The main topic of this paragraph is the triclinium. This sentence is an effective topic sentence for the paragraph because it describes the triclinium.

24. **(B)** *Extensive* is incorrect usage in context. The conjunction "and" effectively links the two independent clauses.

25. **(D)** The given sentence is incorrect. It is not grammatical because the prepositional phrase in the first part of the sentence beginning with "In" and ending with "entertainments" refers to "magnificence and extravagance," which should come immediately after the prepositional phrase. This choice corrects the error.

26. **(B)** The given sentence is not grammatical and makes little sense. This choice corrects the error by making "celebrated for his wealth and profuse expenditure" an appositive phrase referring to Lucullus.

27. **(C)** This choice effectively links the two main ideas expressed in the sentence: one, the fact that Lucullus had a certain standard of expenditure for each triclinium and second, that *as a result* (expressed in choice (C) by the word "so") when he told his servants which hall he wanted to sup in they knew what type of entertainment to prepare.

28. **(B)** This choice corrects the given sentence, which is not grammatical.

29. **(D)** The given sentence makes little sense because it says "The triclinium was twice as long" but doesn't say what it was twice as long as. This choice corrects this error and makes good sense.

30. **(B)** The given sentence after the dash makes little sense; "the upper" can't occupy a table. This choice corrects the error by saying that the upper [part] was occupied by the table and the couches.

31. **(B)** Choice (A) makes no sense in context. "Appropriate to" is the best choice. The decorations were "noble," so it would have been easy for them to be inappropriate to the destination, "yet" they were not.

32. **(D)** Choice (A) does not create a grammatical sentence. Choice (D) corrects this to make a grammatical sentence. Note that this choice creates an independent clause beginning with the subject "each."

33. **(A)** The independent clause beginning with the word *there* is existential. That is, it is pointing out the existence of something. The verb must agree with the plural subject, "shrimps, shellfish, and birds of passage." Note that the word "there" is not the subject of the clause.

34. **(A)** This is the best choice. In context, corruption means "change from original state."

35. **(C)** Choice (A) is not grammatical. Choice (C) casts the verb "throw" in the present perfect tense and makes good sense because the writer's actions ("throwing a ray of light," that is) began in the past and is still continuing at present.

36. **(B)** This sentence follows logically from the preceding sentence. It explains how women can follow the same path to liberation as other groups oppressed by men.

37. **(C)** Choice (A) is not grammatical. This choice is correct because one of the uses of the present progressive is to emphasize that action is continuing over a period of time. Clues to the answer are the verbs "asking" and "sharing."

38. **(D)** This is the only grammatically correct choice; all of the other choices create a run-on sentence. This choice creates two grammatically correct sentences.

39. **(C)** Choice (C) and choice (D) are both grammatically correct. However, choice (C) is better because it is less wordy and follows standard usage. The colon is often used, as it is here, to introduce several ideas. In this instance, "love," "chivalry," and "desire to protect women" all tell what man's "nobler feelings" are.

40. **(B)** This is the best choice because it is clear and concise. Choice (A) and choice (D) are grammatically correct but their meaning is not as clear as that of choice (B).

41. **(C)** This is the only choice that creates two grammatical sentences that make sense.

42. **(D)** This is the only choice that is grammatical and makes good sense. This choice creates an adverb clause of condition (beginning with "had" and ending with "equality") modifying the verb "might have."

43. **(B)** This is the only choice that makes a grammatical sentence. It is required by the structure of the sentence. The preposition *from* earlier in the sentence must be followed by the preposition *to*. (*From* this *to* that.)

44. **(B)** *Conceded* (granted) makes good sense because the author is saying that women have not yet attained equality ("her normal condition") because society has not granted them everything necessary for them to achieve it. Choice (A) would be correct if it was "acquiesced *to*."

Section 3: Math Test (No Calculator)

1. **(A)** Although the absolute value of a number must be greater than or equal to 0, the entire expression, $|m - 2| - 2$ could equal –2. For example, suppose $m = 2$, then:

$$|2 - 2| - 2 = 0 - 2 = -2$$

2. **(C)** Given that $g(x) = 2x + 3$, then $g(3) = 2(3) + 3 = 9$. Since $f(x) = x^2 + 2$, then

$$f(-2) = (-2)^2 + 2 = 6$$

Thus, $g(3) - f(-2) = 9 - 6 = 3$.

Choice (A) is incorrect because it is the sum of $g(x)$ and $f(x)$. Choice (B) is incorrect because it is the value of $g(3)$. Choice (D) is incorrect because it is the result of improper calculation.

3. **(C)** Multiply $x + 4.5y = -12$ by -2. Attain the same coefficient of x but with different signs. Solve by elimination.

$$\begin{aligned} 2x - 3y &= 24 \\ -2(x + 4.5y &= -12) \end{aligned}$$

Solve by eliminating x.

$$\begin{aligned} 2x - 3y &= 24 \\ + -2x - 9y &= 24 \\ \hline -12y &= 48 \\ y &= -4 \end{aligned}$$

Replace y with -4 in $2x - 3y = 24$.

$$\begin{aligned} 2x - 3(-4) &= 24 \\ 2x + 12 &= 24 \\ 2x &= 12 \\ x &= 6 \end{aligned}$$

The product of x and y is $(6)(-4) = -24$
This problem could also have been solved by using the substitution method.

$$\begin{aligned} x + 4.5y &= -12 \\ x &= -4.5y - 12 \end{aligned}$$

$(-4.5y - 12)$ would be substituted for x in $2x - 3y = 24$

4. **(C)** You may have noticed that the length of the shoelace is three times the number of holes. For example a 4-hole lace is 12 inches long and an 8-hole lace is 24 inches long. Therefore, the hiking boot will need shoelaces that are 54 inches long because $18 \times 3 = 54$.

5. **(D)** Substituting for m and n into $3n - m$ results in the following:

$$\begin{aligned} &3(4x^2 + 5x - 7) - (2x^3 + 3x - 11) = \\ &12x^2 + 15x - 21 - 2x^3 - 3x + 11 = \end{aligned}$$

Combine like terms by adding and subtracting those terms with variables raised to the same power.

$$-2x^3 + 12x^2 + 12x - 10$$

6. **(A)** Cross-multiply the proportion and solve for x.

$$\begin{aligned} \frac{1}{3x-1} &= \frac{2}{x} \\ (2)(3x - 1) &= (1)(x) \\ 6x - 2 &= x \\ -2 &= -5x \\ \frac{2}{5} &= x \end{aligned}$$

7. **(D)** Subtract \$2.00 from \$15.75 to count the first quarter mile.

$$\$15.75 - \$2.00 = \$13.75$$

Divide \$13.75 by \$1.25 to calculate the remaining quarter miles.

$$\$13.75 \div \$1.25 = 11$$

The taxi traveled a total of 12 quarter miles. Divide 12 by 4 to find the equivalent number of miles.

$$12 \div 4 = 3$$

8. **(C)** If the system of equations has no solution, each equation has the same slope and a different y-intercept, thus making the lines parallel. In this system of equations, the x's and y's must be multiples of one another.

Find the multiple by dividing $-\frac{10}{3}y$ by $-\frac{5}{9}y$.

$$-\frac{10}{3}y \div -\frac{5}{9}y = 6$$

Multiply $\frac{2}{3}$ by 6 to find the value of b.

$$\frac{2}{3} \times 6 = 4$$

Make sure the constants are different to ensure the lines are parallel. –7(6) does not equal 17 because –42 does not equal 17.

9. **(C)** Square both sides of the equation to get rid of the radical.

$$\sqrt{n-(-4)} = n-2$$
$$(\sqrt{n--4})^2 = (n-2)^2$$
$$n+4 = n^2-4n+4$$
$$0 = n^2-5n$$
$$0 = n(n-5)$$

$n = 0$ or $n - 5 = 0$

$n = 0$ or $n = 5$

Check each solution in the original equation to ascertain any extraneous solutions.

Check 5:

$$\sqrt{5-(-4)} = 5-2$$
$$\sqrt{9} = 3$$
$$3 = 3$$

Check 0:

$$\sqrt{0-(-4)} = 0-2$$
$$\sqrt{4} = -2$$
$$2 \neq -2$$

We accept 5 as the solution and reject 0.

10. **(C)** Let x = the number of points scored in the game.

$$\frac{1}{3}x+\frac{1}{4}x+\frac{1}{3}x+8=x$$
$$\frac{11}{12}x+8=x$$
$$8=\frac{1}{12}x$$
$$96=x$$

11. **(D)** Expand $(x-y)^2$

$$(x-y)^2 = x^2 - 2xy + y^2$$

It was given that $x^2 + y^2 = 12$ and $xy = -13$. Therefore, $-2xy = 26$

$$(x-y)^2 = 12 + 26 = 38$$

Multiply the equation by 2.

$$2(x-y)^2 = (2)(38) = 76$$

12. **(B)** Dish #2 has B bacteria, which is twice the number in dish #1. Therefore, 2A = B. Dish #3 has C bacteria, which is 17 more than B. Given that B = 2A and C = B + 17, then C = 2A + 17.

13. **(C)** The two functions f and g intersect when their x and y values are the same. Set each of the functions equal and solve for x.

$$6x^2 - 24 = -6x^2 + 24$$

Add $6x^2$ and 24 to both sides to isolate x^2.

$$6x^2 - 24 + 6x^2 + 24 = -6x^2 + 24 + 6x^2 + 24$$
$$12x^2 = 48$$
$$x^2 = 4$$

Find the square root of each side of the equation.

$$x^2 = 4$$
$$x = \pm 2$$

Since we are looking for c rather than $-c$, its value is 2.

14. **(B)** Rationalize the denominator by multiplying the numerator and the denominator by $2 + 3i$, the conjugate of $2 - 3i$.

$$\frac{7}{2-3i}\times\frac{2+3i}{2+3i}=$$
$$\frac{7(2+3i)}{4-9i^2}=$$
$$\frac{14+21i}{4+9}=\frac{14+21i}{13}$$

Note that if $i=\sqrt{-1}$, then $i^2=-1$.

15. **(C)** Solve the equation by first dividing all of the terms by 3.

$$(6x^2 + 12x - 15) \div 3 = 0 \div 3$$
$$2x^2 + 4x - 5 = 0$$

The equation cannot be factored so use the quadratic equation to solve.

$$x = \frac{-b \pm \sqrt{b^2 - 4ac}}{2a}$$

$$a = 2 \quad b = 4 \quad c = -5$$

$$\frac{-4 \pm \sqrt{(4)^2 - 4(2)(-5)}}{2(2)}$$

$$\frac{-4 \pm \sqrt{16+40}}{4} =$$

$$\frac{-4 \pm \sqrt{56}}{4} = \frac{-2 \pm \sqrt{14}}{2}$$

16. **140** If a segment connects the midpoints of two sides of a triangle, then the segment (in this case corridor $\overline{AB}$) is both parallel to the base and $\frac{1}{2}$ its length. Multiply one of the bases of the triangular floor by $\frac{1}{2}$.

$$\frac{1}{2} \times 280 = 140$$

17. **5,000**

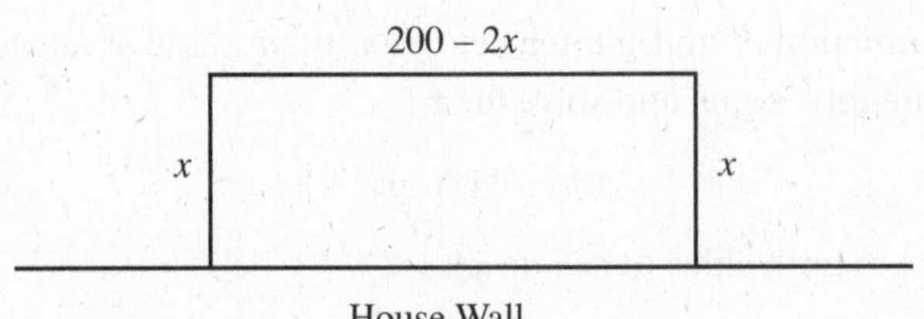

The area of a rectangle is found by using the formula Area = (length)(width). Using the diagram we get

$$f(x) = (200 - 2x)(x) = -2x^2 + 200x$$

The lead term is negative and the function is quadratic, resulting in a parabola that opens down. Its vertex is a maximum of the function which provides the maximum enclosed area of the fence. Begin finding the vertex by using the formula $x = -\frac{b}{2a}$.

$$a = -2 \quad b = 200$$

$$-\frac{200}{2(-2)} = 50$$

Replace x with 50 in $f(x) = -2x^2 + 200x$

$$f(50) = -2(50)^2 + 200(50) = 5{,}000$$

This can be demonstrated with the diagram below.

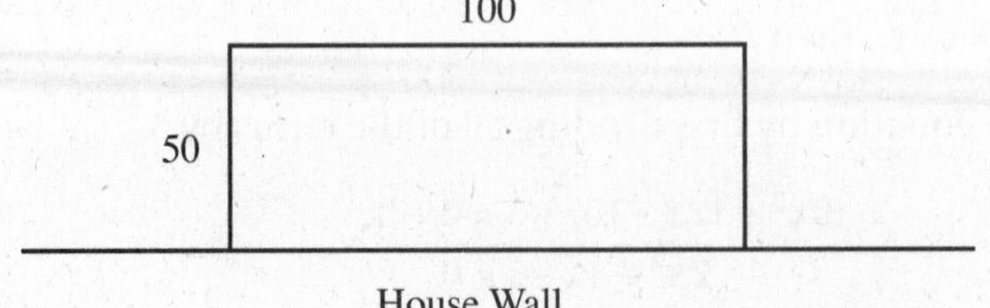

The maximum area enclosed by the fencing is 5,000 square feet. Confirm the calculation by using the formula Area = (length)(width).

$$\text{Area} = 100 \times 50 = 5{,}000$$

18. **6** Begin factoring $x^3 - 6x^2 + 2x - 12 = 0$ by grouping.

$$(x^3 - 6x^2) + (2x - 12) = 0$$

Extract the largest common factor from each of the parentheses.

$$x^2(x - 6) + 2(x - 6) = 0$$

Place x^2 and 2 in its own parentheses.

$$(x^2 + 2)(x - 6) = 0$$

Set each of the parentheses equal to 0.

$$x^2 + 2 = 0 \text{ or } x - 6 = 0$$
$$x^2 = -2 \text{ or } x = 6$$

$x^2 = -2$ becomes $x = \pm i\sqrt{2}$, neither of which is a real number. Therefore, the real solution to $x^3 - 6x^2 + 2x - 12 = 0$ is $x = 6$.

19. **36** $r = 3\sqrt{3}$ and $2r = \sqrt{3x}$, therefore $2r$ also equals $(2)(3\sqrt{3})$ or $6\sqrt{3}$. Set $6\sqrt{3}$ equal to $\sqrt{3x}$ and solve for x.
Remove the radicals by squaring both sides.

$$6\sqrt{3} = \sqrt{3x}$$
$$(6\sqrt{3})^2 = (\sqrt{3x})^2$$
$$108 = 3x$$
$$36 = x$$

20. **2,000** Light travels according to the diagram in a relatively straight line. Thus, use a linear model in the form of $y = mx + b$ to find the time light travels to point E_1. Consider the point where Jupiter is located as the origin leading to $b = 0$.
Let x = distance
Let y = time
Using the information provided in the problem, we have point E_1 at (600, y) and E_2 at (900, y + 1000). Find the slope of the line connecting these two points.

$$\frac{(y+1000)-y}{900-600} = \frac{1000}{300} = \frac{10}{3}$$

The linear model is $y = \frac{10}{3}x$. Find the time light travels by replacing x with the distance from Jupiter to E_1, which is 600 GM.

$$y = \frac{10}{3}(600) = 2000$$

Light travels for 2,000 seconds to reach E_1 from Jupiter.

PRACTICE TEST 1

Section 4: Math Test (Calculator)

1. **(C)** Cross-multiply and solve for x.

$$\frac{m-4}{3}=\frac{x}{9}$$
$$3x=9(m-4)$$
$$x=3(m-4)$$

2. **(C)** The phrase "... at the same rate ..." means use the linear model $y = mx + b$. Find the slope by using the ordered pairs (2, \$2870) and (5, \$7150).

$$m=\frac{y_2-y_1}{x_2-x_1}=\frac{7150-2870}{5-2}=\frac{4280}{3}=1426.67$$

Replace m with 1426.67.

$$y = 1426.67x + b$$

Replace x and y with either point.

$$2870 = 2(1426.67) + b$$
$$16.67 = b$$
$$y = 1426.67x + 16.67$$

Replace x with 78 months, but remember to first convert it to years.

$$78 \text{ months} = 6.5 \text{ years}$$
$$y = 1426.67(6.5) + 16.66$$
$$y = 9{,}290.02$$

\$9,290.02

3. **(B)** Let x = the positive integer

$$x^3 - x^2 = 2x$$
$$x^3 - x^2 - 2x = 0$$
$$x(x^2 - x - 2) = 0$$
$$x(x-2)(x+1) = 0$$
$$x = 0 \quad x-2=0 \quad x+1=0$$
$$x = 0 \quad x=2 \quad x=-1$$

Since x is a positive integer, $x = 2$
If factoring is difficult, try a plug-and-check strategy.

$$(2)^3 - 2^2 = 2(2)$$
$$8 - 4 = 4$$
$$4 = 4$$

4. **(C)** Find the probability of Mr. Tessler choosing a slide of paramecia as his first selection.

$$P(\text{paramecia selected}) = \frac{2}{10}=\frac{1}{5}$$

Next, find the probability of selecting a slide of amoebae. Remember, there are now only 9 slides available since the first slide was removed.

$$P(\text{amoebae}) = \frac{5}{9}$$

Find the probability of selecting a slide of paramecia followed by a slide of amoebae by multiplying the probabilities.

$$\frac{1}{5} \times \frac{5}{9} = \frac{1}{9}$$

5. **(B)** Divide the miles to the Andromeda Galaxy by the miles in a light year to find the light years to the Andromeda Galaxy.

$$\frac{1.3 \times 10^{19}}{5.87 \times 10^{12}} \approx .22 \times 10^{7} = 2.2 \times 10^{6}$$

In scientific notation, the first number is expressed such that $1 \leq x < 10$ and the second number is 10 expressed to a power.

6. **(A)** The cost for m computers at \$18.75 each is \$18.75m. The cost for r keyboards at \$13.25 each is \$13.25r. The cost must be less than \$139, so we arrive at

$$18.75m + 13.25r < 139.$$

Choices (B) and (D) can automatically be eliminated because each features ≤ (less than or equal to). The problem stipulates the cost must be less than \$139.

7. **(D)** The probability of rain on Thursday is 65%. Since the probability of rain on Friday and Saturday is 74% and 31%, respectively, subtract each from 100% to find the probability of no rain on both days.
No rain on Friday: 100% – 74% = 26%
No rain on Saturday: 100% – 31% = 69%
Each day's forecast is independent of the others so multiply the three probabilities.

$$(.65)(.26)(.69) = .1166 \approx 11.7\%.$$

8. **(B)** A system of equations has an infinite number of equations when the lines are the same. For example,

$$x + y = 6$$
$$2x + 2y = 12$$

has infinite solutions because $2(x + y) = (6)(2)$. Both equations are multiples of one another.
Observe the following:

$$7x - 4y = 13$$
$$mx - 10y = 32.5$$
$$(32.5) \div 13 = 2.5$$
$$(-10) \div (-4) = 2.5$$

In order for the system of equations to have infinite solutions, m must be 2.5 times greater than 7.

$$7 \times 2.5 = m$$
$$17.5 = m$$

9. **(D)** The cost of x gallons of water at \$.17/gallon is $.17x$. The tax applied is found by $[.17x + (.073)(.17x)]$ which can be rewritten as $(1.073)(.17x)$. Add the monthly service charge to get

$$f(x) = 31.5 + (1.073)(.17x).$$

10. **(A)** Use the formula $\frac{\text{part}}{\text{whole}} = \frac{n}{100}$ to find the percent of those operating cars that were in the category 6 to 11 years old.

$$6-8: 22.2$$
$$9-11: 16.7$$

The number of cars (in millions) that are between 6 and 11 years old is 38.9 because $22.2 + 16.7 = 38.9$.

Total cars: 104.7

$$\frac{38.9}{104.7} = \frac{n}{100}$$

Cross-multiply and solve for n.

$$104.7n = 38{,}900$$
$$n = 37.2\%$$

11. **(B)** Find the number of cars that were 20 years old and older.

$$(.013)(104.7) = 1.36 \text{ million}$$

Use the formula $\frac{\text{part}}{\text{whole}} = \frac{n}{100}$ to find the percent of cars 12 years old and older that are 20 years old and older.

$$\frac{1.36}{14.4} = \frac{n}{100}$$

Cross-multiply and solve for n.

$$14.4n = 136$$
$$n = 9.4\%$$

12. **(C)** Inverse variation means one variable increases proportionally to the decrease in the other variable. SAT scores generally dropped as daily television/device watching increased.

13. **(D)** The data appear to descend to the right, indicating a negative slope. Therefore, choices (A) and (B) can be eliminated. Choose two points in the center of the data and derive the equation of the line that connects them.

$$(1, 14)\ (2, 12)$$
$$m = \frac{y_2 - y_1}{x_2 - x_1}$$
$$m = \frac{12-14}{2-1}$$
$$m = -2$$
$$y = -2x + b$$

Substitute either point for x and y.

$$14 = -2(1) + b$$
$$16 = b$$

The equation of a line of best fit could be $y = -2x + 16$. Choice (D) is the closest to this equation.

14. **(C)** A = accumulated value of the home over time; P = the purchase price of the home; t = time in years. The formula for the growth of the home over time is the exponential equation $A = P(1.0372)^t$. The addition of 1 and .0372 insures growth in the calculations.

15. **(C)** Input the information provided in the question into the formula $A = P(1.0372)^t$. We substitute 3 for t because three years have elapsed from 2010 to 2013.

$$A = 187{,}650(1.0372)^3 = \$209{,}380$$

16. **(C)** A large outlier skews the value of the mean toward larger values. The following fulfills the description of the data set:

5 8 12 13 292

The mean is 66 but the median is 12. The large value, 292, skewed the mean much higher than any of the other numbers in the set.

17. **(B)** The median of a data set is its middle value when the numbers are arranged in order. Arrange the number of cans in ascending order.

____ ____ 113 116 119

The additional values, x and 108, can appear as follows:

x 108 113 116 119

In this case, the greatest value for x is 107. However, the number of cans can also be arranged in this fashion:

108 x 113 116 119

The greatest value for x in this arrangement is 112. The question asks for the greatest value of x, so we choose choice (B), 112.

Choice (D) is incorrect because it erroneously assumes that x must be less than 108.

18. **(D)** Subtract the area of the square from the area of the circle.
Area of a square: side × side (s^2)

Divide the perimeter by 4 and square that value:

$$\left(\frac{64}{4}\right)^2 = 16^2 = 256$$

The area of the square is 256 square units.

$$\text{Area of a circle} = \pi r^2$$

The diameter of the circle is equal to the length of one of the sides of the square. Each side is 16 so the radius is 8 because the radius of a circle is one-half of the diameter.

$$\pi(8)^2 \approx 201.1$$

Subtract the area of the circle from the area of the square.

$$256 - 201.1 = 54.9$$

Divide the remaining area by 4 to find the shaded area.

$$54.9 \div 4 = 13.73$$

Divide the measure of the shaded area by the area of the square to find the probability of a coin landing in the shaded area.

$$13.73 \div 256 = .053$$

The diagram is assumed to be drawn to scale so choice (A), .363, would appear to be much too large.

19. **(B)** The slopes of perpendicular lines are the opposite reciprocal of one another. Transform $-5x + 6y = -7$ to slope-intercept form to determine its slope.

$$-5x + 6y = -7$$

$$6y = 5x - 7$$

$$y = \frac{5}{6}x - \frac{7}{6}$$

The slope of the line $-5x + 6y = -7$ is $\frac{5}{6}$. The slope of a line perpendicular to $-5x + 6y = -7$ is $-\frac{6}{5}$. Only choice (B) has slope $-\frac{6}{5}$.

$$6x + 5y = 15$$
$$5y = -6x + 15$$
$$y = -\frac{6}{5}x + 3$$

Expressed in slope-intercept form, the slope of $6x + 5y = 15$ is $-\frac{6}{5}$.

Choices (A), (C), and (D) are incorrect because their slopes are $\frac{3}{5}$, $\frac{3}{10}$, and $-\frac{5}{6}$, respectively.

20. **(C)** Find the percentage that is utility expense in 2015.

$$100\% - (14.4 + 41 + 21.6 + 19) = 4\%$$

Set up a proportion comparing an item's percentage of the budget to its dollar expenditure.

$$\frac{21.6}{4{,}100{,}000} = \frac{4}{x}$$

Cross-multiply and solve for x.

$$(21.6)(x) = (4)(4{,}100{,}000)$$
$$21.6x = 16{,}400{,}000$$
$$x = \$759{,}259$$

21. **(A)** The standard deviation is a measure of how far the data set values are from the mean. In the data set for College B, the large majority of the data are in three of the five possible values, which are the three values closest to the mean. In the data set for College A, the data are more spread out, with many values at the minimum and maximum values. Therefore, by observation, the data for College A have a larger standard deviation.

22. **(A)** The percent of high school graduates in 2006 was 73% and in 2012 the percent had increased to 81%. Divide 81 by 73 to find the percent increase.

$$81 \div 73 = 1.109$$

The increase was 10.9%; the closest answer to this figure is 11%.

23. **(D)** The formula indicates the amount of money earned at a savings institution on a \$2,500 deposit, compounded monthly at r%. To find the additional dollars earned at 6% versus 3.2%, find the difference between the annual earnings at each rate.

$2{,}500\left[1+\frac{6}{1{,}200}\right]^{12}$ represents the amount earned each year at 6%.

$2{,}500\left[1+\frac{3.2}{1{,}200}\right]^{12}$ represents the amount earned at 3.2%.

Find their difference by subtracting the smaller expression from the larger.

$$2{,}500\left[1+\frac{6}{1{,}200}\right]^{12}-2{,}500\left[1+\frac{3.2}{1{,}200}\right]^{12}$$

24. **(B)** Inverse variation uses the model $xy = k$ where k is a constant. Since the question stipulates that the square root of x varies inversely with y, use the model $\sqrt{x}y=k$.

$$\sqrt{196}\times -\frac{1}{2}=k$$
$$-7=k$$

Now input $y = -3$ into the equation.

$$\sqrt{x}\times -3=-7$$
$$\sqrt{x}=\frac{7}{3}$$
$$(\sqrt{x})^2=\left(\frac{7}{3}\right)^2$$
$$x=\frac{49}{9}$$

25. **(B)** The graph shows an unmistakable upward rise to the right; as the age increases, so, too, does the distance thrown. Choice (A), which indicates a weak negative correlation in the graph, can be discarded; the graph clearly moves vertically as age increases.

26. **(C)** Find the line of best fit by selecting two points that lie within the data.

$$(12, 100) \quad (15, 200)$$

Find the slope of a line that connects the two points.

$$\frac{y_2-y_1}{x_2-x_1}=\frac{200-100}{15-12}\approx 33.33$$
$$y = 33.33x + b$$

Use either point to find b.

$$100 = 33.33(12) + b$$
$$-299.6 = b$$
$$y = 33.33x - 299.6$$

27. **(C)** Substitute 18 for x in the equation $y = 33.33x - 299.6$.

$$y = 33.33(18) - 299.6 \approx 300 \text{ feet.}$$

28. **(C)** Expand $(2 - 4i)^2$:

$$\begin{aligned}(2-4i)^2 &= 4 - 16i + 16i^2\\ &= 4 - 16i - 16\\ &= -12 - 16i\end{aligned}$$

Multiply $-12 - 16i$ by 3:

$$3(-12 - 16i) = -36 - 48i$$

29. **(D)** If nine students earned an average score of 79%, the class amassed 711 points because $9 \times 79 = 711$. In order for ten students to have an average score of 81, the class must collect 810 points because $10 \times 81 = 810$. Subtracting we get: $810 - 711 = 99$. The tenth student must earn a score of 99% to raise the class average to 81%.

30. **(C)** If the entire class contributed equally, the cost per student, in terms of s and D would be $\frac{D}{s}$. However, 15 of the students do not contribute this sum, so $15\frac{D}{s}$ needs to be split among the remaining $s - 15$ students.

$\frac{15\frac{D}{s}}{s-15}$ can be rewritten as $\left(15\frac{D}{s}\right)\left(\frac{1}{(s-15)}\right)$. Multiplying the numerators and denominators, we arrive at $\frac{15D}{s^2 - 15s}$.

31. **60** Use the formula $d = rt$ (distance = rate $\times$ time) in the form of $t = \frac{d}{r}$.
We get:

Iris: $t = \frac{5 \text{ miles}}{50 \text{ miles per hour}} = \frac{1}{10} \text{ hour } = 6 \text{ minutes}$

Steve: $\frac{5 \text{ miles}}{60 \text{ miles per hour}} = \frac{1}{12} \text{ hour} = 5 \text{ minutes}$

The difference in time is 1 minute or 60 seconds.

32. **848** Replace $P(x)$ with \$9,321,250, the company's profit.

$$\begin{aligned}9{,}321{,}250 &= 11{,}000x - 6{,}750\\ 9{,}328{,}000 &= 11{,}000x\\ 848 &= x\end{aligned}$$

33. **1,786** Kari needs to set the plans equal to each other while leaving the number of minutes as a variable.
Let x = the number of minutes at \$.007 per minute
Plan 1: $24 + .007x$
Plan 2: 36.50

$$\begin{aligned}24 + .007x &= 36.50\\ .007x &= 12.50\\ x &= 1{,}786\end{aligned}$$

At 1,786 minutes, the two data plans have equal monthly costs.

34. **256** The way to calculate the distance of a star is to square the apparent dimness to find the distance. For example, the galaxy that is 1000 times dimmer is 1,000,000 times farther away ($1000^2 = 1{,}000{,}000$). The nebula that is 30 times as dim is 900 times further away ($30^2 = 900$). Therefore a star that is 16 times dimmer than another would be 256 times distant than the brighter star because $16^2 = 256$.

35. **1, 2, 4, 8, or 16** The equation $x^{\frac{y}{4}} = 81$ where x and y are positive integers, can be written as follows:

$$3^4 = 81$$

$$9^2 = 81$$

$$81^1 = 81$$

$$(81^2)^{\frac{1}{2}} = 81$$

$$(81^4)^{\frac{1}{4}} = 81$$

If $x^{\frac{y}{4}} = 81$, and x and y are positive integers, then $\frac{y}{4}$ can equal 4, 2, 1, $\frac{1}{2}$, or $\frac{1}{4}$. Therefore, the value of y can be 16, 8, 4, 2, or 1.

36. **21.6** The area of a sector is found by using the formula

$$A = \frac{m}{360}\pi r^2$$

where m = measure of the central angle and r = length of the radius.
Input the known data and solve for r.

$$139.6 = \frac{34.4}{360}\pi r^2$$

$$465.33 \approx r^2$$

$$21.6 \approx r$$

37. **7.5 or $\frac{15}{2}$** Direct variation calculations can be found by using the model $\frac{y_1}{x_1} = \frac{y_2}{x_2}$.

In the situation with the refracted images, use the model

$$\frac{\text{actual depth}}{\text{apparent depth}} = \frac{\text{actual depth}}{\text{apparent depth}}$$

$$\frac{5}{4} = \frac{n}{6}$$

$$30 = 4n$$

$$7.5 = n$$

38. **2.25** Use the model $\frac{\text{actual depth}}{\text{apparent depth}} = \frac{\text{actual depth}}{\text{apparent depth}}$ to find the actual depth of the keys.

$$\frac{n}{9} = \frac{5}{4}$$

$$45 = 4n$$

$$11.25 = n$$

The question asks for the difference between the actual depth and the apparent depth, so subtract 9 from 11.25.

$$11.25 - 9 = 2.25$$

PRACTICE TEST 1

Section 5: Essay (Optional)

SUGGESTED ESSAY TEST 1

Following is an essay written in response to the prompt. It is unlikely that you would be able to write such a full response in the time allowed, so don't worry if your essay is significantly shorter. Use the suggested essay to see how the task might be approached. For practice, you may wish to rewrite your own essay incorporating some of the points discussed in it.

In this passage Marie Winn discusses the effects that watching television has on children, and suggests an intriguing way of looking at the issue that challenges conventional thinking on the topic. She constructs an argument to support her central contention, which she makes in the first paragraph, that "one is always just watching television when sitting in front of the screen rather than having any other experience."

Winn relies largely on logic to develop this central argument. In the second paragraph she summarizes the views of a group of concerned parents who have worked to reduce violence shown on television as well as the number of commercials. She quotes one of the founders of this group, who expresses the view that children's programs "should meet the specific needs of children." This seems a reasonable enough wish. But Winn follows this quotation with a rhetorical question: "But is it the needs of children which are at stake when parents demand better programs?" This question encourages the reader to question the seemingly obvious assumption that parents who advocate "better" programs for children are motivated primarily by the needs of children. She then makes explicit her own view, suggesting that it is the needs of parents "to find a convenient source of amusement for their offspring" (that is, television) that drives this concern about the types of programs children watch.

Winn is arguing, in other words, that parents allow and even encourage their children to watch television; therefore, children watch a lot of television—which results in parents feeling "anxieties" about this, resulting in parents wanting more "educational" programs to lessen these anxieties.

Although Winn relies primarily on logic, she also makes effective use of language. In the second paragraph, which we just examined, she clearly and concisely summarizes her views by using phrases such as "a convenient source of amusement" and, tellingly, "if the time spent at least seems to be educational."

In the third paragraph Winn turns to what she considers the "real needs" of children that she feels are not met, or not met adequately, by television viewing. She outlines these clearly, using key words—relationships, initiative, communication—to highlight these needs. Her points are given additional force by the use of a semicolon after the description of each need. The semicolon is followed by a brief but uncompromising assertion beginning with the word "television": "television only reduces . . . television provides too easily . . . television retards." The weakness in Winn's argument here is that it offers no evidence for her assertions other than what she and the reader have gathered from their own experiences.

The remainder of the passage discusses "a number of fallacies that have misled parents into thinking that the problem of television will be solved by improving its quality." Winn argues her case clearly and logically. Space does not permit a detailed discussion of the rhetorical techniques she uses here. Worth noting, however, is how she closes the passage in the final sentence. The paragraph is one long sentence that summarizes the main idea of the passage—that television itself is what is harmful to children. This conclusion appeals to the emotions of parents and is a heartfelt call for them to recognize a problem concerning their children and act on it. It is especially effective because, although it is emotional, it is nevertheless logical.

All in all, this is a persuasive piece of writing that logically analyzes an important issue, questions common assumptions about it that are often unquestioningly accepted, and offers a clear solution to a problem. Winn's tone is reasonable throughout but it still conveys a sense of urgency.

Refer to the SAT Essay Rubric on page 23 to analyze and score your essay response. For further guidance on this essay and additional practice and evaluation by teacher and author Philip Geer, contact *info@mentaurs.com*.

ANSWER SHEET
Practice Test 2

Section 1: Reading

1. Ⓐ Ⓑ Ⓒ Ⓓ	14. Ⓐ Ⓑ Ⓒ Ⓓ	27. Ⓐ Ⓑ Ⓒ Ⓓ	40. Ⓐ Ⓑ Ⓒ Ⓓ
2. Ⓐ Ⓑ Ⓒ Ⓓ	15. Ⓐ Ⓑ Ⓒ Ⓓ	28. Ⓐ Ⓑ Ⓒ Ⓓ	41. Ⓐ Ⓑ Ⓒ Ⓓ
3. Ⓐ Ⓑ Ⓒ Ⓓ	16. Ⓐ Ⓑ Ⓒ Ⓓ	29. Ⓐ Ⓑ Ⓒ Ⓓ	42. Ⓐ Ⓑ Ⓒ Ⓓ
4. Ⓐ Ⓑ Ⓒ Ⓓ	17. Ⓐ Ⓑ Ⓒ Ⓓ	30. Ⓐ Ⓑ Ⓒ Ⓓ	43. Ⓐ Ⓑ Ⓒ Ⓓ
5. Ⓐ Ⓑ Ⓒ Ⓓ	18. Ⓐ Ⓑ Ⓒ Ⓓ	31. Ⓐ Ⓑ Ⓒ Ⓓ	44. Ⓐ Ⓑ Ⓒ Ⓓ
6. Ⓐ Ⓑ Ⓒ Ⓓ	19. Ⓐ Ⓑ Ⓒ Ⓓ	32. Ⓐ Ⓑ Ⓒ Ⓓ	45. Ⓐ Ⓑ Ⓒ Ⓓ
7. Ⓐ Ⓑ Ⓒ Ⓓ	20. Ⓐ Ⓑ Ⓒ Ⓓ	33. Ⓐ Ⓑ Ⓒ Ⓓ	46. Ⓐ Ⓑ Ⓒ Ⓓ
8. Ⓐ Ⓑ Ⓒ Ⓓ	21. Ⓐ Ⓑ Ⓒ Ⓓ	34. Ⓐ Ⓑ Ⓒ Ⓓ	47. Ⓐ Ⓑ Ⓒ Ⓓ
9. Ⓐ Ⓑ Ⓒ Ⓓ	22. Ⓐ Ⓑ Ⓒ Ⓓ	35. Ⓐ Ⓑ Ⓒ Ⓓ	48. Ⓐ Ⓑ Ⓒ Ⓓ
10. Ⓐ Ⓑ Ⓒ Ⓓ	23. Ⓐ Ⓑ Ⓒ Ⓓ	36. Ⓐ Ⓑ Ⓒ Ⓓ	49. Ⓐ Ⓑ Ⓒ Ⓓ
11. Ⓐ Ⓑ Ⓒ Ⓓ	24. Ⓐ Ⓑ Ⓒ Ⓓ	37. Ⓐ Ⓑ Ⓒ Ⓓ	50. Ⓐ Ⓑ Ⓒ Ⓓ
12. Ⓐ Ⓑ Ⓒ Ⓓ	25. Ⓐ Ⓑ Ⓒ Ⓓ	38. Ⓐ Ⓑ Ⓒ Ⓓ	51. Ⓐ Ⓑ Ⓒ Ⓓ
13. Ⓐ Ⓑ Ⓒ Ⓓ	26. Ⓐ Ⓑ Ⓒ Ⓓ	39. Ⓐ Ⓑ Ⓒ Ⓓ	52. Ⓐ Ⓑ Ⓒ Ⓓ

Section 2: Writing and Language

1. Ⓐ Ⓑ Ⓒ Ⓓ	12. Ⓐ Ⓑ Ⓒ Ⓓ	23. Ⓐ Ⓑ Ⓒ Ⓓ	34. Ⓐ Ⓑ Ⓒ Ⓓ
2. Ⓐ Ⓑ Ⓒ Ⓓ	13. Ⓐ Ⓑ Ⓒ Ⓓ	24. Ⓐ Ⓑ Ⓒ Ⓓ	35. Ⓐ Ⓑ Ⓒ Ⓓ
3. Ⓐ Ⓑ Ⓒ Ⓓ	14. Ⓐ Ⓑ Ⓒ Ⓓ	25. Ⓐ Ⓑ Ⓒ Ⓓ	36. Ⓐ Ⓑ Ⓒ Ⓓ
4. Ⓐ Ⓑ Ⓒ Ⓓ	15. Ⓐ Ⓑ Ⓒ Ⓓ	26. Ⓐ Ⓑ Ⓒ Ⓓ	37. Ⓐ Ⓑ Ⓒ Ⓓ
5. Ⓐ Ⓑ Ⓒ Ⓓ	16. Ⓐ Ⓑ Ⓒ Ⓓ	27. Ⓐ Ⓑ Ⓒ Ⓓ	38. Ⓐ Ⓑ Ⓒ Ⓓ
6. Ⓐ Ⓑ Ⓒ Ⓓ	17. Ⓐ Ⓑ Ⓒ Ⓓ	28. Ⓐ Ⓑ Ⓒ Ⓓ	39. Ⓐ Ⓑ Ⓒ Ⓓ
7. Ⓐ Ⓑ Ⓒ Ⓓ	18. Ⓐ Ⓑ Ⓒ Ⓓ	29. Ⓐ Ⓑ Ⓒ Ⓓ	40. Ⓐ Ⓑ Ⓒ Ⓓ
8. Ⓐ Ⓑ Ⓒ Ⓓ	19. Ⓐ Ⓑ Ⓒ Ⓓ	30. Ⓐ Ⓑ Ⓒ Ⓓ	41. Ⓐ Ⓑ Ⓒ Ⓓ
9. Ⓐ Ⓑ Ⓒ Ⓓ	20. Ⓐ Ⓑ Ⓒ Ⓓ	31. Ⓐ Ⓑ Ⓒ Ⓓ	42. Ⓐ Ⓑ Ⓒ Ⓓ
10. Ⓐ Ⓑ Ⓒ Ⓓ	21. Ⓐ Ⓑ Ⓒ Ⓓ	32. Ⓐ Ⓑ Ⓒ Ⓓ	43. Ⓐ Ⓑ Ⓒ Ⓓ
11. Ⓐ Ⓑ Ⓒ Ⓓ	22. Ⓐ Ⓑ Ⓒ Ⓓ	33. Ⓐ Ⓑ Ⓒ Ⓓ	44. Ⓐ Ⓑ Ⓒ Ⓓ

ANSWER SHEET
Practice Test 2

Section 3: Math (No Calculator)

1. Ⓐ Ⓑ Ⓒ Ⓓ
2. Ⓐ Ⓑ Ⓒ Ⓓ
3. Ⓐ Ⓑ Ⓒ Ⓓ
4. Ⓐ Ⓑ Ⓒ Ⓓ
5. Ⓐ Ⓑ Ⓒ Ⓓ
6. Ⓐ Ⓑ Ⓒ Ⓓ
7. Ⓐ Ⓑ Ⓒ Ⓓ
8. Ⓐ Ⓑ Ⓒ Ⓓ
9. Ⓐ Ⓑ Ⓒ Ⓓ
10. Ⓐ Ⓑ Ⓒ Ⓓ
11. Ⓐ Ⓑ Ⓒ Ⓓ
12. Ⓐ Ⓑ Ⓒ Ⓓ
13. Ⓐ Ⓑ Ⓒ Ⓓ
14. Ⓐ Ⓑ Ⓒ Ⓓ
15. Ⓐ Ⓑ Ⓒ Ⓓ

16.

17.

18.

19.

20.

ANSWER SHEET
Practice Test 2

Section 4: Math (Calculator)

1. Ⓐ Ⓑ Ⓒ Ⓓ
2. Ⓐ Ⓑ Ⓒ Ⓓ
3. Ⓐ Ⓑ Ⓒ Ⓓ
4. Ⓐ Ⓑ Ⓒ Ⓓ
5. Ⓐ Ⓑ Ⓒ Ⓓ
6. Ⓐ Ⓑ Ⓒ Ⓓ
7. Ⓐ Ⓑ Ⓒ Ⓓ
8. Ⓐ Ⓑ Ⓒ Ⓓ
9. Ⓐ Ⓑ Ⓒ Ⓓ
10. Ⓐ Ⓑ Ⓒ Ⓓ
11. Ⓐ Ⓑ Ⓒ Ⓓ
12. Ⓐ Ⓑ Ⓒ Ⓓ
13. Ⓐ Ⓑ Ⓒ Ⓓ
14. Ⓐ Ⓑ Ⓒ Ⓓ
15. Ⓐ Ⓑ Ⓒ Ⓓ
16. Ⓐ Ⓑ Ⓒ Ⓓ
17. Ⓐ Ⓑ Ⓒ Ⓓ
18. Ⓐ Ⓑ Ⓒ Ⓓ
19. Ⓐ Ⓑ Ⓒ Ⓓ
20. Ⓐ Ⓑ Ⓒ Ⓓ
21. Ⓐ Ⓑ Ⓒ Ⓓ
22. Ⓐ Ⓑ Ⓒ Ⓓ
23. Ⓐ Ⓑ Ⓒ Ⓓ
24. Ⓐ Ⓑ Ⓒ Ⓓ
25. Ⓐ Ⓑ Ⓒ Ⓓ
26. Ⓐ Ⓑ Ⓒ Ⓓ
27. Ⓐ Ⓑ Ⓒ Ⓓ
28. Ⓐ Ⓑ Ⓒ Ⓓ
29. Ⓐ Ⓑ Ⓒ Ⓓ
30. Ⓐ Ⓑ Ⓒ Ⓓ

31.

32.

33.

34.

35.

36.

37.

38.

ANSWER SHEET
Practice Test 2

Essay

PLANNING PAGE

START YOUR ESSAY HERE

READING TEST

65 MINUTES, 52 QUESTIONS

Turn to Section 1 of your answer sheet to answer the questions in this section.

Directions: Following each of the passages (or pairs of passages) below are questions about the passage (or passages). Read each passage carefully. Then, select the best answer for each question based on what is stated in the passage (or passages) and in any graphics that may accompany the passage.

Questions 1–10 are based on the following passage.

This passage is from Dai Sijie, *Balzac and the Little Chinese Seamstress*, © 2001 by Alfred A. Knopf. (English translation Copyright © by Ina Rilke 2001.)

The events portrayed take place during the Cultural Revolution in China. Two boys, the narrator and his friend Luo, have recently been sent by the government to a remote village to work as laborers as part of their "re-education." The stated goal of the Cultural Revolution was to preserve "true" Communist ideology in the country by purging remnants of capitalist and traditional elements from Chinese society, and to re-impose Maoist thought as the dominant ideology within the Party.

The village headman sat cross-legged in the centre of the room, close to the coals burning in a hearth that was hollowed out of the floor; he was inspecting my violin. Among the possessions brought to this mountain village by the two "city youths"—which was how they saw Luo and me—it was the sole item that exuded an air of foreignness, of civilization, and therefore aroused suspicion.

One of the peasants came forward with an oil lamp to facilitate identification of the strange object. The headman held the violin upright and peered into the black interior of the body, like an officious customs officer searching for drugs. Raising the violin to eye level, he shook it, as though convinced something would drop out of the sound holes. His investigation was so enthusiastic I was afraid the strings would break.

Just about everyone in the village had come to the house on stilts way up on the mountain to witness the arrival of the city youths. Men, women and children swarmed inside the cramped room, clung to the windows, jostled each other by the door. When nothing fell out of my violin, the headman held his nose over the sound holes and sniffed long and hard.

Still no clues.

He ran his calloused fingertips over one string, then another . . . . The strange resonance froze the crowd, as if the sound had won some sort of respect.

"It's a toy," said the headman solemnly.

This verdict left us speechless. Luo and I exchanged furtive, anxious glances. Things were not looking good.

One peasant took the "toy" from the headman's hands, drummed with his fists on its back, then passed it to the next man. For a while my violin circulated through the crowd and we—two frail, skinny, exhausted and risible city youths—were ignored. We had

GO ON TO THE NEXT PAGE

been tramping across the mountains all day, and our clothes, faces and hair were streaked with mud. We looked like pathetic little reactionary soldiers from a propaganda film after their capture by a horde of Communist farm workers.

"A stupid toy," a woman commented hoarsely.

"No," the village headman corrected her, "a bourgeois toy."

I felt chilled to the bone despite the fire blazing in the centre of the room.

"A toy from the city," the headman continued, "go on, burn it!"

His command galvanized the crowd. Everyone started talking at once, shouting and reaching out to grab the toy for the privilege of throwing it on the coals.

"Comrade, it's a musical instrument," Luo said as casually as he could, "and my friend here's a fine musician. Truly."

The headman called for the violin and looked it over once more.

Then he held it out to me.

"Forgive me, comrade," I said, embarrassed, "but I'm not that good."

I saw Luo giving me a surreptitious wink. Puzzled, I took my violin and set about tuning it.

"What you are about to hear, comrade, is a Mozart sonata," Luo announced, as coolly as before.

I was dumbfounded. Had he gone mad? All music by Mozart or indeed by any other Western composer had been banned years ago. In my sodden shoes my feet turned to ice. I shivered as the cold tightened its grip on me.

"What's a sonata?" the headman asked warily.

"I don't know," I faltered. "It's Western."

"Is it a song?"

"More or less," I replied evasively.

At that instant the glint of the vigilant Communist reappeared in the headman's eyes, and his voice turned hostile.

"What's the name of this song of yours?"

"Well, it's like a song, but actually it's a sonata."

"I'm asking you what it's called!" he snapped, fixing me with his gaze.

"*Mozart* . . ." I muttered.

"*Mozart* what?"

"*Mozart is Thinking of Chairman Mao,*" Luo broke in.

The audacity! But it worked: as if he had heard something miraculous, the headman's menacing look softened. He crinkled up his eyes in a wide, beatific smile.

"Mozart thinks of Mao all the time," he said.

"Indeed, all the time," agreed Luo.

As soon as I had tightened my bow there was a burst of applause, but I was still nervous. However, as I ran my swollen fingers over the strings, Mozart's phrases came flooding back to me like so many faithful friends. The peasants' faces, so grim a moment before, softened under the influence of Mozart's limpid music like parched earth under a shower, and then, in the dancing light of the oil lamp, they blurred into one.

I played for some time, Luo lit a cigarette and smoked quietly, like a man.

This was our first taste of re-education. Luo was eighteen years old. I was seventeen.

GO ON TO THE NEXT PAGE

1. Until the narrator plays the violin the villagers regard it chiefly as

   (A) a dangerous weapon
   (B) a wondrous, almost magical device
   (C) something alien
   (D) a traditional Chinese musical instrument

2. What word most accurately describes how the narrator views the villagers?

   (A) bourgeois
   (B) materialistic
   (C) reactionary
   (D) uncivilized

3. The narrator says, "Things were not looking good" (lines 37–38) because

   (A) the headman doesn't understand how delicate the violin is, and so the narrator and Luo are afraid that he might accidentally break it
   (B) the headman has discovered the truth about the violin—that it's a toy—and Luo and the narrator are afraid that he will keep it for himself
   (C) the headman has just concluded that the violin is a toy, and therefore something regarded as bourgeois
   (D) Luo and the narrator believe that the headman's verdict about the violin suggests that he has total control of the village

4. The word *coolly* as it is used in line 75 most nearly means

   (A) stylishly
   (B) calmly
   (C) arrogantly
   (D) resignedly

5. What is the most likely reason that the villagers in the crowd regard burning the violin as a "privilege" (line 62)?

   (A) They believe that the person who destroys the violin will be richly rewarded by the headman.
   (B) They see it as an honor to be the person who destroys a symbol of bourgeois decadence.
   (C) They believe that the person who destroys the violin will be likely to become the next headman.
   (D) They believe that the person who destroys the violin will be rewarded in the afterlife.

6. What is the most likely reason that Luo gives the narrator "a surreptitious wink" (line 71)?

   (A) To reassure the narrator that it is all right if his violin playing is not very good.
   (B) To indicate to the narrator that he has a plan, and that the narrator should go along with it.
   (C) To remind the narrator that they should be loyal Communists.
   (D) To warn the narrator that they are in a very difficult situation.

7. The fact that the narrator "took [his] violin and set about tuning it" (lines 72–73) after Luo had winked at him suggests that the narrator

   (A) has no idea at all what Luo was trying to communicate to him by winking at him
   (B) wants to distract the attention of the villagers
   (C) trusts his friend even though he does not understand his plan
   (D) is annoyed with Luo for trying to involve him in a duplicitous plan

GO ON TO THE NEXT PAGE

8. The most likely reason that the narrator exclaims "The audacity!" (line 100) is that
   (A) he believes it is audacious of Luo to interrupt when the headman is waiting for a reply from the narrator
   (B) he thinks that making up a song title called *Mozart is Thinking of Chairman Mao* shows disrespect for one of the great Western classical composers
   (C) he thinks that making up a song title shows disrespect to the headman
   (D) he thinks it is very bold of Luo to make up a song title called *Mozart is Thinking of Chairman Mao* because the headman could have reacted angrily and said that the narrator and Luo were trying to trick him

9. The author makes use of all of the following *except*
   (A) parody
   (B) description of details
   (C) a building up of tension in the narrative
   (D) simile

10. It can be inferred from the fact that Luo "smoked quietly, like a man" (line 119) that
   (A) he is worried about what will happen when the narrator stops playing the Mozart sonata
   (B) he is planning another way to fool the gullible headman
   (C) he is justifiably satisfied with himself for orchestrating a daring and successful plan to gain the favor of the villagers
   (D) he realizes that he has been accepted as a full-fledged adult member of the village

Questions 11–20 are based on the following passage.

This passage is from Irving Kristol, *Reflections of a Neoconservative*, © 1983 by Irving Kristol.

Throughout history, artists and writers have been candidly contemptuous of commercial activity between consenting adults, regarding it as an activity that tends to coarsen and trivialize the human spirit. And since bourgeois society was above all else a commercial society—the first in all of recorded history in which the commercial ethos was sovereign over all others—their exasperation was bound to be all the more acute. Later on, the term "philistinism" would emerge to encapsulate this sentiment.

Though a commercial society may offer artists and writers all sorts of desirable things—freedom of expression especially, popularity and affluence occasionally—it did (and does) deprive them of the status that they naturally feel themselves entitled to. Artists and writers and thinkers always have taken themselves to be Very Important People, and they are outraged by a society that merely tolerates them, no matter how generously.

A commercial society, a society whose civilization is shaped by market transactions, is always likely to reflect the appetites and preferences of common men and women. Each may not have much money, but there are so many of them that their tastes are decisive. Artists and intellectuals see this as an inversion of the natural order of things, since it gives "vulgarity," the power to dominate where and when it can. By their very nature "elitists" (as one now says), they believe that a civilization should be shaped by an aristocracy to which they will

GO ON TO THE NEXT PAGE

be organically attached, no matter how perilously.

In sum, intellectuals and artists will be (as they have been) restive in a bourgeois-capitalist society. The popularity of romanticism in the century after 1750 testifies to this fact, as the artists led an "inner emigration" of the spirit—which, however, left the actual world unchanged. But not all such restiveness found refuge in escapism. Rebellion was an alternative route, as the emergence of various socialist philosophies and movements early in the nineteenth century demonstrated.

Socialism (of whatever kind) is a romantic passion that operates within a rationalist framework. It aims to construct a human community in which everyone places the common good—as defined, necessarily, by an intellectual and moral elite—before his own individual interests and appetites. The intention was not new—there isn't a religion in the world that has failed to preach and expound it. What was new was the belief that such self-denial could be realized, not through a voluntary circumscription of individual appetites, but even while the aggregate of human appetites was being increasingly satisfied by ever-growing material prosperity. "Scientific" socialism promised to remove the conflict between actual and potentially ideal human nature by creating an economy of such abundance that appetite as a social force would, as it were, wither away.

Behind this promise, of course, was the profound belief that modern science—including the social sciences, and especially including scientific economics—would gradually but ineluctably provide humanity with modes of control over nature (and human nature, too) that would permit the modern world radically to transcend all those limitations of the human condition previously taken to be "natural." The trouble with implementing this belief, however, was that the majority of men and women were no more capable of comprehending a "science of society" than they were of practicing austere self-denial. A socialist elite, therefore, was indispensable to mobilize the masses for their own ultimate self-transformation.

The appeal of any such movement to intellectuals is clear enough. As intellectuals, they are qualified candidates for membership in the elite that leads such movements, and they can thus give free expression to their natural impulse for authority and power. They can do so, moreover, within an ideological context, which reassures them that they are disinterestedly serving the "true" interests of the people.

11. The assertion made in lines 1–5 that "Throughout history, artists and writers have been candidly contemptuous of commercial activity between consenting adults, regarding it as an activity that tends to coarsen and trivialize the human spirit" could be best strengthened by

(A) evidence supporting the assertion
(B) an explanation of the word "candidly" (line 2)
(C) a fuller definition of "artists and writers" (line 1)
(D) an explanation of the term "commercial activity" (line 3)

GO ON TO THE NEXT PAGE

12. The phrase “between consenting adults” (lines 3–4) is used to

    (A) exclude commercial activity that is forced upon a person or is necessary for the person’s survival from the sort of commercial activity that artists and writers have contempt for
    (B) remind the reader that all meaningful activity of any sort is between free adults
    (C) suggest that nearly all adults, if given the freedom to do so, resist the urge to engage in commercial activity
    (D) suggest that bourgeois society, more than any other, depends on the freely given consent of adults

13. According to the author, the term “philistinism” (line 11) arose because

    (A) artists and writers became aware that they would increasingly have to participate in commercial activities
    (B) artists and writers became increasingly frustrated and annoyed as society became more commercial and bourgeois
    (C) a new word had to be found to refer to the new commercial ethos that was emerging in the eighteenth century
    (D) artists and writers needed a word to conveniently describe their changing role in bourgeois society

14. In line 30 *decisive* most nearly means

    (A) beyond doubt
    (B) vital
    (C) having the power to decide
    (D) characterized by decision and firmness

15. According to the author, as society became more commercial

    (A) artists and writers became increasingly constrained in their range of subjects
    (B) artists and writers generally tended to follow this trend and increasingly worked only for financial reward
    (C) artists and writers became relatively poorer as compared to people who weren’t artists or writers
    (D) the status of artists and writers became lower

16. Which of the following best describes the author’s attitude about the tastes of common men and women becoming predominant in commercial society?

    (A) Unhappiness that higher art and literature as well as other intellectual pursuits have been devalued in commercial society.
    (B) Resignation to an unfortunate turn of events in history.
    (C) Celebration that at last the voices of common men and women are being heard.
    (D) A non-committal attitude as to whether this is a favorable or unfavorable development.

17. According to the author, romanticism

    (A) led to the creation of socialist philosophies and movements
    (B) culminated in rebellions in the early nineteenth century
    (C) had no effect on the real world
    (D) was most popular among common men and women after 1750

GO ON TO THE NEXT PAGE

18. Which choice provides the best evidence for the answer to the previous question?

(A) lines 1–5 ("Throughout . . . spirit.")
(B) lines 41–45 ("The . . . unchanged.")
(C) lines 51–53 ("Socialism . . . framework.")
(D) lines 72–81 ("Behind . . . natural.'")

19. "Appetite as a social force would, as it were, wither away" (lines 70–71) means

(A) the desire of individuals to have and do what they like would gradually cease to have an effect on the nature of society
(B) common men and women would no longer regard the consumption of goods and services as legitimate
(C) individual taste would gradually be determined by individuals rather than by society
(D) society would gradually come to realize that individual appetites cannot be controlled by intellectual and moral elites

20. In line 98 *disinterestedly* most nearly means

(A) without genuine interest
(B) genuinely
(C) impartially, and not motivated by self-interest
(D) with no emotion

Questions 21–31 are based on the following passages.

Passage 1 is from Samuel P. Huntington, "The Clash of Civilizations?" © 1993 by the Council on Foreign Relations, Inc. Passage 2 is from Albert L. Weeks, "Do Civilizations Hold?" © 1993 by Albert L. Weeks.

PASSAGE 1

Civilization identity will be increasingly important in the future, and the world will be shaped in large measure by the interactions among seven or eight major civilizations. These include Western, Confucian, Japanese, Islamic, Hindu, Slavic-Orthodox, Latin American, and possibly African civilization. The most important conflicts of the future will occur along the cultural fault lines separating these civilizations from one another. Why will this be the case?

First, differences among civilizations are not only real; they are basic. Civilizations are differentiated from each other by history, language, culture, tradition and, most important, religion. The people of different civilizations have different views on the relations between God and man, the individual and the group, the citizen and the state, parents and children, husband and wife, as well as differing views of the relative importance of rights and responsibilities, liberty and authority, equality and hierarchy. These differences are the product of centuries. They will not soon disappear. They are far more fundamental than differences among political ideologies and political regimes. Differences do not necessarily mean conflict, and conflict does not necessarily mean violence. Over the centuries, however, differences among

GO ON TO THE NEXT PAGE

1 1 1

civilizations have generated the most prolonged and the most violent conflicts.

Second, the world is becoming a smaller place. The interactions between peoples of different civilizations are increasing; these increasing interactions intensify civilization consciousness and awareness of differences between civilizations and commonalities within civilizations. Enhanced civilization-consciousness of people, in turn, invigorates differences and animosities stretching or thought to stretch back deep into history.

Third, the processes of economic modernization and social change throughout the world are separating people from longstanding local identities. They also weaken the nation state as a source of identity. In much of the world religion has moved in to fill this gap, often in the form of movements that are labeled "fundamentalist." Such movements are found in Western Christianity, Judaism, Buddhism, and Hinduism, as well as in Islam. In most countries and most religions the people active in fundamentalist movements are young, college-educated, middle-class technicians, professionals, and business persons. The "unsecularization of the world," George Weigel has remarked, "is one of the dominant social facts of life in the late twentieth century." The revival of religion . . . provides a basis for identity and commitment that transcends national boundaries and unites civilizations.

Fourth, the growth of civilization-consciousness is enhanced by the dual role of the West. On the one hand, the West is at a peak of power. At the same time, however, and perhaps as a result, a return to the roots phenomenon is occurring among non-Western civilizations. Increasingly one hears references to trends toward a turning inward and "Asianization" in Japan, the end of the Nehru legacy and the "Hinduization" of India, the failure of Western ideas of socialism and nationalism and hence "re-Islamization" of the Middle East. A West at the peak of its power confronts non-Wests that increasingly have the desire, the will and the resources to shape the world in non-Western ways.

PASSAGE 2

Huntington's classification identifies determinants on a grand scale by "civilizations." His endeavor, however, has its fault lines. The lines are the borders encompassing each distinct nation state and mercilessly chopping the alleged civilizations into pieces. With the cultural and religious glue of these "civilizations" thin and cracked, with the nation state's political regime providing the principal bonds, crisscross fracturing and cancellation of Huntington's macro-scale, somewhat anachronistic fault lines are inevitable.

The world remains fractured along political and possibly geopolitical lines; cultural and historical determinants are a great deal less vital and virulent. Politics, regimes, and ideologies are culturally, historically, and "civilizationally" determined to an extent. But it is willful, day-to-day, crisis-to-crisis, war-to-war political decision-making by nation-state units that remains the single most identifiable determinant of events in the international arena. How else can we explain repeated nation-state "defections" from their collective "civilizations"? As Huntington himself points out, in the Persian Gulf War "one Arab state invaded another and then fought a coalition of Arab, Western, and other states."

GO ON TO THE NEXT PAGE

Raymond Aron described at length the primacy of a nation state's political integrity and independence, its inviolable territoriality and sovereign impermeability. He observed that "men have believed that the fate of cultures was at stake on the battlefields at the same time as the fate of provinces." But, he added, the fact remains that sovereign states "are engaged in a competition for power [and] conquests . . . . In our times the major phenomenon [on the international scene] is the heterogeneity of state units [not] supranational aggregations."

21. The term "cultural fault lines" (line 9) suggests that

(A) like geological continental plates, civilizations are distinct from each other, and sometimes collide
(B) like geological continental plates, civilizations are relatively stable, with little meaningful interaction between them
(C) future civilizational conflict will occur in areas difficult to predict
(D) civilizations are subject to the same laws as all natural processes, such as those governing the movement of the Earth's tectonic plates

22. The word *basic* as it is used in line 13 most nearly means

(A) important
(B) distinct
(C) fundamental
(D) elementary

23. The author of Passage 1 would be most likely to agree with the statement that

(A) differences between cultures nearly always lead to conflict between these cultures
(B) most people in the world identify more strongly with the religion they belong to than the political party they belong to
(C) the differing values of people of different civilizations are more superficial than is generally believed
(D) it is not possible to make meaningful generalizations about the moral and other values of the world's seven or eight major civilizations

24. What would the author of Passage 1 most likely consider to be the most important implication of the statement, "Over the centuries, however, differences among civilizations have generated the most prolonged and the most violent conflicts" (lines 30–33)?

(A) Differences among civilizations rather than differing political ideologies are likely to cause serious future conflict in the world.
(B) All future conflicts among civilizations will be violent and long-lasting.
(C) Differences among civilizations cause wars of great destruction, but these wars serve, paradoxically, to purify and thus strengthen civilizations.
(D) There will ultimately be a major conflict between all the major civilizations of the world resulting in the destruction of all but one of them.

GO ON TO THE NEXT PAGE

25. The author of Passage 1 would most likely agree that

    (A) the growth of trans-national companies is likely to sharply reduce the likelihood of conflict between civilizations
    (B) the wide availability of the World Wide Web has lessened, though not eliminated, the likelihood of major civilizational conflict
    (C) the increased frequency of large movements of people between nations belonging to different civilizations has raised the likelihood of conflict between civilizations
    (D) the availability and affordability of modern air transport has, most importantly, fostered understanding between people of different civilizations

26. According to the author of Passage 1, many young well-educated technicians, professionals, and business persons around the world are turning to religion because

    (A) social change in many countries has brought more people into contact with the major world religions
    (B) economic and technological modernization in poorer countries has given people greater leisure, and thus young people have more opportunity to pursue different spiritual paths
    (C) young people in rapidly developing countries believe that identifying with a major world religion will make them more attractive as employees to multi-national companies
    (D) they identify less strongly with their local traditions and nation, and so seek identity in religion, especially in fundamentalist religious movements

27. The author of Passage 2

    (A) believes that Raymond Aron is correct in his statement that "men have believed that the fate of cultures was at stake on the battlefields at the same time as the fate of provinces."
    (B) believes that the term "civilization" is virtually synonymous with the term "nation-state"
    (C) asserts that ideologies develop independently of civilizations
    (D) suggests that nation-states almost never act to undermine the "civilization" to which they belong

28. The author of Passage 2 says "Politics, regimes, and ideologies are culturally, historically, and 'civilizationally' determined to an extent" (lines 99–102). In the context of the author's main argument, this sentence is most accurately described as

    (A) a central thesis
    (B) a reasonable inference
    (C) a proviso
    (D) a partial concession

29. The meaning of the word *vital* as it is used in line 99 most nearly means

    (A) essential
    (B) fatal
    (C) full of energy
    (D) influential

GO ON TO THE NEXT PAGE

30. The author of Passage 1 would be most likely to respond to the example of the Persian Gulf War cited in Passage 2 (lines 110–112) by saying that
    (A) there will continue to be cases in which nation-states act against the interest of the civilization to which they belong, but the more significant trend is for civilizational loyalty to take precedence over loyalty to the nation-state
    (B) most of the Arab states involved in the Persian Gulf War owe their allegiance primarily to the West, not to Islamic civilization
    (C) the Arab states that allied themselves with the West in the Persian Gulf War were forced to do so for larger geo-political and economic reasons that transcend civilizational concerns
    (D) civilizational loyalty cannot be assessed by the amount of intra-civilizational aggression that occurs

31. The author of Passage 2 most likely put quotation marks around the word *civilizations* in line 85 to
    (A) suggest that it is very possible that what Huntington defines as civilizations are not in actuality civilizations
    (B) make it clear that his definition of civilization is not the same as Huntington's
    (C) suggest the term civilization has no meaning at all
    (D) express his scorn for scholars who use important terms carelessly

Questions 32–41 are based on the following passage.

This passage is from Milton Friend, *Why bother about wildlife disease?*: U.S. Geological Survey Circular 1401, 2014.

What are zoonoses? The common dictionary definition in scientific journals and media coverage of zoonotic disease conveys the limited concept of infectious disease transmissible from animals to humans. However, that perspective is inadequate. Zoonotic disease is multidimensional and ecologically complex, as are many of the pathogens involved. Like those pathogens, the definition of zoonosis has followed an evolutionary path. Here, it is sufficient to recognize that zoonoses are infectious diseases transmissible between vertebrate animals and humans and vice versa. In addition, the animal component has an essential role in maintaining the pathogen in nature for diseases transmitted to humans; for example, foxes and rabies. Humans serve that same role for diseases being transmitted to lower vertebrates; for example, measles and great apes. These revelations have direct ramifications for wildlife conservation.

The general importance of zoonoses for humanity has waxed and waned over time in concert with changing conditions including changes in the number of human cases and (or) exposures associated with enzootic areas, such as chronic disease presence and activity levels, for specific zoonoses. The occurrence of major epizootics or epidemics involving the expansion of established geographic range for specific diseases and (or) the appearance of "new" zoonoses within a geographic area is also of

GO ON TO THE NEXT PAGE

PRACTICE TEST 2

great concern. Rabies is a well-established zoonosis and, except for anthrax, perhaps the next earliest zoonosis to confront humans. The first recorded description of canine rabies dates back to about 500 B.C. Rabies is an important zoonosis in much of the world, because death is the outcome once clinical signs appear. Human deaths from rabies are rare in the United States, but the disease is diagnosed annually in wildlife and other animals where it continues to cause periodic epizootics. A recent major rabies epizootic that occurred among raccoons in the mid-Atlantic and northeastern United States illustrates that even a zoonosis of antiquity can reassert its prominence in the modern era as a challenge for humans and wildlife alike.

Throughout history, zoonoses also have been the cause of humanity at local, regional, and global levels. Globally, an estimated 200–500 million people were sickened during the 1917–19 H1N1 influenza virus "Spanish flu" pandemic, more than 20 million of whom died. The specter of that pandemic contributed greatly to the unprecedented global response following the 1997 diagnoses of highly pathogenic H5N1 avian influenza virus in Asia and the subsequent spread of that virus throughout much of Asia and Europe.

The emergence of highly pathogenic H5N1 is just one of a number of recent Emerging Infectious Diseases (EIDs) that have wildlife roots, including numerous diseases that have caused epizootics of great concern for society. The World Health Organization reported that in 2006, 39.5 million people were currently infected with HIV/AIDS worldwide and that for the next year alone (2007), 18 billion dollars would be needed to prevent future HIV transmission and provide care for those already infected. A myriad of other emerging zoonoses followed HIV/AIDS to the headlines of major newspapers as well as serving as subject matter for major media venues of all types. These diseases have also become a major focus for scientific investigations and the development of specialized programs and facilities to address them.

Some emerging zoonoses cause major economic impacts for agriculture because of their presence in food production species such as poultry (H5N1) and swine (Nipah virus). For example, the highly pathogenic H5N1 avian influenza virus that appeared in Asia during 1997 and reached 51 countries by early 2010 caused billions of dollars in losses for the poultry industries of those countries. West Nile virus (WNV) also stands out because of its geographic spread across the United States and within North America following the 1999 New York City index cases involving human fatalities, fatal cases in horses, and the thousands and thousands of wild birds killed.

Threats from EIDs are unlikely to decrease, because the ever-changing relations between humans and the environment are a major factor driving disease emergence. The separation between the relevance of zoonoses to wildlife management and conservation and to public health issues has rigidly existed in the past but has been greatly eroded by the current wave of EIDs, many of which are zoonoses. Further, the great costs of zoonoses for society demand that these diseases be aggressively dealt with. For example, of the 868 zoonoses identified at the start of the 21st century, a review of 56 of them

GO ON TO THE NEXT PAGE

revealed approximately 2.5 billion cases of human illness and 2.7 million human deaths worldwide per year.

The "Rebirth" of Zoonoses

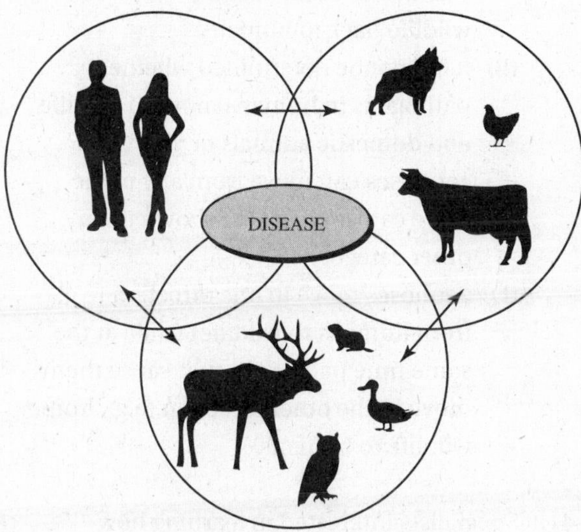

"...emerging zoonotic diseases are among the most important public health threats facing society."

(Mahy and Brown, 2000)

32. According to the author
    - (A) the effects of zoonoses on human beings have remained relatively consistent through human history
    - (B) zoonoses have had little effect on human activities
    - (C) zoonoses have often been the decisive factor in the extinction of civilizations
    - (D) the effects of zoonoses on human beings have varied considerably through human history

33. Which choice provides evidence for the answer to the previous question?
    - (A) "Zoonotic . . . involved." (lines 7–9)
    - (B) "The . . . zoonoses." (lines 24–30)
    - (C) "Human . . . epiczootics." (lines 43–47)
    - (D) "A myriad . . . types." (lines 79–82)

34. The author probably puts the word *new* in quotation marks (line 34) to show that
    - (A) every appearance of a zoonosis involves an entirely new pathogen
    - (B) experts have not been able to determine if any given recent zoonosis is different from previous ones
    - (C) while a given zoonosis might be new to a particular geographic area it is probably not new to Earth
    - (D) zootic diseases are a relatively recent phenomenon in human history

35. The term *epizootics* as it is used in line 31 most nearly means
    - (A) diseases harbored in humans that can be transmitted to animals
    - (B) all diseases affecting animals
    - (C) diseases in animals that occur at a greater than expected rate
    - (D) epidemics that are caused by pathogens harbored in animals and transmitted to humans

36. According to the information provided in the passage, rabies
    - (A) is maintained in nature by animals
    - (B) affects only domesticated animals
    - (C) is no longer a threat to human life
    - (D) cannot be transmitted from an animal to a human

GO ON TO THE NEXT PAGE

37. Which of the following is a reasonable inference that can be made from the information given in the passage?

    (A) Most new zoonoses are the result of the evolution of an entirely new pathogen.
    (B) Pathogens involved in a zoonosis never move outside their geographic area of origin.
    (C) The emergence of an entirely new pathogen that causes diseases in animals that can be transmitted to humans is relatively rare.
    (D) Scientists have been unable to identify the pathogens involved in most zoonoses.

38. The word *specter* as it is used in line 60 most nearly means

    (A) apparition
    (B) haunting image
    (C) effect
    (D) repetition

39. Which of the following could we reasonably infer to be one of the "ramifications for wildlife conservation" (lines 22–23)?

    (A) Authorities acting to prohibit all but the most essential interactions between animals and humans.
    (B) Wildlife conservations coming to realize that eventually all vertebrates except humans will become extinct.
    (C) Authorities acting to outlaw the use of domestic animals to produce food for human consumption.
    (D) Biologists and other specialists more closely monitoring interactions between humans and animals.

40. In the figure on page 143 the arrows indicate that

    (A) all zoonoses move first from humans to domestic animals, then from domestic animals to wildlife, and finally from wildlife back to humans
    (B) it cannot be determined whether pathogens in humans move to wildlife and domestic animals or vice versa
    (C) zoonoses can move from any of the three categories of life shown to any other category
    (D) zoonoses move in one direction (e.g., from humans to wildlife) while at the same time pathogens that cause them move in the other direction (e.g., from wildlife to humans)

41. Specialists interested in learning how zoonotic diseases are spread would probably be least interested in observing activities at

    (A) zoos
    (B) pet shops
    (C) farms
    (D) supermarkets

GO ON TO THE NEXT PAGE

Questions 42–52 are based on the following passage.

The following passage is from Alexis de Tocqueville, *Democracy in America*, translated from French into English by Henry Reeve and originally published in 1835. Alexis de Tocqueville was a French writer and visitor to the United States.

I hold it to be a detestable maxim that, politically speaking, the people have a right to do anything; and yet I have asserted that all authority originates in the will of the majority. Am I, then, in contradiction with myself?

A general law, which bears the name of justice, has been made and sanctioned, not only by a majority of this or that people, but by a majority of mankind. The rights of every people are therefore confined within the limits of what is just. A nation may be considered as a jury which is empowered to represent society at large and to apply justice, which is its law. Ought such a jury, which represents society, to have more power than the society itself whose laws it executes?

When I refuse to obey an unjust law, I do not contest the right of the majority to command, but I simply appeal from the sovereignty of the people to the sovereignty of mankind. Some have not feared to assert that a people can never out step the boundaries of justice and reason in those affairs which are peculiarly its own; and that consequently full power may be given to the majority by which it is represented. But this is the language of a slave.

A majority taken collectively is only an individual, whose opinions, and frequently whose interests, are opposed to those of another individual, who is styled a minority. If it be admitted that a man possessing absolute power may misuse that power by wronging his adversaries, why should not a majority be liable to the same reproach? Men do not change their characters by uniting with one another; nor does their patience in the presence of obstacles increase with their strength. I cannot believe it; the power to do everything, which I should refuse to one of my equals, I will never grant to any number of them.

I do not think that, for the sake of preserving liberty, it is possible to combine several principles in the same government so as really to oppose them to one another. The form of government that is usually termed mixed has always appeared to me a mere chimera. Accurately speaking, there is no such thing as a mixed government in the sense usually given to that word, because in all communities some one principle of action may be discovered which preponderates over the others. England in the eighteenth century, which has been especially cited as an example of this sort of government, was essentially an aristocratic state, although it comprised some great elements of democracy; for the laws and customs of the country were such that the aristocracy could not but preponderate in the long run and direct public affairs according to its own will.

I am therefore of the opinion that social power superior to all others must always be placed somewhere; but I think that liberty is endangered when this power finds no obstacle which can retard its course and give it time to moderate its own vehemence.

Unlimited power is in itself a bad and dangerous thing. Human beings are not competent to exercise it with discretion. There is no power on earth so worthy of

GO ON TO THE NEXT PAGE

honor in itself or clothed with rights so sacred that I would admit its uncontrolled and all-predominant authority. When I see that the right and the means of absolute command are conferred on any power whatever, be it called a people or a king, an aristocracy or a democracy, a monarchy or a republic, I say there is the germ of tyranny, and I seek to live elsewhere, under other laws.

The main evil of the present democratic institutions of the United States does not arise, as is often asserted in Europe, from their weakness, but from their irresistible strength. I am not so much alarmed at the excessive liberty which reigns in that country as at the inadequate securities which one finds there against tyranny; if an individual or a party is wronged in the United States, to whom can he apply for redress? If to public opinion, public opinion constitutes the majority; if to the legislature, it represents the majority and implicitly obeys it; if to the executive power, it is appointed by the majority and serves as a passive tool in its hands. The public force consists of the majority under arms; the jury is the majority invested with the right of hearing judicial cases; and in certain states even the judges are elected by the majority. However iniquitous or absurd the measure of which you complain, you must submit to it as well as you can.

42. The word *sanctioned* as it is used in line 8 most nearly means

(A) disseminated
(B) tolerated
(C) penalized
(D) officially approved

43. The word *people* in line 9 refers to

(A) the members of a particular society
(B) all human beings
(C) the members of the ruling majority in a country
(D) various types of human beings

44. The author says, " The rights of . . . what is just" (lines 10–12). If this is true, then

(A) a person can do something unjust if a majority of people in his or her society approve of it
(B) human rights vary from society to society
(C) people do not have the right to do something unjust
(D) people who act unjustly have no human rights

45. According to the author

(A) it is possible for a majority to establish an unjust law
(B) what is decided by a majority in a society is always just
(C) what is just cannot be decided by human beings
(D) what is just can only be decided by the members of that society for that society

46. The word *principles* as it is used in line 47 most nearly means

(A) standards of proper behavior
(B) basic truths
(C) elements determining intrinsic nature and characteristic behavior
(D) fundamental assumptions

GO ON TO THE NEXT PAGE

1 1 1

47. The author believes that "social power superior to all others must always be placed somewhere [in society]" (lines 66–68) because he thinks that

(A) every society is dominated by its aristocracy
(B) the majority in each society will decide where the dominant interest of the society lies
(C) every society is dominated by a single powerful interest group
(D) every society is unified around one dominant principle

48. Which choice provides the best evidence for the answer to the previous question?

(A) lines 23–26 ("Some . . . own.")
(B) lines 34–37 ("If . . . reproach?")
(C) lines 45–48 ("I . . . another.")
(D) lines 90–95 ("I . . . redress?")

49. The author believes that

(A) once superior power is placed in the hands of a single group, nothing will be able to limit its power
(B) to preserve freedom it is necessary for there to be some opposition to the dominant power group in a society
(C) individual liberty is not possible when a society is dominated by a single principle
(D) individual liberty is only possible when society is dominated by a powerful minority

50. The author makes use of all of the following *except*

(A) rhetorical questions
(B) analogies
(C) examples from history to support his argument
(D) citations of scholarly studies to support his argument

51. Based on what is stated in the passage, which of the following would the author be most likely to favor for the United States?

(A) election of the President by a majority of the popular vote
(B) election of all judges by popular vote
(C) abolition of the national army
(D) appointment of judges to life terms by a non-government body of respected lawyers, judges, and law professors

52. What would be the most appropriate title for this passage?

(A) The Decline of Freedom
(B) Tyranny by the Majority
(C) The Injustices of Democracy
(D) Democracy in Action

STOP

If there is still time remaining, you may review your answers.

2 2 2

WRITING AND LANGUAGE TEST

35 MINUTES, 44 QUESTIONS

Turn to Section 2 of your answer sheet to answer the questions in this section.

Directions: Questions follow each of the passages below. Some questions ask you how the passage might be changed to improve the expression of ideas. Other questions ask you how the passage might be altered to correct errors in grammar, usage, and punctuation. One or more graphics accompany some passages. You will be required to consider these graphics as you answer questions about editing the passage.

There are three types of questions. In the first type, a part of the passage is underlined. The second type is based on a certain part of the passage. The third type is based on the entire passage.

Read each passage. Then, choose the answer to each question that changes the passage so that it is consistent with the conventions of standard written English. One of the answer choices for many questions is "NO CHANGE." Choosing this answer means that you believe the best answer is to make no change in the passage.

Questions 1–11 are based on the following passage and supplementary material.

Mercury Threatens Fish in National Parks

[1] The national park network in the United States ❶ is comprising some of the most pristine and sensitive wilderness in North America. [2] Additionally, variation (up to 20-fold) in site-specific fish THg concentrations within individual parks ❷ suggest that more intensive sampling in some parks will be required to effectively characterize Hg contamination in western national parks. [3] There is concern that via global distribution, Mercury (Hg) contamination could threaten the ecological ❸ virtue of aquatic communities in the parks and the wildlife that depends on it. [4] In this study, we examined Hg concentrations in non-migratory freshwater fish in 86 sites across 21 national parks in the Western United States. [5] Across all parks, sites, and species,

1. (A) NO CHANGE
(B) is comprised of
(C) is being comprised of
(D) comprised of

2. (A) NO CHANGE
(B) suggests
(C) suggesting
(D) having suggested

3. (A) NO CHANGE
(B) morality
(C) ethics
(D) integrity

GO ON TO THE NEXT PAGE

fish total Hg (THg) concentrations ranged from 9.9 to 1,109 nanograms per gram wet weight (ng/g ww) **4** <u>and this means</u> 77.7 ng/g ww. [6] We found substantial variation in fish THg concentrations among and within parks, suggesting that patterns of Hg risk are driven by processes occurring at a combination of scales. **5**

Across all fish sampled, only 5 percent had THg concentrations exceeding a benchmark (200 ng/g ww) associated with **6** <u>malicious</u> responses within the fish themselves. However, Hg concentrations in 35 percent of fish sampled were above a benchmark for risk to highly sensitive avian consumers (90 ng/g ww), and THg concentrations in 68 percent of fish sampled were above exposure levels recommended by the Great Lakes Advisory Group (50 ng/g ww) for unlimited consumption by **7** <u>humans: of</u> the fish assessed for risk to human consumers (that is, species that are large enough to be consumed by recreational or subsistence anglers), only one individual fish from Yosemite National Park had a muscle Hg concentration exceeding the benchmark (950 ng/g ww) **8** <u>at which no human consumption is advised</u>. Zion, Capital Reef, Wrangell-St. Elias, and Lake Clark National Parks all contained sites in which most fish exceeded benchmarks for the protection **9** <u>of human and wildlife health.</u>

4. (A) NO CHANGE
   (B) by means of
   (C) with a mean of
   (D) in means of

5. For the sake of the cohesion of this paragraph, sentence 2 should be placed:
   (A) where it is now
   (B) after sentence 3
   (C) after sentence 4
   (D) after sentence 6

6. (A) NO CHANGE
   (B) murderous
   (C) toxic
   (D) venomous

7. (A) NO CHANGE
   (B) humans; of
   (C) humans, of
   (D) humans. Of

8. (A) NO CHANGE
   (B) where it is advised no humans consume
   (C) which is advised for no human consumption
   (D) which advises no human consumption

9. (A) NO CHANGE
   (B) of human, and, wildlife health.
   (C) of: human and wildlife health.
   (D) of human and wildlife, health.

GO ON TO THE NEXT PAGE

There were no consistent patterns in inter-annual variability across the 10 sites sampled over separate years. Significant differences in mean Hg concentrations were observed at 5 of 10 sites. Fish THg concentrations increased significantly from the first sampling to the second at two sites: ⑩ Sunup Lake and Center Basin Lake. Conversely, fish THg concentrations decreased significantly from the first sampling event to the second in three sites— ⑪ Lake Clark, Mirror Lake, and Ypsilon Lake.

10. Which choice most accurately represents the information in the graph?
    (A) NO CHANGE
    (B) Gladys Lake and Upper Lena Lake
    (C) Sunup Lake and Nanita Lake
    (D) Ypsilon Lake and Sunup Lake

11. Which choice most accurately represents the information in the graph?
    (A) NO CHANGE
    (B) Lake Clark, Poudre Lake, and Ypsilon Lake
    (C) Upper Lena Lake, Poudre Lake, and Ypsilon Lake
    (D) Upper Lena Lake, Mirror Lake, and Lake Clark

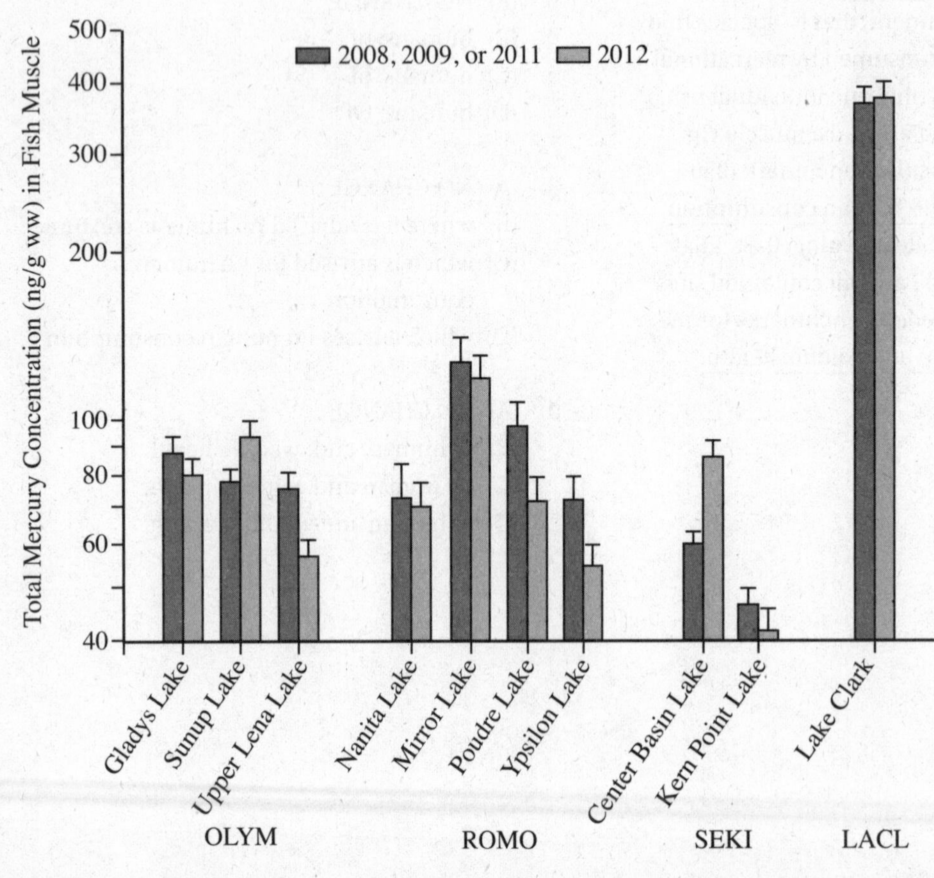

Source: U.S. Geological Survey, Open-file report, 2014-1051

GO ON TO THE NEXT PAGE

Questions 12–22 are based on the following passage.

You're a What? Ornithologist

Ornithologists study birds in their natural habitats or in ⓬ the laboratory and it may also be that they write research reports and proposals for grants, teach classes, present research to the ⓭ public while they have administrative duties related to these activities.

⓮ Many questions about ornithology are best answered by observing birds in the wild during fieldwork. Ornithologists and their students have done fieldwork in locations as remote as the Andes Mountains in South America and as nearby as the forests of southern Ohio and the ⓯ Midwest: fieldwork usually involves surveying, or counting, birds and monitoring their nests. Fieldwork is where many ornithologists learn how to collect data for research. For example, they will watch and record different species foraging to discover where and what they eat. During fieldwork, ornithologists might also attach metal or plastic bands to a bird's leg to help identify individual birds and aid with survival estimates.

[1] Much of the research that ornithologists do is in the lab. [2] But not all ornithologists work outdoors. [3] For example, ⓰ feather collecting during fieldwork are analyzed in the lab for a variety of purposes, including genetic mapping. [4] And some studies of migratory behavior or mate choice might involve observing birds in special cages. [5] Ornithologists often write

12. Select from the following the choice that forms two distinct sentences that make sense.
    (A) laboratory. Besides these things, they may write
    (B) laboratory. Besides, they may also write
    (C) laboratory. And, besides this, they may write
    (D) laboratory. They also may write

13. (A) NO CHANGE
    (B) public, and have
    (C) public, doing all this while having
    (D) public, when having

14. The writer is considering deleting the underlined sentence. Should the writer do this?
    (A) Yes, because it does not relate to the content of the paragraph it would be in.
    (B) Yes, because the information it contains is expressed later in the passage, so it would be redundant.
    (C) No, because it provides detailed information about fieldwork done by ornithologists.
    (D) No, because it is an appropriate topic sentence to introduce the second paragraph, which focuses on fieldwork done by ornithologists.

15. (A) NO CHANGE
    (B) Midwest, fieldwork
    (C) Midwest. Fieldwork
    (D) Midwest; fieldwork

16. (A) NO CHANGE
    (B) collections of feathers
    (C) feathers collected
    (D) feathers, having been collected

GO ON TO THE NEXT PAGE

reports about their research or publish articles in scientific journals focused on biology, ecology, conservation, or **17** managing wildlife. [6] And ornithologists who do research also write grant proposals to seek funding for specific research. **18**

19 Although they educate people through writing about birds, ornithologists share their knowledge by teaching college courses. But education is not limited to teaching college students. Outreach activities **20** did include giving talks and making presentations to natural resources managers of government and other nonprofit organizations as well as to people in public interest groups, bird watching clubs, and schools.

Ornithologists need an advanced degree for most jobs. For most professional jobs, ornithologists need a master's degree that includes a research thesis. Those who want to develop their own research projects, work in high-level management positions, or teach at a university usually need a Ph.D. in **21** a regimen related to their work.

It is estimated that there are about 6,000 ornithologists employed in the United States. **22** For statistics' purposes, they are included among zoologists and wildlife biologists. Their median annual wage is $57,710.

17. (A) NO CHANGE
    (B) wildlife management
    (C) wildlife being managed
    (D) managed wildlife

18. For the sake of the cohesion of this paragraph, sentence 2 should be placed
    (A) where it is now
    (B) before sentence 1
    (C) before sentence 4
    (D) before sentence 6

19. (A) NO CHANGE
    (B) Whether they educate people
    (C) In addition to educating people
    (D) And if people are educated

20. (A) NO CHANGE
    (B) might include
    (C) including
    (D) included

21. (A) NO CHANGE
    (B) an instruction
    (C) a discipline
    (D) a preparation

22. (A) NO CHANGE
    (B) For statistical purposes,
    (C) For statistic purpose,
    (D) For purpose of a statistic

GO ON TO THE NEXT PAGE

Questions 23–33 are based on the following passage.

Understanding Jainism

[1] The oldest continuous monastic tradition in India is Jainism, the path of the Jinas, or victors. [2] This tradition is traced to Vardhamana Mahavira (The Great Hero; ca. 599–527 B.C.), the twenty-fourth and last of the Tirthankaras (Sanskrit for fordmakers). [3] According to legend, Mahavira was born to a **23** family ruling in the town of Vaishali, located in the modern state of Bihar. [4] At the age of thirty, he **24** abdicated his wealthy life and devoted himself to fasting and self-mortification in order to purify his consciousness and discover the meaning of existence. [5] Following the example of the teacher Parshvanatha (ninth century B.C.), he attained enlightenment and spent the rest of his life meditating and teaching a dedicated group of disciples who formed a monastic order following rules **25** he lay down. [6] His life's work complete, he entered a final fast and deliberately died of starvation. [7] He never again dwelt in a house, owned property, **26** nor did he ever wear clothing of any sort. **27**

The ancient belief system of the Jains rests on a concrete understanding of the working of karma, **28** its effects on the living soul (jiva), and the conditions for extinguishing action and the soul's release. According to the Jain view, the soul is a living substance that combines with various kinds of nonliving matter and through action **29** accumulate particles of matter that adhere to it and determine its fate. Most of the matter perceptible to human senses, including all animals and plants, is attached in various degrees to living souls and is in this sense alive. Any action has consequences that necessarily follow

23. (A) NO CHANGE
    (B) ruling family
    (C) a ruler family
    (D) a ruled family

24. (A) NO CHANGE
    (B) renounced
    (C) seceded from
    (D) defected from

25. (A) NO CHANGE
    (B) he had lain
    (C) he has lain
    (D) he laid

26. (A) NO CHANGE
    (B) nor did he wear
    (C) or wore
    (D) nor wore

27. For the sake of the cohesion of this paragraph, sentence 7 should be placed
    (A) where it is
    (B) after sentence 2
    (C) after sentence 3
    (D) after sentence 4

28. (A) NO CHANGE
    (B) its affects on the
    (C) it effects the
    (D) its affecting the

29. (A) NO CHANGE
    (B) accumulates
    (C) accumulated
    (D) accumulating

GO ON TO THE NEXT PAGE

the embodied soul, but the worst accumulations of matter come from violence against other living beings. The ultimate Jain (30) discipline, therefore, rests on complete inactivity and absolute nonviolence (ahimsa) against any living beings. Some Jain monks and nuns wear face masks to avoid accidentally inhaling small organisms, and all practicing believers try to remain (31) vegetarians by extreme renunciation, including the refusal of all food, lies at the heart of a discipline that purges the mind and body of all desires and actions (32) and, as it processes it, burns off the consequences of actions performed in the past. In this sense, Jain renunciants may recognize or (33) bolster deities, but they do not view the *Vedas* as sacred texts and instead concentrate on the atheistic, individual quest for purification and removal of karma. The final goal is the extinguishing of self, a "blowing out" (nirvana) of the individual self.

*The *Vedas* are the oldest scriptures of Hinduism.

30. The word *discipline* most nearly means
    (A) a systematic method to obtain obedience
    (B) punishment to correct undesirable behavior
    (C) training that produces moral improvement
    (D) a branch of learning

31. How should the underlined portions be rewritten?
    (A) NO CHANGE
    (B) vegetarians. Extreme renunciation, including
    (C) vegetarians, extreme renunciation includes
    (D) vegetarians. Extreme renunciation, and this includes

32. (A) NO CHANGE
    (B) and, in the process,
    (C) and processing this
    (D) and with the process of being

33. (A) NO CHANGE
    (B) awe
    (C) revere
    (D) marvel

GO ON TO THE NEXT PAGE

Questions 34–44 are based on the following passage.

What Is Civilization?

[1] To know what civilization is by study and observation is better than to rely upon a formal definition. [2] For instance, it may be used in a narrow sense to indicate the character and quality of the civil relations. [3] Those tribes or nations having a well-developed social order, with government, laws, and other fixed social **34** customs said to be civilized, while those peoples without these characters are assumed to be uncivilized. [4] It may also be considered in a somewhat different sense, when the arts, industries, sciences, and habits of life are stimulated—civilization **35** was determined by the degree in which these are developed. [5] Whichever view is accepted, it involves a contrast of present ideals with past ideals, of an undeveloped with a developed state of human progress. [6] For, indeed, the word is used in so many different ways that it admits of a loose interpretation. **36**

37 But whatever notion we have of civilization, it is difficult to draw a fixed line between civilized and uncivilized peoples. Lewis H. Morgan, in his *Ancient Society*, asserts that civilization began with the phonetic **38** alphabet. He says that all human activity prior to this could be classified as savagery or barbarism. But there is a broader conception of civilization which recognizes all phases of human achievement, from the making of a stone axe to the construction of the airplane; from the rude hut to the magnificent palace; from crude moral and religious conditions to the more

34. (A) NO CHANGE
    (B) customs, and they are said to be civilized,
    (C) customs, said civilized,
    (D) customs are said to be civilized,

35. (A) NO CHANGE
    (B) being
    (C) is being
    (D) has been

36. For the sake of the logic and cohesion of this paragraph, sentence 6 should be placed:

    (A) where it is now
    (B) before sentence 4
    (C) after sentence 4
    (D) before sentence 2

37. The writer is considering deleting the underlined sentence. Should the writer do this?

    (A) Yes, because it is unrelated to the ideas discussed in the second paragraph.
    (B) Yes, because it contradicts what is said in the first paragraph.
    (C) No, because it provides an appropriate link between the first and second paragraphs.
    (D) No, because it provides one more definition of the word "civilization."

38. Which choice most effectively combines the sentences at the underlined portion?

    (A) alphabet that is
    (B) alphabet, and it is his opinion that
    (C) alphabet and that
    (D) alphabet, that is

GO ON TO THE NEXT PAGE

2 2 2

refined conditions of (39) humans in association. If we consider that civilization involves the whole process of human achievement, it must admit of a great variety of qualities and degrees of development; (40) hence it appears to be a relative term applied to the variation of human life. So we might say of the Chinese, the East Indians, and the American Indians, that they each have well-established customs, habits of thought, and standards of life, differing from other nations, (41) which is expressing different types of civilization.

When a member of a primitive tribe invented the bow-and-arrow, (42) or it began to chip a flint nodule in order to make a stone axe, civilization began. As soon as people began to cooperate with one another in obtaining food, building houses, or for protection against wild animals and wild (43) men, that is when they began to treat each other civilly, they were becoming civilized.

39. (A) NO CHANGE
(B) humans associating
(C) human association
(D) association among humans

40. (A) NO CHANGE
(B) furthermore
(C) likewise
(D) finally

41. (A) NO CHANGE
(B) and that is expressing
(C) expressed as
(D) expressing

42. (A) NO CHANGE
(B) or they began
(C) or began
(D) or were beginning

43. For the sake of clarity of meaning and effectiveness of expression, the underlined portion of the sentence should be rewritten as follows:

(A) NO CHANGE
(B) men, that is, when they began to treat each other civilly, they
(C) men—that is, when they began to treat each other civilly—they
(D) men that is when they began to treat each other civilly, they

GO ON TO THE NEXT PAGE

We may say then in reality that civilization has been a continuous process (44) as the first beginning of man's conquest of himself and nature to the modern complexities of social life with its multitude of products of industry and cultural arts.

44. (A) NO CHANGE
(B) from the first beginning of man's conquest of himself and nature to
(C) from the first beginning of man's conquest of himself within
(D) during the first beginning of man's conquest of himself and nature beyond

STOP

If there is still time remaining, you may review your answers.

MATH TEST (NO CALCULATOR)

25 MINUTES, 20 QUESTIONS

Turn to Section 3 of your answer sheet to answer the questions in this section.

Directions: For questions 1–15, solve each problem and choose the best answer from the given options. Fill in the corresponding circle on your answer document. For questions 16–20, solve the problem and fill in the answer on the answer sheet grid. Please use scrap paper to work out your answers.

Notes:

- You **CANNOT** use a calculator on this section.
- All variables and expressions represent real numbers unless indicated otherwise.
- All figures are drawn to scale unless indicated otherwise.
- All figures are in a plane unless indicated otherwise.
- Unless indicated otherwise, the domain of a given function is the set of all real numbers *x* for which the function has real values.

REFERENCE INFORMATION

Area Facts

$A = \ell w$

$A = \frac{1}{2}bh$

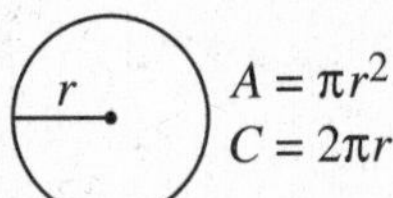

$A = \pi r^2$
$C = 2\pi r$

Volume Facts

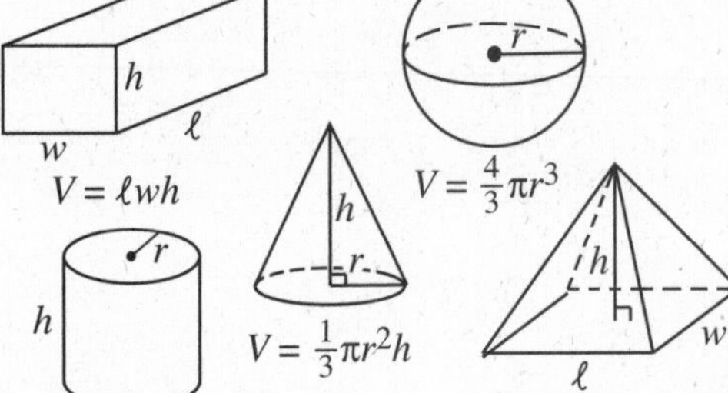

$V = \ell wh$

$V = \frac{4}{3}\pi r^3$

$V = \pi r^2 h$

$V = \frac{1}{3}\pi r^2 h$

$V = \frac{1}{3}\ell wh$

Triangle Facts

$a^2 + b^2 = c^2$

The arc of a circle contains 360°.
The arc of a circle contains 2π radians.
The sum of the measures of the angles in a triangle is 180°.

1. If $\frac{r-2}{6} = n$ and $n = 5$, what is the value of r?

   (A) 28
   (B) 30
   (C) 32
   (D) 42

2. If $i = \sqrt{-1}$, what is the value of $(5 + 3i) + (-4 + 7i)$?

   (A) $1 + 10i$
   (B) $9 + 10i$
   (C) $-41 + 2i$
   (D) $-1 - 5i$

GO ON TO THE NEXT PAGE

3

3. Ted needs to purchase shirts and belts for the costumes in his school's play. He can buy s shirts and b belts but the quantity may not exceed 100 items. Which of the following inequalities represents the conditions of Ted's purchases?

(A) $s + b > 100$
(B) $s + b < 100$
(C) $s + b \leq 100$
(D) $sb \leq 100$

4. $\frac{1}{x} + \frac{3}{x} = \frac{1}{7}$

Jill has employed two painters to paint the outside of her rental apartment. One of the workers paints three times as quickly as the other. Together they paint the apartment in 7 hours. If the equation above models the situation, what does $\frac{3}{x}$ represent?

(A) The entire job if it were done by the faster painter only.
(B) The entire job if it were done by the slower painter only.
(C) The fraction of the job the slower painter completes in one hour.
(D) The fraction of the job the faster painter completes in one hour.

5. What is the result when $3x^2 - 4x + 5$ is subtracted from $3x^3 - 13x + 4$?

(A) $3x^3 - 3x^2 - 9x - 1$
(B) $x^3 - 6x - 1$
(C) $x^5 - 4x^2 - 11$
(D) $3x^3 - 2x^2 - 6x - 9$

6. For what value(s) of x is the following expression undefined?

$$\frac{-5x^2y - 4xy}{6x^2 - 13x - 5}$$

(A) $-1, 5$
(B) 5
(C) $-\frac{1}{3}, \frac{5}{2}$
(D) $\frac{1}{3}, \frac{3}{2}$

7. Which of the following equations has the same x- and y-coordinates of the vertex as $y = 3(x - 4)(x + 6)$?

(A) $y = x^2 - 8x + 15$
(B) $y = 3(x^2 + 4x - 6)$
(C) $y = 3(x + 1)^2 - 75$
(D) $y = 3x^2 + 6x - 10$

8. A square photograph is surrounded by a square frame that is 2 inches wide on each side. If the diagonal of the photograph is 12 inches, what is the area of the frame (in square inches)?

(A) $72 + 48\sqrt{2}$
(B) $16 + 48\sqrt{2}$
(C) 72
(D) $48\sqrt{2}$

9. Which of the following equations represents a line that is parallel to the line with equation $y = \frac{3}{2}x - \frac{7}{4}$?

(A) $6x + 4y = 8$
(B) $-6x + 4y = 11$
(C) $x - 2y = -4$
(D) $3x + 2y = 7$

GO ON TO THE NEXT PAGE

3

10. $n = 3.65 + .35x$
    $m = 4.25 + .15x$

    In the equations above, m and n represent the heights of bamboo plants, in feet, x weeks after September 15. What was the height of the two plants when their heights were equal?

    (A) 1.5
    (B) 3.0
    (C) 4.7
    (D) 4.8

11. $\frac{3i}{2-i}$

    If the expression above is written in the form $a + bi$, where a and b are real numbers, what is the value of a? (Note $i = \sqrt{-1}$)

    (A) −6
    (B) $\frac{6}{5}$
    (C) $-\frac{3}{5}$
    (D) $\frac{5}{3}$

12. If n is a positive rational number, which of the following could be the graph of $y = x^3 + \frac{1}{5}n^n$?

    (A)

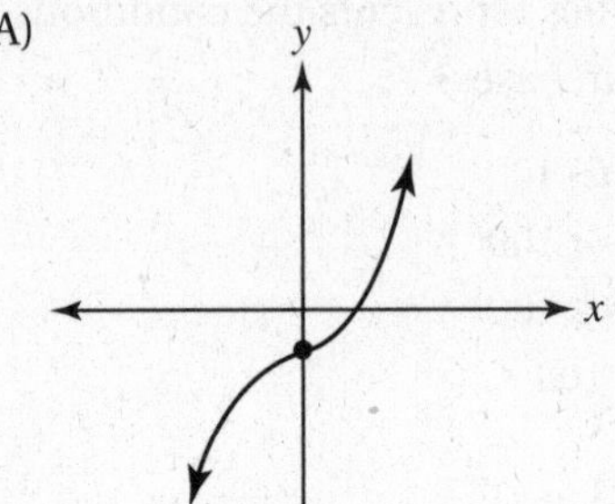

    (B)

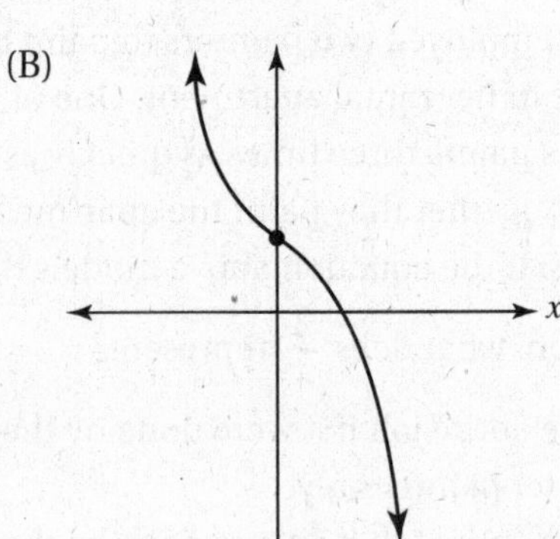

    (C)

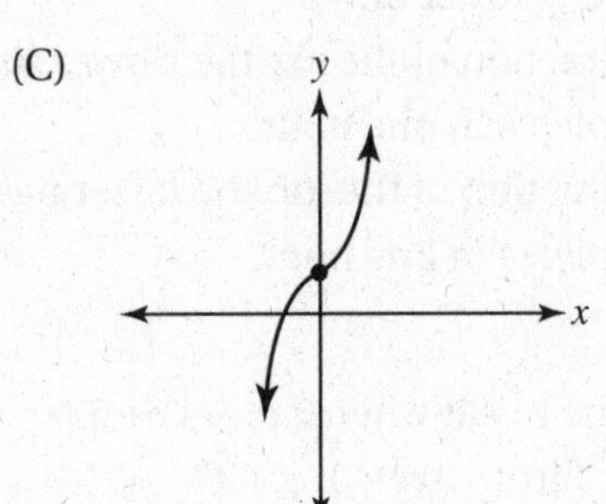

    (D)

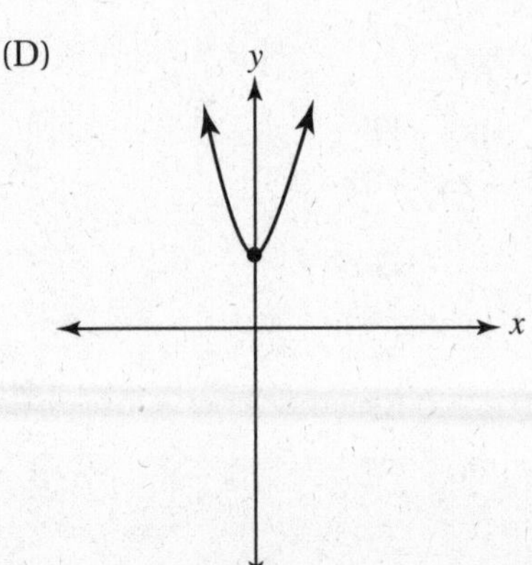

GO ON TO THE NEXT PAGE

13. $h(x) = bx^2 + 30$

For the function h defined above, b is a constant and $h(6) = 138$. What is the value of $h(-4)$?

(A) 24
(B) 64
(C) 78
(D) 86

14. A college currently has 600 students enrolled full time. Of these students, 400 are science majors while 200 are liberal arts majors. If 350 of the students are male, and 250 of the males are science majors, how many female students are liberal arts majors?

(A) 200
(B) 150
(C) 125
(D) 100

15. $P = -1.6x^2 + 2.6xy - 11.4$

The equation above represents a profit function used by an event coordinator at a city museum. In the equation, P represents profit earned, x represents paid admissions $(x > 0)$, and y is any rental discount that is offered. Which of the following represents y in terms of x and P?

(A) $y = \dfrac{1.6xP + 11.4}{2.6x}$

(B) $y = \dfrac{P + 1.6x^2 + 11.4}{2.6x}$

(C) $y = \dfrac{1.6x^2 - 11.4}{2.6x}$

(D) $y = \dfrac{P \pm \sqrt{2.6x}}{11.4}$

GO ON TO THE NEXT PAGE

Grid-in Response Directions

In questions 16–20, first solve the problem, and then enter your answer on the grid provided on the answer sheet. The instructions for entering your answers follow.

- First, write your answer in the boxes at the top of the grid.
- Second, grid your answer in the columns below the boxes.
- Use the fraction bar in the first row or the decimal point in the second row to enter fractions and decimals.

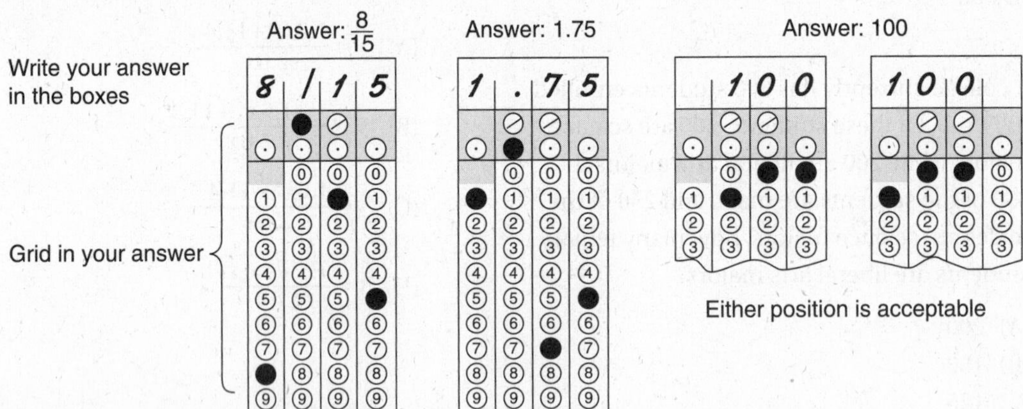

- Grid only one space in each column.
- Entering the answer in the boxes is recommended as an aid in gridding but is not required.
- The machine scoring your exam can read only what you grid, so you **must grid-in your answers correctly to get credit**.
- If a question has more than one correct answer, grid-in only one of them.
- The grid does not have a minus sign; so no answer can be negative.
- A mixed number *must* be converted to an improper fraction or a decimal before it is gridded. Enter $1\frac{1}{4}$ as $\frac{5}{4}$ or 1.25; the machine will interpret 11/4 as $\frac{11}{4}$ and mark it wrong.
- **All decimals must be entered as accurately as possible.** Here are three acceptable ways of gridding

$$\frac{3}{11} = 0.272727\ldots$$

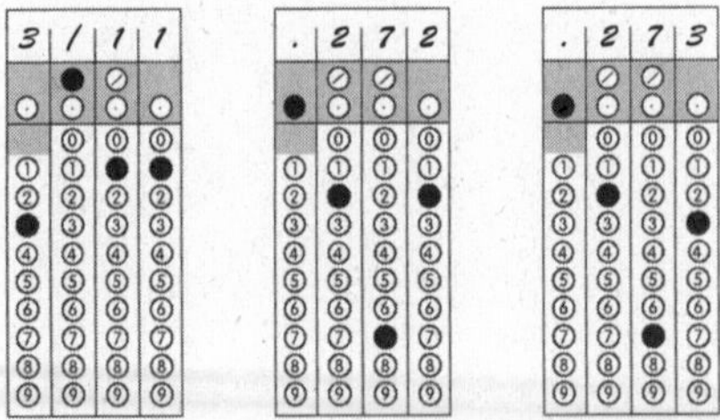

- Note that rounding to .273 is acceptable because you are using the full grid, but you would receive **no credit** for .3 or .27, because they are less accurate.

PRACTICE TEST 2

16. A line passes through the points $(x, 6)$ and $(9, 0)$. If the slope of the line connecting the two points is $\frac{2}{3}$, what is the value of x?

17. Jerry has joined a gymnasium for which he pays dues of $75 each month, plus a daily rate of $10 for each day that he uses the facilities. The function shown below can be used to determine the cost in dollars per month for being a member of this club.

    $f(d) = 75 + 10d$, where d is the number of days.

    Jerry spent $155 in January, $195 in February, and $225 in March. If he spent a total of $850 for the months of January, February, March, and April, what was the total number of days that he spent at the club for those four months?

18. Two sides of a triangle are 7 and 11 inches. If a third side of the triangle is also an integer, what is the product of the smallest and largest values that the side could be?

19. In triangle ABC, the measure of angle B is $90°$, $BC = 80$ and $AC = 100$. Triangle DEF is similar to triangle ABC where vertices D, E, and F correspond with vertices A, B, and C. The scale factor of triangle DEF to triangle ABC is $\frac{1}{10}$. What is the value of $\cos D$?

20. A customer at the produce section of a food store bought cucumbers and heads of lettuce. The quantity she purchased of the heads of lettuce was 6 fewer than 5 times the number of cucumbers. If cucumbers cost $.30 each and a head of lettuce costs $.70 and her cost was $7.20, how many cucumbers did she buy?

If there is still time remaining, you may review your answers.

MATH TEST (CALCULATOR)

55 MINUTES, 38 QUESTIONS

Turn to Section 4 of your answer sheet to answer the questions in this section.

Directions: For questions 1-30, solve each problem and choose the best answer from the given options. Fill in the corresponding circle on your answer document. For questions 31–38, solve the problem and fill in the answer on the answer sheet grid. Please use scrap paper to work out your answers.

Notes:

- The use of a calculator on this section IS permitted.
- All variables and expressions represent real numbers unless indicated otherwise.
- All figures are drawn to scale unless indicated otherwise.
- All figures are in a plane unless indicated otherwise.
- Unless indicated otherwise, the domain of a given function is the set of all real numbers x for which the function has real values.

REFERENCE INFORMATION

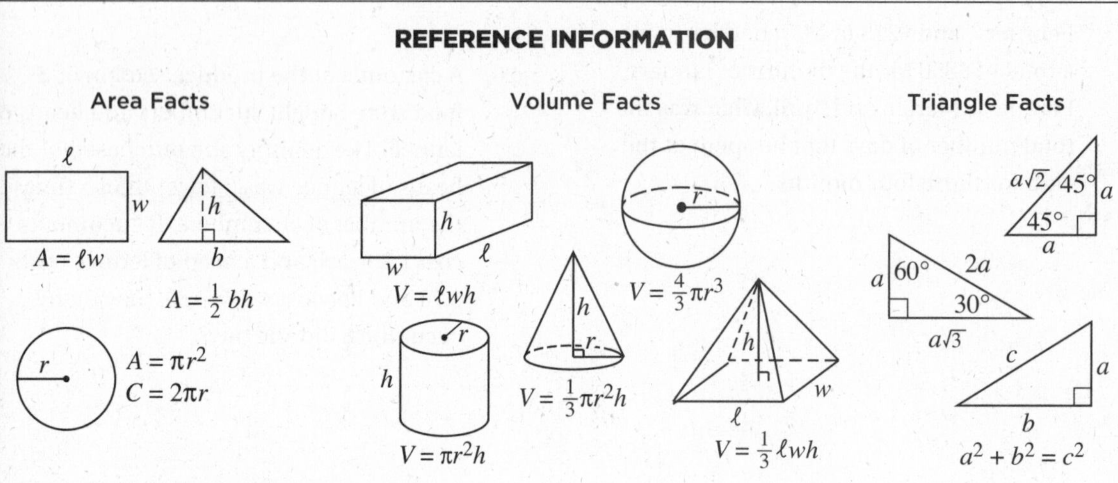

The arc of a circle contains 360°.

The arc of a circle contains 2π radians.

The sum of the measures of the angles in a triangle is 180°.

Questions 1 and 2 refer to the following information.

A graphic novelist earns income directly proportional to the number of books she sells. Her income at a recent book signing was \$1,320 when 800 books were sold.

1. What would be the income for the novelist at a show in which she sold 12,000 books?

(A) \$1,140
(B) \$1,980
(C) \$19,800
(D) \$21,080

GO ON TO THE NEXT PAGE

PRACTICE TEST 2

2. The graphic novelist has to pay certain expenses, called overhead, on all of her sales. The amount of the overhead costs is 32% of the income she earns from book sales. After she pays her overhead costs, what would be her income on sales of 5,000 books?

(A) \$2,640
(B) \$5,610
(C) \$7,610
(D) \$7,620

---

3. In a linear function $f(4) = 6$ and $f(-2) = 14$. What is the value of $f(9)$?

(A) $\frac{20}{3}$
(B) $\frac{2}{3}$
(C) $-\frac{2}{3}$
(D) -3

4. The average (arithmetic mean) of $2x - 4$, $x + 4$, and $3x - 6$ is $x + 4$. What is the value of $-2x + 3$?

(A) -9
(B) -6
(C) 6
(D) 12

5. Shelley is a salesperson for a local furniture store. She receives a \$24.00 commission for every recliner she sells and \$63.00 for every dinette set. If Shelley sells r dinette sets and d recliners during a work shift, which expression represents her pay for that day?

(A) $63r + 24d$
(B) $24r + 63d$
(C) $24r - 63d$
(D) $63r - 24d$

6. The following price sheet indicates the cost of purchasing bottled water.

Quantity	Price
24-pack	\$9.95
12-pack	\$5.95
Individual Bottle	\$1.15

A field trip to the outdoor petting zoo requires that each student have a bottle of water to avoid dehydration. What is the lowest price available for 39 bottles of water?

(A) \$19.35
(B) \$21.30
(C) \$27.20
(D) \$44.85

7. If $n > 0$ then n^2 is

(A) greater than n
(B) equal to n
(C) less than n
(D) there is not enough information to solve this problem.

8. $f(x) = x^2 + 6x - 4$

If the parabola described above is shifted m units to the right and n units up, the new vertex is $(5, -6)$. What is the value of mn^{-1}?

(A) -56
(B) $-\frac{8}{7}$
(C) $\frac{8}{7}$
(D) 56

GO ON TO THE NEXT PAGE

9. A fabric warehouse manager has found that for every 500 square yards of fabric in stock, 13 square yards cannot be sold due to defects. If a recent shipment contained 273 square yards of defective fabric, how many square yards were in the entire shipment?

(A) 10,000
(B) 10,500
(C) 11,000
(D) 23,500

Questions 10 and 11 refer to the graph below.

A botanist was exploring the impact a local red ant population had on local nurseries. An experiment was devised to investigate any correlation between red ant populations and the annual yield of white roses. A scatter plot of the data is shown below.

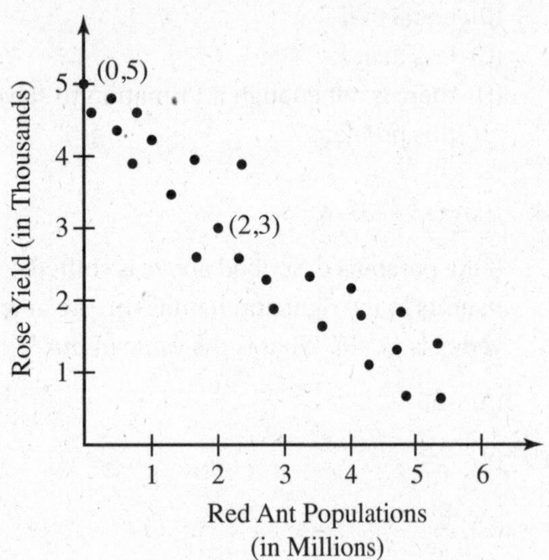

10. A line of best fit is constructed within the data. Which of the following functions best models the data?

(A) $f(x) = -4.88x + 4.66$
(B) $f(x) = 1.15x + 7.88$
(C) $f(x) = 1.27x + 4.88$
(D) $f(x) = -1.14x + 4.88$

11. A grower uses a pesticide that will reduce the ant population by 60%. If the grower currently has five million ants, which of the following is the closest to his rose yield after using the pesticide?

(A) 1,000
(B) 1,800
(C) 3,000
(D) 4,200

Questions 12 and 13 refer to the table below.

Table of the Seven Lightest Chemical Elements (by atomic mass)

Atomic Mass	Name Chemical Element	Symbol	Atomic number
1.0079	Hydrogen	H	1
4.0026	Helium	He	2
6.941	Lithium	Li	3
9.0122	Beryllium	Be	4
10.811	Boron	B	5
12.0107	Carbon	C	6
14.0067	Nitrogen	N	7

12. Which element is approximately equal to the sum of the weights of Helium and Lithium?

(A) Nitrogen
(B) Boron
(C) Beryllium
(D) Lithium

13. Which element is about 30% more massive than Lithium?

(A) Nitrogen
(B) Boron
(C) Beryllium
(D) Hydrogen

GO ON TO THE NEXT PAGE

PRACTICE TEST 2

14. The equation of a circle is shown below.

$x^2 + y^2 - 6y + 4x = 36$

What is the circumference of this circle?

(A) 49π
(B) 36π
(C) 14π
(D) 12π

15. Sammie has done a survey of one hundred 16-year-old Florida students and found that 84% favored including an internship in their schools' curricula. She finds, however, that the margin of error in her survey is 6.9%. What can she do to reduce the margin of error?

(A) check similar surveys in other states
(B) reduce the survey size
(C) increase the survey size
(D) survey other age groups as well

16. The function g is defined by $g(x) = 2x^3 - 8x^2 - bx + 140$. In the xy plane, the graph of g intersects the x-axis at (2, 0), (–5, 0), and (m, 0). What is the value of b?

(A) –44
(B) 4
(C) 31
(D) 62

17. A car travels h hours at a rate of m miles per hour. If the car can travel g miles for each gallon of gasoline used, which equation shows the number of gallons used?

(A) $x = \frac{hm}{g}$

(B) $x = \frac{g}{hm}$

(C) $x = \frac{gh}{m}$

(D) $x = \frac{mg}{h}$

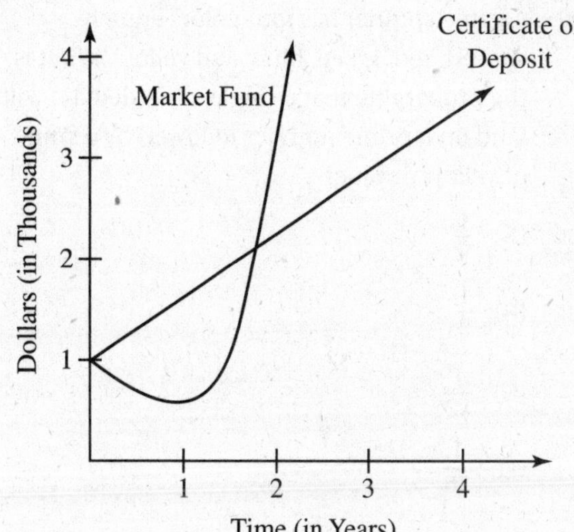

18. Even though she is only twenty-seven years old, Cheryl is interested in beginning a retirement plan. The graph above shows the value of a market fund investment compared to a Certificate of Deposit (CD). Which of the following **cannot** be concluded by Cheryl from the graph?

(A) At one year, the market fund is worth more than the CD.
(B) The market fund shows exponential growth and the CD shows linear growth.
(C) At a point between years 1 and 2, the two funds have the same value.
(D) The initial investment in each account was the same.

19. Which of the following is a step in solving the equation $\sqrt{x-7} = x-7$?

(A) $x - 7 = x - 7$
(B) $2x = 14$
(C) $(x - 8)(x - 7) = 0$
(D) $(x + 7)(x - 6) = 0$

GO ON TO THE NEXT PAGE

20. A game spinner has four colors equally spaced: red, green, blue, and yellow. What is the probability that a single, six-sided die will land on a prime number followed by a spin of yellow or blue?

(A) $\frac{1}{4}$

(B) $\frac{1}{9}$

(C) $\frac{1}{12}$

(D) $\frac{1}{36}$

21. Gold has always been coveted for its aesthetic qualities. However, due to its malleability, it also has many industrial and electronic applications. Gold can be stretched so thinly that a single ounce can cover 100 square yards of surface. How many square feet can be covered with 2.5 ounces of gold?

(A) 2,250 square feet
(B) 1,125 square feet
(C) 750 square feet
(D) 150 square feet

22. A start-up delivery service in Gainesville offers a fee schedule that is indicated in the table below. Each pound (or fraction thereof) costs $2.50 to deliver within a 20-mile radius of downtown Gainesville. A local business owner in the downtown section finds the service cost effective to deliver to suburban clientele at the outskirts of town.

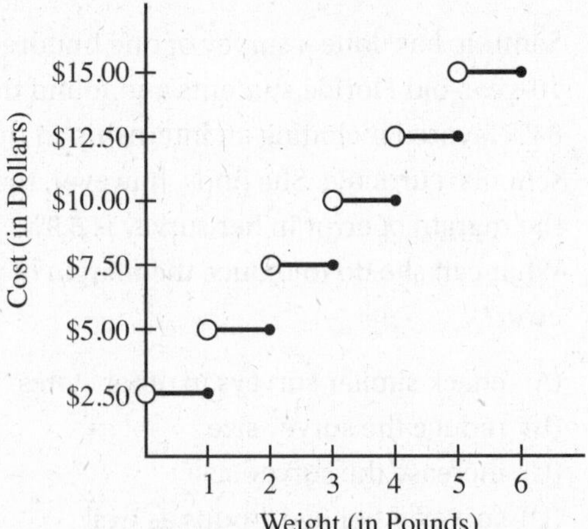

Four recent deliveries had items that weighed the following (in pounds):

2.68 3.11 5.28 4.0

What was the cost to deliver these items?

(A) $37.50
(B) $42.50
(C) $45.00
(D) $52.50

PRACTICE TEST 2

GO ON TO THE NEXT PAGE

23. A learning therapist has shown that students can increase reading levels by increasing required summer reading. She models the increase using the formula $y = 1.09x + .17$, where x represents the current grade reading level and y represents the improvement after the program. Which of the following represents the meaning of 1.09 in the equation?

    (A) The difference between the students who use the program and those who do not.
    (B) The increase in the number of students using the reading program.
    (C) The increase in the reading level plus a constant of .17.
    (D) A 17% increase in reading level.

Questions 24 and 25 refer to the information provided in the table below.

Rank	Country	GDP–per capita (US$)
1	Liechtenstein	141,100
2	Qatar	104,300
3	Luxembourg	81,100
4	Bermuda	69,900
5	Monaco	63,400
6	Singapore	60,500
7	Jersey	57,000
8	Falkland Islands (Islas Malvinas)	55,400
9	Norway	54,200
10	Brunei	50,000

The Gross Domestic Product (GDP) is a measure of a country's wealth. The per-capita income for a country is found by dividing the sum of all of the goods and services that a country produces by the country's population.

24. Which country exceeded the per capita income of Singapore by approximately 4.8%?

    (A) Qatar
    (B) Monaco
    (C) Bermuda
    (D) Norway

25. In 2014, the GDP of Singapore was \$298,000,000,000. Which of the following is the best approximation of the size of Singapore's population?

    (A) 493,000
    (B) 874,000
    (C) 4,900,000
    (D) 6,100,000

	10th	11th
Female	17	18
Male	18	20

26. One lucky student at Bristol High School will be selected to attend a College for Kids camp at Johns Hopkins University. The table above represents the number of students in the 10th and 11th grades at the school. If a student is selected at random, what is the probability that the student will be in 10th grade or a male?

    (A) .753
    (B) .521
    (C) .479
    (D) .472

GO ON TO THE NEXT PAGE

PRACTICE TEST 2

27. A great circle of a sphere contains the sphere's center. If the volume of a sphere is 374 cubic inches, what is the circumference of a great circle on that sphere? (Use $\pi = 3.14$)

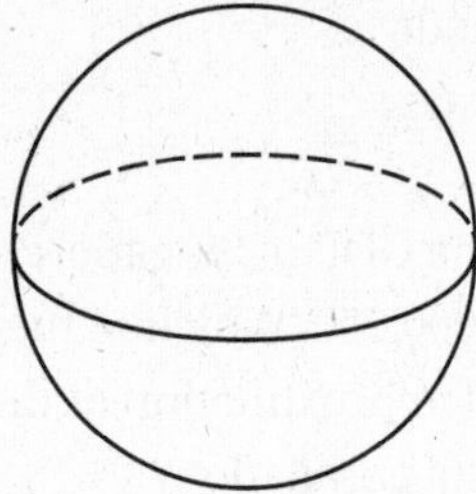

(A) 4.47
(B) 28.07
(C) 56.14
(D) 62.74

Question 28 refers to the information below.

The half-life of an element is the amount of time that elapses until a certain mass of an element or compound decays to one-half its initial amount.

$$A = R_0\left(\frac{1}{2}\right)^x$$

28. A certain compound's half-life can be approximated using the equation above where

R_0 = the initial amount of the compound
A = the amount remaining after x years
x = the time elapsed in years

If 125 grams of the compound is left to decay over 2.3 years, how many grams will remain?

(A) 16.7
(B) 25.4
(C) 29.6
(D) 41.1

29. Twenty-one students entered into a foul shooting contest in basketball. Each student was given five foul shots to attempt. The table below lists the number of foul shots made and the number of students who made that many foul shots.

Successful Foul Shots	Frequency
0	2
1	4
2	4
3	7
4	3
5	1

If a student who successfully shot at least two foul shots was chosen at random, what is the probability that he/she successfully shot exactly 4 foul shots?

(A) $\frac{1}{7}$
(B) $\frac{1}{5}$
(C) $\frac{2}{5}$
(D) $\frac{3}{5}$

Question 30 refers to the system of equations below.

30. $4a + n = 2a - 3$
$4b + m = 2b - 3$

If n is m plus 1, which of the following is true?

(A) a is b minus $\frac{1}{2}$
(B) a is b plus $\frac{1}{2}$
(C) a is b plus 1
(D) a is b minus 2

GO ON TO THE NEXT PAGE

4

Grid-in Response Directions

In questions 31–38, first solve the problem, and then enter your answer on the grid provided on the answer sheet. The instructions for entering your answers follow.

- First, write your answer in the boxes at the top of the grid.
- Second, grid your answer in the columns below the boxes.
- Use the fraction bar in the first row or the decimal point in the second row to enter fractions and decimals.

Answer: $\frac{8}{15}$ Answer: 1.75 Answer: 100

Write your answer in the boxes

8 / 1 5 1 . 7 5 1 0 0 1 0 0

Grid in your answer

Either position is acceptable

- Grid only one space in each column.
- Entering the answer in the boxes is recommended as an aid in gridding but is not required.
- The machine scoring your exam can read only what you grid, so you **must grid-in your answers correctly to get credit**.
- If a question has more than one correct answer, grid-in only one of them.
- The grid does not have a minus sign; so no answer can be negative.
- A mixed number *must* be converted to an improper fraction or a decimal before it is gridded. Enter $1\frac{1}{4}$ as $\frac{5}{4}$ or 1.25; the machine will interpret 11/4 as $\frac{11}{4}$ and mark it wrong.
- **All decimals must be entered as accurately as possible.** Here are three acceptable ways of gridding

$$\frac{3}{11} = 0.272727\ldots$$

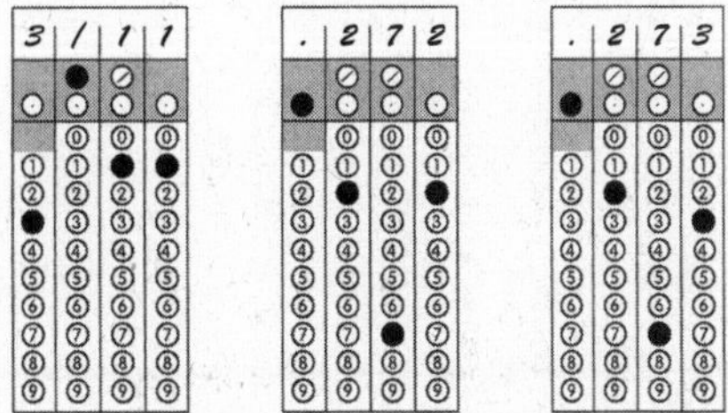

- Note that rounding to .273 is acceptable because you are using the full grid, but you would receive **no credit** for .3 or .27, because they are less accurate.

4  4

31. It's the end of the school year and a tenth grade civics class is planning a barbecue to celebrate. The class has drinks and desserts but needs to plan the number of hamburgers it needs to buy. Hamburger patties are sold in packages of six hamburgers. Hamburger rolls come in packages of eight rolls. What is the smallest number of hamburgers that should be purchased to have no rolls left over from a package?

32. A World History class recently took its mid-term exam. The following table represents the array of scores.

		x	x	
		x	x	
x		x	x	
x	x	x	x	x
20%	**40%**	**60%**	**80%**	**100%**

If a thirteenth student took the exam the next day, what must that score be to arrive at a class mean score of 60%?

33. If $x^3 - 15 = (x - 3)(x^2 + 3x + 9) + m$, what is the value of m?

34. In a circle with center P, central angle MPN has a measure of $\frac{3\pi}{4}$ radians. The area of the sector formed by the central angle MPN is what fraction of the circle?

35. Cindy owns a candy store and sells individual candies as well as mixes. Her most popular mixture is the chocolate and mint collection. The ratio of chocolates to mints in this candy mix is 3 to 5. If she is mixing 7 pounds of the mix, how many pounds are chocolates?

36. $\frac{1}{3}c = 6$

$b - \frac{2}{3}c = -6$

The system of equations has solution (b, c). What is the value of b?

GO ON TO THE NEXT PAGE

Questions 37 and 38 refer to the information provided below.

A merchant is experimenting with discounting prices for men's slacks to raise additional revenue for his business.

37. A merchant sells a pair of slacks called Model 1, for $50 a pair. He is able to sell 40 pairs per month at this price. In order to get money to purchase newer models, the merchant plans to discount this model of slacks by 10%. If the discount yields the sale of 10 additional pairs, how much money will he have gained at the end of the month by discounting this model of slacks?

38. The merchant determined that the additional funds gained from discounting his first model of slacks by 10% was insufficient. He now wants to discount an additional pair of slacks, Model 2, in order to gain a total of $750. In a normal month the Model 2 slacks sell for $65 at 25 pairs per month. If he discounts Model 2 slacks by 25%, how many pairs of this second model must he sell, in addition to the discounted Model 1 slacks, in order to arrive at a $750 gain? (Round your answer to the nearest whole pair.)

STOP

If there is still time remaining, you may review your answers.

ESSAY (OPTIONAL)

Directions: This is your opportunity to show that you can read and understand a passage and write an analysis of that passage. Be sure your essay demonstrates a clear and logical analysis of the passage, using precise language.

On the actual test, you will write your essay on the lines provided in your answer booklet; for now, write your essay on lined paper. Remember to write or print legibly so that others can read what you've written.

You have 50 minutes to read the essay and write a response to the prompt provided.

Carefully read the passage below. As you read, think about how John Davy makes use of

- *reasoning* to develop an argument
- *evidence* to support assertions made
- *language* to persuade the reader

From John Davy, "Has man sold his soul to the computer?" *The Observer. The Observer: Has man sold his soul to the computer?* (circa 1980s) by John Davy (Science Correspondent). The Guardian, 536 Broadway, 6th floor, New York, New York, 10012.

1 Professor Joseph Weizenbaum has been thinking about computers for 20 years or more, working at one of the world's greatest power houses of the new technology, the Department of Computer Science at the Massachusetts Institute of Technology. He occupies a small fifth-floor office, surrounded by some of the world's most advanced computer systems and computer scientists, looking rather like Albert Einstein before his hair went white. If we consider what he now thinks about computers, we should be surprised that his hair is not white, too. He is regarded by many around him as a heretical and a dangerous dissident. He is increasingly convinced that we are sleep-walking into a technology whose real influence, unless we wake up, will be far more malign than benign. "I'm coming close to believing," he told me, "that the computer is inherently anti-human—an invention of the devil."

2 According to Weizenbaum, computers induce powerful delusional thinking in quite normal people. One dangerous delusion is that computers are "revolutionizing" our lives. In fact, says Professor Weizenbaum, far from generating social change, they have been mainly used so far to preserve traditional structures, and operate them on a much larger scale. And, says Professor Weizenbaum, they prevent us asking fundamental questions about the needs the systems are supposed to serve. The operators of the system are increasingly insulated from the realities of poverty, unemployment, or war by a mesh of impersonal electronic vested interests.

3 Still more sinister is the delusion that computers can make "judgments." During the Vietnam War, says Professor Weizenbaum, "computers operated by officers who had not the slightest idea of what went on inside their machines effectively chose which villages were to be bombed." Many large systems now in use have been built up cumulatively, so that no one knows all the rules by which they are operating. "Decisions" may be made by computers whose programs nobody can any longer take responsibility for.

4 Behind these dilemmas of computers and society, Weizenbaum sees more subtle and sinister influences on our own psyche. "The computer programmer," he says, "is the creator of universes for which he alone is the law giver." He is in effect a designer of games, a maker of model universes in which he rules. The computer games now invading our homes allow us to wage wars, destroy cities, and do violence to opponents in toy worlds safely separated from real life. What is the addictive power of such games?

5 Brooding on all this at MIT, Professor Weizenbaum wonders whether, instead of asking about the effects of technology on society, we should look at the effect of society on technology. In the 1960s he and his colleagues were wondering what would happen if computers became really cheap. No one believed they would get so cheap so quickly. "We talk about all kinds of possible uses. None of us foresaw that the main consumer market would be for computer games."

6 He has been looking at earlier examples of technological euphoria. Take medicine. Huge machines coupled to computers are installed for more precise location of brain tumors. "Brain tumor location is 97th on the list of current pressing medical problems," says Professor Weizenbaum. Technology makes us ask, not what problems most need solutions, but "what problems exist for which this machine is a solution? Where medicine is practiced for profit, the automation of medicine is a godsend."

7 The computer embodies games we have constructed and for which we have made the rules. As such, they are tools for what Professor Weizenbaum calls "instrumental reason"—that form of thinking which reduces all understanding of the world to the question of whether we can manipulate it. "Programming is very seductive," says Weizenbaum, "especially for beginners." Students quickly acquire basic techniques and feel themselves in charge of an electronic universe. But in fact, "they are like people who have mastered the rudiments of a foreign language, but have absolutely nothing to say in it." Here is where real education for the computer age must begin, Weizenbaum believes. The central task is not the acquisition of programming skills, but the realization of the whole human being. What distinguishes us from a computer? "Courage," says Professor Weizenbaum, "trust, endurance, creativity."

8 A friend driving me to the airport, hearing I was going to see Professor Weizenbaum, described a scene she had witnessed that day in the supermarket. A customer was in dispute with a girl operating an electronic till. "It must be right," said the girl. "That machine is smarter than I am." The girl at the next till turned to her fiercely and said, "If you think that you're dead." Which girl should we see as our hope for the future? Professor Weizenbaum has no doubt of the answer. Do we?

Write an essay explaining how John Davy constructs an argument to convince the reader of the validity of the view held by Professor Joseph Weizenbaum that computers are more harmful than beneficial to human beings. Describe and analyze how Davy uses one or more of the elements of persuasive writing listed in the box on page 174 to strengthen his argument. You may also discuss other writing techniques used by the author.

Your essay should not state your opinion on the topic discussed in the passage, but rather analyze how Davy constructs an argument to persuade the reader.

ANSWER KEY
Practice Test 2

Section 1: Reading

1.	**C**	14.	**C**	27.	**A**	40.	**C**
2.	**D**	15.	**D**	28.	**D**	41.	**D**
3.	**C**	16.	**D**	29.	**C**	42.	**D**
4.	**B**	17.	**C**	30.	**A**	43.	**A**
5.	**B**	18.	**B**	31.	**A**	44.	**C**
6.	**B**	19.	**A**	32.	**D**	45.	**A**
7.	**C**	20.	**C**	33.	**B**	46.	**C**
8.	**D**	21.	**A**	34.	**C**	47.	**C**
9.	**A**	22.	**C**	35.	**D**	48.	**C**
10.	**C**	23.	**B**	36.	**A**	49.	**B**
11.	**A**	24.	**A**	37.	**C**	50.	**D**
12.	**A**	25.	**C**	38.	**B**	51.	**D**
13.	**B**	26.	**D**	39.	**D**	52.	**B**

Number Correct ______

Number Incorrect ______

Section 2: Writing and Language

1.	**B**	12.	**D**	23.	**B**	34.	**D**
2.	**B**	13.	**B**	24.	**B**	35.	**B**
3.	**D**	14.	**D**	25.	**D**	36.	**D**
4.	**C**	15.	**C**	26.	**C**	37.	**C**
5.	**D**	16.	**C**	27.	**D**	38.	**C**
6.	**C**	17.	**B**	28.	**A**	39.	**C**
7.	**D**	18.	**B**	29.	**B**	40.	**A**
8.	**A**	19.	**C**	30.	**C**	41.	**D**
9.	**A**	20.	**B**	31.	**B**	42.	**C**
10.	**A**	21.	**C**	32.	**B**	43.	**C**
11.	**C**	22.	**B**	33.	**C**	44.	**B**

Number Correct ______

Number Incorrect ______

ANSWER KEY
Practice Test 2

Section 3: Math (No Calculator)

1. **C**
2. **A**
3. **C**
4. **D**
5. **A**
6. **C**
7. **C**
8. **B**
9. **B**
10. **C**
11. **C**
12. **C**
13. **C**
14. **D**
15. **B**

16. **18**

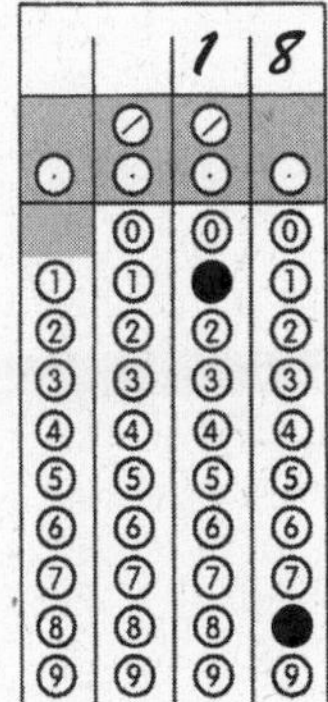

17. **55**

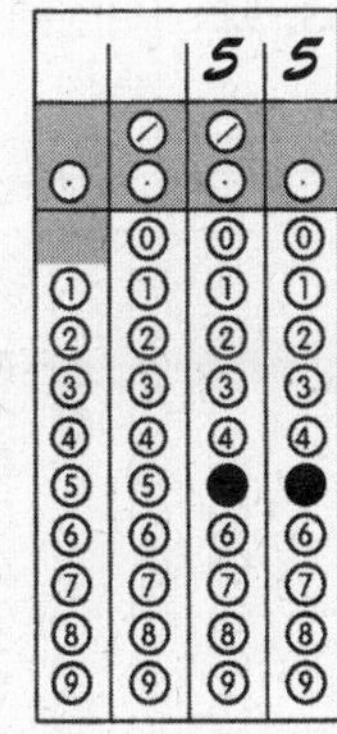

18. **85**

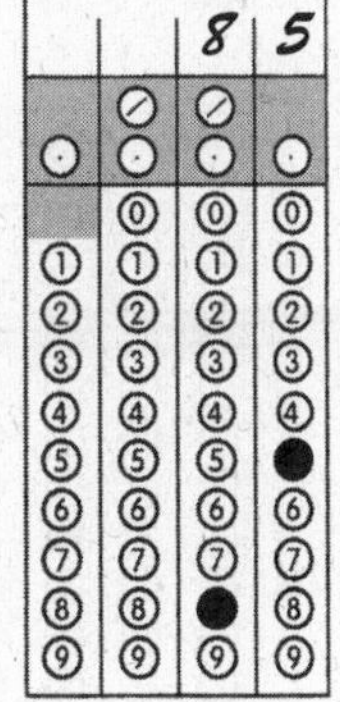

19. **3/5** or **.6**

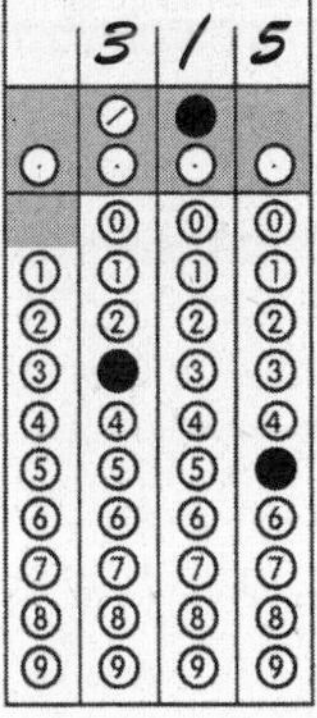

or

20. **3**

Number Correct ______

Number Incorrect ______

ANSWER KEY
Practice Test 2

Section 4: Math (Calculator)

1. **C**
2. **B**
3. **C**
4. **A**
5. **A**
6. **A**
7. **D**
8. **C**
9. **B**
10. **D**
11. **C**
12. **B**
13. **C**
14. **C**
15. **C**
16. **D**
17. **A**
18. **A**
19. **C**
20. **A**
21. **A**
22. **B**
23. **C**
24. **B**
25. **C**
26. **A**
27. **B**
28. **B**
29. **B**
30. **A**

31. **24**

32. **40**

33. **12**

34. **3/8** or **.375**

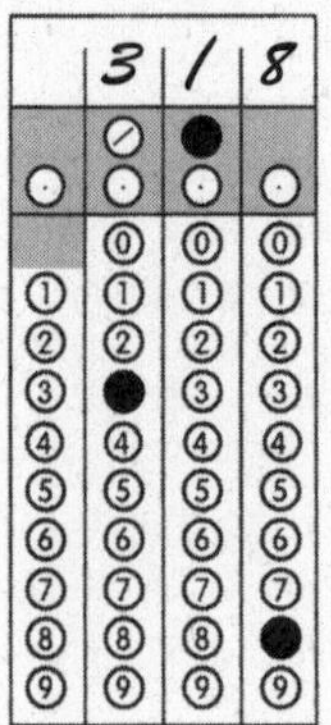

or

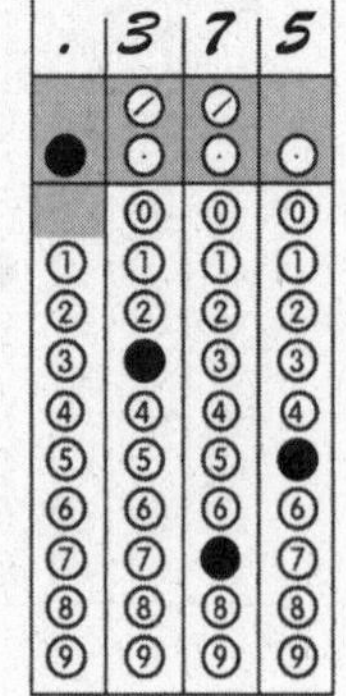

ANSWER KEY
Practice Test 2

35. **21/8** or **2.62** or **2.63**

or

or

36. **6**

37. **250**

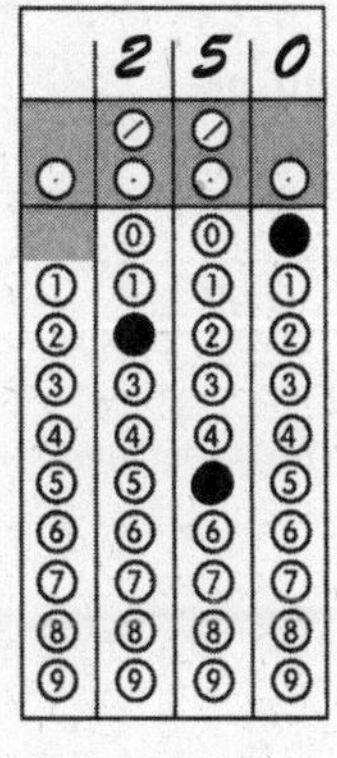

38. **44**

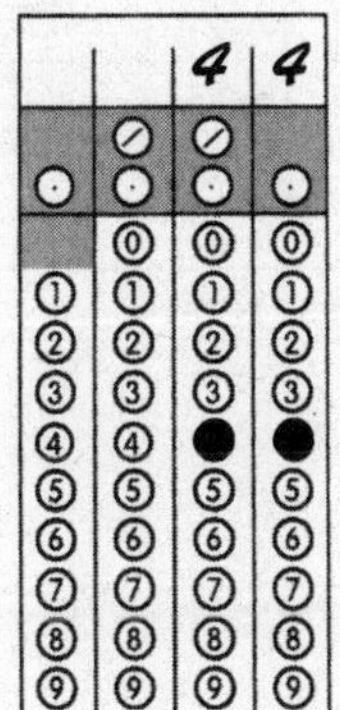

Number Correct _______

Number Incorrect _______

SCORE ANALYSIS

Reading and Writing Test

Section 1: Reading ________ = ________ (A)
correct raw score

Section 2: Writing ________ = ________ (B)
correct raw score

To find your Reading and Writing test scores, consult the chart below: find the ranges in which your raw scores lie and read across to find the ranges of your test scores.

________ + ________ = ________ (C)
range of reading test scores | range of writing test scores | range of reading + writing test scores

To find the range of your Reading and Writing Scaled Score, multiply (C) by 10.

Test Scores for the Reading and Writing Sections

Reading Raw Score	Writing Raw Score	Test Score
44-52	39-44	35-40
36-43	33-38	31-34
30-35	28-32	28-30
24-29	22-27	24-27
19-23	17-21	21-23
14-18	13-16	19-20
9-13	9-12	16-18
5-8	5-8	13-15
less than 5	less than 5	10-12

Math Test

Section 3: ________ = ________ (D)
correct raw score

Section 4: ________ = ________ (E)
correct raw score

Total Math raw score: (D) + (E) = ________

To find your Math Scaled Score, consult the chart below: find the range in which your raw score lies and read across to find the range for your scaled score.

Scaled Scores for the Math Test

Raw Score	Scaled Score
50-58	700-800
44-49	650-690
38-43	600-640
32-37	550-590
26-31	500-540

Raw Score	Scaled Score
20-25	450-490
15-19	400-440
11-14	350-390
7-10	300-340
less than 7	200-290

ANSWER EXPLANATIONS

Section 1: Reading Test

1. **(C)** In lines 7–10 the narrator says, "It [the violin] was the sole item that exuded an air of foreignness. . . ." In line 13, it is described as a "strange object" in the eyes of the villagers. The headman "[holds] his nose over the sound holes and sniffed long and hard" (lines 28–29), but the villagers have no idea what it is until the headman strums a few strings and the violin produces a sound. The only term the villagers have for the violin is "toy." Choice (B) is too positive to describe the villagers' attitude to the violin; they are suspicious of it.

2. **(D)** The narrator says that the violin was the only item Luo and he had that "exuded an air of . . . civilization, and therefore aroused suspicion" (lines 8–10). We can infer from this that the narrator regards the villagers as uncivilized.

3. **(C)** After examining the violin thoroughly, the headman concludes that it's a toy. The narrator says, "This verdict left us speechless" (line 36). The narrator says, "Things were not looking good" (lines 37–38) because he knows that the villagers, as loyal Communists, would regard them as bourgeois.

4. **(B)** In context, *coolly* means "calmly." Earlier the narrator said that Luo spoke to the headman "as casually as he could" (line 64).

5. **(B)** We can infer from their comments and behavior that the villagers see themselves as loyal Communists, which means they follow Communist ideology and condemn bourgeois (middle class) values and pastimes, such as playing Western music, as decadent. Thus, the villagers would see it as an honor to be the person who destroys a symbol of bourgeois decadence. The sentence "We looked like . . . Communist farm workers" (lines 47–50) strongly suggests that the villagers are Communists and that the narrator and Luo are "reactionary" (the latter suggests they are bourgeois). Further clues are that the headman condemns the violin as "a bourgeois toy" (line 54) and that the narrator describes the headman as "the vigilant Communist" (lines 88–89).

6. **(B)** In light of what happens after Luo winks at the narrator, we can infer that Luo winked at the narrator to indicate that he had a plan and that the narrator should follow it. Evidently, Luo's plan was to announce that the narrator would play "a Mozart sonata" (line 75) and then say that the sonata was called *Mozart is Thinking of Chairman Mao.*

7. **(C)** The narrator says he was "puzzled" (line 72) by Luo's wink, but he nevertheless takes his violin and tunes it. This suggests he trusts his friend to act intelligently and responsibly even though the narrator does not know what his friend is planning to do.

8. **(D)** We can infer this because we know that the narrator realizes that he and Luo are in a tense, dangerous situation in which they are dependent on the headman.

9. **(A)** Parody is not used in the passage. (B) There is a lot of description of details; for example,"his calloused fingertips" (line 31). (C) Tension is built up until the climax at the end of the passage. (D) There are several similes; for example, "Mozart's phrases came flooding back to me like so many faithful friends" (lines 110–112).

10. **(C)** The narrator says that Luo was only eighteen years old when the events recounted in the passage occurred. It can be inferred that when Luo lights a cigarette and smokes it while the narrator plays the violin for the villagers he is feeling satisfied with the successful outcome of his daring plan. The fact that the narrator describes Luo as smoking "quietly, like a man" suggests that he has just undergone an experience that made him more mature and that he is aware that he has become more mature.

11. **(A)** The assertion is about a matter of fact, and thus historical evidence would strengthen the assertion. Examples of this attitude on the part of artists and writers could be given.

12. **(A)** We can infer that the writer does not think that artists and writers would have contempt for commercial activity that is forced upon a person or that is necessary for their survival.

13. **(B)** The phrase "this sentiment" (line 12) refers to the "exasperation" (line 10) of artists and writers with highly commercial society. *Philistinism* (line 11)—*an attitude of smug ignorance and conventionalism toward artistic and cultural values*—neatly describes the attitude that artists and writers found exasperating.

14. **(C)** In context, *decisive* (line 30) means "having the power to decide." The author is explaining that in commercial society the tastes of common people are the most influential ones in determining the prevailing tastes of a society.

15. **(D)** In lines 6–9 ("And since . . . over all others . . .") we are told that bourgeois society was the first in which the "commercial ethos" was dominant, so we can infer that the author is discussing a time at which the society was becoming more commercial. In lines 16–19 we are told that "[commercial society] did (and does) deprive [artists and writers] of the status that they naturally feel themselves entitled to."

16. **(D)** The author is concerned mainly with describing the attitudes of artists and writers and their place in bourgeois society. In lines 24–27 he says "A commercial society, a society whose civilization is shaped by market transactions, is always likely to reflect the appetites and preferences of common men and women." He does not express a view on whether this was a favorable or unfavorable development. His main concern is to describe its effect on artists and writers.

17. **(C)** The author says, "The popularity of romanticism in the century after 1750 testifies to this fact, as the artists led an 'inner emigration' of the spirit—which, however, left the actual world unchanged" (lines 41–45).

18. **(B)** Lines 41–45 ("The . . . unchanged") provide the best evidence. The author says that the activities of artists embracing romanticism did not affect the "actual world."

19. **(A)** The phrase "social force" refers to anything that affects the nature of society. According to the author, socialists believed that the creation of great material abundance would mean that the demand for goods and services, "appetite" (line 70) would no longer affect the nature of society.

20. **(C)** In context, "disinterestedly" means *impartially, not motivated by self-interest.* The author is saying that one of the reasons that "scientific socialism" (line 66) is an appealing ideology to intellectuals is that it supports their belief that they are not exercising control over others because they enjoy power or prestige but because they

want to help "mobilize the masses for their own ultimate self-transformation" (lines 87–88).

21. **(A)** "Fault lines" is a term in geology that refers to the place where two tectonic plates meet. The use of the term to refer to civilizations compares civilizations to continental plates, suggesting that, like continental plates, civilizations are distinct entities that sometimes collide, causing conflict between them.

22. **(C)** We can infer that the author uses the word *basic* to mean *fundamental* because immediately after the sentence in which he uses the word, he describes differences among civilizations that, in his view, determine the essential nature of civilizations: "Civilizations are differentiated . . . equality and hierarchy" (lines 13–24). Also, in line 26 he refers to the differences as "fundamental."

23. **(B)** The author says, "Civilizations are differentiated from each other by history, language, culture, tradition and, *most important, religion*" (lines 13–16) and "[These differences] are far more fundamental than differences among political ideologies . . ." (lines 26–28). We can infer from this that the author believes that most people identify more strongly with their religion than with their political party.

24. **(A)** The author is arguing that what he considers the most fundamental differences among civilizations (as described in lines 13–24; "Civilizations are differentiated . . . equality and hierarchy") have "over the centuries . . . generated the most prolonged and the most violent conflicts" (lines 30–33). Since the passage is mainly concerned with the cause of future conflict, it makes sense that the author would consider the most important implication of the statement to be that differences among civilizations rather than differing political ideologies will cause serious future conflict in the world.

25. **(C)** The author says, "The interactions between peoples of different civilizations are increasing; these interactions intensify civilization consciousness and awareness of differences between civilizations and commonalities within civilizations" (lines 35–40). In lines 40–43 the author says, "Enhanced civilization-consciousness of people, in turn, invigorates differences and animosities stretching or thought to stretch back deep into history." From this information we can infer that the author would be very likely to agree that the increased large movements of large numbers of people belonging to different civilizations from one civilization to another has increased the likelihood of conflict between civilizations.

26. **(D)** The author says, "The processes of economic modernization and social change throughout the world are separating people from longstanding local identities . . . In much of the world religion has moved in to fill this gap . . . . In most countries and most religions the people active in fundamentalist movements are young, college-educated, middle-class technicians, professionals, and business persons" (lines 44–59).

27. **(A)** The author of Passage 2 believes Raymond Aron's statement is correct because he agrees with Aron that although culture and civilization are important to people and play a part in determining events in the international arena, nation-states play the decisive role in determining such events.

28. **(D)** The author's main argument is that "It is willful, day-to-day, crisis-to-crisis, war-to-war political decision-making by nation-state units that remains the single most identifiable determinant of events in the international arena" (lines 102–106) In this context, the statement in lines 99–102 is most accurately described as a "partial concession" to Huntington's argument that politics, regimes, and ideologies are determined by culture, history, and civilization. The author says Huntington's argument is true "*to an extent*" (line 102), a statement that can be described as a partial concession to Huntington's argument.

29. **(C)** In context, *vital* means "full of energy." The author is explaining his view that political rather than cultural and historical factors have the most important role in determining events in "the world area." Thus, it makes sense that he describes the cultural and historical factors as less full of energy.

30. **(A)** The author of Passage 1 does not argue that *all* conflict is at present caused by conflicts between civilizations or that this will be true in the future. He argues that "the world will be shaped *in large measure* by the interactions among seven or eight major civilizations" (lines 2–4) and that "the most important conflicts of the future will occur along the cultural fault lines separating these civilizations from one another" (lines 8–11). Thus, he would be likely to say that the Persian Gulf War is an example of nation-states putting their interests ahead of the interests of the civilization to which they belong, but that this one example does not invalidate his argument that civilizational loyalty is becoming more important than loyalty to the nation-state in causing conflict in the world.

31. **(A)** After describing Huntington's classification as "[identifying] determinants [of international events] on a grand scale by 'civilizations'" (lines 83–85), the author of Passage 2 describes what he sees as the difficulties with Huntington's classification: "His endeavor, however, has its own fault lines. The lines are the borders encompassing each distinct nation and mercilessly chopping the alleged civilizations into pieces" (lines 85–89). From this we can infer that the author of Passage 2 has serious doubts about whether the term "civilization" can be applied to the entities described as such by Huntington.

32. **(D)** In lines 24–26 the author says, "The general importance of zoonoses for humanity has waxed and waned over time in concert with changing conditions . . . ."

33. **(B)** These lines provide the best evidence, as stated above.

34. **(C)** In his discussion of zoonoses the author makes clear that zoonoses are "maintain[ed] in nature" (lines 16–17) in certain animals and humans, so it can be inferred that all (or at least nearly all) zoonoses are not actually new in the sense that they didn't exist previously. In lines 24–36 the author discusses how zoonoses vary in range and says that a zoonosis can appear in an area that had not previously existed; in this sense it is "new."

35. **(D)** If we know what an epidemic is we can infer that an epizootic is an epidemic caused by zoonotic pathogens.

36. **(A)** The author says "Rabies is a well-established zoonosis and, except for anthrax, perhaps the earliest zoonosis to confront humans" (lines 36–39).

37. **(C)** As discussed in the explanation to question 3, all (or nearly all) zoonoses exist in nature (that is, in humans or animals). The author does not discuss how often new zoonoses occur, but his discussion strongly suggests that it does not occur frequently.

38. **(B)** From the context we can infer that *specter* must mean "haunting image" because it is used to refer to the Spanish flu that killed and sickened so many people.

39. **(D)** The "revelations" (line 22) the author refers to is the knowledge humanity has gained about zoonoses. Later in the passage he describes a number of zoonoses that have had a serious effect on human and animal health. In lines 103–107 he says, "Threats . . . emergence." Thus it can be inferred that one of the ramifications (implications or effects) for wildlife managers will be that it will play an increasing role in monitoring human-animal interaction that can lead to zoonotic disease.

40. **(C)** The three arrows all point in two directions, indicating that zoonoses can move from humans to domestic animals and vice versa, from wildlife to domestic animals and vice versa, and from wildlife to humans and vice versa.

41. **(D)** We can infer this because at zoos, pet shops, and farms there is a great deal of interaction between animals and humans, which can lead to the transmission of zoonotic disease from humans to animals or vice versa.

42. **(D)** In context *sanctioned* means "officially approved." The author says that a "majority of mankind" has approved a law (justice).

43. **(A)** The author says a law has been approved "not only by a majority of this or that people, but by a majority of mankind" (lines 8–10).

44. **(C)** This statement means that peoples' rights cannot include any that are not just. Thus, people do not have a right to do something that is not just.

45. **(A)** The author asks, "If it be admitted that a man possessing absolute power may misuse that power by wronging his adversaries, why should not a majority be liable to the same reproach?" (lines 34–37). This rhetorical question makes the point that the majority can take actions, such as passing laws, that "wrong" people. Such laws would be unjust.

46. **(C)** The sentence in which the word *principles* is used begins a discussion of the composition of government. Thus, we can infer that the word means the elements that make up a government.

47. **(C)** In the previous paragraph (lines 45–65; "I . . . will") the author argues that it is not possible to create a government in such a way that one "principle of action" (line 55) dominates. It follows from this that some group will dominate the society.

48. **(C)** These lines provide the best evidence for the answer to the previous question.

49. **(B)** The author says "I think that liberty is endangered when this power [the dominant social power] finds no obstacle which can retard its course and give it time to moderate its own vehemence" (lines 68–71).

50. **(D)** Scholarly studies are not cited. All the others are used.

51. **(D)** The author believes that in order to preserve justice and liberty in a democracy, it is necessary for there to be institutions that can check the power of the majority. In the

final paragraph of the passage he argues that this is particularly true of the United States where "democratic institutions" are very strong. He says that the majority controls all of the institutions of society, such as the legislature and juries. He says that in some states "even" judges are elected by the majority. Thus, it can be inferred that he would probably support the appointment of judges to create an institution to protect the rights of the minority.

52. **(B)** As mentioned in the explanation to the previous question, the author believes that in America the majority controls all of the institutions of society. We can infer that he believes that unless there are institutions capable of checking the power of these majority-dominated institutions there would be a tyranny of the majority, in which the rights of minorities are infringed. Thus, "Tyranny by the Majority" would be an appropriate title for this passage.

Section 2: Writing and Language Test

1. **(B)** This is the only grammatically correct choice.
2. **(B)** *Suggests* is correct because this verb must agree in number with the simple subject, "variation." Note that the words "concentrations" and "parks" are the objects of prepositional phrases and so can be ignored when choosing the correct verb form for this question.
3. **(D)** This choice makes good sense in context; in context *integrity* means "being unimpaired."
4. **(C)** This makes good sense in context, in which a range of mercury contamination is being described. In this context, *mean* means "arithmetic mean" (average).
5. **(D)** This is the best choice because sentence 2 adds information directly relevant to that given in sentence 6 and makes a suggestion based on findings mentioned in both sentences. The word "additionally" in sentence 2 provides a clue to the answer to this question.
6. **(C)** In context, *toxic* means "caused by poison." This is the best choice because the topic of the passage is mercury contamination.
7. **(D)** This is the best choice because it creates two sentences, each giving information about a related but separate topic.
8. **(A)** The phrase "at which" refers to "the benchmark 950 ng/g ww." A benchmark is "a standard of reference against which things can be compared."
9. **(A)** This is the correct choice because it is correctly punctuated. "Of human and wildlife health" is a prepositional phrase in which the noun *health* is the object. The adjectives *human* and *wildlife* modify the noun *health.*
10. **(A)** This can be seen by comparing the increase or decrease of mercury concentrations at each location. This is shown in the bar graph.
11. **(C)** As in the previous question, the answer can be seen by comparing the increase or decrease in mercury concentration at each location.

12. **(D)** All of the choices are grammatical. However, the best answer is choice (D), which creates two clear and concise sentences.

13. **(B)** Choice (A) is grammatical but creates a sentence that is awkward and has an unclear meaning. Choice (D) is not grammatical. Choice (C) is grammatical but wordy. Choice (B) is clear and concise.

14. **(D)** This sentence is an effective topic sentence to introduce the paragraph it is in. It also helps link the first paragraph to the second paragraph.

15. **(C)** This is the best choice. It creates two clear and grammatical sentences. Choice (A) is incorrect because the information given after the colon does not relate directly to the information given before the colon. Choice (B) creates a run-on sentence. Choice (D) is acceptable but is not as good a choice as choice (C) because a semicolon is normally used to create a sentence containing two independent clauses containing closely related information. In this case two quite separate points are made, so a period is a better choice.

16. **(C)** This is the best choice in context. Choice (A) and choice (B) do not make sense. Choice (D) is acceptable but is wordy and awkward.

17. **(B)** The underlined phrase *managing wildlife* is one of four in a series of topics, so to maintain parallelism standard usage requires that all of the nouns be in the same form.

18. **(B)** This is the best choice because sentence 2 provides a good transition between the second paragraph, which is about fieldwork (outdoor work), and the third paragraph, which is about lab work (indoor work).

19. **(C)** This is the only choice that is grammatical and makes good sense. The author is stating another way ornithologists educate people. Choice (A) is grammatical but does not make sense because "although" signals a contrast but there is no contrast made in the sentence.

20. **(B)** This is the best choice because the author is stating some of the things that outreach activities *might* be. Choice (A) is grammatical, but the past tense verb *did* makes no sense in context because the author is describing ongoing activities or activities that have been done in the past, are being done in the present, and almost certainly will be done in the future rather than something done only in the past.

21. **(C)** This is the correct choice in context, which requires a word meaning a "field of knowledge." A Ph.D. in a relevant discipline is required for certain occupations related to ornithology.

22. **(B)** This choice is correct because the phrase "For statistical purposes" is an adverbial prepositional phrase that modifies the verb *included* and it is standard usage. Note that a comma is not required after such introductory phrases but is correct to use in such cases and often useful in making the meaning clear.

23. **(B)** This is the correct expression. Choice (A) and choice (C) are not standard idiomatic usage.

24. **(B)** This is the best choice because it means "formally renounced." None of the other choices is correct usage in context.

25. **(D)** This choice is correct because "laid" is the simple past tense, which is correct in this context. Note that "lain" is the past participle of a different verb, "lie."

26. **(C)** Choice (A) is grammatical but wordy because the phrase "nor did he ever" is unnecessary as the words "never again" earlier in the sentence apply to all three verbs—"dwelt," "owned," and "wore."

27. **(D)** This is the best choice because sentence 4 describes what Mahavira did to "purify his consciousness and discover the meaning of existence." To do this he "renounced" his wealthy life and fasted. It follows that he would never live in a house again, and so forth.

28. **(A)** This is the only grammatically correct choice. Note that the simple subjects of the prepositional phrase beginning with "of" and ending with "release" are "working," "effects," and "conditions," which means they are (correctly) parallel.

29. **(B)** Choice (B) is the only grammatically correct choice. The subject of the two verbs "combines" and "accumulates" in the clause beginning with "that combines" and ending with "matter" is the pronoun "that." The verbs must agree with the subject in number.

30. **(C)** This choice makes the best sense. The sentence immediately before the one in which the word "discipline" appears describes how action, especially violence, has consequences for the soul. It therefore makes sense that the next sentence would describe training based on inactivity and nonviolence to make a moral improvement.

31. **(B)** The given sentence is not grammatical. Choice (B) creates two grammatical sentences. Choice (D) is grammatically correct, but it is awkward and not standard usage.

32. **(B)** This is the only choice that is grammatical and makes sense.

33. **(C)** This is the correct choice in the context, which requires a verb meaning "regard with reverence and profound honor."

34. **(D)** This is the only choice that is grammatical.

35. **(B)** This is the only choice that is grammatical. It changes the verb "was" to the present participle of be, "being," creating a participial phrase modifying the noun "civilization."

36. **(D)** This is the correct answer because sentence 6 follows logically from sentence 1 and because sentence 2 gives an example of something mentioned in sentence 2.

37. **(C)** This sentence helps to relate what is discussed in the first paragraph to what is discussed in the second paragraph. The words "but whatever notion we have of civilization" refer back to what has been discussed in the first paragraph, and the rest of the sentence introduces the subject of the second paragraph.

38. **(C)** This is the best choice because it makes a compound sentence with two independent clauses linked by the coordinating conjunction "and." Note that a comma must be put before the word *and* because this choice creates a compound sentence. Choice (B) is acceptable but unnecessarily wordy in that there is no need to say "it is his opinion" because this is evident from the context.

39. **(C)** This is the standard phrase in this context. Choice (A) and choice (D) are non-standard and a bit wordy.

40. **(A)** This is the correct choice because what comes after the word *hence* is a consequence of what comes before the word *hence.*

41. **(D)** This is the only grammatically correct choice. The subjects of the verb *expressing* are "customs," "habits," and "standards."

42. **(C)** This is the only grammatically correct choice. In the phrase "or began" it is understood that the action is performed by "a member." "It" is incorrect because "it" cannot be used to refer to a person.

43. **(C)** This is the only choice that makes good sense and is grammatical. The adverb clause "when they began to treat each other civilly," together with the phrase "that is," is set off by dashes. The material set off by dashes amplifies what has just been said. Note that this use of dashes is often effective, but dashes should be used sparingly in formal writing.

44. **(B)** The construction *from* [something] *to* [something else] is required: *from* "the beginning of man's conquest ..." *to* "the modern complexities ... ."

Section 3: Math Test (No Calculator)

1. **(C)** Substitute 5 for n as provided in the original equation.

$$\frac{r-2}{6}=5$$

Next, multiply both sides of the equation by 6 to isolate $r-2$.

$$(6)\frac{r-2}{6}=5(6)$$
$$r-2=30$$

Add 2 to both sides of the equation.

$$r-2+2=30+2$$
$$r=32$$

2. **(A)** Simplify $(5 + 3i) + (-4 + 7i)$ by combining the real components of the expression first.

$$5+-4=1$$

Next, combine the imaginary components.

$$3i+7i=10i$$

Add the two components with the real number followed by the imaginary.

$$1+10i$$

3. **(C)** The number of shirts (s) and belts (b) cannot exceed 100 items, but they can be equal to that sum. We therefore add the two quantities and ensure that they could not exceed 100 items.

$$s+b\leq 100$$

Choices (A) and (B) can be eliminated at once. The question suggests that the number of items cannot exceed 100 items. That implies the number of items could be equal to 100 but not more. Therefore, the symbol "≤" is needed, but using "<" would be incorrect.

PRACTICE TEST 2

4. **(D)**

$$\frac{1}{x}+\frac{3}{x}=\frac{1}{7}$$

The model above shows the portion of the work completed in one hour because $\frac{1}{7}$ is 1 hour of the 7 needed to complete the job. Since one worker can work 3 times more quickly than the other, her time is represented by $\frac{3}{x}$. The slower worker would accomplish solely $\frac{1}{x}$ of the entire job in 1 hour.

5. **(A)** When adding or subtracting algebraic expressions, combine only like terms. Like terms are those that have the same variables raised to the same power.

$$(3x^3 - 13x + 4) - (3x^2 - 4x + 5) =$$
$$3x^3 - 3x^2 +(-13x + 4x) + (4 - 5) =$$
$$3x^3 - 3x^2 - 9x - 1$$

When adding and subtracting polynomials, we only combine like terms; we do not add exponents unless we are multiplying. Thus, choice (C) with an exponent of 5 should be immediately eliminated.

6. **(C)** Division by 0 is undefined. Set $6x^2 - 13x - 5$ equal to 0 and solve.

$$6x^2 - 13x - 5 = 0$$

Solve by factoring.

$$(3x + 1)(2x - 5) = 0$$

Set each of the parentheses equal to 0 and solve for the variable.

$$3x + 1 = 0 \text{ or } 2x - 5 = 0$$
$$3x = -1 \text{ or } 2x = 5$$
$$x = -\frac{1}{3} \quad x = \frac{5}{2}$$

$\frac{-5x^2y-4xy}{6x^2-13x-5}$ is undefined when $x=-\frac{1}{3}$ $x=\frac{5}{2}$

7. **(C)** Find the coordinates of the vertex of $3(x - 4)(x + 6)$ by multiplying.

$$y = 3(x - 4)(x + 6)$$
$$y = 3(x^2 + 2x - 24)$$

Begin to transform the equation from standard form to graphing form. First, move –24 to the right of the parentheses, remembering to first multiply it by 3.

$$y = 3(x^2 + 2x) - (24)(3)$$
$$y = 3(x^2 + 2x) - 72$$

Complete the square by squaring $\frac{b}{2}$. Remember to multiply that value by 3.

$$y = 3(x^2 + 2x + 1) - 72 - (3 \times -1)$$
$$y = 3(x^2 + 2x + 1) - 72 - 3$$
$$y = 3(x + 1)^2 - 75$$

The equation is now in graphing form. The vertex is (–1, –75).

8. **(B)** The diagonal of a square creates two isosceles right triangles. Use the Pythagorean theorem to find the length of a side of the square.

$$x^2 + x^2 = 12^2$$
$$2x^2 = 144$$
$$x^2 = 72$$

The area of the square photograph is 72 square inches because the formula for area requires us to multiply adjacent sides. However, we need to find the length of a side to find the frame's dimensions.

$$x^2 = 72$$
$$x = 6\sqrt{2}$$

Each side of the square photograph is $6\sqrt{2}$. Add 4 to $6\sqrt{2}$ because there is a 2 inch border on each side of the photograph. We now know that each side of the frame is $6\sqrt{2} + 4$. Multiply that value by itself to find the area surrounded by the frame.

$$(6\sqrt{2} + 4)^2 = 88 + 48\sqrt{2}$$

Find the area of the frame by subtracting the area of the square photograph from the area surrounded by the frame.

$$88 + 48\sqrt{2} - 72 = 16 + 48\sqrt{2}$$

9. **(B)** Parallel lines have the same slope but distinct y-intercepts. The equation $y = \frac{3}{2}x - \frac{7}{4}$ has slope $\frac{3}{2}$ and y-intercept $-\frac{7}{4}$. Transform each of the equations to slope-intercept form, $y = mx + b$, to compare slopes and y-intercepts. Choice (B) offers the following:

$$-6x + 4y = 11$$

Transform to slope-intercept form by isolating y:

$$-6x + 6x + 4y = 6x + 11$$
$$4y = 6x + 11$$

Divide both sides of the equation by 4.

$$\frac{4}{4}y = \frac{6}{4}x + \frac{11}{4}$$
$$y = \frac{3}{2}x + \frac{11}{4}$$
$$m = \frac{3}{2} \quad b = \frac{11}{4}$$

$y = \frac{3}{2}x + \frac{11}{4}$ and $y = \frac{3}{2}x - \frac{7}{4}$ have the same slope but different y-intercepts so the two lines are parallel.

10. **(C)**

$$n = 3.65 + .35x$$
$$m = 4.25 + .15x$$

Setting $m = n$ will provide the number of weeks that passed when the two plants were the same height.

$$3.65 + .35x = 4.25 + .15x$$

Solve for x.

$$3.65 + .35x = 4.25 + .15x$$
$$.2x = .6$$
$$x = 3$$

After 3 weeks passed, the two plants were identical heights. Replace x with 3 in either equation to find the height when they were the same.

$$3.65 + .35(3) = 4.7$$

The two plants were both 4.7 feet three weeks after September 15.

11. **(C)** Rationalize the denominator by multiplying the numerator and the denominator by $2 + i$.

$$\frac{3i}{2-i} \times \frac{2+i}{2+i} =$$

$$\frac{6i+3i^2}{4-i^2}$$

Substitute -1 for i^2 into the expression.

$$\frac{6i+3(-1)}{4-(-1)} = \frac{6i-3}{5}$$

$\frac{6i-3}{5}$ can be rewritten in the form of $a + bi$ as $-\frac{3}{5} + \frac{6i}{5}$. Therefore, $a = -\frac{3}{5}$.

12. **(C)** The parent graph of $y = x^3$ is an S-shaped curve. Its end behavior approaches $-\infty$ as x assumes smaller values and ∞ for larger values. Its y-intercept is 0 because when $x = 0$, $y = 0$. Adding a positive rational number shifts the parent graph vertically; its y-intercept will be greater than 0. Choice (C) illustrates such a graph.

13. **(C)** Replace $h(x)$ with 138 and x with 6 in order to find b.

$$138 = b(6)^2 + 30$$
$$138 = 36b + 30$$
$$108 = 36b$$
$$3 = b$$

Replace b with 3 to find $h(-4)$.

$$h(-4) = 3(-4)^2 + 30$$
$$h(-4) = 78$$

14. **(D)** Since 350 of the students are males, 250 are females (600 – 350 = 250). Given that 250 of the males are science majors, the remaining science majors, 150, must be female (400 – 250 = 150). Thus, if 150 of the 250 females are science majors, the remaining 100 must be liberal arts majors.

15. **(B)** Use the basic steps of algebra to isolate y.

STEP 1 Add $1.6x^2$ and 11.4 to both sides of the equation.

$$P = -1.6x^2 + 2.6xy - 11.4$$
$$P + 1.6x^2 + 11.4 = -1.6x^2 + 2.6xy - 11.4 + 1.6x^2 + 11.4$$
$$P + 1.6x^2 + 11.4 = 2.6xy$$

STEP 2 Divide both sides of the equation by $2.6x$

$$\frac{P + 1.6x^2 + 11.4}{2.6x} = \frac{2.6xy}{2.6x}$$
$$\frac{P + 1.6x^2 + 11.4}{2.6x} = y$$

16. **18** The slope of a line can be found by using the formula $\frac{rise}{run}$ or $\frac{y_2 - y_1}{x_2 - x_1}$. Substitute (9, 0) for x_2 and y_2 and $(x, 6)$ for x_1 and y_1. Set the value of that fraction to $\frac{2}{3}$, the slope of the line connecting these two points.

$$\frac{0-6}{9-x} = \frac{2}{3}$$
$$\frac{-6}{9-x} = \frac{2}{3}$$

Cross-multiply and solve for x.

$$2(9 - x) = (-3)(6)$$
$$18 - 2x = -18$$
$$-2x = -36$$
$$x = 18$$

17. **55** The dollar amount in April was \$850 – \$155 – \$195 – \$225 = \$275. The number of days for January can be found by solving the equation $155 = 75 + 10d$. Subtract 75 from each side to get $80 = 10d$. Then $d = 8$. In a similar manner, the number of days for each of February, March, and April can be determined by solving the equations $195 = 75 + 10d$, $225 = 75 + 10d$, and $275 = 75 + 10d$, respectively. We find that Jerry spent 12 days in February, 15 days in March, and 20 days in April. Thus, the total number of days spent at the club was $8 + 12 + 15 + 20 = 55$.

18. **85** The sum of two sides of a triangle is always larger than the length of the third side. Suppose that 11 is the measure of the longest side. Then $7 + x > 11$ and $x > 4$. The smallest integer that satisfies this inequality is 5.
Suppose the largest side is unknown, then $7 + 11 > x$ and $18 > x$. The largest value that satisfies this inequality is 17. Therefore the product of the smallest value, 5, and the largest value, 17, is $5 \times 17 = 85$.

19. $\frac{3}{5}$ **or .6** The scale factor of triangle *DEF* to triangle *ABC* is $\frac{1}{10}$, so multiply the sides of triangle *ABC* by $\frac{1}{10}$.

$$(100)\left(\frac{1}{10}\right) = 10 = DF$$

$$(80)\left(\frac{1}{10}\right) = 8 = EF$$

Use the Pythagorean theorem to calculate the length of *DE*.

$$a^2 + 8^2 = 10^2$$
$$a^2 = 36$$
$$a = 6$$

The cosine function is found by using the ratio $\cos x = \frac{\text{adjacent side}}{\text{hypotenuse}}$. The side adjacent to angle *D* is 6 and the hypotenuse is 10 so $\frac{\text{adjacent side}}{\text{hypotenuse}} = \frac{3}{5} = .6$.

20. **3** This question can be answered by using a system of equations. "The quantity she purchased of the heads of lettuce was 6 fewer than 5 times the number of cucumbers" can be translated as $h + 6 = 5c$. Each head of lettuce costs \$.70 and each cucumber costs \$.30, so the cost for the vegetables, in terms of *c* and *h*, is $.3c + .7h$. Given that the cost of the purchase was \$7.20, we get the second equation in the system of equations.

$$.3c + .7h = 7.2$$

Transform $h + 6 = 5c$ to $h = 5c - 6$, and replace that value for h in $.3c + .7h = 7.2$.

$$.3c + .7(5c - 6) = 7.2$$
$$.3c + 3.5c - 4.2 = 7.2$$
$$3.8c = 11.4$$
$$c = 3$$

Section 4: Math Test (Calculator)

1. **(C)** Use the ratio of books sold to income earned to create a proportion.

$$\frac{800}{1320} = \frac{12{,}000}{x}$$

Cross-multiply and solve for *x*.

$$(800)(x) = (1{,}320)(12{,}000)$$
$$800x = 15{,}840{,}000$$
$$x = \$19{,}800$$

The graphic novelist would earn \$19,800 on sales of 12,000 books.
Choices (A) and (B) can be eliminated immediately. Each is much too close to the initial \$1,320 earned when 800 books were sold. Clearly, selling 12,000 books should yield a significantly higher figure as offered in choices (C) and (D).

2. **(B)** Use the ratio of books sold: income earned once again.

$$\frac{800}{1320}=\frac{5000}{x}$$

Cross-multiply and solve for x.

$$(1320)(5000) = (800)(x)$$
$$6{,}600{,}000 = 800x$$
$$8250 = x$$

The income earned before overhead costs are subtracted is $8,250. Subtract 32% of that amount to find the novelist's net income.
$8250 – (8250)(.32) = $5,610. Note that choice (A) is incorrect because it represents the expenses, not the net income.

3. **(C)** A linear function that contains $f(4) = 6$ and $f(-2) = 14$ indicates that the points (4, 6) and (–2, 14) satisfy the function. Use these points to find the slope of the function.

$$m=\frac{y_2-y_1}{x_2-x_1}=\frac{14-6}{-2-4}=-\frac{4}{3}$$

Use the point-slope form of a line to create the linear function.

$$y-y_1=m(x-x_1)$$

Substitute either point for x and y.

$$y-6=-\frac{4}{3}(x-4)$$

Substitute 9 for x to find $f(9)$.

$$y-6=-\frac{4}{3}(9-4)$$
$$y-6=-\frac{20}{3}$$
$$y=-\frac{2}{3}$$

Therefore $f(9)=-\frac{2}{3}$

4. **(A)** Add the three terms and divide the sum by 3. Set this value equal to $x + 4$, the average.

$$\frac{2x-4+x+4+3x-6}{3}=x+4$$
$$\frac{6x-6}{3}=x+4$$
$$6x-6=3x+12$$
$$3x=18$$
$$x=6$$

Replace x with 6 in $-2x + 3$.

$$-2(6)+3=-9.$$

5. **(A)** If Shelley sold 10 recliners and 10 dinette sets, her commission would be 10(24) + 10(63) = 870. In other words, multiply each commission by the number of units sold of a particular item. If she sold r dinette sets and d recliners, her commission would be $63r + 24d$.

6. **(A)** Calculate the cost per bottle of a 24-pack and a 12-pack.

$$\$9.95 \div 24 \approx \$.41 \text{ per bottle}$$
$$\$5.95 \div 12 \approx \$.50 \text{ per bottle}$$

Minimize the cost by purchasing one 24-pack, one 12-pack, and three individual bottles.

$$\$9.95 + \$5.95 + (3 \times \$1.15) = \$19.35$$

Choice (D) can be eliminated at once. It is the cost of 39 bottles of water sold at the most expensive price, $1.15 per bottle.

7. **(D)** Consider the three conditions that each satisfy $n > 0$:
(a) Let $n = 2$, then $n^2 = 4$

$$n^2 > n$$

(b) Let $n = 1$, then $n^2 = 1$

$$n^2 = n$$

(c) let $n = \frac{1}{2}$, then $n^2 = \frac{1}{4}$

$$n^2 < n$$

Without more information about n, we cannot make a conclusion about n^2.

8. **(C)** Assess the vertex of $f(x) = x^2 + 6x - 4$ by transforming to graphing form.

$$f(x) = x^2 + 6x - 4$$
$$f(x) = x^2 + 6x + 9 - 4 - 9$$
$$f(x) = (x + 3)^2 - 13$$

The vertex of the parabola is (–3, –13). A shift to a vertex located at (5, –6) means the graph shifted 8 units to the right (m) and 7 units up (n). If $m = 8$ and $n = 7$, then

$$mn^{-1} = (8)\left(\frac{1}{7}\right) = \frac{8}{7}$$

9. **(B)** Form a proportion using the ratio $\frac{\text{defects}}{\text{total shipment}}$

$$\frac{13}{500} = \frac{273}{n}$$

Cross-multiply and solve for n.

$$13n = (273)(500)$$
$$13n = 136{,}500$$
$$n = 10{,}500$$

A shipment of 10,500 square yards of fabric would produce 273 square yards of defective fabric.

10. **(D)** The data roughly correspond to a line with a negative slope, so only choices (A) and (D) should be considered. Using the points (0, 5) and (2, 3) we can get a sense of the slope:

$$\frac{\text{rise}}{\text{run}} = \frac{5-3}{0-2} = -1$$

Choice (D) is more closely aligned with slope –1. Choices (B) and (C) can be eliminated at once. The data appear to descend to the right as the number of ants increase, thus indicating a negative slope. Choices (B) and (C) incorrectly show positive slopes.

11. **(C)** After the grower uses the pesticide, his ant population will be reduced by 60%. Find 60% of 5,000,000 and subtract that amount from 5,000,000.

$$5{,}000{,}000 - (.60)(5{,}000{,}000) = 2{,}000{,}000$$

The graph indicates the point (2, 3) is on the line of best fit. Thus, when the grower has 2,000,000 ants, he can expect a yield of 3,000 roses.

12. **(B)** The combined weights of Helium and Lithium are 4.0026 + 6.941 = 10.9436. The weight of Boron is 10.811. That value is the closest to the combined weights of Helium and Lithium among the answer choices.

13. **(C)** The atomic weight of Lithium is 6.941. Multiply that number by .30 and add it to the weight of Lithium.

$$6.941 + (.30)(6.941) = 9.023$$

Of the elements listed in the table, Beryllium, with a weight of 9.0122, is approximately 30% heavier than Lithium.

14. **(C)** Change the equation of the circle to graphing form by completing the square for x and y. The general form of a circle in graphing form is $(x-h)^2 + (y-k)^2 = r^2$, where (h, k) is the circle's center, and r is its radius.

$$x^2 + y^2 - 6y + 4x = 36$$
$$(x^2 + 4x + 4) + (y^2 - 6y + 9) = 49$$
$$(x+2)^2 + (y-3)^2 = 49$$

The radius squared, r^2, is 49 so r is 7. Replace the measure of the radius, r, in the circumference formula.

$$C = 2\pi r$$
$$C = (2)(\pi)(7) = 14\pi$$

Choice (A) can be eliminated as it represents the area, not the circumference, of the circle.

15. **(C)** If Sammie interviewed every 16-year-old in Florida, she would have no margin of error: she would have all of the data! Thus, the larger the sample size, the smaller the margin of error. Sammie ought to interview additional students to reduce the margin of error in the sample.

16. **(D)** Use any of the given zeroes to solve for b. In the zero (2, 0), $x = 2$ and $y = 0$. Substitute both in $g(x) = 2x^3 - 8x^2 - bx + 140$.

$$0 = 2(2)^3 - 8(2)^2 - b(2) + 140$$
$$0 = 124 - 2b$$
$$2b = 124$$
$$b = 62$$

17. **(A)** Imagine the following:

$$h = 4 \text{ hours}$$
$$m = 60 \text{ miles per hour}$$
$$g = 20 \text{ miles per gallon}$$

The number of gallons used would be:

$$[(4 \text{ hours})(60 \text{ miles per hour})]/20 \text{ miles per gallon} =$$
$$240 \text{ miles}/20 \text{ miles per gallon} = 12 \text{ gallons}$$

Thus, $x = \dfrac{hm}{g}$, which represents the number of gallons used.

18. **(A)** At one year, the market fund was worth \$600 and the CD was valued at \$1,600. Thus, choice (A) cannot be concluded because it states incorrectly that the market fund is worth more than the CD.

19. **(C)** Square both sides of the equation to remove the radical.

$$(\sqrt{x-7})^2 = (x-7)^2$$
$$x - 7 = x^2 - 14x + 49$$
$$x = x^2 - 14x + 56$$
$$x^2 - 15x + 56 = 0$$
$$(x-7)(x-8) = 0$$

This last step reflects answer choice (C).

20. **(A)** Find the probability that a single, six-sided die will land on a prime number:

$$p\,(\text{prime number}) = \frac{2,3,5}{1,2,3,4,5,6} = \frac{1}{2}$$

Remember, 1 is not a prime number.
Find the probability that the spinner will land on yellow or blue.

$$\frac{\text{yellow,blue}}{\text{red,green,blue,yellow}} = \frac{1}{2}$$

The two events, landing on a prime number and spinning yellow or blue, are independent so multiply the probabilities.

$$\frac{1}{2} \times \frac{1}{2} = \frac{1}{4}$$

21. **(A)** An ounce of gold covers 100 square yards of surface but the question requires the answer to be in square feet.

$$1 \text{ yard} = 3 \text{ feet}$$

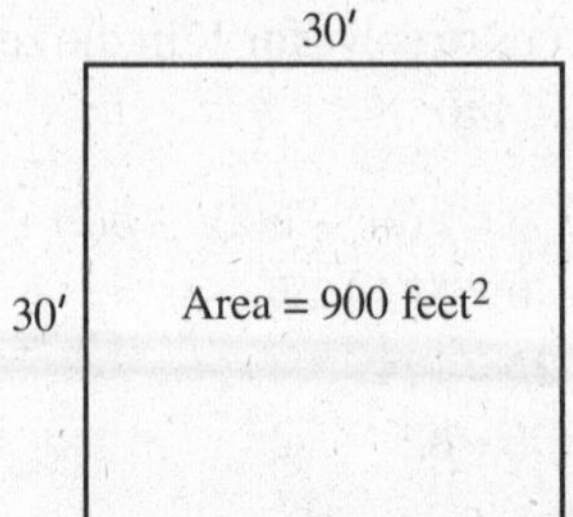

30′

30′ Area = 900 feet^2

100 square yards is equivalent to 900 square feet, so one ounce of gold covers 900 square feet. Multiply 900 by 2.5 to find the area covered by 2.5 ounces of gold.

$$2.5 \times 900 = 2{,}250 \text{ square feet.}$$

22. **(B)** Based on the fee schedule outlined in the graph, the business owner incurs the following delivery fees:

2.68 pounds cost \$7.50
3.11 pounds cost \$10.00
5.28 pounds cost \$15.00
4.0 pounds cost \$10.00

Adding the different costs, the sum of the costs of the delivery is \$42.50

23. **(C)** The learning therapist has demonstrated that her program increases students' reading levels. 1.09 in the equation ensures growth. For example, if a student is in the second grade and uses the program, we get the following:

$$x = 2$$
$$y = 1.09(2) + .17$$
$$y = 2.35$$

This means a student in second grade would read at a level more than 3 months in advance (assuming a 10-month school year) of students who are not in the reading program.

24. **(B)** The per-capita income of Singapore is \$60,500. Multiply that value by .048 and add it to \$60,500.

$$\$60{,}500 + (.048)(\$60{,}500) = \$63{,}404$$

At \$63,400, Monaco's per capita income is closest to this value.

25. **(C)** The GDP is found by multiplying the total value of goods and services that a country produces. Use the formula GDP = (per capita income)(population).
Let x = the population size

$$298{,}000{,}000{,}000 = 60{,}500\ (x)$$
$$x = 4{,}925{,}619.$$

Choice (C), 4,900,000 is the closest to this value.

26. **(A)** Use the probability formula:

$$P(x) = \frac{\text{desired outcomes}}{\text{all outcomes}}$$

There are 35 tenth graders and 38 boys. However, some of the tenth graders are boys and should not be counted twice. Thus:

P(10th grader or boy) = [(number of 10th graders) + (number of boys) – (number of 10th grade boys)] ÷ (total number of students)

P(10th grader or boy) = (35 + 38 – 18) ÷ (73)

P(10th grader or boy) = 55 ÷ 73 = .753

27. **(B)** Find the radius of the sphere by using the formula $V = \frac{4}{3}\pi r^3$.

$$374 = \frac{4}{3}(3.14)r^3$$
$$374 = 4.19r^3$$
$$89.26 = r^3$$
$$4.47 = r$$

The circumference of a circle is found by using the formula $C = 2\pi r$.

$$C = (2)(4.47)(3.14) = 28.07$$

Once you have calculated the length of the radius of the sphere, choice (A) can be eliminated. 4.47 is the radius of the circle, not its circumference.

28. **(B)**

$$A = R_0\left(\frac{1}{2}\right)^x$$

Input 2.3 for the number of years, x, and 125 for R_0 the initial amount of the compound.

$$A = 125\left(\frac{1}{2}\right)^{2.3}$$
$$A = 25.4$$

After 2.3 years, 125 grams of the compound will be reduced to 25.4 grams.

29. **(B)** Find the probability of selecting a student who successfully shot four foul shots by using the formula $\frac{\text{favored outcomes}}{\text{all outcomes}}$.

There are a total of 15 students who successfully shot two or more foul shots. Of those 15 students, 3 made exactly 4 baskets. Therefore $\frac{3}{15}$, or $\frac{1}{5}$, of the students in the sample made exactly 4 baskets.

30. **(A)** Subtract the two equations and combine like terms.

$$\begin{array}{r} 4a + n = 2a - 3 \\ -\ 4b + m = 2b - 3 \\ \hline 4a - 4b + n - m = 2a - 2b \\ 2a - 2b + n - m = 0 \end{array}$$

Substitute $m + 1$ for n.

$$2a - 2b + m + 1 - m = 0$$
$$2a - 2b + 1 = 0$$
$$2a - 2b = -1$$
$$a - b = -\frac{1}{2}$$
$$a = b - \frac{1}{2}$$

31. **24** The least number of hamburgers and rolls to buy is the least common multiple (LCM) of 6 and 8. Multiply 6 and 8 by 1, 2, 3, and so on to find the least common multiple.

6: 6, 12, 18, **24**, 30
8: 8, 16, **24**, 32

24 is the LCM of 6 and 8

In order to buy hamburger patties and rolls without any left over, 24 of each should be purchased.

32. **40** Add the scores of all twelve of the students.

$$(2 \times 20) + (1 \times 40) + (4 \times 60) + (4 \times 80) + (1 \times 100) = 740$$

In order for 13 students to average 60%, the class must amass 780 points because $13 \times 60 = 780$.
Since the first 12 students accumulated 740 points, then the thirteenth student must score a 40% on his/her test because $780 - 740 = 40$.

33. **12** Use the model for factoring the difference of cubes:

$$a^3 - b^3 = (a - b)(a^2 + ab + b^2).$$

$(x - 3)(x^2 + 3x + 9)$ is the factored form of $x^3 - 27$.
Substituting $x^3 - 27$ for $(x - 3)(x^2 + 3x + 9)$ gets $x^3 - 15 = x^3 - 27 + m$

$$12 = m$$

34. $\mathbf{\frac{3}{8}}$ **or .375** The area of a circle is surrounded by an angle of measure 2π radians. Find the ratio of the central angle, $\frac{3\pi}{4}$, to the entire circle.

$$\frac{\frac{3\pi}{4}}{\frac{2\pi}{1}} = \frac{3\pi}{4} \times \frac{1}{2\pi} = \frac{3}{8} \text{ or } .375$$

35. $\mathbf{\frac{21}{8}}$ **or 2.62 or 2.63** Since the ratio of chocolates to mints is 3 to 5, the ratio of chocolates to the mix is $\frac{3}{3+5} = \frac{3}{8}$. Remember, there are 8 parts to the mix: 3 parts chocolate and 5 parts mints. Multiply 7 pounds by $\frac{3}{8}$ to find the number of pounds of chocolates in a 7-pound mix.

$$\frac{3}{8} \times 7 = \frac{21}{8} \text{ or } 2.62 \text{ or } 2.63$$

PRACTICE TEST 2

36. **6**

$$\frac{1}{3}c=6$$
$$b-\frac{2}{3}c=-6$$

Solve for c in the first equation.

$$\frac{1}{3}c=6$$
$$(3)\left(\frac{1}{3}c=6\right)(3)$$
$$c=18$$

Substitute 18 for c in the second equation and solve for b.

$$b-\frac{2}{3}c=-6$$
$$b-\left(\frac{2}{3}\right)(18)=-6$$
$$b-12=-6$$
$$b=6$$

37. **250** Normally the merchant sells 40 pairs of slacks at \$50 a pair, so find the revenue from selling 40 pairs.

$$\$50 \times 40 = \$2{,}000$$

Next determine the price of the slacks with the 10% applied.

$$\$50 - (.10)(50) = \$45$$

Since 50 pairs of slacks were sold at the new discounted price of \$45, multiply these together to get the total earnings for that month.

$$50 \times \$45 = \$2{,}250$$

The last step is to subtract this value from the earnings in a normal month.

$$\$2{,}250 - \$2{,}000 = \$250$$

38. **44** The first step is to determine how much additional money is needed from the sale of Model 2 slacks. Model 1 slacks give additional capital of \$250. Subtracting \$250 from \$750, we arrive at \$500 as the amount needed. Next find out how much money is normally received from the Model 2 slacks.

$$\$65 \times 25 \text{ pairs of slacks} = \$1{,}625$$

\$1,625 + \$500 = \$2,125 is the amount of money needed from the sale of Model 2 slacks. Find the price of Model 2 slacks after the discount of 25%.

$$\$65 \times 75\% = \$48.75$$

Let n = number of slacks needed to sell

$$\$48.75n = \$2{,}125$$
$$n = 43.58$$

Round up to 44 pairs of slacks. 44 pairs of Model 2 slacks must be sold so the merchant can earn a total of \$750 extra from the sale of Model 1 and Model 2 slacks.

Section 5: Essay (Optional)

SUGGESTED ESSAY TEST 2

Following is an essay written in response to the prompt. It is unlikely that you would be able to write such a full response in the time allowed, so don't worry if your essay is significantly shorter. Use the suggested essay to see how the task might be approached. For practice, you may wish to rewrite your own essay incorporating some of the points discussed in it.

John Davy carefully constructs this passage to convince the reader of Professor Weizenbaum's view that computers will cause humans more harm than benefit. To do this he uses a number of rhetorical techniques, which will be discussed below. First, though, let us look at the central argument and its logic. Note that Professor Weizenbaum—and also, presumably, John Davy—is not arguing that computers are completely bad for humans. Instead, he points to what he regards as some of the dangers they pose, focusing on what he calls the "delusional thinking" (paragraph two) they create.

According to the introductory material this passage was an article in a newspaper. Normally, as it seems in this case, a mass circulation periodical does not publish articles that rigorously examine all sides of an issue. Rather, most articles seek to raise important issues in an interesting and provocative way, as does this one. Thus, it is not a weakness of the passage that it does not examine counter-arguments, of which there are many—for example, how computers have allowed us to predict the weather better and facilitated scientific research.

Let us now turn to the rhetorical techniques Davy employs. Central to his construction of the passage is the use of the journalistic technique of quoting an authority he has interviewed. Davy uses direct quotations and paraphrases to clearly and succinctly present Professor Weizenbaum's views. In the first paragraph he uses this technique to introduce the focus of the passage—that computers are "more malign than benign"—and follows this with a provocative direct quotation: "I'm coming close to believing that the computer is inherently anti-human—an invention of the devil." We should also note here the effective use of the technique of sensationalism—"an invention of the devil." This statement gets our attention because it is not the sort of statement normally made in discussions of science and technology.

PRACTICE TEST 2

We shall return to the use of quotations and paraphrases later. Let us next examine how Davy constructs the first paragraph. He builds this paragraph so that Professor Weizenbaum can be viewed as a respected authority conducting a lonely battle against powerful institutions in society: "[He works at] one of the world's greatest powerhouses of the new technology . . . at the Massachusetts Institute of Technology"; "[He is] surrounded by some of the world's most advanced computer systems [and looks] rather like Albert Einstein"; "he is regarded by many around him as a heretical and dangerous dissident." This portrayal of Professor Weizenbaum makes Davy's subsequent quotes and paraphrases of Professor Weizenbaum—which form the central structure of the article—very persuasive because the reader continually has this portrayal in mind.

Paragraph two is introduced by a paraphrase of Professor Weizenbaum about "delusional thinking" (which we mentioned earlier)—an arresting and challenging description—caused by computers. The rest of the passage neatly summarizes Professor Weizenbaum's view that computers, far from causing fundamental change, as "deluded" people think, have actually fostered the status quo.

In the third paragraph Davy uses the example of the Vietnam War to illustrate the "delusion" that computers can make decisions. This is effective because most people know something about the extensive bombing carried out by American forces in Vietnam, often against civilians. Thus, the depiction of computers choosing "which villages ... to be bombed" powerfully highlights the catastrophic consequences of this delusion.

In paragraph four Davy turns to a "subtle and sinister influence on our psyche"—computer games. The quotation from Professor Weizenbaum, "The computer programmer is the creator of universes for which he alone is the lawgiver," powerfully introduces a moral consideration. The description of computer games "invading our homes" dramatizes how ubiquitous and damaging such games have become and evokes an image of people wasting hour after hour on such games. The use of the word "invading," which has many negative connotations, stresses how dangerous the threat is. Davy emphasizes the powerful influence of these games on us by saying they "allow us to wage wars, destroy cities, and do violence to opponents in toy worlds safely separated from real life." He does not mean that we really wage war. Rather, what he suggests is that such simulations might gradually blind us—in our "toy worlds safely separated from real life"—to the reality of war and other forms of violence. Davy closes the paragraph with a rhetorical question—"What is the addictive power of such games?"—which stresses the idea that we cannot tell what the ultimate effect of computer games will be on humanity.

Space does not permit a full analysis of paragraphs five, six, and seven, but a few specific strategies should be mentioned. "Technological euphoria" (paragraph six) is an evocative phrase neatly describing the widespread love (worship?) of computers. Also in paragraph six is the effective citing of evidence—"brain tumor location is 97th"—to support a point. Notable in paragraph seven is the use of an analogy between beginning language learners and beginning computer programmers to illustrate the idea of instrumental reasoning.

Many writers would be content to use the final paragraph to recapitulate the argument, reminding readers of the central point. Davy, however, does not summarize what he has said earlier. What he does do is remind the reader of the central point—the dangers to humanity represented by computers. He does this through the use of an anecdote about two girls, one embodying the notion that computers are "smarter than [us]" and the other the view that this belief will destroy humanity—"if you think that you're dead." This down-to-earth anecdote about ordinary people in everyday life helps bring home the reality of the influence of computers. Two rhetorical questions close the passage. Especially effective is the short one at the very end: "Do we. . .?" This challenges the reader to confront the issues raised and, like Professor Weizenbaum, take a stand on them.

Refer to the SAT Essay Rubric on page 23 to analyze and score your essay response. For further guidance on this essay and additional practice and evaluation by teacher and author Philip Geer, contact *info@mentaurs.com*.

ANSWER SHEET
Practice Test 3

Section 1: Reading

1. Ⓐ Ⓑ Ⓒ Ⓓ
2. Ⓐ Ⓑ Ⓒ Ⓓ
3. Ⓐ Ⓑ Ⓒ Ⓓ
4. Ⓐ Ⓑ Ⓒ Ⓓ
5. Ⓐ Ⓑ Ⓒ Ⓓ
6. Ⓐ Ⓑ Ⓒ Ⓓ
7. Ⓐ Ⓑ Ⓒ Ⓓ
8. Ⓐ Ⓑ Ⓒ Ⓓ
9. Ⓐ Ⓑ Ⓒ Ⓓ
10. Ⓐ Ⓑ Ⓒ Ⓓ
11. Ⓐ Ⓑ Ⓒ Ⓓ
12. Ⓐ Ⓑ Ⓒ Ⓓ
13. Ⓐ Ⓑ Ⓒ Ⓓ
14. Ⓐ Ⓑ Ⓒ Ⓓ
15. Ⓐ Ⓑ Ⓒ Ⓓ
16. Ⓐ Ⓑ Ⓒ Ⓓ
17. Ⓐ Ⓑ Ⓒ Ⓓ
18. Ⓐ Ⓑ Ⓒ Ⓓ
19. Ⓐ Ⓑ Ⓒ Ⓓ
20. Ⓐ Ⓑ Ⓒ Ⓓ
21. Ⓐ Ⓑ Ⓒ Ⓓ
22. Ⓐ Ⓑ Ⓒ Ⓓ
23. Ⓐ Ⓑ Ⓒ Ⓓ
24. Ⓐ Ⓑ Ⓒ Ⓓ
25. Ⓐ Ⓑ Ⓒ Ⓓ
26. Ⓐ Ⓑ Ⓒ Ⓓ
27. Ⓐ Ⓑ Ⓒ Ⓓ
28. Ⓐ Ⓑ Ⓒ Ⓓ
29. Ⓐ Ⓑ Ⓒ Ⓓ
30. Ⓐ Ⓑ Ⓒ Ⓓ
31. Ⓐ Ⓑ Ⓒ Ⓓ
32. Ⓐ Ⓑ Ⓒ Ⓓ
33. Ⓐ Ⓑ Ⓒ Ⓓ
34. Ⓐ Ⓑ Ⓒ Ⓓ
35. Ⓐ Ⓑ Ⓒ Ⓓ
36. Ⓐ Ⓑ Ⓒ Ⓓ
37. Ⓐ Ⓑ Ⓒ Ⓓ
38. Ⓐ Ⓑ Ⓒ Ⓓ
39. Ⓐ Ⓑ Ⓒ Ⓓ
40. Ⓐ Ⓑ Ⓒ Ⓓ
41. Ⓐ Ⓑ Ⓒ Ⓓ
42. Ⓐ Ⓑ Ⓒ Ⓓ
43. Ⓐ Ⓑ Ⓒ Ⓓ
44. Ⓐ Ⓑ Ⓒ Ⓓ
45. Ⓐ Ⓑ Ⓒ Ⓓ
46. Ⓐ Ⓑ Ⓒ Ⓓ
47. Ⓐ Ⓑ Ⓒ Ⓓ
48. Ⓐ Ⓑ Ⓒ Ⓓ
49. Ⓐ Ⓑ Ⓒ Ⓓ
50. Ⓐ Ⓑ Ⓒ Ⓓ
51. Ⓐ Ⓑ Ⓒ Ⓓ
52. Ⓐ Ⓑ Ⓒ Ⓓ

Section 2: Writing and Language

1. Ⓐ Ⓑ Ⓒ Ⓓ
2. Ⓐ Ⓑ Ⓒ Ⓓ
3. Ⓐ Ⓑ Ⓒ Ⓓ
4. Ⓐ Ⓑ Ⓒ Ⓓ
5. Ⓐ Ⓑ Ⓒ Ⓓ
6. Ⓐ Ⓑ Ⓒ Ⓓ
7. Ⓐ Ⓑ Ⓒ Ⓓ
8. Ⓐ Ⓑ Ⓒ Ⓓ
9. Ⓐ Ⓑ Ⓒ Ⓓ
10. Ⓐ Ⓑ Ⓒ Ⓓ
11. Ⓐ Ⓑ Ⓒ Ⓓ
12. Ⓐ Ⓑ Ⓒ Ⓓ
13. Ⓐ Ⓑ Ⓒ Ⓓ
14. Ⓐ Ⓑ Ⓒ Ⓓ
15. Ⓐ Ⓑ Ⓒ Ⓓ
16. Ⓐ Ⓑ Ⓒ Ⓓ
17. Ⓐ Ⓑ Ⓒ Ⓓ
18. Ⓐ Ⓑ Ⓒ Ⓓ
19. Ⓐ Ⓑ Ⓒ Ⓓ
20. Ⓐ Ⓑ Ⓒ Ⓓ
21. Ⓐ Ⓑ Ⓒ Ⓓ
22. Ⓐ Ⓑ Ⓒ Ⓓ
23. Ⓐ Ⓑ Ⓒ Ⓓ
24. Ⓐ Ⓑ Ⓒ Ⓓ
25. Ⓐ Ⓑ Ⓒ Ⓓ
26. Ⓐ Ⓑ Ⓒ Ⓓ
27. Ⓐ Ⓑ Ⓒ Ⓓ
28. Ⓐ Ⓑ Ⓒ Ⓓ
29. Ⓐ Ⓑ Ⓒ Ⓓ
30. Ⓐ Ⓑ Ⓒ Ⓓ
31. Ⓐ Ⓑ Ⓒ Ⓓ
32. Ⓐ Ⓑ Ⓒ Ⓓ
33. Ⓐ Ⓑ Ⓒ Ⓓ
34. Ⓐ Ⓑ Ⓒ Ⓓ
35. Ⓐ Ⓑ Ⓒ Ⓓ
36. Ⓐ Ⓑ Ⓒ Ⓓ
37. Ⓐ Ⓑ Ⓒ Ⓓ
38. Ⓐ Ⓑ Ⓒ Ⓓ
39. Ⓐ Ⓑ Ⓒ Ⓓ
40. Ⓐ Ⓑ Ⓒ Ⓓ
41. Ⓐ Ⓑ Ⓒ Ⓓ
42. Ⓐ Ⓑ Ⓒ Ⓓ
43. Ⓐ Ⓑ Ⓒ Ⓓ
44. Ⓐ Ⓑ Ⓒ Ⓓ

ANSWER SHEET
Practice Test 3

Section 3: Math (No Calculator)

1. Ⓐ Ⓑ Ⓒ Ⓓ
2. Ⓐ Ⓑ Ⓒ Ⓓ
3. Ⓐ Ⓑ Ⓒ Ⓓ
4. Ⓐ Ⓑ Ⓒ Ⓓ
5. Ⓐ Ⓑ Ⓒ Ⓓ
6. Ⓐ Ⓑ Ⓒ Ⓓ
7. Ⓐ Ⓑ Ⓒ Ⓓ
8. Ⓐ Ⓑ Ⓒ Ⓓ
9. Ⓐ Ⓑ Ⓒ Ⓓ
10. Ⓐ Ⓑ Ⓒ Ⓓ
11. Ⓐ Ⓑ Ⓒ Ⓓ
12. Ⓐ Ⓑ Ⓒ Ⓓ
13. Ⓐ Ⓑ Ⓒ Ⓓ
14. Ⓐ Ⓑ Ⓒ Ⓓ
15. Ⓐ Ⓑ Ⓒ Ⓓ

16.

17.

18.

19.

20.

ANSWER SHEET

Practice Test 3

Section 4: Math (Calculator)

1. Ⓐ Ⓑ Ⓒ Ⓓ
2. Ⓐ Ⓑ Ⓒ Ⓓ
3. Ⓐ Ⓑ Ⓒ Ⓓ
4. Ⓐ Ⓑ Ⓒ Ⓓ
5. Ⓐ Ⓑ Ⓒ Ⓓ
6. Ⓐ Ⓑ Ⓒ Ⓓ
7. Ⓐ Ⓑ Ⓒ Ⓓ
8. Ⓐ Ⓑ Ⓒ Ⓓ
9. Ⓐ Ⓑ Ⓒ Ⓓ
10. Ⓐ Ⓑ Ⓒ Ⓓ
11. Ⓐ Ⓑ Ⓒ Ⓓ
12. Ⓐ Ⓑ Ⓒ Ⓓ
13. Ⓐ Ⓑ Ⓒ Ⓓ
14. Ⓐ Ⓑ Ⓒ Ⓓ
15. Ⓐ Ⓑ Ⓒ Ⓓ
16. Ⓐ Ⓑ Ⓒ Ⓓ
17. Ⓐ Ⓑ Ⓒ Ⓓ
18. Ⓐ Ⓑ Ⓒ Ⓓ
19. Ⓐ Ⓑ Ⓒ Ⓓ
20. Ⓐ Ⓑ Ⓒ Ⓓ
21. Ⓐ Ⓑ Ⓒ Ⓓ
22. Ⓐ Ⓑ Ⓒ Ⓓ
23. Ⓐ Ⓑ Ⓒ Ⓓ
24. Ⓐ Ⓑ Ⓒ Ⓓ
25. Ⓐ Ⓑ Ⓒ Ⓓ
26. Ⓐ Ⓑ Ⓒ Ⓓ
27. Ⓐ Ⓑ Ⓒ Ⓓ
28. Ⓐ Ⓑ Ⓒ Ⓓ
29. Ⓐ Ⓑ Ⓒ Ⓓ
30. Ⓐ Ⓑ Ⓒ Ⓓ

31.

32.

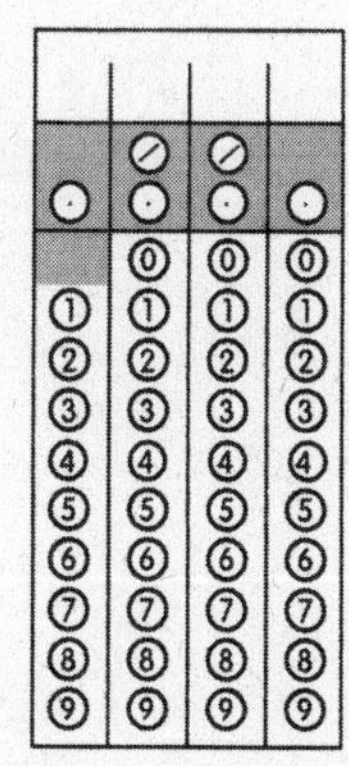

33.

34.

35.

36.

37.

38.

ANSWER SHEET
Practice Test 3

Essay

PLANNING PAGE

START YOUR ESSAY HERE

  1

READING TEST

65 MINUTES, 52 QUESTIONS

Turn to Section 1 of your answer sheet to answer the questions in this section.

Directions: Following each of the passages (or pairs of passages) below are questions about the passage (or passages). Read each passage carefully. Then, select the best answer for each question based on what is stated in the passage (or passages) and in any graphics that may accompany the passage.

Questions 1–10 are based on the following passage.

This passage is from Sir Arthur Conan Doyle, *The Great Boer War*, published in 1900.

Take a community of Dutchmen of the type of those who defended themselves for fifty years against all the power of Spain at a time when Spain was the greatest power in the world. Intermix with them a strain of those inflexible French Huguenots who gave up home and fortune and left their country for ever at the time of the revocation of the Edict of Nantes. The product must obviously be one of the most rugged, virile, unconquerable races ever seen upon earth. Take this formidable people and train them for seven generations in constant warfare against savage men and ferocious beasts, in circumstances under which no weakling could survive, place them so that they acquire exceptional skill with weapons and in horsemanship, give them a country which is eminently suited to the tactics of the huntsman, the marksman, and the rider. Then, finally, put a finer temper upon their military qualities by a dour fatalistic Old Testament religion and an ardent and consuming patriotism. Combine all these qualities and all these impulses in one individual, and you have the modern Boer—the most formidable antagonist who ever crossed the path of Imperial Britain. Our military history has largely consisted in our conflicts with France, but Napoleon and all his veterans have never treated us so roughly as these hard-bitten farmers with their ancient theology and their inconveniently modern rifles.

Look at the map of South Africa, and there, in the very center of the British possessions, like the stone in a peach, lies the great stretch of the two republics, a mighty domain for so small a people. How came they there? Who are these Teutonic folk who have burrowed so deeply into Africa? No one can know or appreciate the Boer who does not know his past, for he is what his past has made him.

It was in 1652 that the Dutch made their first lodgment at the Cape of Good Hope. The Portuguese had been there before them, but, repelled by the evil weather, and lured forwards by rumors of gold, they had passed the true seat of empire and had voyaged further to settle along the eastern coast. Some gold there was, but not much, and the Portuguese settlements have never been sources of wealth to the mother country. The coast upon which they settled reeked with malaria. A hundred miles of poisonous marsh separated it from the healthy inland plateau. For centuries these pioneers of South African colonization strove to obtain some further

GO ON TO THE NEXT PAGE

footing, but save along the courses of the rivers they made little progress. Fierce natives and an enervating climate barred their way.

But it was different with the Dutch. That very rudeness of climate which had so impressed the Portuguese adventurer was the source of their success. Cold and poverty and storm are the nurses of the qualities which make for empire. It is the men from the bleak and barren lands who master the children of the light and the heat. And so the Dutchmen at the Cape prospered and grew stronger in that robust climate. They did not penetrate far inland, for they were few in number and all they wanted was to be found close at hand. But they built themselves houses, and they supplied the Dutch East India Company with food and water and pushed their settlements up the long slopes which lead to the great central plateau.

For a hundred more years the history of the colony was a record of the gradual spreading of the Afrikaners over the huge expanse of veld which lay to the north of them. Cattle raising became an industry, but in a country where six acres can hardly support a sheep, large farms are necessary for even small herds. The diseases which follow the white man had in Africa, been fatal to the natives, and an epidemic of smallpox cleared the country for the newcomers. Further and further north they pushed. Already the settlers were showing that independence of control and that detachment from Europe which has been their most prominent characteristic. Even the sway of the Dutch Company had caused them to revolt. The local rising, however, was hardly noticed in the universal cataclysm which followed the French Revolution. After twenty years, during which the world was shaken by the titanic struggle between England and France the Cape Colony was added in 1814 to the British Empire.

1. Which of the following, according to the author, did *not* go into the making of "the modern Boer" (line 26)?

   (A) Dutch ancestry
   (B) seven generations of constant warfare
   (C) a country well-suited to the tactics the Boer were good at
   (D) a religion that valued pleasure above all else

2. What does the author mean by "treated us so roughly" (line 31)?

   (A) was such a difficult foe to defeat on the battlefield
   (B) denied us vital exports of farm products
   (C) insulted our national honor
   (D) slaughtered so many of our helpless women and children

3. What does the writer mean when he describes the Boers' rifles as "inconveniently modern" (lines 33–34)?

   (A) The Boers' rifles were up-to-date but poorly designed.
   (B) The Boers' rifles were very effective.
   (C) The Boers' rifles were effective but inconveniently stored so that there was difficulty in getting them to the troops before battle.
   (D) The Boers' rifles were old-fashioned.

GO ON TO THE NEXT PAGE

4. The word *nurses* as it is used in line 66 most nearly means
   - (A) things that foster certain characteristics in people
   - (B) persons trained to look after the sick and injured
   - (C) persons who are skilled in conserving precious resources
   - (D) foods that are nutritious in a cold, inhospitable climate

5. What, according to the author, was the main reason that the Dutch, rather than the Portuguese, succeeded in establishing a successful colony in Africa?
   - (A) The Dutch had more financial support from their mother country.
   - (B) The Dutch were more ruthless than the Portuguese.
   - (C) The Dutch were stronger than the Portuguese because they were from a harsher climate.
   - (D) The religion of the Dutch placed more emphasis on colonization of other lands than did that of the Portuguese.

6. Which of the following words best describes the attitude of the writer toward the Boers?
   - (A) skeptical
   - (B) admiring
   - (C) hostile
   - (D) neutral

7. The word *temper* as it is used in line 21 most nearly means
   - (A) irritability
   - (B) hardness
   - (C) resilience
   - (D) disposition

8. The word *consuming* as it is used in line 24 most nearly means
   - (A) reckless
   - (B) self-destructive
   - (C) deeply felt
   - (D) wasteful

9. Which of the following would the author be *least* likely to say is a characteristic of the modern Boer?
   - (A) readiness to compromise
   - (B) independent spirit
   - (C) determination
   - (D) patriotism

10. The author does which of the following?
    - (A) questions the premises of some of his central assertions
    - (B) recounts historical events
    - (C) cites authorities to support some of his assertions
    - (D) contrasts his view of the Boer with that of other writers

GO ON TO THE NEXT PAGE

Questions 11–20 are based on the following passage.

This passage is from Simon Singh, *Fermat's Enigma*, © 1997 by Simon Singh.

The periodical cicadas, most notably *Magicicada septendecim*, have the longest life cycle of any insect. Their unique life cycle begins underground, where the nymphs patiently suck the juice from the roots of trees. Then, after 17 years of waiting, the adult cicadas emerge from the ground, swarm in vast numbers, and temporarily swamp the landscape. Within a few weeks they mate, lay their eggs, and die.

The question that puzzled biologists was, *Why is the cicada's life cycle so long*? And is there any significance to the life cycle being a prime number of years? Another species, *Magicicada tredecim*, swarms every 13 years, implying that life cycles lasting a prime number of years offer some evolutionary advantage.

One theory suggests that the cicada has a parasite that also goes through a lengthy life cycle and that the cicada is trying to avoid. If the parasite has a life cycle of, say, 2 years then the cicada wants to avoid a life cycle that is divisible by 2, otherwise the parasite and the cicada will regularly coincide. Similarly, if the parasite has a life cycle of 3 years then the cicada wants to avoid a life cycle that is divisible by 3, otherwise the parasite and the cicada will once again regularly coincide. Ultimately, to avoid meeting its parasite the cicadas' best strategy is to have a long life cycle lasting a prime number of years. Because nothing will divide into 17, *Magicicada septendecim* will rarely meet its parasite. If the parasite has a 2-year life cycle they will meet only every 34 years, and if it has a longer life cycle, say 16 years, then they will meet only every 272 (16 × 17) years.

In order to fight back, the parasite has only two life cycles that will increase the frequency of coincidences—the annual cycle and the same 17-year cycle as the cicada. However, the parasite is unlikely to survive reappearing 17 years in a row, because for the first 16 appearances there will be no cicadas for it to parasitize. On the other hand, in order to reach the 17-year life cycle, the generations of parasites would first have to evolve through the 16-year life cycle. This would mean at some stage of evolution the parasite and cicada would not coincide for 272 years! In either case the cicada's long prime life cycle protects it.

This might explain why the alleged parasite has never been found! In the race to keep up with the cicada, the parasite probably kept extending its life cycle until it hit the 16-year hurdle. Then it failed to coincide for 272 years, by which time the lack of coinciding with cicadas had driven it to extinction. The result is a cicada with a 17-year life cycle, which it no longer needs because its parasite no longer exists.

11. As it is used in line 3 *unique* most nearly means

(A) one of a kind
(B) strange
(C) interesting
(D) solitary

12. Which word best describes the author's use of the word *patiently* in line 5?

(A) humorous
(B) ironic
(C) anthropomorphic
(D) exaggerated

GO ON TO THE NEXT PAGE

13. Which of the following is the main likely intended audience of this passage?

    (A) biologists
    (B) laypersons interested in biology
    (C) children
    (D) journalists

14. Scientists theorize that cicadas have a 17-year life cycle because

    (A) 17 years is the optimum length of time for cicadas to most efficiently use available food and other resources in order to reproduce
    (B) no parasite species can survive 17 years without reproducing
    (C) it evolved as the most advantageous way for cicadas to co-exist with a parasite that has now become extinct
    (D) it evolved as a successful defense against a parasite that no longer exists

15. The reason *Magicicada tredecim* has a 13-year life cycle rather than a 17-year one is probably because

    (A) it is a less advanced species than *Magicicada septendecim*
    (B) two species of cicada having the same life cycle would create unnecessary competition for both species, so one evolved a different long prime number life cycle
    (C) its parasite became extinct so it had no need to evolve a life cycle lasting a longer prime number of years
    (D) it has a parasite with a 16-year life cycle, which means that it will meet its parasite only once every 208 (16×13) years

16. According to the theory described in the passage, which of the following statements is *not* true?

    (A) The cicada wants to decrease the frequency with which its life cycle coincides with its parasite.
    (B) The cicada's parasite wants to increase the frequency with which its life cycle coincides with that of the cicadas.
    (C) For the cicada's parasite, the longer the life cycle of the cicadas the better.
    (D) To avoid meeting its parasite it is advantageous for cicadas to have a life cycle lasting a prime number of years.

17. Which of the following lines provides the best evidence for the answer to the previous question?

    (A) lines 1–3 ("The . . . insect.")
    (B) lines 19–21 ("One . . . avoid.")
    (C) lines 30–33 ("Ultimately . . . years. ")
    (D) lines 44–47 ("However . . . parasitize.")

18. Which of the following most accurately describes the explanation given in the passage for the fact that *Magicicada septendecim* has a 17-year life cycle?

    (A) It is based on a scientific theory that has reasonably good empirical and theoretical support.
    (B) It is based entirely on conjecture.
    (C) It is based on a scientific theory that has good theoretical support but no empirical support.
    (D) It is based on a theory with excellent empirical support but almost no theoretical support.

GO ON TO THE NEXT PAGE

19. If an organism is discovered that parasitizes *Magicicada septendecim* it would
    (A) totally invalidate the theory that *Magicicada septendecim* evolved a long life cycle lasting a prime number of years to protect itself from a parasite
    (B) demonstrate conclusively that *Magicicada septendecim* evolved a long life cycle lasting a prime number of years in order to protect itself from a parasite
    (C) suggest that the theory that *Magicicada septendecim* evolved a long life cycle lasting a prime number of years to protect itself from a parasite might not be true
    (D) show conclusively that certain parasites can survive 272 years without a host to parasitize

20. The passage does all of the following *except*
    (A) pose questions about an observed phenomenon
    (B) formulate hypotheses
    (C) cite specific scientific papers dealing with the phenomena discussed
    (D) make use of deductive reasoning

Questions 21–31 are based on the following passages.

Passage 1 is from "Sustainability and Renewable Resources" by Steven Hayward, Ph.D., Elizabeth Fowler, and Laura Steadman. Copyright © 2000 by the Mackinac Center for Public Policy, Midland, Michigan.

Passage 2 is from OECD/Nuclear Energy Agency (2000), "Nuclear Energy in a Sustainable Development Perspective," *www.oecd-nea.org/sd.*

PASSAGE 1

Sustainability of renewable resources can be defined in different ways. Maintaining the economic output of an ecosystem (e.g., in a commercially exploited forest) is one option and maintaining the integrity of the whole ecosystem (e.g., in an old-growth forest) is another possibility. In addition to the immediate value associated with its economic outputs, the ecosystem that supports the resource flows may have option values for possible future uses, and existence values simply because people value its continued existence. Ecosystems have information value as working models of complex interacting life-sustaining systems, about which we still have much to learn. Option and existence values are less tangible and more difficult to measure than the immediate economic output, but may be of comparable importance, especially in a long-term perspective.

Renewable resources are subject to a variety of stresses, often more powerful than those acting on non-renewables. They are inexhaustible in the sense that they can be continually recycled, but this does not mean they are infinite in amount and does

GO ON TO THE NEXT PAGE

not prevent their degradation. Renewable resources, including air, water, and land, are subject to pressures for different uses, which may be incompatible. Air and water are particularly susceptible to pollutants because of the ease with which they can be used as open-access resources for receiving and disseminating waste. Habitat for plant and animal species may be very sensitive to environmental impacts, and easily destroyed. Thus renewable resources should be seen as finite and vulnerable to pressures.

For example, a river system can be dedicated to a variety of purposes: power generation, drinking water, irrigation, industrial use, sport and commercial fishing, recreation in various forms such as rafting and canoeing, swimming, sailing or motor-boating on lakes and reservoirs, scenery for hikers and campers, sites for resorts or cottages, or pure wilderness. Once dedicated, it cannot be used again without disturbing the constituencies that use its features and whose property values depend on them. Some of these uses may degrade the quality of the water, or spoil it for other uses. In some cases, so much water is withdrawn for various uses that not much reaches the sea or ocean—the Nile and the Colorado are in this condition at times. This in turn can have an impact on coastal currents and water quality, salinity of water in the delta, etc. Policy for renewable resources, including pricing policy, should reflect their scarcity value, multiple uses, and susceptibility to degradation or irreversible loss.

PASSAGE 2

Many instances of unsustainable resource use can be attributed not only to a lack of a well-functioning market, but to perverse institutional or legal incentives, such as a lack of property rights to resources, or (especially in underdeveloped nations) a lack of ready resource alternatives. Groundwater resources in the U.S., for instance, are often overused because of subsidies, a lack of tradable rights to water ("use it or lose it"), and a lack of clear property rights to water tables. Overfishing in the oceans provides a better example. It is easy to imagine that cattle might be scarce, just as buffalo became scarce, if they were owned in common and were taken from one vast domain, rather than being privately owned on separate ranches. While the exact analogue to barbed wire for fishing grounds in the ocean may be hard to conceive, assigning ownership rights to the ocean should not be much more difficult than assigning ownership rights to the radio frequency spectrum, as is currently being done throughout the world.

The United States should encourage developing nations to follow this general strategy. Much of the destruction of forest resources that is of present concern is due to unsound government policies that private owners would not likely have undertaken to the same extent, if at all. Al Gore notes in Earth in the Balance: "the most serious examples of environmental degradation in the world today are tragedies that were created or actively encouraged by governments—usually in pursuit of some notion that a dramatic reordering of the material world would enhance the greater good."

There is much enthusiasm for "getting the incentives right." This produces nods of agreement on the general level, and furious disagreement about its specific application. "Getting the incentives right" should mean chiefly assigning property

GO ON TO THE NEXT PAGE

rights to environmental goods, rather than using government power to set the "correct price" for the use of a commonly held environmental good. Any so-called "market-based incentive" policy that involves government setting the "correct price" to establish a "level playing field" is inherently flawed, because it misunderstands the nature of markets and prices. The government will always lack the necessary knowledge to set the "right" price, and such policies will usually introduce new distortions into the marketplace that will likely be counterproductive and wasteful of resources.

21. The term "option values" as it is used in line 11 refers to

    (A) optional financial transactions
    (B) uses other than the present ones to which an ecosystem could be put
    (C) commercial worth
    (D) values that can be converted to cash under certain circumstances

22. According to the author of Passage 1, a renewable resource such as land is "inexhaustible" (line 25) but not "infinite in amount" (line 27). This means that a particular resource, such as a 10-acre tract of land,

    (A) can be used for activities without worrying about the effects of these activities on it for the foreseeable future
    (B) can be put to an infinite number of uses but eventually it will have no value for anything
    (C) can be used for first one purpose, then another, and another, and so on indefinitely, but the total amount of land cannot be increased
    (D) is inexhaustible in that the supply of land is infinite, but there are so many types of uses to which it can be put that it ultimately will not be worthwhile maintaining

23. According to the author of Passage 1, once a river system is reserved for certain uses

    (A) it can never be used for any other purpose
    (B) it can be used for other purposes, but this will affect those already using it
    (C) it is always harmful to the river's ecosystem to change those uses
    (D) it is inevitable that water quality in the system will be degraded

GO ON TO THE NEXT PAGE

24. Which of the following provides evidence for the answer to the previous question?
    (A) "Renewable . . . . non-renewables." (lines 22–24)
    (B) "Air . . . waste." (lines 31–35)
    (C) "Once . . . them." (lines 48–51)
    (D) "This . . . etc." (lines 57–59)

25. As it is used in line 66 *perverse* most nearly means
    (A) convoluted
    (B) corrupt
    (C) caused by selfishness
    (D) arising from obstinate persistence in an error

26. According to the author of Passage 2, a lack of tradable rights to water encourages people with rights to water to
    (A) speculate on price rises for water
    (B) use other unsustainable resources in place of water
    (C) conserve the water they have
    (D) use the water they have rights to

27. We can infer that the author of Passage 2 believes that cattle might become scarce if they "were owned in common and were taken from one vast domain" (lines 78–79) because
    (A) people would have little incentive to conserve cattle
    (B) cattle would be much easier to kill
    (C) fatal diseases would spread easily through the cattle population
    (D) private ownership is always better than common or public ownership

28. According to the information provided in the passage, we can infer that the author of Passage 2 believes that
    (A) one of the most important roles of government in the conservation of unsustainable resources is to assign property rights to environmental goods
    (B) if property rights are assigned to environmental goods there will be no more instances of unsustainable resource use
    (C) the private market has no role in the conservation of unsustainable resources
    (D) only government has the expertise, access to information, and manpower to set the price of a commonly held economic good

GO ON TO THE NEXT PAGE

29. Passage 1 and Passage 2 differ in that

(A) Passage 1 provides four definitions of sustainability of renewable resources; Passage 2 discusses several examples of unsustainable resource use
(B) Passage 1 describes the difficulties involved in promoting the sustainable use of resources; Passage 2 discusses some important concepts related to the sustainable use of resources and argues for more government involvement in the conservation of resources
(C) Passage 1 outlines a policy for encouraging the sustainable use of resources; Passage 2 discusses the role of government in preserving the environment through promoting the sustainable use of resources
(D) Passage 1 discusses various issues related to the sustainability of renewable resources and makes some general recommendations about the issue; Passage 2 analyzes certain examples of unsustainable resource use and makes firm recommendations about how some such problems in this area can be corrected

30. What comment would the author of Passage 1 be most likely to make about the suggestion in Passage 2 that ownership rights should be assigned to the ocean?

(A) It might have some merit but the results would have to be closely monitored because habitats could be destroyed and what is done by one owner could have a great effect on the areas of the ocean owned by others.
(B) It has some merit, but ownership rights to the ocean should be given only for fishing.
(C) It would be an excellent idea both for fostering economic activity and for environmental conservation.
(D) It is a good idea as long as owners are prohibited from oil exploration and promise to provide scientists with information on the effects of their commercial activities on the ecosystem.

31. Based on the information provided in Passage 1 and Passage 2, which of the following would most accurately reflect the probable views of the author of Passage 1 about the main argument made in Passage 2?

(A) He would say that a market-based approach should be encouraged in some instances, but that there are many problems related to the sustainability of renewable resources that cannot be solved by this approach alone.
(B) He would agree with it with certain relatively minor reservations.
(C) He would say that it is entirely misguided because the free market has no place in the conservation of resources.
(D) He would say that it is unrealistic because most governments will not grant property rights to resources.

GO ON TO THE NEXT PAGE

Questions 32–42 are based on the following passage.

This passage is from David Alpaugh, "What Poets Can Learn from Songwriters," © 2011 by David Alpaugh, © 2011 *Scene4 Magazine.*

In *Finishing The Hat,* Stephen Sondheim zeroes in on the essential difference between the art of the lyricist and that of the poet: "Poetry doesn't need music," he writes, "lyrics do." Poetry is the art of "concision," written to stand on its own; lyrics, the art of "expansion," written to accommodate music.

And yet, the line between song and poem is not as firm as Sondheim suggests. William Blake called his greatest books of poetry *Songs of Innocence* and *Songs of Experience.* Walt Whitman called the opening poem of *Leaves of Grass* "Song of Myself." In both cases, their work straddles the line between the genres. Blake's

Piping down the valleys wild,
Piping songs of pleasant glee,
On a cloud I saw a child,
And he laughing said to me

practically begs to be set to music, and has been by more than one composer. Whitman's great elegy, beginning

In the dooryard fronting an old farm-house near the white-wash'd palings,
Stands the lilac-bush tall-growing . . .

is one of the loveliest "songs" in the Kurt Weill / Langston Hughes musical, *Street Scene.*

Perhaps the most significant divergence between these sister arts today is the way in which poets and songwriters imagine their audiences.

Whereas poetry is aimed almost exclusively at a limited number of fellow poets, hundreds of millions of men and women listen to songs on iPods and smart phones and millions more sing them in showers, kitchens, and karaoke bars.

Poets who want to achieve wider readership might consider the qualities that attract millions of intelligent men and women to their sister art. First in importance, the primary mission of the poem should be the same as the primary mission of the song: *to make the listener want to hear the song again and again!*

If I'm satisfied with listening to a song once the song is a failure! Yet, how many times have I heard poets introduce their poems with words like these:

"I think I may have read this poem here before. If so, I hope you'll bear with me. Hopefully there are others here who haven't heard it."

Imagine Paul Simon saying, "If there's anyone here who has already heard 'Bridge Over Troubled Water' I apologize for boring you with it again." If Frost came back from the grave would audiences shout, "We only want to hear new work, Robert. Don't you dare read 'Birches' or 'The Road Not Taken'!" Frost acknowledged poetry's ambition to be heard again and again when he explained that his goal was "to lodge a few poems where they will be hard to get rid of."

Too many poets programmatically eschew the memory cues songwriters unabashedly use to accomplish this mission. After talking to writing students, conditioned by their professors to tolerate no rhyme or meter in poetry, James Fenton suggests (in American Scholar) that they would "be happier if they

GO ON TO THE NEXT PAGE

accepted that the person who was studying creative writing, with the aim of producing poetry, was the same person who had a car full of country and western tapes, or whatever the music was that delighted them."

The aversion to rhyme and meter, Fenton implies, is an artificially-acquired, counter-intuitive, schizophrenic taste. The popularity of rap, rock, and country music, as well as the power of advertising, remind us that our desire for repetition is based on pulse and heartbeat and the nature of the human brain. It's suicidal for poets to reject their own biology!

Still, I hear critics admonishing me for ignoring the singing elephant in the room. It's not the lyric, they protest, but the music that makes us want to hear a song again and again. And music is something poets do not have in their arsenal.

Or do they? To be sure, poets cannot rely on actual musical tones; still the poems I love (formal or open) have a quasi-melodic structure that has an effect not unlike melody proper.

Melody seizes us, picks us up, and holds us with the progression of its tones, never putting us back on the ground until the final notes stops vibrating. Great poems use purely verbal elements—syllables, words, accent—to build a rhetorical arc that provides a similar experience.

At a time when too many poets have so purged their "poetry" of repetition and melody that it reads and sounds like outright prose, songwriters continue to satisfy a human craving that cannot and should not be denied. Whether or not poets can again become relevant to non-practitioners of their art may depend on how well they listen to their big sister.

32. Which of the following statements about Stephen Sondheim's description of the difference between the art of the lyricist and that of the poet would the author of this passage be most likely to agree with?

(A) It is simplistic, but contains an element of truth.
(B) It expresses a truth about only one relatively minor aspect of the difference between the two arts.
(C) It is fundamentally true, yet at times the difference between them is not so clear.
(D) It is impossible to meaningfully generalize either about lyrics or poetry.

33. The author quotes lines from Blake's *Songs of Innocence* in order to

(A) illustrate how very different a poem is from a lyric
(B) provide an example of a poem that is very much like a lyric
(C) show that only a simple poem can successfully be set to music
(D) show that there is no difference between melody in music and repetition in poetry

34. According to the author, one of the main reasons that poems are not as popular as songs is that

(A) poets tend to write for a limited audience, whereas songwriters tend to write for a mass audience
(B) poets are not sufficiently trained in music theory and composition
(C) poems have become too complex for most people to understand
(D) poems have become too much like songs, thus losing the distinctiveness that gives them their appeal

GO ON TO THE NEXT PAGE

35. Which of the following provides evidence for the answer to the previous question?

(A) "Whereas . . . bars." (lines 33–38)
(B) "After . . . them.'" (lines 68–77)
(C) "The . . . biology!" (lines 80–86)
(D) "At . . . denied." (lines 105–110)

36. The meaning of the phrase "programmatically eschew" as it is used in line 66 is most nearly

(A) automatically embrace as part of a program
(B) slavishly copy
(C) avoid something because one thinks it is conformist
(D) avoid something because it isn't part of one's customary system

37. The quotation by James Fenton "[They would] be happier if they accepted that the person who was studying creative writing, with the aim of producing poetry, was the same person who had a car full of country and western tapes, or whatever the music was that delighted them" (lines 72–77) suggests that

(A) more music lovers should enroll in writing courses aimed at producing poets
(B) writing students should listen to more music
(C) writing students wanting to become poets tend not to draw on their knowledge and appreciation of music in their attempts to produce poetry
(D) writing students are not happy because their professors do not allow them to draw on their knowledge and appreciation of music in their writing of poetry

38. As it is used in line 80 *schizophrenic* most nearly means

(A) characterized by delusional thought patterns
(B) characterized by the coexistence of antagonistic qualities
(C) outside the bounds of what is normally accepted
(D) mentally unstable

39. The phrase "singing elephant in the room" as it is used in line 88 can be described accurately by all of the following words *except*

(A) metaphorical
(B) jocular
(C) colorful
(D) elegiac

40. As it is used in line 97 "melody proper" most nearly means

(A) musical melody
(B) properly used melody
(C) poetic "melody"
(D) melody like that in old-time songs

GO ON TO THE NEXT PAGE

41. In the last line of the passage the author says, "Whether or not poets can again become relevant to non-practitioners of their art may depend on how well they listen to their big sister" (lines 110–113).

    The author is most likely suggesting that

    (A) to significantly increase their popularity of their work among people who are not poets themselves, poets should strongly consider learning some of the techniques that songwriters use and employing them when they write poetry
    (B) to become popular outside poetry circles poets should write poems just like song lyrics
    (C) how popular a poet becomes depends on how sophisticated his or her musical tastes are
    (D) young poets must heed the advice of senior poets, including listening to popular music to develop their sense of rhythm and melody

42. Based on the information in the passage, the author would be most likely to agree with the statement that

    (A) a poem can be both excellent and popular
    (B) popular poetry is almost by definition bad poetry
    (C) the more like a song a poem becomes the better it is
    (D) a poem without a lot of "musical" qualities cannot be a good poem

Questions 43–52 are based on the following passage.

This passage is from Preston Dyches, "Cassini Catches Titan Naked in the Solar Wind," NASA News and Features, January 28, 2015.

Researchers studying data from NASA's Cassini mission have observed that Saturn's largest moon, Titan, behaves much like Venus, Mars, or a comet when exposed to the raw power of the solar wind. The observations suggest that unmagnetized bodies like Titan might interact with the solar wind in the same basic ways, regardless of their nature or distance from the sun.

Titan is large enough that it could be considered a planet if it orbited the sun on its own, and a flyby of the giant moon in Dec. 2013 simulated that scenario, from Cassini's vantage point. The encounter was unique within Cassini's mission, as it was the only time the spacecraft has observed Titan in a pristine state, outside the region of space dominated by Saturn's magnetic field, called its magnetosphere.

"We observed that Titan interacts with the solar wind very much like Mars, if you moved it to the distance of Saturn," said Cesar Bertucci of the Institute of Astronomy and Space Physics in Buenos Aires, who led the research with colleagues from the Cassini mission. "We thought Titan in this state would look different. We certainly were surprised," he said.

GO ON TO THE NEXT PAGE

The solar wind is a fast-flowing gale of charged particles that continually streams outward from the sun, flowing around the planets like islands in a river. Studying the effects of the solar wind at other planets helps scientists understand how the sun's activity affects their atmospheres. These effects can include modification of an atmosphere's chemistry as well as its gradual loss to space.

Titan spends about 95 percent of the time within Saturn's magnetosphere. But during a Cassini flyby on Dec. 1, 2013, the giant moon happened to be on the sunward side of Saturn when a powerful outburst of solar activity reached the planet. The strong surge in the solar wind so compressed the sun-facing side of Saturn's magnetosphere that the bubble's outer edge was pushed inside the orbit of Titan. This left the moon exposed to, and unprotected from, the raging stream of energetic solar particles.

Using its magnetometer instrument, which is akin to an exquisitely sensitive compass, Cassini has observed Titan many times during the mission's decade in the Saturn system, but always within Saturn's magnetosphere. The spacecraft has not been able to detect a magnetic field coming from Titan itself. In its usual state, Titan is cloaked in Saturn's magnetic field.

This time the influence of Saturn was not present, allowing Cassini's magnetometer to observe Titan as it interacted directly with the solar wind. The special circumstance allowed Bertucci and colleagues to study the shockwave that formed around Titan where the full-force solar wind rammed into the moon's atmosphere.

At Earth, our planet's powerful magnetic field acts as a shield against the solar wind, helping to protect our atmosphere from being stripped away. In the case of Venus, Mars, and comets—none of which is protected by a global magnetic field—the solar wind drapes around the objects themselves, interacting directly with their atmospheres (or in the comet's case, its coma). Cassini saw the same thing at Titan. Researchers thought they would have to treat Titan's response to the solar wind with a unique approach because the chemistry of the hazy moon's dense atmosphere is highly complex. But Cassini's observations of a naked Titan hinted at a more elegant solution. "This could mean we can use the same tools to study how vastly different worlds, in different parts of the solar system, interact with the wind from the sun," Bertucci said.

Bertucci noted that the list of similarly unmagnetized bodies might include the dwarf planet Pluto, to be visited this year for the first time by NASA's New Horizons spacecraft.

"After nearly a decade in orbit, the Cassini mission has revealed once again that the Saturn system is full of surprises," said Michele Dougherty, principal investigator of the Cassini magnetometer at Imperial College, London. "After more than a hundred flybys, we have finally encountered Titan out in the solar wind, which will allow us to better understand how such moons maintain or lose their atmospheres."

GO ON TO THE NEXT PAGE

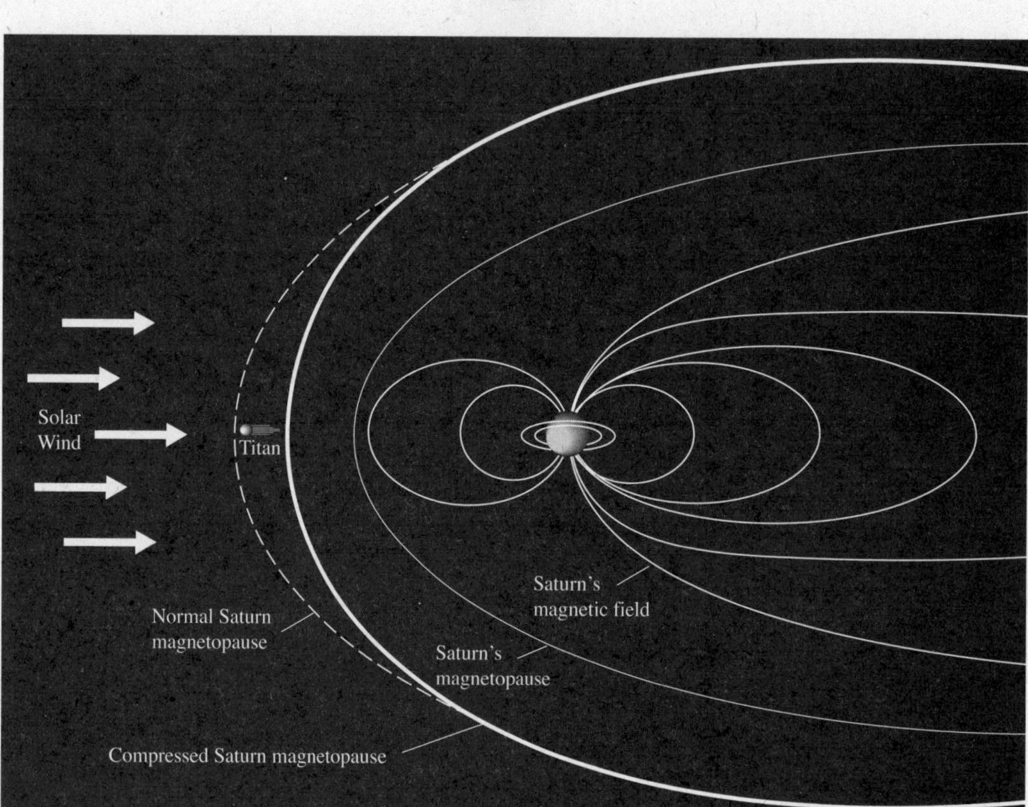

Source: "Cassini Catches Titan Naked in the Solar Wind," NASA News and Features, January 28, 2015.

43. According to the author

(A) all planets have a magnetosphere
(B) only Earth has a magnetosphere
(C) the Earth and Saturn have a magnetosphere
(D) only comets have a magnetosphere

44. Which of the following provide evidence for the answer to the previous question?

(A) "The . . . sun." (lines 5–9) and "Bertucci . . . spacecraft." (lines 89–93)
(B) "dominated . . . magnetosphere" (lines 18–19) and "At . . . away." (lines 68–71)
(C) "The . . . river." (lines 29–32) and "The . . . itself." (lines 56–58)
(D) "The . . . Titan." (lines 44–48) and "In . . . coma." (lines 71–77)

45. From the information provided we can infer that

(A) the strength of the solar wind varies
(B) the solar wind does not affect the atmosphere of planets in orbit around the sun
(C) the solar wind is stronger at Saturn than at Earth
(D) no known force can affect the solar wind

46. Which of the following provide evidence for the answer to the previous question?

(A) "The . . . sun." (lines 5–9)
(B) "The . . . river." (lines 29–32)
(C) "The . . . Titan." (lines 44–48)
(D) "Researchers . . . complex." (lines 78–82)

GO ON TO THE NEXT PAGE

1

47. Which of the following provides the best summary of the passage?

    (A) "Researchers . . . sun." (lines 1–9)
    (B) "We . . . said." (lines 20–28)
    (C) "Using . . . field." (lines 51–59)
    (D) "Researchers . . . said." (lines 78–88)

48. The word *elegant* as it is used in line 83 most nearly means

    (A) complex
    (B) tasteful and distinguished
    (C) ingenious and simple
    (D) stylish

49. In the drawing Titan is pictured

    (A) inside Saturn's magnetic field
    (B) outside Saturn's compressed magnetosphere
    (C) outside Saturn's normal magnetosphere
    (D) halfway between the sun and Saturn

50. The author most likely used the word *naked* in line 83 to

    (A) shock the reader
    (B) relate scientific findings to famous mythological figures
    (C) help the reader picture Titan as a god
    (D) dramatize the event described

51. The author makes use of all of the following *except*

    (A) quotations from experts
    (B) figurative language
    (C) description of natural phenomena
    (D) rhetorical questions

52. The author says "The spacecraft has not been able to detect a magnetic field coming from Titan itself. In its usual state, Titan is cloaked in Saturn's magnetic field" (lines 56–59). From this we can infer that

    (A) Titan may have a magnetic field that is difficult to detect because of Saturn's powerful magnetic field
    (B) Titan definitely does not have its own magnetic field
    (C) Titan definitely has its own magnetic field
    (D) scientists will never be able to determine if Titan has its own magnetic field

STOP

If there is still time remaining, you may review your answers.

WRITING AND LANGUAGE TEST

35 MINUTES, 44 QUESTIONS

Turn to Section 2 of your answer sheet to answer the questions in this section.

Directions: Questions follow each of the passages below. Some questions ask you how the passage might be changed to improve the expression of ideas. Other questions ask you how the passage might be altered to correct errors in grammar, usage, and punctuation. One or more graphics accompany some passages. You will be required to consider these graphics as you answer questions about editing the passage.

There are three types of questions. In the first type, a part of the passage is underlined. The second type is based on a certain part of the passage. The third type is based on the entire passage.

Read each passage. Then, choose the answer to each question that changes the passage so that it is consistent with the conventions of standard written English. One of the answer choices for many questions is "NO CHANGE." Choosing this answer means that you believe the best answer is to make no change in the passage.

Questions 1–11 are based on the following passage.

Drawing in Ancient Egypt

Of the system upon which drawing was taught by the Egyptian masters, we know nothing. **1** It was learning experience to determine the general proportions of the body, and the invariable relations of the various parts one with another; but they never troubled themselves to tabulate those proportions, or **2** reducing them to a system. Nothing in what remains to us of their **3** works that justify the belief that they ever possessed a canon based upon the length of the human finger or foot. Theirs was a teaching of routine, and not of

1. For the sake of clarity of expression and meaning, the underlined portion of the sentence should be written as follows:
   - (A) as it is now
   - (B) Learning experience determining
   - (C) Learning experience, determining
   - (D) They had learned from experience to determine

2. (A) NO CHANGE
   - (B) to reduce
   - (C) having reduced
   - (D) have to reduce

3. (A) NO CHANGE
   - (B) works justifies
   - (C) working justifies
   - (D) workings justify

GO ON TO THE NEXT PAGE

theory. Models executed by the master ❹ copied over and over again by his pupils, until they could reproduce them with absolute exactness. That they also studied from life is shown by the facility with which they seized a likeness, or ❺ converted the characteristics and movements of different kinds of animals. They made their first attempts upon slabs of limestone, on drawing boards covered with a coat of red or white stucco, or on the backs of old manuscripts of no value. New papyrus was too dear to be spoiled by the scrawls of tyros. ❻ They had neither pencil nor stylus. They were making use of the reed, the end of which, when steeped in water, opened out into small fibers, and made a more or less fine brush according to the size of the stem. The palette was of thin wood, in shape a rectangular oblong, with a groove ❼ where to lay the brush at the lower end. At the upper end were two or more

4. (A) NO CHANGE
   (B) copy
   (C) to copy
   (D) were copied

5. (A) NO CHANGE
   (B) yielded
   (C) rendered
   (D) furnished

6. Which choice most effectively combines the underlined sentences?
   (A) They had neither pencil nor stylus, they made use of the reed, the end of which, when steeped in water, opened out into small fibers, and made a more or less fine brush according to the size of the stem.
   (B) Having neither pencil nor stylus, made use of the reed, the end of which, when steeped in water, opened out into small fibers, making a more or less fine brush according to the size of the stem.
   (C) Having neither pencil nor stylus, they made use of the reed, the end of which, when steeped in water, opened out into small fibers, and made a more or less fine brush according to the size of the stem.
   (D) They had neither pencil nor stylus, they were making use of the reed, the end of which, when steeped in water, it opened out into small fibers, this made a more or less fine brush according to the size of the stem.

7. (A) NO CHANGE
   (B) which
   (C) in which
   (D) when

GO ON TO THE NEXT PAGE

cup-like hollows, each fitted with a cake of **8** ink; black and red being the colors most in use. A tiny pestle and mortar for color-grinding, and a cup of water in which to clip and wash the brush, **9** completing the apparatus of the student. Palette in hand, **10** squatted cross-legged before his copy, and, without any kind of support for his wrist, endeavored to reproduce the outline in black. The master looked **11** across his work when done, and corrected the errors in red ink.

8. (A) NO CHANGE
   (B) ink black and red
   (C) ink—black and red
   (D) ink (black and red)

9. (A) NO CHANGE
   (B) completed
   (C) completes
   (D) having completed

10. (A) NO CHANGE
    (B) squatting
    (C) he squatted
    (D) a squat

11. (A) NO CHANGE
    (B) past
    (C) around
    (D) over

GO ON TO THE NEXT PAGE

Questions 12–22 are based on the following passage.

You're a What? Acupuncturist

Got a headache? It could be your liver. And as part of your treatment, Jon Simon might stick a needle in your toe. Jon is an acupuncturist. He uses needles, herbs, and other devices to treat ailments such as headaches, back problems, and foot pain. Through his work, Jon **12** alleges Oriental medicine's centuries-old precept that the body is interconnected—head to toe and everything in between. It's a complex approach to well-being, he says, not a quick fix: "Acupuncture is more than just sticking needles in somebody's **13** body, its a whole system of healing."

Patients begin visits to Jon's New York City office by completing a form to describe their **14** condition, Jon reviews the form and then in an interview with the patient focuses on specific symptoms. "It may seem like I'm asking a bunch of unrelated questions," he says, "but I'm trying to find the nature of the complaint." Based on information gathered from the form and the interview, Jon **15** has recommended treatment.

The most common acupuncture treatment is **16** needling strategically inserting and manipulating thin, solid needles at specific points along the skin. Other treatment methods, often used in conjunction with needling, **17** including the prescriptions of herbs or herb mixtures; acupressure, which involves massaging instead of needling acupuncture points; and recommendations for lifestyle changes, such as dietary modifications and exercise. Jon usually gives a brief description of Oriental medicine **18** in case patients understand

12. (A) NO CHANGE
    (B) pleads
    (C) advocates
    (D) bears

13. (A) NO CHANGE
    (B) body. Its
    (C) body its
    (D) body. It's

14. For the sake of clarity of meaning and expression, the underlined portion of the sentence should be written as follows:
    (A) as it is now
    (B) condition. Jon reviews the form and then, in an interview with the patient, focuses
    (C) condition, Jon reviewing the form and then in an interview with the patient focusing
    (D) condition. Jon, reviewing the form, and then in an interview with the patient, focuses

15. (A) NO CHANGE
    (B) is recommending
    (C) had recommended
    (D) recommends

16. (A) NO CHANGE
    (B) needling: strategically
    (C) needling; strategically
    (D) needling. Strategically

17. (A) NO CHANGE
    (B) including the prescribing of
    (C) include prescriptions of
    (D) include to prescribe

18. (A) NO CHANGE
    (B) so that
    (C) whether
    (D) which

GO ON TO THE NEXT PAGE

2 2 2

his suggested treatment. 19 Pain or illness results when the flow of energy is disrupted; by stimulating meridians via specific points on the skin, acupuncture eliminates disruption and restores balance.

[1] A study in the November 1998 Journal of the American Medical Association reports that between 1990 and 1997, patient visits to practitioners of alternative medicine increased about 47 percent. [2] And in a survey published in the January 2001 American Demographics, 70 percent of respondents had tried at least 1 of 8 selected forms of alternative medicine, including acupuncture. [3] 20 Surprisingly, the number of acupuncturists also has risen. [4] According to the Acupuncture and Oriental Medicine Alliance, the number of 21 licensed acupuncturists nearly tripled in less than a decade: from 525 in 1992 to 14,228 in 2000. [5] Data show that acupuncture and other forms of traditional Oriental medicine are gaining popularity as a treatment choice. 22

19. At this point the writer is considering adding the following sentence.

Oriental medicine is based on the principle that human energy circulates along interconnected pathways known as meridians.

Should the writer make this addition here?

(A) Yes, because this sentence effectively links the preceding sentence to the following sentence. This sentence describes the principle of oriental medicine. The following sentence describes how illness results when processes this principle describes are disrupted.
(B) Yes, because this sentence describes more precisely than the preceding sentence how patients can better understand the principle of Oriental medicine.
(C) No, because this sentence is not directly relevant to the main topic of the passage, which is acupuncture.
(D) No, because this principle is disputed by Western medicine.

20. (A) NO CHANGE
(B) Likely
(C) Inexplicably
(D) Not surprisingly

21. (A) NO CHANGE
(B) licensing acupuncturists
(C) license acupuncturists
(D) acupuncturists with license

22. For the sake of the cohesion of this paragraph, sentence 5 should be placed:

(A) where it is now
(B) before sentence 1
(C) after sentence 1
(D) after sentence 3

GO ON TO THE NEXT PAGE

Questions 23–33 are based on the following passage.

Stained Glass

[1]

Stained glass is not one of the arts in which the method of production reveals itself at the first glance. Indeed, so few people when looking at a stained-glass window, whether a gorgeous and solemn one of the thirteenth or fourteenth century, or a crude and vulgar one of the nineteenth, realize the long and laborious process by which the result, good or bad, has been obtained. ㉓

[2]

㉔ One hears it so often spoken of as "painted glass" that it is not surprising that there should be a good deal of misconception on the point. It must be clearly understood then that the color effects ㉕ which are the glorious art are not directly produced by painting at all, but by the ㉖ window building up of a multitude of small pieces of white and colored glass—glass, that is, colored in the making, and of which the artist must choose the exact shades he needs, cut them out to shape, and ㉗ fitting them together to form his design, using a separate piece for every color or shade of color.

Think about the passage as a whole as you answer question 23.

23. To make the passage most logical, paragraph 1 should be placed
    - (A) where it is now
    - (B) after paragraph 2
    - (C) after paragraph 3
    - (D) after paragraph 4

24. The writer is considering deleting the underlined sentence. Should the writer do this?
    - (A) Yes, because the passage is mainly about the history of stained glass, not about how it is made.
    - (B) Yes, because no evidence is provided to support the assertion that stained glass is "so often spoken of as 'painted glass.' "
    - (C) No, because the following sentence would not make good sense if this sentence were deleted. The following sentence explains the "misconception" mentioned in this sentence.
    - (D) No, because the focus of the passage is on common misconceptions about stained glass and this sentence introduces this topic.

25. (A) NO CHANGE
    - (B) which are the glory of the art
    - (C) which, glorifying the art,
    - (D) which are glorious of the art

26. (A) NO CHANGE
    - (B) window, it has been built up
    - (C) window's being built up
    - (D) window when building up

27. (A) NO CHANGE
    - (B) having been fit together
    - (C) he fits them together
    - (D) fit them together

GO ON TO THE NEXT PAGE

[3]

In twelfth and thirteenth century windows many of these pieces are only half an inch wide and from one to two inches long, and few are bigger than the palm of one's hand; so the reader can **28** humor himself, if he wishes, in trying to calculate the number of pieces in one of the huge windows of this date in the Cathedral of Canterbury, York, or Chartres, **29** and the labor that has involved this, the initial stage of the process.

[4]

When the window is finished these pieces are put together like a puzzle and joined by grooved strips of lead soldered at the joints, just as any "lattice" window is put together; but before this **30** is done the details of the design—features, folds of drapery, patterns, and so on—are painted on the glass in an opaque brownish enamel made of oxide of iron and other metals ground up with a "soft" glass (glass with a low melting-point). This is mixed with oil or gum and water in order to apply it, and then the glass is placed in a kiln and "fired" till the enamel is fused on and, if well fired, becomes part of the glass **31** itself, the only "painting" involved in the production of a stained-glass window. **32** Its' effect, in the hand of an artist, is to decorate and enrich what would **33** otherwise be somewhat crude and papery in effect.

28. (A) NO CHANGE
(B) content
(C) amuse
(D) accommodate

29. (A) NO CHANGE
(B) and the labor involved in this,
(C) and the labor in which this is involved,
(D) and the involving labor of this,

30. (A) NO CHANGE
(B) has
(C) is being
(D) had been

31. Rewrite the underlined portion of the sentence to make two distinct sentences that make sense

(A) itself. Only the "painting" is
(B) itself. The only "painting" is
(C) itself. This is the only "painting"
(D) itself. The "painting" is only

32. (A) NO CHANGE
(B) It's
(C) Its
(D) It is

33. (A) NO CHANGE
(B) nevertheless
(C) subsequently
(D) accordingly

GO ON TO THE NEXT PAGE

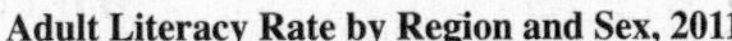

Questions 34–44 are based on the following passage and supplementary material.

Global Trends in Literacy

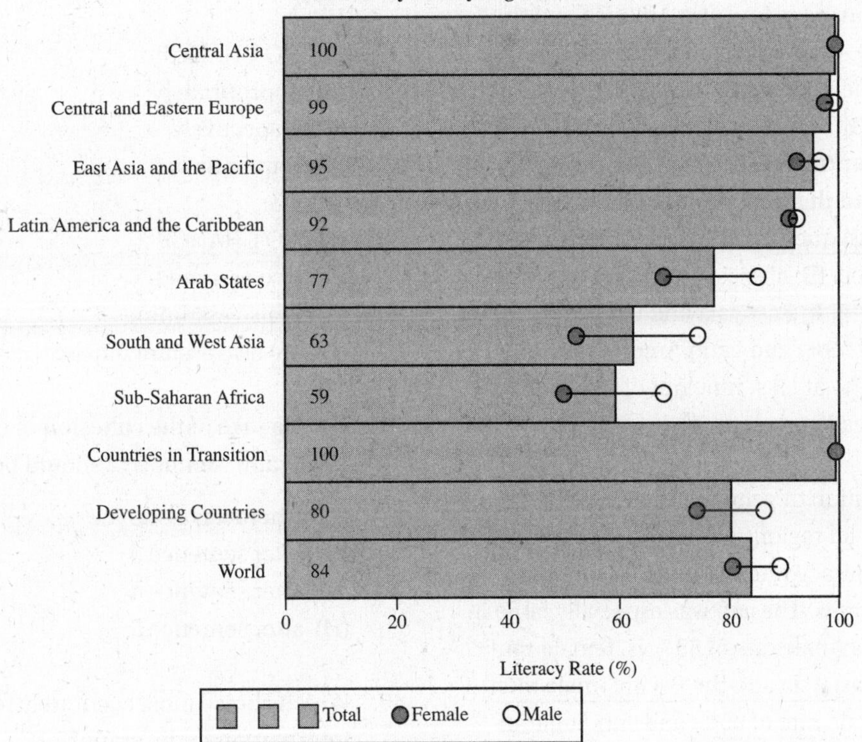

Note: 2011 data refer to the period 2005–2011.
Source: UNESCO Institute for Statistics, May 2013.

In 2011, the global adult literacy rate for the population aged 15 years and older was (34) <u>74%</u>. Regional averages of the adult literacy rate in 2011 were calculated for 151 countries and territories from eight regions, except (35) <u>North America and Western Europe</u> due to the limited number of countries in the region that report literacy rates.

34. Which choice most accurately represents the information in the graph?
    (A) NO CHANGE
    (B) 64%
    (C) 84%
    (D) 94%

35. Which choice most accurately represents the information in the graph?
    (A) NO CHANGE
    (B) East Asia and the Pacific
    (C) Sub-Saharan Africa
    (D) South and West Asia

GO ON TO THE NEXT PAGE

[1] Adult literacy rates were below the global average in South and West Asia (63%) and sub-Saharan Africa (59%), where more than one-third of adults could not read and write. [2] However, the average for Latin America and the Caribbean (36) evades lower literacy rates in the Caribbean, where the adult literacy rate was only 69% in 2011. [3] Two regions, Central and Eastern Europe and Central Asia, were at or near universal literacy, with adult literacy rates of 99% and 100%, (37) consequently. [4] North America and Western Europe (38) also assumes near universal adult literacy. [5] In East Asia and the Pacific (adult literacy rate of 95%) and Latin America and the Caribbean (92%) at least nine out of ten adults were able to read and write. (39)

An examination of gender-disaggregated data reveals that in all regions with data, except Central Asia, female literacy rates were (40) higher than male literacy rates. The gap was especially large in the Arab States (male rate of 85% vs. female rate of 68%), (41) East Asia and the Pacific (male rate of 92% vs. female rate of 90%) and sub-Saharan Africa (male rate of 68% vs. female rate of 51%). Globally, 89% of men and 80% of women were able to read and write in 2011.

36. (A) NO CHANGE
(B) harbors
(C) conceals
(D) curbs

37. (A) NO CHANGE
(B) appropriately
(C) respectively
(D) sequentially

38. (A) NO CHANGE
(B) also assumed
(C) is also assuming
(D) are also assumed to be

39. For the sake of the cohesion of this paragraph, sentence 2 should be placed:
(A) where it is now
(B) after sentence 3
(C) after sentence 4
(D) after sentence 5

40. Which choice most accurately represents the information in the graph?
(A) NO CHANGE
(B) lower than
(C) similar to
(D) related to

41. Which choice most accurately represents the information in the graph?
(A) NO CHANGE
(B) South and West Asia (male rate of 74% vs. female rate of 52%)
(C) Latin America and the Caribbean (male rate of 93% vs. female rate of 92%)
(D) Central and Eastern Europe (male rate of 99% vs. female rate of 98%)

GO ON TO THE NEXT PAGE

Adult literacy rates are projected to increase in almost all regions between 2011 and 2015. The exception is Central and Eastern Europe, where projections **42** implicate a small drop in adult literacy by one-half of a percentage point. The global adult literacy rate is projected to reach 86% in 2015, meaning that the target global literacy rate of 91%, a goal adopted by the World Education Forum in 2000, would be missed by 5%. Sub-Saharan Africa is projected to be **43** furthest from the 2015 target, and South and West Asia is projected to also come below the target for 2015. Central and Eastern Europe, Central Asia, and East Asia and the Pacific are projected to **44** reach, or come within one percentage point of the 2015 target.

42. (A) NO CHANGE
(B) insinuate
(C) connote
(D) indicate

43. (A) NO CHANGE
(B) above
(C) right on
(D) within

44. (A) NO CHANGE
(B) reach or come within
(C) reach or come, within
(D) reach; or come within

STOP

If there is still time remaining, you may review your answers.

MATH TEST (NO CALCULATOR)

25 MINUTES, 20 QUESTIONS

Turn to Section 3 of your answer sheet to answer the questions in this section.

Directions: For questions 1-15, solve each problem and choose the best answer from the given options. Fill in the corresponding circle on your answer document. For questions 16-20, solve the problem and fill in the answer on the answer sheet grid. Please use scrap paper to work out your answers.

Notes:

- You **CANNOT** use a calculator on this section.
- All variables and expressions represent real numbers unless indicated otherwise.
- All figures are drawn to scale unless indicated otherwise.
- All figures are in a plane unless indicated otherwise.
- Unless indicated otherwise, the domain of a given function is the set of all real numbers *x* for which the function has real values.

REFERENCE INFORMATION

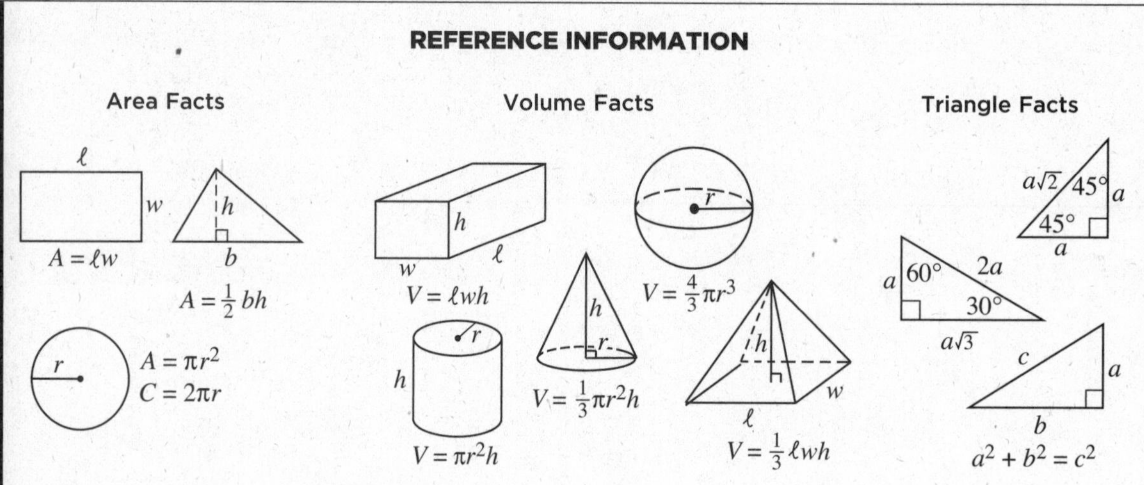

The arc of a circle contains 360°.
The arc of a circle contains 2π radians.
The sum of the measures of the angles in a triangle is 180°.

GO ON TO THE NEXT PAGE

1. Charles is conducting a survey regarding a proposed recreational center in his town. He finds the cost of the survey is expensive and must find a way to reduce the cost. Which of the following is the best way to reduce his costs?

(A) Interview more people to get more detailed information
(B) Accept a wider margin of error in the survey
(C) Interview people about topics other than the proposed recreational center
(D) Accept a narrower margin of error in the survey

2. Simplify $-2\left(\frac{x^2-8x-180}{x+10}\right)$ if $x \neq -10$

(A) $x-18$
(B) $-2x+36$
(C) $-2x^2+x$
(D) $x+10$

3. If $(x+n)^2 = x^2 + 19x + n^2$, what is the value of n^2?

(A) 361
(B) $\frac{361}{2}$
(C) $\frac{361}{4}$
(D) 38

4. Brian and Richard stand back-to-back. Each boy takes 5 equally spaced steps, in opposite directions from the starting location. At this point, Richard walks to where Brian is now and does so in 9 steps. How many times bigger are Richard's steps than Brian's steps?

(A) $\frac{4}{5}$
(B) $\frac{5}{4}$
(C) $\frac{7}{4}$
(D) 2

5. If M represents the number of prime numbers less than 25 and r is their range, what is $2M-r$?

(A) −3
(B) 3
(C) 8.9
(D) 27

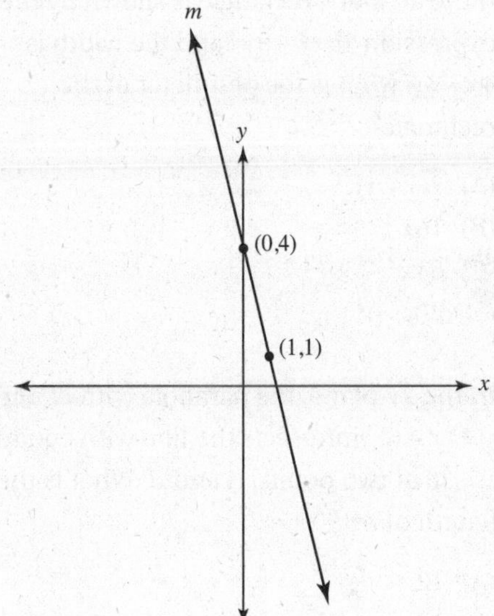

6. If line m (see diagram above) is translated down 4 units and right 5 units, what is the slope of the new line?

(A) −3
(B) $-\frac{15}{7}$
(C) $-\frac{3}{8}$
(D) $-\frac{5}{7}$

7. If $f(x) = x^3 - 7$ and $g(x) = 2x + 5$, what is $g(f^{-1}(20))$?

(A) −4
(B) −3
(C) 11
(D) 13

GO ON TO THE NEXT PAGE

8. If $2x + 3y = 17$ and $5x - 7y = 31$, what is the value of $\frac{7x-4y}{8}$?

(A) 6
(B) 7
(C) 8
(D) 12

9. If the area of a rectangle is shown by the expression $16x^2 - 9y^2$ and the width is $4x - 3y$, what is the perimeter of the rectangle?

(A) $4(x + y)$
(B) $16x$
(C) $64x^2 - 36y^2$
(D) $2(x + y)$

10. In the xy-plane, the parabola with equation $y = (x - 6)^2$ intersects the line with equation $y = 36$ at two points, A and B. What is the length of AB?

(A) 12
(B) 16
(C) 24
(D) 48

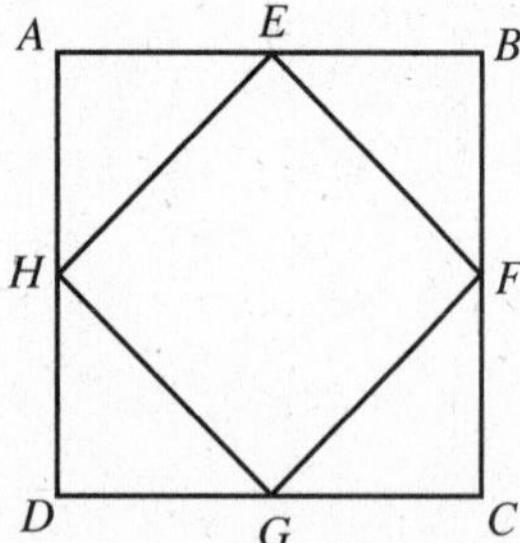

11. Square $EHGF$ lies within square $ABCD$ with E, F, G, and H all being midpoints. If the area of square $EHGF$ is 64 units squared, what is the area of square $ABCD$ (in square units)?

(A) 36
(B) 64
(C) $96\sqrt{2}$
(D) 128

12. In a 10-question true/false test, what is the probability of guessing correctly on exactly two of the questions from 6 through 8?

(A) $\frac{1}{3}$
(B) $\frac{3}{8}$
(C) $\frac{2}{3}$
(D) $\frac{7}{8}$

13. $2x^2 + y^2 = 360$
$y = 4x$

What is the value of x^2?

(A) 12
(B) 15
(C) 18
(D) 20

14. What are the solutions to $2x^2 + 8x - 12 = 0$?

(A) $x = -4 \pm 3\sqrt{10}$
(B) $x = -3 + \frac{\sqrt{10}}{10}$
(C) $x = -2 \pm \sqrt{10}$
(D) $x = 2 \pm \sqrt{10}$

15. $(ax - 7)(bx + 5) = 6x^2 + cx - 35$. If $ab = 6$ and $a - b = -1$ what are two possible values of c?

(A) $c = 2$ or $c = -4$
(B) $c = -11$ or $c = -1$
(C) $c = -2$ or $c = 4$
(D) $c = 12$ or $c = -5$

GO ON TO THE NEXT PAGE

Grid-in Response Directions

In questions 16–20, first solve the problem, and then enter your answer on the grid provided on the answer sheet. The instructions for entering your answers follow.

- First, write your answer in the boxes at the top of the grid.
- Second, grid your answer in the columns below the boxes.
- Use the fraction bar in the first row or the decimal point in the second row to enter fractions and decimals.

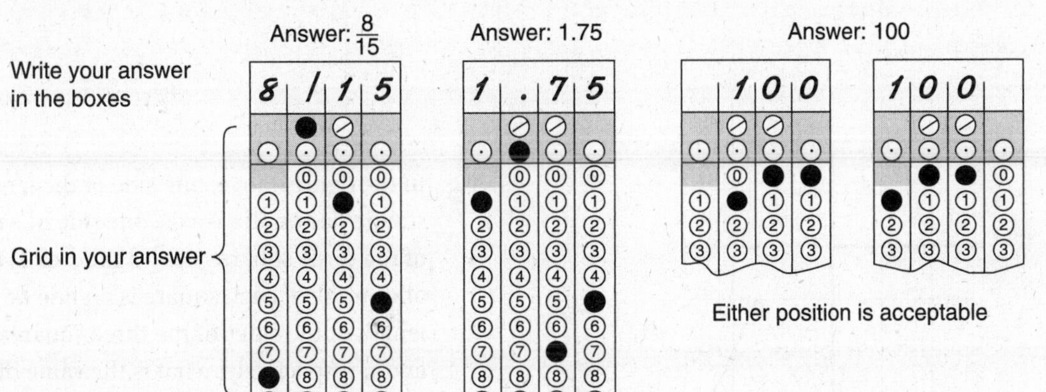

- Grid only one space in each column.
- Entering the answer in the boxes is recommended as an aid in gridding but is not required.
- The machine scoring your exam can read only what you grid, so you **must grid-in your answers correctly to get credit.**
- If a question has more than one correct answer, grid-in only one of them.
- The grid does not have a minus sign; so no answer can be negative.
- A mixed number *must* be converted to an improper fraction or a decimal before it is gridded. Enter $1\frac{1}{4}$ as $\frac{5}{4}$ or 1.25; the machine will interpret 11/4 as $\frac{11}{4}$ and mark it wrong.
- **All decimals must be entered as accurately as possible.** Here are three acceptable ways of gridding

$$\frac{3}{11} = 0.272727\ldots$$

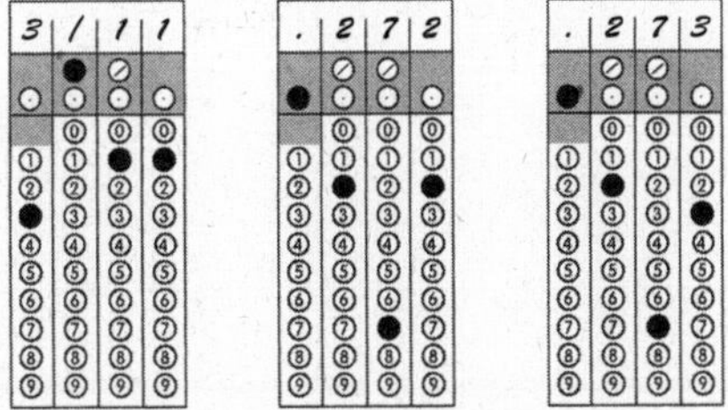

- Note that rounding to .273 is acceptable because you are using the full grid, but you would receive **no credit** for .3 or .27, because they are less accurate.

16. Jamie is considering two different companies to rent him a mobile home trailer for one day. One service charges $30 per day and $0.25 per mile. The other service charges $40 per day and $0.20 per mile. At what number of miles is the cost for the two services equal?

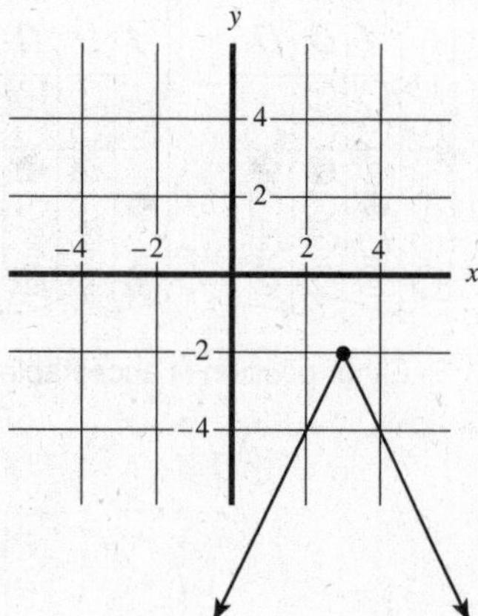

17. The graph of $f(x) = -2|x - m| + n$ is shown. What is the value of $-mn^{-1}$?

18. In a right triangle one of the acute angles measures $x°$, where $\sin x° = \frac{5}{8}$. What is the value of $\cos(90° - x°)$?

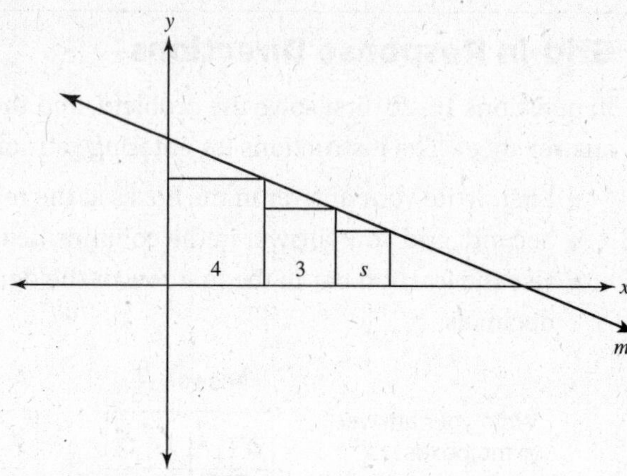

19. In the figure above, one side of the largest square lies on the y-axis, one side of each of the three squares lies on the x-axis, and one vertex of each square is on line m. If the length of the sides of the three squares is 4, 3, and s, respectively, what is the value of s?

20. A function, r, is defined as $r(n) = (n - 7)[(n + 1) - 7][(n + 2) - 7] \ldots [(n + 100) - 7]$ where n is an integer. What is the value of $r(1)$?

If there is still time remaining, you may review your answers.

MATH TEST (CALCULATOR)

55 MINUTES, 38 QUESTIONS

Turn to Section 4 of your answer sheet to answer the questions in this section.

Directions: For questions 1–30, solve each problem and choose the best answer from the given options. Fill in the corresponding circle on your answer document. For questions 31–38, solve the problem and fill in the answer on the answer sheet grid. Please use scrap paper to work out your answers.

Notes:

- The use of a calculator on this section IS permitted.
- All variables and expressions represent real numbers unless indicated otherwise.
- All figures are drawn to scale unless indicated otherwise.
- All figures are in a plane unless indicated otherwise.
- Unless indicated otherwise, the domain of a given function is the set of all real numbers x for which the function has real values.

REFERENCE INFORMATION

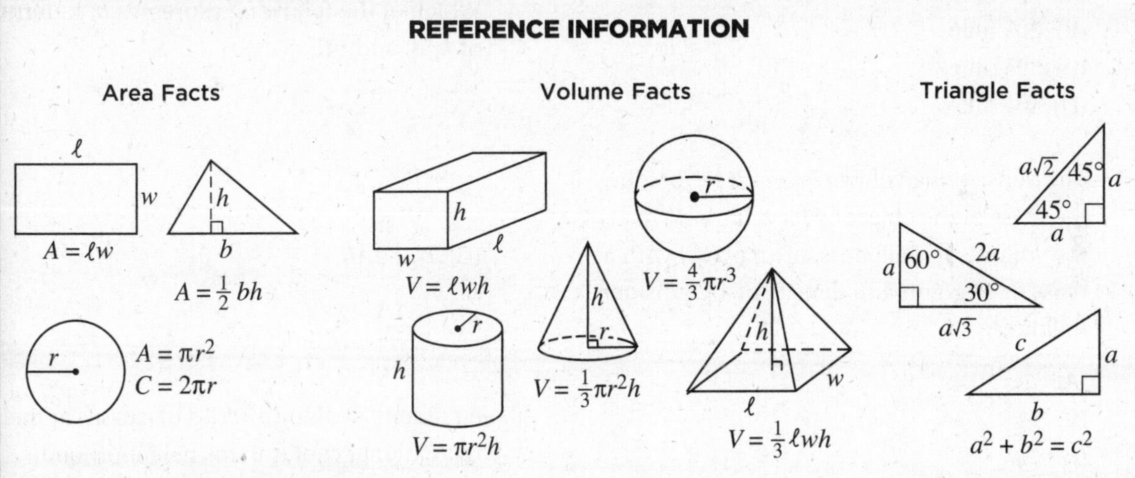

The arc of a circle contains 360°.

The arc of a circle contains 2π radians.

The sum of the measures of the angles in a triangle is 180°.

GO ON TO THE NEXT PAGE

1. Warren has a streaming video account with an online movie channel. His cost for each movie he rents is $2.25 and his monthly membership fee is $4.00. If his invoice for the past month was $24.25, how many movies did Warren rent?

(A) 6
(B) 7
(C) 8
(D) 9

2. The legend on a map shows that 1 inch = 80 miles. The distance on a map shows that Hartford, Connecticut and Roanoke, Virginia are 5.05 inches apart. What is the actual distance between the two cities?

(A) 80 miles
(B) 205 miles
(C) 395 miles
(D) 404 miles

3. The density of an object is found by dividing the mass of the object by its volume. What is the volume, in milliliters, of an object with a mass of 48 grams and density of 4 grams per milliliter?

(A) 12
(B) 14
(C) 16
(D) 24

4. A customer service call center for a credit card company asks 1 in 8 of the callers to take a survey at the conclusion of the call. Approximately 20% of those solicited consent to the survey. If 400 callers were serviced between 2:00 and 3:00 one afternoon and 20% of the callers consented to the survey, how many callers did **not** consent to the survey?

(A) 20
(B) 30
(C) 35
(D) 40

5. The formula for the area of a trapezoid is

$$A = \frac{1}{2}(h)(b_1 + b_2)$$

Which of the following expresses b_1 in terms of h, A, and b_2?

(A) $\frac{2A}{h} - b_2$

(B) $\frac{h}{2A} - b_2$

(C) $b_2 + 2Ah$

(D) $\left(\frac{A}{2h}\right) - b_2$

6. A student is taking a series of classes at the recreational center in his neighborhood. Each class has a monthly fee of $5.75 and there is a single monthly membership cost of $11.50. If the total cost for March was $51.75, how many classes were taken?

(A) 5
(B) 6
(C) 7
(D) 8

GO ON TO THE NEXT PAGE

7. If $2p - 4 \geq 6$, what is the least possible value of $2p + 4$?

(A) 7
(B) 14
(C) 21
(D) 28

8. Circle P has center (4, –2). The point A (7, 3) lies on the circle. What is the area of circle P?

(A) 24π
(B) 34π
(C) 54π
(D) 64π

Questions 9 and 10 refer to the graph below.

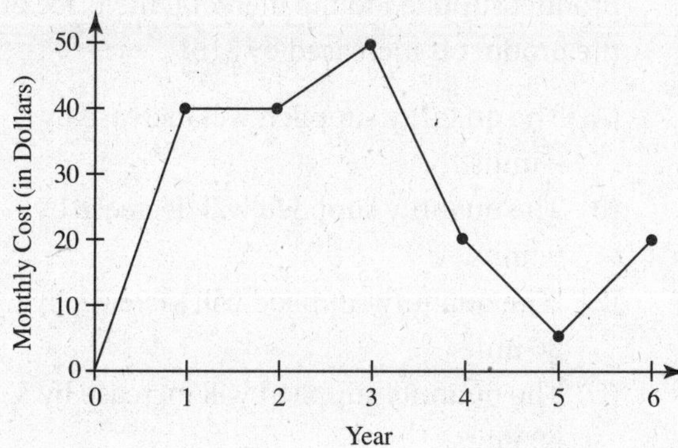

The monthly costs of certain internet plans have varied greatly over the six year period as illustrated in the graph.

9. What was the largest percent drop in price from one year to another?

(A) 25
(B) 50
(C) 75
(D) 85

10. What was the greatest decrease in internet plan price in the graph?

(A) \$40
(B) \$30
(C) \$25
(D) \$10

---

11. Given that $4a - 3b = 12$ and $6a + 8b = 17$, what is the value of $2a + b$?

(A) $\frac{29}{5}$
(B) $\frac{16}{5}$
(C) $-\frac{18}{5}$
(D) –9

12. Friendly Car Service charges a flat rate of \$1.50 and \$.55 per mile. Mustafa has only \$11 to spend on his ride. Write an inequality that represents the maximum distance that Mustafa can travel.

(A) $.55m - 1.50 \leq 11$
(B) $.55m + 1.50 \leq 11$
(C) $1.50m + .55 \geq 11$
(D) $.55m + 1.50 \geq 11$

13. Pham is interested in starting a 4H Club at her high school. She randomly sampled a group of 200 students and found that 31.5% of the students in her sample thought that starting a club was a good idea. If her high school has 1,145 students enrolled, approximately how many will consider that starting the 4H club was a good idea?

(A) 360
(B) 340
(C) 280
(D) 225

GO ON TO THE NEXT PAGE

Questions 14 and 15 refer to the graph below.

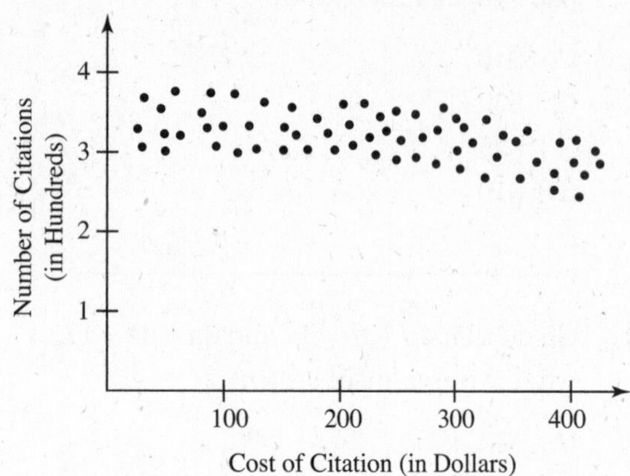

14. The graph shows the number of drivers who have been caught texting while driving and the fines that were levied against them. Which of the following can be concluded from the graph?

    (A) There is a strong negative correlation between higher fines and the number of drivers cited for texting while driving.
    (B) There is a weak negative correlation between higher fines and the number of drivers cited for texting while driving.
    (C) There is a strong positive correlation between higher fines and the number of drivers cited for texting while driving.
    (D) There is no correlation between higher fines and the number of drivers cited for texting while driving.

15. Based on the data from the graph, which of the following would be useful in reducing texting while driving?

    (A) Reduce the fines for citations
    (B) Increase the fines for citations
    (C) Launch a series of commercials illustrating the dangers of texting while driving
    (D) Maintain the fine amount for a period of 18 months

Questions 16 and 17 refer to the following information.

$$S(x) = \frac{3}{5}x + 60$$

$$D(x) = 240 - x$$

The quantity of a product supplied to the public and the quantity of a product that is demanded by the public are each functions of the product's price. The functions above model the estimated supply and demand of a particular product. The function $S(x)$ gives the quantity of the product supplied to the market when the price is x dollars and the function $D(x)$ indicates the quantity of the product demanded when its price is x dollars.

16. What will be the effect on the quantity of the product supplied to the market if the price of the product is increased by \$15?

    (A) The quantity supplied will increase by 9 units.
    (B) The quantity supplied will decrease by 9 units.
    (C) The quantity supplied will increase by 36 units.
    (D) The quantity supplied will increase by 69 units.

17. At what price will the supply of the product be equal to the demand for the product?

    (A) \$202.50
    (B) \$180.00
    (C) \$127.50
    (D) \$112.50

GO ON TO THE NEXT PAGE

Questions 18 and 19 refer to the table below.

A recent marathon featured runners of many different ages. The table below shows a listing of the participants as categorized by age and place in the race.

Age	Under 20	20–29	30–39	40–49	50–69	70 and Over	Total
Top 10 Finisher	2	6	1	1	0	0	10
Finished in place 11 to 40	11	11	5	3	0	0	30
Finished after 40th Place	5	8	23	31	43	12	122
Total	18	25	29	35	43	12	162

18. What percent of the top forty finishers came from the 30 to 39 age group?

(A) 8%
(B) 10%
(C) 15%
(D) 18%

19. What is the difference between the percent of runners under 20 years of age who finished in places 11 to 40 and the percent of runners age 40 to 49 who also finished in places 11 through 40?

(A) 52.5%
(B) 46.4%
(C) 34.2%
(D) 31.1%

x	1	2	3
$g(x)$	3	5	7

x	3	4	5
$h(x)$	8	16	24

20. Values for $g(x)$ and $h(x)$ are listed above. What is the value for the $h(g(2))$?

(A) 24
(B) 36
(C) 48
(D) 72

21. $|m - 3| = 12$
$|n + 7| = 22$

In the equations above, $m < 0$ and $n < 0$. What is the value of $m - n$?

(A) 14
(B) 18
(C) 20
(D) 24

Questions 22 and 23 refer to the table below.

A mariner wants to purchase a sailboat and needs to finance some of the cost. The chart below provides the monthly payments per $1000 borrowed.

Monthly payment per $1000 borrowed

Annual Interest Rate	Number of Payments		
	36	48	60
5%	$29.97	$23.03	$18.87
8%	$31.34	$24.41	$20.28
10%	$32.27	$25.36	$21.24
12%	$33.22	$26.34	$22.24

22. The boat the mariner is interested in purchasing costs $8,795. The mariner wants to borrow $6,500 and pay for the balance in cash. What would the monthly payment be if a financing plan at 10%, paid off in 36 monthly payments is selected?

(A) $167.32
(B) $179.33
(C) $209.76
(D) $318.43

23. A boat vendor is offering a 5% rate for 36, 48, or 60 months. If the mariner can afford a $300 monthly payment, which of the following is closest to the price that can be paid for a sailboat?

(A) $10,000
(B) $13,000
(C) $14,000
(D) $15,000

24. Homeowners want to create a circular rock garden that measures 20 feet in diameter. Reference materials state that the space for the garden needs to be 3" deep. The rocks they wish to buy cost $80 per cubic yard and must be purchased in whole cubic yards. How much will they have to spend on rocks?

(A) $480
(B) $400
(C) $320
(D) $240

25. A Boy Scout troop in Des Moines is practicing its marching order in the upcoming Memorial Day parade. The troop leader wants the boys to march in neat rows, the same number in each row. When the leader tries four in a row, the last row has three. When he tries five boys in a row, the last row has four. In desperation, he tries to line up six boys in a row, only to find five in the last row. What is the least number of boys that could be in the troop?

(A) 11
(B) 14
(C) 59
(D) 119

26. Seven students draw numbered cards, each with a value that is a positive integer. The mean of their selections is 14. What is the largest number any student could have drawn?

(A) 92
(B) 70
(C) 28
(D) 14

GO ON TO THE NEXT PAGE

27. The golden ratio compares dimensions that are appealing to the eye. Sometimes the golden ratio appears in nature but more frequently in painting and architecture. The ratio has been defined as $\frac{1+\sqrt{5}}{2}:1$ which corresponds to length:width.

A new downtown cultural center is being planned for construction in 2017. The city planners hope to construct the main amphitheater using the golden ratio. If the proposed width of the amphitheater is to be 87 meters, what will be its length? (Round your answer to the nearest meter.)

(A) 211
(B) 176
(C) 157
(D) 141

Questions 28 and 29 refer to the data below.

	BMI
Underweight	Below 18.5
Normal	18.5–24.9
Overweight	25.0–29.9
Obesity	30.0 and Above

Body Mass Index is a calculation that measures obesity and the potential for serious health risks such as strokes and heart attacks. The BMI can be found by using the following formula:

$$\frac{\text{weight (pounds)}}{\text{height}^2 \text{ (inches)}} \times 703$$

28. What is the category of BMI of a patient who weighs 182 pounds and is 5'10"?

(A) Underweight
(B) Normal
(C) Overweight
(D) Obesity

29. What is the weight of a patient who is 6 feet tall and has the lowest BMI that is categorized as obese? (Round to the nearest pound)

(A) 194
(B) 221
(C) 231
(D) 241

---

30. Sam was babysitting his three-year-old brother Josh. When Sam wasn't watching, Josh had taken the aquarium and tipped it on its side so the water level was as shown below. When Sam found Josh, he quickly grabbed the tank and returned it to a horizontal position. What was the height of the water in the aquarium when it was in a horizontal position if the dimensions of the tank are 100 cm long, 60 cm wide, and 40 cm high?

(C is the midpoint of AB)

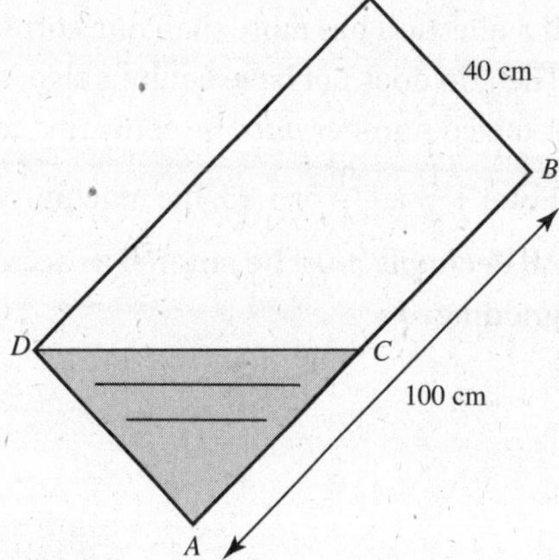

(A) 10
(B) 20
(C) 30
(D) 40

PRACTICE TEST 3

GO ON TO THE NEXT PAGE

Grid-in Response Directions

In questions 31–38, first solve the problem, and then enter your answer on the grid provided on the answer sheet. The instructions for entering your answers follow.

- First, write your answer in the boxes at the top of the grid.
- Second, grid your answer in the columns below the boxes.
- Use the fraction bar in the first row or the decimal point in the second row to enter fractions and decimals.

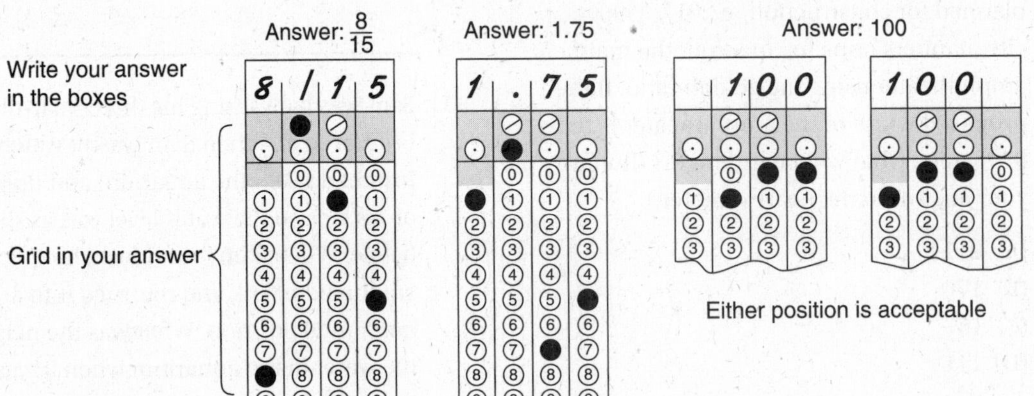

- Grid only one space in each column.
- Entering the answer in the boxes is recommended as an aid in gridding but is not required.
- The machine scoring your exam can read only what you grid, so you **must grid-in your answers correctly to get credit.**
- If a question has more than one correct answer, grid-in only one of them.
- The grid does not have a minus sign; so no answer can be negative.
- A mixed number *must* be converted to an improper fraction or a decimal before it is gridded. Enter $1\frac{1}{4}$ as $\frac{5}{4}$ or 1.25; the machine will interpret 11/4 as $\frac{11}{4}$ and mark it wrong.
- **All decimals must be entered as accurately as possible.** Here are three acceptable ways of gridding

$$\frac{3}{11} = 0.272727\ldots$$

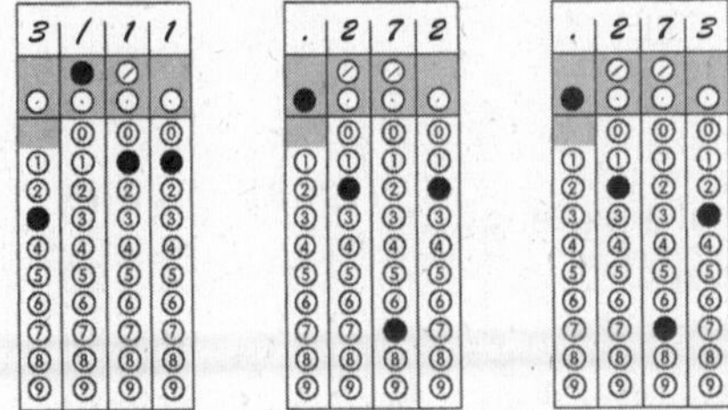

- Note that rounding to .273 is acceptable because you are using the full grid, but you would receive **no credit** for .3 or .27, because they are less accurate.

$$6x - 7y = \frac{37}{2}$$
$$ax - \frac{21}{2}y = \frac{111}{4}$$

31. In the above system of equations a is a constant. What value for a gives the system of equations infinite solutions?

	7th grade	8th grade	9th grade
Girls	191	215	174
Boys	162	219	181

32. The data above represents students categorized by gender and grade at a local middle school. If a student is selected at random, what is the probability the student is not an eighth-grade girl (round your answer to the nearest hundredth)?

33. A furniture manufacturer of office chairs uses the following profit function:

    $P(x) = -.08x^2 + 23.1x + 500$, where x represents the number of chairs that are manufactured and $P(x)$ is profit in dollars. What is the most profitable number of chairs to manufacture (round your answer to the nearest whole number)?

$$\left(\frac{1}{3}\right)^{x-2} = (27)^{3-x}$$

34. Given the equation above, what is the value of $2x + 11$?

35. A small wooden bridge has a maximum carrying capacity of 15,000 pounds. Three cars are currently crossing the bridge, each with a mean weight of 3,250 pounds. What is the greatest weight a fourth car or truck can have and still cross the bridge safely?

36. Students at a local art school wish to create a Styrofoam pyramid. The pyramid will have a rectangular base that measures 6 feet by 8 feet and will have a height that measures 12 feet. If each cubic foot weighs 4 ounces and the cost per pound of Styrofoam is $.50 per pound, what will be the cost to create the pyramid? (Note: 16 ounces = 1 pound) (Ignore the $ sign)

PRACTICE TEST 3

GO ON TO THE NEXT PAGE

Questions 37 and 38 refer to the information below.

Objects above the Earth's surface weigh less than objects on the Earth's surface due to the effects of gravity. Scientists use the following formula when considering the weight of satellites orbiting Earth.

$$W(h) = m\left(\frac{4000}{4000+h}\right)^2$$

where m equals the weight of an object at sea level and h is its height in miles above sea level.

37. A NOAH weather satellite is in a decaying orbit around Earth. In anticipation of this development, the engineers that built the satellite created the vehicle to be light enough to completely disintegrate as it descended to Earth. Thus the scientists created the weather satellite to weigh 50 pounds when it orbited at 22,000 miles. What was the weight of the satellite on Earth before it was launched into space (round your answer to the nearest pound)?

38. Susan is flying in a military test jet that can fly several miles higher than a passenger jet. At sea level, she weighs 120 pounds. At what height will she weigh 119.5 pounds (round your answer to the nearest hundredth of a mile)?

If there is still time remaining, you may review your answers.

ESSAY (OPTIONAL)

Directions: This is your opportunity to show that you can read and understand a passage and write an analysis of that passage. Be sure your essay demonstrates a clear and logical analysis of the passage, using precise language.

On the actual test, you will write your essay on the lines provided in your answer booklet; for now, write your essay on lined paper. Remember to write or print legibly so that others can read what you've written.

You have 50 minutes to read the essay and write a response to the prompt provided.

Carefully read the passage below. As you read, think about how Erich Fromm makes use of

- *reasoning* to develop an argument
- *evidence* to support assertions made
- *language* to persuade the reader

From Erich Fromm, *Escape from Freedom*, Henry Holt, 1941.

1 Modern man's feeling of isolation and powerlessness is increased by the character which all his human relationships have assumed. The concrete relationship of one individual to another has lost its direct and human character and has assumed a spirit of manipulation and instrumentality. In all social and personal relations the laws of the market are the rule. It is obvious that the relationship between competitors has to be based on mutual human indifference. Otherwise any one of them would be paralyzed in the fulfillment of his economic tasks—to fight each other and not to refrain from the actual economic destruction of each other if necessary.

2 The relationship between employer and employee is permeated by the same spirit of indifference. They both use each other for the pursuit of their economic interests; their relationship is one in which both are means to an end, both are instrumental to each other. It is not a relationship of two human beings who have any interest in the other outside of this mutual usefulness. The same instrumentality is the rule in the relationship between the businessman and his customer. The customer is an object to be manipulated, not a concrete person whose aims the businessman is interested to satisfy. The attitude toward work has the quality of instrumentality; in contrast to a medieval artisan the modern manufacturer is not primarily interested in what he produces; he produces essentially in order to make a profit from his capital investment, and what he produces depends essentially on the market which promises that the investment of capital in a certain branch will prove to be profitable.

3 Not only the economic, but also the personal relations between men have this character of alienation; instead of relations between human beings, they assume the character of relations between things. But perhaps the most important and the most devastating instance of this spirit of instrumentality and alienation is the individual's relationship to his own self. Man does not only sell commodities, he sells himself and feels himself to be a commodity. The manual laborer sells his physical energy; the businessman, the physician, the clerical employee, sell their "personality." They have to have a "personality" if they are to sell their products or services. This personality should be pleasing, but besides that its possessor should meet a number of other requirements: he should have energy, initiative, this, that, or the other, as his particular position may require. As with any other commodity it is the market which decides the value of these human qualities, yes, even their very existence. If there is no use for the qualities a person offers, he has none; just as an unsalable commodity is valueless though it might have its use value. Thus, the self-confidence, the "feeling of self," is merely an indication of what others think of the person. It is not he who is convinced of his value regardless of popularity and his success on the market. If he is sought after, he is somebody; if he is not popular, he is simply nobody. This dependence of self-esteem on the success of the "personality" is the reason why for modern man popularity has this tremendous importance. On it depends not only whether or not one goes ahead in practical matters, but also whether one can keep up one's self-esteem or whether one falls into the abyss of inferiority feelings.

Write an essay explaining how Erich Fromm constructs an argument to convince the reader that people in modern society are alienated both from themselves and from other people. Describe and analyze how Fromm uses one or more of the elements of persuasive writing listed on page 257 to strengthen his argument. You may also discuss other writing techniques used by the author.

Your essay should not state your opinion on the topic discussed in the passage, but rather analyze how Fromm constructs an argument to persuade the reader.

ANSWER KEY

Practice Test 3

Section 1: Reading

1. **D**
2. **A**
3. **B**
4. **A**
5. **C**
6. **B**
7. **C**
8. **C**
9. **A**
10. **B**
11. **A**
12. **C**
13. **B**
14. **D**
15. **C**
16. **C**
17. **C**
18. **C**
19. **C**
20. **C**
21. **B**
22. **C**
23. **B**
24. **C**
25. **D**
26. **D**
27. **A**
28. **A**
29. **D**
30. **A**
31. **A**
32. **C**
33. **B**
34. **A**
35. **A**
36. **D**
37. **C**
38. **B**
39. **D**
40. **A**
41. **A**
42. **A**
43. **C**
44. **B**
45. **A**
46. **C**
47. **A**
48. **C**
49. **B**
50. **D**
51. **D**
52. **A**

Number Correct ______

Number Incorrect ______

Section 2: Writing and Language

1. **D**
2. **B**
3. **B**
4. **D**
5. **C**
6. **C**
7. **C**
8. **C**
9. **B**
10. **C**
11. **D**
12. **C**
13. **D**
14. **B**
15. **D**
16. **B**
17. **C**
18. **B**
19. **A**
20. **D**
21. **A**
22. **B**
23. **A**
24. **C**
25. **B**
26. **C**
27. **D**
28. **C**
29. **B**
30. **A**
31. **C**
32. **C**
33. **A**
34. **C**
35. **A**
36. **C**
37. **C**
38. **D**
39. **D**
40. **B**
41. **B**
42. **D**
43. **A**
44. **B**

Number Correct ______

Number Incorrect ______

ANSWER KEY
Practice Test 3

Section 3: Math (No Calculator)

1. **B**	5. **A**	9. **B**	13. **D**
2. **B**	6. **A**	10. **A**	14. **C**
3. **C**	7. **C**	11. **D**	15. **B**
4. **B**	8. **A**	12. **B**	

16. **200**

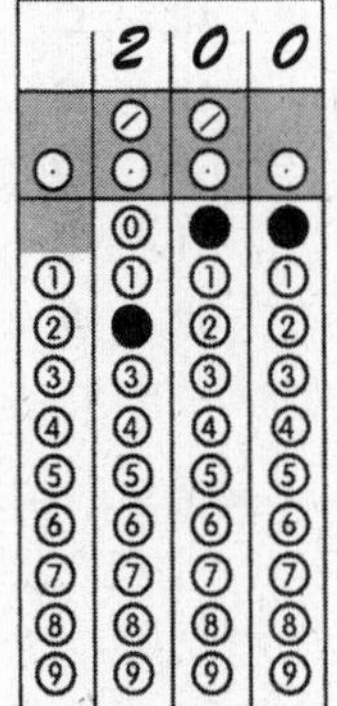

17. **3/2** or **1.5**

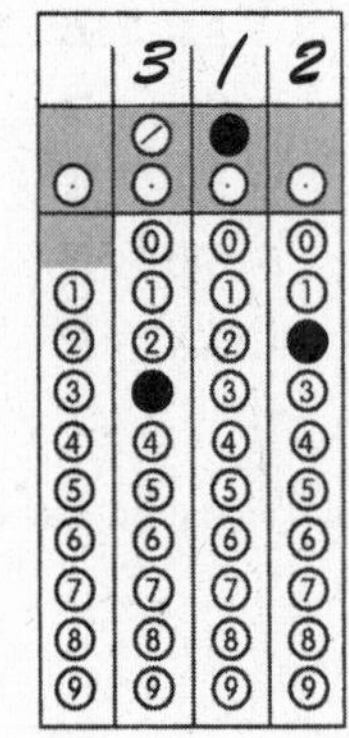

or

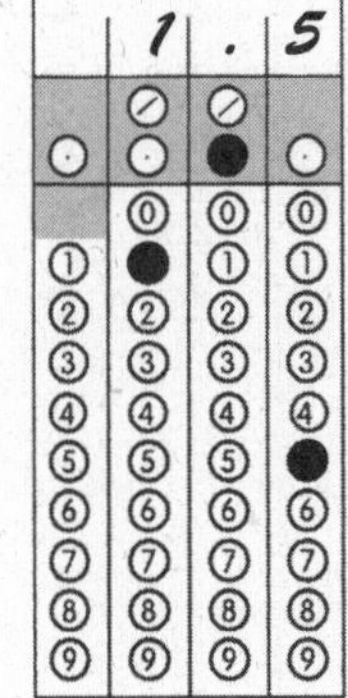

18. **5/8** or **.625**

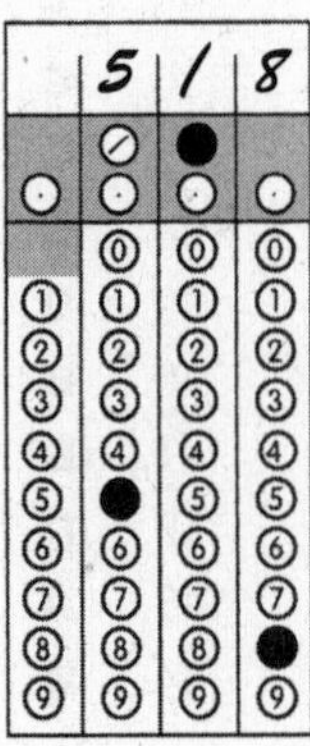

or

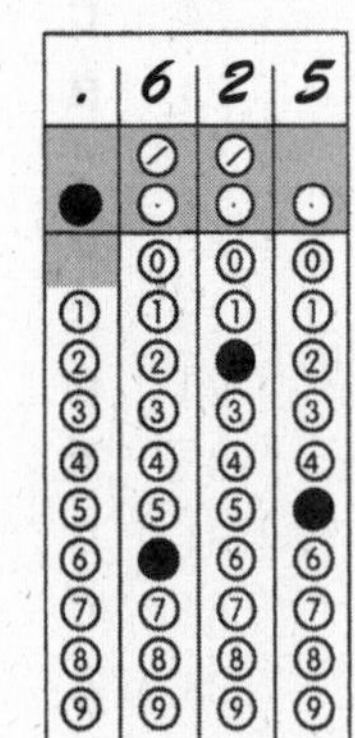

19. **9/4** or **2.25**

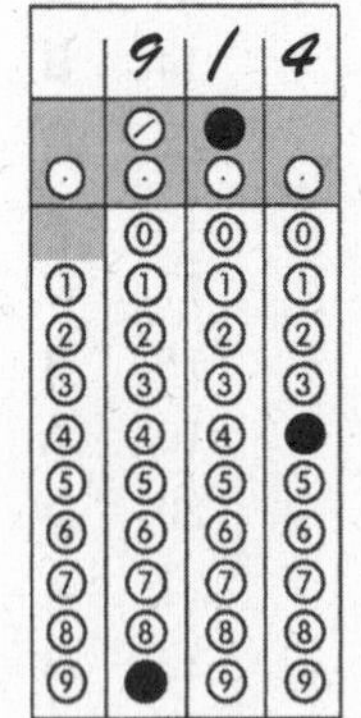

or

ANSWER KEY
Practice Test 3

20. **0**

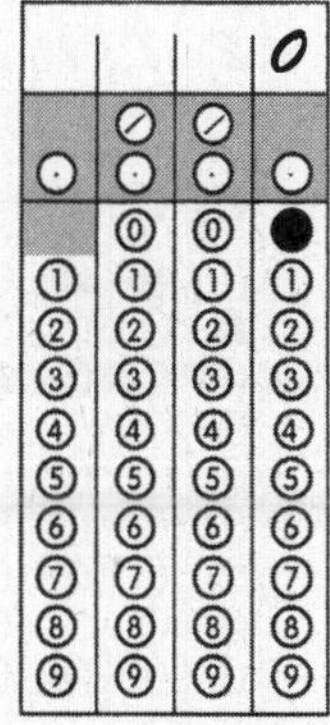

Number Correct ______

Number Incorrect ______

Section 4: Math (Calculator)

1.	**D**	7.	**B**	13.	**A**	19.	**A**	25.	**C**
2.	**D**	8.	**B**	14.	**B**	20.	**A**	26.	**A**
3.	**A**	9.	**C**	15.	**C**	21.	**C**	27.	**D**
4.	**D**	10.	**B**	16.	**A**	22.	**C**	28.	**C**
5.	**A**	11.	**A**	17.	**D**	23.	**D**	29.	**B**
6.	**C**	12.	**B**	18.	**C**	24.	**D**	30.	**A**

31. **9**

32. **.81**

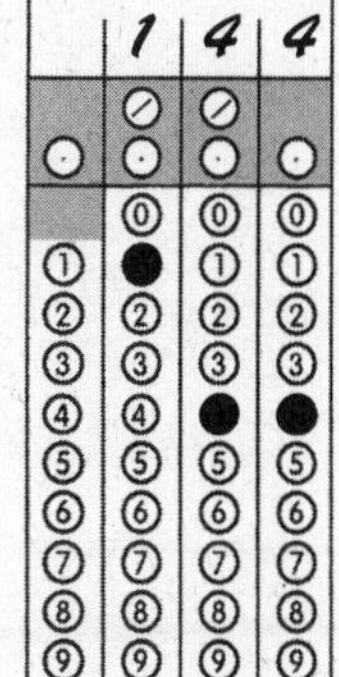

33. **144**

34. **18**

ANSWER KEY
Practice Test 3

35. **5,250**

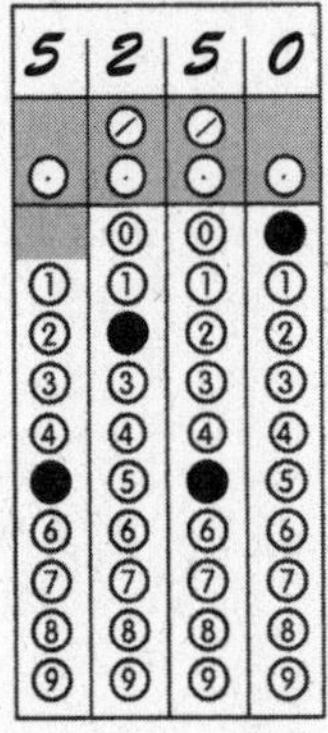

36. **24.0** or **24**

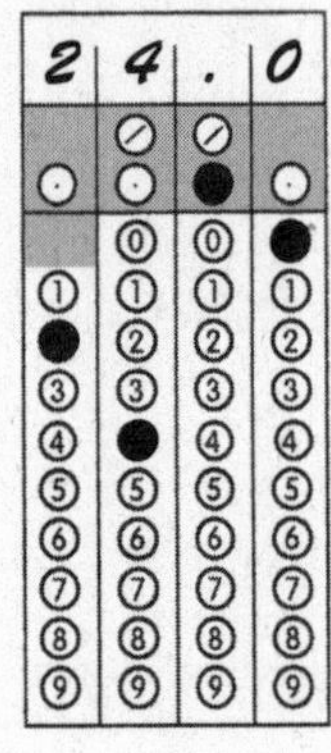

or

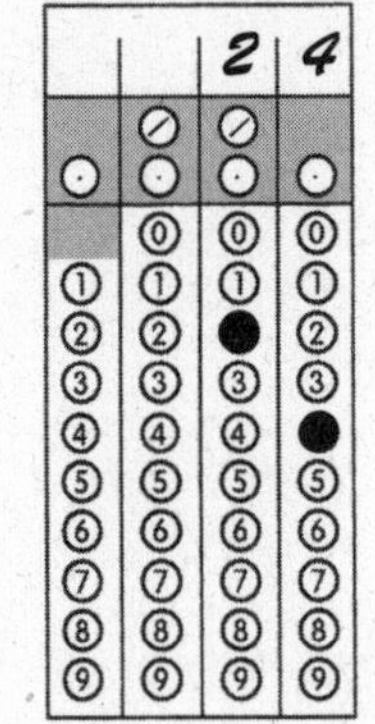

37. **2,113**

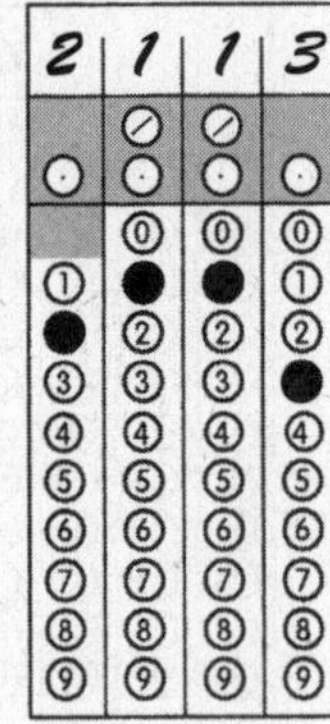

38. **8.02**

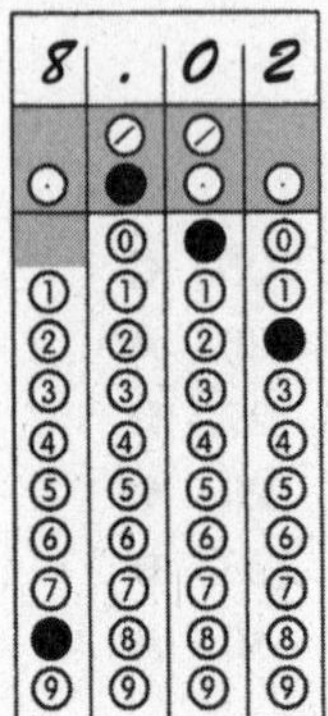

Number Correct ______

Number Incorrect ______

SCORE ANALYSIS

Reading and Writing Test

Section 1: Reading ________ = ________ (A)
correct raw score

Section 2: Writing ________ = ________ (B)
correct raw score

To find your Reading and Writing test scores, consult the chart below: find the ranges in which your raw scores lie and read across to find the ranges of your test scores.

________ + ________ = ________ (C)
range of reading test scores range of writing test scores range of reading + writing test scores

To find the range of your Reading and Writing Scaled Score, multiply (C) by 10.

Test Scores for the Reading and Writing Sections

Reading Raw Score	Writing Raw Score	Test Score
44-52	39-44	35-40
36-43	33-38	31-34
30-35	28-32	28-30
24-29	22-27	24-27
19-23	17-21	21-23
14-18	13-16	19-20
9-13	9-12	16-18
5-8	5-8	13-15
less than 5	less than 5	10-12

Math Test

Section 3: ________ = ________ (D)
correct raw score

Section 4: ________ = ________ (E)
correct raw score

Total Math raw score: (D) + (E) = ________

To find your Math Scaled Score, consult the chart below: find the range in which your raw score lies and read across to find the range for your scaled score.

Scaled Scores for the Math Test

Raw Score	Scaled Score	Raw Score	Scaled Score
50-58	700-800	20-25	450-490
44-49	650-690	15-19	400-440
38-43	600-640	11-14	350-390
32-37	550-590	7-10	300-340
26-31	500-540	less than 7	200-290

ANSWER EXPLANATIONS

Section 1: Reading Test

1. **(D)** The author says that Boers had "a dour fatalistic Old Testament religion" (lines 22–23). The word *dour* means stern and gloomy.

2. **(A)** In lines 30–34 the author is comparing Napoleon's troops with Boer soldiers, so in context this phrase refers to the fact that the Boer soldiers were harder for the British to defeat than Napoleon's troops.

3. **(B)** As discussed in lines 24–28, the author says the Boers were very difficult foes on the battlefield, so it makes sense that they would have very effective rifles. The word *inconveniently* is used humorously, referring to the word *ancient* in the phrase "ancient theology" (line 33).

4. **(A)** The author says "cold and poverty and storm are the nurses of the qualities which make for empire" (lines 65–67). Clearly he means that cold, poverty, and hardship fostered these characteristics in the Boer. In these lines he explains this: "It . . . climate" (lines 67–71).

5. **(C)** In lines 62–71 ("But it was . . . that robust climate"), the author explains why the Dutch succeeded where the Portuguese had not.

6. **(B)** Throughout the passage the writer has an admiring attitude toward the Boers. This is well illustrated in the first paragraph, in which the author describes the origin and qualities of the Boers.

7. **(C)** *Temper* in context means resilience.

8. **(C)** *Consuming* in context means "deeply felt."

9. **(A)** All of the other characteristics are either mentioned or implied. However, there is no suggestion that the modern Boers are willing to compromise.

10. **(B)** The author mainly recounts events in the course of describing the history of the Boers.

11. **(A)** *Unique* means "one of a kind." It can be inferred from the author's description of periodical cicadas that they are one of a kind.

12. **(C)** The cicada nymphs are described as *patiently* sucking the juice from the tree roots. Attributing patience to a non-human can be described as *anthropomorphic.*

13. **(B)** The likely intended audience is laypersons interested in biology because it describes an interesting theory in biology. It is a bit informal and not highly technical, so (A) can be ruled out. It is too advanced for (C) children. There is no reason to think (D) journalists in particular would be interested in it.

14. **(D)** The theory is outlined in lines 19–39.

15. **(C)** We can infer this from the theory described in lines 19–39. As described in the theory, the parasite must keep extending its life cycle to keep up with the cicada's increasing life cycle. The parasite thus must have become extinct after *Magicicada tredecim's* life cycle became 13 years.

16. **(C)** This is not true because according to the theory described in the passage the longer the cicada's life cycle is the more difficult it will be for its parasite to survive.

17. **(C)** The author says that the cicadas' best strategy for avoiding their parasites is to have a long life cycle. This contradicts the statement in choice (C) from question 16 that the parasite benefits from the fact that the cicadas have a long life cycle. Thus, (C) provides the best evidence to answer question 17.

18. **(C)** The theory explains the phenomenon very well. The fact that the parasite has not been found (line 56) suggests that it does not exist but does not provide what scientists consider to be empirical evidence because they believe that a lack of evidence should not be considered evidence.

19. **(C)** As mentioned in question 8, the fact that the parasite has not been found provides good support for the theory. The discovery of the parasite would be strong evidence against the theory, but it would not invalidate it because it is possible that the parasite survived even though it had to make it through the difficult 272-year period mentioned in line 60 without a cicada to parasitize.

20. **(C)** The passage does not cite scientific studies. It does all of the others.

21. **(B)** The phrase "for possible future uses" (line 11) signals that values (which means "uses") in the future are being referred to.

22. **(C)** "They can be continually recycled" (lines 25–26) signals that land can be used successively for an infinite number of purposes. "Does not mean they are infinite in amount" (lines 26–27) indicates that the amount of land cannot be increased.

23. **(B)** "Once dedicated, [a river system] cannot be used again without disturbing the constituencies that use its features" (lines 48–50).

24. **(C)** This provides good evidence. The sentence says that once a river system is dedicated, it cannot be used for other purposes without affecting those already using it.

25. **(D)** In context, "perverse" means *arising from obstinate persistence in an error.* The author is saying that often unsustainable resource use is encouraged by policies that continue despite evidence that they do not work.

26. **(D)** The author uses groundwater resources in the U.S. as an example of a situation in which there exist "perverse institutional or legal incentives" (lines 66–67). The phrase "use it or lose it" (line 73) immediately after "a lack of tradable rights to water" (lines 72–73) signals that the author is saying that because people can't trade water rights they have an incentive to use the water they have before others gain access to it and use it through digging wells.

27. **(A)** The author cites the example of cattle to illustrate the principle that private ownership often results in more effective conservation of resources than public ownership. We can infer that the author believes that cattle might become scarce if they were owned in common because individuals would have little incentive to care for cattle and limit the number of cattle they consume. (In fact, the author might argue that people would have an incentive to kill as many cattle as they can before others do.)

28. **(A)** The author argues throughout the passage that in many cases assigning ownership rights is the most effective way to conserve unsustainable resources. In lines 103–104

PRACTICE TEST 3

he says, "Getting the incentives right" should mean chiefly assigning property rights to environmental goods.

29. **(D)** This is the most accurate characterization of each passage.

30. **(A)** The author of Passage 1 says, "Air and water are particularly susceptible to pollutants because of the ease with which they can be used as open-access resources for receiving and disseminating waste" (lines 31–35). Thus, he would probably argue for close monitoring of the result of assigning ownership rights. In his discussion of the example of a river system, the author stresses that the various uses it is put to can have a great effect on other uses it has, on the system itself, and on things outside the system related to it. Thus, it is likely he would be concerned about the effects of the activity of one owner on the parts of the ocean owned by others.

31. **(A)** The author of Passage 1 does not discuss the value of a market-based approach, but there is no reason to think that he would rule out some use of a market-based approach if the results achieved by it were carefully monitored and the approach helped to effectively sustain renewable resources. However, he would also be likely to say that granting ownership rights cannot be the sole solution in the case of resources that have many, and often competing, uses, such as a river system. He says (in lines 60–63), "Policy for renewable . . . or irreversible loss."

32. **(C)** The author says Stephen Sondheim "zeroes in on the *essential* differences between the art of the lyricist and that of the poet" (lines 2–3) but he also says, "And yet, the line between song and poem is not as firm as Sondheim suggests" (lines 8–9).

33. **(B)** The author says, "[Blake's *Songs of Innocence* and *Songs of Experience* and Whitman's 'Song of Myself' straddle] the line between genres" (lines 14–15). He then quotes from *Songs of Innocence* and says the lines "practically [beg] to be set to music" (line 20).

34. **(A)** The author says, "Whereas poetry is aimed almost exclusively at a limited number of fellow poets, hundreds of millions of men and women listen to songs . . . " (lines 33–36).

35. **(A)** This is the best choice because it provides clear evidence for the answer to the previous question. It is reasonable to infer that material written for a small, specialized audience will have less appeal than material written for a broad audience.

36. **(D)** As it is used in line 66 "eschew" means *avoid* and "programmatically" means *following a set system.* The writer is saying that many poets follow a set system of avoiding the use of memory cues that songwriters employ.

37. **(C)** Robert Fenton is suggesting that writing students tend to be one "person"—that is, think in a certain way—when listening to music and another "person" when writing poems, and thus do not apply what they know about music to their writing of poetry.

38. **(B)** In context, "schizophrenic" refers to taste that is divided by two antagonistic qualities. We can infer that one of these qualities is a liking for rhyme, meter, and other "musical" qualities in poetry, and the other is a dislike for these qualities. A clue to the meaning is Robert Fenton's reference to "the person" in line 73 and "the same person" in line 75, suggesting a division in taste in one person.

39. **(D)** The expression "elephant in the room" is a (C) *colorful* and (A) *metaphorical* idiom meaning *an obvious truth that is being ignored.* The author's adjective "singing" is a (B) *jocular* (joking) reference to the idea that it's the music, not the lyric, that makes a person want to hear a song again. (D) *Elegiac* (related to an elegy or mourning) is the correct answer because the expression has nothing to do with an elegy or mourning.

40. **(A)** The author says, "Poets cannot rely on actual musical tones; still the poems I love . . . have a quasi-melodic structure that has an effect not unlike melody proper" (lines 93–97). The author is saying that some poems have an effect that is very similar to musical melody.

41. **(A)** In the sentence preceding the last line ("At a time . . . not be denied;" lines 105–110) the author says that poets are no longer using repetition and melody, but that songwriters continue to use these techniques, which help make their songs popular. It makes sense, therefore, that in the last sentence the author is suggesting that to become more widely popular poets should use some of the techniques of their "big sister" (line 113)—that is, songwriting.

42. **(A)** One of the author's main points is that poets can use some of the techniques of songwriters to make their poems more popular. There is nothing in the passage to suggest that the author believes that a poem cannot be both excellent and popular.

43. **(C)** In lines 17–19 the author mentions, "The region of space dominated by Saturn's magnetic field, called its magnetosphere." In lines 68–69 he mentions "our planet's powerful magnetic field."

44. **(B)** As mentioned in the explanation to the previous question, these lines tell us that the Earth and Saturn have a magnetosphere.

45. **(A)** In lines 43–44 the author mentions "A powerful outburst of solar activity," from which we can infer that the strength of the solar wind varies. Also, in lines 44–45 he mentions, "The strong surge in the solar wind."

46. **(C)** Of the choices given, this sentence provides the best evidence.

47. **(A)** The author summarizes a theory based on observations. Both the observations and the theory are elaborated upon in the rest of the passage.

48. **(C)** The possible solution discussed can be described as "elegant" because it does not require a "unique approach" (line 80) to explain Titan's response to the solar wind. Scientists typically describe an approach as elegant when it offers an ingenious solution that is simple yet can be applied to complex and varied phenomena.

49. **(B)** The arrows in the diagram depict the intense burst of solar wind compressing Saturn's normal magnetosphere so that Titan is outside of Saturn's magnetosphere.

50. **(D)** The adjective "naked" refers to the fact that sometimes Titan is not within Saturn's magnetosphere and thus is unprotected from the solar wind. Using the word *naked* instead of *unprotected* helps make the occurrence seem more dramatic, in part because Titan is also a god.

51. **(D)** The author does not use any rhetorical questions.

52. **(A)** We can infer that Titan may have a magnetic field because the author says Cassini has only observed Titan when it was within Saturn's powerful magnetosphere. The fact that a magnetic field coming from Titan has not been found does not mean it does not exist. Titan may have a magnetic field that is relatively weak and thus difficult to detect due to interference from Saturn's powerful magnetic field. The author does not mention whether Cassini looked for a magnetic field coming from Titan when Titan was outside Saturn's magnetic field, but presumably the intense solar wind that existed at this time would have made the detection of a weak magnetic field difficult.

Section 2: Writing and Language Test

1. **(D)** This is the correct choice because it creates a grammatical sentence that follows logically from the preceding sentence. In this choice "they" refers to the "Egyptian masters" in the previous sentence. Both sentences are correctly cast in the past tense. The other choices do not create grammatical sentences that make good sense.

2. **(B)** This choice creates a grammatical sentence that makes good sense. Note that the infinitive phrase "to reduce them to a system," like the preceding infinitive phrase "to tabulate those properties," is the object of the verb "troubled." None of the other choices creates a grammatical sentence.

3. **(B)** The adjective prepositional phrase "in what remains to us of their work" modifies the noun "nothing," which is the subject of the sentence. "Justifies" is the correct verb form because it agrees in number with the subject, "nothing."

4. **(D)** The past tense is correct because the sentence is describing what the pupils did in the past. "Were copied" agrees with the subject, "models," in number.

5. **(C)** In context "rendered" means "represented in drawing." This makes sense because this sentence, like the previous sentence, is describing how the students improved their ability to depict things.

6. **(C)** This is the only choice that creates a grammatical sentence. The participial phrase "having neither pencil nor stylus" modifies the noun "they," creating a clear sentence that makes good sense.

7. **(C)** This choice creates the phrasal preposition "in which," which refers to the object of the preceding prepositional phrase, "groove." A grammatical and coherent sentence is created.

8. **(C)** Choice (A) is incorrect because a semicolon can only join two independent clauses, and in this case the part of the sentence after the semicolon is not an independent clause. Choice (B) is not grammatical. Choice (D) makes little sense. Choice (C) is correct because a dash can be used to introduce additional information about a topic, which in this case is "ink." Note that the words after the dash do not have to create an independent clause as they must after a semicolon.

9. **(B)** The past tense of the verb "complete" makes good sense in context because actions in the past are being described.

10. **(C)** Past action is being described, so the past tense "squatted" is correct. A subject of the verb "squatted" is needed. Choice (B) provides this subject—"he."

11. **(D)** This is the correct choice because the context requires the phrasal verb *looked over*, which means "examined."

12. **(C)** This is the best choice because Jon *advocates* (supports) that the body is interconnected by practicing acupuncture, which is based on this idea.

13. **(D)** This is the only grammatically correct choice. It corrects the run-on sentence by creating a new sentence. Note that "it's" is the contraction of "it is."

14. **(B)** This is grammatical and makes good sense. Choice (A) and choice (C) create run-on sentences. Choice (D) is not grammatical.

15. **(D)** The present tense is correct because recommending treatment is something that Jon does regularly.

16. **(B)** This choice creates an effective sentence in which the practice of needling is clearly explained. The colon is used appropriately to set off the explanation of an important procedure.

17. **(C)** This is the only choice that creates a grammatical sentence. Choice (A) and choice (B) are incorrect because they do not create an independent clause, which is necessary before the semicolon. Choice (D) does not make sense.

18. **(B)** This choice is the best choice because it makes sense that the reason Jon gives patients an explanation of Oriental medicine is to help them understand the treatment.

19. **(A)** As mentioned in the correct answer, this sentence provides a logical link between the previous sentence and the following sentence. It describes the principle of Oriental medicine, which makes sense because in the previous sentence the writer says, "Jon usually gives a brief description of Oriental medicine." The following sentence describes how illnesses occur when the processes this principle describes are disrupted.

20. **(D)** This is the best choice because the first sentence of the paragraph says that visits to practitioners of alternative medicine increased.

21. **(A)** This is the standard expression in this context. Choice (D) is acceptable but somewhat awkward; it is also rather ambiguous because "with licenses" could mean they have a license for some other activity or field.

22. **(B)** This makes the best sense because it is an effective topic sentence for the paragraph, which is about the increasing popularity of acupuncture and other forms of traditional Oriental medicine.

23. **(A)** This is the correct answer because paragraph 1 serves as an introduction to the passage. It introduces the topic of stained glass and how it is produced. The following three paragraphs elaborate on this topic.

24. **(C)** As mentioned in the correct answer, this sentence is necessary for the sentence following it to make good sense.

25. **(B)** This is the only choice that is grammatical and makes sense. The passage is about what the author calls the "gorgeous" (line 5) stained glass of the thirteenth or fourteenth century, so it makes sense that he would describe the color effects very favorably.

26. **(C)** This is the only choice that is grammatical. The participial phrase "being built up" modifies *window*, the object of the prepositional phrase beginning with "by."

27. **(D)** Parallelism requires that the verb "fit" be in the present tense. This can be seen by looking at the two preceding verbs in the series: The artist must *choose*... [and] *cut*."

28. **(C)** In context "amuse" means "provide interesting occupation." This makes good sense because it would amuse the reader to make the calculations mentioned.

29. **(B)** This is the correct choice because it is grammatical and makes sense.

30. **(A)** The present tense is correct in context because a statement of fact is being made.

31. **(C)** The given sentence is a run-on sentence. This choice corrects the error and is the only choice that makes sense in context.

32. **(C)** *Its* is correct because the context requires the possessive form of the personal pronoun *it*. Choice (A) is incorrect because *its'* is not how the possessive form of *it* is formed. Choice (B) is incorrect because *it's* is the contracted form of *it is*, which makes no sense in context. Similarly, choice (D) is incorrect.

33. **(A)** This is the correct choice because the context requires the adverb *otherwise*, which here means "under other circumstances."

34. **(C)** This can be seen in the bar graph. The precise percentage is given on the left side of each bar.

35. **(A)** This is stated in the first paragraph of explanation of the bar graph.

36. **(C)** This is the best choice. It makes sense because only one literacy rate is given for the category "Latin America and the Caribbean," so there is no way to determine the literacy rate in each separate area.

37. **(C)** *Respectively* is used correctly to tell us that 99% applies to Central and Eastern Europe and that 100% applies to Central Asia.

38. **(D)** This is the only choice that is grammatical and makes good sense.

39. **(D)** This is the best choice because sentence 2 provides more detailed information about literacy rates in Latin America and the Caribbean, which is the subject of sentence 5.

40. **(B)** This can be seen both in the bar graph and in the paragraph in which this question appears.

41. **(B)** This information is given in the bar graph.

42. **(D)** This is the best choice in context. The first sentence of the paragraph says that literacy rates are "projected to increase in all regions." The second sentence says that Central and Eastern Europe is "an exception," so it makes sense that there are projections of "a small drop in adult literacy."

43. **(A)** The answer to this question can be arrived at by a process of elimination. Choices (B), (C), and (D) can be eliminated because the sentence says "South and West Asia is projected to *also* come below the target for 2015." This means that Sub-Saharan Africa is also predicted to come below the target.

44. **(B)** This is the only choice that makes sense in context.

Section 3: Math Test (No Calculator)

1. **(B)** If Charles interviewed everyone in town, there would be no margin of error—he would have all of the data! Therefore accepting a wider margin of error by interviewing fewer people reduces the number of surveys and the costs as well.

2. **(B)** Factor and cancel as needed.

$$-2\left(\frac{x^2-8x-180}{x+10}\right)=$$

$$-2\left(\frac{(x+10)(x-18)}{x+10}\right)=$$

$$-2(x-18)=-2x+36$$

3. **(C)** Find the value of n^2 by completing the square in $x^2 + 19x + n^2$.

Multiply 19 by $\frac{1}{2}$ and square the product.

$$x^2 + 19x + n^2 = x^2+19x+\left(\frac{19}{2}\right)^2=x^2+19x+\frac{361}{4}$$

$$n^2=\frac{361}{4}$$

Choice (B) can be eliminated at once since the denominator, 2, is not a perfect square.

4. **(B)** Brian and Richard take 5 steps apart and then Richard walks to Brian in 9 steps. The diagram below illustrates these events.

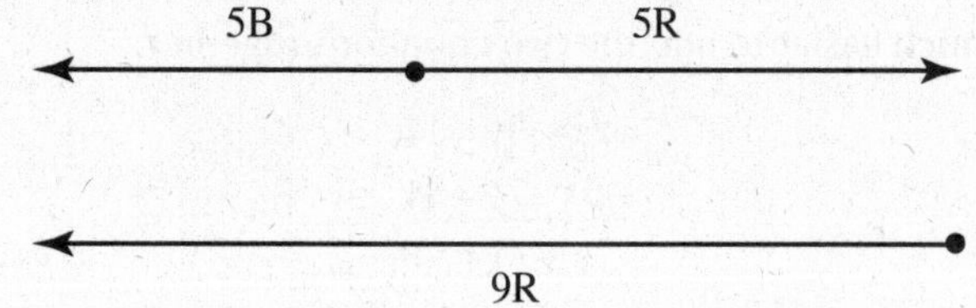

We conclude the following:

$$5R+5B=9R$$

$$5B=4R$$

$$\frac{5}{4}B=R$$

Each of Richard's steps is $\frac{5}{4}$ the size of Brian's.

5. **(A)** The prime numbers less than 25 are: 2, 3, 5, 7, 11, 13, 17, 19, 23. There are nine prime numbers less than 25, so M = 9. Find the range of this set of numbers by subtracting the lowest value from the highest.

$$23-2=21$$

The range of the numbers is 21, so $r = 21$

$$2M-r=2(9)-21=-3$$

6. **(A)** The slope of a line is found by using the formula $m = \frac{y_2 - y_1}{x_2 - x_1}$.

$$(0, 4)\ (1, 1)$$

$$\frac{1-4}{1-0} = -3$$

The line in the diagram has a slope that measures –3. Translating the line moves all the points in the same direction creating a parallel line. Parallel lines have the same slope so the translated line will also have a slope of –3.

7. **(C)** Find $f^{-1}(x)$

$$f(x) = x^3 - 7$$
$$y = x^3 - 7$$

Reverse the positions of x and y to find $f^{-1}(x)$. Then begin to solve for y.

$$x = y^3 - 7$$
$$x + 7 = y^3$$
$$\sqrt[3]{x+7} = y = f^{-1}(x)$$

Replace x with 20 in $f^{-1}(x)$.

$$f^{-1}(20) = \sqrt[3]{20+7} = 3$$

Replace x with 3 in $g(x)$.

$$g(3) = 2(3) + 5 = 11$$

8. **(A)** Although this system of equations can be solved via the substitution or elimination method, it is much easier to add the two equations together.

$$2x + 3y = 17$$
$$+\ 5x - 7y = 31$$
$$7x - 4y = 48$$

$$\frac{7x-4y}{8} = \frac{48}{8} = 6$$

9. **(B)** Factoring $16x^2 - 9y^2$ gives $(4x + 3y)(4x - 3y)$. The area of a rectangle is given by the formula Area = (length) (width) or $A = lw$. Since $4x - 3y$ is the width, $4x + 3y$ is the length. The perimeter of a rectangle is found by using perimeter = $2l + 2w$.

$$2(4x + 3y) + 2(4x - 3y) = 8x + 6y + 8x - 6y = 16x$$

10. **(A)** The intersections of two lines, parabolas, etc. are those points that satisfy both equations. In this case, the parabola $y = (x - 6)^2$ intersects the horizontal line $y = 36$. Since both equations are equal to y, set each of them equal to one another.

$$36 = (x - 6)^2$$

Solve this equation by finding the square root of each side of the equation.

$$36 = (x-6)^2$$
$$\sqrt{36} = \sqrt{(x-6)^2}$$
$$\pm 6 = x - 6$$
$$x = 12 \text{ or } x = 0$$

The points of intersection are (12, 36) and (0, 36). Although we can use the distance formula to find the distance between these two points, intuitively, they lie along the line $y = 36$. Subtract the x-coordinates to find the distance between the two points.

$$12 - 0 = 12$$

The length of AB, then, is 12.

11. **(D)** Square *EFGH* has an area that measures 64 square units which means each side is 8 units. All four of the triangles are isosceles right triangles with hypotenuse 8. Using the formula for a 45-45-90 triangle, both legs of each right triangle are therefore $4\sqrt{2}$ units. Each side of square *ABCD*, then, is $8\sqrt{2}$ units long. The formula for the area of a square is Area = s^2, where s is the measure of a side.

$$\text{Area} = s^2$$
$$\text{Area} = (8\sqrt{2})^2 = 128$$

The figures can be assumed to be to scale as there is no note indicating otherwise. We therefore can deduce square *ABCD* is larger than square *EFGH*. Thus, choices (A) 36, and (B) 64 can be immediately eliminated.

12. **(B)** A total of 8 outcomes are possible when guessing among 3 questions:
Let C = the answers guessed correctly
Let I = the answers guessed incorrectly

CCC, CCI, CIC, CII, ICC, ICI, IIC, and III

Of the 8 possible outcomes, 3 contain exactly two correct guesses (and therefore one incorrect guess). Therefore, the probability of guessing correctly on exactly two of the three questions among questions 6 through 8 is $\frac{3}{8}$.

13. **(D)** Substitute $4x$ for y in $2x^2 + y^2 = 360$.

$$2x^2 + (4x)^2 = 360$$
$$2x^2 + 16x^2 = 360$$
$$18x^2 = 360$$
$$x^2 = 20$$

14. **(C)** Divide both sides of the equation by 2, the *GCF* of $2x^2 + 8x - 12$.

$$(2x^2 + 8x - 12) \div 2 = 0 \div 2$$
$$x^2 + 4x - 6 = 0$$

The equation does not factor so solve by using the quadratic equation.

$$x = \frac{-b \pm \sqrt{b^2 - 4ac}}{2a}$$

$$a = 1 \quad b = 4 \quad c = -6$$

$$x = \frac{-4 \pm \sqrt{(4)^2 - 4(1)(-6)}}{2(1)}$$

$$x = \frac{-4 \pm \sqrt{40}}{2}$$

$$x = \frac{-4 \pm 2\sqrt{10}}{2}$$

$$x = -2 \pm \sqrt{10}$$

15. **(B)**

$$(ax - 7)(bx + 5) = 6x^2 + cx - 35$$

Solve for a or b in $a - b = -1$ and create a system of equations.

$$a - b = -1 \text{ so } a = b - 1$$

Substitute $b - 1$ for a in $ab = 6$.

$$(b - 1)b = 6$$
$$b^2 - b = 6$$
$$b^2 - b - 6 = 0$$

Factor and solve for b.

$$(b + 2)(b - 3) = 0$$
$$b + 2 = 0 \text{ or } b - 3 = 0$$
$$b = -2 \text{ or } b = 3$$

Find a when $b = 3$ or $b = -2$.

$$ab = 6$$
$$3a = 6$$
$$a = 2$$

When $b = 3$ $a = 2$

$$ab = 6$$
$$-2a = 6$$
$$a = -3$$

When $b = -2$ $a = -3$

Solve for c when a and b are 2 and 3, respectively.

$$(2x - 7)(3x + 5) = 6x^2 - 11x - 35$$
$$c = -11$$

Solve for c when a and b are -3 and -2, respectively.

$$(-3x - 7)(-2x + 5) = 6x^2 - x - 35$$
$$c = -1$$

You only have to solve for one of the values of c. Choice (B) is the only one that has either of the correct solutions to the question.

16. **200** Let x = the number of miles for the two trailer rental costs to be equal.

$$40 + 0.20x = 30 + 0.25x$$
$$40 + 0.20x - 0.20x = 30 + 0.25x - 0.20x$$
$$40 = 30 + 0.05x$$
$$10 = 0.05x$$
$$200 = x$$

17. **$\frac{3}{2}$ or 1.5** The graph of an absolute value function is in the form $f(x) = a|x - h| + k$ where (h, k) is the vertex. In the function $f(x) = -2|x - m| + n$, $m = h$ and $n = k$. The graph shows the vertex is $(3, -2)$ so $m = 3$ and $n = -2$. Therefore, $-mn^{-1} = -(3)\left(-\frac{1}{2}\right) = \frac{3}{2}$.

18. $\frac{5}{8}$ **or .625** By the complementary angle relationship for sine and cosine, $\sin(x°) = \cos(90° - x°)$. Therefore, $\cos(90° - x°) = \frac{5}{8}$.

Either the fraction $\frac{5}{8}$ or its decimal equivalent, .625 may be gridded in as the correct answer.

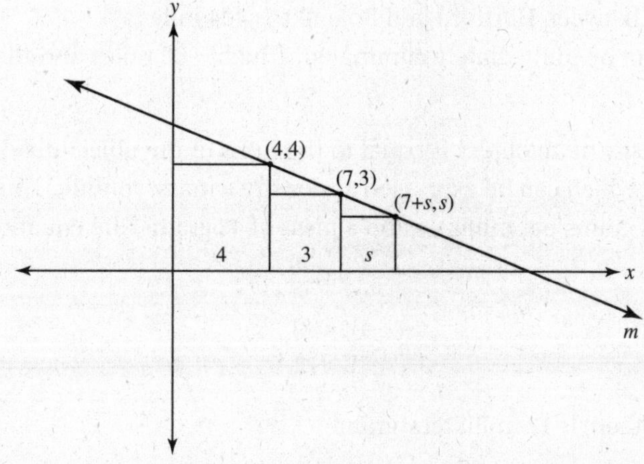

19. $\frac{9}{4}$ **or 2.25** Using the first two points of line *m*, we get the slope is $\frac{3-4}{7-4} = -\frac{1}{3}$. Using the second and third points we get the slope as $\frac{s-3}{(7+s)-7} = \frac{s-3}{s}$. Since $\frac{s-3}{s} = -\frac{1}{3}$, cross-multiply and solve for *s*.

$$\frac{s-3}{s} = -\frac{1}{3}$$
$$s(-1) = (3)(s - 3)$$
$$-s = 3s - 9$$
$$4s = 9$$
$$s = \frac{9}{4} \text{ or } 2.25$$

20. **0** Replace *n* with 1 in *r*(*n*).

$$(1 - 7)(2 - 7)(3 - 7)(4 - 7)(5 - 7)(6 - 7)(7 - 7)\ldots$$

The function progresses to 7 – 7, which equals 0. The product of 0 and any other number is 0.

Section 4: Math Test (Calculator)

1. **(D)** Let *x* equal the number of movies rented by Warren in the past month.

$$2.25x + 4 = 24.25$$
$$2.25x = 20.25$$

Divide both sides of the equation by 2.25.

$$\frac{2.25x}{2.25} = \frac{20.25}{2.25}$$
$$x = 9$$

2. **(D)** Use the proportion $\frac{\text{map distance}}{\text{actual distance}} = \frac{\text{map distance}}{\text{actual distance}}$ to answer the question.

$$\frac{1}{80} = \frac{5.05}{d}$$
$$1 \times d = 80 \times 5.05$$
$$d = 404$$

The distance between Hartford and Roanoke is 404 miles.
Choice (A) can be immediately eliminated; 1 inch = 80 miles and the map shows 5.05 inches.

3. **(A)** The density of an object is equal to the mass of the object divided by the volume of the object, which can be expressed as density = mass/volume. Thus, if an object has a density of 4 grams per milliliter and a mass of 48 grams, the equation becomes:

$$4 = \frac{48}{V}$$
$$4V = 48$$
$$V = 12$$

The volume, then, is 12 milliliters/gram.

4. **(D)** If 1 in 8 callers were solicited for the survey, then one-eighth of the callers were asked to participate. Thus, one-eighth of 400 callers is 50 callers. Since 20% of the callers consented to the survey, then 80% did not want to take part. Find 80% of 50 by multiplying 50 by .8.

$$50 \times .8 = 40$$

5. **(A)** Begin to isolate b_1 by multiplying the area formula by 2.

$$A = \frac{1}{2}(h)(b_1 + b_2)$$
$$(2)A = \frac{1}{2}(h)(b_1 + b_2)(2)$$
$$2A = (h)(b_1 + b_2)$$

Divide both sides of the equation by h, the height of the trapezoid.

$$\frac{2A}{h} = \frac{(h)(b_1 + b_2)}{h}$$
$$\frac{2A}{h} = b_1 + b_2$$

Subtract b_2 from both sides of the equation.

$$\frac{2A}{h} - b_2 = b_1$$

6. **(C)** Since the number of classes the student took is unknown, let x equal that value. Adding the monthly cost we get the following equation:

$$5.75x + 11.50 = 51.75$$

Subtract 11.50 from both sides.

$$5.75x + 11.50 - 11.50 = 51.75 - 11.50$$
$$5.75x = 40.25$$

Divide each side of the equation by 5.75 to isolate x.

$$5.75x \div 5.75 = 40.25 \div 5.75$$
$$x = 7$$

7. **(B)** Solve $2p - 4 \geq 6$ and assess its least value.

$$2p - 4 + 4 \geq 6 + 4$$
$$2p \geq 10$$
$$p \geq 5$$

Substitute 5 into the expression $2p + 4$ to calculate its least value.

$$2(5) + 4 = 14$$

8. **(B)** Use the distance formula to find the distance from the center to point A.

$$d = \sqrt{(x_1 - x_2)^2 + (y_1 - y_2)^2}$$
$$d = \sqrt{(4-7)^2 + (-2-3)^2} = \sqrt{34}$$

The formula for the area of a circle is $A = \pi r^2$. Replace r with $\sqrt{34}$ to find the area of the circle.

$$A = \pi(\sqrt{34})^2 = 34\pi$$

9. **(C)** The greatest drop, as a percentage, occurred between years 4 and 5.

Year 4: \$20
Year 5: \$5

Use the formula $\frac{\text{decrease}}{\text{original}} = \frac{n}{100}$ to find the percent decrease.

$$\frac{15}{20} = \frac{n}{100}$$
$$20n = 1{,}500$$
$$n = 75\%$$

10. **(B)** In year 3, the internet plan price was \$50. In year 4, the plan price decreased to \$20.

$$50 - 20 = 30$$

11. **(A)** Stack the equations vertically.

$$4a - 3b = 12$$
$$6a + 8b = 17$$

Although the system of equations can be solved via the substitution or elimination methods, it is easier to simply add the two equations.

$$\begin{array}{r} 4a - 3b = 12 \\ +\ 6a + 8b = 17 \\ \hline 10a + 5b = 29 \end{array}$$

Divide the sum by 5.

$$\frac{10a}{5} + \frac{5b}{5} = \frac{29}{5}$$
$$2a + b = \frac{29}{5}$$

12. **(B)** Let m equal the number of miles. Multiply m by the cost per mile, and add the fixed charge of $1.50 per transaction.

$$.55m + 1.50$$

This amount can be no more than $11 since that is all the money that Mustafa has.

$$.55m + 1.50 \leq 11$$

Choices (C) and (D) can immediately be eliminated as they express inequalities permitting costs no lower than $11. Mustafa has only $11 to spend.

13. **(A)** Because Pham surveyed a random sample of the students in her school, her sample was representative of the entire high school. Thus, the percent of students in the entire high school expected to prefer starting a 4H Club is appropriately estimated by the percent of students who preferred it in the sample, 31.5%. Thus, of the 1,145 students in the high school, approximately $1,145 \times 0.315 = 360.7$ students would be expected to prefer starting the 4H Club. Of the choices given, this is closest to 360.

14. **(B)** Although the number of students cited for texting while driving is reduced slightly as higher fees are levied, a line of best fit would show only a mild negative slope. Thus, there is a weak negative correlation between higher fines and the number of students cited for texting while driving.

15. **(C)** It has been shown that increasing the cost of a texting citation has only a modest impact on the number of citations issued. Some other plan is needed to decrease the number of offenders. Perhaps a series of commercials showing the traffic fatalities caused by texters would enhance the program to reduce texting while driving.

16. **(A)** The quantity of the product supplied to the public is modeled by the function $S(x) = \frac{3}{5}x + 60$. If the price of the product is increased by $15, the function becomes $S(x + 15) = \frac{3}{5}(x + 15) + 60$. To find the impact of increasing the price of the product by $15, subtract $S(x)$ from $S(x + 15)$.

$$S(x + 15) = \frac{3}{5}x + 9 + 60$$

$$= \frac{3}{5}x + 69$$

$$S(x) = \frac{3}{5}x + 60$$

$$S(x + 15) - S(x) = \left(\frac{3}{5}x + 69\right) - \left(\frac{3}{5}x + 60\right) = 9$$

An increase of $15 in the price of the product yields an increase of 9 units of the product that is supplied to the public.

17. **(D)**

$$S(x) = \frac{3}{5}x + 60$$
$$D(x) = 240 - x$$

To find the price of the product in which its demand equals supply, set the supply and demand functions equal to one another and solve for x.

$$\frac{3}{5}x + 60 = 240 - x$$
$$\frac{8}{5}x = 180$$
$$x = \$112.50$$

Choices (A), (B), and (C) yield prices in which the supply and demand functions are not equal.

18. **(C)** Of the runners who placed in the top 40, 6 were in the age group of 30 to 39. One runner in that age group finished in the top 10 and 5 others finished somewhere in places between 11 and 40. Divide 6 by 40 to get .15 which, when expressed as a percent, is 15%.

19. **(A)** The number of runners under 20 years of age who placed in positions 11 through 40 was 11. Given that the total number of runners in that age group was 18, the percent who finished in places 11 through 40 is 61.1%. The number of runners between the ages of 40 and 49 who also finished in places 11 through 40 was 3. Given that a total of 35 runners were in this category, the percent of those runners who finished in places 11 through 40 was 8.6%. The difference between 61.1% and 8.6% is 52.5%.

20. **(A)** Using the values chart, note that when $x = 2$, $g(2) = 5$. Now, check the $h(x)$ values chart for $x = 5$. We find $h(5) = 24$. Therefore, $h(g(2)) = 24$.

21. **(C)** Solve each absolute value equation:

$$|m - 3| = 12$$

Therefore:

$$m - 3 = 12 \text{ or } m - 3 = -12$$
$$m = 15 \text{ or } m = -9$$

Therefore:

$$|n + 7| = 22$$
$$n + 7 = 22 \text{ or } n + 7 = -22$$
$$n = 15 \text{ or } n = -29$$

Since m and n are both less than 0, select –9 and –29 for m and n, respectively.

$$m - n = -9 - (-29) = 20$$

22. **(C)** The mariner is borrowing \$6,500, which is 6.5 increments of \$1,000. At 36 payments with a rate of 10%, the cost is \$32.27 per \$1,000. Multiply 6.5 by \$32.27 to find the monthly payment.

$$\$32.27 \times 6.5 = \$209.76$$

23. **(D)** In order to maximize the amount that can be spent on a boat, the mariner must find the lowest payment per $1,000 loaned. At a rate of 5% for 60 months, the cost per $1,000 is $18.87. Divide $300 by $18.87 to find the most that can be spent on a sailboat.

$$\$300 \div \$18.87 = \$15.898$$
$$15.898 \times \$1{,}000 = \$15{,}898$$

The closest answer is choice (D), $15,000.

24. **(D)** Convert everything into yards.

$$3 \text{ inches} = .08 \text{ yards}$$
$$10 \text{ foot radius} = 3.33 \text{ yards}$$
$$\pi = 3.14$$

Use the formula $V = \pi r^2 h$, the volume of a cylinder, to determine how much rock is needed if 3.33 yards is the radius and .08 yards is the height.

$$3.14 \times 3.33^2 \times .08 = 3.14 \times 11.09 \times .08 = 2.79 \text{ cubic yards}$$

Rounding to the nearest cubic yard, the homeowners must purchase 3 cubic yards of rock.

$$3 \text{ cubic yards} \times \$80 = \$240$$

25. **(C)** Whether the rows contained 4, 5, or 6 boys, the last row was always one short. Suppose the number of boys in the group is r, then $r + 1$ would be the quantity that is divisible by 4, 5, and 6. Find the least common multiple of 4, 5, and 6 and set the value equal to $r + 1$.
The least common multiple of 4, 5, and 6 is 60, so $r + 1 = 60$. Therefore, r must be 59, the least number of boys that could be in the Boy Scout troop.

26. **(A)** Find the sum of the cards by multiplying the mean by the number of cards:

$$7 \times 14 = 98$$

To maximize the value of a single card, minimize the value of the other cards by assigning each a value of 1:

$$1 + 1 + 1 + 1 + 1 + 1 + 92 = 98$$

27. **(D)** Use a proportion to find the length of the proposed amphitheater in the downtown cultural center. This operation can be facilitated by approximating the length in decimal form.
$\frac{1+\sqrt{5}}{2}$:1 is approximately equal to 1.62 : 1. Use this ratio substituting 87 for the width.

$$\frac{1.62}{1} = \frac{x}{87}$$

Cross-multiply and solve for x.

$$x = (1.62)(87) = 140.94$$

140.94 rounded to the nearest meter is 141.
Choice (A) can be eliminated quickly (and possibly choice (B) as well). Once it is determined that the golden ratio is about 1.62:1, 211 would surely seem more than twice as large as 87.

28. **(C)** Use the BMI formula with the provided data to assess the patient's BMI number. Remember to convert the height to inches: 5 feet 10 inches equals 70 inches.

$$\frac{182}{70^2} \times 703 = 26.11$$

A patient with a BMI of 26.11 is classified as overweight.

29. **(B)** Use the BMI formula using the provided data to assess the patient's BMI weight. Remember to convert the height to inches: 6 feet equals 72 inches. The lowest BMI categorized as obese is 30.0.
Let x = the patient's weight.

$$\frac{x}{72^2} \times 703 = 30$$
$$.136x = 30$$
$$x \approx 221$$

30. **(A)** Find the volume of the tank by multiplying its length by its width and depth.

$$100 \times 60 \times 40 = 240{,}000 \text{ cm}^3$$

The tilted tank in the diagram demonstrates that the water in the aquarium represents $\frac{1}{4}$ of the tank's volume. Therefore the volume of the water is $\left(\frac{1}{4}\right)(240{,}000) = 60{,}000$ cm^3. Once the tank is replaced on its horizontal axis we find the width is still 60 cm, the length is still 100 cm but the water's height is unknown. Let x = the height of the water in the tank and replace the volume with 60,000.

$$(100)(60)(x) = 60{,}000$$
$$6{,}000x = 60{,}000$$
$$x = 10$$

31. **9** A system of equations yields an infinite number of solutions when the equations are equivalent. For example:

$$x + y = 6$$
$$2x + 2y = 12$$

has infinite solutions because

$$(2x + 2y = 12) \div 2 = x + y = 6$$

Dividing, we get:

$$-\frac{21}{2}y \div -7y = 1.5$$
$$\frac{111}{4} \div \frac{37}{2} = 1.5$$

Each term in the second equation is 1.5 times the corresponding term in the first equation. The value of a is 9 because $6 \times 1.5 = 9$.

32. **.81** Find the probability that the student selected is an eighth-grade girl and subtract that value from 1.0.

$$\frac{\text{eighth-grade girl}}{\text{all students}} = \frac{215}{1142} = .188$$

Subtract .188 from 1.0 to find the probability that the student selected is not an eighth-grade girl.

$$1.0 - .188 = .812$$

The answer, .812, rounds to .81.

33. **144** The profit function, $P(x) = -.08x^2 + 23.1x + 500$, is a parabola that opens down. The vertex is a maximum with the x-coordinate representing the most profitable number of chairs to manufacture. Find the x-coordinate by using the formula for finding the axis of symmetry, $x = -\frac{b}{2a}$.

$$a = -.08 \quad b = 23.1$$

$$x = -\frac{23.1}{2(-.08)} = 144.375 \approx 144$$

34. **18** Solve for x by changing each base to 3.

$$\left(\frac{1}{3}\right)^{x-2} = (27)^{3-x}$$

$$(3^{-1})^{x-2} = (3^3)^{3-x}$$

$$-x + 2 = 9 - 3x$$

$$-7 = -2x$$

$$\frac{7}{2} = x$$

or

$$3.5 = x$$

Substitute 3.5 for x in $2x + 11$.

$$(2)(3.5) + 11 = 18$$

35. **5,250 pounds** Find the weight of the three cars currently crossing the bridge. Subtract that sum from 15,000, the carrying capacity of the bridge. Since the average weight of the three cars is 3,250 pounds, multiply that value by 3 to find the weight of all three.

$$3 \times 3{,}250 = 9{,}750$$

Subtract 9,750 from 15,000 to find the maximum allowable weight for a fourth car or truck.

$$15{,}000 - 9{,}750 = 5{,}250$$

36. **24.0** or **24** Find the volume of the pyramid using the formula $V = \frac{1}{3}Bh$, where B is the base area of the pyramid and h is its height.
Use the formula Area = (length)(width) to find the base area.

$$\text{Area} = 6 \times 8 = 48 \text{ square feet}$$

Replace B with 48 in the volume formula.

$$V = \left(\frac{1}{3}\right)(48)(12) = 192$$

The pyramid has a volume that measures 192 cubic feet. Since each cubic foot weighs 4 ounces, multiply 192 by 4 to find its weight in ounces.

$$192 \times 4 = 768.$$

Divide 768 by 16, the number of ounces in a pound, to find the weight of the pyramid in pounds.

$$768 \div 16 = 48$$

Multiply 48 by .50 to find the cost for the Styrofoam to make the pyramid.

$$48 \times \$.50 = \$24.00$$

37. **2,113** Replace $W(h)$ with 50 and h with 22,000 in $W(h) = m\left(\frac{4000}{4000+h}\right)^2$

$$50 = m\left(\frac{4000}{26000}\right)^2$$

$$50 = m\left(\frac{2}{13}\right)^2$$

$$\left(\frac{169}{4}\right)50 = m\left(\frac{\cancel{4}}{\cancel{169}}\right)\left(\frac{\cancel{169}}{\cancel{4}}\right)$$

$$2{,}112.5 = m$$

The question asks to round to the nearest pound, so the answer is 2,113 pounds.

38. **8.02** Substitute Susan's sea level weight, 120 pounds, for m and her weight in the jet, $W(h)$ with 119.5.

$$119.5 = 120\left(\frac{4000}{4000+h}\right)^2$$

Divide both sides of the equation by 120.

$$.996 = \left(\frac{4000}{4000+h}\right)^2$$

Find the square root of both sides of the equation.

$$.998 = \frac{4000}{4000+h}$$

Begin to solve for h.

$$.998(4000 + h) = 4{,}000$$

$$3{,}992 + .998h = 4{,}000$$

$$.998h = 8$$

$$h = 8.02$$

Section 5: Essay (Optional)

SUGGESTED ESSAY TEST 3

Following is an essay written in response to the prompt. It is unlikely that you would be able to write such a full response in the time allowed, so don't worry if your essay is significantly shorter. Use the suggested essay to see how the task might be approached. For practice, you may wish to rewrite your own essay incorporating some of the points discussed in it.

The introductory material says that the passage is from a book. Evidently this passage is from a continuation of an exposition by Erich Fromm on "modern man's feeling of isolation and powerlessness" (as stated in the first sentence). This passage focuses on "the character all human relationships have assumed" and how they have, in the author's view, increased man's "feeling of isolation and powerlessness."

Fromm carefully organizes his points through the use of paragraphs. The first paragraph introduces, in the second sentence, the focus of the rest of the passage: how human relationships have "assumed a spirit of manipulation and instrumentality." The remainder of the first paragraph is about the modern relationship between competitors. The second paragraph discusses changed relationships between employer and employee, businessman and customer, and manufacturer and product, while the third paragraph focuses on "the individual's relationship to his own self."

Another device Fromm uses to organize—and also reinforce—his points is the repetition of a key word, "instrumentality," which is used five times. This word helps unify the passage because it is the key concept running through his argument—that people have become for each other, in effect, "things" to be used to achieve desired ends.

Let us examine Fromm's argument more closely. As just mentioned, the key unifying idea of the piece is "instrumentality." Fromm's thesis is that the primacy of the market economy in modern life makes it necessary for people to treat, to an unprecedented extent, other people as things to be used for economic gain. Fromm supports this contention by citing the relationships between people engaged in various economic activities. A criticism of this argument that can be made is that he does not give many examples in his comparison of present human economic relationships to those in the past. Were such relationships really so different in the past? He does provide the example of the "medieval artisan" as someone who was "primarily interested in what he produce[d]." However, it can be pointed out that there are still quite a few craftsmen who take pride in their work and in what they produce. It should be noted that Fromm qualifies his assertion about the modern manufacturer with the words "primarily" and "essentially," which acknowledges the fact that the issue is a matter of degree, not one that is all or nothing.

In the final paragraph Fromm turns to the subject of man's relationship to himself in the modern market economy. The main idea is well expressed in this carefully crafted sentence, which uses parallel structure and the repetition of key words—sells, himself, commodity/commodities: "Man not only sells commodities, he sells himself and feels himself to be a commodity." Here, I believe, Fromm's argument is the most convincing. Especially effective is the description of how people must take on various "personalities" to be successful in the modern market economy: "he should have energy, initiative, this, that, or the other." The words "this, that, or the other" are somewhat sarcastic and convincingly convey the idea that the qualities a person takes on are superficial and unimportant in themselves.

Also persuasive is the argument after this that modern man depends heavily on the popularity he gains from his personality. This is neatly expressed: "If he is sought after, he is somebody; if he is not popular, he is simply nobody." Fromm emphasizes the contrast here by using two independent clauses beginning with "if," joined by a semicolon. Note the contrasting ending words "somebody" and "nobody."

In conclusion, this is a thought-provoking passage that emphasizes one side of an issue with a considerable degree of effectiveness. It has been carefully constructed, through organization, sentence structure, word choice, and other devices, to persuade the reader of the validity of the claims made.

Refer to the SAT Essay Rubric on page 23 to analyze and score your essay response. For further guidance on this essay and additional practice and evaluation by teacher and author Philip Geer, contact *info@mentaurs.com*.

ANSWER SHEET
Practice Test 4

Section 1: Reading

1. Ⓐ Ⓑ Ⓒ Ⓓ	14. Ⓐ Ⓑ Ⓒ Ⓓ	27. Ⓐ Ⓑ Ⓒ Ⓓ	40. Ⓐ Ⓑ Ⓒ Ⓓ
2. Ⓐ Ⓑ Ⓒ Ⓓ	15. Ⓐ Ⓑ Ⓒ Ⓓ	28. Ⓐ Ⓑ Ⓒ Ⓓ	41. Ⓐ Ⓑ Ⓒ Ⓓ
3. Ⓐ Ⓑ Ⓒ Ⓓ	16. Ⓐ Ⓑ Ⓒ Ⓓ	29. Ⓐ Ⓑ Ⓒ Ⓓ	42. Ⓐ Ⓑ Ⓒ Ⓓ
4. Ⓐ Ⓑ Ⓒ Ⓓ	17. Ⓐ Ⓑ Ⓒ Ⓓ	30. Ⓐ Ⓑ Ⓒ Ⓓ	43. Ⓐ Ⓑ Ⓒ Ⓓ
5. Ⓐ Ⓑ Ⓒ Ⓓ	18. Ⓐ Ⓑ Ⓒ Ⓓ	31. Ⓐ Ⓑ Ⓒ Ⓓ	44. Ⓐ Ⓑ Ⓒ Ⓓ
6. Ⓐ Ⓑ Ⓒ Ⓓ	19. Ⓐ Ⓑ Ⓒ Ⓓ	32. Ⓐ Ⓑ Ⓒ Ⓓ	45. Ⓐ Ⓑ Ⓒ Ⓓ
7. Ⓐ Ⓑ Ⓒ Ⓓ	20. Ⓐ Ⓑ Ⓒ Ⓓ	33. Ⓐ Ⓑ Ⓒ Ⓓ	46. Ⓐ Ⓑ Ⓒ Ⓓ
8. Ⓐ Ⓑ Ⓒ Ⓓ	21. Ⓐ Ⓑ Ⓒ Ⓓ	34. Ⓐ Ⓑ Ⓒ Ⓓ	47. Ⓐ Ⓑ Ⓒ Ⓓ
9. Ⓐ Ⓑ Ⓒ Ⓓ	22. Ⓐ Ⓑ Ⓒ Ⓓ	35. Ⓐ Ⓑ Ⓒ Ⓓ	48. Ⓐ Ⓑ Ⓒ Ⓓ
10. Ⓐ Ⓑ Ⓒ Ⓓ	23. Ⓐ Ⓑ Ⓒ Ⓓ	36. Ⓐ Ⓑ Ⓒ Ⓓ	49. Ⓐ Ⓑ Ⓒ Ⓓ
11. Ⓐ Ⓑ Ⓒ Ⓓ	24. Ⓐ Ⓑ Ⓒ Ⓓ	37. Ⓐ Ⓑ Ⓒ Ⓓ	50. Ⓐ Ⓑ Ⓒ Ⓓ
12. Ⓐ Ⓑ Ⓒ Ⓓ	25. Ⓐ Ⓑ Ⓒ Ⓓ	38. Ⓐ Ⓑ Ⓒ Ⓓ	51. Ⓐ Ⓑ Ⓒ Ⓓ
13. Ⓐ Ⓑ Ⓒ Ⓓ	26. Ⓐ Ⓑ Ⓒ Ⓓ	39. Ⓐ Ⓑ Ⓒ Ⓓ	52. Ⓐ Ⓑ Ⓒ Ⓓ

Section 2: Writing and Language

1. Ⓐ Ⓑ Ⓒ Ⓓ	12. Ⓐ Ⓑ Ⓒ Ⓓ	23. Ⓐ Ⓑ Ⓒ Ⓓ	34. Ⓐ Ⓑ Ⓒ Ⓓ
2. Ⓐ Ⓑ Ⓒ Ⓓ	13. Ⓐ Ⓑ Ⓒ Ⓓ	24. Ⓐ Ⓑ Ⓒ Ⓓ	35. Ⓐ Ⓑ Ⓒ Ⓓ
3. Ⓐ Ⓑ Ⓒ Ⓓ	14. Ⓐ Ⓑ Ⓒ Ⓓ	25. Ⓐ Ⓑ Ⓒ Ⓓ	36. Ⓐ Ⓑ Ⓒ Ⓓ
4. Ⓐ Ⓑ Ⓒ Ⓓ	15. Ⓐ Ⓑ Ⓒ Ⓓ	26. Ⓐ Ⓑ Ⓒ Ⓓ	37. Ⓐ Ⓑ Ⓒ Ⓓ
5. Ⓐ Ⓑ Ⓒ Ⓓ	16. Ⓐ Ⓑ Ⓒ Ⓓ	27. Ⓐ Ⓑ Ⓒ Ⓓ	38. Ⓐ Ⓑ Ⓒ Ⓓ
6. Ⓐ Ⓑ Ⓒ Ⓓ	17. Ⓐ Ⓑ Ⓒ Ⓓ	28. Ⓐ Ⓑ Ⓒ Ⓓ	39. Ⓐ Ⓑ Ⓒ Ⓓ
7. Ⓐ Ⓑ Ⓒ Ⓓ	18. Ⓐ Ⓑ Ⓒ Ⓓ	29. Ⓐ Ⓑ Ⓒ Ⓓ	40. Ⓐ Ⓑ Ⓒ Ⓓ
8. Ⓐ Ⓑ Ⓒ Ⓓ	19. Ⓐ Ⓑ Ⓒ Ⓓ	30. Ⓐ Ⓑ Ⓒ Ⓓ	41. Ⓐ Ⓑ Ⓒ Ⓓ
9. Ⓐ Ⓑ Ⓒ Ⓓ	20. Ⓐ Ⓑ Ⓒ Ⓓ	31. Ⓐ Ⓑ Ⓒ Ⓓ	42. Ⓐ Ⓑ Ⓒ Ⓓ
10. Ⓐ Ⓑ Ⓒ Ⓓ	21. Ⓐ Ⓑ Ⓒ Ⓓ	32. Ⓐ Ⓑ Ⓒ Ⓓ	43. Ⓐ Ⓑ Ⓒ Ⓓ
11. Ⓐ Ⓑ Ⓒ Ⓓ	22. Ⓐ Ⓑ Ⓒ Ⓓ	33. Ⓐ Ⓑ Ⓒ Ⓓ	44. Ⓐ Ⓑ Ⓒ Ⓓ

ANSWER SHEET
Practice Test 4

Section 3: Math (No Calculator)

1. Ⓐ Ⓑ Ⓒ Ⓓ
2. Ⓐ Ⓑ Ⓒ Ⓓ
3. Ⓐ Ⓑ Ⓒ Ⓓ
4. Ⓐ Ⓑ Ⓒ Ⓓ
5. Ⓐ Ⓑ Ⓒ Ⓓ
6. Ⓐ Ⓑ Ⓒ Ⓓ
7. Ⓐ Ⓑ Ⓒ Ⓓ
8. Ⓐ Ⓑ Ⓒ Ⓓ
9. Ⓐ Ⓑ Ⓒ Ⓓ
10. Ⓐ Ⓑ Ⓒ Ⓓ
11. Ⓐ Ⓑ Ⓒ Ⓓ
12. Ⓐ Ⓑ Ⓒ Ⓓ
13. Ⓐ Ⓑ Ⓒ Ⓓ
14. Ⓐ Ⓑ Ⓒ Ⓓ
15. Ⓐ Ⓑ Ⓒ Ⓓ

16.

17.

18.

19.

20.

ANSWER SHEET
Practice Test 4

Section 4: Math (Calculator)

1. Ⓐ Ⓑ Ⓒ Ⓓ
2. Ⓐ Ⓑ Ⓒ Ⓓ
3. Ⓐ Ⓑ Ⓒ Ⓓ
4. Ⓐ Ⓑ Ⓒ Ⓓ
5. Ⓐ Ⓑ Ⓒ Ⓓ
6. Ⓐ Ⓑ Ⓒ Ⓓ
7. Ⓐ Ⓑ Ⓒ Ⓓ
8. Ⓐ Ⓑ Ⓒ Ⓓ
9. Ⓐ Ⓑ Ⓒ Ⓓ
10. Ⓐ Ⓑ Ⓒ Ⓓ
11. Ⓐ Ⓑ Ⓒ Ⓓ
12. Ⓐ Ⓑ Ⓒ Ⓓ
13. Ⓐ Ⓑ Ⓒ Ⓓ
14. Ⓐ Ⓑ Ⓒ Ⓓ
15. Ⓐ Ⓑ Ⓒ Ⓓ
16. Ⓐ Ⓑ Ⓒ Ⓓ
17. Ⓐ Ⓑ Ⓒ Ⓓ
18. Ⓐ Ⓑ Ⓒ Ⓓ
19. Ⓐ Ⓑ Ⓒ Ⓓ
20. Ⓐ Ⓑ Ⓒ Ⓓ
21. Ⓐ Ⓑ Ⓒ Ⓓ
22. Ⓐ Ⓑ Ⓒ Ⓓ
23. Ⓐ Ⓑ Ⓒ Ⓓ
24. Ⓐ Ⓑ Ⓒ Ⓓ
25. Ⓐ Ⓑ Ⓒ Ⓓ
26. Ⓐ Ⓑ Ⓒ Ⓓ
27. Ⓐ Ⓑ Ⓒ Ⓓ
28. Ⓐ Ⓑ Ⓒ Ⓓ
29. Ⓐ Ⓑ Ⓒ Ⓓ
30. Ⓐ Ⓑ Ⓒ Ⓓ

31.

32.

33.

34.

35.

36.

37.

38.

ANSWER SHEET
Practice Test 4

Essay

PLANNING PAGE

START YOUR ESSAY HERE

READING TEST

65 MINUTES, 52 QUESTIONS

Turn to Section 1 of your answer sheet to answer the questions in this section.

Directions: Following each of the passages (or pairs of passages) below are questions about the passage (or passages). Read each passage carefully. Then, select the best answer for each question based on what is stated in the passage (or passages) and in any graphics that may accompany the passage.

Questions 1–10 are based on the following passage.

This passage is from John Okada, *No-No Boy*, published by the University of Washington Press, Copyright © 2001.

First, the real Japanese-Japanese were rounded up. These real Japanese-Japanese were Japanese nationals who had the misfortune to be diplomats and businessmen and visiting professors. They were put on a boat and sent back to Japan.

Then the alien Japanese, the ones who had been in America for two, three, or even four decades, were screened, and those found to be too actively Japanese were transported to the hinterlands and put in a camp.

The security screen was sifted once more and, this time, the lesser lights were similarly plucked and deposited. An old man, too old, too feeble, and too scared, was caught in the net. In his pocket was a little, black book. He had been a collector for the Japan-Help-the-Poor-and-Starving—and Flooded-Out-and-Homeless-and-Crippled-and-What-Have-You Fund. "Yamada-san, 50 American cents; Okada-san, two American dollars; Watanabe-san, 24 American cents; Takizaki-san, skip this month because boy broke leg"; and so on down the page. Yamada-san, Okada-san, Watanabe-san, Takizaki-san, and so on down the page were whisked away from their homes while weeping families wept until the tears must surely have been wept dry, and then wept some more.

By now, the snowball was big enough to wipe out the rising sun. The big rising sun would take a little more time, but the little rising sun which was the Japanese in countless Japanese communities in the coastal states of Washington, Oregon, and California presented no problem. The whisking and transporting of Japanese and the construction of camps with barbed wire and ominous towers supporting fully armed soldiers in places like Idaho and Wyoming and Arizona, places which even Hollywood scorned for background, had become skills which demanded the utmost of America's great organizing ability.

And so, a few months after the seventh day of December of the year nineteen forty-one, the only Japanese left on the west coast of the United States was Matsusaburo Inabukuro who, while it has been forgotten whether he was Japanese-American or American-Japanese, picked up an "I am Chinese"—not American or American-Chinese or Chinese-American but "I am Chinese"—button and got a job in a California shipyard.

GO ON TO THE NEXT PAGE

Two years later a good Japanese-American who had volunteered for the army sat smoking in the belly of a B-24 on his way back to Guam from a reconnaissance flight to Japan. His job was to listen through his earphones, which were attached to a high-frequency set, and jot down air-ground messages spoken by Japanese-Japanese in Japanese planes and in Japanese radio shacks.

The lieutenant who operated the radar-detection equipment was a blond giant from Nebraska.

The lieutenant from Nebraska said: "Where you from?"

The Japanese-American who was an American soldier answered: "No place in particular."

"You got folks?"

"Yeah, I got folks."

"Where at?"

"Wyoming, out in the desert."

"Farmers, huh?"

"Not quite."

"What's that mean?"

"Well, it's this way . . . ." And then the Japanese-American whose folks were still Japanese-Japanese, or else they would not be in a camp with barbed wire and watchtowers with soldiers holding rifles, told the blond giant from Nebraska about the removal of the Japanese from the Coast, which was called the evacuation, and about the concentration camps, which were called relocation centers.

The lieutenant listened and he didn't believe it. He said: "That's funny. Now, tell me again."

The Japanese-American soldier of the American army told it again and didn't change a word.

The lieutenant believed him this time. "Hell's bells," he exclaimed, "if they'd done that to me, I wouldn't be sitting in the belly of a broken-down B-24 going back to Guam from a reconnaissance mission to Japan."

"I got reasons," said the Japanese-American soldier soberly.

1. As it is used in line 11 *hinterlands* most nearly means

(A) lands outside the continental United States
(B) a special area outside the border of the United States
(C) camps within the United States for housing people displaced by order of the United States government
(D) a region remote from urban areas

2. As it is used in line 14 *lights* most nearly means

(A) enemy soldiers
(B) notable people
(C) rebels
(D) inspiring speakers

3. The *snowball* mentioned in line 32 most likely refers to

(A) the accumulating tears of Japanese family members who have seen their relatives moved to relocation camps
(B) the steadily increasing, accumulating efforts of Americans to defeat the Japanese
(C) the steadily growing efforts of Americans to relocate Japanese aliens living in America
(D) the steadily accumulating efforts of Japanese aliens living in America to return to Japan to fight for their country

GO ON TO THE NEXT PAGE

1 1 1

4. Which of the following words best describes the author's tone in lines 38–46?

"The whisking and transporting of Japanese and the construction of camps with barbed wire and ominous towers supporting fully armed soldiers in places like Idaho and Wyoming and Arizona, places which even Hollywood scorned for background, had become skills which demanded the utmost of America's great organizing ability."

(A) jocular
(B) sarcastic
(C) apologetic
(D) solemn

5. We can infer that the "I am Chinese" button that Matsusaburo Inabukuro wore helped him get a job because

(A) people believed that he wasn't Japanese
(B) people thought he was a Japanese person trying to make people believe he was a Chinese person
(C) people believed that a Chinese person in America was likely to be an American citizen
(D) people thought that he was a Chinese alien

6. The author would be most likely to describe the term "relocation center" (line 92) as

(A) hyperbole
(B) an understatement
(C) a euphemism
(D) a cliché

7. As it is used in line 94 *funny* most nearly means

(A) strange
(B) exaggerated
(C) humorous
(D) not true

8. The author uses all of the following *except*

(A) irony
(B) humor
(C) metaphor
(D) extrapolation

9. At the time of this account the narrator's parents are

(A) living on their farm in Wyoming
(B) living in Japan
(C) living in a relocation camp in Wyoming
(D) deceased

10. Which of the following provides evidence for the answer to the previous question?

(A) "By . . . problem." (lines 32–38)
(B) "The . . . ability." (lines 38–46)
(C) "'You . . . centers.'" (lines 76–92)
(D) "'The . . . Japan.'" (lines 99–103)

GO ON TO THE NEXT PAGE

Questions 11–21 are based on the following passage.

This passage is from Freeman Dyson, *Disturbing the Universe*. Copyright © 1979 by Freeman J. Dyson.

There are some striking examples in the laws of nuclear physics of numerical accidents that seem to conspire to make the universe habitable. The strength of the attractive nuclear force is just sufficient to overcome the electrical repulsion between the positive charges in the nuclei of ordinary atoms such as oxygen or iron. But the nuclear forces are not quite strong enough to bind together two protons (hydrogen nuclei) into a bound system which would be called a diproton if it existed. If the nuclear forces had been slightly stronger than they are, the diproton would exist and almost all the hydrogen in the universe would have been combined into diprotons and heavier nuclei. Hydrogen would be a rare element, and stars like the sun, which live for a long time by the slow burning of hydrogen in their cores, could not exist. On the other hand, if the nuclear forces had been substantially weaker than they are, hydrogen could not burn at all and there would be no heavy elements. If, as seems likely, the evolution of life requires a star like the sun, supplying energy at a constant rate for billions of years, then the strength of nuclear forces had to lie within a rather narrow range to make life possible.

A similar but independent numerical accident appears in connection with the weak interaction by which hydrogen actually burns in the sun. The weak interaction is millions of times weaker than the nuclear force. It is just weak enough so that the hydrogen in the sun burns at a slow and steady rate. If the weak interaction were much stronger or much weaker, any forms of life dependent on sunlike stars would again be in difficulties.

The facts of astronomy include some other numerical accidents that work to our advantage. For example, the universe is built on such a scale that the average distance between stars in an average galaxy like ours is about twenty million million miles—an extravagantly large distance by human standards If a scientist asserts that the stars at these immense distances have a decisive effect on the possibility of human existence, he will be suspected of being a believer in astrology. But it happens to be true that we could not have survived if the average distance between stars were only two million million miles instead of twenty. If the distances had been smaller by a factor of ten, there would have been a high probability that another star, at some time during the four billion years that the earth has existed, would have passed by the sun close enough to disrupt with its gravitational field the orbits of the planets. To destroy life on earth, it would not be necessary to pull the earth out of the solar system. It would be sufficient to pull the earth into a moderately eccentric elliptical orbit.

All the rich diversity of organic chemistry depends on a delicate balance between electrical and quantum-mechanical forces. The balance exists only because the laws of physics include an "exclusion principle" which forbids two electrons to occupy the same state. If the laws were changed so that electrons no longer excluded each other, none of our essential chemistry would survive. There are many other lucky accidents in atomic physics. Without such accidents, water could not exist as a liquid,

GO ON TO THE NEXT PAGE

chains of carbon atoms could not form complex organic molecules, and hydrogen atoms could not form breakable bridges between molecules.

I conclude from the existence of these accidents of physics and astronomy that the universe is an unexpectedly hospitable place for living creatures to make their home. Being a scientist, trained in the habits of thought and language of the twentieth century rather than the eighteenth, I do not claim that the architecture of the universe proves the existence of God. I claim only that the architecture of the universe is consistent with the hypothesis that mind plays an essential role in its functioning.

11. According to the author, if the nuclear forces in atoms had been slightly stronger than they are
 (A) there would be many more stars like the Sun than there are
 (B) the universe would be made up of over 99% hydrogen
 (C) most of the hydrogen in the universe would have burned up
 (D) stars like the Sun would not exist

12. As it is used in line 46 *extravagantly* most nearly means
 (A) erroneously
 (B) imprudently
 (C) incomprehensibly
 (D) in a way that exceeds a reasonable amount

13. The author most likely refers to astrology in line 51 to
 (A) show that he is familiar with ways of thinking outside of conventional science
 (B) support his assertion that stars greatly affect human beings
 (C) emphasize how remarkable it is that faraway stars affect life on Earth
 (D) support his contention that faraway stars can come near the Sun and disrupt the Earth's orbit around it

14. As it is used in line 48 *decisive* most nearly means
 (A) resolute
 (B) important
 (C) extreme
 (D) conclusive

15. According to the author, which of the following does not contribute to making the universe "an unexpectedly hospitable place for living creatures to make their home" (lines 84–86)?
 (A) the "exclusion principle" forbids two electrons to occupy the same state
 (B) the strength of the attractive nuclear force lies within a narrow range
 (C) hydrogen atoms cannot form breakable bridges between molecules
 (D) the average distance between stars in galaxies like the Milky Way is about twenty million million miles rather than only two million million miles

GO ON TO THE NEXT PAGE

16. Which of the following provides the evidence to answer the previous question?

(A) "If . . . nuclei." (lines 12–16)
(B) "On . . . elements." (lines 20–23)
(C) "If . . . difficulties." (lines 36–39)
(D) "Without . . . . molecules." (lines 76–81)

17. The phrase "habits of thought" as it is used in lines 86–87 most nearly means

(A) recurrent patterns of thinking
(B) scientific thinking
(C) unconscious thinking
(D) philosophical thinking

18. The author's tone in the passage is most accurately described as

(A) measured and reasonable
(B) mildly amused
(C) deeply skeptical
(D) indignant

19. Which of the following, if it occurred, would support the conclusion reached by the author?

(A) the discovery of a diproton
(B) proof that no organic compounds exist on planets in several nearby solar systems
(C) the discovery of life on a planet in orbit around another star in our galaxy
(D) the discovery that stars like the Sun are burning hydrogen at a rapidly increasing rate

20. The author would be most likely to agree that the argument he makes in this passage

(A) shows conclusively that the universe was designed by some super-human agency
(B) offers good but far from decisive support for philosophers who argue that the highly ordered structure of the universe proves the existence of God
(C) demonstrates the futility of speculating about how and why the universe was created
(D) strongly suggests that life exists on some planets in solar systems near to Earth

21. Which of the following does the author make use of in his argument?

(A) paradox
(B) understatement
(C) inductive reasoning
(D) concession

GO ON TO THE NEXT PAGE

Questions 22–32 are based on the following passage.

This passage is from Lewis Thomas, *The Medusa and the Snail*, copyright ©1974.

It is customary to place the date for the beginnings of modern medicine somewhere in the mid-1930s, with the entry of sulfonamides and penicillin into the pharmacopoeia, and it is usual to ascribe to these events the force of a revolution in medical practice. This is what things seemed like at the time. Medicine was upheaved, revolutionized indeed. Therapy had been discovered for great numbers of patients whose illnesses had previously been untreatable. Cures were now available. It seemed a totally new world. Doctors could now cure disease, and this was astonishing, most of all to the doctors themselves.

It was a major occurrence in medicine, and a triumph for biological science applied to medicine but perhaps not a revolution after all, looking back from this distance. For the real revolution in medicine, which set the stage for antibiotics and whatever else we have in the way of effective therapy today, had already occurred one hundred years before penicillin. It did not begin with the introduction of science into medicine. That came years later. Like a good many revolutions this one began with the destruction of dogma. It was discovered, sometime in the 1830s, that the greater part of medicine was nonsense.

The history of medicine has never been a particularly attractive subject in medical education, and one reason for this is that it is so unrelievedly deplorable a story. For century after century, all the way into the remote millennia of its origins, medicine got along by sheer guesswork and the crudest sort of empiricism. It is hard to conceive of a less scientific enterprise among human endeavors. Virtually anything that could be thought up for treatment of disease was tried out at one time or another, and once tried, lasted decades or even centuries before being given up. It was, in retrospect, the most frivolous and irresponsible kind of human experimentation, based on nothing but trial and error, and usually resulting in precisely that sequence. Bleeding, purging, cupping, the administration of infusions of every known plant, solutions of every known metal, every conceivable diet including total fasting, most of these based on the weirdest imaginings about the cause of disease, concocted out of nothing but thin air—this was the heritage of medicine until a little over a century ago. It is astounding that the profession survived so long, and got away with so much with so little outcry. Almost everyone seems to have been taken in. Evidently, one had to be a born skeptic to see through the old nonsense. Most people were convinced of the magical powers of medicine and put up with it.

Then, sometime in the early nineteenth century, it was realized by a few of the leading figures in medicine that almost all of the complicated treatments then available for disease did not really work, and the suggestion was made by several courageous physicians that most of them actually did more harm than good. Simultaneously, the surprising discovery was made that certain diseases were self-limited, got better by themselves, possessed a "natural history." It is hard for us now to imagine the magnitude of this discovery and its effect on the practice of medicine. That long habit, extending back into the distant past, had been to treat

GO ON TO THE NEXT PAGE

everything with something, and it was taken for granted that every disease demanded treatment and might in fact end fatally if not treated. In a sober essay written on this topic in 1876, Professor Edward H. Clarke reviewed what he regarded as the major scientific accomplishment of medicine in the preceding fifty years, which consisted of studies proving that patients with typhoid and typhus fever could recover all by themselves, without medical intervention, and often did better for being untreated than when they received the bizarre herbs, heavy metal and fomentations that were popular at that time. Delirium tremens, a disorder long believed to be fatal in all cases unless subjected to constant and aggressive medical intervention, was observed to subside by itself more readily in patients left untreated, with a substantially improved rate of survival.

Gradually, over succeeding decades, the traditional therapeutic ritual of medicine was given up, and what came to be called the "art of medicine" emerged to take its place. In retrospect, this art was really the beginning of the science of medicine. It was based on meticulous, objective, even cool observations of sick people. From this endeavor we learned the details of the natural history of illness, so that, for example, it came to be understood that typhoid and typhus were really two entirely separate, unrelated disorders, with quite different causes. Accurate diagnosis became the central purpose and justification for medicine, and as the methods for diagnosis improved, accurate prognosis also became possible.

22. As it is used in line 5 *pharmacopoeia* most nearly means

(A) collection of drugs approved by the government for medical use
(B) accepted medical practice
(C) stock of medical drugs
(D) knowledge of doctors

23. Why, according to the author, were doctors astonished around the mid-1930s?

(A) They were amazed that drugs were able to cure diseases.
(B) Cures were becoming available for some illnesses, whereas before these doctors had little capacity to cure illnesses.
(C) The practice of medicine was being revolutionized by a bold young breed of doctors.
(D) They were surprised that people still had so much respect for doctors and medicine.

24. Which of the following is part of the "dogma" referred to in line 28?

(A) Every illness must be treated.
(B) Every illness ends in the patient's death if it is not treated.
(C) Some diseases get better if left untreated.
(D) Accurate diagnosis, not treatment, is the most important purpose of medicine.

GO ON TO THE NEXT PAGE

25. As it is used in lines 37–38 the phrase "the crudest sort of empiricism" most nearly means

(A) acquisition of scientific knowledge by careful experimentation
(B) extremely impolite experimentation on patients
(C) very unsophisticated use of observation and experimentation to gain knowledge
(D) the use of powerful drugs without a scientific understanding of their compositions

26. What is the most likely reason that the author says, "It is astounding that the profession survived so long" (lines 56–57)?

(A) He believes that being a doctor in the time before the development of modern medicine was extremely demanding, and he's amazed that so few doctors left the medical profession.
(B) He believes it is very surprising that the medical profession was not assimilated into the larger field of biological science, as the latter field made huge advances in the early years of the twentieth century.
(C) He believes it is remarkable that a profession that was so poor at doing its job was so popular.
(D) He believes it is amazing that the medical profession was not more appreciated by the public before the mid-1930s.

27. As it is used in line 60 *skeptic* most nearly means

(A) person of very high intelligence
(B) cynical person
(C) person who analyzes things objectively
(D) person who questions generally accepted ideas

28. It can be inferred that the author describes "several physicians" as "courageous" (line 69) because

(A) he believes that it took courage for physicians to risk injuring their own health by administering new drugs to patients
(B) he believes that it took courage for physicians to suggest that the methods used in their profession were almost completely wrong, since doing so would make them unpopular with other members of the profession and possibly endanger their standing in the medical profession
(C) he believes that it took courage for physicians to suggest that the profession should try new methods of treating patients
(D) he believes that it took courage for such physicians to admit to their fellow professionals that they had been wrong in their criticism of accepted medical practice

29. The author describes the "discovery" mentioned in line 72 as "surprising" because

(A) Doctors at the time believed that medical intervention in illness was generally unhelpful.
(B) Doctors at the time believed that there were some diseases that could not be cured.
(C) Most people, including doctors, believed that all illnesses had to be treated.
(D) Medicine has advanced so much since the early nineteenth century that it is surprising that such a discovery was made then.

GO ON TO THE NEXT PAGE

30. Which of the following provides evidence for the answer to the previous question?

(A) "Doctors . . . themselves." (lines 13–15)
(B) " Virtually . . . up." (lines 40–44)
(C) "Simultaneously . . . 'history.'" (lines 71–74)
(D) "That . . . treated." (lines 77–82)

31. The word that best describes the "the major scientific accomplishment of medicine in the preceding fifty years" (lines 84–86) is

(A) ironic
(B) unsubstantiated
(C) humorous
(D) unethical

32. As it is used in line 95 *aggressive* most nearly means

(A) dangerous
(B) destructive
(C) very intensive
(D) hostile

This passage is from Elizabeth Zubritsky, "NASA Finds Friction from Tides Could Help Distant Earths Survive, and Thrive," NASA's Goddard Space Flight Center.

Questions 33–42 are based on the following passage.

As anybody who has started a campfire by rubbing sticks knows, friction generates heat. Now, computer modeling by NASA scientists shows that friction could be the key to survival for some distant Earth-sized planets traveling in dangerous orbits.

The findings are consistent with observations that Earth-sized planets appear to be very common in other star systems. Although heat can be a destructive force for some planets, the right amount of friction, and therefore heat, can be helpful and perhaps create conditions for habitability.

"We found some unexpected good news for planets in vulnerable orbits," said Wade Henning, a scientist working at NASA and lead author of the new study. "It turns out these planets will often experience just enough friction to move them out of harm's way and into safer, more-circular orbits more quickly than previously predicted."

Simulations of young planetary systems indicate that giant planets often upset the orbits of smaller inner worlds. Even if those interactions aren't immediately catastrophic, they can leave a planet in a treacherous eccentric orbit—a very elliptical course that raises the odds of crossing paths with another body, being absorbed by the host star, or getting ejected from the system.

Another potential peril of a highly eccentric orbit is the amount of tidal stress a planet may undergo as it draws very close to its star and then retreats away. Near the star, the gravitational force is powerful enough

GO ON TO THE NEXT PAGE

to deform the planet, while in more distant reaches of the orbit, the planet can ease back into shape. This flexing action produces friction, which generates heat. In extreme cases, tidal stress can produce enough heat to liquefy the planet.

In this new study Henning and his colleague Terry Hurford explored the effects of tidal stresses on planets that have multiple layers, such as rocky crust, mantle or iron core. One conclusion of the study is that some planets could move into a safer orbit about 10 to 100 times faster than previously expected—in as a little as a few hundred thousand years, instead of the more typical rate of several million years. Such planets would be driven close to the point of melting or, at least, would have a nearly melted layer, similar to the one right below Earth's crust. Their interior temperatures could range from moderately warmer than our planet is today up to the point of having modest-sized magma oceans.

The transition to a circular orbit would be speedy because an almost-melted layer would flex easily, generating a lot of friction-induced heat. As the planet threw off that heat, it would lose energy at a fast rate and relax quickly into a circular orbit. (Later, tidal heating would turn off, and the planet's surface could become safe to walk on.) In contrast, a world that had completely melted would be so fluid that it would produce little friction. Before this study, that is what researchers expected to happen to planets undergoing strong tidal stresses. Cold, stiff planets tend to resist the tidal stress and release energy very slowly. In fact, Henning and Hurford found that many of them actually generate less friction than previously thought. This may be especially true for planets farther from their stars. If these worlds are not crowded by other bodies, they may be stable in their eccentric orbits for a long time. "In this case, the longer, non-circular orbits could increase the 'habitable zone,' because the tidal stress will remain an energy source for longer periods of time," said Hurford. "This is great for dim stars or ice worlds with subsurface oceans."

Surprisingly, another way for a terrestrial planet to achieve high amounts of heating is to be covered in a very thick ice shell, similar to an extreme "snowball Earth." Although a sheet of ice is a slippery, low-friction surface, an ice layer thousands of miles thick would be very springy. A shell like this would have just the right properties to respond strongly to tidal stress, generating a lot of heat. (The high pressures inside these planets could prevent all but the topmost layers from turning into liquid water.)

The researchers found that the very responsive layers of ice or almost-melted material could be relatively thin, just a few hundred miles deep in some cases, yet still dominate the global behavior. The team modeled planets that are the size of Earth and up to two-and-a-half times larger. Henning added that superEarths—planets at the high end of this size range—likely would experience stronger tidal stresses and potentially could benefit more from the resulting friction and heating.

GO ON TO THE NEXT PAGE

1 1 1

Planets in eccentric orbits can experience powerful tidal forces. A planet covered by a very thick ice shell (left) is springy enough to flex a great deal, generating a lot of internal friction and heat. Some terrestrial planets (right) also will flex, especially with partially molten inner layers.

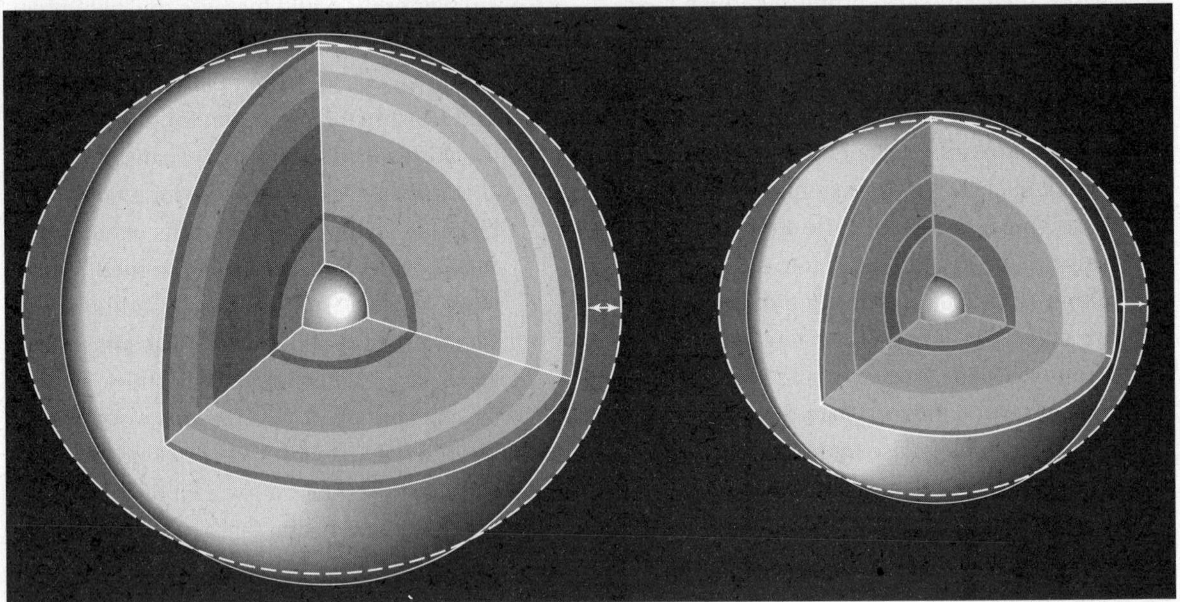

Credit: NASA's Goodard Space Flight Center

33. The data gathered in the study conducted by Wade Henning and his colleague and described in the passage was obtained by

    (A) telescopic observation of planets in orbit around stars
    (B) simulations run on computers
    (C) a review of past studies
    (D) all of the above

34. Which choice provides the best evidence for the answer to the previous question?

    (A) lines 3–6 ("Now . . . orbits.")
    (B) lines 31–34 ("Another . . . away.")
    (C) lines 59–62 ("The . . . heat.")
    (D) lines 98–102 (The . . . behavior.")

35. The word *dangerous* in line 6 most nearly means

    (A) likely to cause harm
    (B) threatening
    (C) risky
    (D) certain to be destroyed

36. The author most likely refers to making a campfire to

    (A) help the reader visualize a phenomenon
    (B) show that terrestrial and astronomical phenomena are fundamentally different
    (C) create humor
    (D) introduce a mystery that will be explained later in the passage

GO ON TO THE NEXT PAGE

37. Which of the following is the main phenomenon discussed in the passage that may prevent a young planet from developing into a habitable planet?

(A) tidal stress
(B) an eccentric orbit
(C) absorption by a star
(D) collision or near collision with other bodies

38. Based on the information in the passage, which of the following conclusions would the authors of the study discussed in the passage probably believe to be most likely?

(A) Nearly all of the Earth-size planets in a typical star system are in a circular orbit.
(B) Earth-size planets are rare.
(C) All of the Earth-size planets that exist in other star systems were once in elliptical orbits around their host star.
(D) Some of the Earth-like planets in other star systems have always been in a circular orbit, while others were previously in elliptical orbits.

39. Which word most accurately describes the phenomenon described in lines 86–94 ("Surprisingly . . . heat.")?

(A) paradoxical
(B) inexplicable
(C) simple
(D) mysterious

40. Based on the information in the passage, which of the following statements would the authors of the study described in the passage be most likely to agree with?

(A) The composition of Earth-size planets in other systems is important for scientists to understand and should be investigated further.
(B) Planets in eccentric orbits can never be habitable.
(C) Once a planet melts it can never become habitable.
(D) Tidal friction is the main process driving the formation of Earth-size habitable planets.

41. The most appropriate title for the passage would be

(A) How Earth-like Planets Are Created
(B) Evidence Found that Friction from Tides Could Help Earth-like Planets Survive
(C) The Possibility of Life on Earth-size Planets
(D) Proof Found that Habitable Earth-size Planets Are Common

42. The study discussed in this passage would be most likely to appear

(A) in a science magazine for the general public
(B) in a weekly news magazine
(C) in a professional astronomy journal
(D) in a NASA newsletter for high school science students

GO ON TO THE NEXT PAGE

Questions 43–52 are based on the following passage.

This passage is from John L. O'Sullivan, "The Great Nation of Futurity." It was originally published in 1839.

The American people having derived their origin from many other nations, and the Declaration of National Independence being entirely based on the great principle of human equality, these facts demonstrate at once our disconnected position as regards any other nation; that we have, in reality, but little connection with the past history of any of them, and still less with all antiquity, its glories, or its crimes. On the contrary, our national birth was the beginning of a new history, the formation and progress of an untried political system, which separates us from the past and connects us with the future only; and so far as regards the entire development of the natural rights of man, in moral, political, and national life, we may confidently assume that our country is destined to be the great nation of futurity.

It is so destined because the principle upon which a nation is organized fixes its destiny, and that of equality is perfect, is universal. It presides in all the operations of the physical world, and it is also the conscious law of the soul—the self-evident dictates of morality, which accurately defines the duty of man to man, and consequently man's rights as man. Besides, the truthful annals of any nation furnish abundant evidence that its happiness, its greatness, its duration, were always proportionate to the democratic equality in its system of government.

What friend of human liberty, civilization, and refinement can cast his view over the past history of the monarchies and aristocracies of antiquity, and not deplore that they ever existed? What philanthropist can contemplate the oppressions, the cruelties, and injustice inflicted by them on the masses of mankind, and not turn with moral horror from the retrospect?

America is destined for better deeds. It is our unparalleled glory that we have no reminiscences of battle fields but in defense of humanity, of the oppressed of all nations, of the rights of conscience, the rights of personal enfranchisement. Our annals describe no scenes of horrid carnage, where men were led on by hundreds of thousands to slay one another, dupes and victims to emperors, kings, nobles, demons in the human form called heroes. We have had patriots to defend our homes, our liberties, but no aspirants to crowns or thrones; nor have the American people ever suffered themselves to be led on by wicked ambition to depopulate the land, to spread desolation far and wide, that a human being might be placed on a seat of supremacy.

We have no interest in the scenes of antiquity, only as lessons of avoidance of nearly all their examples. The expansive future is our arena, and for our history. We are entering on its untrodden space, with the truths of God in our minds, beneficent objects in our hearts, and with a clear conscience unsullied by the past. We are the nation of human progress, and who will, what can, set limits to our onward march? Providence is with us, and no earthly power can. We point to the everlasting truth on the first page of our national declaration, and we proclaim to the millions of other lands, that "the gates of hell"—the powers of aristocracy and monarchy—"shall not prevail against it."

GO ON TO THE NEXT PAGE

The far-reaching, the boundless future will be the era of American greatness. In its magnificent domain of space and time, the nation of many nations is destined to manifest to mankind the excellence of divine principles; to establish on earth the noblest temple ever dedicated to the worship of the Most High—the Sacred and the True.

Its floor shall be a hemisphere—its roof the firmament of the star-studded heavens, and its congregation a Union of many Republics, comprising hundreds of happy millions, calling, owning no man master, but governed by God's natural and moral law of equality, the law of brotherhood—of "peace and good will amongst men."...

We are the nation of progress, of individual freedom, of universal enfranchisement. We must onward to the fulfillment of our mission—to the entire development of the principle of our organization—freedom of conscience, freedom of person, freedom of trade and business pursuits, universality of freedom and equality. This is our high destiny, and we must accomplish it. All this will be our future history, to establish on earth the moral dignity and salvation of man—the immutable truth and beneficence of God. For this blessed mission to the nations of the world, which are shut out from the life-giving light of truth, has America been chosen.

43. The passage can best be described as

(A) a discussion of the historical origins of American values
(B) an endeavor to reconcile political and religious ideals
(C) an effort to put America's place in the world in historical perspective
(D) an attempt to rally readers around a belief

44. The word *suffered* as it is used in line 56 most nearly means

(A) felt guilty
(B) endured pain
(C) objected to
(D) permitted

45. Which statement would the author be most likely to agree with?

(A) Democracy is the best form of government.
(B) War is never justified.
(C) Nothing can be learned from history.
(D) Religious ideals have no place in a nation's politics.

46. Which choice provides the best evidence for the answer to the previous question?

(A) lines 1–10 ("The . . . crimes.")
(B) lines 34–38 ("What . . . existed?")
(C) lines 28–33 ("Besides . . . government.")
(D) lines 93–95 ("We . . . enfranchisement.")

47. The word *philanthropist* as it is used in line 38 most nearly means

(A) kind person
(B) person who gives money to help others
(C) historian specializing in the study of monarchies
(D) lover of humankind

GO ON TO THE NEXT PAGE

48. Which of the following does the author make use of to persuade the reader of his views?

    (A) rhetorical questions
    (B) quotations from America's Founding Fathers
    (C) studies by political scientists
    (D) careful analysis of the underlying assumptions made in the course of his argument

49. The meaning of the word *objects* as it is used in line 67 most nearly means

    (A) focuses of attention
    (B) things perceptible to the senses
    (C) goals
    (D) gifts

50. Which of the following is the most accurate summary of the main argument of the passage?

    (A) America is destined to be a perfect Republic with freedom and equality for all, something no other nation could achieve.
    (B) America's future greatness is assured, but no one can predict what form this greatness will take.
    (C) Because America is unique in being founded on the principles of freedom and equality it has a sacred duty to manifest them and spread them to other nations.
    (D) Although America is exceptional among nation states in some ways, it cannot escape the ultimate fate of all nations—decline, and, finally, death.

51. The author's tone can most accurately be described as

    (A) ironic and understated
    (B) derisive
    (C) enthusiastic and serious
    (D) dispassionate

52. The most appropriate title for this passage would be

    (A) The Republican Form of Government
    (B) America's Sacred Mission
    (C) Democracy and Equality
    (D) The Influence of Religious Ideas on American Government and Politics

If there is still time remaining, you may review your answers.

WRITING AND LANGUAGE TEST

35 MINUTES, 44 QUESTIONS

Turn to Section 2 of your answer sheet to answer the questions in this section.

Directions: Questions follow each of the passages below. Some questions ask you how the passage might be changed to improve the expression of ideas. Other questions ask you how the passage might be altered to correct errors in grammar, usage, and punctuation. One or more graphics accompany some passages. You will be required to consider these graphics as you answer questions about editing the passage.

There are three types of questions. In the first type, a part of the passage is underlined. The second type is based on a certain part of the passage. The third type is based on the entire passage.

Read each passage. Then, choose the answer to each question that changes the passage so that it is consistent with the conventions of standard written English. One of the answer choices for many questions is "NO CHANGE." Choosing this answer means that you believe the best answer is to make no change in the passage.

Questions 1–11 are based on the following passage and supplementary material.

Toxoplasmosis

Toxoplasmosis is a zoonotic protozoal disease of humans and animals caused by the coccidian parasite *Toxoplasma gondii* (*T. gondii*). Infection by *T. gondii* is widely prevalent in ❶ humans, in spite of nearly one-third of humanity having been exposed to this parasite. Although toxoplasmosis usually does not cause clinical illness in healthy people, it can cause debilitating disease in congenitally infected infants.

[1] Since 1937 *T. gondii* has become recognized as a significant cause of disease in infants and children, as well as adults who may suffer from delayed conditions originating from congenital infections. [2] Because about 90 percent of these infants usually do not show any signs of the disease at birth, the effects of the infection may not be ❷ foreseen until later in childhood or

1. For the sake of clarity of meaning and effectiveness of expression, the underlined portion of the sentence should be written as follows:
   (A) NO CHANGE
   (B) humans, despite the fact that one-third of humanity has been exposed
   (C) humans, one-third of humanity exposed
   (D) humans, and nearly one-third of humanity has been exposed

2. (A) NO CHANGE
   (B) disclosed
   (C) recognized
   (D) unveiled

GO ON TO THE NEXT PAGE

adulthood. [3] Early identification of infants at risk of infection or disease **3** is vital except for limiting the financial and social costs of people suffering the effects of the infection. [4] In the United States 400–4,000 infants are born each year with congenital toxoplasmosis. **4**

5 The organism is transmitted during gestation when the mother becomes infected for the first time while the mother rarely has symptoms of infection. She does have parasites in the blood temporarily. Focal lesions develop in the placenta and the fetus may become infected. At first there is generalized infection in the fetus. Later, infection is cleared from the visceral tissues and may localize in the central nervous system.

3. (A) NO CHANGE
   (B) is vital to limiting
   (C) vitally limited
   (D) vitally has a limit on

4. For the sake of the cohesion of this paragraph, sentence 4 should be placed:
   (A) where it is now
   (B) before sentence 1
   (C) before sentence 2
   (D) before sentence 3

5. For the sake of clarity of meaning and effectiveness of expression, the underlined sentences should be written as follows:
   (A) NO CHANGE
   (B) The organism, transmitted during gestation when the mother becomes infected for the first time, rarely has symptoms of infection, but there are parasites in the blood temporarily.
   (C) The organism is transmitted during gestation. Rarely having symptoms of infection, the mother is infected for the first time, but there are parasites in the blood temporarily.
   (D) The organism is transmitted during gestation when the mother becomes infected for the first time. While the mother rarely has symptoms of infection, she does have parasites in the blood temporarily.

GO ON TO THE NEXT PAGE

Risk of congenital infection and development of clinical signs by duration of gestation at maternal seroconversion.

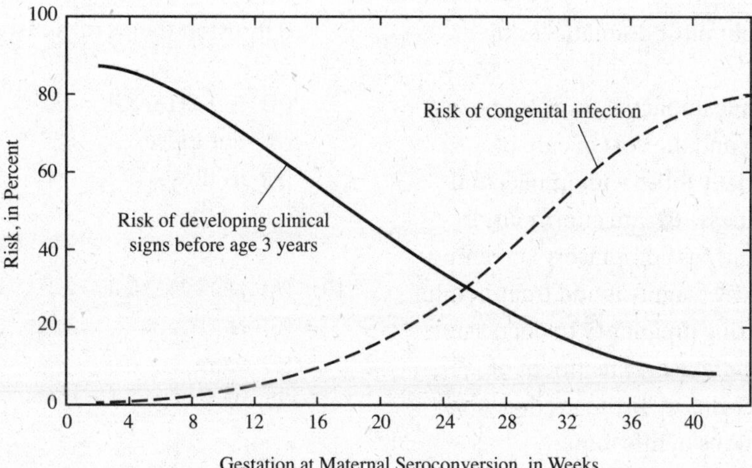

Source: U.S. Geological Survey, Circular 1389, 2014.

The risk of congenital infection is lowest when maternal infection is during the first trimester and highest when infection is during the third trimester. **6** Also, the risk of developing clinical signs before age 3 years is lower when congenital infection occurs during the first trimester than it is when the infection occurs during the third trimester (see graph above).

A wide **7** spectrum of pregnancy outcomes and clinical diseases can occur as a result of congenital toxoplasmosis, including spontaneous abortion and stillbirth, as well as birth defects in live born infants such as hydrocephalus (accumulation of cerebrospinal fluid in the brain), microcephalus (abnormally small brain for age), intracerebral calcification,

6. Which choice most accurately and effectively represents the information in the graph?
   (A) NO CHANGE
   (B) However, the risk of developing clinical signs before age 3 years is higher when congenital infection occurs during the first trimester than it is when the infection occurs during the third trimester.
   (C) However, the risk of developing clinical signs before age 3 years increases when congenital infection occurs in the second or third trimesters instead of the first trimester.
   (D) The risk of developing clinical signs before age 3 is the same whether congenital infection occurs during the first, second, or third trimesters.

7. (A) NO CHANGE
   (B) catalogue
   (C) horizon
   (D) panorama

GO ON TO THE NEXT PAGE

convulsions, 8 diminishing of vision, and retinochoroiditis (inflammation of the inner layers of the eye). 9 Listing these, hydrocephalus is the least common but most dramatic lesion of toxoplasmosis.

The socioeconomic impact of toxoplasmosis on human suffering and the cost of care of sick children, especially those with intellectual disability and blindness, 10 are enormous. In some European countries compulsory screening programs ensure early diagnosis and treatment of women infected during pregnancy to decrease 11 migration to their fetuses. Treatment of infected neonates begins at birth to reduce the potential complications of infection.

8. (A) NO CHANGE
   (B) vision diminishing
   (C) diminished vision
   (D) vision that is diminished

9. (A) NO CHANGE
   (B) For these,
   (C) In these,
   (D) Of these,

10. (A) NO CHANGE
   (B) is
   (C) were
   (D) was

11. (A) NO CHANGE
   (B) distribution
   (C) communication
   (D) transmission

GO ON TO THE NEXT PAGE

Questions 12–22 are based on the following passage and supplementary material.

Aiming for a Ph.D.?

⓬ Desiring a doctorate for thousands of students outweighs concern about the job market that awaits after graduation. Most Ph.D. candidates are willing to ⓭ direct themselves to intensive research and study because they enjoy the subject matter. Statistics also show other, more ⓮ tangible payoffs for Ph.D. recipients when they enter the labor force. Unemployment rates are consistently lower and earnings are significantly higher for people with a Ph.D. degree ⓯ than people with lower levels of educational attainment. Doctoral degree holders in 2001 had an unemployment rate of slightly more than 1 percent and median annual earnings of $66,000—considerably better than the 3.7-percent unemployment rate and $30,300 median earnings of the population aged 25 and older. Prior to embarking on doctoral studies, many students already ⓰ were completing several years of formal study in their chosen field. The Survey of Earned Doctorates shows that in 2000, more than half of all Ph.D. recipients held a bachelor's degree in the same subject as that of their doctoral study—and nearly three-fourths held a master's.

According to the same survey, the total number of new research doctorates awarded each year ⓱ had grown about 10 percent between

12. For the sake of clarity of meaning and clarity of expression, the underlined portion of the sentence should be written as follows:

(A) As it is now
(B) Thousands of students desire a doctorate, outweighing
(C) For thousands of students, the desire for a doctorate outweighs
(D) Thousands of students who desire a doctorate outweigh

13. (A) As it is now
(B) allocate
(C) appropriate
(D) dedicate

14. (A) NO CHANGE
(B) tactile
(C) tangential
(D) corporeal

15. (A) NO CHANGE
(B) than people having
(C) than those people with
(D) than they are for people with

16. (A) NO CHANGE
(B) have completed
(C) had completed
(D) complete

17. Which choice most accurately and effectively represents the information in the graph?

(A) NO CHANGE
(B) grew about 20 percent
(C) grew about 40 percent
(D) grew about 60 percent

GO ON TO THE NEXT PAGE

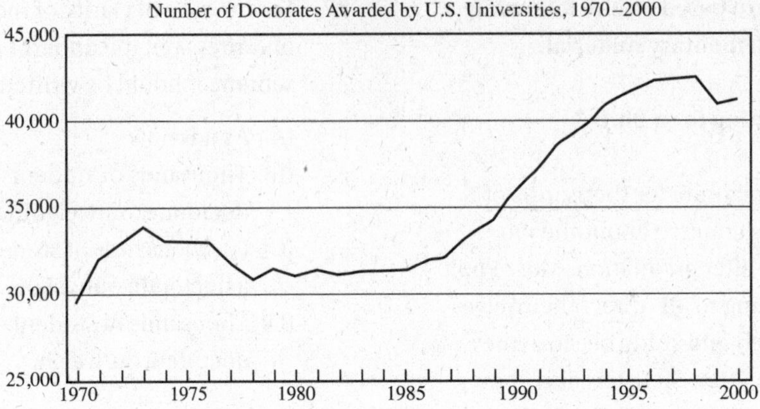

Source: National Science Foundation/SRS, Survey of Earned Doctorates

1970 and 2000 (see graph above). Of these research doctorates, about 95 percent are Ph.D.'s. After rising steadily from **18** <u>the late 1970s into</u> the 1990s, the total number of degrees awarded stabilized.

Between 1970 and 2000, there have been changes by field of study in the numbers of Ph.D. degrees granted. Generally, fields with the greatest increases in the numbers of doctoral degrees **19** <u>awarding</u> also had the most job growth.

[1] In 1999, about 405,000 people held doctorates in the natural sciences and engineering, according to the National Science Foundation's Survey of Doctorate Recipients. [2] **20** <u>Relating to</u> the fields that exhibited gains, biological sciences and health sciences experienced relatively steady increases in the numbers of doctoral degrees awarded. [3] Computer science, first measured in 1978, showed similar increases, **21** <u>and this demonstrated</u>

18. (A) NO CHANGE
    (B) from 1970 to
    (C) from 1980 to
    (D) the late 1980s into

19. (A) NO CHANGE
    (B) award
    (C) awarded
    (D) awards

20. (A) NO CHANGE
    (B) In all
    (C) Speaking of
    (D) Of

21. (A) NO CHANGE
    (B) demonstrated
    (C) demonstrating
    (D) a demonstration of

GO ON TO THE NEXT PAGE

particularly strong growth from 1980 to 1990. [4] Engineering had large decreases in the number of degrees awarded from 1970 to 1980 but experienced significant increases in the following decades. [5] Between 1970 and 2000, some fields gained a relative share of doctorates awarded; others lost ground. [6] In physics and astronomy, chemistry, and mathematics, the numbers of doctorates awarded in 2000 were below 1970 levels in those fields. (22)

22. For the sake of the logic and cohesion of this paragraph, sentence 5 should be placed

(A) where it is now
(B) after sentence 1
(C) after sentence 2
(D) after sentence 6

GO ON TO THE NEXT PAGE

Questions 23–33 are based on the following passage.

Sargon the Great

[1] The first great Semitic empire in Babylonia was that founded by the famous Sargon of Akkad. [2] (23) As the case with many popular heroes and monarchs whose deeds are remembered in song and story—for example, Perseus, Oedipus, Cyrus, Romulus—the early years of Sargon were passed in (24) ambiguity. [3] Sargon is, in fact, one of the "fatal children." [4] He was, legend stated, born in concealment and sent adrift, like Moses, in an ark of bulrushes on the waters of the Euphrates, whence he was rescued and brought up by one Akki, a husbandman. [5] But the time of his recognition at length arrived, and he received the crown of Babylonia. [6] His foreign conquests were extensive. [7] On four successive occasions he invaded Syria and Palestine, which he succeeded in welding into a single empire with Babylonia. [8] (25) He, pressing his victories to the margin of the Mediterranean, erected upon its shores statues of himself as a symbol of his conquests. (26)

Even at this comparatively early time (3800 B.C.) the resources of the country had been well exploited by its Semitic conquerors, and their absorption of the Sumerian civilization had permitted them to make very considerable progress in the enlightened arts. Some of their work in bas-relief, and even in (27) the less if equally difficult craft of gem-cutting, is among

23. (A) NO CHANGE
(B) As is the case with
(C) As the case of
(D) The same as

24. (A) NO CHANGE
(B) camouflage
(C) suppression
(D) obscurity

25. For the sake of clarity of meaning and effectiveness of expression, the sentence should be rewritten as follows:

(A) NO CHANGE
(B) He erected upon its shores, pressing his victories to the margin of the Mediterranean, statues of himself as a symbol of his conquests.
(C) He erected upon its shores statues of himself where he pressed his victories, to the margin of the Mediterranean, as a symbol of his conquests.
(D) Pressing his victories to the margin of the Mediterranean, he erected upon its shores statues of himself as a symbol of his conquests.

26. For the sake of the cohesion of this paragraph, sentence 3 should be placed

(A) where it is now
(B) after sentence 4
(C) after sentence 5
(D) after sentence 6

27. (A) NO CHANGE
(B) the lesser if
(C) the least if
(D) at least an

GO ON TO THE NEXT PAGE

the finest efforts of Babylonian art. Nor were they deficient in more 28 efficient fields. They constructed roads through the most important portions of the empire, 29 along with a service of posts carried messages at stated intervals, the letters conveyed by these being stamped or franked by clay seals, bearing the name of Sargon.

Sargon is also famous as the first founder of a Babylonian library. This library appears to have contained works of a most surprising nature, 30 considering the period at which it was instituted. One of these was entitled The Observations of Bel, and consisted of no less than seventy-two books dealing with astronomical matters of considerable 31 complexity, it registered and described the appearances of comets, conjunctions of the sun and moon, and the phases of the planet Venus, besides recording many eclipses. This wonderful work 32 had been long afterward translated into Greek by the Babylonian historian Berossus, and it demonstrates the great antiquity of Babylonian astronomical science even at this very early epoch. Another famous work contained in the library of Sargon dealt with omens, the manner of casting them, and their 33 interpretation; a very important side-issue of Babylonian magico-religious practice.

28. (A) NO CHANGE
(B) realistic
(C) utilitarian
(D) productive

29. (A) NO CHANGE
(B) along this
(C) along which
(D) along

30. (A) NO CHANGE
(B) without considering
(C) in consideration of
(D) in considering

31. (A) NO CHANGE
(B) complexity; it registered
(C) complexity, having been registered
(D) complexity, registered

32. (A) NO CHANGE
(B) has been
(C) was
(D) being

33. (A) NO CHANGE
(B) interpretation—a
(C) interpretation; A
(D) interpretation. A

GO ON TO THE NEXT PAGE

Questions 34–44 are based on the following passage.

The Art of Fiction

[1] One is sometimes asked about the "obstacles" that confront young writers who are trying to do good work. [2] I should say the greatest obstacles that writers today have to get over, are the dazzling journalistic successes of twenty years (34) ago, they were stories that surprised and delighted by their sharp photographic detail and that were really nothing more than lively pieces of reporting. [3] The whole aim of that school of writing was novelty—never a very important thing in art. [4] They gave us, altogether, poor standards—taught us to multiply our ideas instead of to condense them. [5] They tried to make a story out of every theme that occurred to them and to get returns on every situation that suggested itself. [6] They got returns, of a kind. [7] But their work, when one (35) was looking back on it, now that the novelty upon which they counted so much is gone, is journalistic and thin. [8] The especial merit of a good reportorial story is that it shall be intensely interesting and (36) apparent today and shall have lost its point by tomorrow. (37)

(38) That, indeed, is very nearly the whole of the higher artistic process: finding what conventions of form and what detail one can do without and

34. (A) NO CHANGE
(B) ago. Stories that surprised and delighted
(C) ago, stories that surprised and delighted
(D) ago, surprising and delightful stories

35. (A) NO CHANGE
(B) had looked
(C) has looked
(D) looks

36. (A) NO CHANGE
(B) consequential
(C) influential
(D) pertinent

37. For the sake of the logic and cohesion of this paragraph, sentence 6 should be placed
(A) where it is now
(B) after sentence 2
(C) after sentence 4
(D) after sentence 7

38. At this point, the writer is considering adding the following sentence.

Art, it seems to me, should simplify.

Should the writer make this addition here?

(A) Yes, because this sentence clearly and concisely presents a view of "the higher artistic process" that is at odds with the view of the writer.
(B) Yes, because the sentence concisely and effectively summarizes the focus of the second paragraph, which is the importance of simplification in art.
(C) No, because this sentence is a summary of the first paragraph, so it should be the last sentence of that paragraph.
(D) No, because based on what the writer says in the rest of the passage, this sentence overstates her argument about art.

GO ON TO THE NEXT PAGE

yet preserve the spirit of the whole—so that all that one has suppressed and cut away is there to the reader's consciousness as much as if it were **39** in type on the page. Millet had done hundreds of sketches of peasants sowing grain, some of them very complicated and interesting, but when **40** he comes to paint the spirit of them all into one picture, "The Sower," the composition is so simple that it seems inevitable. **41** Previously, all the discarded sketches that went before made the picture what it finally became, and the process was all the time one of simplifying, of sacrificing many conceptions good in themselves for one that was better and more universal.

Any first rate novel or story must have in it the strength of a dozen fairly good stories that **42** have been a sacrifice to it. A good workman can't be a cheap workman; he can't be stingy about wasting material, and he cannot compromise. Writing ought either to be the manufacture of stories for which there is a market demand—a business as safe and commendable as making soap or breakfast foods—or it should be an art, which is always a search for something for which there is no market demand, something new and untried, where the values are **43** introverted and have nothing to do with standardized values. **44**

39. (A) NO CHANGE
 (B) a typing on the page.
 (C) a type of page.
 (D) a page of typing.

40. (A) NO CHANGE
 (B) has come
 (C) came
 (D) is coming

41. (A) NO CHANGE
 (B) All the previous sketches, discarded,
 (C) All the sketches, previously discarded,
 (D) All the discarded sketches that went before

42. (A) NO CHANGE
 (B) sacrificing to it
 (C) have been sacrificed to it
 (D) were made a sacrifice to it

43. (A) NO CHANGE
 (B) intrinsic
 (C) congenital
 (D) ingrained

44. Which choice most effectively establishes the main topic of the paragraph?
 (A) techniques of writing
 (B) making money as a writer
 (C) writing as an art
 (D) the writer and her readers

STOP

If there is still time remaining, you may review your answers.

3  3

MATH TEST (NO CALCULATOR)

25 MINUTES, 20 QUESTIONS

Turn to Section 3 of your answer sheet to answer the questions in this section.

Directions: For questions 1–15, solve each problem and choose the best answer from the given options. Fill in the corresponding circle on your answer document. For questions 16–20, solve the problem and fill in the answer on the answer sheet grid. Please use scrap paper to work out your answers.

Notes:

- You **CANNOT** use a calculator on this section.
- All variables and expressions represent real numbers unless indicated otherwise.
- All figures are drawn to scale unless indicated otherwise.
- All figures are in a plane unless indicated otherwise.
- Unless indicated otherwise, the domain of a given function is the set of all real numbers *x* for which the function has real values.

REFERENCE INFORMATION

Area Facts | **Volume Facts** | **Triangle Facts**

ℓ, w

$A = \ell w$

h, b

$A = \frac{1}{2}bh$

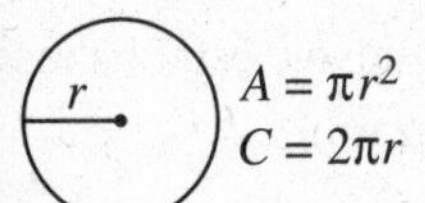

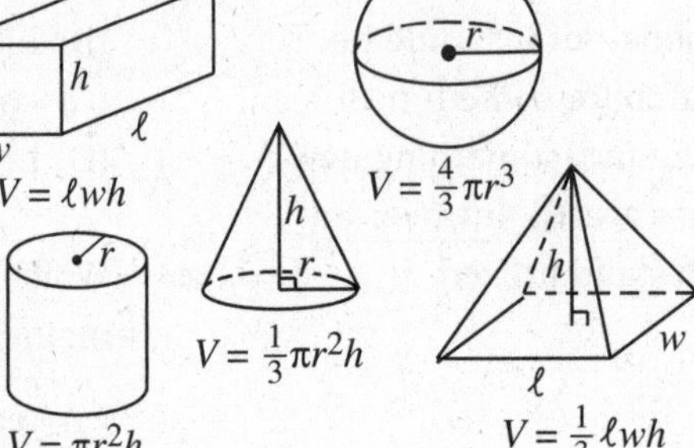

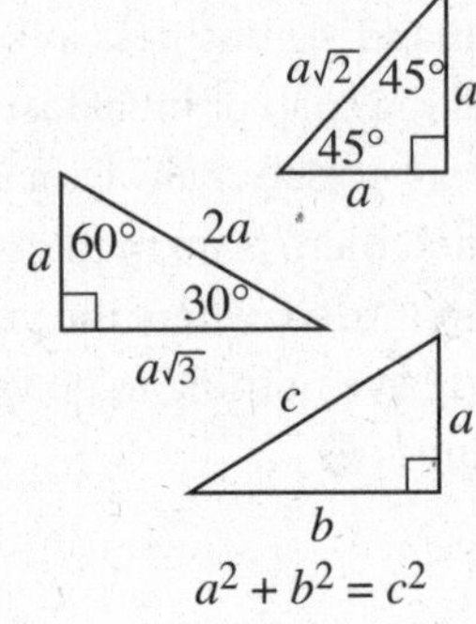

The arc of a circle contains 360°.
The arc of a circle contains 2π radians.
The sum of the measures of the angles in a triangle is 180°.

1. The product of an integer, *n*, and 5, increased by 12 is –13. What is the value of *n*?

(A) 25
(B) 5
(C) $\frac{1}{5}$
(D) –5

2. If $i = \sqrt{-1}$, what is the value of $(7 - 2i) + (4 - 5i)$?

(A) $4i$
(B) $11 - 7i$
(C) $7 - 11i$
(D) $-77i^2$

GO ON TO THE NEXT PAGE

3

3. Alan had a big day catching 17 fish. He is concerned, however, about the weight of all of the fish. The average weight of the 17 fish he caught is f pounds. What would be the weight of the 17 fish if they were placed in a single container?

(A) $\frac{17}{f}$

(B) $\frac{f}{17}$

(C) $17f$

(D) $f + 17$

4. Jorge earns a weekly allowance of \$10, and he gets \$8 for every chore he does at his home. During a recent week, Jorge was paid \$106 for his allowance and chores. How many chores did he do?

(A) 12
(B) 11
(C) 9
(D) 7

5. $-4xy^2 - 2xy + xy - 8mn + mn$

Which of the following is equivalent to the expression above?

(A) $-5x^3y^3 - 8m^2n^2$
(B) $-5x^3y - 7m^2n^2$
(C) $32y - 8$
(D) $-4xy^2 - xy - 7mn$

6. A small city was incorporated in the year Y. Every 15 years, the town doubled in size. How many times larger was the town in year $Y + 90$ than it was in year Y?

(A) 16
(B) 32
(C) 64
(D) It cannot be determined because the initial population is unknown.

7. If $\frac{m}{n} = 7$, what is the value of $\frac{2n}{m}$?

(A) 14

(B) $\frac{7}{2}$

(C) $\frac{2}{7}$

(D) $\frac{1}{7}$

8.
$$y = \frac{2}{5}x - 3$$
$$2x - 5y = 7$$

The linear equations above form lines that are

(A) parallel
(B) perpendicular
(C) parallel and perpendicular
(D) neither parallel nor perpendicular

9. Which of the following is true about the graph of the equation $y = 4(x - 3)^2 + 13$?

(A) The graph is wider than the graph of $y = (x - 3)^2 + 13$.
(B) It has no real roots.
(C) Its minimum value is –3.
(D) Its roots are $x = 3$ and $x = -13$.

GO ON TO THE NEXT PAGE

3

10. $V = 7.5 + .75x$
$C = 1.25x$

Sarah is an art teacher who wants to purchase calligraphy pens for her students. Visionary Arts (V) charges a delivery fee of $7.50 plus $.75 for each pen. Cramer's Art Supply charges $1.25 per pen with free delivery. What number of pens would need to be purchased such that the two deals are equivalent?

(A) 8
(B) 10
(C) 15
(D) 20

11. A line in the xy-plane passes through the origin and has a slope of $\frac{1}{9}$. Which of the following points lies on the line?

(A) (−6, 12)
(B) (−4, 36)
(C) $\left(3, \frac{1}{3}\right)$
(D) $\left(-\frac{1}{3}, 3\right)$

12. Which of the following is equivalent to $\dfrac{1}{\frac{1}{x+4}+\frac{1}{x+6}}$?

(A) $x^2 + 10x + 24$
(B) $\dfrac{1}{\frac{1}{x+12}}$
(C) $\dfrac{x^2+10x+24}{2x+10}$
(D) $\dfrac{x+4}{x+6}$

13. If $12x - 3y = 5$, what is the value of $\dfrac{16^{3x}}{8^y}$?

(A) 4
(B) 16
(C) 32
(D) 64

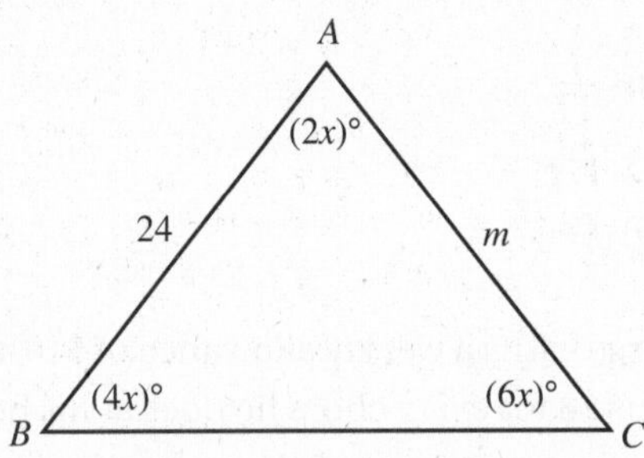

Figure Not Drawn to Scale

14. In $\triangle ABC$, what is the value of m?

(A) 12
(B) $12\sqrt{3}$
(C) $12\sqrt{2}$
(D) $3\sqrt{6}$

15. Which of the following is equal to $\left(\frac{m}{2}+n\right)^2$?

(A) $\dfrac{m^2}{2}+n^2$
(B) $\dfrac{m^2}{4}+mn+n^2$
(C) $\dfrac{m^2}{2}+mn+\dfrac{n^2}{4}$
(D) $m+\dfrac{mn}{2}+n$

GO ON TO THE NEXT PAGE

3

Grid-in Response Directions

In questions 16–20, first solve the problem, and then enter your answer on the grid provided on the answer sheet. The instructions for entering your answers follow.

- First, write your answer in the boxes at the top of the grid.
- Second, grid your answer in the columns below the boxes.
- Use the fraction bar in the first row or the decimal point in the second row to enter fractions and decimals.

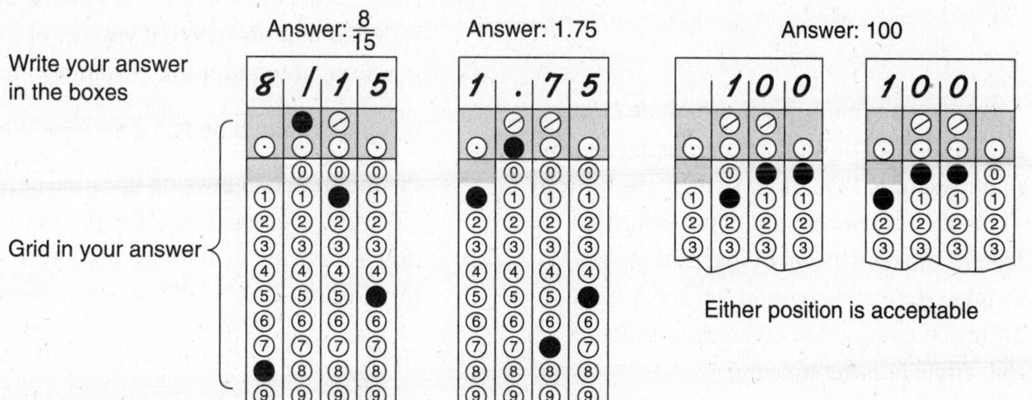

- Grid only one space in each column.
- Entering the answer in the boxes is recommended as an aid in gridding but is not required.
- The machine scoring your exam can read only what you grid, so you **must grid-in your answers correctly to get credit**.
- If a question has more than one correct answer, grid-in only one of them.
- The grid does not have a minus sign; so no answer can be negative.
- A mixed number *must* be converted to an improper fraction or a decimal before it is gridded. Enter $1\frac{1}{4}$ as $\frac{5}{4}$ or 1.25; the machine will interpret 11/4 as $\frac{11}{4}$ and mark it wrong.
- **All decimals must be entered as accurately as possible.** Here are three acceptable ways of gridding

$$\frac{3}{11} = 0.272727\ldots$$

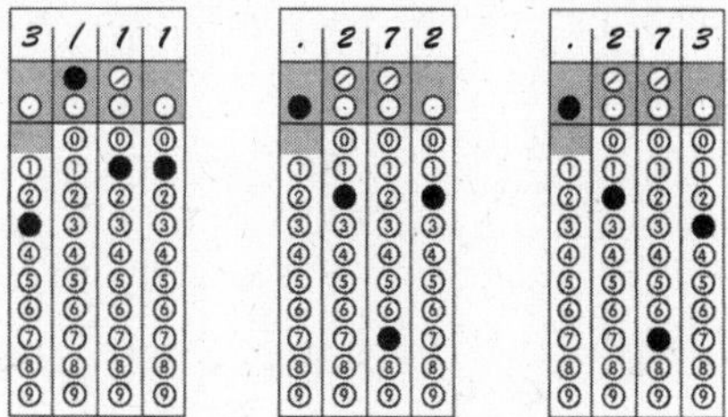

- Note that rounding to .273 is acceptable because you are using the full grid, but you would receive **no credit** for .3 or .27, because they are less accurate.

PRACTICE TEST 4

3

16. Kareem has purchased a hybrid automobile that has an average fuel efficiency of 40 miles per gallon. He recently filled his 12-gallon tank yesterday but it now registers $\frac{3}{4}$ full. How many miles did Kareem drive if his mileage reflected his average fuel efficiency?

17. A gymnast has a routine in which he sways back and forth on a high bar, making an arc that measures 135°. As he swings, the bottom of his shoes create an arc that measures 9 feet. At the conclusion of his routine, he swings completely around for one full circle around the bar. What is the circumference of that circle (answer in feet)?

18. If $\frac{1}{5}x+\frac{5}{8}y=2$, then $8x+25y=$?

19. In a right triangle, one angle measures $n°$ where $\sin(n°) = \frac{7}{9}$. What is $\cos(90 - n)°$?

20. New drivers must learn that braking distance is dependent on speed. If you travel x miles per hour, your stopping distance in feet can be approximated by $f(x) = x + \frac{x^2}{20}$. What is the difference in braking distance between a driver traveling at 60 miles per hour and a driver traveling at 40 miles per hour? (Answer in feet.)

STOP

If there is still time remaining, you may review your answers.

4  4

MATH TEST (CALCULATOR)

55 MINUTES, 38 QUESTIONS

Turn to Section 4 of your answer sheet to answer the questions in this section.

Directions: For questions 1–30, solve each problem and choose the best answer from the given options. Fill in the corresponding circle on your answer document. For questions 31–38, solve the problem and fill in the answer on the answer sheet grid. Please use scrap paper to work out your answers.

Notes:

- The use of a calculator on this section IS permitted.
- All variables and expressions represent real numbers unless indicated otherwise.
- All figures are drawn to scale unless indicated otherwise.
- All figures are in a plane unless indicated otherwise.
- Unless indicated otherwise, the domain of a given function is the set of all real numbers x for which the function has real values.

REFERENCE INFORMATION

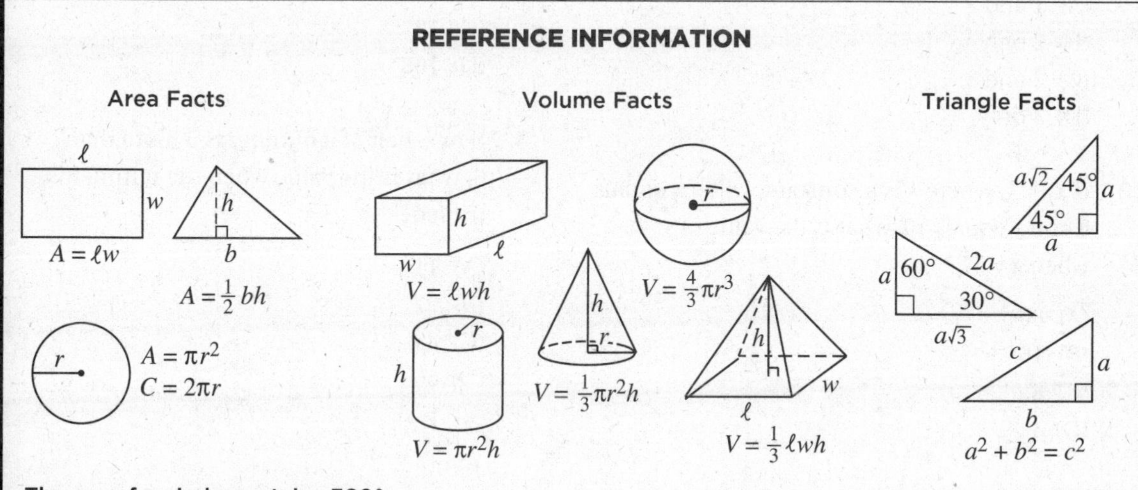

The arc of a circle contains 360°.

The arc of a circle contains 2π radians.

The sum of the measures of the angles in a triangle is 180°.

GO ON TO THE NEXT PAGE

4

4

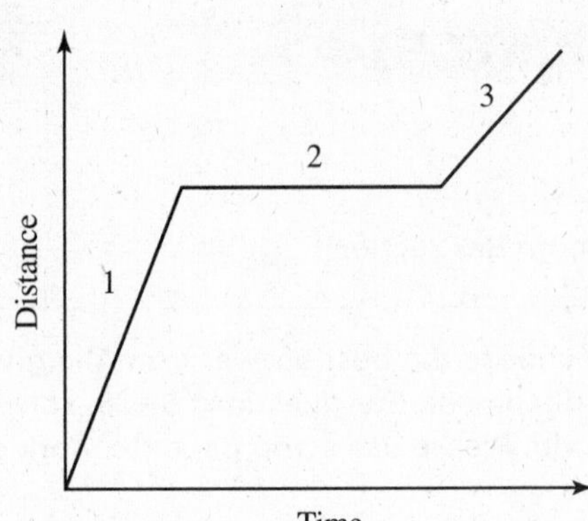

1. Thomas rides his bike to the park and then sits down on a bench to rest. After his rest, he jogs several miles. Which part(s) of the graph represents the time he spent sitting on the bench?

(A) 1 and 2
(B) 2 only
(C) 2 and 3
(D) 3 only

2. If $xy = k$, where k is a constant, when x equals 8 and y equals 10, what is the value of y when $x = 5$?

(A) 80
(B) 16
(C) 8
(D) 4

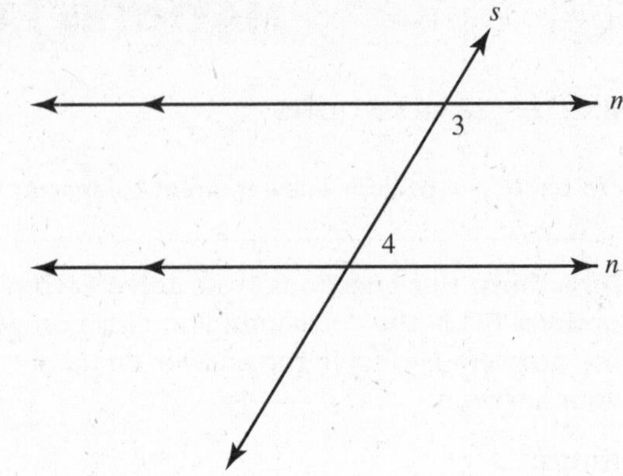

3. In the figure above, lines m and n are parallel. If $m\angle 3 = (3x)°$ and $m\angle 4 = (2x)°$, what is the measure of $m\angle 4$?

(A) 36°
(B) 48°
(C) 72°
(D) 108°

4. If one-half of a number is 5 more than 6, what is the value when the number is tripled?

(A) 11
(B) 22
(C) 33
(D) 66

GO ON TO THE NEXT PAGE

5. Which of the following graphs shows a strong positive association between t and w?

(A)

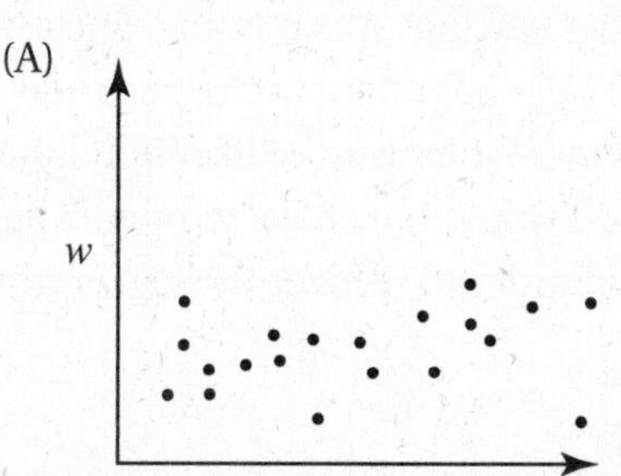

(B)

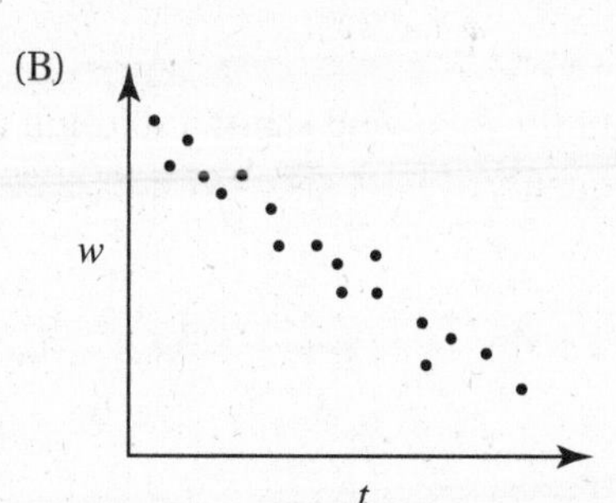

(C)

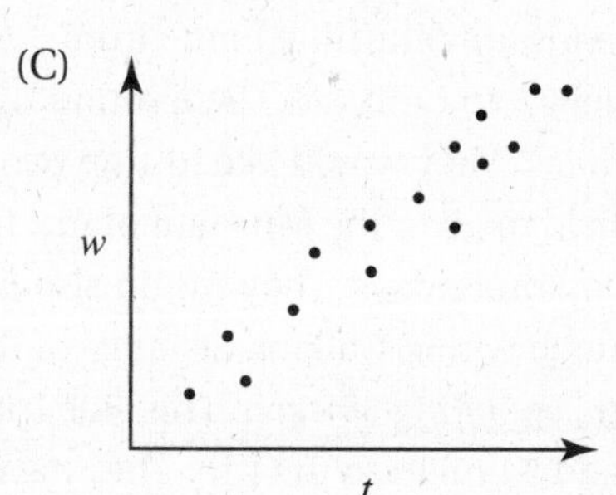

(D)

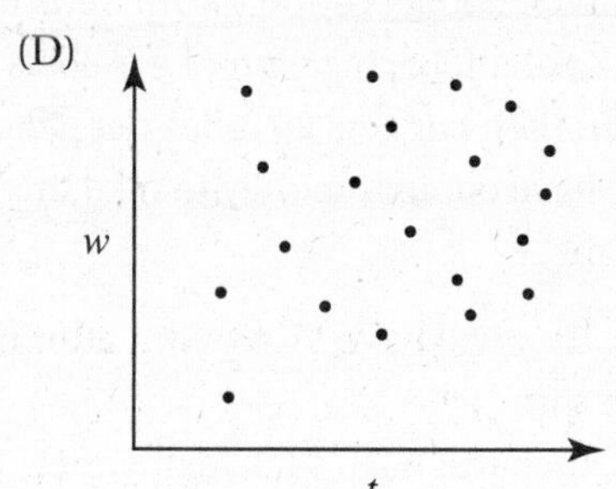

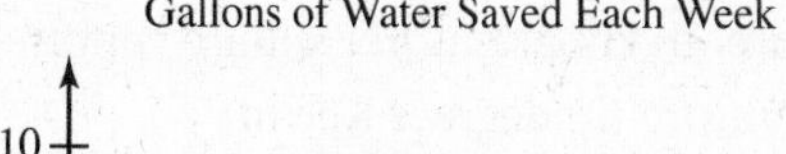

1 hectogram = 100 grams
100 centigrams = 1 gram

6. A popular snack is packaged in 2 hectogram containers. If a customer ate $\frac{1}{4}$ of one of these containers, how many centigrams did he/she consume?

(A) 50
(B) 100
(C) 1,000
(D) 5,000

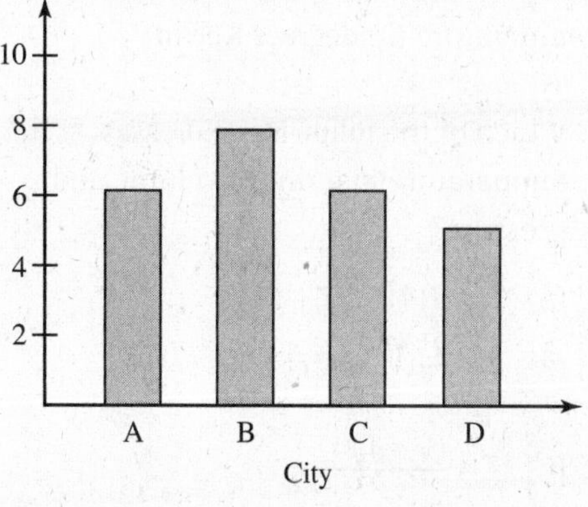

7. Certain cities in the southwestern United States are experimenting with water-saving plumbing. If the total gallons saved as expressed in the graph above equal 25,000 gallons, what is an appropriate label for the vertical axis?

(A) Gallons saved (in tens)
(B) Gallons saved (in hundreds)
(C) Gallons saved (in thousands)
(D) Gallons saved (in hundred thousands)

GO ON TO THE NEXT PAGE

8. What value(s) of n satisfies $|n + 11| \geq -12$?

(A) $-1 \leq n \leq 1$
(B) $n \geq 11$ or $n \leq -23$
(C) there is no value n
(D) all real numbers

Questions 9 and 10 refer to the following information.

An enclosed volume of a certain gas is shown by the following equation:

$$V = \frac{.7T}{P} + 3.77$$

where
V = volume of the gas (in cubic centimeters)
P = pressure (in kilograms per square centimeter)
T = temperature (in degrees Kelvin)

9. Which of the following expresses temperature in terms of volume and pressure?

(A) $T = (P - V)(.7) - 3.77$
(B) $T = \frac{P}{.7}(V - 3.77)$
(C) $T = \frac{(V + 3.77)}{P}$
(D) $T = \frac{P}{V - 3.77}$

10. Find the temperature (in degrees Kelvin) when the volume of the gas is 8,000 cubic centimeters and the pressure is 1.2 kg/cm^2.

(A) 7,407
(B) 8,176
(C) 13,708
(D) 16,511

11. Brittany was packing bags for shipping. She had packed 42 bags before she realized that one of her earrings was missing. She asked Todd to help her open up the bags and find her earring. What was the likelihood that she and Todd would only have to open 7 bags apiece in order to recover the lost earring?

(A) 33%
(B) 17%
(C) 50%
(D) 18%

12. Which of the following is **not** a solution of the inequality $-7x + 4 \leq 4x - 5$?

(A) 0
(B) 1
(C) 3
(D) 4

13. Two friends are returning home from Vacaville, CA to Carlsbad, CA, a round trip of 984 miles. They would like to stop over in Bakersfield to go to the Museum of Art, free admission on Fridays. They would also like to eat lunch within walking distance of the museum, spending $8 each. This side trip would add 54 miles to the trip. They have designated a budget of $90 for the return trip to Carlsbad. Each gallon of gas costs $3.64 and their car gets 26 miles per gallon. Do they have enough money to take this extra stop?

(A) Yes, they will have $7.43 extra after the side trip.
(B) Yes, they will have $4.32 extra after the side trip.
(C) No, they will need an additional $2.44.
(D) No, they will need an additional $8.73.

GO ON TO THE NEXT PAGE

Presidential Candidate	Vice Presidential Candidate	Political Party	Popular Vote		Electoral Vote	
Barack H. Obama	Joseph R. Biden, Jr.	Democratic	65,918,507	51.01%	332	61.7%
Willard Mitt Romney	Paul Ryan	Republican	60,934,407	47.15%	206	38.3%
Gary Johnson	James P. Gray	Libertarian	1,275,923	0.99%	0	0.0%
Jill Stein	Cheri Honkala	Green	469,015	0.36%	0	0.0%
Other (+)	—	—	637,706	0.49%	0	0.0%
Total			129,235,558		538	

14. The results of the 2012 presidential election are listed above. If all of the Libertarian, Green, and Other votes were cast for former governor Romney, what would have been true about the vote difference between Obama and Romney?

    (A) Romney would have earned the presidency by a total of 2,601,456 votes.
    (B) Obama's margin of victory would have been cut by 2,382,644 votes.
    (C) Obama would have won the election by 3,135,721 votes.
    (D) The difference between the candidates' vote totals would have been so slim that a recount would have been in order as had happened in 2000.

15. A plumbing service charges a fixed fee for a house call in addition to its hourly rate. A 2-hour call costs $114 and a call for 4.5 hours costs $194. What is the cost of the hourly rate?

    (A) $80
    (B) $75.50
    (C) $65
    (D) $32

PRACTICE TEST 4

GO ON TO THE NEXT PAGE

Questions 16–18 refer to the table below.

Daily Statistics for June 2015												
Day	**Hits**		**Files**		**Pages**		**Visits**		**Sites**		**KBytes**	
1	**327**	6.35%	**274**	6.62%	**250**	7.29%	**85**	7.58%	**60**	8.97%	**2203**	4.87%
2	**432**	8.39%	**383**	9.25%	**349**	10.17%	**64**	5.71%	**57**	8.52%	**2506**	5.54%
3	**283**	5.49%	**235**	5.68%	**181**	5.28%	**56**	5.00%	**50**	7.47%	**2332**	5.15%
4	**249**	4.83%	**208**	5.03%	**143**	4.17%	**47**	4.19%	**56**	8.37%	**2816**	6.22%
5	**265**	5.14%	**164**	3.96%	**134**	3.91%	**39**	3.48%	**44**	6.58%	**1644**	3.63%
6	**165**	3.20%	**142**	3.43%	**114**	3.32%	**45**	4.01%	**42**	6.28%	**1425**	3.15%
7	**250**	4.85%	**155**	3.74%	**134**	3.91%	**50**	4.46%	**51**	7.62%	**1621**	3.58%

The table above is a statistics page for an educational website. The visits, files, and other data are shown for the first week of June 2015. The owner of the educational site is wondering how to effectively reach more viewers.

16. Which of the following can be concluded from the table?

    (A) The number of visits exceeds the number of sites each day.
    (B) On day 7, the ratio of hits to files is greater than the ratio of files to pages.
    (C) The ratio of KBytes to sites is greater on day 6 than on day 1.
    (D) The ratio of pages to visits is never less than 3 : 1.

17. What is the median number of visits in the first seven days of June 2015?

    (A) 85
    (B) 47
    (C) 56
    (D) 50

18. If R is the range of the File category and r is the range of the KByte category, what is the value of $2r - R$?

    (A) 3,126
    (B) 2,541
    (C) 254
    (D) −249

19. Two brothers remembered their first high school job. In their first week, Rick earned \$4.50 per hour while Jay earned \$5.25 per hour. They worked a total of 44 hours and their combined wage was \$202.50. How many hours did Rick work that week?

    (A) 10
    (B) 17
    (C) 34
    (D) 38

GO ON TO THE NEXT PAGE

20. Briana bought a pair of running shoes at a 25% discount off of the original price. The total she paid the cashier was r dollars, which includes an 8% sales tax on the discounted price. Which of the following represents the original price of the running shoes in terms of r?

    (A) $.81r$

    (B) $\frac{r}{.75}$

    (C) $(.75)(1.08)r$

    (D) $\frac{r}{(1.08)(.75)}$

Questions 21 and 22 refer to the information provided below.

The metabolic rate r (in kilocalories per day) of any mammal can be modeled by using the formula $r = km^{\frac{3}{4}}$ where k is a constant and m is the mass in kilograms of the mammal. The formula $s = \frac{km^{\frac{3}{4}}}{m}$ is used to find the specific metabolic rate which measures the rate per unit of mass.

21. If the weight of a great walrus is 1,000 kilograms, and its metabolic rate is 18,500 kilocalories per day, what is the value of k in the metabolic rate formula?

    (A) 134.74
    (B) 104.03
    (C) 94.42
    (D) 41.53

22. Using the k value from question 21, find the specific metabolic rate of the great walrus.

    (A) 4.47
    (B) 4.03
    (C) 18.50
    (D) 23.47

23. A central angle in a circle has a measure of 34.4° and the measure of the area of its sector is 139.6 square units. To the nearest tenth of a unit, what is the measure of the circle's radius?

    (A) 19.4
    (B) 21.6
    (C) 27.3
    (D) 29.7

Questions 24 and 25 refer to the information below.

$$h = -4.9t^2 + 32t$$

The equation above shows the height of a ball thrown upward from ground level with an initial velocity of 32 meters per second.

24. After approximately how many seconds will the ball hit the ground?

    (A) 5.6
    (B) 6.5
    (C) 7.4
    (D) 8.2

25. After how many seconds will the ball be 18 meters in the air?

    (A) 2.2
    (B) 4.3
    (C) .6 and 5.9
    (D) .6 or 6.3

GO ON TO THE NEXT PAGE

26. The mean of seven numbers is x. What must be added to the sum of the numbers to increase the mean of the seven numbers by $\frac{4}{7}$?

(A) $\frac{19}{7}$

(B) 4

(C) $\frac{29}{7}$

(D) 8

27. In the xy-plane, the graph of a circle is $2x^2 + 8x + 2y^2 + 12y = 36$. What is the diameter of the circle?

(A) $\sqrt{31}$

(B) $2\sqrt{31}$

(C) $\sqrt{62}$

(D) $2\sqrt{62}$

28. Which of the following is an equivalent form of the function h, such that the minimum value of h appears as a constant or coefficient?

$h(x) = (x - 8)(x + 2)$

(A) $h(x) = x^2 - 6x - 16$
(B) $h(x) = x^2 + 6x - 16$
(C) $h(x) = (x - 3)^2 - 25$
(D) $h(x) = (x + 3)^2 - 25$

29. If $x^3 - 20 = (x + 5)(x^2 - 5x + 25) + m$, what is the value of m?

(A) 65
(B) 10
(C) 5
(D) −145

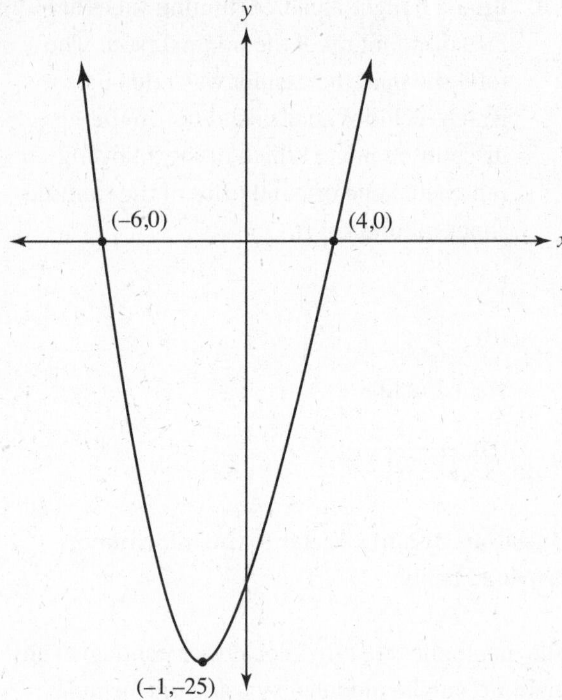

30. Which of the following equations is equivalent to the parabola with equation $y = (x - 4)(x + 6)$?

(A) $y = (x + 1)^2 - 25$
(B) $y = (x - 1)^2 + 25$
(C) $y = (x + 3)(x - 8)$
(D) $y = (x + 12)(x - 2)$

GO ON TO THE NEXT PAGE

Grid-in Response Directions

In questions 31–38, first solve the problem, and then enter your answer on the grid provided on the answer sheet. The instructions for entering your answers follow.

- First, write your answer in the boxes at the top of the grid.
- Second, grid your answer in the columns below the boxes.
- Use the fraction bar in the first row or the decimal point in the second row to enter fractions and decimals.

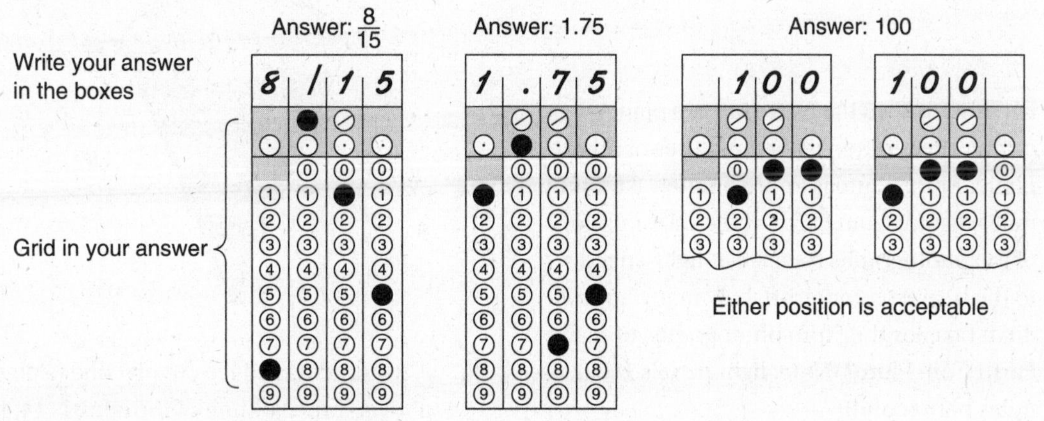

- Grid only one space in each column.
- Entering the answer in the boxes is recommended as an aid in gridding but is not required.
- The machine scoring your exam can read only what you grid, so you **must grid-in your answers correctly to get credit**.
- If a question has more than one correct answer, grid-in only one of them.
- The grid does not have a minus sign; so no answer can be negative.
- A mixed number *must* be converted to an improper fraction or a decimal before it is gridded. Enter $1\frac{1}{4}$ as $\frac{5}{4}$ or 1.25; the machine will interpret 11/4 as $\frac{11}{4}$ and mark it wrong.
- **All decimals must be entered as accurately as possible.** Here are three acceptable ways of gridding

$$\frac{3}{11} = 0.272727\ldots$$

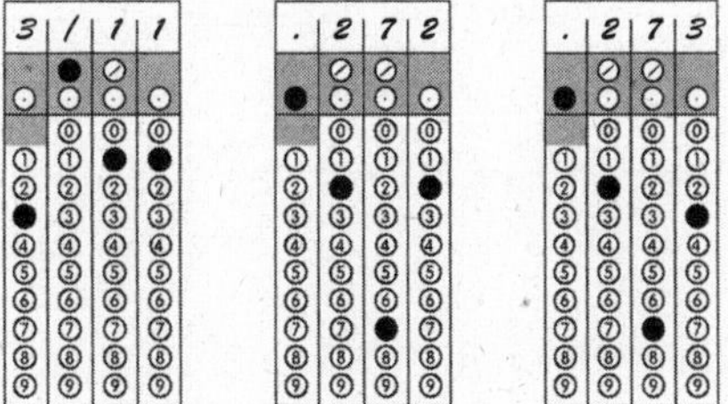

- Note that rounding to .273 is acceptable because you are using the full grid, but you would receive **no credit** for .3 or .27, because they are less accurate.

PRACTICE TEST 4

31. A pair of hiking boots sells for \$80.00. After one week, the vendor reduced the cost of the boots by 20%. After two weeks, he raised the current price by 20%. What is the cost of the hiking boots after two weeks? (Ignore the \$ sign)

32. On July 15, 2015 the New Horizon planet orbiter transmitted its first pictures of minor planet Pluto. Pluto is approximately 3 billion miles distant from Earth. If the transmission of the photographs traveled at light-speed, to the nearest hundredth, how many hours did it take for the Pluto photographs to reach Earth from Pluto? (Note: light travels 186,000 miles per second)

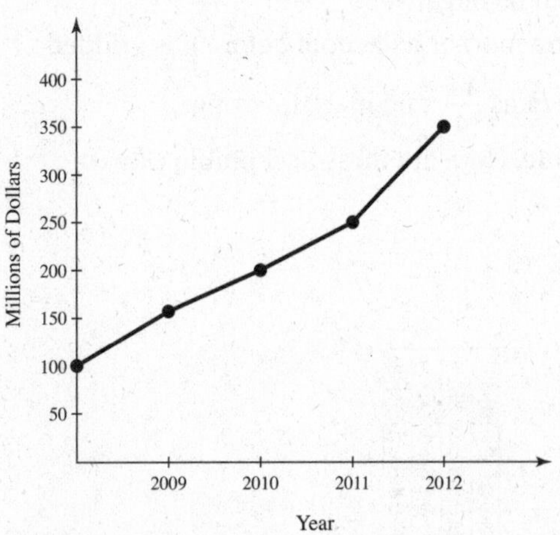

33. The County Education Budget is shown in the graph above. According to the line graph, the budget in 2010 is what fraction of the budget in 2012?

34. If $g(x) = 2(x^2 - 6)$ and $f(x) = x^2 - 5$, what does $g(f(5)) - f(g(-3))$ equal?

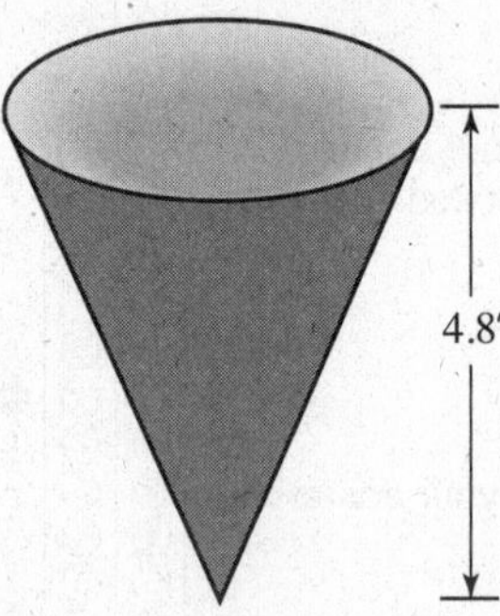

35. A waffle-flavored ice cream cone is pictured above. If the volume of the cone is 14.4π cubic inches, what is the diameter of the cone (in inches)?

36. $$f(x)=\frac{1}{2(x-3)^2+4(x-3)+2}$$

For what value of x is the function f undefined?

GO ON TO THE NEXT PAGE

Questions 37 and 38 refer to the information below.

An annuity is a fixed income stream paid out over an agreed upon period of time. A $1,000,000 insurance payment is an annuity if it is paid out over a period of time in fixed installments. The insurance company may offer the payee a lump sum payout called the present value of the annuity. The formula to calculate the present value of an annuity is as follows.

$$P = A(1+\frac{r}{n})^{-nt}$$

P = the present value of the payout
A = the dollars that would have been received over time
t = time in years
r = the interest rate expressed as a decimal
n = compounding periods each year

37. Jorge and his brothers have inherited a pension plan from their grandfather. The plan will pay each grandchild $10,000 over the course of a ten-year period. Jorge chooses to accept the present value of the inheritance at 8% compounded monthly. How much should he expect his payout to be? (Round your answer to the nearest dollar.)

38. Samantha received a cash annuity as a gift for college graduation. The annuity would pay an interest rate of 3.5% over a 5-year period compounded quarterly. Samantha elected to receive the present value of the annuity, which totaled $1,621. To the nearest dollar, what would have been the payout of the annuity if she chose to accept the 5-year payout terms?

If there is still time remaining, you may review your answers.

ESSAY (OPTIONAL)

Directions: This is your opportunity to show that you can read and understand a passage and write an analysis of that passage. Be sure your essay demonstrates a clear and logical analysis of the passage, using precise language.

On the actual test, you will write your essay on the lines provided in your answer booklet; for now, write your essay on lined paper. Remember to write or print legibly so that others can read what you've written.

You have 50 minutes to read the essay and write a response to the prompt provided.

Carefully read the passage below. As you read, think about how Lyall Watson makes use of

- *reasoning* to develop an argument
- *evidence* to support assertions made
- *language* to persuade the reader

From the Introduction to *Supernature,* by Lyall Watson, Coronet Books, 1974.

1 Science no longer holds any absolute truths. Even the discipline of physics, whose laws once went unchallenged, has had to submit to the indignity of an Uncertainty Principle. In this climate of disbelief, we have begun to doubt even fundamental propositions, and the old distinction between natural and supernatural has become meaningless.

2 I find this tremendously exciting. The picture of science as a jigsaw puzzle, with a finite number of pieces that would one day all be slotted neatly into place, has never been appealing. Experience indicates that things are not like that at all. Every new development in the microscope reveals further minute detail in structures once thought to be indivisible. Each enlargement in the power of the telescope adds thousands of galaxies to a list already so long that it is meaningless to all but mathematicians. Even research into what once seemed to be simple behavior patterns has a way of going on forever.

3 Fifty years ago naturalists were content with the observation that bats catch moths. Then came the discovery that bats produce sounds inaudible to the human ear and use echoes to locate their prey. Now it appears that not only do moths have soundproofing, but that they have ears specifically designed to listen in to an approaching enemy transmitter. To counter this advance, bats developed an irregular flight path, which confused the moths until they in turn came up with an ultrasonic jamming device. But bats still catch moths, and it can only be a matter of time before research discovers the next development in this escalating drama of nature.

4 All the best science has soft edges, limits that are still obscure and extend without interruption into areas that are wholly inexplicable. On the fringe, between those things that we understand as normal occurrences and those that are completely paranormal and defy explanation, are a cluster of semi-normal phenomena. Between nature and the supernatural are a host of happenings that I choose to describe as Supernature. It is with these go-betweens that this book is concerned.

5 In the course of a fairly catholic education in most of the life sciences, there have been many moments when the syllabus brushed up against something strange, shied away, and tried to pretend that it had not happened. These loose ends have always worried me and have now accumulated to a point where I am forced to go back and attempt to pick some of them up and try to relate them to the rest of my experience. Viewed together, they begin to make some kind of sense, but I must emphasize that this is very much a beginning and in no way a definitive study. I am resigned to the fact that my synthesis goes so far beyond the bounds of established practice that many scientists will find it outrageous, while at the same time it does not go nearly far enough to satisfy believers in everything occult. This is what bridges are about. I hope that there can be some kind of meeting in the middle.

6 The supernatural is usually defined as that which is not explicable by the known forces of nature. Supernature knows no bounds. Too often we see only what we expect to see: our view of the world is restricted by the blinkers of our limited experience; but it need not be this way. Supernature is nature with all it flavors intact, waiting to be tasted. I offer it as logical extension of the present state of science, as a solution to some of the problems with which traditional science cannot cope and as an analgesic to modern man.

7 I hope that it will prove to be more than that. Few aspects of human behavior are so persistent as our need to believe in things unseen—and as a biologist, I find it hard to accept that this is purely fortuitous. The belief, or the strange things to which this belief is so stubbornly attached, must have real survival value, and I think that we are rapidly approaching a situation in which this value will become apparent. As man uses up the resources of the world, he is going to have to rely more and more on his own. Many of these are at the moment concealed in the occult—a word that simply means "secret knowledge" and is a very good description of something that we have known all along but have been hiding from ourselves.

8 This natural history of the supernatural is designed to extend the traditional five senses into areas where others have been operating undercover. It is an attempt to fit all nature, the known and the unknown, into the body of Supernature and to show that, of all the faculties we possess, none is more important at this time than a wide-eyed sense of wonder.

Write an essay explaining how Lyall Watson constructs an argument to convince the reader that it is important for human beings to recognize the existence of "Supernature" and study it. Describe and analyze how Watson uses one or more of the elements of persuasive writing listed in the box on page 338 to strengthen his argument. You may also discuss other writing techniques used by the author.

Your essay should not state your opinion on the topic discussed in the passage, but rather analyze how Watson constructs an argument to persuade the reader.

ANSWER KEY
Practice Test 4

Section 1: Reading

1.	**D**	14.	**D**	27.	**D**	40.	**A**
2.	**B**	15.	**C**	28.	**B**	41.	**B**
3.	**B**	16.	**C**	29.	**C**	42.	**C**
4.	**B**	17.	**A**	30.	**D**	43.	**D**
5.	**A**	18.	**A**	31.	**A**	44.	**D**
6.	**C**	19.	**C**	32.	**C**	45.	**A**
7.	**A**	20.	**B**	33.	**B**	46.	**C**
8.	**D**	21.	**C**	34.	**A**	47.	**D**
9.	**C**	22.	**C**	35.	**A**	48.	**A**
10.	**C**	23.	**B**	36.	**A**	49.	**C**
11.	**D**	24.	**A**	37.	**B**	50.	**C**
12.	**D**	25.	**C**	38.	**D**	51.	**C**
13.	**C**	26.	**C**	39.	**A**	52.	**B**

Number Correct ______

Number Incorrect ______

Section 2: Writing and Language

1.	**D**	12.	**C**	23.	**B**	34.	**C**
2.	**C**	13.	**D**	24.	**D**	35.	**D**
3.	**B**	14.	**A**	25.	**D**	36.	**D**
4.	**C**	15.	**D**	26.	**A**	37.	**A**
5.	**D**	16.	**B**	27.	**B**	38.	**B**
6.	**B**	17.	**C**	28.	**C**	39.	**A**
7.	**A**	18.	**D**	29.	**C**	40.	**C**
8.	**C**	19.	**C**	30.	**A**	41.	**D**
9.	**D**	20.	**D**	31.	**B**	42.	**C**
10.	**A**	21.	**C**	32.	**C**	43.	**B**
11.	**D**	22.	**B**	33.	**B**	44.	**C**

Number Correct ______

Number Incorrect ______

ANSWER KEY
Practice Test 4

Section 3: Math (No Calculator)

1. **D**
2. **B**
3. **C**
4. **A**
5. **D**
6. **C**
7. **C**
8. **A**
9. **B**
10. **C**
11. **C**
12. **C**
13. **C**
14. **B**
15. **B**

16. **120**

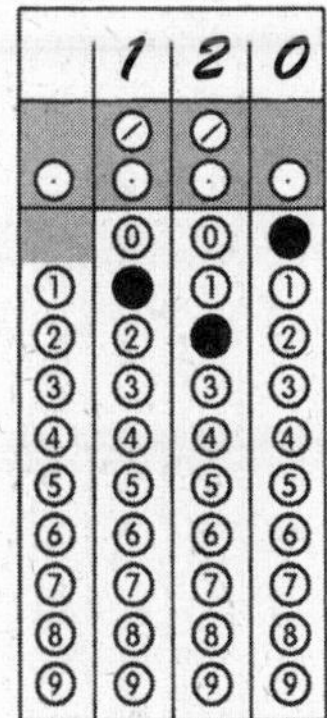

17. **24**

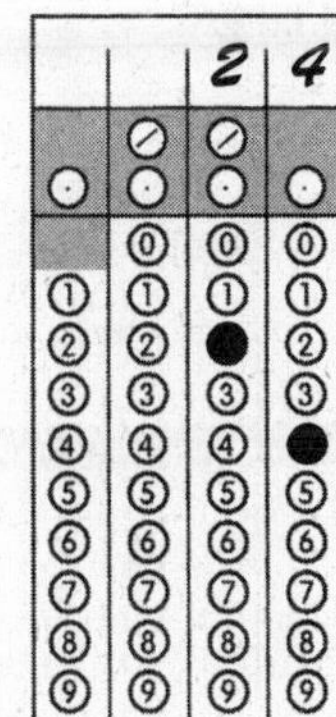

18. **80**

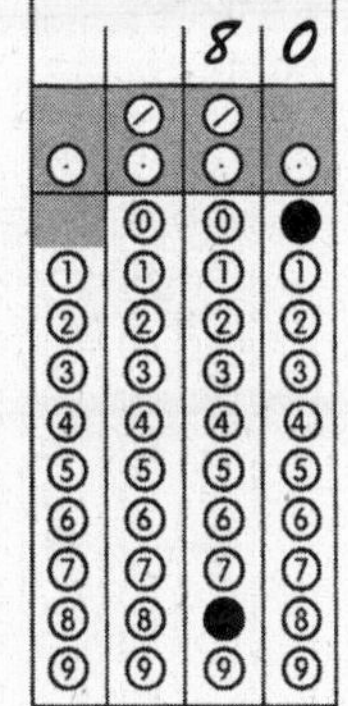

19. **7/9**

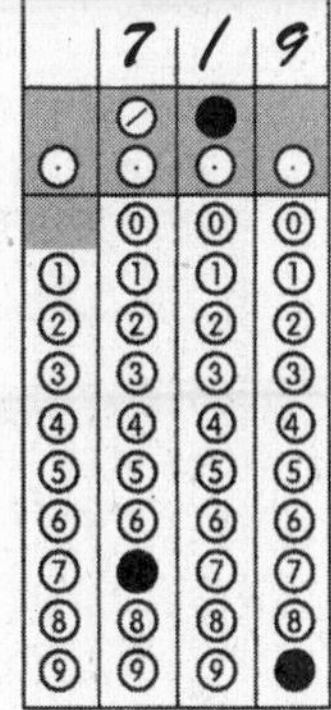

20. **120**

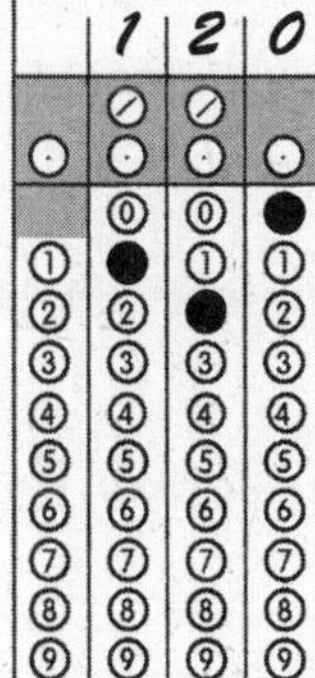

Number Correct ______

Number Incorrect ______

PRACTICE TEST 4

ANSWER KEY
Practice Test 4

Section 4: Math (Calculator)

1. **B**	7. **C**	13. **C**	19. **D**	25. **C**
2. **B**	8. **D**	14. **B**	20. **D**	26. **B**
3. **C**	9. **B**	15. **D**	21. **B**	27. **B**
4. **D**	10. **C**	16. **B**	22. **C**	28. **C**
5. **C**	11. **A**	17. **D**	23. **B**	29. **D**
6. **D**	12. **A**	18. **B**	24. **B**	30. **A**

31. **76.8**

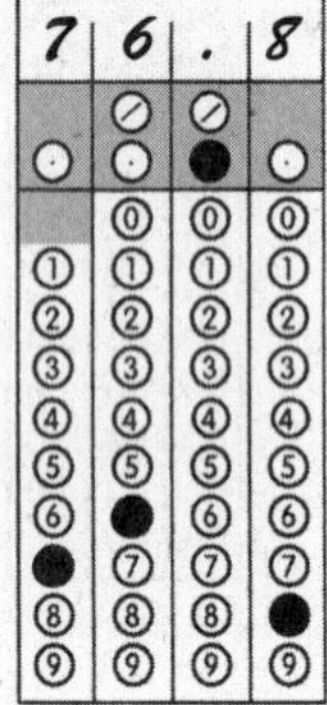

32. **4.48**

33. **4/7**

34. **757**

35. **6**

36. **2**

37. **4,505**

38. **1,930**

Number Correct ______

Number Incorrect ______

SCORE ANALYSIS

Reading and Writing Test

Section 1: Reading ________ = ________ (A)
correct raw score

Section 2: Writing ________ = ________ (B)
correct raw score

To find your Reading and Writing test scores, consult the chart below: find the ranges in which your raw scores lie and read across to find the ranges of your test scores.

________ + ________ = ________ (C)
range of reading test scores | range of writing test scores | range of reading + writing test scores

To find the range of your Reading and Writing Scaled Score, multiply (C) by 10.

Test Scores for the Reading and Writing Sections

Reading Raw Score	Writing Raw Score	Test Score
44-52	39-44	35-40
36-43	33-38	31-34
30-35	28-32	28-30
24-29	22-27	24-27
19-23	17-21	21-23
14-18	13-16	19-20
9-13	9-12	16-18
5-8	5-8	13-15
less than 5	less than 5	10-12

Math Test

Section 3: ________ = ________ (D)
correct raw score

Section 4: ________ = ________ (E)
correct raw score

Total Math raw score: (D) + (E) = ________

To find your Math Scaled Score, consult the chart below: find the range in which your raw score lies and read across to find the range for your scaled score.

Scaled Scores for the Math Test

Raw Score	Scaled Score
50-58	700-800
44-49	650-690
38-43	600-640
32-37	550-590
26-31	500-540

Raw Score	Scaled Score
20-25	450-490
15-19	400-440
11-14	350-390
7-10	300-340
less than 7	200-290

PRACTICE TEST 4

ANSWER EXPLANATIONS

Section 1: Reading Test

1. **(D)** *Hinterlands* means *remote country regions* and makes good sense in context.
2. **(B)** *Lights* means people in context because the author is describing how Japanese people in America were put in camps.
3. **(B)** Presumably, the image of the snowball was used by the author in an earlier part of the book from which this passage was taken. However, it can be inferred that the "snowball" mentioned in line 32 refers to the accumulating efforts of Americans to destroy the Japanese because the author is describing the steps taken by Americans to prevent Japanese nationals, Japanese aliens, and Japanese-Americans in America from aiding Japan in the war against America. He says, "The snowball was big enough to wipe out the rising sun" (lines 32–33), suggesting that these efforts had stopped the Japanese threat on American soil.
4. **(B)** *Sarcastic* (characterized by words that mean the opposite of what they seem to mean and are intended to mock) is the best choice. It is likely that the author is being sarcastic because it would not require "the utmost of America's great organizing ability" (lines 45–46) to construct camps and put people in them as described in the passage.
5. **(A)** Because America was at war with Japan, it makes sense that some people would hire a person that they believed was Chinese but not a person they believed to be Japanese.
6. **(C)** A *euphemism* (a word or phrase used in place of a term that might be considered too direct, unpleasant, or offensive) is the best choice because "relocation center" can be seen as a pleasant way of saying "concentration camp" (lines 91–92).
7. **(A)** *Strange* is the best choice because the lieutenant says, "That's funny," after he is told about the removal of the Japanese from the Coast and the construction of relocation centers for them. The narrator says, "He didn't believe it" (lines 93–94), suggesting that the lieutenant thought it was strange that this was being done.
8. **(D)** There is no extrapolation (estimation by projection of known information) in the passage.
9. **(C)** The answer can be inferred from the information in lines 76–92 ("You . . . centers").
10. **(C)** This provides the best evidence for the answer to the previous question because it can be inferred from the conversation between the radio operator and the narrator that the narrator's parents are living in a relocation camp in Wyoming. In response to the radio operator's question "Farmers, huh?" the narrator replies "Not quite" and then explains how his parents and others have been moved to relocation camps.
11. **(D)** The author says, "If the nuclear forces had been slightly stronger than they are . . . hydrogen would be a rare element, and stars like the sun . . . could not exist" (lines 12–20).
12. **(D)** The author uses the word *extravagantly* to emphasize that the stars in an average galaxy are separated by a distance that is far greater than appears to be necessary.

13. **(C)** After referring to astrology, the author says, "But it happens to be true that we could not have survived if the average distance between stars were only two million million miles instead of twenty" (lines 51–54). It makes sense that the author refers to astrology to stress how remarkable it is that faraway stars affect life on Earth because astrology also says that faraway stars affect life on Earth.

14. **(D)** The main argument in the passage is that the universe seems designed for life, so it is reasonable that the word "decisive" in line 48 means *conclusive.* The author is saying that without the great distances between stars life would be impossible.

15. **(C)** The author says, "Without such accidents . . . hydrogen atoms could not form breakable bridges between molecules" (lines 76–81).

16. **(C)** These lines provide the best evidence. The author is providing an example of an accident that helps make the universe hospitable. He says that the fact that "hydrogen atoms form breakable bridges between molecules" is such an example.

17. **(A)** The author says he is "a scientist, trained in the habits of thought and language of the twentieth century rather than the eighteenth" (lines 86–88). He is contrasting the way a twentieth century scientist is trained to think with the way people were trained to think in the eighteenth century. Such training produces "habits of thought"—that is, recurrent patterns of thinking.

18. **(A)** The author's tone is measured and reasonable. It is not amused, skeptical, or indignant.

19. **(C)** The author says, "I conclude from the existence of these accidents of physics and astronomy that the universe is an unexpectedly hospitable place for living creatures to make their home" (lines 82–86). The discovery of life on a planet of another star in our galaxy would provide evidence that life is not unique to Earth.

20. **(B)** The author says, "I do not claim that the architecture of the universe proves the existence of God. I claim only that the architecture of the universe is consistent with the hypothesis that mind plays an essential role in its functioning" (lines 88–93). The author would probably agree that what he calls the "accidents" of physics and astronomy suggest fairly strongly that the universe was designed, presumably by some powerful agency, such as God.

21. **(C)** Inductive reasoning is the process of deriving general principles from particular facts. The author makes extensive use of this in his argument. He does not use understatement, paradox, or concession.

22. **(C)** The words "the entry of sulfonamides and penicillin" signal that *pharmacopoeia* refers to a stock of medical drugs.

23. **(B)** The author says, "Therapy [new and effective drugs] had been discovered for great numbers of patients whose illnesses had previously been untreatable" (lines 9–12) and "Doctors could now cure disease, and this was astonishing, most of all to the doctors themselves" (lines 13–15).

24. **(A)** The author says, "That long habit . . . had been to treat everything with something" (lines 77–79).

25. **(C)** *Crudest* means "very unsophisticated" and *empiricism* is "the use of observation and experimentation to gain knowledge."

26. **(C)** Before commenting, "It is astounding that the profession survived so long" (lines 56–57), the author describes how medicine was practiced throughout most of history. He describes this practice as "irresponsible" (line 45), as having no scientific basis, and as often harming patients more than helping them.

27. **(D)** A *skeptic* is a person who questions generally accepted ideas. The author says that Montaigne (a sixteenth century French essayist) saw through "the old nonsense" (established medical practice, that is) because he was a skeptic.

28. **(B)** It makes sense that the author believes it took courage for physicians to suggest that their profession was using faulty methods because members of a field who criticize their profession would be likely to be regarded as disloyal by other members of the field.

29. **(C)** The author says, "It is hard for us now to imagine the magnitude of this discovery and its effect on the practice of medicine. That long habit . . . had been to treat everything with something, and it was taken for granted that every disease demanded treatment" (lines 74–81). The discovery that certain diseases are self-limited was surprising because it contradicted what nearly everyone thought.

30. **(D)** These lines provide the best evidence for the answer to the previous question. The discovery that most diseases improve without treatment was surprising because most doctors believed that treatment was necessary for every disease.

31. **(A)** *Ironic* (involving an incongruity between what might be expected and what actually occurs) is the best word to describe the accomplishment because it is ironic that the major scientific accomplishment of medicine, which exists to cure people of disease, is the discovery that patients often are better off without medical treatment.

32. **(C)** In context, *aggressive* refers to *very intensive* medical treatment.

33. **(B)** In line 3 the author refers to "computer modeling by NASA scientists." Also, in line 22 she refers to "simulations of young planetary systems."

34. **(A)** This provides the best evidence for the answer to the previous question.

35. **(A)** In context, *dangerous* means "likely to cause harm." This can be inferred because the sentence in which the word *dangerous* is used is about "the key to survival for some . . . planets" (lines 4–5). A dangerous orbit is one likly to cause harm to the planet in that orbit.

36. **(A)** The reference to a common terrestrial experience helps the reader to visualize a process governed by the same fundamental physical laws but on a far larger scale.

37. **(B)** The passage is about a process (tidal friction) that may help young planets in dangerous orbits achieve a safer orbit. In lines 24–27 the author describes how giant planets can interrupt the orbits of smaller planets and says, "Even if those interactions aren't immediately catastrophic, they can leave a planet in a treacherous eccentric orbit." She then goes on to describe some of the effects on the planet of having an eccentric orbit.

38. **(D)** In lines 8–9 the author says that "Earth-sized planets appear to be very common in other star systems." In lines 22–24 she says, "simulations of young planetary systems indicate that giant planets often upset the orbits of smaller inner worlds." She then goes on to describe a theory that explains how tidal friction may help some Earth-sized planets in elliptical orbits return to circular orbits. We can infer from this information that since their creation some Earth-sized planets have always been in a circular orbit, others have always been in an elliptical orbit, some were once in a circular orbit but are now in an elliptical orbit, and still others once were in an elliptical orbit but have since returned to a circular orbit.

39. **(A)** It can be described as paradoxical because a thick covering of something very cold—ice—helps the planet become warmer.

40. **(A)** Choices (B), (C), and (D) are not supported by information in the passage. It can be inferred that the authors of the study described in the passage would be likely to agree with this statement because much of their study deals with this subject. Further study appears to be important because much of the phenomena described is theoretical and more data is needed to explain it fully.

41. **(B)** This accurately summarizes the main topic of the passage.

42. **(C)** Because the study was by NASA scientists, we can infer that it was technical in nature and written for a specialized journal, such as an astronomy journal, read by professional scientists. The passage itself, in contrast, could have been written by any of the other three choices because the passage describes the scientists' findings and theories in a non-technical way.

43. **(D)** Throughout the passage the author argues for his belief that America "is destined to be the great nation of futurity" (lines 18–19).

44. **(D)** From context, it can be inferred that *suffered* means "permitted." The author is saying what Americans have never permitted themselves to do.

45. **(A)** The author says, "Besides . . . government" (lines 28–33).

46. **(C)** This provides the best evidence. The author says that the more "democratic equality" a country has, the greater it is. We can infer from this that he believes that democracy is the best form of government.

47. **(D)** It makes sense that a lover of mankind would be horrified by the suffering inflicted on people by monarchies and aristocracies.

48. **(A)** The author uses two rhetorical questions in the third paragraph (lines 34–42). The two rhetorical questions in succession are an effective way to advance his argument.

49. **(C)** It makes sense that *objects* means "goals" because the author is discussing America's "expansive future" mentioned in lines 63–64.

50. **(C)** This is the best summary of the passage. A good restatement of it is found in the last paragraph.

51. **(C)** The author is advancing a serious argument with enthusiasm.

52. **(B)** The author's main argument is that America's destiny is to become a great democratic nation, spreading democracy to other countries. As mentioned in the explanation of question 50, a summary of the passage is found in the final paragraph, in which the author discusses America's "blessed mission to the nations of the world."

Section 2: Writing and Language Test

1. **(D)** Choices (A) and (B) do not make sense. Choice (C) is not grammatical. Choice (D) is grammatical and creates a sentence that makes good sense. A clue to the answer is the word *prevalent*.
2. **(C)** Choice (A) makes no sense because the effects of the infection can't be "foreseen" at a "later" time; they can only be foreseen at an earlier time. Choice (B) makes some sense, but the word *disclosed* is used to refer to a situation in which someone knows something but has not said what it is, which is not the case here. Choice (D) has the same meaning as choice (B) in context, and so also is not correct. Choice (C) makes good sense because the sentence says "about 90 percent of these infants usually do not show any signs of the disease at birth."
3. **(B)** This is the best choice. It is grammatical and makes good sense.
4. **(C)** Sentence 4 follows logically from sentence 1, which says "*T. gondi* has become recognized as a significant cause of disease in infants and children. Sentence 2 mentions "about 90 percent of these infants," which is a reference to the "400–4,000 infants" mentioned in sentence 4, so sentence 2 follows logically from sentence 4.
5. **(D)** This is the only choice that makes good sense.
6. **(B)** From the graph it can be seen that the risk of developing clinical signs before age 3 is higher when congenital infection occurs during the first trimester than it is when infection occurs during the third trimester. Also, the preceding sentence says that "the risk of congenital infection is *lowest* when maternal infection is during the first trimester and *highest* when infection is during the third trimester." Choice (B) is the correct answer because it describes a contrast (signaled by the word *however*) with what is described in the preceding sentence.
7. **(A)** *Spectrum*, which means "range" in context, is the best choice in context. A clue is the long list of "outcomes" and "diseases" given later in the sentence.
8. **(C)** The outcomes and diseases listed are all nouns (sometimes modified by an adjective), so in order to maintain parallelism, the answer for this blank should also be a noun. The noun *vision* modified by the adjective *diminished* is the best choice.
9. **(D)** This is the correct choice because it signals that one of the diseases listed in the previous sentence will be discussed in the sentence.
10. **(A)** The simple present tense is correct in context because a statement of fact is being made.
11. **(D)** This is the correct choice because it is standard usage in this context.
12. **(C)** Choice (A) makes some sense but creates a very awkward and ambiguous sentence. Choice (B) is grammatical but makes little sense. Choice (D) also is grammatical but

makes little sense. Choice (C) is correct because it creates a clear and grammatical sentence.

13. **(D)** *Dedicate,* which in context means "commit oneself to a course of action," is the best choice. A clue is the words "because they enjoy the subject matter," which suggest that the Ph.D. candidates do the research and study more because of this than other motivations.

14. **(A)** *Tangible* (concrete) is the best choice. The author is comparing such "payoffs"—better employment and earning prospects—to the intangible motivations mentioned in the previous sentence.

15. **(D)** The given Choice (A) creates a sentence with faulty parallelism because "rates" and "earnings" are compared to "people." Choice (D) corrects this error. In "they are for people with" the pronoun *they* refers to "rates" and "earnings."

16. **(B)** This is the best choice. The present perfect tense is used here because the action ("completing several years of study") was done in the past and continues to be done at present.

17. **(C)** This information is given in the chart.

18. **(D)** This information is given in the chart.

19. **(C)** The participial is the correct choice. It modifies the noun *degrees,* telling us what type of degrees they are.

20. **(D)** This is the best choice because it is idiomatic and makes sense. Choice (C) could be considered acceptable, but it is too informal for the context, which is a formal article.

21. **(C)** This choice creates a grammatical sentence that makes good sense.

22. **(B)** Sentence 5 follows logically from sentence 1 and introduces the topic (gains and losses of shares of doctorates awarded) elaborated on in sentences 2–6.

23. **(B)** This is the standard expression in this sort of context.

24. **(D)** This is the only choice that fits contextually, idiomatically, and grammatically. *Obscurity* in this context means "state of being little known."

25. **(D)** This is the best choice because it is clear and grammatical. The nonrestrictive participial phrase beginning with "Pressing" and ending with "Mediterranean" modifies the pronoun "he." Choice (A) is grammatical but not as effectively expressed as choice (D).

26. **(A)** This is the best choice because sentence 3 helps to link sentence 2 and sentence 4.

27. **(B)** This is the correct choice because in this context "lesser" is an adjective meaning "lower in importance or esteem."

28. **(C)** This is the best choice in context because the author is contrasting "the enlightened arts" discussed in the preceding sentences to practical fields such as road building. In this context utilitarian means "practical."

29. **(C)** This is the correct choice because the phrase *along which* begins a prepositional phrase modifying the noun "roads." Note that "through the most important parts of the empire" is also a prepositional phrase modifying the noun "roads." Choice (A) does

not create a grammatical sentence because there is not a relative pronoun ("that" or "which") before the verb "carried."

30. **(A)** This is the only choice that is idiomatically correct and makes sense.

31. **(B)** This is the best choice because the independent clause after the semicolon further describes the book mentioned in the independent clause before the semicolon, focusing on the "astronomical matters of considerable complexity" dealt with in the book.

32. **(C)** The simple past tense *was* is correct in context. Choice (A) is incorrect because the work was translated at a time in the past later, not earlier, than the time in the past the author is generally referring to in the paragraph.

33. **(B)** This is the correct choice because it correctly punctuates the sentence. A dash is used correctly to signal that what follows the dash is amplifying material.

34. **(C)** This choice is correct because it creates a dependent clause providing more information about the "dazzling journalistic successes" mentioned earlier in the sentence.

35. **(D)** The simple present tense is correct in context. The author is making a generalization.

36. **(D)** This is the best choice because in context pertinent means "relevant." A clue is the words "shall have lost its point by tomorrow;" "lost its point" means "lost its relevance."

37. **(A)** This is the best choice because sentence 6 follows logically from sentence 5, which describes what the earlier writers attempted to do, providing a link to sentence 7, which evaluates the success of these attempts.

38. **(B)** This sentence is a concise and accurate statement of the view the writer expands on in the second paragraph. It should be added here because it serves as an effective topic sentence of the paragraph.

39. **(A)** This is the correct idiom in context.

40. **(C)** The simple past tense is correct in context because in this sentence the action described moves from an earlier time in the past ("had done," which is cast in the past perfect tense) to a more recent time in the past.

41. **(D)** This is the correct choice. It is clear and grammatical. Choice (A) makes no sense. Choice (C) makes sense and is grammatical; however, it is awkward.

42. **(C)** This is the best choice because it creates a grammatical sentence that makes good sense. Choice (A) and choice (D) are grammatically correct but are not as suitable as choice (C) because they suggest that the "fairly good stories" have been sacrificed to the "first rate novel or story" as an act of devotion.

43. **(B)** *Intrinsic,* which means *inherent* in context, is the best choice. Choices (C) and (D) have similar meanings but are not suitable in context.

44. **(C)** The focus of the paragraph is on writing as an art.

Section 3: Math Test (No Calculator)

1. **(D)** The product of two values is the result of multiplying them. "Increased by" means use addition. We therefore arrive at the equation:

$$5n + 12 = -13$$

Begin isolating the variable by subtracting 12 from both sides of the equation.

$$5n + 12 - 12 = -13 - 12$$
$$5n = -25$$

Complete the problem by dividing both sides of the equation by 5.

$$\frac{5n}{5} = -\frac{25}{5}$$
$$n = -5$$

Check your solution by replacing n with -5 in the equation we have created.

$$5(-5) + 12 = -13$$
$$-25 + 12 = -13$$
$$-13 = -13$$

2. **(B)** Each complex number is expressed in the form $a + bi$ where a is the real component and bi is the imaginary. Add the real components together and then add the imaginary components.

$$(7 - 2i) + (4 - 5i)$$
$$(7 + 4) + (-2i - 5i)$$
$$11 - 7i$$

3. **(C)** Although it is possible that no single fish weighs f pounds, on average each one weighs that amount. To find the total weight of 17 fish, each with a weight of f pounds, multiply the number of fish, 17, by its average weight, f.

$$17 \times f = 17f$$

4. **(A)** Let n represent the number of chores Jorge performed in the week in which he earned \$106. Including Jorge's weekly allowance we come up with the following equation:

$$10 + 8n = 106$$
$$8n = 96$$
$$n = 12$$

Jorge performed 12 chores the week he was paid \$106.

5. **(D)** Combine like terms by adding and subtracting the coefficients. Like terms are those that contain the same variable(s) raised to the same power(s). In this example, the following are the like terms:

$$-2xy,\ xy \text{ and } -8mn \text{ and } mn$$
$$-4xy^2 - 2xy + xy - 8mn + mn = -4xy^2 - xy - 7mn$$

Remember, a term such as mn is understood to have a coefficient of 1.

6. **(C)** The year $Y + 90$ means 90 years had elapsed since year Y. The town doubled in size every 15 years so it doubled a total of 6 times because $90 \div 15 = 6$. Given that doubling means multiply by 2, the town was 2^6 as large as it was in year Y. $2^6 = 64$, so the town was 64 times larger than it was in year Y. Choice (D) suggests we need to know the original size of the population, but that fact is irrelevant. Whatever its size was in year Y, we only need to know how many times larger it became in year $Y + 90$.

7. **(C)** If $\frac{m}{n} = 7$ then $\frac{n}{m} = \frac{1}{7}$. $\frac{2n}{m}$ can be interpreted as $(2)\left(\frac{n}{m}\right)$. Since $\frac{n}{m} = \frac{1}{7}$, then double that value, $\frac{2n}{m}$, must equal $\frac{2}{7}$.

8. **(A)** Parallel lines have the same slope but different y-intercepts.

$$y = \frac{2}{5}x - 3$$
$$2x - 5y = 7$$

Convert the second equation to slope-intercept form to compare the slopes of the equations.

$$\begin{aligned} 2x - 5y &= 7 \\ -5y &= -2x + 7 \\ \frac{-5}{-5}y &= \frac{-2}{-5}x + \frac{7}{-5} \\ y &= \frac{2}{5}x - \frac{7}{5} \end{aligned}$$

The slope of both lines is $\frac{2}{5}$ and the y-intercepts are different, so the lines are parallel. Choice (C) can automatically be eliminated; two lines cannot be both parallel and perpendicular.

9. **(B)** One way to solve this problem is to let $y = 0$. Doing so will let us find the roots of the equation.

$$\begin{aligned} 0 &= 4(x-3)^2 + 13 \\ -13 &= 4(x-3)^2 \\ -\frac{13}{4} &= (x-3)^2 \\ \pm\sqrt{-\frac{13}{4}} &= x - 3 \\ 3 \pm \frac{i\sqrt{13}}{2} &= x \end{aligned}$$

PRACTICE TEST 4

The equation has no real roots, solely imaginary ones. Another way to solve this question is to quickly sketch the graph.

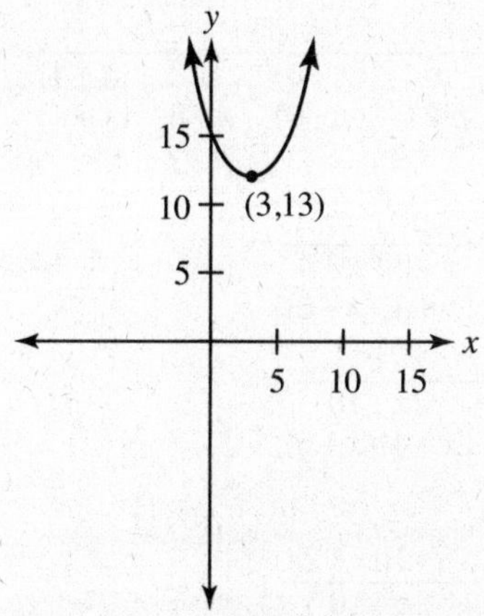

The entire parabola is above the x-axis so its roots are imaginary.

10. **(C)** Set both purchase plans equal to one another to calculate the number of pens which make both deals equal in cost.

$$7.5 + .75x = 1.25x$$

$$7.5 = .5x$$

$$15 = x$$

Purchasing 15 pens gives the same price at Visionary Arts and Cramer's Art Supply. Check your answer.

$$\$7.50 + \$.75(15) = \$18.75$$

$$\$1.25(15) = \$18.75$$

11. **(C)** A line that passes through the origin with a slope of $\frac{1}{9}$ has an equation of $y = \frac{1}{9}x + 0$, or more simply $y = \frac{1}{9}x$. The point $\left(3, \frac{1}{3}\right)$ satisfies the equation.

$$y = \frac{1}{9}x$$

$$\frac{1}{3} = \left(\frac{1}{9}\right)(3)$$

$$\frac{1}{3} = \frac{1}{3}$$

PRACTICE TEST 4

12. **(C)** Multiply $\frac{1}{x+4}$ by $\frac{x+6}{x+6}$ and $\frac{1}{x+6}$ by $\frac{x+4}{x+4}$.

$$\frac{1}{\frac{1}{x+4}\times\frac{(x+6)}{(x+6)}+\frac{1}{x+6}\times\frac{(x+4)}{(x+4)}}=$$

$$\frac{1}{\frac{x+6+x+4}{(x+4)(x+6)}}=$$

$$\frac{1}{\frac{2x+10}{(x+4)(x+6)}}=$$

$$\frac{x^2+10x+24}{2x+10}$$

13. **(C)** Convert the numerator and the denominator to base 2.

$$\frac{16^{3x}}{8^y}=\frac{(2^4)^{3x}}{(2^3)^y}=\frac{2^{12x}}{2^{3y}}$$

When dividing terms with the same base, subtract the exponents.

$$\frac{2^{12x}}{2^{3y}}=2^{12x-3y}$$

Since $12x-3y=5$, then $2^{12x-3y}=2^5=32$

14. **(B)** Find the measure of each angle by solving for x.

$$\begin{aligned}6x+4x+2x&=180\\12x&=180\\x&=15\\2x&=30\\4x&=60\\6x&=90\end{aligned}$$

$\triangle ABC$ is a 30-60-90 triangle. The hypotenuse measures 24 so m measures $12\sqrt{3}$ because it is opposite the 60° angle.

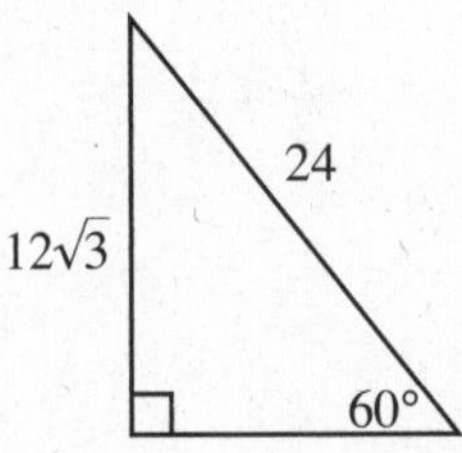

15. **(B)** Use the model $(a+b)^2=a^2+2ab+b^2$ to expand the trinomial $\left(\frac{m}{2}+n\right)^2$.

$$\left(\frac{m}{2}\right)^2+2\left(\frac{m}{2}n\right)+(n)^2=\frac{m^2}{4}+mn+n^2$$

PRACTICE TEST 4

The correct answer could also be found using the FOIL method of multiplication.

$$\left(\frac{m}{2}+n\right)^2 = \left(\frac{m}{2}+n\right)\left(\frac{m}{2}+n\right)$$

$$= \frac{m^2}{4} + \frac{mn}{2} + \frac{mn}{2} + n^2$$

$$= \frac{m^2}{4} + mn + n^2$$

Choices (A), (C), and (D) are the results of improperly expanding the trinomial $\left(\frac{m}{2}+n\right)^2$.

16. **120** Kareem's gas tank registered $\frac{3}{4}$ full, which means he has used $\frac{1}{4}$ of his full tank, which has a capacity of 12 gallons. Multiply $\frac{1}{4}$ by 12 to find how many gallons Kareem used.

$$\frac{1}{4} \times 12 = 3$$

Kareem used 3 gallons of gas and each gallon provided him 40 miles, so he drove a total of 120 miles.

17. **24** A circle measures 360°. Find what portion a 135° arc is of a circle and then use that information to create a proportion. It will be useful to reduce $\frac{135}{360}$ to $\frac{3}{8}$.

$$\frac{3}{8}=\frac{9}{x}$$
$$3x=72$$
$$x=24$$

18. **80** Multiply $\frac{1}{5}x+\frac{5}{8}y=2$ by 40, the least common multiple (LCM) of 5 and 8.

$$(40)\left(\frac{1}{5}x+\frac{5}{8}y=2\right)$$
$$8x + 25y = 80$$

19. $\mathbf{\frac{7}{9}}$ The acute angles in a right triangle are complementary. The complementary theorem states that sin x = cos(90 – x). Since sin $n°$ = $\frac{7}{9}$ then cos(90 – $n°$) also equals $\frac{7}{9}$.

20. **120** Input 60 and 40 for x in the braking distance formula, then find their difference.

$$f(x)=x+\frac{x^2}{20}$$
$$f(60)=60+\frac{60^2}{20}=240$$
$$f(40)=40+\frac{40^2}{20}=120$$
$$240-120=120$$

Section 4: Math Test (Calculator)

1. **(B)** Part 2 of the graph is flat, indicating that time passed but no additional distance was covered. Sections 1 and 3 show both time and distance were covered over each interval as evidenced by the upward behavior of the graph.

2. **(B)** Input the known data for x and y to find k.

$$(8)(10) = k$$
$$80 = k$$

Replace x with 5 and k with 80 and solve for y.

$$5y = 80$$
$$y = 16$$

3. **(C)** $\angle 3$ and $\angle 4$ are consecutive interior angles. When lines are parallel, consecutive interior angles are supplementary. Find their sum and set that value equal to 180°.

$$3x + 2x = 180$$
$$5x = 180$$
$$x = 36$$

The measure of $\angle 4$ is $(2x)°$, so replace x with 36 and solve.

$$(2)(36) = 72$$

The figure is drawn to scale and angle 4 seems to be acute, so choice (D), 108°, can be eliminated at once.

4. **(D)** Let n = the number
"... one-half of a number is 5 more than 6" translates into the following equation:

$$\frac{1}{2}n = 5 + 6$$

Solve for n as you normally would.

$$\frac{1}{2}n = 11$$
$$2\left(\frac{1}{2}n = 11\right)2$$
$$n = 22$$

The question requires tripling the value of n so multiply 22 by 3.

$$3 \times 22 = 66$$

5. **(C)** A strong positive association means when t values increase, w values increase. Choice (C) shows this relationship while choice (B) shows a strong negative association. The other two graphs show a weak association and no association.

6. **(D)** One hectogram equals 100 grams, so 2 hectograms equal 200 grams. The customer consumed $\frac{1}{4}$ of one container, so 50 grams of the snack was consumed $\left(\frac{1}{4} \times 200 = 50\right)$. Each gram equals 100 centigrams, so multiply 50 by 100 to find the amount consumed expressed as centigrams.

$$50 \times 100 = 5{,}000$$

7. **(C)** The sum of the measures of the bars in the graph is 25 units. Given that the four cities saved 25,000 gallons of water, the vertical axis should read *Gallons saved (in thousands)* because 25,000 ÷ 25 = 1,000.

8. **(D)** The absolute value of a quantity is greater than or equal to 0. Therefore, any value of n satisfies $|n + 11| \geq -12$. The solution set to the inequality, then, is all real numbers.

9. **(B)** Isolate T by subtracting 3.77 from each side of $V = \frac{.7T}{P} + 3.77$.

$$V = \frac{.7T}{P} + 3.77$$
$$V - 3.77 = \frac{.7T}{P}$$

Multiply both sides of the equation by $\frac{P}{.7}$, the reciprocal of $\frac{.7}{P}$.

$$\left(\frac{P}{.7}\right)(V - 3.77) = \frac{.7T}{P}\left(\frac{P}{.7}\right)$$
$$\left(\frac{P}{.7}\right)(V - 3.77) = T$$

10. **(C)** Use the formula $V = \frac{.7T}{P} + 3.77$ and input 8,000 for V and 1.2 for P.

$$8000 = \frac{.7T}{1.2} + 3.77$$
$$7996.23 = \frac{.7T}{1.2}$$

Multiply each side of the equation by $\frac{1.2}{.7}$, the reciprocal of $\frac{.7}{1.2}$.

$$\frac{1.2}{.7}\left(7996.23 = \frac{.7T}{1.2}\right)\frac{1.2}{.7}$$
$$13{,}708 \approx T$$

11. **(A)** Using the probability event formula, divide the number of events by the total number of outcomes. Todd and Brittany each have a $\frac{7}{42}$ chance to recover the lost earring.

$$\frac{7}{42} + \frac{7}{42} = \frac{14}{42} = \frac{1}{3}$$

A $\frac{1}{3}$ probability of success translates to approximately 33%.

12. **(A)** Simplify by subtracting $4x$ from both sides of the inequality.

$$-7x + 4 \leq 4x - 5$$
$$-11x + 4 \leq -5$$

Subtract 4 from both sides of the inequality.

$$-11x \leq -9$$

PRACTICE TEST 4

Divide both sides of the inequality by –11 remembering to reverse the direction of the inequality sign.

$$\frac{-11x}{-11} \le \frac{-9}{-11}$$
$$x \ge \frac{9}{11}$$

The answer choice (A) 0, does not satisfy the inequality.

13. **(C)** The return trip from Vacaville to Carlsbad is 492 miles. Add 54 miles to get a total of 546 miles. Divide this number by 26 miles to the gallon which comes out to 21 gallons. Multiply 21 by \$3.64 which comes to \$76.44. Add \$16 for the two lunches to \$76.44 which brings the cost to \$92.44. The friends had allocated \$90 for the cost of the return trip, so the side trip and the two lunches will exceed their budget by \$2.44

14. **(B)** President Obama's margin of victory over former governor Romney was a total of 4,984,100 votes (65,918,507 – 60,934,407 = 4,984,100). However, if all of the other votes, other than those cast for Obama, went to Romney, Romney's new vote total would have been 63,317,051. With this new total, Romney would have earned 2,601,456 fewer votes than the victor. Had Romney accumulated all of the Green, Libertarian, and Other votes, his margin of loss would have been reduced by 2,382,646 because 4,984,100 – 2,601,456 = 2,382,644.

15. **(D)** Use a linear model in the form of $y = mx + b$ to solve this question.

$$\begin{gathered}\text{Let } x = \text{number of hours}\\ y = \text{the cost of the visit}\\ b = \text{fee for the house call}\\ 114 = 2x + b \Rightarrow 114 - 2x = b\\ 194 = 4.5x + b \Rightarrow 194 - 4.5x = b\end{gathered}$$

Since both equations are expressed as a function of b, set the two values equal.

$$\begin{gathered}114 - 2x = 194 - 4.5x\\ 2.5x = 80\\ x = 32\end{gathered}$$

16. **(B)** On day 7, the ratio of hits to files is greater than the ratio of files to pages. Note the ratio of hits to files:

$$\frac{250}{155} \approx 1.61$$

The ratio of files to pages is $\frac{155}{134} \approx 1.16$.

$$1.61 > 1.16$$

Choices (A), (C), and (D) cannot be supported by the data in the table.

17. **(D)** The median is the middle value when the numbers are arranged in order. The numbers are arranged in order below.

39 45 47 50 56 64 85

The value in the middle, 50, is the median.

18. **(B)** The range of a group of numbers is found by finding the difference between the greatest and least values.
The range of the Files is 383 – 142 = 241

$$R = 241$$

The range of the KBytes is 2,816 – 1,425 = 1,391

$$r = 1{,}391$$

Find $2r - R$ by substituting 241 and 1,381 for R and r, respectively.

$$(2)(1{,}391) - 241 = 2{,}541$$

19. **(D)** Use a system of equations to answer this question.
Let r = Rick's number of hours worked
Let j = Jay's number of hours worked
They worked a total of 44 hours, so $r + j = 44$. Assign the monetary value of each boy's work to get the second equation, $4.5r + 5.25j = 202.5$. Our system of equations, then, is

$$r + j = 44$$
$$4.5r + 5.25j = 202.5$$

Use substitution or elimination to solve for r, Rick's hours worked. Transform $r + j = 44$ to $j = 44 - r$ and substitute the value into the second equation.

$$4.5r + 5.25(44 - r) = 202.5$$
$$4.5r + 231 - 5.25r = 202.5$$
$$-.75r + 231 = 202.5$$
$$-.75r = -28.5$$
$$r = 38$$

20. **(D)** Let x be the original price of the running shoes, in dollars. The discounted price is 25 percent off the original price, so $x - 0.25x = 0.75x$ is the discounted price, in dollars. The tax is 8 percent of the discounted price, so $0.08(0.75x)$ is the tax on the purchase, in dollars. The price r, in dollars, that Briana paid the cashier is the sum of the discounted price and the tax:

$$r = 0.75x + (0.08)(0.75x)$$

which can be rewritten as $r = 1.08(0.75x)$. Therefore, the original price, x, of the running shoes, in dollars, can be written as $\frac{r}{(1.08)(.75)}$.

21. **(B)** Input the known data and solve for k.

$$r = km^{\frac{3}{4}}$$

$$18{,}500 = k(1000)^{\frac{3}{4}}$$
$$18{,}500 = k(177.83)$$
$$104.03 = k$$

22. **(C)** Input the known data, including the value of k from question 21, and solve for s, the specific metabolic rate.

$$s = \frac{km^{\frac{3}{4}}}{m}$$

$$s = \frac{104.03(1000)^{\frac{3}{4}}}{1000} = 18.50$$

23. **(B)** The area of a sector is found by using the formula $A = \frac{m}{360}\pi r^2$ where m = measure of the central angle and r = length of the radius. Input the known data and solve for r.

$$139.6 = \frac{34.4}{360}\pi r^2$$
$$465.03 \approx r^2$$
$$21.6 \approx r$$

24. **(B)** The ball hits the ground when the height is 0 feet. Let h equal 0 and solve for t.

$$0 = -4.9t^2 + 32t$$
$$0 = t(-4.9t + 32)$$
$$t = 0 \text{ or } -4.9t + 32 = 0$$
$$t = 0 \text{ or } t = 6.5$$

The initial value of $t = 0$ represents the time before the ball was thrown.

25. **(C)** Replace h with 18 as the height the ball attains. Use the formula $h = -4.9t^2 + 32t$.

$$18 = -4.9t^2 + 32t$$

Set the equation equal to 0 and solve for t.

$$-4.9t^2 + 32t - 18 = 0$$

The equation does not factor, so use the quadratic formula $\frac{-b \pm \sqrt{b^2 - 4ac}}{2a}$.

Let $a = -4.9$ $b = 32$ $c = -18$

After using the quadratic formula, we arrive at two different answers, .6 and 5.9. We get two different answers because after .6 seconds the ball attains a height of 18 meters and rises higher. As the ball returns to earth, it reaches 18 meters high again, 5.9 seconds after it was thrown into the air.

26. **(B)** Let $x = 1$ (or any easy number). Therefore, the sum of the seven numbers must be $7 \times 1 = 7$.

Since $x = 1$, then $x + \frac{4}{7} = 1\frac{4}{7}$. The sum of the seven numbers with mean $1\frac{4}{7}$ is $7 \times 1\frac{4}{7} = 11$.

In order to increase the mean of the seven numbers by $\frac{4}{7}$, the sum of the numbers must be increased by 4.

27. **(B)** The graphing form of a circle is $(x-h)^2+(y-k)^2=r^2$ where:

(h, k) is the center of the circle
r is the radius of the circle

Divide by 2 to simplify the equation:

$$(2x^2+8x+2y^2+12y)\div 2=36\div 2$$
$$x^2+4x+y^2+6y=18$$

Next, complete the square for both the x and y components of the equation.

$$x^2+4x+4+y^2+6y+9=18+4+9$$

Factor the left side of the equation and simplify the left.

$$(x+2)^2+(y+3)^2=31$$

In this circle, $r^2=31$ so $r=\sqrt{31}$. The question requires the diameter of the circle, so multiply the radius by 2.

$$2\times\sqrt{31}=2\sqrt{31}$$

28. **(C)** Transform $h(x)=(x-8)(x+2)$ to graphing form by multiplying the parentheses.

$$h(x)=(x-8)(x+2)=x^2-6x-16$$

Move −16 to the far right of the equation as you complete the square. Remember as you add a value to complete the square, that same value must be subtracted from −16.

$$h(x)=x^2-6x-16$$
$$h(x)=x^2-6x+9-16-9$$
$$h(x)=(x-3)^2-25$$

The vertex of the parabola is (3, −25) and the minimum value is −25.

29. **(D)** $(x+5)(x^2-5x+25)$ is the factored form of x^3+125. Replace $(x+5)(x^2-5x+25)$ with x^3+125 and solve for m.

$$x^3-20=x^3+125+m$$
$$-145=m$$

30. **(A)** Transform the equation to graphing form $y=(x-h)^2+k$, where (h, k) represent the parabola's vertex.

$$y=(x-4)(x+6)$$
$$y=x^2+2x-24$$

Move −24 to the far right of the equation.

$$y=x^2+2x-24$$

Complete the square by dividing b by 2 and squaring that quantity.

$$b=2\text{ so }\left(\frac{2}{2}\right)^2=1$$

Add 1 to $2x$, remembering to subtract 1 from −24.

$$y=(x^2+2x+1)-24-1$$

Factor and combine like terms.

$$y = (x + 1)^2 - 25$$

Looking at the graph, we could also have identified the vertex as (−1, −25), which confirms that choice (A) is the correct answer.

31. **76.80** Find the cost of the boots after one week:

$$\$80.00 - (.20)(\$80.00) = \$64.00$$

Add 20% to $64.00 to find the cost after two weeks.

$$\$64.00 + (.20)(\$64.00) = \$76.80$$

32. **4.48** Find the quotient of 3 billion and 186,000 to find the number of seconds elapsed between the transmission and reception of the photos (these are known as "light seconds").

$$3{,}000{,}000{,}000 \div 186{,}000 = 16{,}129 \text{ seconds}$$

There are 60 seconds in a minute and 60 minutes in an hour so there are 3,600 seconds in one hour ($60 \times 60 = 3{,}600$). Divide 16,129 by 3,600 to find the number of hours needed to successfully transmit photographs from Pluto to Earth.

$$16{,}129 \div 3{,}600 = 4.48 \text{ hours.}$$

33. $\mathbf{\frac{4}{7}}$ The County Education Budget for 2010 was $200,000,000. By 2012, the budget had increased to $350,000,000. Divide $200,000,000 by $350,000,000 to find what fraction 2010's figure is of 2012's. $\frac{200{,}000{,}000}{350{,}000{,}000} = \frac{4}{7}$

34. **757** Find $g(f(5))$ by first finding $f(5)$.

$$f(5) = (5^2) - 5 = 20$$

Next find $g(20)$.

$$g(20) = 2(20^2 - 6) = 788$$

We find that $g(f(5)) = 788$
Repeat the process with $f(g(-3))$.
Find $g(-3)$.

$$2[(-3)^2 - 6] = 6$$

Next, find $f(6)$.

$$6^2 - 5 = 31$$

We find $f(g(-3)) = 31$. Find the difference between $g(f(5))$ and $f(g(-3))$.

$$788 - 31 = 757$$

35. **6** The volume of a cone is found by using the formula $V = \frac{1}{3}\pi r^2 h$, where r is the radius of the circular base and h is the height. Input the known data and solve for r.

$$14.4\pi = \frac{1}{3}\pi r^2(4.8)$$
$$14.4 = 1.6r^2$$
$$9 = r^2$$
$$3 = r$$

The question asks for the diameter, so multiply the radius, 3, by 2.

$$2 \times 3 = 6$$

36. **2** Simplify the denominator.

$$f(x) = \frac{1}{2(x-3)^2+4(x-3)+2}$$
$$f(x) = \frac{1}{2x^2-12x+18+4x-12+2}$$
$$f(x) = \frac{1}{2x^2-8x+8}$$
$$f(x) = \frac{1}{2(x-4x+4)}$$
$$f(x) = \frac{1}{2(x-2)^2}$$

Division by 0 is not allowed. Set $x - 2$ equal to 0 to find the restriction on

$$x - 2 = 0$$
$$x = 2$$

37. **4,505** Use the present value formula and input the known information.

$$P = A\left(1+\frac{r}{n}\right)^{-nt}$$
$$P = 10{,}000\left(1+\frac{.08}{12}\right)^{(-12)(10)} = 4{,}505$$

Jorge can expect to receive $4,505 as the present value of his $10,000 ten-year annuity.

38. **1,930** Input the known information into the present value formula and solve for A.

$$P = A\left(1+\frac{r}{n}\right)^{-nt}$$
$$1{,}621 = A\left(1+\frac{.035}{4}\right)^{-(4)(5)}$$
$$1{,}621 = .84A$$
$$1{,}930 = A$$

Samantha would have earned $1,930 if she had elected to receive her gift as an annuity.

Section 5: Essay (Optional)

SUGGESTED ESSAY TEST 4

Following is an essay written in response to the prompt. It is unlikely that you would be able to write such a full response in the time allowed, so don't worry if your essay is significantly shorter. Use the suggested essay to see how the task might be approached. For practice, you may wish to rewrite your own essay incorporating some of the points discussed in it.

According to the introductory material this passage is from an introduction to a book called Supernature. We can infer that the passage is written by the author of the book by statements such as, "Between nature and the supernatural are a host of happenings that I choose to describe as Supernature. It is with these go-betweens that this book is concerned."

Lyell Watson's main contention is that there exist important phenomena outside the understanding of today's science and that these phenomena should be studied. By its nature this is a contention that is extremely difficult to prove (or disprove, for that matter). Watson therefore does not try to prove his contention. Rather, he advances arguments to persuade us that it is very possible that "Supernature" exists.

Let us now examine Watson's reasoning and the supporting evidence he offers for his contention that Supernature exists and is worth our attention. He argues that the Uncertainty Principle has called into question the idea that statements can be made about nature with certainty, which can be seen as allowing room for the existence of phenomena outside what is now regarded by science as nature. This is a fairly strong argument. The other good argument he makes is that it seems reasonable that the existence of belief in "things unseen" must have evolved ("survival value") for a purpose. These two arguments offer some support for his main contention but are very far from proving it.

The other main supporting argument Watson makes is that science keeps making discoveries, such as the finding of new galaxies and discoveries about the ongoing battle between moths and bats. These examples do not directly support his contention because these discoveries are not of a fundamentally different nature from earlier discoveries and thus are not evidence for "Supernature." However, it does support the idea that nature is not "finite," which in turn lends some support

PRACTICE TEST 4

to the idea that phenomena outside the current understanding of science exist.

Let us now focus on how Lyell Watson uses language and reasoning to advance his argument. Watson uses a number of rhetorical strategies to construct this passage. One of the main techniques he uses is alternately making statements in the third person and in the first person. This allows him to make assertions and then comment on them from his, or sometimes our, point of view. This variety helps make the piece interesting, and the first person introduces a personal, informal tone that engages the reader.

Let us next examine the first two paragraphs more closely to see how the strategy just discussed, as well as other rhetorical strategies, are employed. The first paragraph begins with a bold statement that contradicts conventional thinking: "Science no longer holds any absolute truth." This short, simple, yet challenging assertion catches our interest. Watson immediately supports the statement with evidence, citing the Uncertainty Principle (which we have already discussed). He says physics "has had to submit to the indignity of an Uncertainty Principle," which introduces an element of humor and mild sarcasm because physics is personified as losing its dignity. The following statement switches so that it is made in the first-person plural "we," which serves to include the reader in the discussion.

The second paragraph begins with a statement that is similar in some ways to the opening sentence of the first paragraph. It is short and gets our attention. In this way it parallels the first sentence of the first paragraph, helping to link the two paragraphs. However, it is different in that it is in the first-person singular: "I find this tremendously exciting." This personal touch helps capture the reader's interest in what to some people might seem a rather dry subject. The rest of the paragraph is a series of straightforward, unadorned statements supporting the thesis advanced in the first paragraph that "science no longer holds any absolute truths." These statements provide relevant examples of how one discovery leads to another in science. They are appropriate in this context because they illustrate the point in a way that a non-scientist can understand. Another device used here is the analogy cited (as false) in the first sentence of the paragraph between science and a jigsaw puzzle: "The picture of science as a jigsaw puzzle with a finite number of pieces that would one day all be slotted neatly into place, has never been appealing." Visualizing science as a jigsaw puzzle helps to persuade the reader that this is a simplistic view of nature and science. The phrase "slotted neatly into place" is mildly sarcastic, emphasizing the simplistic nature of the view.

In the third paragraph Watson follows the rather general supporting statements made in the second paragraph with a detailed description of a situation that suggests nature is not finite. No explicit transition from the preceding paragraph is used. Rather, Watson relies on the logic of his argument to enable the reader to follow his reasoning. Also, he continues using the same plain style used in the previous paragraph. This approach works because it relies on reasoning rather than language "tricks." The one rhetorical flourish in the paragraph—"this escalating drama of nature"—is effective in part because it contrasts with the straightforward language of the rest of the paragraph.

Space does not permit a detailed analysis of the rest of the passage. It employs the same general strategy used in the first three paragraphs: reliance on logical argument and alternating between first person and third person. Watson uses these and other techniques to create an intriguing but far from conclusive argument for the existence of something—"Supernature"—that many, perhaps most, people would regard as unscientific and nonexistent.

Refer to the SAT Essay Rubric on page 23 to analyze and score your essay response. For further guidance on this essay and additional practice and evaluation by teacher and author Philip Geer, contact *info@mentaurs.com*.

ANSWER SHEET
Practice Test 5

Section 1: Reading

1. Ⓐ Ⓑ Ⓒ Ⓓ	14. Ⓐ Ⓑ Ⓒ Ⓓ	27. Ⓐ Ⓑ Ⓒ Ⓓ	40. Ⓐ Ⓑ Ⓒ Ⓓ
2. Ⓐ Ⓑ Ⓒ Ⓓ	15. Ⓐ Ⓑ Ⓒ Ⓓ	28. Ⓐ Ⓑ Ⓒ Ⓓ	41. Ⓐ Ⓑ Ⓒ Ⓓ
3. Ⓐ Ⓑ Ⓒ Ⓓ	16. Ⓐ Ⓑ Ⓒ Ⓓ	29. Ⓐ Ⓑ Ⓒ Ⓓ	42. Ⓐ Ⓑ Ⓒ Ⓓ
4. Ⓐ Ⓑ Ⓒ Ⓓ	17. Ⓐ Ⓑ Ⓒ Ⓓ	30. Ⓐ Ⓑ Ⓒ Ⓓ	43. Ⓐ Ⓑ Ⓒ Ⓓ
5. Ⓐ Ⓑ Ⓒ Ⓓ	18. Ⓐ Ⓑ Ⓒ Ⓓ	31. Ⓐ Ⓑ Ⓒ Ⓓ	44. Ⓐ Ⓑ Ⓒ Ⓓ
6. Ⓐ Ⓑ Ⓒ Ⓓ	19. Ⓐ Ⓑ Ⓒ Ⓓ	32. Ⓐ Ⓑ Ⓒ Ⓓ	45. Ⓐ Ⓑ Ⓒ Ⓓ
7. Ⓐ Ⓑ Ⓒ Ⓓ	20. Ⓐ Ⓑ Ⓒ Ⓓ	33. Ⓐ Ⓑ Ⓒ Ⓓ	46. Ⓐ Ⓑ Ⓒ Ⓓ
8. Ⓐ Ⓑ Ⓒ Ⓓ	21. Ⓐ Ⓑ Ⓒ Ⓓ	34. Ⓐ Ⓑ Ⓒ Ⓓ	47. Ⓐ Ⓑ Ⓒ Ⓓ
9. Ⓐ Ⓑ Ⓒ Ⓓ	22. Ⓐ Ⓑ Ⓒ Ⓓ	35. Ⓐ Ⓑ Ⓒ Ⓓ	48. Ⓐ Ⓑ Ⓒ Ⓓ
10. Ⓐ Ⓑ Ⓒ Ⓓ	23. Ⓐ Ⓑ Ⓒ Ⓓ	36. Ⓐ Ⓑ Ⓒ Ⓓ	49. Ⓐ Ⓑ Ⓒ Ⓓ
11. Ⓐ Ⓑ Ⓒ Ⓓ	24. Ⓐ Ⓑ Ⓒ Ⓓ	37. Ⓐ Ⓑ Ⓒ Ⓓ	50. Ⓐ Ⓑ Ⓒ Ⓓ
12. Ⓐ Ⓑ Ⓒ Ⓓ	25. Ⓐ Ⓑ Ⓒ Ⓓ	38. Ⓐ Ⓑ Ⓒ Ⓓ	51. Ⓐ Ⓑ Ⓒ Ⓓ
13. Ⓐ Ⓑ Ⓒ Ⓓ	26. Ⓐ Ⓑ Ⓒ Ⓓ	39. Ⓐ Ⓑ Ⓒ Ⓓ	52. Ⓐ Ⓑ Ⓒ Ⓓ

Section 2: Writing and Language

1. Ⓐ Ⓑ Ⓒ Ⓓ	12. Ⓐ Ⓑ Ⓒ Ⓓ	23. Ⓐ Ⓑ Ⓒ Ⓓ	34. Ⓐ Ⓑ Ⓒ Ⓓ
2. Ⓐ Ⓑ Ⓒ Ⓓ	13. Ⓐ Ⓑ Ⓒ Ⓓ	24. Ⓐ Ⓑ Ⓒ Ⓓ	35. Ⓐ Ⓑ Ⓒ Ⓓ
3. Ⓐ Ⓑ Ⓒ Ⓓ	14. Ⓐ Ⓑ Ⓒ Ⓓ	25. Ⓐ Ⓑ Ⓒ Ⓓ	36. Ⓐ Ⓑ Ⓒ Ⓓ
4. Ⓐ Ⓑ Ⓒ Ⓓ	15. Ⓐ Ⓑ Ⓒ Ⓓ	26. Ⓐ Ⓑ Ⓒ Ⓓ	37. Ⓐ Ⓑ Ⓒ Ⓓ
5. Ⓐ Ⓑ Ⓒ Ⓓ	16. Ⓐ Ⓑ Ⓒ Ⓓ	27. Ⓐ Ⓑ Ⓒ Ⓓ	38. Ⓐ Ⓑ Ⓒ Ⓓ
6. Ⓐ Ⓑ Ⓒ Ⓓ	17. Ⓐ Ⓑ Ⓒ Ⓓ	28. Ⓐ Ⓑ Ⓒ Ⓓ	39. Ⓐ Ⓑ Ⓒ Ⓓ
7. Ⓐ Ⓑ Ⓒ Ⓓ	18. Ⓐ Ⓑ Ⓒ Ⓓ	29. Ⓐ Ⓑ Ⓒ Ⓓ	40. Ⓐ Ⓑ Ⓒ Ⓓ
8. Ⓐ Ⓑ Ⓒ Ⓓ	19. Ⓐ Ⓑ Ⓒ Ⓓ	30. Ⓐ Ⓑ Ⓒ Ⓓ	41. Ⓐ Ⓑ Ⓒ Ⓓ
9. Ⓐ Ⓑ Ⓒ Ⓓ	20. Ⓐ Ⓑ Ⓒ Ⓓ	31. Ⓐ Ⓑ Ⓒ Ⓓ	42. Ⓐ Ⓑ Ⓒ Ⓓ
10. Ⓐ Ⓑ Ⓒ Ⓓ	21. Ⓐ Ⓑ Ⓒ Ⓓ	32. Ⓐ Ⓑ Ⓒ Ⓓ	43. Ⓐ Ⓑ Ⓒ Ⓓ
11. Ⓐ Ⓑ Ⓒ Ⓓ	22. Ⓐ Ⓑ Ⓒ Ⓓ	33. Ⓐ Ⓑ Ⓒ Ⓓ	44. Ⓐ Ⓑ Ⓒ Ⓓ

ANSWER SHEET
Practice Test 5

Section 3: Math (No Calculator)

1. Ⓐ Ⓑ Ⓒ Ⓓ
2. Ⓐ Ⓑ Ⓒ Ⓓ
3. Ⓐ Ⓑ Ⓒ Ⓓ
4. Ⓐ Ⓑ Ⓒ Ⓓ
5. Ⓐ Ⓑ Ⓒ Ⓓ
6. Ⓐ Ⓑ Ⓒ Ⓓ
7. Ⓐ Ⓑ Ⓒ Ⓓ
8. Ⓐ Ⓑ Ⓒ Ⓓ
9. Ⓐ Ⓑ Ⓒ Ⓓ
10. Ⓐ Ⓑ Ⓒ Ⓓ
11. Ⓐ Ⓑ Ⓒ Ⓓ
12. Ⓐ Ⓑ Ⓒ Ⓓ
13. Ⓐ Ⓑ Ⓒ Ⓓ
14. Ⓐ Ⓑ Ⓒ Ⓓ
15. Ⓐ Ⓑ Ⓒ Ⓓ

16.

	⊘	⊘	
⊙	⊙	⊙	⊙
	⓪	⓪	⓪
①	①	①	①
②	②	②	②
③	③	③	③
④	④	④	④
⑤	⑤	⑤	⑤
⑥	⑥	⑥	⑥
⑦	⑦	⑦	⑦
⑧	⑧	⑧	⑧
⑨	⑨	⑨	⑨

17.

	⊘	⊘	
⊙	⊙	⊙	⊙
	⓪	⓪	⓪
①	①	①	①
②	②	②	②
③	③	③	③
④	④	④	④
⑤	⑤	⑤	⑤
⑥	⑥	⑥	⑥
⑦	⑦	⑦	⑦
⑧	⑧	⑧	⑧
⑨	⑨	⑨	⑨

18.

	⊘	⊘	
⊙	⊙	⊙	⊙
	⓪	⓪	⓪
①	①	①	①
②	②	②	②
③	③	③	③
④	④	④	④
⑤	⑤	⑤	⑤
⑥	⑥	⑥	⑥
⑦	⑦	⑦	⑦
⑧	⑧	⑧	⑧
⑨	⑨	⑨	⑨

19.

	⊘	⊘	
⊙	⊙	⊙	⊙
	⓪	⓪	⓪
①	①	①	①
②	②	②	②
③	③	③	③
④	④	④	④
⑤	⑤	⑤	⑤
⑥	⑥	⑥	⑥
⑦	⑦	⑦	⑦
⑧	⑧	⑧	⑧
⑨	⑨	⑨	⑨

20.

	⊘	⊘	
⊙	⊙	⊙	⊙
	⓪	⓪	⓪
①	①	①	①
②	②	②	②
③	③	③	③
④	④	④	④
⑤	⑤	⑤	⑤
⑥	⑥	⑥	⑥
⑦	⑦	⑦	⑦
⑧	⑧	⑧	⑧
⑨	⑨	⑨	⑨

ANSWER SHEET
Practice Test 5

Section 4: Math (Calculator)

1. Ⓐ Ⓑ Ⓒ Ⓓ	9. Ⓐ Ⓑ Ⓒ Ⓓ	17. Ⓐ Ⓑ Ⓒ Ⓓ	25. Ⓐ Ⓑ Ⓒ Ⓓ
2. Ⓐ Ⓑ Ⓒ Ⓓ	10. Ⓐ Ⓑ Ⓒ Ⓓ	18. Ⓐ Ⓑ Ⓒ Ⓓ	26. Ⓐ Ⓑ Ⓒ Ⓓ
3. Ⓐ Ⓑ Ⓒ Ⓓ	11. Ⓐ Ⓑ Ⓒ Ⓓ	19. Ⓐ Ⓑ Ⓒ Ⓓ	27. Ⓐ Ⓑ Ⓒ Ⓓ
4. Ⓐ Ⓑ Ⓒ Ⓓ	12. Ⓐ Ⓑ Ⓒ Ⓓ	20. Ⓐ Ⓑ Ⓒ Ⓓ	28. Ⓐ Ⓑ Ⓒ Ⓓ
5. Ⓐ Ⓑ Ⓒ Ⓓ	13. Ⓐ Ⓑ Ⓒ Ⓓ	21. Ⓐ Ⓑ Ⓒ Ⓓ	29. Ⓐ Ⓑ Ⓒ Ⓓ
6. Ⓐ Ⓑ Ⓒ Ⓓ	14. Ⓐ Ⓑ Ⓒ Ⓓ	22. Ⓐ Ⓑ Ⓒ Ⓓ	30. Ⓐ Ⓑ Ⓒ Ⓓ
7. Ⓐ Ⓑ Ⓒ Ⓓ	15. Ⓐ Ⓑ Ⓒ Ⓓ	23. Ⓐ Ⓑ Ⓒ Ⓓ	
8. Ⓐ Ⓑ Ⓒ Ⓓ	16. Ⓐ Ⓑ Ⓒ Ⓓ	24. Ⓐ Ⓑ Ⓒ Ⓓ	

31. 32. 33. 34.

35. 36. 37. 38.

ANSWER SHEET
Practice Test 5

Essay

PLANNING PAGE

START YOUR ESSAY HERE

 1 1

READING TEST

65 MINUTES, 52 QUESTIONS

Turn to Section 1 of your answer sheet to answer the questions in this section.

Directions: Following each of the passages (or pairs of passages) below are questions about the passage (or passages). Read each passage carefully. Then, select the best answer for each question based on what is stated in the passage (or passages) and in any graphics that may accompany the passage.

Questions 1–10 are based on the following passage.

This passage is from Henry Van Dyke, *The Americanism of Washington.* It was originally published in 1906.

"Professedly prudent" is the phrase that I have chosen to apply to Benjamin Franklin. For the one thing that is clear, as we turn to look at him and the other men who stood with Washington, is that, whatever their philosophical professions may have been, they were not controlled by prudence. They were really imprudent, and at heart willing to take all risks of poverty and death in a struggle whose cause was just though its issue was dubious. If it be rashness to commit honor and life and property to a great adventure for the general good, then these men were rash to the verge of recklessness. They refused no peril, they withheld no sacrifice, in the following of their ideal.

I hear John Dickinson saying: "It is not our duty to leave wealth to our children, but it is our duty to leave liberty to them. We have counted the cost of this contest, and we find nothing so dreadful as voluntary slavery." I see Samuel Adams, impoverished, living upon a pittance, hardly able to provide a decent coat for his back, rejecting with scorn the offer of a profitable office, wealth, a title even, to win him from his allegiance to the cause of America. I see Robert Morris, the wealthy merchant, opening his purse and pledging his credit to support the Revolution, and later devoting all his fortune and his energy to restore and establish the financial honor of the Republic, with the memorable words, "The United States may command all that I have, except my integrity." I hear the proud John Adams saying to his wife, "I have accepted a seat in the House of Representatives, and thereby have consented to my own ruin, to your ruin, and the ruin of our children;" and I hear her reply, with the tears running down her face, "Well, I am willing in this cause to run all risks with you, and be ruined with you, if you are ruined." I see Benjamin Franklin, in the Congress of 1776, already past his seventieth year, prosperous, famous, by far the most celebrated man in America, accepting without demur the difficult and dangerous mission to France, and whispering to his friend, Dr. Rush, "I am old and good for nothing, but as the store-keepers say of their remnants of cloth, 'I am but a fag-end, and you may have me for what you please.'"

Here is a man who will illustrate and prove, perhaps better than any other of those who stood with Washington, the point at which I am aiming. There was none of the

GO ON TO THE NEXT PAGE

glamour of romance about old Ben Franklin. He was shrewd, canny, humorous. The chivalric Southerners disliked his philosophy, and the solemn New-Englanders mistrusted his jokes. He made no extravagant claims for his own motives, and some of his ways were not distinctly ideal. He was full of prudential proverbs, and claimed to be a follower of the theory of enlightened self-interest. But there was not a faculty of his wise old head which he did not put at the service of his country, nor was there a pulse of his slow and steady heart which did not beat loyal to the cause of freedom.

He forfeited profitable office and sure preferment under the crown, for hard work, uncertain pay, and certain peril in behalf of the colonies. He followed the inexorable logic, step by step, which led him from the natural rights of his countrymen to their liberty, from their liberty to their independence. He endured with a grim humor the revilings of those whom he called "malevolent critics and bug-writers." He broke with his old and dear associates in England, writing to one of them, "You and I were long friends; you are now my enemy and I am Yours, B. Franklin."

1. In applying the term "professedly prudent" (line 1) to Benjamin Franklin, the author is suggesting that

(A) Benjamin Franklin claimed to be prudent but in many ways was not
(B) Benjamin Franklin did not claim to be prudent
(C) historians are unsure whether Benjamin Franklin was prudent or not
(D) Benjamin Franklin was prudent in professional matters

2. As it is used in line 6 *professions* most nearly means

(A) fields of study
(B) misgivings
(C) occupations
(D) avowals of belief

3. As it is used in line 11 *issue* most nearly means

(A) offspring
(B) moral principle
(C) outcome
(D) controversial topic

4. The author most likely quotes Robert Morris' words, "The United States may command all that I have, except my integrity" (lines 34–35) to suggest that Robert Morris

(A) had no integrity
(B) was not loyal to the United States
(C) was a person of both great integrity and great patriotism
(D) was not completely reliable

5. As it is used in line 47 *celebrated* most nearly means

(A) iconoclastic
(B) highly decorated for military service
(C) intrepid
(D) known and praised widely

6. Based on the information in the passage, which of the following is *not* true of Benjamin Franklin?

(A) He was wise.
(B) He believed deeply in natural rights and liberty.
(C) He never went to Europe.
(D) He was widely admired in his country.

GO ON TO THE NEXT PAGE

7. According to the information given in the passage, Benjamin Franklin said that he
   (A) was motivated by what would benefit him
   (B) was motivated to action by the highest ideals
   (C) was chivalrous
   (D) was the most useful person that his country could send on a mission to France

8. The most appropriate title of this passage would be
   (A) Ben Franklin: A Study in Prudence
   (B) Benjamin Franklin: An American Hero
   (C) John Dickinson, Robert Morris, John Adams, and Benjamin Franklin: Flawed Heroes of the American Revolution
   (D) Benjamin Franklin's Theory of Enlightened Self-interest

9. The quotation from Benjamin Franklin's letter in lines 83–85 ("You and I were long friends; you are now my enemy and I am Yours") is primarily intended to show
   (A) how upset Benjamin Franklin was after his decision to support American independence
   (B) that Benjamin Franklin was a less than perfect man
   (C) that some of Benjamin Franklin's friends in England did not have a good character
   (D) that Benjamin Franklin was so patriotic that he sacrificed friendships for his love of country

10. The author makes use of all of the following *except*
    (A) quotations
    (B) understatement
    (C) description
    (D) assertion of fact

Questions 11–20 are based on the following passage.

This passage is from Suparna Choudhury, "Culturing the adolescent brain: what can neuroscience learn from anthropology?" in *Social Cognitive and Affective Neuroscience*, 2010.

If we assume that a transitional period of the life cycle, akin to adolescence, organized around puberty and of variable length, exists almost universally, the next question is what forms it takes and whether its features, too, are universal. Ethnographic research in Samoa conducted by anthropologist Margaret Mead brought the issue of cultural difference in the experience of adolescence to the fore. Her book, *Coming of Age in Samoa,* famously challenged Hall's "storm and stress" model and argued that Samoan culture influenced psychological development of girls in such a way that the transition from childhood to adulthood was smooth and lacked the "natural" turbulence with which it had been characterized by the evolutionary view. Unlike American culture, Samoan culture, she argued, did not place judgments and pressures on adolescents and was more relaxed, for example, in its views about sexuality.

All of these factors were thought to make Samoan adolescence relatively tranquil and enjoyable and led to Mead's assertion of the primacy of nurture over nature. While Derek Freeman later critiqued Mead's culturally deterministic approach for a number of methodological reasons her ethnographic approach has been important for subsequent cross-cultural approaches to adolescence. Since then, a sizeable literature in psychology and anthropology has developed which has addressed cross-cultural differences in adolescence.

GO ON TO THE NEXT PAGE

Schlegel and Barry's cross-cultural study of adolescents in tribal and traditional societies using data collected from over 175 societies around the world demonstrated that adolescence as a distinctive, socially marked stage of life is ubiquitous. These researchers put forward a biosocial theory, arguing that the social stage of adolescence is a response to the development of the reproductive capacity. Most notably, however, these cross-cultural studies challenge the notion that features of "storm and stress" and a period of psychological crisis are universal inevitabilities in adolescence. For example, while mild forms of antisocial behavior were present in some societies, it was certainly not generalizable as a feature. Similarly, aggressive and violent behavior occurred in a minority of cultures and when present was heavily gendered with aggression in girls being particularly low. Cross-cultural researchers stress that the *meanings* of developmental tasks associated with adolescence such as the establishment of independence or autonomy may differ according to culture, and may be subject to change over time. For example, developing independence in some cultures may mean taking on duties to care for siblings or elders, and not necessarily separating from adults and orienting towards peers. Based on a study comparing five cultures that could be contrasted as "traditional" and "modern" or "collectivistic" and "individualistic," Trommsdorff suggested that "turbulent" features such as intergenerational conflict stem from the focus on attaining independence from parents during this period and are linked to cultural values of individualism in Western societies. Certainly, in many cultures, particularly in pre-industrial societies, adolescence is not marked by such a characterization or psychological turmoil, and thus, both the characterization and length of this life stage vary according to culture. Puberty, too, which is clearly grounded in biology across cultures, interacts with the local environment. Menarche, which marks the beginning of puberty in girls, is occurring increasingly early in industrialized countries such as Japan or the USA. This finding may be connected to changes in dietary intake. Even if puberty could be the biological marker of the start of adolescence in every culture, the end point is less clear.

In summary, adolescence conceptualized as a prolonged period of identity development linked to increased autonomy, intergenerational conflict, peer-relatedness and social psychological anxieties, is not the norm across cultures.

Indeed, these features seem to depend on degrees of individualism, social/economic role expectations, gender and class. A historical appreciation of adolescence as a category of science as well as cross-cultural investigations of the experience of adolescence demonstrates that characteristics associated with this developmental stage may not only have biological bases but also social and cultural origins.

11. As it is used in line 27 *critiqued* most nearly means

(A) criticized
(B) extolled
(C) evaluated objectively
(D) imitated

GO ON TO THE NEXT PAGE

12. According to the author of the passage, from her observation that adolescence in Samoa is different from adolescence in America, Margaret Mead argued that
    (A) Samoan culture is different from American culture
    (B) culture has a larger part in shaping human behavior than does genetics
    (C) girls are treated better in Samoa than they are in America
    (D) people go through the same basic life experiences in all societies but do so at different times in their lives

13. According to the author, Schlegel and Barry's cross-cultural study of adolescents in tribal and traditional societies showed that
    (A) the phenomenon of adolescence is found everywhere
    (B) adolescence is a time of great conflict in every society
    (C) anti-social behavior always increases during adolescence
    (D) adolescent boys become aggressive in every society

14. In line 49 *inevitabilities* most nearly means
    (A) stages of life
    (B) assumptions
    (C) unavoidable occurrences
    (D) rare happenings

15. In line 55 *gendered* most nearly means
    (A) free of bias toward either males or females
    (B) based on genetics
    (C) characteristic of one gender
    (D) seen from a male perspective

16. Trommsdorff, whose study is cited in the passage, would most likely agree that
    (A) modern cultures are "collectivistic"
    (B) individualistic cultures are "traditional" cultures
    (C) adolescents in "collectivist" cultures do not argue with their parents as much as adolescents in "individualistic" cultures do
    (D) adolescents in "collectivist" societies never become fully adult because they never achieve independence from their parents

17. Which of the following lines offers the best evidence for the answer to question 16?
    (A) "Schlegel . . . ubiquitous." (lines 36–41)
    (B) "Cross-cultural . . . time." (lines 57–62)
    (C) "Based . . . societies." (lines 66–75)
    (D) "In . . . cultures." (lines 92–97)

18. Based on what is said in the passage, it can be inferred that its author most likely believes that
    (A) one of the main features of adolescence everywhere is rebellion by young people against parental authority
    (B) adolescence as a distinct period of life is unique to industrialized societies
    (C) adolescence occurs in every culture (or at least nearly every culture), but the form that it takes varies from culture to culture
    (D) adolescence as a distinct period of life occurs only in "individualistic" societies

GO ON TO THE NEXT PAGE

19. The point of view of the author of the passage is that of
    (A) a proponent of the view that nature is predominant in human development
    (B) an objective commentator on an important issue in social science
    (C) a strong critic of the view that a young person's culture largely determines his or her experience of adolescence
    (D) an advocate for the rights of people in pre-industrial societies

20. The author makes use of all of the following *except*
    (A) assumption
    (B) qualification
    (C) citing of research
    (D) humor

Questions 21–31 are based on the following passage.

This passage is from Gilbert Highet, *The Art of Teaching*, copyright 1950 by Gilbert Highet.

The first professional higher educators in the Western world were the group of brilliant talkers and keen thinkers who appeared in Greece during the fifth century B.C. They were called "sophists."

They were exclusively lecturers. All that we hear of them shows them as phenomenally graceful and subtle talkers, usually to fairly large audiences. In that they are the direct ancestors of the modern "authority" who tours the large cities giving a carefully prepared speech in which his own personal power or charm is combined with well-spaced jokes and memorable epigrams, the whole varying very little from one repetition to another. Like him, they were highly paid and widely advertised and welcomed by a reception committee and entertained by ambitious hosts. But unlike him, some of them professed to be authorities on everything. They said they could lecture on any subject under the sun. Often they were challenged to speak on odd and difficult topics, and accepted the dare. However, they did not pretend to know more facts than others, but rather to be able to think and talk better. In that, perhaps, they are the ancestors of the modern journalists who have the knack of turning out a bright and interesting article on any new subject, without using special or expert information. The sophists dazzled everyone without convincing anyone of anything positive. They argued unsystematically and unfairly, but painted over the gaps in their reasoning with glossy rhetoric. They had few constructive

GO ON TO THE NEXT PAGE

ideas, and won most applause by taking traditional notions and showing they were based on convention rather than logic. They demonstrated that almost anything could be proved by a fast talker—sometimes they made a powerful speech on one side of a question in the morning, and an equally powerful speech on the opposite side in the afternoon.

To some of his contemporaries Socrates looked like a sophist. But he distrusted and opposed the sophists wherever possible. They made carefully prepared continuous speeches; he only asked questions. They took rich fees for their teaching; he refused regular payment, living and dying poor. They were elegantly dressed, with secretaries and servants. Socrates wore the workingman's clothes, bare feet and smock. They spoke in specially prepared lecture-halls; he talked to people at street-corners and in the gymnasium, where every afternoon the young men exercised, and old men talked. Socrates said he trained people to think. The sophists said they knew everything and were ready to explain it. Socrates said he knew nothing and was trying to find out.

The sophists were the first lecturers. Socrates was the first tutor. His invention was more radical than theirs. Speeches such as they delivered could be heard elsewhere—in the new democratic law-courts, where clever orators tried to sway large juries by dozens of newly developed oratorical tricks, and in the theaters, where tragic kings, queens, gods, and heroes accused and defied one another in mortal tirades, and in the assemblies of the people, where any citizen could speak on the destinies of Athens. And traveling virtuosi like the sophists were fairly common in other fields—touring musicians, painters, and eminent poets, were all welcome in Greek cities and at the rich court of the "tyrants." It was not too hard, then for the sophists to work out a performance of their own, as brilliant and sometimes as impermanent as a harpist's recital. The innovations Socrates made were to use ordinary conversation as a method of teaching, and to act on one society only, his own city of Athens, instead of detaching himself and traveling. And he made the other fellow do most of the talking. He merely asked questions.

But anyone who has watched a cross-examination in court knows that this is more difficult than making a prepared speech. Socrates questioned all sorts, from schoolboys to elderly capitalists, from orthodox middle-of-the-road citizens to extremists, friends and enemies, critics and admirers, the famous and the obscure, prostitutes and politicians, average Athenians and famous visitors. It was incredibly difficult for him to adapt himself to so many different characters and outlooks, and yet we know that he did. Socrates looked ugly. He had good manners, but no aristocratic polish. Yet he was able to talk to the cleverest and the toughest minds of this age and to convince them that they knew no more than he did. His methods were, first, the modest declaration of his own ignorance—which imperceptibly flattered the other man and made him eager to explain to such an intelligent but naive inquirer; second, his adaptability—which showed him the side on which each man could be best approached; and, third, his unfailing good humor—which allowed him always to keep the conversation going and at crises, when the other lost his temper, to dominate it.

GO ON TO THE NEXT PAGE

21. The author would be most likely to say that modern journalists often produce articles that are
    (A) not authoritative
    (B) poorly written
    (C) insipid
    (D) not understandable by readers who are not experts in the subject of the article

22. The phrase "glossy rhetoric" as it is used in line 36 most nearly means
    (A) colorful language
    (B) elaborate language with little meaning
    (C) specious conclusions
    (D) fascinating but distracting details

23. According to the author all of the following were true about the sophists *except*
    (A) they made speeches that had been prepared in advance
    (B) they were well paid
    (C) some of them said that they were experts on everything
    (D) they were always scrupulously fair in argument

24. It can be inferred that the author believes that Socrates "opposed the sophists wherever possible" (line 48) because he believes that Socrates
    (A) was seeking the truth, whereas the sophists had little concern for the truth
    (B) resented the popularity of the sophists
    (C) believed that emphasizing his rivalry with the sophists would help make him popular
    (D) tended to attack anyone with views and methods different from his own

25. According to the author, all of the following contributed to the acceptance and success of the sophists *except*
    (A) they were articulate
    (B) speeches of high quality by others besides sophists were common in Athens
    (C) they and similar traveling virtuosos were welcomed by the wealthy rulers
    (D) they offered people clear and profound new answers to their philosophical perplexities

26. The most appropriate title for this passage would be
    (A) The Sophists and Socrates
    (B) The Greek World at the Time of Socrates
    (C) The Influence of the Sophists on Socrates
    (D) Socrates: A Man in Search of Truth

27. Based on the information in the passage, which of the following statements would Socrates have been *least* likely to agree with?
    (A) It is more important to seek the truth than to impress other people.
    (B) The truth is often hidden by language.
    (C) Many people do not carefully examine their beliefs and assumptions.
    (D) Most truths have already been discovered.

28. The word *naive* as it is used in line 111 most nearly means
    (A) innocent
    (B) guileless
    (C) uninformed
    (D) credulous

GO ON TO THE NEXT PAGE

29. It can be inferred that people with whom Socrates was discussing ideas sometimes lost their temper because
    (A) they became frustrated at their inability to refute Socrates' arguments
    (B) they regarded Socrates' debating tactics as unfair
    (C) they became upset because Socrates could not understand their argument
    (D) Socrates continually insulted them

30. Based on the author's description of Socrates, it can be inferred that Socrates possessed which of the following qualities not mentioned in the passage?
    (A) the ability to write entertaining dramatic literature
    (B) an excellent understanding of human nature
    (C) an ability to charm women
    (E) great legal acumen

31. Which of the following provides evidence for the answer to the previous question?
    (A) "Socrates . . . out." (lines 60–63)
    (B) "The . . . only" (lines 83–86)
    (C) "And . . . talking." (lines 87–88)
    (D) "It . . . did." (lines 99–102)

Questions 32–42 are based on the following passage.

This passage is from Milton Friend, "Why bother about wildlife disease?" U.S. Geological Survey Circular 1401, 2014.

The animal life of urban environments varies greatly from one geographic area to another and with season of the year. Nevertheless, it is useful to consider the general composition of urban fauna and their disease dynamics. For free-ranging wild birds, there is considerable interfacing between resident and transient populations during seasonal migration periods. Spring dispersal of wild mammals may also result in some infusion of dispersed young into and through urban areas. This interfacing of previously disparate cohorts of the same and other wildlife species provides fresh opportunities for pathogen transfers resulting in disease events. Furthermore, the infection of transient cohorts by their resident urban cohorts can facilitate disease transfer to other areas as those migrants continue their journey. The spread of West Nile virus (see map on page 384) is a graphic example of the ability of birds to expand the enzootic* range of infectious disease great distances.

Duck plague first appeared in North America in 1967 as the cause for a major epizootic** in the Long Island, New York white Pekin duck industry. The subsequent eradication of duck plague from the commercial duck industry of the United States has been followed by numerous duck

*maintained in the population without the need for external inputs
** a disease that appears as new cases in a given animal population, during a given period, at a rate that substantially exceeds what is expected based on recent experience

GO ON TO THE NEXT PAGE

Reports of West Nile Fever in the United States, 1999–2003

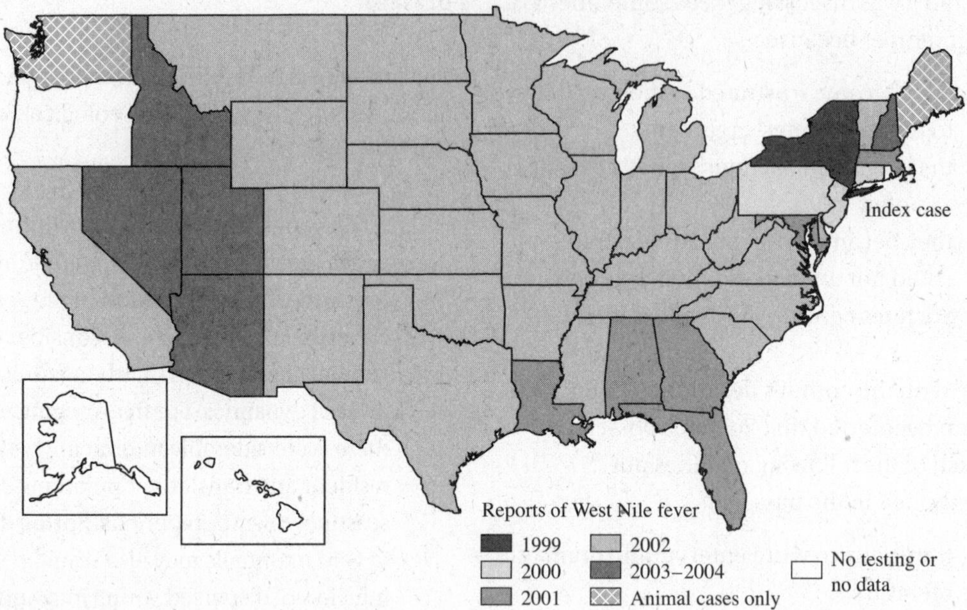

Source: U.S. Geological Survey Circular 1401

plague epizootics in urban, migratory, and other waterfowl flocks across the nation. In addition, there have been two large-scale epizootics involving migratory waterfowl.

Aggressive actions taken to combat urban waterfowl duck plague epizootics may have contributed to the rare documentation of duck plague in migratory waterfowl populations despite recurring outbreaks in a variety of urban and suburban captive and free ranging wildlife populations. However, in some instances the culling of urban waterfowl collections infected by duck plague has been vigorously opposed by various segments of society. That opposition highlights one of the difficulties associated with wildlife disease management within urban environments; companion animal status conferred upon these waterfowl by segments of the public may interfere with needed disease control actions and facilitate disease establishment and spread when eradication was possible.

Another disease dynamic of increased importance within urban environments is the transfer of pathogens between wildlife and companion animals (dogs and cats). A recent study of urban areas in California has disclosed that domestic cats, wild bobcats and mountain lions that live in the same area share the same diseases. The passage of those pathogens from wildlife to domestic cats provides a vehicle for bringing those diseases into the home, thereby bridging an "infection gap" between people and wildlife. Rabies, plague, and tularemia are among the diseases of wildlife that cats and dogs have brought into the home. There is also potential for companion animals to transmit their pathogens to free-ranging wildlife. The establishment of parvovirus and heartworm infections in wolves and wildlife rabies in the United States are examples of disease transfers from infected dogs to wild mammals.

GO ON TO THE NEXT PAGE

Pathogen-laden feces are a common means for disease transmission. Infection of the southern sea otter with toxoplasmosis is an example of the transfer of an infectious pathogen from the domestic cat to a marine mammal (via runoff into the nearshore environment with contaminated cat feces). In addition, during 2008 an *Escherichia coli* outbreak among a cluster of children was traced to elk droppings on football fields near Denver, Colorado and resulted in a decision to cancel football games on fields close to where elk graze. Urban waterfowl commonly litter park areas and golf courses with their feces. That type of contamination periodically results in public health agencies closing public swimming areas because of *E. coli* from waterfowl feces. An extremely hazardous feces shed parasite is *Echinococcus multilocularis,* a tapeworm of foxes. People who accidentally ingest the eggs of this parasite may develop alveolar hydatid disease. Because dogs and cats can also become infected and serve as definitive hosts, usually by feeding on infected small rodents (intermediate hosts), they can bring the parasite to one's home as well as to public areas where companion animals are walked or allowed to roam.

Urban environments are important wildlife habitats and need to be managed in ways that benefit free-ranging wildlife. Furthermore, human attitudes towards wildlife will increasingly be shaped by human experiences in urban environments, because this is where most within urbanized society now interface with wildlife. Thus, it is imperative that wildlife disease be adequately addressed in these environments so that wildlife continue to be cherished.

32. Which of the following would be an appropriate title for this passage?

(A) Managing the Urban Wildlife Habitat
(B) Urban and Suburban Diseases
(C) Diseases in Urban Areas
(D) Urban Fauna and Disease

33. The word *dynamics* as it is used in line 6 most nearly means

(A) variations in intensity
(B) the forces and motions that characterize a system
(C) continuous changes
(D) powerful forces

34. The "aggressive actions taken to combat urban waterfowl duck plague epizootics" (lines 35–36) most likely included

(A) prohibiting people from photographing waterfowl in urban environments
(B) culling of at least some of the infected animals
(C) tagging waterfowl to track their movements
(D) encouraging people to care for such waterfowl, and, if possible, keep them as pets

35. Which of the following provides evidence for the answer to the previous question?

(A) "The . . . nation." (lines 27–32)
(B) "Aggressive . . . populations." (lines 35–41)
(C) "However . . . society." (lines 42–45)
(D) "That . . . possible." (lines 45–53)

GO ON TO THE NEXT PAGE

36. According to the author, a difficulty faced by authorities in charge of wildlife management in urban areas is that
    (A) people in urban areas often have little interest in wildlife
    (B) many people in urban areas take action to destroy non-indigenous wildlife
    (C) quite a few people can become quite emotionally attached to animals and seek to protect them despite the need for disease control measures
    (D) the interests of fishermen, hunters, and wildlife conservationists seldom coincide

37. Which of the following provides evidence for the answer to the previous question?
    (A) "For . . . periods." (lines 6–9)
    (B) "Furthermore . . . distances." (lines 16–23)
    (C) "That . . . possible." (lines 45–53)
    (D) "Furthermore . . . wildlife." (lines 108–112)

38. The word *interfacing* as it is used in line 7 most nearly means
    (A) interfering
    (B) fighting
    (C) mating
    (D) interacting

39. According to the author, pet dogs and cats in urban areas
    (A) are immune to the diseases of wildlife in their area
    (B) are rapidly beginning to share the characteristics of wildlife in their area
    (C) frequently bring disease-causing agents from wildlife into homes but never bring disease-causing agents to wildlife
    (D) sometimes bring diseases into homes and can also bring their disease-causing agents to wildlife

40. Based on the information in the passage, which of the following statements would the author be likely to agree with?
    (A) Based on past experience in urban areas, there is little that wildlife managers and public health officials can do to stop the spread of disease between animals and humans.
    (B) As the world becomes more urbanized it is important for wildlife managers and public health professionals to work closely together to monitor and control human and animal disease.
    (C) Zoos must be abolished to reduce the spread of disease from captive animals to wild animals.
    (D) The health of resident wildlife in urban environments has little to do with the health of free-ranging wildlife.

41. According to the map, in what year(s) was the spread of West Nile fever the most extensive in the United States?
    (A) 2000
    (B) 2001
    (C) 2002
    (D) 2003–2004

42. The author does all of the following *except*
    (A) cite studies
    (B) provide examples
    (C) quote recognized experts
    (D) describe processes

GO ON TO THE NEXT PAGE

Questions 43–52 are based on the following passage.

This passage is from Charles Darwin, *The Autobiography of Charles Darwin*, originally published in 1887.

In one respect my mind has changed during the last twenty or thirty years. Up to the age of thirty, poetry of many kinds gave me great pleasure, and even as a schoolboy I took intense delight in Shakespeare. Formerly, pictures gave me considerable, and music very great delight. But now for many years I cannot endure to read a line of poetry: I have tried lately to read Shakespeare, and found it intolerably dull. I have also almost lost my taste for pictures. On the other hand, novels which are works of the imagination, though not of a very high order, have been for years a wonderful pleasure to me, and I often bless all novelists. I like all if moderately good, and if they do not end unhappily—against which a law ought to be passed.

This lamentable loss of the higher aesthetic tastes is all the odder, as books on history, biographies, and travels (independently of any scientific facts which they may contain), and essays on all sorts of subjects interest me as much as ever they did. My mind seems to have become a kind of machine for grinding general laws out of large collections of facts, but why this should have caused the atrophy of that part of the brain alone, on which the higher tastes depend, I cannot conceive. A man with a mind more highly organized or better constituted than mine, would not, I suppose, have thus suffered; and if I had to live my life again, I would have made a rule to read some poetry and listen to some music at least once every week; for perhaps the parts of my brain now atrophied would thus have been kept active through use.

I have no great quickness of apprehension or wit which is so remarkable in some clever men. I am therefore a poor critic: a paper or book, when first read, generally excites my admiration, and it is only after considerable reflection that I perceive the weak points. My power to follow a long and purely abstract train of thought is very limited; and therefore I could never have succeeded with metaphysics or mathematics. My memory is extensive, yet hazy: it suffices to make me cautious by vaguely telling me that I have observed or read something opposed to the conclusion which I am drawing, or on the other hand in favor of it; and after a time I can generally recollect where to search for my authority.

Some of my critics have said, "Oh, he is a good observer, but he has no power of reasoning!" I do not think that this can be true, for *The Origin of Species* is one long argument from the beginning to the end, and it has convinced not a few able men. No one could have written it without having some power of reasoning. I have a fair share of invention, and of common sense, but not in any higher degree.

On the favorable side of the balance, I think that I am superior to the common run of men in noticing things which easily escape attention, and in observing them carefully. My industry has been nearly as great as it could have been in the observation and collection of facts. From my early youth I have had the strongest desire to understand or explain whatever I observed,—that is to group all facts under some general laws. These causes combined have given me the patience to reflect or ponder for any number of years over any unexplained problem. I am

GO ON TO THE NEXT PAGE

not apt to follow blindly the lead of other men. I have steadily endeavored to keep my mind free so as to give up any hypothesis, however much beloved (and I cannot resist forming one on every subject), as soon as facts are shown to be opposed to it. Indeed, I have had no choice but to act in this manner, for with the exception of the Coral Reefs, I cannot remember a single first-formed hypothesis which had not after a time to be given up or greatly modified. This has naturally led me to distrust greatly deductive reasoning in the mixed sciences. On the other hand, I am not very skeptical,—a frame of mind which I believe to be injurious to the progress of science. A good deal of skepticism in a scientific man is advisable to avoid much loss of time, but I have met with not a few men, who have often thus been deterred from experiment or observations, which would have proved directly or indirectly serviceable.

43. When the author writes "against which a law ought to be passed" (line 17), he is most likely being

(A) satirical
(B) serious
(C) jocular
(D) sarcastic

44. Which of the following would the author probably have most enjoyed doing when he was the age at which he wrote this passage?

(A) reading a poem by William Wordsworth
(B) reading a play by William Shakespeare
(C) reading an essay on English history
(D) studying advanced mathematics

45. The author says "independently of any scientific facts which they may contain" (lines 21–22). This is most likely intended to make clear that

(A) he is interested in reading books on history, biographies, and travels for their intrinsic merit and not only for the scientific facts they may contain
(B) he is interested in reading books on history, biographies, and travels only for the scientific facts they contained
(C) books on history, biographies, and travels do not contain any scientific facts
(D) facts found in books on history, biographies, and travels cannot be related to the facts found by science

46. The author believes that he has considerable ability in all of the following areas *except*

(A) thinking independently
(B) evaluating the worth of hypotheses he has formed
(C) quickly evaluating the worth of a book or paper written by someone else
(D) observing carefully

47. Which of the following provides evidence for the answer to the previous question?

(A) "My . . . conceive." (lines 24–29)
(B) "I . . . points." (lines 38–43)
(C) "On . . . carefully." (lines 65–68)
(D) "On . . . science." (lines 90–93)

48. Which of the following best characterizes the main process the author says he employs in his study of nature?

(A) skepticism
(B) deduction
(C) induction
(D) impartiality

GO ON TO THE NEXT PAGE

49. The word *apprehension* as it is used in line 38 most nearly means

    (A) trepidation
    (B) diligence
    (C) understanding
    (D) anticipation

50. The author believes that

    (A) the more skeptical a scientist is the better the scientist he or she will be
    (B) a scientist must be somewhat skeptical but not excessively so
    (C) skepticism has no place in science
    (D) skepticism is irrelevant to the pursuit of scientific research

51. Which of the following provides evidence for the answer to the previous question?

    (A) "My . . . mathematics." (lines 44–47)
    (B) "I . . . degree." (lines 62–64)
    (C) "I . . . men." (lines 77–79)
    (D) "On . . . serviceable." (lines 90–99)

52. The word *invention* as it is used in line 63 most nearly means

    (A) discovery
    (B) mechanical aptitude
    (C) insight
    (D) creativity

STOP

If there is still time remaining, you may review your answers.

2 2 2

WRITING AND LANGUAGE TEST

35 MINUTES, 44 QUESTIONS

Turn to Section 2 of your answer sheet to answer the questions in this section.

Directions: Questions follow each of the passages below. Some questions ask you how the passage might be changed to improve the expression of ideas. Other questions ask you how the passage might be altered to correct errors in grammar, usage, and punctuation. One or more graphics accompany some passages. You will be required to consider these graphics as you answer questions about editing the passage.

There are three types of questions. In the first type, a part of the passage is underlined. The second type is based on a certain part of the passage. The third type is based on the entire passage.

Read each passage. Then, choose the answer to each question that changes the passage so that it is consistent with the conventions of standard written English. One of the answer choices for many questions is "NO CHANGE." Choosing this answer means that you believe the best answer is to make no change in the passage.

Questions 1–11 are based on the following passage and supplementary material.

Millions of Jobs in Healthcare

In career news, healthcare is everywhere. (1) Because the healthcare industry is projected to add more jobs—over 4 million—than any other industry between 2012 and 2022, according to the U.S. Bureau of Labor Statistics (BLS). And it is projected to be among the fastest-growing industries in the economy.

In 2013, there were more than 15.8 million jobs in healthcare industries, according to BLS. Hospitals (2) purported the largest number of jobs in healthcare, about 39 percent of total healthcare employment in 2013. Offices of health practitioners

1. (A) NO CHANGE
(B) That's because
(C) The cause of this is that
(D) This is caused by the fact that

2. (A) NO CHANGE
(B) explained
(C) accounted for
(D) professed

GO ON TO THE NEXT PAGE

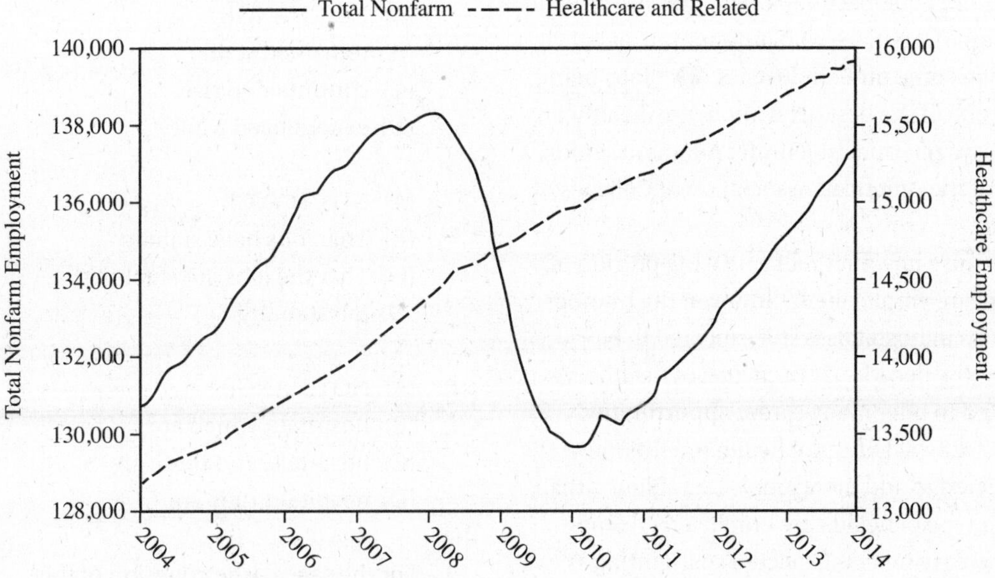

Note: Healthcare and related include series CEU6562000101, CEU9091622001, CEU9092262201, and CEU9093262201, January 2014 data are preliminary.
Source: U.S. Bureau of Labor Statistics, Current Employment Statistics (wage and salary employment, seasonally adjusted).

made up about 26 percent, **3** only nursing and residential care facilities made up about 20 percent of healthcare jobs. Home healthcare services, and outpatient, laboratory, and other **4** ambulatory care services each had about 8 percent of healthcare jobs in 2013.

Employment in the healthcare industry **5** will be growing steadily for years, BLS data show (see graph). This growth is due, in part, to people depending on health services no matter what the economic climate. Even when total U.S. employment fell during the 2007–09 recession, for

3. (A) NO CHANGE
   (B) at the same time
   (C) yet
   (D) while

4. (A) NO CHANGE
   (B) itinerant
   (C) roving
   (D) migratory

5. Which choice most accurately and effectively represents the information in the graph?
   (A) NO CHANGE
   (B) has been growing
   (C) is to grow
   (D) was grown

GO ON TO THE NEXT PAGE

example, healthcare employment **6** had only a slight fall. And because healthcare-related jobs often require personal interaction, they are difficult to outsource or replace with automation, as happens in some other industries. **7** "Jobs being stable is one of the best parts about any healthcare career," says pharmacist Jennifer Adams, a senior director at the American Association of Colleges of Pharmacy.

[1] Because hospitals make up a big portion of all healthcare employment, however, the number of new jobs in hospitals is still expected to be large over the decade. [2] Each area of healthcare is expected to offer many career opportunities through 2022. [3] Offices of health practitioners are projected to add more jobs—1.2 million—than any other type of healthcare employer. [4] Some of this increase reflects expected cost-cutting efforts to shift demand for health services away from **8** hospitals being relatively expensive. **9**

Home healthcare services **10** are projected to be the fastest growing detailed industry in the economy, with employment projected to increase by almost 60 percent between 2012 and 2022. As greater numbers of older people seek care that allows them to stay in their homes and maintain their independence, the need for workers in home healthcare services is expected to **11** extend.

6. Which choice most accurately represents the information in the graph?
   (A) NO CHANGE
   (B) remained stable
   (C) continued to rise
   (D) experienced a lull

7. (A) NO CHANGE
   (B) That jobs have stability
   (C) That the jobs are stable
   (D) Job stability

8. (A) NO CHANGE
   (B) hospitals, which are
   (C) hospitals, and these are
   (D) hospitals, they are

9. For the sake of the cohesion of this paragraph, sentence 1 should be placed:
   (A) where it is now
   (B) after sentence 2
   (C) after sentence 3
   (D) after sentence 4

10. (A) NO CHANGE
    (B) will project to be
    (C) were projected to be
    (D) is projected to be

11. (A) NO CHANGE
    (B) elevate
    (C) amplify
    (D) expand

GO ON TO THE NEXT PAGE

Questions 12–22 are based on the following passage.

Ohiyesa: The Winner

The author of this book was born in a teepee of buffalo hide near Redwood Falls, Minnesota, during the winter of 1858. (12) His father was a full-blooded Sioux called "Many Lightnings," his mother, the granddaughter of Chief "Cloud Man" of the Sioux and daughter of a well-known army officer, she died shortly after his birth. He was named Ohiyesa (The Winner).

[1] The knowledge thus gained of life's realities and the secrets of nature, as well as of the idealistic philosophy of the Indian, has always been regarded by the author as a most valuable part of his education. [2] The baby was reared to boyhood by the care of his grandmother. [3] When he was four years old, the so-called "Minnesota massacre" of 1862 separated him from his father and elder brothers and only sister, and drove him with a (13) residue of the eastern Sioux into exile in Manitoba. [4] For more than ten years, he lived the original nomadic life of his people in the family of an uncle, from whom he received the Spartan training of an Indian youth of that day. (14)

12. Select from the following the choice that forms two distinct sentences that make sense:

    (A) His father, a full-blooded Sioux, was called "Many Lightnings." His mother was the granddaughter of Chief "Cloud Man" of the Sioux, and she was also the daughter of a well-known army officer, she died shortly after his birth.
    (B) His father was a full-blooded Sioux. He was called "Many Lightnings" and his mother was the granddaughter of Chief "Cloud Man" of the Sioux and daughter of a well-known army officer who died shortly after birth.
    (C) His father, he was a full-blooded Sioux called "Many Lightnings" and his mother was the granddaughter of Chief "Cloud Man" of the Sioux. She was also the daughter of a well-known army officer, dying shortly after his birth.
    (D) His father was a full-blooded Sioux called "Many Lightnings." His mother, the granddaughter of Chief "Cloud Man" of the Sioux and daughter of a well-known army officer, died shortly after his birth.

13. (A) NO CHANGE
    (B) remnant
    (C) shred
    (D) trace

14. For the sake of the cohesion of this paragraph, sentence 1 should be placed:

    (A) where it is now
    (B) after sentence 2
    (C) after sentence 3
    (D) after sentence 4

GO ON TO THE NEXT PAGE

2 2 2

When Ohiyesa had reached the age of fifteen years, and had been presented with a flint-lock musket in token of his arrival at the estate of young manhood, he was astonished by the reappearance of the father whose **15** considered death at the hands of white men he had been taught that he must some day avenge. He learned that this father had adopted the religion and customs of the hated **16** race, and had come to take home his youngest son.

Ohiyesa's new home was a pioneer log cabin on a farm at Flandreau, Dakota Territory, **17** that a small group of progressive Indians had taken up homesteads like white men **18** and had earnings of an independent livelihood. His long hair was cropped, he was put into a suit of citizen's clothing and sent off to a mission day school. **19** First he was reluctant, he soon became interested, and two years later voluntarily walked 150 miles to attend a larger and better school at Santee, Nebraska, where he made rapid progress under the veteran missionary educator, Dr. Alfred L. Riggs, and was soon advanced to the preparatory department of Beloit College, Wisconsin. **20** Although the boy named himself Charles Alexander, his father had adopted his wife's English name of Eastman.

15. (A) NO CHANGE
    (B) regarded
    (C) implied
    (D) supposed

16. (A) NO CHANGE
    (B) race and comes
    (C) race, being come
    (D) race, and would come

17. (A) NO CHANGE
    (B) where
    (C) whereby
    (D) from this

18. (A) NO CHANGE
    (B) whose earnings were
    (C) and were earning
    (D) so that they earned

19. (A) NO CHANGE
    (B) Being that he was first reluctant,
    (C) At first reluctant,
    (D) Reluctant first,

20. For the sake of clarity of meaning and effectiveness of expression, the sentence should be rewritten as follows:

    (A) NO CHANGE
    (B) His father had adopted his wife's English name of Eastman, and the boy named himself Charles Alexander.
    (C) The boy named himself Charles Alexander, the father having adopted his wife's English name of Eastman.
    (D) His father had adopted his wife's English name, Eastman, the boy having named himself Charles Alexander.

GO ON TO THE NEXT PAGE

After two years at Beloit, young Eastman went on to Knox College, Illinois; then east to Kimball Union Academy in New Hampshire, and to Dartmouth College, where Indians had found a special welcome since colonial days. He was graduated from Dartmouth in 1887, and went immediately to Boston University, where he took the medical course, and was graduated in ㉑ 1890 as orator of his class. The entire time spent in primary, preparatory, college, and professional education, including the ㉒ ability of the English language, was seventeen years, or about two years less than is required by the average white youth.

21. (A) NO CHANGE
    (B) 1890 orator
    (C) 1890 by orator
    (D) 1890 with orator

22. (A) NO CHANGE
    (B) mastery
    (C) agility
    (D) digestion

GO ON TO THE NEXT PAGE

Questions 23–33 are based on the following passage.

Exploration of Cuba

23 For a considerable time after the last visit of Columbus, Cuba was strangely neglected by the enterprising explorers and conquistadors of Spain. Hispaniola became the chief colony and centre of Spanish authority in the 24 Antilles. It for many years was far outranking Cuba in interest and importance. It does not appear that for more than a dozen years after the last visit of Columbus any attempt whatever was made to colonize or to explore the great island, if indeed it was so much as voluntarily visited. 25 Frequently doubtless navigators passed near its shores, on their way to and from Darien and the Venezuelan coast, and occasionally stress of weather on the "stormy Caribbean" or actual shipwreck compelled some to land upon it. Such involuntary landings were presumably made either in the neighborhood of the Zapata Peninsula, or, still more probably, not exactly upon Cuba at all but upon the southern shore of the tributary Isle of Pines. 26 In spite of this, the voyagers carried back to Hispaniola or to Spain the not unnatural report that Cuba consisted of nothing but swamps; this report of course did

23. The writer is considering deleting the underlined sentence. Should the writer do this?
    (A) Yes, because this sentence focuses on Cuba, whereas the rest of the passage largely focuses on Hispaniola.
    (B) Yes, because no evidence is cited to support the claim that "Cuba was strangely neglected by the enterprising explorers and conquistadors of Spain."
    (C) No, because this sentence is a concise and accurate statement of the main topic of the passage, which is how and why "Cuba was strangely neglected by the enterprising explorers and conquistadors of Spain."
    (D) No, because this sentence introduces the main topic of the passage, which is the conquistadors of Spain.

24. Which choice most effectively combines the sentences at the underlined portion?
    (A) Antilles—far outranked Cuba for many years
    (B) Antilles, and it for many years far outranked Cuba
    (C) Antilles, it was for many years far outranking Cuba
    (D) Antilles in which, for many years, it was far out outranking Cuba

25. (A) NO CHANGE
    (B) Frequently navigators without doubts passed
    (C) Navigators, frequently doubtless, passed
    (D) Navigators doubtless frequently passed

26. (A) NO CHANGE
    (B) In such a case
    (C) In consequence
    (D) In like fashion

GO ON TO THE NEXT PAGE

not inspire others with zeal to visit so unfavorable a place.

[1] For a similar space of time, too, the delusion that Cuba was a part of the continent generally prevailed. [2] It is true that on a map of Juan de la Cosa's, to which the date of 1500 **27** attributed, Cuba is indicated to be an island. [3] But the date is not certain, by any means; and it is notorious that more than one early cartographer drew upon imagination as well as upon **28** ascertained geographical facts. [4] There is no proof, however, that this **29** has been more than a rumor. [5] Somewhat more significant is the fact that Peter Martyr spoke of Cuba as an island, and said that some sailors pretended to have circumnavigated it. [6] What seems certain is that as late as 1508 the best authorities were ignorant whether Cuba was an island or mainland, and that not until that time was the question settled. **30**

Columbus **31** had succeeded in authority in Hispaniola by Francisco de Bobadilla, and the latter in turn had in 1501 given way to Nicholas de Ovando. It does not appear that Ovando sought to colonize Cuba. But he did wish to determine its extent, and whether it was insular or continental, and he commissioned Sebastian de Ocampo to explore the coasts of the country and, if he found it to be an island, to circumnavigate it. **32** This was done by Ocampo, returning to Hispaniola in the fall of 1508 with the report that he had sailed completely round Cuba. On the way, he said, he had made occasional landings, and **33** founded the whole island to be inhabited by a kindly and intelligent people, well disposed toward Spain.

27. (A) NO CHANGE
    (B) is attributed
    (C) attributes
    (D) was attributing

28. (A) NO CHANGE
    (B) classified
    (C) resolved
    (D) pinpointed

29. (A) NO CHANGE
    (B) should be
    (C) is
    (D) was

30. For the sake of clarity of meaning and effectiveness of expression, sentence 4 should be placed:
    (A) where it is now
    (B) after sentence 5
    (C) after sentence 1
    (D) after sentence 2

31. (A) NO CHANGE
    (B) succeeded
    (C) had been succeeded
    (D) had been succeeding

32. (A) NO CHANGE
    (B) This Ocampo, he did it, and returned
    (C) This Ocampo did, returning
    (D) This Ocampo did, he returned

33. (A) NO CHANGE
    (B) finding
    (C) finds
    (D) had found

GO ON TO THE NEXT PAGE

Questions 34–44 are based on the following passage.

Hydro-meteorological Hazards in Indonesia

[1] **34** Indonesia lies between the Indian Ocean and the Pacific Ocean, positioned on the equator, and has more than 13,000 islands, most of which are small islands. [2] Although the typhoons rarely hit these areas directly, the effects they generate around the ocean are still powerful enough to have adverse impacts on these communities. [3] The majority of the population is made up of coastal and small island communities, which are exposed to a number of hydro-meteorological hazards, such as sea storms (cyclones and typhoons), coastal abrasion, strong winds, floods, droughts, and climate change impacts. [4] Coastal areas around Aceh, Southern Java, the north coast of Sulawesi and Eastern Nusa Tenggara **35** have an experience with a number of typhoons every year. **36**

In the last decades, the combination of land subsidence and sea level rise has been observed in several places in Indonesia. One of the areas most affected by the sea level rise is the north coast of Central **37** Java: with the impacts of sea level rise also observed in several coastal villages in Eastern Nusa Temggara. Unlike the city of Jakarta in Central Java, which is constructing giant sea walls to **38** mollify the increasing sea level, other areas in Indonesia are far from ready to cope with the effects of climate change.

34. For the sake of clarity of meaning and effectiveness of expression, the underlined portion of the sentence should be written as follows:
    (A) as it is now
    (B) Positioned on the equator, Indonesia lies between the Indian Ocean and the Pacific Ocean and has
    (C) Indonesia lies, positioned on the equator, between the Indian Ocean and the Pacific Ocean and has
    (D) Indonesia's position lies on the equator between the Indian Ocean and the Pacific Ocean, having

35. (A) NO CHANGE
    (B) had experienced
    (C) have the experience of
    (D) experience

36. For the sake of the cohesion of this paragraph, sentence 2 should be placed:
    (A) where it is now
    (B) before sentence 1
    (C) after sentence 3
    (D) after sentence 4

37. (A) NO CHANGE
    (B) Java, with the impacts
    (C) Java; with the impacts
    (D) Java, the impacts

38. (A) NO CHANGE
    (B) allay
    (C) mitigate
    (D) temper

GO ON TO THE NEXT PAGE

Bedono village, located on the north coast of Central Java Province, is an example which illustrates the vulnerability of coastal communities to hydro-meteorological hazards and the impacts of climate (39) change before 1995. Most people in this village cultivated rice on paddy fields. However, in the past ten years, all the paddy fields have been submerged by intruding sea water, forcing people to change their land into fish ponds. The villagers have also had to elevate their houses to avoid sea water at every high tide.

The Pulo Aceh islands are located on the northern tip of Sumatra Island in Aceh province, which is prone to hydro-meteorological hazards and the impacts of climate change. Between 2002 and 2011, 25 cases of extreme waves and coastal erosion, and 49 cases of strong winds were reported in the province. Pulo Aceh islanders have had to adapt and (40) entertain sea (41) storms, and strong winds are generated around the Andaman Sea and the Indian Ocean. Extreme sea weather often disrupts transportation between the islands and mainland Sumatra, cutting communities off from the (42) mainland and they leave them isolated for several days. Inadequate communication and transportation infrastructure also contributes to the difficulties faced by these communities. They do have their own local and indigenous knowledge to anticipate hydro-meteorological hazards, (43) some of which is similar to knowledge found in other parts of Indonesia. (44)

39. (A) NO CHANGE
(B) change: before 1995, most
(C) change. Before 1995, most
(D) change; before 1995, most

40. (A) NO CHANGE
(B) assume
(C) conjecture
(D) anticipate

41. (A) NO CHANGE
(B) storms, and strong winds generate
(C) storms and strong winds generated
(D) storms and strong winds generate

42. (A) NO CHANGE
(B) mainland and leaving them
(C) mainland, they are left
(D) mainland, left

43. (A) NO CHANGE
(B) similarly
(C) being similar
(D) of which is similar

44. Which choice most effectively establishes the main point of the paragraph?
(A) The Pulo Aceh islands are often cut off from mainland Indonesia.
(B) The Pulo Aceh islands are subject to a variety of extreme weather events that make life difficult for people there.
(C) The Pulo Aceh islands on Sumatra Island, Indonesia, have poor transportation and communication facilities, making life difficult for residents during severe storms.
(D) The devastating impact of climate change is seen clearly in the Pulo Aceh islands illustrated by numerous examples.

If there is still time remaining, you may review your answers.

MATH TEST (NO CALCULATOR)

25 MINUTES, 20 QUESTIONS

Turn to Section 3 of your answer sheet to answer the questions in this section.

Directions: For questions 1-15, solve each problem and choose the best answer from the given options. Fill in the corresponding circle on your answer document. For questions 16–20, solve the problem and fill in the answer on the answer sheet grid. Please use scrap paper to work out your answers.

Notes:

- You **CANNOT** use a calculator on this section.
- All variables and expressions represent real numbers unless indicated otherwise.
- All figures are drawn to scale unless indicated otherwise.
- All figures are in a plane unless indicated otherwise.
- Unless indicated otherwise, the domain of a given function is the set of all real numbers x for which the function has real values.

REFERENCE INFORMATION

Area Facts

$A = \ell w$

$A = \frac{1}{2}bh$

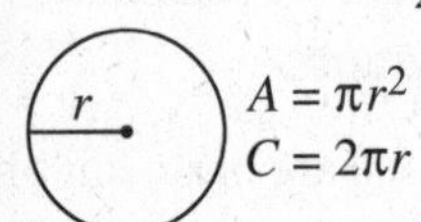

Volume Facts

$V = \ell wh$

$V = \frac{4}{3}\pi r^3$

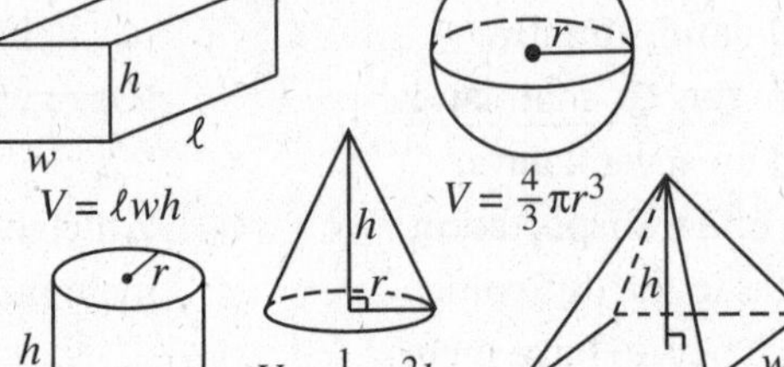

$V = \pi r^2 h$

$V = \frac{1}{3}\ell wh$

Triangle Facts

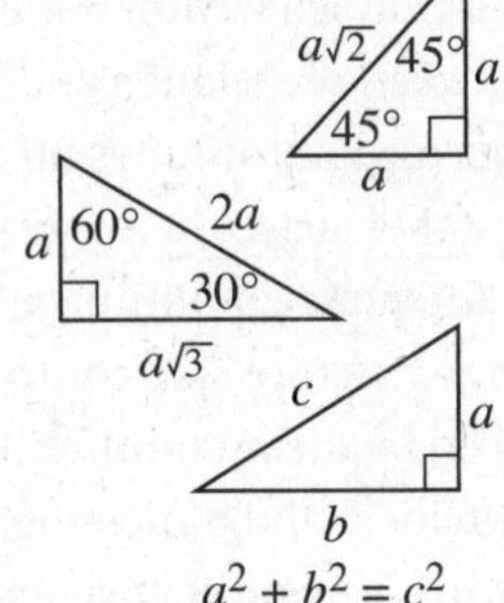

The arc of a circle contains 360°.
The arc of a circle contains 2π radians.
The sum of the measures of the angles in a triangle is 180°.

1. If $7n = 42$, what is the value of $4n - 11$?

(A) 13
(B) 16
(C) 17
(D) 19

2. Which of the following is equal to $(m^{\frac{1}{3}})^2$?

(A) $\sqrt{m^{\frac{1}{6}}}$
(B) $\sqrt[3]{m^2}$
(C) $\sqrt{m^3}$
(D) $m\sqrt{m}$

GO ON TO THE NEXT PAGE

3. A marathon runner can run m miles at d miles per hour in h hours. The formula for the distance she runs is $hd = m$. If m is a constant, which of the following conclusions is correct?

(A) when d increases, h increases
(B) when d decreases, h decreases
(C) as h increases, d decreases
(D) d will never increase but m can increase or decrease

4. If the area of a square is doubled, how many times longer is a side of the larger square than is the length of the smaller square?

(A) 4
(B) 2
(C) $\sqrt{3}$
(D) $\sqrt{2}$

5. If $\frac{6}{n} = \frac{18}{n+24}$, what is the value of $\frac{n}{12}$?

(A) 1
(B) 1.5
(C) 2
(D) 4.5

$$3x + 6y = 14$$
$$2x + 5y = -11$$

6. If (x, y) is a solution to the system of equations above, what is the value of $x + y$?

(A) 3
(B) 17.5
(C) 24
(D) 25

x	$f(x)$
0	5
2	3
4	1
5	0
8	−2

7. The function f is defined by a polynomial. Some values of x and $f(x)$ are shown in the table above. Which of the following must be a factor of $f(x)$?

(A) x
(B) $x - 3$
(C) $x - 5$
(D) $x - 8$

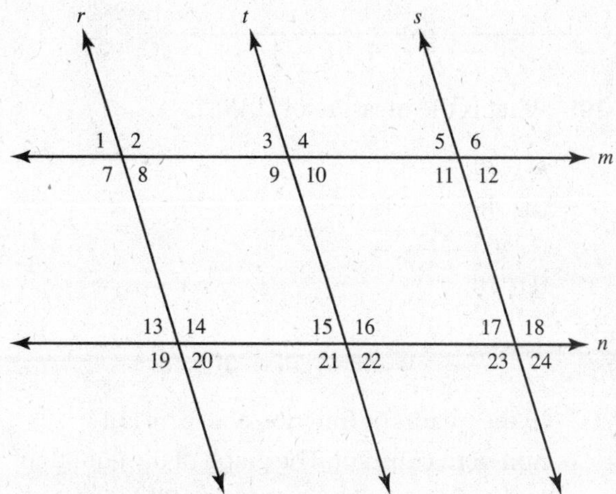

8. In the diagram above, $r \parallel t \parallel s$ and $m \parallel n$. If the measure of $\angle 3 = (2m + 18)°$ and the measure of $\angle 2 = (4m + 42)°$, what is the measure of $\angle 18$?

(A) 122°
(B) 61°
(C) 58°
(D) 20°

GO ON TO THE NEXT PAGE

$$5x+3y=-10$$
$$bx-4.5y=13.5$$

9. In the system of equations above, b is a constant and x and y are variables. For what value of b will the system of equations have no solution?

(A) −10
(B) −7.5
(C) 2.5
(D) 4

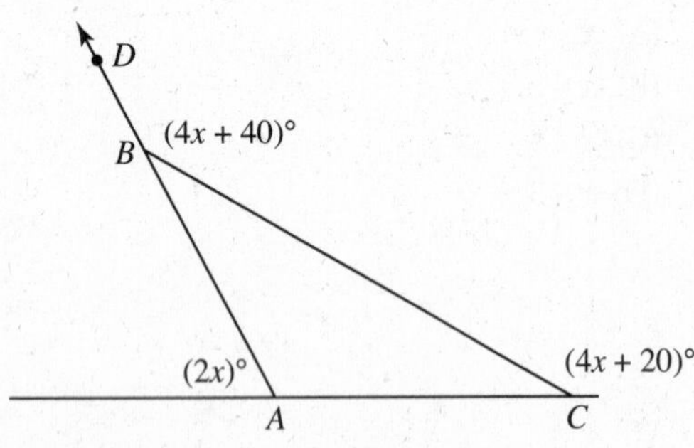

10. What is the measure of $\angle ABC$?

(A) 20
(B) 40
(C) 65
(D) 70

$$y=m(x+3)(x-5)$$

11. In the quadratic function above, m is a non-zero constant. The graph of the equation in the xy-plane has vertex (e, f). Which of the following is the value of f?

(A) $16m$
(B) $4m$
(C) $-4m$
(D) $-16m$

12. What is the value of x if $x=\dfrac{w^2+2w+1}{\dfrac{w+1}{3}}$

(A) $\dfrac{3}{w+1}$

(B) $3(w+1)$

(C) $\dfrac{1}{3w+1}$

(D) $\dfrac{\frac{1}{w}}{3+w}$

13. Which of the following is equivalent to $25^{\frac{3}{4}}$?

(A) $5\sqrt{5}$
(B) $\sqrt[3]{25}$
(C) $5\sqrt[3]{25}$
(D) 37.5

GO ON TO THE NEXT PAGE

3

$$F = \frac{9}{5}C + 32$$

14. The equation above shows how a temperature, C, measured in degrees Celsius, relates to a temperature, F, in degrees Fahrenheit. Based on the equation, which of the following must be true?

  I. An increase in temperature of 1 degree Celsius is equivalent to an increase of 1.8 degrees Fahrenheit.
  II. A temperature of 5° F is equivalent to –15°C.
  III. A temperature of 20°C is equivalent to 62°F.

(A) I only
(B) I and II
(C) I and III
(D) III only

15. The expression $\frac{4n+6}{n-4}$ is equivalent to which of the following?

(A) $-\frac{4+6}{4}$

(B) $4-\frac{6}{4}$

(C) $4+\frac{6}{n-4}$

(D) $4+\frac{22}{n-4}$

GO ON TO THE NEXT PAGE

Grid-in Response Directions

In questions 16–20, first solve the problem, and then enter your answer on the grid provided on the answer sheet. The instructions for entering your answers follow.

- First, write your answer in the boxes at the top of the grid.
- Second, grid your answer in the columns below the boxes.
- Use the fraction bar in the first row or the decimal point in the second row to enter fractions and decimals.

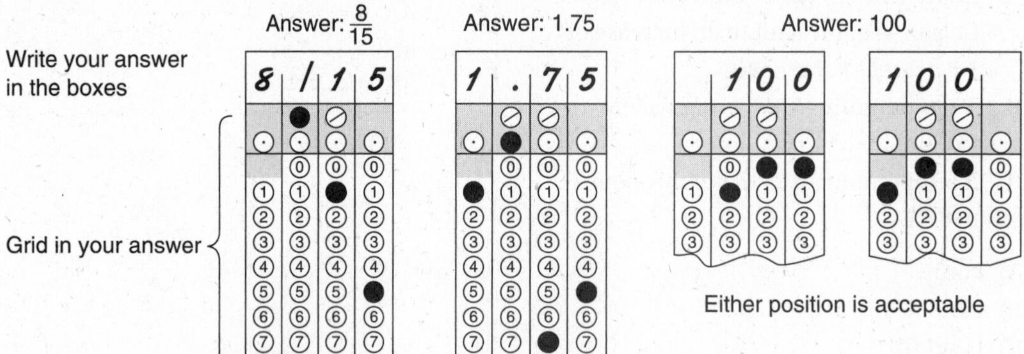

- Grid only one space in each column.
- Entering the answer in the boxes is recommended as an aid in gridding but is not required.
- The machine scoring your exam can read only what you grid, so you **must grid-in your answers correctly to get credit.**
- If a question has more than one correct answer, grid-in only one of them.
- The grid does not have a minus sign; so no answer can be negative.
- A mixed number *must* be converted to an improper fraction or a decimal before it is gridded. Enter $1\frac{1}{4}$ as $\frac{5}{4}$ or 1.25; the machine will interpret 11/4 as $\frac{11}{4}$ and mark it wrong.
- **All decimals must be entered as accurately as possible.** Here are three acceptable ways of gridding

$$\frac{3}{11} = 0.272727\ldots$$

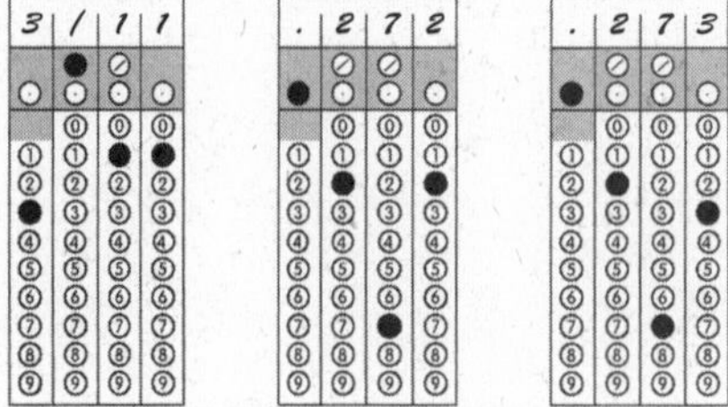

- Note that rounding to .273 is acceptable because you are using the full grid, but you would receive **no credit** for .3 or .27, because they are less accurate.

16. If $m^2 - 6m + 8 = 0$, what is *one* possible value of $\frac{1}{m}$?

17. What is the radius of the circle whose equation is $x^2 + 6y + y^2 - 4x = 12$?

18. What is *one* possible value for the compound inequality $-8 \leq 2x - 8 < 8$?

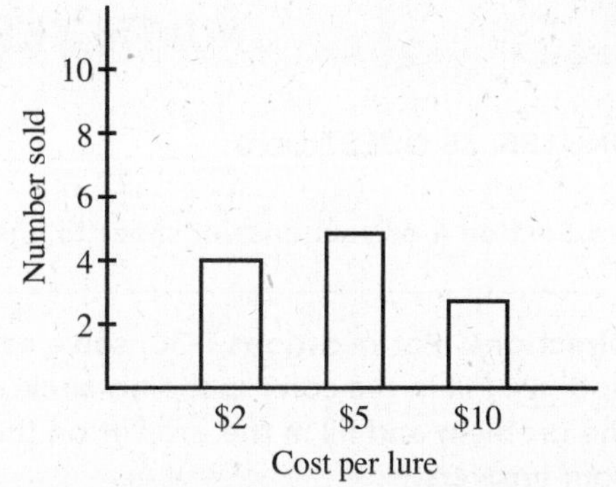

19. The bar graph above represents the fishing lures sold in a sales competition sponsored by the seller.

What is the median cost of the lures sold?

20. An academic quiz show features local high school students. Each correctly answered question nets the team one point and an incorrectly answered question results in a two-point deduction. If a team scored 38 points on a fifty-question quiz, how many questions did it answer incorrectly?

STOP

If there is still time remaining, you may review your answers.

MATH TEST (CALCULATOR)

55 MINUTES, 38 QUESTIONS

Turn to Section 4 of your answer sheet to answer the questions in this section.

Directions: For questions 1–30, solve each problem and choose the best answer from the given options. Fill in the corresponding circle on your answer document. For questions 31–38, solve the problem and fill in the answer on the answer sheet grid. Please use scrap paper to work out your answers.

Notes:

- The use of a calculator on this section IS permitted.
- All variables and expressions represent real numbers unless indicated otherwise.
- All figures are drawn to scale unless indicated otherwise.
- All figures are in a plane unless indicated otherwise.
- Unless indicated otherwise, the domain of a given function is the set of all real numbers x for which the function has real values.

REFERENCE INFORMATION

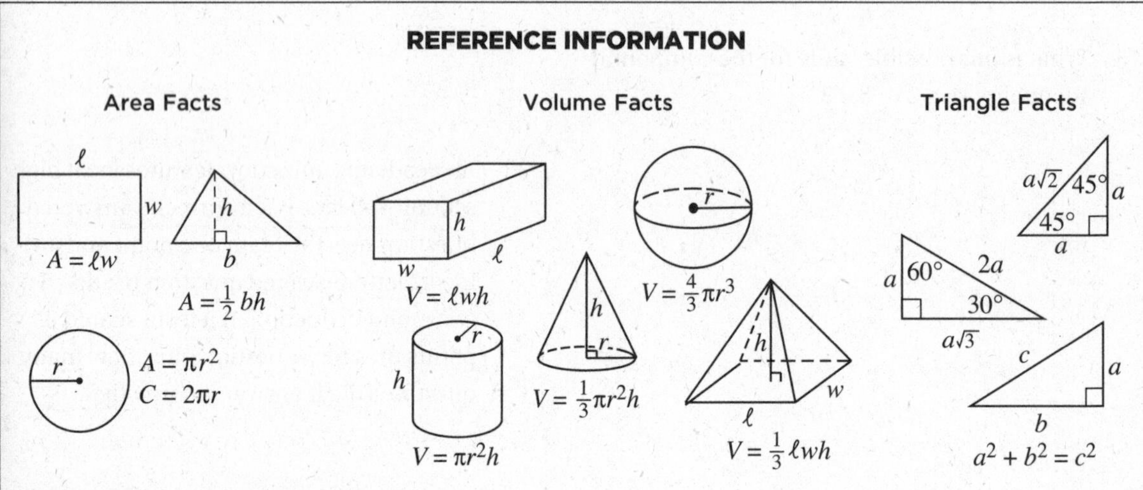

The arc of a circle contains 360°.

The arc of a circle contains 2π radians.

The sum of the measures of the angles in a triangle is 180°.

GO ON TO THE NEXT PAGE

1. Anita climbed 5 flights of stairs because the elevator was in disrepair. If each staircase had 16 stairs and she reached the top stair of the 5th flight in 5 minutes and 20 seconds, what was the mean time spent climbing each stair?

(A) 3 seconds
(B) 4 seconds
(C) 5 seconds
(D) 6 seconds

	Boy	Girl	Total
Swim	12	14	26
Water Polo	16	15	31
Total	28	29	57

2. The above chart represents the students who are members of a high school's swim and water polo teams.

The water polo and swim teams are having a Spring Banquet. One of the team members will be chosen as athlete of the year. What is the probability the person chosen will be a member of the water polo team or a boy?

(A) $\frac{31}{57}$

(B) $\frac{43}{57}$

(C) $\frac{52}{57}$

(D) $\frac{55}{57}$

Questions 3 and 4 refer to the information below.

The graph below shows the number of domestic bee farms in the metropolitan Atlanta area from 2005 to 2010.

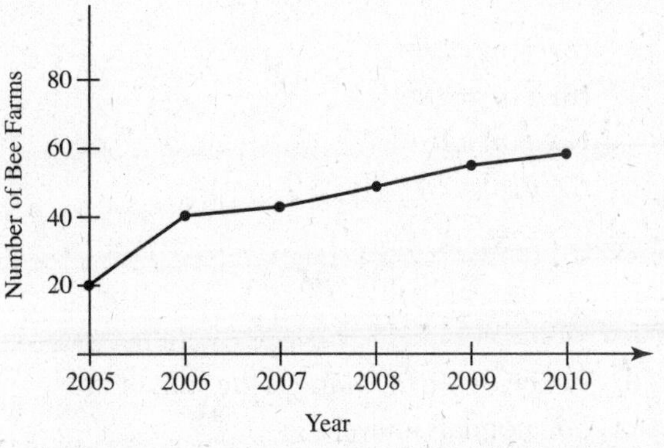

3. Based on the graph, which of the following describes the trend in the number of domestic bee farms in the Atlanta area?

(A) exponential growth between 2005 and 2010
(B) continued but modest growth after 2006
(C) an increase until 2007 followed by a gradual decline after that year
(D) a dramatic decrease after 2008

4. What was the annual increase in domestic bee farms from 2005 to 2010?

(A) 5%
(B) 20%
(C) 40%
(D) 60%

GO ON TO THE NEXT PAGE

PRACTICE TEST 5

n	1	2	3	4
$r(n)$	–1	1	3	5

5. The table above shows some values of the linear function *r*. Which of the following defines *r*?

(A) $r(n) = 2n + 3$
(B) $r(n) = 3n - 5$
(C) $r(n) = n - 3$
(D) $r(n) = 2n - 3$

$$4x^2 + 5x - 6$$
$$3x^2 + x - 11$$

6. Which of the following is the sum of the polynomials above?

(A) $x^2 + 4x + 5$
(B) $x^2 + 6x - 17$
(C) $7x^2 + 6x - 17$
(D) $7x^4 + 6x^2 - 17$

7. If $\frac{5}{9}n = \frac{7}{20}$, what is the value of n?

(A) $\frac{16}{25}$

(B) $\frac{27}{50}$

(C) $\frac{17}{25}$

(D) $\frac{63}{100}$

8. A swearing-in ceremony for new American citizens is scheduled for early 2017. Although tickets are free, seating is scarce. The event planners use the following formula to ration the distribution of tickets.

$T(x) = -.4x^2 + 9x + 11$ where x represents the number of days that tickets are available for distribution.

How many days after the tickets are made available will the peak number of tickets be distributed and what will be the number of tickets distributed on that day?

(A) 11 days, 62 tickets
(B) 12 days, 11 tickets
(C) 19 days, 38 tickets
(D) 38 days, 19 tickets

9. Gina runs 28 meters in 4.7 seconds. If she continues to run at this rate, which of the following is the closest to the distance (in meters) she will run in 2.4 minutes?

(A) 269 meters
(B) 542 meters
(C) 653 meters
(D) 858 meters

GO ON TO THE NEXT PAGE

Questions 10 and 11 refer to the information below.

The following table represents federal spending for NASA for the years 1958 through 1963.

NASA spending since 1958

Year	NASA fed outlay, $ in millions	Total US fed spending, $ in millions	NASA as % of US spending	President	Party
1958	89	71,936	0.1	Dwight D. Eisenhower	Rep
1959	145	80,697	0.2	Dwight D. Eisenhower	Rep
1960	401	76,539	0.5	Dwight D. Eisenhower	Rep
1961	744	81,515	0.9	John F. Kennedy	Dem
1962	1,257	106,821	1.18	John F. Kennedy	Dem
1963	2,552	111,316	2.28	Lyndon B. Johnson	Dem

10. Which of the following can be concluded about the information portrayed in the table?

(A) From 1958 until 1963, spending on NASA as a percentage of the US budget increased nearly 2,200%.
(B) Between 1962 and 1963 spending on NASA virtually tripled.
(C) In 1963, real spending on NASA exceeded the $1 billion mark for the first time.
(D) The total dollars spent each year from 1958 to 1963 decreased.

11. Total US spending in 1962 was about how many times larger than the NASA budget in 1958?

(A) 77 times
(B) 88 times
(C) 650 times
(D) 1,200 times

GO ON TO THE NEXT PAGE

Questions 12 and 13 refer to the following information.

An investment of $7,500 in a certain piece of artwork has depreciated in value. The investor uses the following formula to calculate the value of her investment.

$A = P(1 - r)^t$

where
A = the accumulated value over time
P = the initial price of the artwork
r = rate of decrease expressed as a decimal
t = time in years

12. Which of the following equations models the value of the artwork if it has devalued at 4.6% annually for 3.5 years?

(A) $A = 7{,}500(.965)^{3.5}$
(B) $A = 7{,}500(1.035)^{3.5}$
(C) $A = 7{,}500(1.046)^{3.5}$
(D) $A = 7{,}500(.954)^{3.5}$

13. Three years after the purchase date, the value of the artwork had declined to $6,511.88. If the depreciation has occurred at a 4.6% annual rate, what was its value five years later?

(A) $5,145.75
(B) $5,337.62
(C) $5,476.39
(D) $6,126.63

14. A clinical study was devised to see if a new procedure was an effective early detector of skin cancer. A group of 500 patients participated but only 250, group A, received the treatment. The other 250 participants, group B, received the standard procedure which is 45% effective. Group A was treated with the new procedure, resulting in 79% effectiveness. Based on the design and results of the study, which of the following is an appropriate conclusion?

(A) The study size was too small to make a conclusion.
(B) The new early detection program is better than any other available program.
(C) The new early detection program was more effective than the current standard procedure.
(D) The new procedure will help all patients in danger of skin cancer.

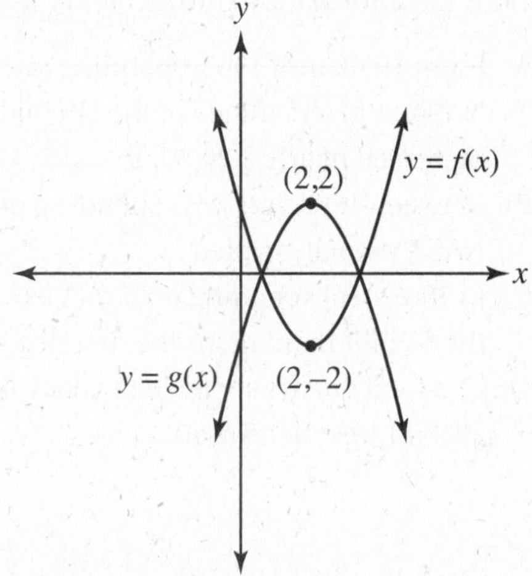

15. Graphs of the functions f and g are shown in the xy-plane. What is the value of $f(2) + g(2)$?

(A) 0
(B) 1
(C) 2
(D) 3

GO ON TO THE NEXT PAGE

Questions 16 and 17 refer to the information below.

The term light-year refers to the distance light travels in one year.

16. If light travels 186,000 miles per second, which of the following is closest to the distance from Earth to Sirius, 8 light-years distant?

(A) 47 billion miles
(B) 198 billion miles
(C) 9 trillion miles
(D) 50 trillion miles

17. If light travels 186,000 miles per second, how far does light travel in one-billionth of a second (note: 1 mile = 5,280 feet)?

(A) 10 miles
(B) 1 mile
(C) 1 foot
(D) 0.01 feet

---

18. An airline company is calculating its passenger cost for a trans-Atlantic flight. The plane flies approximately 3,000 miles at an average air speed of 500 miles per hour. The cost is given by the following function.

$$C(x) = 100 + \frac{x}{10} + \frac{36{,}000}{x}$$

where x is the ground speed. Ground speed is defined as air speed ± wind speed.

What is the airline's cost if there is no wind during the flight?

(A) \$176
(B) \$222
(C) \$358
(D) \$422

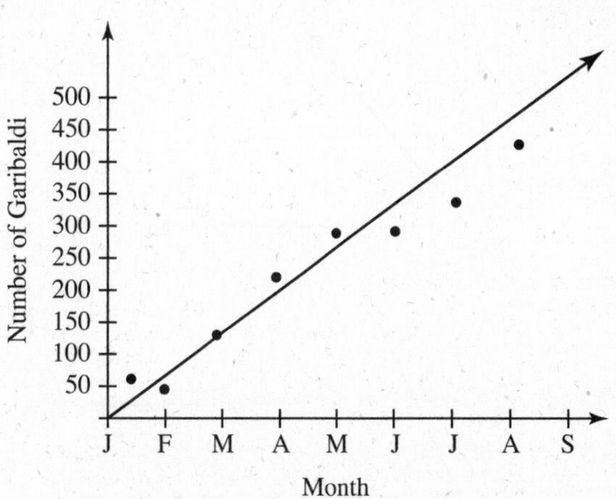

19. Garibaldi are bright orange fish that are closely related to goldfish. They are frequently found in the waters of the eastern Pacific Ocean. In different coastal California lagoons, researchers counted the number of Garibaldi found per cubic mile of ocean. The graph of that study is shown above along with a line of best fit.

In August, what was the difference between the number predicted by the line of best fit and the actual number of Garibaldi that were counted?

(A) 120
(B) 100
(C) 60
(D) 50

20. The sum of three numbers is 780. One of the numbers, n, is 50% more than the sum of the other two numbers. What is the value of n?

(A) 144
(B) 312
(C) 424
(D) 468

GO ON TO THE NEXT PAGE

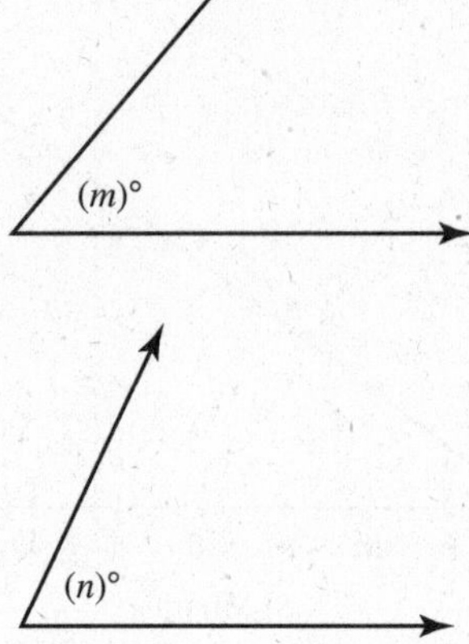

Note: Figures not drawn to scale

21. The angles shown above are complementary and $\sin(m°) = \cos(n°)$. If $m = (3x - 12)°$ and $n = (6x - 18)°$, what is the value of x?

    (A) $13.\overline{3}$
    (B) 20.6
    (C) 30.25
    (D) 40.3

22. Ms. Garcia has a jar containing m milliliters of a solution for her chemistry class. If she gives 8 milliliters to each student, she will have 6 milliliters left over. If she provides 10 milliliters to each student, she will need an additional 16 milliliters. How many students are in her class?

    (A) 10
    (B) 11
    (C) 17
    (D) 22

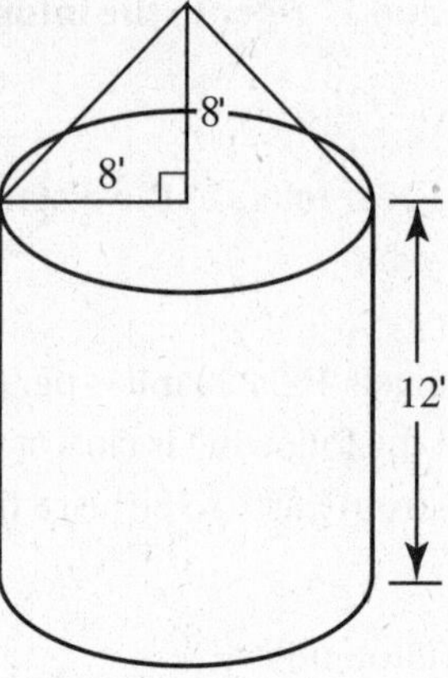

Height of Cylinder: 12′

Radius of Cylinder: 8′

Radius of Cone: 8′

Height of Cone: 8′

23. The diagram above represents a grain silo with a right cylindrical base and a top in the shape of a right cone. The owner believes he needs a new silo which will store 10% more grain than his existing silo. Which of the following represents the volume of the new silo (in cubic feet)?

    (A) 2,123
    (B) 2,678
    (C) 2,948
    (D) 3,243

24. In the xy-plane, the line determined by $(6, m)$ and $(m, 54)$ passes through the origin. Which of the following could be the value of m?

    (A) 2
    (B) 18
    (C) 36
    (D) 48

GO ON TO THE NEXT PAGE

25. The length of a rectangle was reduced by 10% and the width by x%. If the resulting dimensions reduced the area by 32.5%, what is the value of x?

(A) 25
(B) 21
(C) 18
(D) 13

26. A collectible vinyl record made in 1948 has appreciated in value about 12% every five years. If the record was worth \$7,000 in 1980, which of the following expressions represents its value in 2005?

(A) $7,000(.12)^5$
(B) $7,000(.12)^{25}$
(C) $7,000(1.12)^{25}$
(D) $7,000(1.12)^5$

27. Alice loves rope licorice. She is offered the three following deals:

Deal 1: She can buy licorice ropes at a rate of \$5.40 per yard.
Deal 2: She can buy licorice ropes for \$1.92 per foot.
Deal 3: She can buy licorice ropes for \$.14 per inch.

Alice wants to buy 1.5 yards of licorice rope at the lowest price. What deal should she select?

(Note: 1 yard = 3 feet; 1 foot = 12 inches)

(A) Deal 1
(B) Deal 2
(C) Deal 3
(D) Deals 1 and 3 provide equal prices for the licorice

$$2x^{\frac{2}{3}} = 6^{\frac{1}{2}}$$

28. In the equation above, what is the value of x?

(A) $\frac{27}{8}$
(B) $\left(\frac{27}{8}\right)^{\frac{1}{4}}$
(C) $\left(\frac{8}{27}\right)^{\frac{1}{4}}$
(D) $\frac{16}{27}$

29. Let $g(x) = \frac{\sqrt{x^2-4}}{x^2-3}$. For how many integers, x, is $g(x)$ not defined?

(A) none
(B) 1
(C) 2
(D) 3

30. The value p varies directly with q^{-1}. If $p = \frac{1}{6}$ when $q = \frac{5}{8}$, what is the value of p when $q = 18$?

(A) $\frac{864}{5}$
(B) $\frac{7}{24}$
(C) $\frac{5}{864}$
(D) $-\frac{8}{135}$

PRACTICE TEST 5

GO ON TO THE NEXT PAGE

Grid-in Response Directions

In questions 31–38, first solve the problem, and then enter your answer on the grid provided on the answer sheet. The instructions for entering your answers follow.

- First, write your answer in the boxes at the top of the grid.
- Second, grid your answer in the columns below the boxes.
- Use the fraction bar in the first row or the decimal point in the second row to enter fractions and decimals.

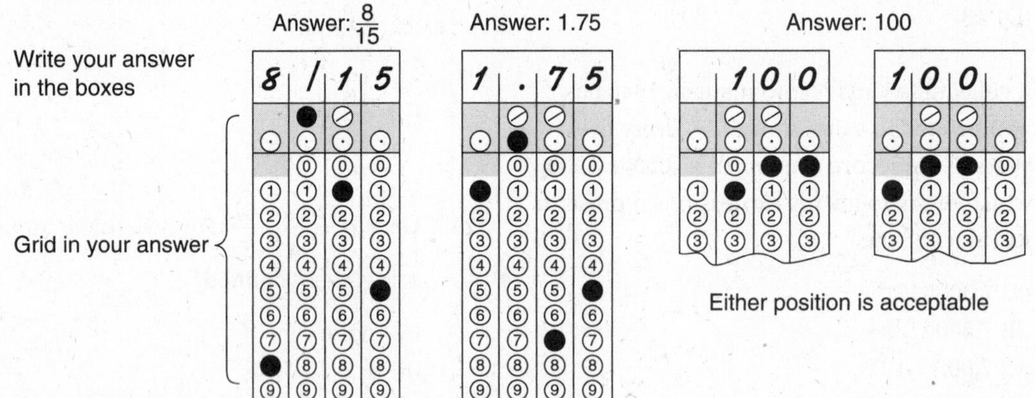

- Grid only one space in each column.
- Entering the answer in the boxes is recommended as an aid in gridding but is not required.
- The machine scoring your exam can read only what you grid, so you **must grid-in your answers correctly to get credit**.
- If a question has more than one correct answer, grid-in only one of them.
- The grid does not have a minus sign; so no answer can be negative.
- A mixed number *must* be converted to an improper fraction or a decimal before it is gridded. Enter $1\frac{1}{4}$ as $\frac{5}{4}$ or 1.25; the machine will interpret 11/4 as $\frac{11}{4}$ and mark it wrong.
- **All decimals must be entered as accurately as possible.** Here are three acceptable ways of gridding

$$\frac{3}{11} = 0.272727\ldots$$

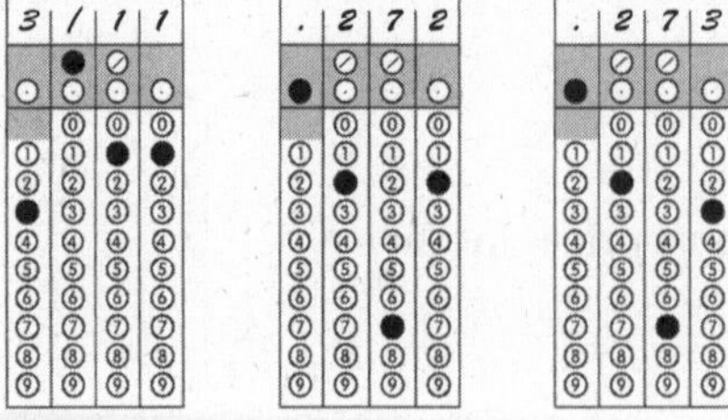

- Note that rounding to .273 is acceptable because you are using the full grid, but you would receive **no credit** for .3 or .27, because they are less accurate.

31. Belts cost \$11 and blouses cost \$18. If Kara spends at least \$51 but no more than \$62 for x belts and one blouse, what is *one* possible value of x?

$$(-8x^2 + 15x - 2) - 3(2x^2 + 4x - 2)$$

32. If the expression above is written in the form of $ax^2 + bx + c$, where a, b, and c are constants, what is the value of b?

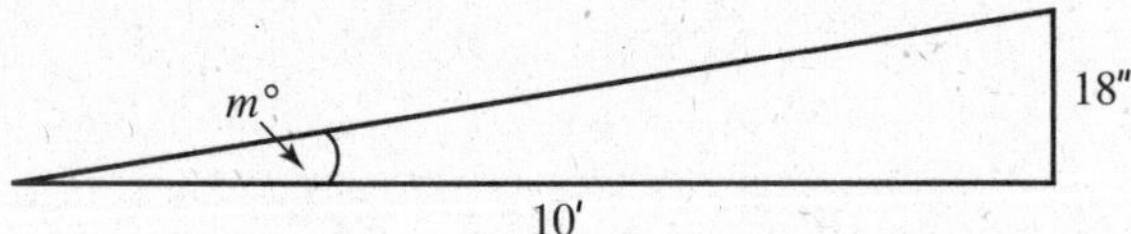

33. OSHA has determined that an entrance ramp to a store used by those with disabilities cannot exceed a certain grade. The diagram shows an example of a ramp that is at the highest degree of elevation and is still code-compliant. What is the highest degree of elevation for an OSHA code entrance ramp to a store (round your answer to the nearest hundredth of a degree)?

34. A new movie recently scored an average rating of 4.3 stars out of 5 from its first 12 reviewers. If the next two reviewers each give the movie a 5-star review, what will the new average rating be?

$$A = 25m + 275$$

35. Terrence has made an initial deposit into his bank account. Each month after his initial deposit he has deposited a fixed amount into the account. The equation above represents the amount, A, he has in dollars after he has made m monthly deposits. According to this equation, what was the initial deposit Terrence made into his account?

36. The points (2, 7) and (−3, 37) lie on the graph of $y = ax^2 - 4x + 7$. What is the value of a?

GO ON TO THE NEXT PAGE

Questions 37 and 38 refer to the following information.

The theory of special relativity suggests that an observer moving at great speed experiences the flow of time much more slowly than an observer on Earth. The following formula is used to calculate what is known as time dilation.

$$F(t) = \frac{t}{\sqrt{1-v^2}}$$

In the formula, t represents some unit of time and v represents velocity as some fraction of light-speed. For example, an observer counts one second in a rocket ship traveling at 60% of the speed of light while an observer on Earth measures 1.25 seconds.

37. If an observer traveling at 80% the speed of light counts off one second, how many seconds will be counted by an observer on Earth?

38. An observer on Earth measures 2 seconds, while an observer traveling at a fraction of light-speed measures 1 second. What fraction of light-speed was the moving observer traveling?

If there is still time remaining, you may review your answers.

ESSAY (OPTIONAL)

Directions: This is your opportunity to show that you can read and understand a passage and write an analysis of that passage. Be sure your essay demonstrates a clear and logical analysis of the passage, using precise language.

On the actual test, you will write your essay on the lines provided in your answer booklet; for now, write your essay on lined paper. Remember to write or print legibly so that others can read what you've written.

You have 50 minutes to read the essay and write a response to the prompt provided.

Carefully read the passage below. As you read, think about how John Holt makes use of

- *reasoning* to develop an argument
- *evidence* to support assertions made
- *language* to persuade the reader

From John Holt, *The Underachieving School*, Pitman Books Ltd., 1968

1 True learning—learning that is permanent and useful, that leads to intelligent action and further learning—can arise only out of the experience, interests, and concerns of the learner.

2 Every child, without exception, has an innate and unquenchable drive to understand the world in which he lives and to gain freedom and competence in it. Whatever truly adds to his understanding, his capacity for growth and pleasure, his powers, his sense of his own freedom, dignity and worth may be said to be true education. Education is something a person gets for himself, not that which someone else gives or does to him.

3 What young people need and want to get from their education is: one, a greater understanding of the world around them; two, a greater development of themselves; three, a chance to find their work, that is, a way in which they may use their own unique tastes and talents to grapple with the real problems of the world around them and to serve the cause of humanity.

4 Our society asks schools to do three things for and to children: one, pass on the traditions and higher values of our own culture; two, acquaint the child with the world in which he lives; three, prepare the child for employment and, if possible, success. All of these tasks have traditionally been done by the society, the community itself, none of them is done well by schools. None of them can or ought to be done by the schools solely or exclusively. One reason the schools are in trouble is that they have been given too many functions that are not properly or exclusively theirs.

5 Schools should be a resource, but not the only resource, from which children, but not only children, can take what they need and want to carry on the business of their own education. Schools should be places where people go to find out the things they want to find out and develop the skills they want to develop. The child who is educating himself, and if he doesn't no one else will, should be free, like the adult, to decide when and how much and in what way he wants to make use of whatever resources the schools can offer him. There are an infinite number of roads to education; each learner should and must be free to choose, to find, to make his own.

6 Children want and need and deserve and should be given, as soon as they want it, a chance to be useful in society. It is an offence to humanity to deny a child, or anyone of age, who wants to do useful work the opportunity to do it. The distinction, indeed opposition, we have made between education and work is arbitrary, unreal, and unhealthy.

7 Unless we have faith in the child's eagerness and ability to grow and learn, we cannot help and can only harm his education.

> Write an essay explaining how John Holt constructs an argument to convince the reader that true learning can only occur when education centers on the needs and interests of the learner. Describe and analyze how Holt uses one or more of the elements of persuasive writing listed in the box on page 417 to strengthen his argument. You may also discuss other writing techniques used by the author.
>
> Your essay should not state your opinion on the topic discussed in the passage, but rather analyze how Holt constructs an argument to persuade the reader.

ANSWER KEY
Practice Test 5

Section 1: Reading

1.	**A**	14.	**C**	27.	**D**	40.	**B**
2.	**D**	15.	**C**	28.	**C**	41.	**C**
3.	**C**	16.	**C**	29.	**A**	42.	**C**
4.	**C**	17.	**C**	30.	**B**	43.	**C**
5.	**D**	18.	**C**	31.	**D**	44.	**C**
6.	**C**	19.	**B**	32.	**D**	45.	**A**
7.	**A**	20.	**D**	33.	**B**	46.	**C**
8.	**B**	21.	**A**	34.	**B**	47.	**B**
9.	**D**	22.	**B**	35.	**B**	48.	**C**
10.	**B**	23.	**D**	36.	**C**	49.	**C**
11.	**A**	24.	**A**	37.	**C**	50.	**B**
12.	**B**	25.	**D**	38.	**D**	51.	**D**
13.	**A**	26.	**A**	39.	**D**	52.	**D**

Number Correct _______

Number Incorrect _______

Section 2: Writing and Language

1.	**B**	12.	**D**	23.	**C**	34.	**B**
2.	**C**	13.	**B**	24.	**B**	35.	**D**
3.	**D**	14.	**D**	25.	**D**	36.	**D**
4.	**A**	15.	**D**	26.	**C**	37.	**B**
5.	**B**	16.	**A**	27.	**B**	38.	**C**
6.	**C**	17.	**B**	28.	**A**	39.	**C**
7.	**D**	18.	**C**	29.	**D**	40.	**D**
8.	**B**	19.	**C**	30.	**B**	41.	**C**
9.	**D**	20.	**B**	31.	**C**	42.	**B**
10.	**D**	21.	**A**	32.	**C**	43.	**A**
11.	**D**	22.	**B**	33.	**D**	44.	**B**

Number Correct _______

Number Incorrect _______

ANSWER KEY
Practice Test 5

Section 3: Math (No Calculator)

1. **A**
2. **B**
3. **C**
4. **D**
5. **A**
6. **D**
7. **C**
8. **A**
9. **B**
10. **A**
11. **D**
12. **B**
13. **A**
14. **B**
15. **D**

16. **1/4** or **1/2**

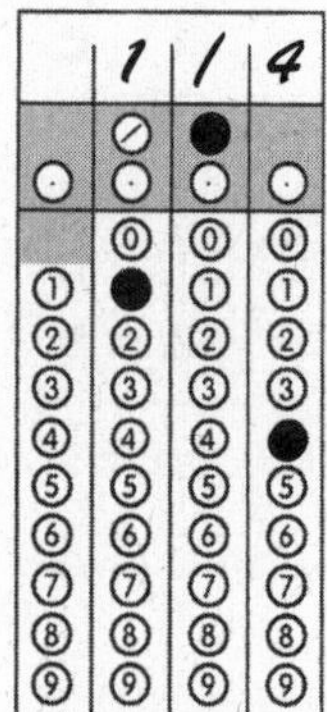

or

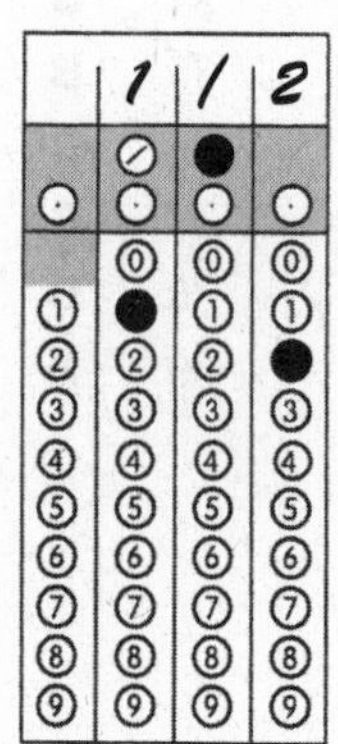

17. **5**

18. **Answers may vary.**
$0 \le x < 8$

19. **5**

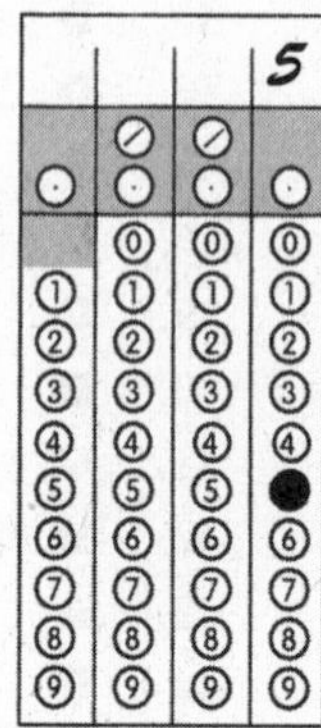

20. **4**

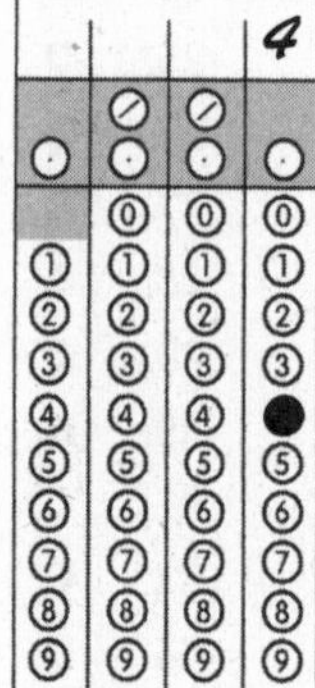

Number Correct ______

Number Incorrect ______

ANSWER KEY
Practice Test 5

Section 4: Math (Calculator)

1. **B**
2. **B**
3. **B**
4. **C**
5. **D**
6. **C**
7. **D**
8. **A**
9. **D**
10. **A**
11. **D**
12. **D**
13. **A**
14. **C**
15. **A**
16. **D**
17. **C**
18. **B**
19. **D**
20. **D**
21. **A**
22. **B**
23. **D**
24. **B**
25. **A**
26. **D**
27. **C**
28. **B**
29. **D**
30. **C**

31. **3** or **4**

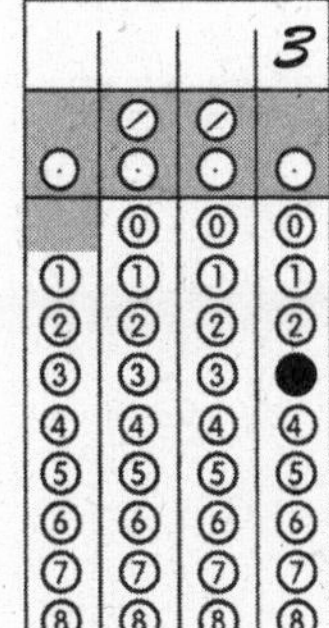

or

32. **3**

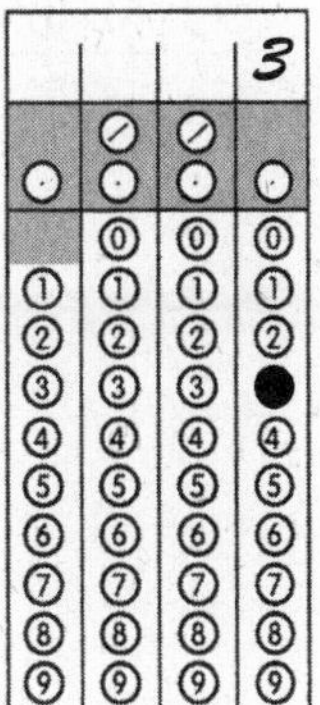

33. **8.53**

34. **4.4**

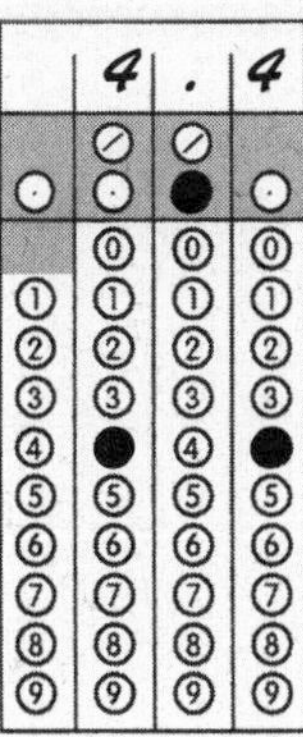

35. **275**

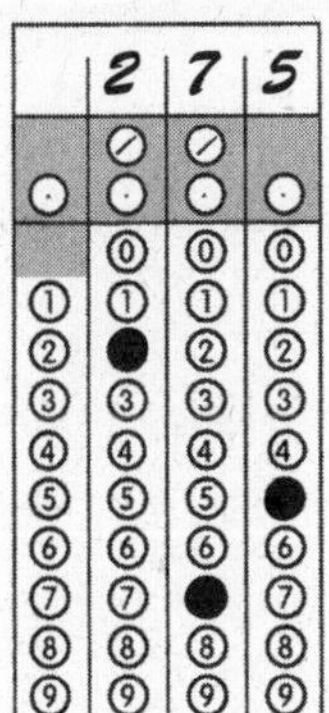

36. **2**

ANSWER KEY
Practice Test 5

37. **1.66** or **1.67** or **5/3**

1 . 6 6 or 1 . 6 7 or 5 / 3

38. **.866**

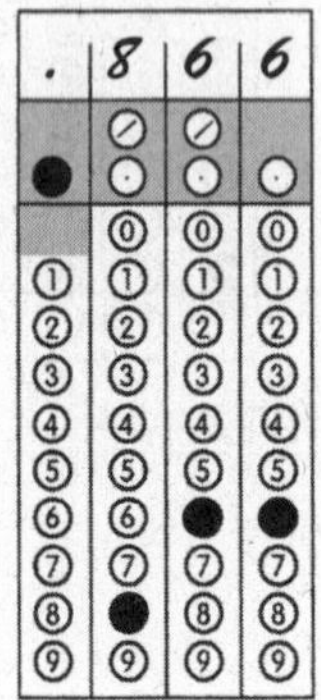

Number Correct ______

Number Incorrect ______

SCORE ANALYSIS

Reading and Writing Test

Section 1: Reading ________ = ________ (A)
correct raw score

Section 2: Writing ________ = ________ (B)
correct raw score

To find your Reading and Writing test scores, consult the chart below: find the ranges in which your raw scores lie and read across to find the ranges of your test scores.

________ + ________ = ________ (C)
range of reading test scores | range of writing test scores | range of reading + writing test scores

To find the range of your Reading and Writing Scaled Score, multiply (C) by 10.

Test Scores for the Reading and Writing Sections

Reading Raw Score	Writing Raw Score	Test Score
44-52	39-44	35-40
36-43	33-38	31-34
30-35	28-32	28-30
24-29	22-27	24-27
19-23	17-21	21-23
14-18	13-16	19-20
9-13	9-12	16-18
5-8	5-8	13-15
less than 5	less than 5	10-12

Math Test

Section 3: ________ = ________ (D)
correct raw score

Section 4: ________ = ________ (E)
correct raw score

Total Math raw score: (D) + (E) = ________

To find your Math Scaled Score, consult the chart below: find the range in which your raw score lies and read across to find the range for your scaled score.

Scaled Scores for the Math Test

Raw Score	Scaled Score	Raw Score	Scaled Score
50-58	700-800	20-25	450-490
44-49	650-690	15-19	400-440
38-43	600-640	11-14	350-390
32-37	550-590	7-10	300-340
26-31	500-540	less than 7	200-290

PRACTICE TEST 5

ANSWER EXPLANATIONS

Section 1: Reading Test

1. **(A)** The author says, "Whatever their [Franklin's and the other men's who stood with Washington] philosophical professions may have been, they were not controlled by prudence" (lines 5–7). The word "professions" in this context means *avowals of belief.* The phrase "professedly prudent" means that Franklin professed—that is *avowed*—to be *prudent* (cautious and sensible).

2. **(D)** As stated in the previous explanation, *professions* in this context means *avowals of belief.*

3. **(C)** The author says, "They were . . . willing to take all risks . . . in a struggle whose course was just though its issue was dubious" (lines 8–11). It makes sense that the word "issue" means *outcome* here because a struggle results in an outcome.

4. **(C)** It can be inferred that the author quotes these words to show that Robert Morris had great integrity and patriotism because Morris said he will do anything asked of him by his country unless it would mean a loss of his integrity.

5. **(D)** In context, the word "celebrated" means *known and praised widely.*

6. **(C)** The author says, "I see Benjamin Franklin . . . accepting without demur the difficult and dangerous mission to France" (lines 44–49).

7. **(A)** The author says that Benjamin Franklin "claimed to be a follower of the theory of enlightened self-interest" (lines 65–66).

8. **(B)** This is the best title because the passage concentrates on the important role Benjamin Franklin had in American history and the sacrifices he made for America.

9. **(D)** The quotation referred to is in the last sentence of a paragraph (lines 72–85; "He . . . Franklin") describing the great sacrifices that Benjamin Franklin made for his country.

10. **(B)** The author makes use of all of the choices except *understatement* (intentional lack of emphasis in expression).

11. **(A)** The author says, "While Derek Freeman later critiqued Mead's culturally deterministic approach" (lines 26–28), so we can infer that by "critique" the author means "criticized."

12. **(B)** The author says, "All of these factors were thought to make Samoan adolescence relatively tranquil and enjoyable and led to Mead's assertion of the primacy of nurture over nature" (lines 23–26). "Nurture" refers to cultural influences and "nature" refers to the influence of a person's genetic make-up.

13. **(A)** The author says, "Schlegel and Barry's cross-cultural study of adolescents . . . demonstrated that adolescence . . . is ubiquitous" (lines 36–41). In context, "ubiquitous" means *existing everywhere.*

14. **(C)** In context, the word "inevitabilities" (line 49) means *unavoidable occurrences.*

15. **(C)** In context, the word "gendered" (line 55) means *characteristic of one gender.* The phrase "with aggression in girls being particularly low" (lines 55–56) provides a clue to the meaning.

16. **(C)** According to the author, based on a study "Trommsdorff suggested that 'turbulent' features such as intergenerational conflict stem from the focus on attaining independence from parents during this period and are linked to cultural values of individualism in Western societies" (lines 70–75). From this it can be inferred that Trommsdorff would probably agree that adolescents in individualistic cultures would be more likely to argue with their parents than adolescents in collective cultures.

17. **(C)** These lines provide the best evidence because they state what Trommsdorff suggested about adolescence in collectivist and individualistic cultures.

18. **(C)** The author says, "If we assume that a transitional period of the life cycle, akin to adolescence, organized around puberty and of variable length, exists almost universally . . ." (lines 1–6). The author also says, "Adolescence conceptualized as a prolonged period of identity development linked to increased autonomy, intergenerational conflict, peer-relatedness and social psychological anxieties, is not the norm across cultures" (lines 92–97).

19. **(B)** The author objectively evaluates what social science has discovered about adolescence and reaches a conclusion about an important issue concerning it.

20. **(D)** Humor is not used in the passage.

21. **(A)** The author says modern journalists can produce articles "without using . . . expert information" (line 31). It can be inferred that he would say that modern journalists often produce articles that are not authoritative because such articles require expert information that journalists normally do not have.

22. **(B)** "Rhetoric" in context means *language that is elaborate but has little meaning.* The author says the sophists used rhetoric to hide the gaps in their logic. The adjective "glossy" means *slick* or *smooth,* suggesting that the sophist used rhetoric to, metaphorically, paint over the gaps in their reasoning with slick language.

23. **(D)** The author says the sophists "argued unsystematically and unfairly" (line 34).

24. **(A)** The author believes that Socrates "opposed the sophists wherever possible" because he believes that Socrates, unlike the sophists, was seeking the truth. This can be inferred from what the author says about the sophists and about Socrates. First, the sophists: "The sophists dazzled everyone without convincing anyone of anything positive. They argued unsystematically and unfairly . . . . They had few constructive ideas . . . . They demonstrated that almost anything could be proved by a fast talker" (lines 32–41). Second, Socrates: "He distrusted . . . the sophists (lines 47–48); "He only asked questions" (line 50); "Socrates said he knew nothing and was trying to find out" (lines 62–63). It is thus reasonable that the author believes that Socrates opposed the sophists because he believed that they not only were not seeking the truth, but they were also detrimental to the search for the truth.

25. **(D)** The other choices are mentioned in lines 66–83. It is unlikely that the sophists had new philosophical answers that helped them become successful because the author says that the sophists "dazzled without convincing anyone of anything positive" (lines 32–33) and "had few constructive ideas" (lines 36–37), and generally were not concerned with finding the truth.

26. **(A)** This is the best choice because the passage is mainly concerned with the sophists and Socrates.

27. **(D)** According to the author, "Socrates said he knew nothing and was trying to find out" (lines 62–63) He spent his life questioning all sorts of people "and to convinc[ing] them that they knew no more than he did" (lines 105–107). Thus, it is very unlikely that Socrates would believe that most truths have been discovered.

28. **(C)** In context, the word "naive" means *uninformed.* This can be inferred because the author says that Socrates convinced people they "knew no more than he did" (lines 106–107) by first telling them that he knew nothing. This made the person eager to explain to Socrates because they believed he was "intelligent" (line 111) but uninformed.

29. **(A)** The author describes Socrates' "unfailing good humor—which allowed him to . . . keep the conversation going and at crises when the other lost his temper, to dominate it" (lines 114–117).

30. **(B)** The author says that "Socrates questioned all sorts" (line 93) of people and that he adapted to them (lines 99–102; "It . . . did"). He also says that Socrates' "adaptability . . . showed him the side on which each man could be best approached" (lines 112–113). We can infer from this information about Socrates that he had an excellent understanding of human nature because it would have been difficult for him to adapt to so many people without it.

31. **(D)** This provides the best evidence for the answer to the previous question for reasons explained in the explanation to question 30.

32. **(D)** The primary concern of the passage is disease in animals (fauna) in urban areas.

33. **(B)** The author is describing the processes by which diseases are spread among animals as a result of their movement. This system is a dynamic one, with continual changes in the interactions among animals.

34. **(B)** The author is advancing a theory that measures taken to control urban waterfowl duck plague epizootics resulted in very few ("rare"—line 37) cases of duck plague in migratory ducks. In lines 42–45 ("However . . . society"), he discusses "culling" of urban waterfowl.

35. **(B)** As discussed in the explanation of the answer to the previous question, the author is suggesting that culling of infected waterfowl in urban waterfowl populations resulted in fewer occasions for the spread of disease to migratory waterfowl.

36. **(C)** In lines 48–49 the author says that some people living in urban areas regard resident waterfowl as companions ("companion animal status [is] conferred"). We can infer from this that many of these people would actively oppose the culling of resident waterfowl because of their emotional attachment to these animals, making wildlife management and disease control difficult.

37. **(C)** These lines provide the best evidence for the answer to the previous question because they describe a difficulty sometimes encountered in managing wildlife in urban areas.

38. **(D)** The author is discussing disease "dynamics" (line 6) in urban fauna. These dynamics involve the movement of animals, resulting in interaction between different populations of animals.

39. **(D)** The author describes these processes in lines 54–71.

40. **(B)** We can infer that the author would agree with this statement because throughout the passage he describes some of the complex interactions in urban areas among various animal populations and between animal populations and humans that sometimes result in the spread of disease. In lines 105–115 ("Urban . . . cherished"), he stresses the importance of managing wildlife in urban areas. We can therefore infer that he would agree that increased urbanization requires effective cooperation between wildlife managers and public health officials.

41. **(C)** West Nile fever spread to more states in 2002 than in the other years.

42. **(C)** The author does not quote "recognized experts."

43. **(C)** The author says he has liked the novels that have been read to him "if they do not end unhappily" (line 16). He is most likely being *jocular* (humorous) because it is very unlikely that he would believe that a law should be passed against novels ending unhappily.

44. **(C)** The author says that he still enjoys "books on history, biographies, and travels . . . and essays on all sorts of subjects" (lines 19–23). It is thus likely that the author would enjoy reading an essay on English history. He says he no longer enjoys choices (A) and (B), and it is unlikely that he would enjoy choice (D) *studying advanced mathematics* because he says, "My power to follow a long and purely abstract train of thought is very limited; and therefore I could never have succeeded with . . . mathematics" (lines 44–47).

45. **(A)** The author's main point in the sentence is that his loss of "the higher aesthetic tastes" is strange in view of the fact that he is still able to appreciate essays on history and so forth. The words in parentheses are thus presumably intended mainly to make it clear that he is interested in such essays for their intrinsic merit and not only for the scientific facts they may contain.

46. **(C)** The author says, "I have no great quickness of apprehension or wit . . . I am therefore a poor critic: a paper or book, when first read, generally excites my admiration, and it is only after considerable reflection that I perceive the weak points" (lines 38–43).

47. **(B)** These lines provide the best evidence for the answer to the previous question.

48. **(C)** Induction is *the process of deriving general principles from particular facts.* The author says that "My mind seems to have become a kind of machine for grinding general laws out of large collections of facts" (lines 24–26). He also says, "I have had the strongest desire to understand or explain whatever I observed,—that is, to group all facts under some general laws" (lines 71–74). Finally, he says, "This has naturally led to distrust greatly deductive reasoning in the mixed sciences" (lines 88–90).

49. **(C)** The author is describing his intellectual abilities, so the meaning he intends by the word "apprehension" must be *understanding.*

50. **(B)** The author says, "I am not very skeptical,—a frame of mind which I believe to be injurious to the progress of science. A good deal of skepticism in a scientific man is

advisable to avoid much loss of time, but [some men] have often thus been deterred from experiment or observations, which would have proved directly or indirectly serviceable" (lines 91–99).

51. **(D)** These lines provide the best evidence for the answer to the previous question.

52. **(D)** The writer is describing his intellectual abilities. He has already discussed his "power of reasoning" (line 62), so it is unlikely that "invention" refers to choice (C) logical ability. Therefore, the meaning of the word "invention" as it is used in line 63 is *creativity*.

Section 2: Writing and Language Test

1. **(B)** All of the choices are grammatically correct because they all correct the error, which is that the clause beginning with "Because" and ending with "BLS" is not an independent clause and thus is not a complete sentence. However, choice (B) is the best choice because it is the most clear and concise.

2. **(C)** This is the only choice that makes good sense in context.

3. **(D)** This is the best choice because the context requires a conjunction linking the two parts of the sentences. The second part of the sentence provides more of the same type of information as given in the first part of the sentence, so the word *while* used as a conjunction meaning *and* is correct.

4. **(A)** This is the correct choice because in this context *ambulatory* means "of medical care or services provided on an outpatient basis." "Outpatient care" and "laboratory [care]" are examples of such medical care.

5. **(B)** This is the correct choice. Some form of the past tense is required because growth in the healthcare industry in the past is being discussed. This is confirmed by the data shown in the chart. Choice (D) is a past tense verb but is not a good choice because it makes little sense. Choice (B) is grammatical and makes good sense because the verb is cast in the past progressive tense, which is used to show that some action (in this case, growth in employment) was in process during a period of time in the past.

6. **(C)** It can be seen from the graph that healthcare employment continued to increase steadily between 2007 and 2009.

7. **(D)** All of the choices are grammatically correct and make sense in context. However, this is the best choice because it is clear and concise. In the phrase *job stability* the word *job* functions as an adjective modifying the noun *stability*.

8. **(B)** Choice (A) is grammatical (if *hospitals* was changed to *hospitals'*) but makes little sense. Choice (C) is grammatical but awkward. Choice (D) is incorrect because it creates a run-on sentence. Choice (B) is the best choice because it creates a clear and grammatical sentence: the focus of the sentence is cost-cutting efforts; the nonrestrictive adjective clause beginning with *which* modifies the noun *hospitals*, telling us something about them in relation to cost-cutting.

9. **(D)** This is the best choice because sentence 1 does not make sense as the first sentence of this paragraph because it provides additional information about the topic that sentence 4 is about. Moving sentence 1 so that it comes after sentence 4 makes sentence

2 the first sentence of the paragraph, which makes sense because it is an appropriate topic sentence.

10. **(D)** This is the only choice that is grammatical and makes good sense. Note that the phrase "home healthcare services" is singular because in the context of the passage it is a category within the healthcare industry.

11. **(D)** This is the correct choice because it is standard usage in this context.

12. **(D)** The second sentence in choice (A) is a run-on sentence, so this is incorrect. Choice (B) does not make sense because an army officer cannot die shortly after birth. Choice (C) contains a grammatical error; "His father, he . . . ." Choice (D) is grammatical and clear.

13. **(B)** The correct choice is *remnant,* which in context means "a small surviving group of people." Choice (A) makes sense but *residue* is not used to refer to people.

14. **(D)** This is the correct choice because sentence 4 describes how Ohiyesa "lived the original nomadic life of his people." Sentence 1 follows logically from this because it explains "the knowledge thus gained" from this experience.

15. **(D)** This choice makes good sense because Ohiyesa "was astonished by the reappearance of his father."

16. **(A)** This choice is correct because the present perfect tense is used here correctly to indicate that Ohiyesa's father came home at an earlier point in time than the point in time at which he learned about it.

17. **(B)** In this context, *where* is a conjunction meaning "at which place." It refers to "Flandreau, Dakota Territory."

18. **(C)** This is the correct choice in context because the past progressive tense indicates that the group of Indians were earning their living over a period of time in the past.

19. **(C)** This is the correct choice in context. *At first reluctant* is a standard phrase meaning "Although [he] was reluctant at first." It makes good sense because the sentence goes on to say "he soon became interested."

20. **(B)** Choices (A) and (C) do not make sense. Choice (D) makes sense but is unclear because it suggests a relationship between the father's action and the boy's action that is not specified. Choice (B) is the best choice because it is clear and grammatical.

21. **(A)** This is the idiomatically correct choice.

22. **(B)** This is the correct choice because it is standard usage in this context.

23. **(C)** This statement clearly summarizes the main subject of the passage, which is that Spanish explorers and conquistadors paid little attention to Cuba.

24. **(B)** This is the only grammatically correct choice. It creates a compound sentence, whereas the other choices do not make a grammatical sentence.

25. **(D)** This is the only choice that is grammatical and makes good sense in context.

26. **(C)** *In consequence* makes the best sense because the sentence that this phrase introduces describes a report brought back to Hispaniola or Spain as a *consequence* of what is described in the previous sentence.

27. **(B)** The linking verb "is" is necessary to create a grammatical sentence. None of the other choices is grammatically correct.

28. **(A)** *Ascertained*, which in context means "determined with certainty," is the correct choice. *Ascertained* in context is a participial adjective modifying the noun "facts."

29. **(D)** The simple past tense is the correct tense in context. The writer is referring to events in the past.

30. **(B)** This is the best placement for sentence 4 because sentence 5 describes "somewhat more significant" evidence in support of the belief that people knew that Cuba was an island. Sentence 4 follows logically from this because it suggests that this evidence may be based on a rumor.

31. **(C)** This is the only choice that is grammatical and makes sense in context. In this context *succeeded* means "came after and took the place of." The past perfect "had been succeeded" is correct because the writer is talking about a time period before the one he was talking about in the previous paragraph. Note that the verb must be in the passive voice (indicated by *been*, the past participle of *be*) because Francisco de Bobadilla performed the action, as indicated by the preposition "by."

32. **(C)** Choice (B) is grammatically correct, but it creates a clumsy sentence. Choice (C) creates a clear and grammatical sentence.

33. **(D)** This is the correct choice. The past perfect tense is the appropriate tense here because the sentence is recounting what Sebastian de Ocampo *said* (simple past tense; earlier event) he *had found* (past perfect tense; later event).

34. **(B)** Choice (A) creates an ungrammatical sentence. This corrects the error by placing the participial phrase "positioned on the equator" in the beginning of the sentence. In addition to being grammatical, this choice puts emphasis on what is in context important—Indonesia's position.

35. **(D)** Choice (B) is incorrect because the past tense is not suitable in this context because a statement of fact is being made, which requires the present tense. Choices (A) and (C) are grammatical but not idiomatic.

36. **(D)** This is the best choice because sentence 2 follows naturally from sentence 4, describing the effects of the typhoons mentioned in sentence 4. Also, sentence 2 makes little sense placed after sentence 1; whereas sentence 3 makes good sense after sentence 1.

37. **(B)** Choice (A) is not correct because it creates an ungrammatical sentence in which the second part of the sentence is a dependent clause rather than an independent clause. Choice (B) corrects this error and creates a grammatically correct sentence. Choice (C) is incorrect because a dependent clause cannot come after a semicolon. Choice (D) is incorrect because a run-on sentence is created.

38. **(C)** *Mitigate* (moderate in force) is the best choice in context. It is unlikely that the sea walls will solve the problem; rather it is likely that the sea walls will make the effects of the typhoons less damaging.

39. **(C)** Choice (A) makes little sense. Choice (C) is the best choice in context. Although choice (B) and choice (D) each create a grammatical sentence that makes sense, choice

(C) is best because the sentence now beginning "Before . . ." expresses a new idea rather than one closely related to the previous sentence.

40. **(D)** This is the only choice that makes good sense in context and is grammatical. In this context *anticipate* means "act in advance so as to mitigate."

41. **(C)** This is the only choice that creates a grammatical sentence. "Sea storms and strong winds" becomes the object of the verbs "adapt" and "entertain," creating a grammatical sentence.

42. **(B)** Choices (A), (C), and (D) are not grammatical. Choice (B) corrects the error by creating a participial phrase beginning with "cutting."

43. **(A)** Choices (B), (C), and (D) are not grammatical. Choice (A) creates a sentence that is grammatical and makes good sense.

44. **(B)** This is the focus of the paragraph. The other choices are mentioned in relation to this main topic.

Section 3: Math Test (No Calculator)

1. **(A)** Solve for n in $7n = 42$ and replace that value in $4n - 11$.

$$7n = 42$$
$$n = 6$$
$$4(6) - 11 = 13$$

2. **(B)** When raising an exponent to another, multiply the exponents.

$$(m^{\frac{1}{3}})^2 = m^{\frac{2}{3}}$$

Rational exponents can be expressed as radicals: the numerator is the exponent and the denominator is the root.

$$m^{\frac{2}{3}} = \sqrt[3]{m^2}$$

The root, 3, exceeds the exponent, 2, so $\sqrt[3]{m^2}$ is simplified to its lowest term.

3. **(C)** Use simple values for m, d, and h to find the correct conclusion.
Let $m = 12$
$hd = m$

h	d
1	12
2	6
3	4
4	3
6	2
12	1

As h increases, d decreases.

4. **(D)** Imagine a square that has an area of 4 square units. Since the area of a square is found by using the formula $A = s^2$ (where s is the length of a side), then each side of the square is 2 because $\sqrt{4} = 2$. If the area of the larger square is double the smaller, then its area must be 8. Find the square root of 8 to find the length of a side.

$$\sqrt{8} = 2\sqrt{2}$$

When the area of a square is doubled, each side length increases by a factor of $\sqrt{2}$.

5. **(A)** Cross-multiply and solve for n.

$$\frac{6}{n} = \frac{18}{n+24}$$
$$6(n+24) = (18)(n)$$
$$6n + 144 = 18n$$
$$144 = 12n$$
$$12 = n$$

Find the value of $\frac{n}{12}$ by substituting 12 for n.

$$\frac{12}{12} = 1$$

6. **(D)** Although the system of equations can be solved by using elimination or substitution, it is easier to subtract the equations.

$$\begin{array}{r} 3x + 6y = 14 \\ -(2x + 5y = -11) \\ \hline x + y = 25 \end{array}$$

7. **(C)** A polynomial has a zero x if $f(x) = 0$. The chart indicates (5, 0) satisfies the function, so $f(5) = 0$ and $x = 5$. Subtracting 5 from both sides of the equation we get $x - 5 = 0$. Therefore, $x - 5$ is a factor of $f(x)$.

8. **(A)** Angle 2 and $\angle 3$ are consecutive interior angles, so their sum is 180°. Solve for m by setting their sum equal to 180.

$$(2m + 18) + (4m + 42) = 180$$
$$6m + 60 = 180$$
$$6m = 120$$
$$m = 20$$

Substitute 20 for m and find the measure of $\angle 2$.

$$(4)(20) + 42 = 122$$

Angle 2 and $\angle 6$ are corresponding angles so their measures are equal. Angle 6 and $\angle 18$ are corresponding angles so their measures are also the same. Using the transitive property, we find that the measure of $\angle 2$ equals the measure of $\angle 6$, which equals the measure of $\angle 18$, which all equal 122°.

There are several alternate ways to solve this problem but the easiest way is visually. The diagram is drawn to scale and $\angle 18$ appears to be obtuse. Solely choice (A), 122°, appears to have a measure greater than 90°.

9. **(B)** A system of equations has no solution when the equations are parallel lines. Parallel lines have the same slope but different y-intercepts. Convert $5x + 3y = -10$ to slope-intercept form to inspect the slope and y-intercept.

$$5x + 3y = -10$$
$$3y = -5x - 10$$
$$y = -\frac{5}{3}x - \frac{10}{3}$$

Substitute -7.5 for b and convert to slope-intercept form.

$$-7.5x - 4.5y = 13.5$$
$$-4.5y = 7.5x + 13.5$$
$$y = -\frac{5}{3}x - 3$$

The equations $y = -\frac{5}{3}x - \frac{10}{3}$ and $y = -\frac{5}{3}x - 3$ are parallel lines because their slopes are the same but the y-intercepts are different. When $b = -7.5$, the system of equations has no solution.

10. **(A)** The sum of the measures of the exterior angles of a polygon is 360°. Add the exterior angles of $\triangle ABC$ and set them equal to 360 to find x.

$$(4x + 40) + (4x + 20) + 2x = 360$$
$$10x + 60 = 360$$
$$10x = 300$$
$$x = 30$$

$\angle DBC$ and $\angle ABC$ are supplementary angles; their sum is 180°.

$$\angle DBC = 4x + 40 = 4(30) + 40 = 160$$

Therefore, $m\angle ABC + 160 = 180$ and $m\angle ABC = 20$

11. **(D)** Use FOIL to expand the quantities in the parentheses.

$$y = m(x + 3)\,(x - 5) = m(x^2 - 2x - 15)$$

Multiply each term in the parentheses by m.

$$m(x^2 - 2x - 15) = mx^2 - 2xm - 15m$$

Find the value of e by using the formula $e = -\frac{b}{2a}$ (this is also the formula for finding the axis of symmetry of a parabola).

$$e = -\frac{b}{2a} = -\frac{(-2m)}{2m} = 1$$

Find f by replacing x with 1 in $mx^2 - 2xm - 15m$.

$$m(1)^2 - 2(1)m - 15m = -16m$$

The value of f in the vertex is $-16m$.

12. **(B)** Factor the numerator of the complex fraction.

$$\frac{\frac{w^2+2w+1}{w+1}}{3} = \frac{\frac{(w+1)(w+1)}{w+1}}{3}$$

When dividing a complex fraction, invert the denominator and multiply that quantity with the numerator.

$$\frac{(w+1)(w+1)}{\frac{w+1}{3}}=(w+1)(w+1)\left(\frac{3}{w+1}\right)$$

Cross-divide as needed.

$$(w+1)(w+1)\left(\frac{3}{w+1}\right)=3(w+1)$$

13. **(A)** Transform $25^{\frac{3}{4}}$ to $(5^2)^{\frac{3}{4}}$, which equals $5^{\frac{6}{4}}=5^{\frac{3}{2}}$.
When a number is raised to a rational power, the numerator serves as the power of the number and the denominator is its root. Therefore, raise 5 to the third power and find the square root of that quantity.

$$\sqrt{5^3}=\sqrt{125}=5\sqrt{5}$$

Choices (B) and (C) are incorrect because $25^{\frac{3}{4}}$ transforms to a square root, not a cube root. Choice (D) is incorrect because it multiplies 25 by $\frac{3}{2}$ rather than raising it to the $\frac{3}{4}$ power.

14. **(B)** Verify the accuracy of the statements.
I. An increase in temperature Celsius is equivalent to an increase of 1.8 degrees Fahrenheit.
Use $C=1$ and $C=2$

$$\frac{9}{5}(1)+32=33.8$$
$$\frac{9}{5}(2)+32=35.6$$
$$35.6-33.8=1.8$$

Statement I is true.
II. A temperature of 5°F is equivalent to –15°C.

$$5=\frac{9}{5}C+32$$
$$-27=\frac{9}{5}C$$
$$-15=C$$

Statement II is correct.

III. A temperature of 20°C is equivalent to 62°F.

$$\frac{9}{5}(20)+32=68$$

Statement III is incorrect. Statements I and II are correct and statement III is incorrect.

15. **(D)** Use long division to assess the equivalent statement.

$$\begin{array}{r} 4+\dfrac{22}{n-4} \\ n-4\overline{)\ 4n+6} \\ \underline{4n-16} \\ 22 \end{array}$$

$4+\dfrac{22}{n-4}$ is equivalent to $\dfrac{4n+6}{n-4}$.

16. $\mathbf{\frac{1}{4}}$ **or** $\mathbf{\frac{1}{2}}$

Solve for m.

$$m^2-6m+8=0$$
$$(m-4)(m-2)=0$$
$$m-4=0 \text{ or } m-2=0$$
$$m=4 \text{ or } m=2$$

$\dfrac{1}{m}$ equals $\dfrac{1}{4}$ *or* $\dfrac{1}{2}$.

17. **5** Complete the square for both x and y.

$$x^2+6y+y^2-4x=12$$
$$x^2-4x+y^2+6y=12$$
$$x^2-4x+4+y^2+6y+9=12+4+9$$
$$(x-2)^2+(y+3)^2=25$$

The graphing form of a circle is $(x-h)^2+(y-k)^2=r^2$. Since $r^2=25$, $r=5$.

18. **Answers may vary.** $\mathbf{0 \leq x < 8}$

Solve the compound inequality by writing it as two separate inequalities.

$$\begin{array}{lcl} -8 \leq 2x-8 & \textit{and} & 2x-8<8 \\ 0 \leq 2x & & 2x<16 \\ 0 \leq x & & x<8 \end{array}$$

$$0 \leq x < 8$$

19. **5** The median of a data set is the middle value when data are arranged in order. Array the number of lures sold; there are four \$2 lures, five \$5 lures, and three \$10 lures.

2 2 2 2 5 5 5 5 5 10 10 10

The middle numbers are both 5's, so find their mean.

$$(5+5)\div 2=5$$

20. **4** There are two ways this question can be solved.

Method 1: System of equations.

Let x = questions answered correctly
Let y = questions answered incorrectly

There are 50 questions, so the first equation is $x + y = 50$. Since two points are deducted for each incorrect answer, we get $x - 2y = 38$. Solve by subtracting the equations.

$$\begin{array}{r} x + y = 50 \\ \underline{-(x - 2y = 38)} \\ 3y = 12 \\ y = 4 \end{array}$$

There were 4 incorrectly answered questions.

An alternate method to solve the problem is by using trial and error. Suppose 40 questions were answered correctly and 10 questions were answered incorrectly.

$40(1) - 10(2) = 20$; Too many incorrect answers.

Try 48 questions answered correctly and 2 questions answered incorrectly.

$48(1) - 2(2) = 44$; Too few questions answered incorrectly.

Try the correct answer 46 questions answered correctly and 4 questions answered incorrectly.

$$46(1) - 4(2) = 38$$

Section 4: Math Test (Calculator)

1. **(B)** Anita climbed 5 flights of stairs, each flight containing 16 steps. The total number of stairs she climbed is 80 stairs. Her effort used five minutes and 20 seconds, which is a total of 320 seconds. Divide the number of seconds by the number of stairs to find the mean time spent climbing a single stair.

$$320 \div 80 = 4 \text{ seconds per stair}$$

2. **(B)** Find the probability that the athlete will be a boy or a water polo member. Avoid double counting by subtracting the boys who are on the water polo team.

$$\text{boys: } \frac{28}{57} \qquad \text{water polo members: } \frac{31}{57}$$

$$\text{boys on the water polo team: } \frac{16}{57}$$

$$\frac{28}{57} + \frac{31}{57} - \frac{16}{57} = \frac{43}{57}$$

3. **(B)** From 2005 to 2006, there was a 100% growth (from 20 to 40). After 2006, however, the graph shows about a 5% increase per year.

4. **(C)** In 2005, there were 20 bee farms in the metropolitan Atlanta area. By 2016, that number gradually increased to 60, an increase of 40 additional farms. Find the total increase as a percentage by using the formula $\frac{\text{increase}}{\text{original}} = \frac{n}{100}$.

$$\frac{40}{20} = \frac{n}{100}$$

$$20n = 4{,}000$$

$$n = 200$$

The increase as a percentage from 2005 to 2010 is 200%. Divide that number by 5 to find the annual increase:

$$200 \div 5 = 40$$

5. **(D)** Use the formula $\frac{\text{rise}}{\text{run}}$ to find the slope of the linear function. As n increases by 1, $r(n)$ increases by 2. Thus, $r(n) = 2n + b$ with b representing the y-intercept. Input any of the points to calculate b.

$$(4, 5)$$

$$5 = 2(4) + b$$
$$5 = 8 + b$$
$$-3 = b$$
$$r(n) = 2n - 3$$

6. **(C)** Polynomials are added by combining like terms. Like terms have the same variable(s) raised to equivalent exponents.

$$\begin{array}{r} 4x^2 + 5x - 6 \\ +\ 3x^2 + x - 11 \\ \hline 7x^2 + 6x - 17 \end{array}$$

Note that when like terms are added, coefficients are combined but the exponents remain the same.

7. **(D)** Isolate n by multiplying both sides of the equation by $\frac{9}{5}$.

$$\frac{9}{5}\left(\frac{5}{9}n\right) = \left(\frac{7}{20}\right)\frac{9}{5}$$
$$n = \frac{63}{100}$$

8. **(A)** Use the formula for the axis of symmetry of a parabola to find which day will result in the greatest distribution of tickets.

$$x = -\frac{b}{2a}$$
$$x = -\frac{9}{2(-.4)} \approx 11$$

Input 11 for x in $T(x) = -.4x^2 + 9x + 11$ to find the number of tickets distributed on day 11.

$$T(11) = -.4(11)^2 + 9(11) + 11 = 62 \text{ tickets.}$$

9. **(D)** Use the proportion $\frac{\text{distance}}{\text{time}} = \frac{\text{distance}}{\text{time}}$ to find how far Gina will run in 2.4 minutes. Since the original ratio is stated in seconds, convert 2.4 minutes into seconds. 2.4 minutes = 2.4(60) = 144 seconds.

$$\frac{28}{4.7} = \frac{n}{144}$$
$$4.7n = (144)(28)$$
$$4.7n = 4{,}032$$
$$n \approx 858$$

10. **(A)** The percent of the U.S. budget was .1% in 1958. By 1963, the percentage of the U.S. budget rose to 2.28%. Use the formula $\frac{\text{increase}}{\text{original}} = \frac{n}{100}$ to find the percent increase.

Increase = 2.28 −.1 = 2.18

$$\frac{2.18}{.1} = \frac{n}{100}$$
$$218 = .1n$$
$$n = 2{,}180\%$$

Choice (A), 2,200%, is the closest to this figure.

11. **(D)** U.S. spending in 1962 was $106,821,000,000. The NASA budget in 1958 was $89,000,000. Divide 106,821,000 by 89,000,000 to calculate how many times larger the 1962 U.S. spending was than the 1958 NASA budget.

$$106{,}821{,}000{,}000 \div 89{,}000{,}000 = 1{,}200.23.$$

Choice (D), 1,200, is the closest.

12. **(D)** Use $7500(.954)^{3.5}$ to represent the depreciated value of the artwork. Each year the piece loses 4.6% of its value, so place 1 – .046 in the parentheses which simplifies to .954. Show 3.5 years of compounding decline by placing 3.5 in the exponential position. Choices (B) and (C) can be eliminated immediately because each demonstrates growth, not depreciation.

13. **(A)** Five years after the three-year value is a total of eight years beyond the purchase date. Let $t = 8$

$$A = 7500(.954)^8 = \$5{,}145.75$$

14. **(C)** The study size, 250 per group, is large enough to conclude that the new early detection program is more effective than the standard procedure. However, since the new procedure compared its results to solely the standard procedure, no conclusion can be made about alternate procedures for early detection of skin cancer.

15. **(A)** From the graph, $g(2)$ yields a value of 2 while $f(2)$ yields a value of −2. In other words:

$$f(2) = -2$$
$$g(2) = 2$$

Thus, $f(2) + g(2) = -2 + 2 = 0$

16. **(D)** Find the number of seconds in one year.

(365 days) × (24 hours in a day) × (60 minutes in an hour) × (60 seconds in a minute) = 31,536,000 seconds in one year.

Next, find the product of 31,536,000 and 186,000 to find how many miles light travels in one year.

$$186{,}000 \times 31{,}536{,}000 = 5{,}860{,}000{,}000{,}000 \text{ (about 6 trillion miles)}$$

Multiply 5,860,000,000,000 by 8 to find the number of miles to Sirius.

$$5{,}860{,}000{,}000{,}000 \times 8 = 46.9 \text{ trillion}$$

Choice (D), 50 trillion, was the closest to this figure.

17. **(C)** Divide 186,000 miles by one billion. Scientific notation will facilitate this process.

$$\frac{1.86\times10^5}{1\times10^9}=1.86\times10^{-4}=.000186$$

In one billionth of a second, light travels .000186 miles. Multiply .000186 by 5,280 feet, the number of feet in a mile.

$$.000186\times5{,}280=.98\text{ feet.}$$

.98 feet is closest to choice (C) 1 foot.

18. **(B)** Ground speed is defined as air speed ± wind speed. If there is no wind, then the ground speed is the air speed because 500 ± 0 = 500.

$$C(500)=100+\frac{500}{10}+\frac{36{,}000}{500}=222$$

19. **(D)** The line of best fit predicts 450 Garibaldi would be counted per cubic mile in August. The actual number that was counted, however, was 400. Find the difference by subtracting 400 from 450.

$$450-400=50.$$

20. **(D)** If n is the largest of the three numbers, then $780-n$ is the sum of the other two. Since n is 50% greater than the sum of the smaller numbers, we arrive at:

$$\begin{aligned}n&=1.5(780-n)\\n&=1170-1.5n\\2.5n&=1170\\n&=468\end{aligned}$$

$$(.6)(780)=468$$

21. **(A)** Since the angles are complementary and $\sin(m^\circ)=\cos(n^\circ)$, it follows from the complementary angle property of sines and cosines that $m+n=90$. Substituting $3x-12$ for m and $6x-18$ for n gives $(3x-12)+(6x-18)=90$, which simplifies to $9x-30=90$. Therefore, $9x=120$, and $x=13.\overline{3}$.

22. **(B)** Let x equal the number of students in the chemistry class. When providing 8 milliliters per student we get $m=8x+6$. This reflects the fact that 6 milliliters are left over from the jar containing m milliliters. When Ms. Garcia wished to provide 10 milliliters per student, she required an additional 16 milliliters to ensure each student had the same amount. This situation is represented by the equation $m=10x-16$. Since $8x+6$ and $10x-16$ both equal m, set each expression equal to one another.

$$\begin{aligned}10x-16&=8x+6\\2x&=22\\x&=11\end{aligned}$$

There are 11 students in Ms. Garcia's chemistry class.

23. **(D)** Find the volume of the cylinder and the cone and add 10% to that sum.
Volume of a cylinder, πr^2h: $\pi(8^2)(12)=2{,}412$

Volume of a cone, $\frac{1}{3}\pi r^2h=\frac{1}{3}\pi(8^2)(8)=536$

Add the two quantities to find the volume of the silo.

$$2{,}412 + 536 = 2{,}948$$

The farmer needs 10% more space so find 10% of 2,948 and add it to 2,948.

$$2{,}948 + (.10)(2{,}948) = 3{,}243$$

Once the volume of the silo has been determined to be 2,948 you don't need to finish the calculation. Only choice (D), 3,243, is larger than 2,948.

24. **(B)** In order for the line containing (6, m) and (m, 54) to pass through the origin, each point must share the slope that connects it to the origin. Use the formula $\frac{\text{rise}}{\text{run}}$ for both points and set the quantities equal.

$$\frac{m}{6} = \frac{54}{m}$$

Cross-multiply and solve for m.

$$m^2 = 324$$
$$m = 18 \text{ or } m = -18$$

Although both 18 and −18 are solutions to the equation, only 18 was provided as an answer choice.

25. **(A)** The area of a rectangle is found by using the formula $A = lw$ where l and w are the length and width, respectively. Reducing the length by 10% gives $.9l$. Reducing the width by x% gives us $(1.0 -.01x)w$. The new dimensions reduce the area by 32.5% so the new area is $.675A$. Use a system of equations to find x.

$$A = lw$$
$$.675A = .9l(1.0 - .01x)w$$

Multiply $.9l$ and $(1.0 - .01x)w$.

$$.675A = .9lw - .009lwx$$

Substitute A for lw in the second equation.

$$.675A = .9A - .009Ax$$
$$.675A - .9A = -.009Ax$$
$$-.225A = -.009Ax$$

Divide both sides by A and solve for x.

$$-.225 = -.009x$$
$$25 = x$$

The width in the original rectangle was reduced by 25%.

26. **(D)** From 1980 to 2005, the record appreciated 12% five times. Twenty-five years had elapsed and the record grew in value every 5 years. We add 1.0 to .12 to ensure growth. Thus, choices (A) and (B) are eliminated because each would represent depreciation.

27. **(C)** There are three different measures of length in this situation: yards, feet, and inches. In order to accurately decide which deal is the best, convert all the deals into the same unit of measure. Since inches are the smallest unit of measure, let's convert all the units into inches. But first, a reminder about unit conversion from grade school:

$$1 \text{ yard} = 3 \text{ feet}$$
$$1 \text{ foot} = 12 \text{ inches}$$

We can also deduce the following:

$$1 \text{ yard} = 36 \text{ inches}$$

Solve each deal as a cost per inch:
Deal 1: 1 yard for \$5.40 means 36 inches for \$5.40. Therefore, \$5.40 ÷ 36 = \$.15 per inch.
Deal 2: 1 foot for \$1.92 means 12 inches for \$1.92. Therefore, \$1.92 ÷ 12 = \$.16 per inch
Deal 3: 1 inch for \$.14
Deal 3 is the most economical.

28. **(B)** Begin isolating x by raising both sides of the equation to the sixth power.

$$2x^{\frac{2}{3}} = 6^{\frac{1}{2}}$$
$$(2x^{\frac{2}{3}})^6 = (6^{\frac{1}{2}})^6$$
$$64x^4 = 6^3$$
$$64x^4 = 216$$

Divide both sides of the equation by 64.

$$\frac{64x^4}{64} = \frac{216}{64}$$
$$x^4 = \frac{27}{8}$$

Raise both sides of the equation to the $\frac{1}{4}$th power.

$$(x^4)^{\frac{1}{4}} = \left(\frac{27}{8}\right)^{\frac{1}{4}}$$
$$x = \left(\frac{27}{8}\right)^{\frac{1}{4}}$$

29. **(D)** $g(x)$ is not defined by any value x that makes $x^2 - 3$ equal to 0 or $x^2 - 4 < 0$.
$x^2 - 3 = 0$ only if $x = \sqrt{3}$ or $x = -\sqrt{3}$, neither of which are integers.
$x^2 - 4 < 0$ for $-2 < x < 2$. The only integers that satisfy this inequality are −1, 0, and 1.
Therefore, there are three integers for which $g(x)$ is not defined.

30. **(C)** For direct variation, use the model

$$\frac{p_1}{q^{-1}_1} = \frac{p_2}{q^{-1}_2}$$

Remember, $q^{-1} = \frac{1}{q}$.

$$\frac{\frac{1}{6}}{\frac{8}{5}} = \frac{p_2}{\frac{1}{18}}$$

Cross-multiply and solve for p_2.

$$\frac{8}{5}p_2 = \left(\frac{1}{6}\right)\left(\frac{1}{18}\right)$$

$$p_2 = \frac{5}{864}$$

31. **3** or **4** Subtract \$18 from \$51 and \$62 to find the amount of money Kara may have spent on belts.

$$51 - 18 = 33$$
$$62 - 18 = 44$$

Kara may have spent between \$33 and \$44 for belts. Given that each belt cost \$11, Kara could have purchased 3 or 4 belts.

32. **3** Multiply $2x^2 + 4x - 2$ by 3.

$$3(2x^2 + 4x - 2) = 6x^2 + 12x - 6$$

Subtract $6x^2 + 12x - 6$ from $-8x^2 + 15x - 2$.

$$(-8x^2 + 15x - 2) - (6x^2 + 12x - 6) = -14x^2 + 3x + 4$$

$3x$ represents the bx term in $ax^2 + bx + c$ so $b = 3$.

33. **8.53** The ramp pictured in the diagram is a right triangle. Note the base is measured in feet while the height is measured in inches. Convert 18 inches to feet so both of the triangle's dimensions use the same label.

1 foot = 12 inches so 18 inches equals 1.5 feet.

The side opposite the angle of elevation and the adjacent side to that angle are both known, so use the tangent function to calculate the measure of the angle.

$$\tan^{-1}\left(\frac{1.5}{10}\right) \approx 8.53°$$

34. **4.4** Find the total points amassed by the first 12 reviews by multiplying 12 by the 4.3, the average review.

$$12 \times 4.3 = 51.6$$

Add 10 to 51.6 to include the two additional 5-star reviews.

$$51.6 + 10 = 61.6$$

Divide 61.6 by 14, the total number of reviewers.

$$61.6 \div 14 = 4.4$$

35. **275** After his initial deposit, Terrence made fixed monthly deposits. Consider the initial deposit to have occurred in month zero, prior to the start of the monthly deposits.

$$\text{Let } m = 0$$
$$A = 25(0) + 275$$
$$A = 275$$

Terrence made an initial deposit of $275.

36. **2** Substitute either (2, 7) or (–3, 37) for x and y and solve for a.

$$7 = (a)(2)^2 - (4)(2) + 7$$
$$7 = 4a - 8 + 7$$
$$8 = 4a$$
$$2 = a$$

37. **1.66 or 1.67 or $\frac{5}{3}$** Input 80% for v into the formula of special relativity.

$$F(t) = \frac{t}{\sqrt{1-v^2}}$$

$$F(1) = \frac{1}{\sqrt{1-.8^2}} = 1.\overline{66}$$

38. **.866** Input 1 and 2 for t and $F(t)$, respectively, into the special relativity formula.

$$F(t) = \frac{t}{\sqrt{1-v^2}}$$
$$2 = \frac{1}{\sqrt{1-v^2}}$$
$$2(\sqrt{1-v^2}) = 1$$
$$\sqrt{1-v^2} = .5$$
$$(\sqrt{1-v^2})^2 = (.5)^2$$
$$1-v^2 = .25$$
$$-v^2 = -.75$$
$$v = .866$$

Section 5: Essay (Optional)

SUGGESTED ESSAY TEST 5

Following is an essay written in response to the prompt. It is unlikely that you would be able to write such a full response in the time allowed, so don't worry if your essay is significantly shorter. Use the suggested essay to see how the task might be approached. For practice, you may wish to rewrite your own essay incorporating some of the points discussed in it.

John Holt constructs a persuasive argument that students must be the focus of education if what he calls "true learning" is to take place. To do this he employs a number of rhetorical techniques.

Holt builds his argument around straightforward assertions made in relatively short sentences using simple, concrete words. This style helps give the piece a down-to-earth, realistic tone. He offers little in the way of supporting evidence, instead relying on the logic of his argument. In some ways the piece is like a speech—a heartfelt expression of an argument without questioning of premises or making references to complicated real-life examples to distract from his main points.

Let us look more closely at each paragraph to further analyze how the passage is constructed. The first paragraph begins with the effective short phrase "true learning," which is immediately defined. This definition is set off by dashes, making it stand out. The rest of the paragraph states the thesis of the argument clearly. The shortness of the paragraph helps make the central thesis stand out in the reader's mind.

Paragraph two elaborates on the thesis stated in the first paragraph. It employs several techniques. It begins, "Every child, without exception. . ." The phrase "without exception" stresses the fact that all children are included. The second sentence (beginning with "whatever") adds variety in length and structure. It uses repetition—"his" is used four times—to add emphasis.

Paragraphs three and four are similar to each other in that they are more matter-of-fact and less passionate than the first two paragraphs. Each uses the device of listing the main points made, which puts stress on these points and creates variety in sentence structure, helping to hold the reader's interest. Paragraph three focuses on the needs of the child. Paragraph four then states the tasks society gives to schools. This structure encourages the reader to think about how well schools are meeting the needs of students.

The argument in paragraph four that schools have failed because they have been given too many tasks is a strong one. Especially convincing is the sentence, "All of these tasks have traditionally been done by the society, the community itself." This is a reasonable argument because it seems unlikely that schools could adapt successfully so quickly to the greatly increased demands on them. Holt uses repetition of the word "none" at the beginning of the next two sentences to emphasize his point, contrasting the point made in these sentences with the point made in the sentence just quoted, beginning with "all."

In paragraph five Holt explicitly states how he thinks children should be educated and what the role of schools should be. In light of his definition of "true learning" (and "true education") and the failure of schools in this regard, his argument makes good sense. An effective rhetorical technique used in this paragraph is in the first sentence, beginning with "Schools." He uses a parallel structure—"but not the only"—and then "but not only" to emphasize that there is great variation in both education resources and the people for whom they provide. A weakness in the argument here is that one can reasonably ask if a child can make good decisions about "when and how much and in what way" he or she should be educated. The assumption of this paragraph that there is no difference between adults and children needs to be examined.

Despite some weaknesses, such as the one just noted above, this piece succeeds fairly well in convincing the reader that true learning must center on the needs of the student. Holt concludes, in the final two paragraphs, with an appeal to emotion—our concern for our children. In the first sentence of paragraph six he uses repetition and rhythm—"want and need and deserve"—in this appeal. In the next sentence he uses the phrase "an offense to humanity," raising the issue to a moral one. The next sentence continues the hard-hitting appeal to emotion with the words "arbitrary, unreal, and unhealthy."

The final paragraph, like the first paragraph, is only one sentence, in this case a warning of the consequences if we fail to strive for "true learning." The juxtaposition of the words "help" and "harm" stresses the result of action, on the one hand, and, on the other hand, inaction. This short final appeal to our concern for children effectively concludes the piece.

Refer to the SAT Essay Rubric on page 23 to analyze and score your essay response. For further guidance on this essay and additional practice and evaluation by teacher and author Philip Geer, contact *info@mentaurs.com*.

ANSWER SHEET
Practice Test 6

Section 1: Reading

1. Ⓐ Ⓑ Ⓒ Ⓓ	14. Ⓐ Ⓑ Ⓒ Ⓓ	27. Ⓐ Ⓑ Ⓒ Ⓓ	40. Ⓐ Ⓑ Ⓒ Ⓓ
2. Ⓐ Ⓑ Ⓒ Ⓓ	15. Ⓐ Ⓑ Ⓒ Ⓓ	28. Ⓐ Ⓑ Ⓒ Ⓓ	41. Ⓐ Ⓑ Ⓒ Ⓓ
3. Ⓐ Ⓑ Ⓒ Ⓓ	16. Ⓐ Ⓑ Ⓒ Ⓓ	29. Ⓐ Ⓑ Ⓒ Ⓓ	42. Ⓐ Ⓑ Ⓒ Ⓓ
4. Ⓐ Ⓑ Ⓒ Ⓓ	17. Ⓐ Ⓑ Ⓒ Ⓓ	30. Ⓐ Ⓑ Ⓒ Ⓓ	43. Ⓐ Ⓑ Ⓒ Ⓓ
5. Ⓐ Ⓑ Ⓒ Ⓓ	18. Ⓐ Ⓑ Ⓒ Ⓓ	31. Ⓐ Ⓑ Ⓒ Ⓓ	44. Ⓐ Ⓑ Ⓒ Ⓓ
6. Ⓐ Ⓑ Ⓒ Ⓓ	19. Ⓐ Ⓑ Ⓒ Ⓓ	32. Ⓐ Ⓑ Ⓒ Ⓓ	45. Ⓐ Ⓑ Ⓒ Ⓓ
7. Ⓐ Ⓑ Ⓒ Ⓓ	20. Ⓐ Ⓑ Ⓒ Ⓓ	33. Ⓐ Ⓑ Ⓒ Ⓓ	46. Ⓐ Ⓑ Ⓒ Ⓓ
8. Ⓐ Ⓑ Ⓒ Ⓓ	21. Ⓐ Ⓑ Ⓒ Ⓓ	34. Ⓐ Ⓑ Ⓒ Ⓓ	47. Ⓐ Ⓑ Ⓒ Ⓓ
9. Ⓐ Ⓑ Ⓒ Ⓓ	22. Ⓐ Ⓑ Ⓒ Ⓓ	35. Ⓐ Ⓑ Ⓒ Ⓓ	48. Ⓐ Ⓑ Ⓒ Ⓓ
10. Ⓐ Ⓑ Ⓒ Ⓓ	23. Ⓐ Ⓑ Ⓒ Ⓓ	36. Ⓐ Ⓑ Ⓒ Ⓓ	49. Ⓐ Ⓑ Ⓒ Ⓓ
11. Ⓐ Ⓑ Ⓒ Ⓓ	24. Ⓐ Ⓑ Ⓒ Ⓓ	37. Ⓐ Ⓑ Ⓒ Ⓓ	50. Ⓐ Ⓑ Ⓒ Ⓓ
12. Ⓐ Ⓑ Ⓒ Ⓓ	25. Ⓐ Ⓑ Ⓒ Ⓓ	38. Ⓐ Ⓑ Ⓒ Ⓓ	51. Ⓐ Ⓑ Ⓒ Ⓓ
13. Ⓐ Ⓑ Ⓒ Ⓓ	26. Ⓐ Ⓑ Ⓒ Ⓓ	39. Ⓐ Ⓑ Ⓒ Ⓓ	52. Ⓐ Ⓑ Ⓒ Ⓓ

Section 2: Writing and Language

1. Ⓐ Ⓑ Ⓒ Ⓓ	12. Ⓐ Ⓑ Ⓒ Ⓓ	23. Ⓐ Ⓑ Ⓒ Ⓓ	34. Ⓐ Ⓑ Ⓒ Ⓓ
2. Ⓐ Ⓑ Ⓒ Ⓓ	13. Ⓐ Ⓑ Ⓒ Ⓓ	24. Ⓐ Ⓑ Ⓒ Ⓓ	35. Ⓐ Ⓑ Ⓒ Ⓓ
3. Ⓐ Ⓑ Ⓒ Ⓓ	14. Ⓐ Ⓑ Ⓒ Ⓓ	25. Ⓐ Ⓑ Ⓒ Ⓓ	36. Ⓐ Ⓑ Ⓒ Ⓓ
4. Ⓐ Ⓑ Ⓒ Ⓓ	15. Ⓐ Ⓑ Ⓒ Ⓓ	26. Ⓐ Ⓑ Ⓒ Ⓓ	37. Ⓐ Ⓑ Ⓒ Ⓓ
5. Ⓐ Ⓑ Ⓒ Ⓓ	16. Ⓐ Ⓑ Ⓒ Ⓓ	27. Ⓐ Ⓑ Ⓒ Ⓓ	38. Ⓐ Ⓑ Ⓒ Ⓓ
6. Ⓐ Ⓑ Ⓒ Ⓓ	17. Ⓐ Ⓑ Ⓒ Ⓓ	28. Ⓐ Ⓑ Ⓒ Ⓓ	39. Ⓐ Ⓑ Ⓒ Ⓓ
7. Ⓐ Ⓑ Ⓒ Ⓓ	18. Ⓐ Ⓑ Ⓒ Ⓓ	29. Ⓐ Ⓑ Ⓒ Ⓓ	40. Ⓐ Ⓑ Ⓒ Ⓓ
8. Ⓐ Ⓑ Ⓒ Ⓓ	19. Ⓐ Ⓑ Ⓒ Ⓓ	30. Ⓐ Ⓑ Ⓒ Ⓓ	41. Ⓐ Ⓑ Ⓒ Ⓓ
9. Ⓐ Ⓑ Ⓒ Ⓓ	20. Ⓐ Ⓑ Ⓒ Ⓓ	31. Ⓐ Ⓑ Ⓒ Ⓓ	42. Ⓐ Ⓑ Ⓒ Ⓓ
10. Ⓐ Ⓑ Ⓒ Ⓓ	21. Ⓐ Ⓑ Ⓒ Ⓓ	32. Ⓐ Ⓑ Ⓒ Ⓓ	43. Ⓐ Ⓑ Ⓒ Ⓓ
11. Ⓐ Ⓑ Ⓒ Ⓓ	22. Ⓐ Ⓑ Ⓒ Ⓓ	33. Ⓐ Ⓑ Ⓒ Ⓓ	44. Ⓐ Ⓑ Ⓒ Ⓓ

ANSWER SHEET
Practice Test 6

Section 3: Math (No Calculator)

1. Ⓐ Ⓑ Ⓒ Ⓓ
2. Ⓐ Ⓑ Ⓒ Ⓓ
3. Ⓐ Ⓑ Ⓒ Ⓓ
4. Ⓐ Ⓑ Ⓒ Ⓓ
5. Ⓐ Ⓑ Ⓒ Ⓓ
6. Ⓐ Ⓑ Ⓒ Ⓓ
7. Ⓐ Ⓑ Ⓒ Ⓓ
8. Ⓐ Ⓑ Ⓒ Ⓓ
9. Ⓐ Ⓑ Ⓒ Ⓓ
10. Ⓐ Ⓑ Ⓒ Ⓓ
11. Ⓐ Ⓑ Ⓒ Ⓓ
12. Ⓐ Ⓑ Ⓒ Ⓓ
13. Ⓐ Ⓑ Ⓒ Ⓓ
14. Ⓐ Ⓑ Ⓒ Ⓓ
15. Ⓐ Ⓑ Ⓒ Ⓓ

16.

17.

18.

19.

20.

ANSWER SHEET
Practice Test 6

Section 4: Math (Calculator)

1. Ⓐ Ⓑ Ⓒ Ⓓ
2. Ⓐ Ⓑ Ⓒ Ⓓ
3. Ⓐ Ⓑ Ⓒ Ⓓ
4. Ⓐ Ⓑ Ⓒ Ⓓ
5. Ⓐ Ⓑ Ⓒ Ⓓ
6. Ⓐ Ⓑ Ⓒ Ⓓ
7. Ⓐ Ⓑ Ⓒ Ⓓ
8. Ⓐ Ⓑ Ⓒ Ⓓ
9. Ⓐ Ⓑ Ⓒ Ⓓ
10. Ⓐ Ⓑ Ⓒ Ⓓ
11. Ⓐ Ⓑ Ⓒ Ⓓ
12. Ⓐ Ⓑ Ⓒ Ⓓ
13. Ⓐ Ⓑ Ⓒ Ⓓ
14. Ⓐ Ⓑ Ⓒ Ⓓ
15. Ⓐ Ⓑ Ⓒ Ⓓ
16. Ⓐ Ⓑ Ⓒ Ⓓ
17. Ⓐ Ⓑ Ⓒ Ⓓ
18. Ⓐ Ⓑ Ⓒ Ⓓ
19. Ⓐ Ⓑ Ⓒ Ⓓ
20. Ⓐ Ⓑ Ⓒ Ⓓ
21. Ⓐ Ⓑ Ⓒ Ⓓ
22. Ⓐ Ⓑ Ⓒ Ⓓ
23. Ⓐ Ⓑ Ⓒ Ⓓ
24. Ⓐ Ⓑ Ⓒ Ⓓ
25. Ⓐ Ⓑ Ⓒ Ⓓ
26. Ⓐ Ⓑ Ⓒ Ⓓ
27. Ⓐ Ⓑ Ⓒ Ⓓ
28. Ⓐ Ⓑ Ⓒ Ⓓ
29. Ⓐ Ⓑ Ⓒ Ⓓ
30. Ⓐ Ⓑ Ⓒ Ⓓ

31.

32.

33.

34.

35.

36.

37.

38.

ANSWER SHEET
Practice Test 6

Essay

PLANNING PAGE

START YOUR ESSAY HERE

1 1 1

READING TEST

65 MINUTES, 52 QUESTIONS

Turn to Section 1 of your answer sheet to answer the questions in this section.

Directions: Following each of the passages (or pairs of passages) below are questions about the passage (or passages). Read each passage carefully. Then, select the best answer for each question based on what is stated in the passage (or passages) and in any graphics that may accompany the passage.

Questions 1–11 are based on the following passages.

Passage 1 is from "Hotspots: Mantle Thermal Plumes" in *This Dynamic Earth: The Story of Plate Tectonics* by Jacqueline Kious and Robert I. Tilling, U.S. Geological Survey, 1996.

Passage 2 is from "Scientists Locate Deep Origins of Hawaiian Hotspots," press release 09-232, December 3, 2009, National Science Foundation.

PASSAGE 1

The vast majority of earthquakes and volcanic eruptions occur near tectonic plate boundaries, but there are some exceptions. For example, the Hawaiian Islands, which are entirely of volcanic origin, have formed in the middle of the Pacific Ocean more than 3,200 km from the nearest plate boundary. How do the Hawaiian Islands and other volcanoes that form in the interior of plates fit into the plate-tectonics picture?

In 1963, J. Tuzo Wilson came up with an ingenious idea that became known as the "hotspot" theory. Wilson noted that in certain locations around the world, such as Hawaii, volcanism has been active for very long periods of time. This could only happen, he reasoned, if relatively small, long-lasting, and exceptionally hot regions—called hotspots—existed below the plates that would provide localized sources of high heat energy (thermal plumes) to sustain volcanism. Wilson hypothesized that the distinctive linear shape of the Hawaiian Island-Emperor Seamounts chain resulted from the Pacific Plate moving over a deep, stationary hotspot in the mantle, located beneath the present-day position of the Island of Hawaii. Heat from this hotspot produced a persistent source of magma by partly melting the overriding Pacific Plate. The magma, which is lighter than the surrounding solid rock, then rises through the mantle and crust to erupt onto the seafloor, forming an active seamount. Over time, countless eruptions cause the seamount to grow until it finally emerges above sea level to form an island volcano. Continuing plate movement eventually carries the island beyond the hotspot, cutting it off from the magma source, and volcanism ceases. As one island volcano becomes extinct, another develops over the hotspot, and the cycle is repeated. This process of volcano growth and death, over many millions of years, has left a long trail of volcanic islands and seamounts across the Pacific Ocean floor.

According to Wilson's hotspot theory, the volcanoes of the Hawaiian chain should get progressively older and become more eroded the farther they travel beyond the

GO ON TO THE NEXT PAGE

PRACTICE TEST 6

hotspot. The oldest volcanic rocks on Kauai, the northwesternmost inhabited Hawaiian island, are about 5.5 million years old and are deeply eroded. By comparison, on the "Big Island" of Hawaii—southeasternmost in the chain—the oldest exposed rocks are less than 0.7 million years old and new volcanic rock is continually being formed.

PASSAGE 2

The Hawaiian Islands are one of the outstanding volcanic features on Earth, but their origins have been shrouded in mystery. Still in debate has been a theory proposed 40 years ago, which states that mid-tectonic plate hotspots such as Hawaii are generated by upwelling plumes of lava from the base of Earth's lower mantle.

A team of scientists put the theory to the test. They deployed a large network of sea-floor seismometers in Hawaii, through an expedition called the Plume-Lithosphere Undersea Melt Experiment (PLUME), opening up a window into the Earth. PLUME allowed scientists to obtain the best picture yet of a mantle plume originating from the lower mantle, and revealed Hawaii's deep roots.

"The hypothesis that hotspots like Hawaii originate from mantle plumes is one of the longest-standing and most controversial topics in geology," says Dr. Robert Detrick. "This experiment combining large numbers of broadband seismometers on the seafloor with instruments on land has provided the most persuasive evidence yet for the existence of a mantle plume extending into the lower mantle beneath Hawaii."

The project involved four oceanographic research cruises to deploy and recover ocean bottom seismometers at 73 sites, and a concurrent deployment of land seismometers on the main Hawaiian Islands. The large seafloor network yielded unprecedented results in a remote oceanic region. The seismometers were used to record the timing of seismic shear waves from large earthquakes around the world. This information was used to determine whether seismic waves travel more slowly through hot rock as they pass beneath Hawaii.

Combining the timing measurements from earthquakes recorded on many seismometers allowed scientists to construct a sophisticated 3-dimensional image of the Hawaiian mantle. In the upper mantle, the Hawaiian Islands are underlain by low shear-wave velocities, linked with hotter-than-average material from an upwelling plume. Low velocities continue down into the Earth's transition zone, at 410 to 660 km depth, and extend even deeper into the Earth's lower mantle down to at least 1,500 km depth.

The location of the Hawaiian Islands in the middle of the Pacific Ocean had hampered past efforts to resolve its deep structure. Seismometer deployments limited to land sites on the islands did not provide sufficient coverage for high-resolution imaging, and Hawaii is also far from the most active circum-Pacific zones of earthquakes. Therefore, scientists turned to a more technologically challenging, marine approach by placing temporary instrumentation on the seafloor to record seismic waves.

Results of the project make a strong case for the existence of a deep mantle plume.

GO ON TO THE NEXT PAGE

1. Passage 1 provides information explaining all of the following *except*

   (A) the process by which an island is formed over a hotspot
   (B) the cause of hotspots
   (C) why volcanic rocks on Kauai are deeply eroded, whereas those on the Big Island are not
   (D) why the volcanoes of the Hawaiian chain become progressively older as one moves north along the chain

2. According to J. Tuzo Wilson's "hotspot" theory, the fact that volcanic rock is regularly being formed on the "Big Island" suggests that

   (A) the "Big Island" is situated over a hotspot
   (B) the reason that the "Big Island" is larger than the other islands in the Hawaiian Island chain is that it alone was formed as a result of a hotspot
   (C) volcanism is a relatively recent phenomenon on the "Big Island"
   (D) the Pacific Plate is much nearer to the ocean surface in the area of the "Big Island" than it is in the areas of the other Hawaiian Islands

3. Which of the following is true about J. Tuzo Wilson's "hotspot" theory?

   (A) There is no place in it for the mechanism of plate tectonics.
   (B) It incorporates some features of plate tectonics but largely supersedes it as a theory explaining the cause of volcanoes around the world.
   (C) It envisions hotspots as occurring only in the area of the Hawaiian Island-Emperor Seamounts chain.
   (D) It does not claim to explain the origin of all volcanoes in the world.

4. Which of the following sequences best describes the chronological order of the thought process by which J. Tuzo Wilson most likely came up with the "hotspot" theory?

   (A) observation, deduction, formation of hypothesis
   (B) observation, induction, formation of hypothesis
   (C) observation, formation of hypothesis, testing of hypothesis
   (D) formation of hypothesis, deduction, observation

5. According to the "hotspot" theory, the reason that some Hawaiian Islands are older than other Hawaiian Islands is that

   (A) hotspots move steadily below the Earth's crust, creating island volcanoes at different times
   (B) the Pacific tectonic plate continuously moves, causing one island volcano to form over a hotspot, then another, and so on
   (C) erosion has worn away much of the material from the older islands, such as Kauai
   (D) there are several hotspots, of varying ages, below the Pacific tectonic plate in the area of the Hawaiian Islands; the oldest islands were created by the oldest hotspots and the youngest islands were created by the youngest hotspots

6. Which choice provides the best evidence for the answer to the previous question?

   (A) (lines 4–10) "For . . . picture?"
   (B) (lines 11–15) "Wilson . . . volcanism"
   (C) (lines 30–37) "The . . . volcano."
   (D) (lines 37–42) "Continuing . . . repeated."

GO ON TO THE NEXT PAGE

7. In line 72, the word *window* is used

(A) hyperbolically
(B) literally
(C) ironically
(D) metaphorically

8. It can be inferred that the earthquakes mentioned in line 102

(A) were caused by the eruption of volcanoes in the Hawaiian Islands
(B) were caused by mid-tectonic hotspots
(C) were largely or entirely unrelated to geological activity on or near the Hawaiian Islands
(D) occurred simultaneously

9. The word *resolve* as it is used in line 115 most nearly means

(A) speculate about
(B) to render visible and distinct
(C) scientifically establish the facts about
(D) solve

10. Both passages are primarily concerned with the question of

(A) what causes deep mantle plumes
(B) what causes volcanic islands to form in the middle of tectonic plates
(C) what caused volcanism to occur in the area of the Hawaiian Islands
(D) what caused the "Big Island" of Hawaii to form

11. Which best describes the relationship between Passage 1 and Passage 2?

(A) Passage 1 describes a theory in detail and provides some evidence for it; Passage 2 describes two experiments that have been done to test the theory described in Passage 1.
(B) Passage 1 describes two competing theories and the evidence for one of them; Passage 2 evaluates the two theories described in Passage 1 and reaches a conclusion about which one is better supported by the evidence.
(C) Passage 1 describes the main geological processes involved in creating the Hawaiian Islands; Passage 2 describes an experiment done to gather information about these processes.
(D) Passage 1 describes a theory in considerable detail and provides some evidence for it; Passage 2 describes an experiment that produced good evidence supporting the theory described in Passage 1.

GO ON TO THE NEXT PAGE

Questions 12–21 are based on the following passage.

This passage is from W. E. B. Du Bois, *The Souls of Black Folk*, originally published in 1903.

Being a problem is a strange experience,—peculiar even for one who has never been anything else, save perhaps in babyhood and in Europe. It is in the early days of rollicking boyhood that the revelation first bursts upon one, all in a day, as it were. I remember well when the shadow swept across me. I was a little thing, away up in the hills of New England, where the dark Housatonic winds between Hoosac and Taghkanic to the sea. In a wee wooden schoolhouse, something put it into the boys' and girls' heads to buy gorgeous visiting-cards—ten cents a package—and exchange. The exchange was merry, till one girl, a tall newcomer, refused my card,—refused it peremptorily, with a glance. Then it dawned upon me with a certain suddenness that I was different from the others; or like, mayhap, in heart and life and longing, but shut out from their world by a vast veil. I had thereafter no desire to tear down that veil, to creep through; I held all beyond it in common contempt, and lived above it in a region of blue sky and great wandering shadows. That sky was bluest when I could beat my mates at examination-time, or beat them at a foot-race, or even beat their stringy heads. Alas, with the years all this fine contempt began to fade; for the words I longed for, and all their dazzling opportunities, were theirs, not mine. But they should not keep these prizes, I said; some, all, I would wrest from them. Just how I would do it I could never decide: by reading law, by healing the sick, by telling the wonderful tales that swam in my head,—some way. With other black boys the strife was not so fiercely sunny: their youth shrunk into tasteless sycophancy, or into silent hatred of the pale world about them and mocking distrust of everything white; or wasted itself in a bitter cry, Why did God make me an outcast and a stranger in mine own house? The shades of the prison-house closed round about us all: walls strait and stubborn to the whitest, but relentlessly narrow, tall, and unscalable to sons of night who must plod darkly on in resignation, or beat unavailing palms against the stone, or steadily, half hopelessly, watch the streak of blue above.

After the Egyptian and Indian, the Greek and Roman, the Teuton and Mongolian, the Negro is a sort of seventh son, born with a veil, and gifted with second-sight in this American world,—a world which yields him no true self-consciousness, but only lets him see himself through the revelation of the other world. It is a peculiar sensation, this double-consciousness, this sense of always looking at one's self through the eyes of others, of measuring one's soul by the tape of a world that looks on in amused contempt and pity. One ever feels his twoness,—an American, a Negro; two souls, two thoughts, two unreconciled strivings; two warring ideals in one dark body, whose dogged strength alone keeps it from being torn asunder.

The history of the American Negro is the history of this strife,—this longing to attain self-conscious manhood, to merge his double self into a better and truer self. In this merging he wishes neither of the older selves to be lost. He would not Africanize America, for America has too much to teach the world and Africa. He would not bleach his Negro soul in a flood of white Americanism, for he knows that Negro blood has a message

GO ON TO THE NEXT PAGE

for the world. He simply wishes to make it possible for a man to be both a Negro and an American, without being cursed and spit upon by his fellows, without having the doors of Opportunity closed roughly in his face.

This, then, is the end of his striving: to be a co-worker in the kingdom of culture, to escape both death and isolation, to husband and use his best powers and his latent genius.

12. The word *revelation* in line 5 refers to
    (A) the author's realization that despite their different skin color whites and blacks are fundamentally the same
    (B) the author's realization that blacks are not part of the white people's world
    (C) the author's learning that not everyone is kind
    (D) the author's realization that he could beat his white classmates at examinations and in a foot-race

13. From his experience with the visiting-cards the narrator learns that
    (A) as a black man he is fundamentally different from white people
    (B) white people accept all blacks except him
    (C) he is fundamentally the same as white people but separated from them by their attitudes toward blacks
    (D) white boys but not white girls accept him

14. According to the narrator, the other black boys at his school
    (A) were largely unaware of the attitude of white people toward blacks
    (B) often reacted violently to their bad treatment by white people
    (C) came to either kowtow to white people, hate the world of white people, or become bitter
    (D) learned to accept that they were different and would never have the opportunities that white people did

15. Which choice provides the best evidence for the answer to the previous question?
    (A) (lines 4–6) "It . . . were."
    (B) (lines 21–25) "I . . . shadows."
    (C) (lines 36–43) "With . . . house?"
    (D) (lines 43–50) "The . . . above."

16. The author's use of the word *stubborn* in line 45 suggests that he believed that
    (A) there were more obstacles for white people than there were for black people
    (B) black people were, in general, more stubborn than white people in following the accepted way of thinking of the time
    (C) white people were generally more stubborn than black people in following the accepted way of thinking of the time
    (D) white people were confined by prevailing attitudes and limited opportunities, but could overcome these with sufficient effort

GO ON TO THE NEXT PAGE

17. The phrase "second-sight" in line 54 refers to
    (A) the unique ability of Negroes to visualize future events
    (B) an awareness of the injustice of how the whites treat Negroes
    (C) the whites' view of the world
    (D) a mystical ability to perceive reality directly

18. The word *end* as it is used in line 84 most nearly means
    (A) conclusion
    (B) closing stages
    (C) result
    (D) goal

19. The author makes use of all of the following except
    (A) rhetorical question
    (B) symbolism
    (C) anecdote
    (D) appeal to authority

20. The most appropriate title of this passage would be
    (A) Blacks Can Never Be Fully American
    (B) Blacks Must Give Up Their Heritage to Be Truly American
    (C) The Problem of Black Identity in America
    (D) The Black Experience in America

21. Which of the following phrases is not used symbolically in the passage?
    (A) "vast veil" (line 21)
    (B) "blue sky" (line 24)
    (C) "prison-house" (line 44)
    (D) "latent genius" (line 87)

Questions 22–31 are based on the following passage.

This passage is from Joseph Conrad, *Lord Jim*, originally published in 1917.

He was an inch, perhaps two, under six feet, powerfully built, and he advanced straight at you with a slight stoop of the shoulders, head forward, and a fixed from-under stare which made you think of a charging bull. His voice was deep, loud, and his manner displayed a kind of dogged self-assertion which had nothing aggressive in it. It seemed a necessity, and it was directed apparently as much at himself as at anybody else. He was spotlessly neat, appareled in immaculate white from shoes to hat, and in the various Eastern ports where he got his living as a ship-chandler's water-clerk he was very popular.

A water-clerk need not pass an examination in anything under the sun, but he must have Ability in the abstract and demonstrate it practically. His work consists in racing under sail, steam, or oars against other water-clerks for any ship about to anchor, greeting her captain cheerily, forcing upon him a card—the business card of the ship-chandler—and on his first visit on shore piloting him firmly but without ostentation to a vast, cavern-like shop which is full of things that are eaten and drunk on board ship; where you can get everything to make her seaworthy and beautiful, from a set of chain-hooks for her cable to a book of gold-leaf for the carvings of her stern; and where her commander is received like a brother by a ship-chandler he has never seen before. There is a cool parlor, easy-chairs, bottles, cigars, writing implements, a copy of harbor regulations, and a warmth of welcome that

GO ON TO THE NEXT PAGE

melts the salt of a three months' passage out of a seaman's heart. The connection thus begun is kept up, as long as the ship remains in harbor, by the daily visits of the water-clerk. To the captain he is faithful like a friend and attentive like a son, with the patience of Job, the unselfish devotion of a woman, and the jollity of a boon companion. Later on the bill is sent in. It is a beautiful and humane occupation. Therefore good water-clerks are scarce. When a water-clerk who possesses Ability in the abstract has also the advantage of having been brought up to the sea, he is worth to his employer a lot of money and some humoring. Jim had always good wages and as much humoring as would have bought the fidelity of a fiend. Nevertheless, with black ingratitude he would throw up the job suddenly and depart. To his employers the reasons he gave were obviously inadequate. They said 'Confounded fool!' as soon as his back was turned. This was their criticism on his exquisite sensibility.

To the white men in the waterside business and to the captains of ships he was just Jim—nothing more. He had, of course, another name, but he was anxious that it should not be pronounced. His incognito, which had as many holes as a sieve, was not meant to hide a personality but a fact. When the fact broke through the incognito he would leave suddenly the seaport where he happened to be at the time and go to another—generally farther east. He kept to seaports because he was a seaman in exile from the sea, and had Ability in the abstract, which is good for no other work but that of a water-clerk. He retreated in good order towards the rising sun, and the fact followed him casually but inevitably. Thus in the course of years he was known successively in Bombay, in Calcutta, in Rangoon, in Penang, in Batavia—and in each of these halting-places was just Jim the water-clerk. Afterwards, when his keen perception of the Intolerable drove him away for good from seaports and white men, even into the virgin forest, the Malays of the jungle village, where he had elected to conceal his deplorable faculty, added a word to the monosyllable of his incognito. They called him Tuan Jim: as one might say—Lord Jim.

22. The word *humoring* as it is used in line 51 most nearly means

(A) amusing
(B) teasing
(C) entertaining
(D) indulging

23. The phrase "fidelity of a fiend" (line 53) most nearly means

(A) loyalty of a devil
(B) faithfulness of a fanatic
(C) respect and love of a good woman
(D) devotion of a friend

24. Commenting on Jim's occupation, the author says "It is a beautiful and humane occupation. Therefore good water-clerks are scarce" (lines 45–47).

Which of the following words most accurately describes this comment?

(A) exaggerated
(B) tongue-in-cheek
(C) drily humorous
(D) fatuous

GO ON TO THE NEXT PAGE

1 1 1

25. Why does Jim regularly give up the job he has in a particular port and move to another port to take up a similar position?

(A) He becomes tired of living under a false name.
(B) A secret about him becomes known in the area.
(C) He wants to advance his career.
(D) When his real identity becomes known, people shower him with honors (such as calling him "Lord"), which he finds so embarrassing that he has to leave.

26. Which of the following lines provide the best evidence for the answer to the previous question?

(A) (lines 1–15) "He . . . popular."
(B) (lines 53–55) "Nevertheless . . . depart."
(C) (lines 67–70) "When . . . east."
(D) (lines 76–80) "Thus . . . water-clerk."

27. What does the author mean by "His incognito . . . had as many holes as a sieve" (lines 64–65)?

(A) Jim often lets his real identity leak out deliberately.
(B) Jim's false name was able to hide his real personality effectively because it was open to many interpretations.
(C) Jim's false identity was able to keep "the fact" (line 66) but not his real name secret.
(D) Jim's false identity did a poor job of keeping people from learning his real identity.

28. The "fact" mentioned in lines 67 and 75 most likely refers to

(A) something disreputable that Jim did
(B) Jim's real name
(C) the fact that Jim had no formal qualification for the position of water-clerk
(D) the fact that Jim had been exiled from the sea

29. According to the passage, Jim is

(A) effeminate and extremely neat in appearance
(B) lonely and aggressive
(C) powerfully built and popular
(D) academically gifted, especially in abstract subjects

30. Which of the following lines provides the best evidence for the answer to the previous question?

(A) (lines 6–9) "His . . . it." and (lines 41–44) "To . . . companion."
(B) (lines 1–2) "He . . . built" and (lines 11–15) "He . . . popular."
(C) (lines 51–53) "Jim . . . fiend." and (lines 60–62) "To . . . more."
(D) (lines 47–51) "When . . . humoring." and (lines 62–64) "He . . . pronounced."

31. The word *casually* as it is used in line 76 most nearly means

(A) lazily
(B) cautiously
(C) unobtrusively
(D) informally

GO ON TO THE NEXT PAGE

Questions 32–41 are based on the following passage.

This passage is from Charles A. Eastman (Ohiyesa), *The Indian Today: The Past and Future of The First American*, originally published in 1915.

The original attitude of the American Indian toward the Eternal, the "Great Mystery" that surrounds and embraces us, was as simple as it was exalted. To him it was the supreme conception, bringing with it the fullest measure of joy and satisfaction possible in this life.

The worship of the "Great Mystery" was silent, solitary, free from all self-seeking. It was silent, because all speech is of necessity feeble and imperfect; therefore the souls of my ancestors ascended to God in wordless adoration. It was solitary, because they believed that He is nearer to us in solitude, and there were no priests authorized to come between a man and his Maker. None might exhort or confess or in any way meddle with the religious experience of another. Among us all men were created sons of God and stood erect, as conscious of their divinity. Our faith might not be formulated in creeds, nor forced upon any who were unwilling to receive it; hence there was no preaching, proselytizing, nor persecution, neither were there any scoffers or atheists.

There were no temples or shrines among us save those of nature. Being a natural man, the Indian was intensely poetical. He would deem it sacrilege to build a house for Him who may be met face to face in the mysterious, shadowy aisles of the primeval forest, or on the sunlit bosom of virgin prairies, upon dizzy spires and pinnacles of naked rock, and yonder in the jeweled vault of the night sky! He who enrobes Himself in filmy veils of cloud, there on the rim of the visible world where our Great-Grandfather Sun kindles his evening camp-fire, He who rides upon the rigorous wind of the north, or breathes forth His spirit upon aromatic southern airs, whose war-canoe is launched upon majestic rivers and inland seas—He needs no lesser cathedral!

That solitary communion with the Unseen which was the highest expression of our religious life is partly described in the word *bambeday*, literally "mysterious feeling," which has been variously translated "fasting" and "dreaming." It may better be interpreted as "consciousness of the divine."

The first bambeday, or religious retreat, marked an epoch in the life of the youth. Having first prepared himself by means of the purifying vapor-bath, and cast off as far as possible all human or fleshly influences, the young man sought out the noblest height, the most commanding summit in all the surrounding region. Knowing that God sets no value upon material things, he took with him no offerings or sacrifices other than symbolic objects, such as paints and tobacco. Wishing to appear before Him in all humility, he wore no clothing save his moccasins and loincloth. At the solemn hour of sunrise or sunset he took up his position, overlooking the glories of earth and facing the "Great Mystery," and there he remained, naked, erect, silent, and motionless, exposed to the elements and forces of His arming, for a night and a day to two days and nights. In this holy trance or ecstasy the Indian mystic found his highest happiness and the motive power of his existence.

The native American has been generally despised by his white conquerors for his poverty and simplicity. They forget, perhaps, that his religion forbade the accumulation

GO ON TO THE NEXT PAGE

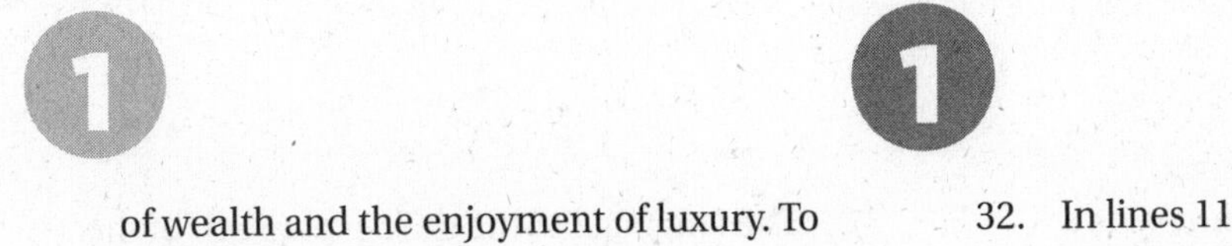

of wealth and the enjoyment of luxury. To him, as to other single-minded men in every age and race, from Diogenes to the brothers of Saint Francis, the love of possessions has appeared a snare, and the burdens of a complex society a source of needless peril and temptation. Furthermore, it was the rule of his life to share the fruits of his skill and success with his less fortunate brothers. Thus he kept his spirit free from the clog of pride, cupidity, or envy, and carried out, as he believed, the divine decree—a matter profoundly important to him.

It was not, then, wholly from ignorance or improvidence that he failed to establish permanent towns and to develop a material civilization. To the untutored sage, the concentration of population was the prolific mother of all evils, moral no less than physical. He argued that food is good, while surfeit kills; that love is good, but lust destroys; and not less dreaded than the pestilence following upon crowded and unsanitary dwellings was the loss of spiritual power inseparable from too close contact with one's fellow men. All who have lived much out of doors know that there is a magnetic and nervous force that accumulates in solitude and that is quickly dissipated by life in a crowd; and even his enemies have recognized the fact that for a certain innate power and self-poise, wholly independent of circumstances, the American Indian is unsurpassed among men.

32. In lines 11–13 the author says "the souls of my ancestors ascended to God in wordless adoration." What does he most likely mean by this?

(A) that the souls of his dead ancestors went to be with God in heaven
(B) that the souls of his dead ancestors could not communicate their experience of God to others upon their return from heaven
(C) that his dead ancestors worshipped God using no language and that their souls grew closer to God
(D) that no one can describe God because He is beyond human understanding

33. We can reasonably infer that the author uses the word *original* (line 1) to suggest that

(A) the early attitudes of American Indians toward the "Great Mystery" was not as truly spiritual as it later became
(B) the attitudes of American Indians toward the "Great Mystery" cannot be described in words
(C) the attitudes of American Indians toward the "Great Mystery" was very creative
(D) American Indians' view of the "Great Mystery" changed from what it was earlier

34. The most likely reason the author uses a variety of capitalized names for God is to
    (A) communicate the idea that God cannot be assigned any one name and that humans conceive of God in a variety of ways
    (B) show that American Indians' idea of God was not sophisticated
    (C) remind the reader that the word God is different in the languages of the various Indian tribes
    (D) convince the reader of his view that because American Indians had many different names for God they did not truly understand him

35. The second paragraph of the passage (lines 8–25) can most accurately be regarded as containing
    (A) a thinly disguised attack on religion in all its forms
    (B) a defense of all traditional religious beliefs and practices
    (C) an implicit criticism of organized religions such as Christianity
    (D) a call to American Indians to abandon their traditional religious beliefs

36. The author most likely uses exclamation marks in the third paragraph (lines 26–43) to
    (A) convey a sense of religious ecstasy
    (B) convince the reader that he is correct in his description of the religious views of American Indians
    (C) break up the monotony created by ending sentences with a period
    (D) alert the reader that his view might contain exaggerations

37. The language of the third paragraph of the passage (lines 26–43) can most accurately be described as
    (A) understated
    (B) euphemistic
    (C) ironic
    (D) rhapsodic

38. The word *epoch* as it is used in line 52 most nearly means
    (A) a past event
    (B) a historical event
    (C) an important event
    (D) an important period of time in the past

39. Which of the following would the author of the passage be most likely to agree with?
    (A) Native Americans were conquered by white people because they lacked courage in battle.
    (B) Native Americans alone possess true spirituality.
    (C) Native Americans did not develop complex technology because they lacked the intelligence to do so.
    (D) There is much to admire about Native Americans.

40. Which of the following provides the best evidence for the answer to the above question?
    (A) (lines 21–25) "Our . . . atheists."
    (B) (lines 62–64) "Wishing . . . loincloth."
    (C) (lines 74–76) "The . . . simplicity."
    (D) (lines 107–111) "and . . . men."

GO ON TO THE NEXT PAGE

41. The phrase "untutored sage" (line 94) most nearly means

   (A) a wise person who lacks formal education
   (B) a wise person who has not received religious instruction from tribal elders
   (C) a teacher pretending to be knowledgeable who in reality has little knowledge
   (D) a foolish person

Questions 42– 52 are based on the following passage.

This passage is from Anne Fadiman, *Ex Libris: Confessions of a Common Reader.* Copyright © 1998 by Anne Fadiman.

I call the "to each his own" quandary the His'er Problem, after a solution originally proposed by Chicago school superintendent Ella Young in 1912: "To each his'er own." I'm sorry. I just can't. My reactionary self has aesthetic as well as grammatical standards, and *his'er* is hideous. Unlike *Ms., his'er* could never become reflexive. (I might interject here that when I posed the His'er Problem to my brother, who was raised in the same grammatical hothouse as I, he surprised me by saying, "I won't say *his'er*. That would be a capitulation to barbarism. But I would be willing to consider a more rhythmically acceptable neologism such as *hyr* or *hes*, which would be preferable to having to avoid *his* by plotting each sentence in advance like a military campaign.")

What about "to each his or her own"? I do resort to that construction occasionally, but I find the double pronoun an ungainly burden. More frequently I recast the entire sentence in the plural, although "to all their own" is slightly off pitch. Even a phrase that is not stylistically disfigured—for example, "all writers worth their salt," which is only marginally more lumpish than "every writer worth his salt"—loses its specificity, that fleeting moment in which the reader conjures up an individual writer instead of a faceless throng.

But I can't go back. I said "to each his own" until about five years ago, believing what my sixth-grade grammar textbook, *Easy English Exercises*, had told me: that "or

GO ON TO THE NEXT PAGE

her" was "understood," just as womankind was understood to be lurking somewhere within "mankind." I no longer understand. The other day I came across the following sentence by my beloved role model, E.B. White: "There is one thing the essayist cannot do—he cannot indulge himself in deceit or concealment, for he will be found out in no time." I felt the door slamming in my face so fast I could feel the wind against my cheek. "But he meant to include you!" some of you may be murmuring. "It was understood!"

I don't think so. Long ago, my father wrote something similar: "The best essays [do not] develop original themes. They develop original men, their composers." Since my father, unlike E.B. White, is still around to testify, I called him up last night and said, "Be honest. What was really in your mind when you wrote those sentences?" He replied, "Males. I was thinking about males. I viewed the world of literature—indeed, the entire world of artistic creation—as a world of males, and so did most writers. Any writer of fifty years ago who denies that is lying. Any male writer, I mean."

I believe that although my father and E.B. White were not misogynists, they didn't really see women, and their language reflected and reinforced that blind spot. Our invisibility was brought home to me fifteen years ago, after *Thunder Out of China*, a 1946 best-seller about China's role in the Second World War, was reissued in paperback. Its co-authors were Theodore H. White and Annalee Jacoby, my mother. In his foreword to the new edition, Harrison Salisbury mentioned White nineteen times and my mother once.

For as long as anyone can remember, my father has called every woman who is more than ten years his junior a girl. Since he is now ninety-one, that covers a lot of women. He would never call a man over the age of eighteen a boy. I have tried to persuade him to mend his ways, but the word is ingrained, and he means it gallantly. He truly believes that inside every stout, white-haired woman of eighty there is the glimmer of that fresh and lissome thing, a girl.

If my father were still writing essays, every full-grown "girl" would probably be transformed by an editor's pencil into a "woman." The same thing would happen to E.B. White. In an essay called "The Sea and the Wind That Blows," White described a small sailing craft as "shaped less like a box than like a fish or a bird or a girl." I don't think he meant a ten-year-old girl. I think he meant a girl old enough to be called a woman. But if he had compared that boat to a woman, his slim little craft, as well as his sentence, would have been forever slowed.

What I am saying here is very simple. Changing our language to make men and women equal has a cost. That doesn't mean it shouldn't be done. High prices are attached to many things that are on the whole worth doing. It does mean that the loss of our heedless grace should be mourned, and then accepted with all the civility we can muster, by every writer worth his'er salt.

GO ON TO THE NEXT PAGE

42. The author says that she and her brother were "raised in the same grammatical hothouse" (lines 10–11). By this she most likely means to suggest that

(A) as children she and her brother continually fought with each other about questions of grammar
(B) she and her brother were sent to schools that emphasized the importance of correct grammar
(C) she and her brother were brought up by parents who were very concerned with correct grammar and did everything they could to make sure that their children knew and cared about correct grammar
(D) she and her brother were raised in a family that placed so much emphasis on grammar that it ruined their ability to appreciate beautiful prose

43. The most likely reason that the author was "surprised" (line 11) by her brother's response when she posed the His'er Problem to him is that

(A) she did not believe that he would object to saying "his'er"
(B) she thought he was not concerned with the issue because it mainly concerns women
(C) she thought he would object to saying "hyr" or "hes" because they sound bad
(D) she thought he would object to using any new word

44. The word *neologism* as it is used in line 15 most nearly means

(A) new word
(B) contraction
(C) pronoun
(D) correct word

45. The phrase "see women" as it is used in line 64 most nearly means

(A) regard women as human beings
(B) notice women
(C) take women seriously
(D) have women as friends

46. The author's "reactionary self" (line 5) would most likely write

(A) "her book"
(B) "his book"
(C) "his or her book"
(D) "his'er book"

GO ON TO THE NEXT PAGE

47. The author comments on a sentence E.B. White wrote in an essay: "But if he had compared that boat to a woman, his slim little craft, as well as his sentence, would have been forever slowed" (lines 94–97). The author most likely means to suggest by this comment that if E.B. White had written "woman" instead of "girl"

(A) his sentence would have illustrated clearly that he was not sexist
(B) his sentence would have illustrated the truth of the view that although changing language to make it gender neutral has a cost, the cost is worth it
(C) his sentence would not have been as graceful and as effective at conveying its meaning
(D) like the boat in his sentence, his career as a writer would have been slowed

48. The phrase "heedless grace" (line 104) refers to

(A) elegant writing that is not concerned with treating women as the equals of men
(B) awkward language
(C) writing that appears to be aesthetically pleasing but that is really ugly
(D) refusal to be concerned with sexist language

49. The phrase "all the civility we can muster" (line 105) suggests that

(A) writers are essentially selfish in that all they really care about is writing well
(B) female writers will be able to adapt more easily than male writers to using gender-neutral language
(C) few writers will be able to write well using gender-neutral language
(D) it will not be easy for writers to accept the need to change their writing habits to avoid sexist language

50. The most likely reason that the author uses the expression "his'er" in line 106 is to

(A) use some humor to remind the reader of the ongoing difficulties writers face in deciding how to deal with the His'er Problem
(B) demonstrate that the only solution to the His'er Problem is to use clumsy, unappealing language
(C) show that she agrees with Ella Young's suggestion about how to deal with the His'er Problem after all
(D) show that it doesn't really matter whether we say *he or she* or *his'er* or *hyr* or *hes* or any of the other suggestions that have been made about how to deal with the His'er Problem

GO ON TO THE NEXT PAGE

1 1 1

51. Which of the following statements would the author of the passage be most likely to agree with?

(A) The need to use the English language in a gender-neutral way has imposed an unfair and unnecessary burden on writers.
(B) The English language should not be used to promote social or political objectives.
(C) Writers should make some effort to use gender-neutral language, but should not let it significantly affect the style of their writing.
(D) Writers should make every effort to use language that treats men and women equally, even if their writing loses much of its grace as a result.

52. Based on what she says in the passage, the author would be most likely to believe that the best way to change the sentence "Every writer should watch his P's and Q's when referring to male and female human beings" to make it gender neutral would be

(A) all writers, regardless of his or her gender, should watch his or her P's and Q's when referring to male and female human beings
(B) all writers should watch their P's and Q's when referring to male and female human beings
(C) every writer should watch his'er P's and Q's when referring to male and female human beings
(D) every writer should watch her P's and Q's when referring to male and female human beings

STOP

If there is still time remaining, you may review your answers.

2 2 2

WRITING AND LANGUAGE TEST

35 MINUTES, 44 QUESTIONS

Turn to Section 2 of your answer sheet to answer the questions in this section.

Directions: Questions follow each of the passages below. Some questions ask you how the passage might be changed to improve the expression of ideas. Other questions ask you how the passage might be altered to correct errors in grammar, usage, and punctuation. One or more graphics accompany some passages. You will be required to consider these graphics as you answer questions about editing the passage.

There are three types of questions. In the first type, a part of the passage is underlined. The second type is based on a certain part of the passage. The third type is based on the entire passage.

Read each passage. Then, choose the answer to each question that changes the passage so that it is consistent with the conventions of standard written English. One of the answer choices for many questions is "NO CHANGE." Choosing this answer means that you believe the best answer is to make no change in the passage.

Questions 1–11 are based on the following passage and supplementary material.

Malaria in the United States

[1]

Malaria in humans is caused by infection with one or more of several species of **1** *Plasmodium*, the infection is being transmitted by the bite of an infective female *Anopheles* mosquito. *P. falciparum* and *P. vivax* species **2** cause the most infections worldwide.

[2]

The majority of reported malaria cases diagnosed each year in the United States are imported from regions where malaria transmission is known to occur, **3** since congenital infections and infections resulting from exposure to blood or blood products also are reported.

1. For the sake of clarity of expression and meaning the underlined portion of the sentence should be written as follows:
   - (A) *Plasmodium.* The infection has its transmission
   - (B) *Plasmodium,* the infection being transmitted
   - (C) *Plasmodium.* The infection is transmitted
   - (D) *Plasmodium,* it is transmitted

2. (A) NO CHANGE
   (B) causes
   (C) causing
   (D) being causes of

3. (A) NO CHANGE
   (B) in fact
   (C) and therefore
   (D) although

GO ON TO THE NEXT PAGE

PRACTICE TEST 6

[3]

In 2010, the Centers for Disease Control and Prevention (CDC) received 1,691 **4** reports. They are concerning cases of malaria among persons in the United States, representing a 14% increase from the 1,484 cases reported with onset of symptoms in 2009. Additionally, the number of cases reported in 2010 are the largest number of malaria cases that have been reported in the United States since 1980 (N = 1,864). In 2010, a total of 1,131 cases **5** will have occurred among U.S. residents, 368 cases among foreign residents, and 192 cases among patients with unknown or unreported resident status.

[4]

Among the 1,691 reported cases, 1,688 were classified as imported cases; one transfusion-related case and two **6** unaccustomed cases were reported. Information on region of **7** procurement was known for 88% of the imported cases. Of 1,479 imported cases for which the region of acquisition was known, 959 (65%) were acquired in Africa, 285 (19%) in Asia, 230 (15%) in the Americas, and five (0.3%) in Oceania. The majority of cases reported in the United States among persons who indicated travel to Africa

4. Rewrite the underlined portion of the two sentences to form one complete sentence that makes sense.
   (A) reports, these concern
   (B) reports which are concerning
   (C) reports concerning
   (D) reports, and they concern

5. (A) NO CHANGE
   (B) occurred
   (C) occur
   (D) would occur

6. (A) NO CHANGE
   (B) serious
   (C) cryptic
   (D) veiled

7. (A) NO CHANGE
   (B) accession
   (C) accretion
   (D) acquisition

GO ON TO THE NEXT PAGE

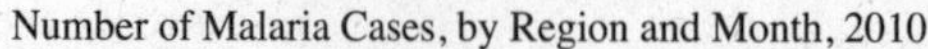

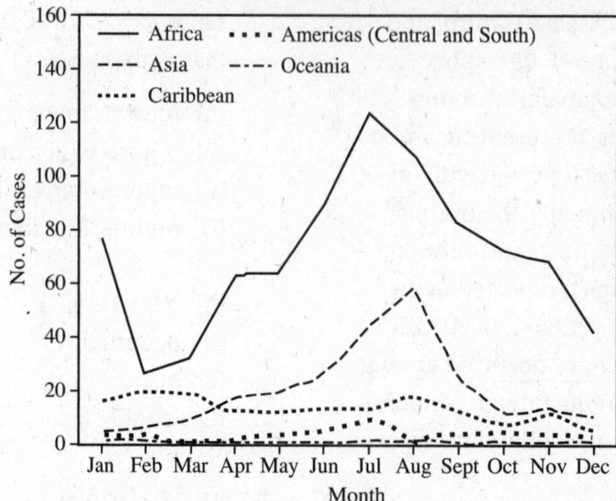

Source: Centers for Disease Control and Prevention, "Malaria Surveillance—United States, 2010."

peaked in ❽ February and July (see above graph). These peaks likely correlated with peak travel times to African destinations related to winter and early summer holidays. The majority of cases reported in the United States among those who indicated travel to Asia (most of whom had traveled to India) peaked in August, followed by a smaller peak in ❾ December (see above graph).

[5]

Among the 1,388 imported malaria cases with an identified *Plasmodium* species, the interval between both the date of arrival in the United States and onset of illness was known for 1,002 cases. Onset of symptoms began before arrival in the United States for 109 ❿ patients; the remaining 893 patients experienced malaria symptoms on or after arrival to the United States. ⓫

8. Which choice most accurately represents the information in the graph?

(A) NO CHANGE
(B) January
(C) June
(D) November

9. (A) NO CHANGE
(B) October
(C) November
(D) February

10. (A) NO CHANGE
(B) patients: the remaining
(C) patients, there remained
(D) patients, the remainder of

Think about the passage as a whole as you answer question 11.

11. To make the passage most logical, paragraph 5 should be placed

(A) where it is now
(B) before paragraph 2
(C) before paragraph 3
(D) before paragraph 4

GO ON TO THE NEXT PAGE

Questions 12–22 are based on the following passage and supplementary material.

Wanted: Trained Teachers

Universal primary education (UPE) will remain a distant dream for millions of ⓬ living children in countries without enough teachers in classrooms. Current discussions of the post-2015 development agenda include a target to ⓭ brace the supply and training of teachers as part of efforts to ensure that every child learns in a stimulating and supportive classroom environment.

⓮ In help to formulate and monitor possible post-2015 education targets, the Unesco Institute of Statistics (UIS) has released a new set of projections of the demand and supply of primary teachers at the global and national levels. According to the data, countries needed to recruit a total of 4 million teachers to achieve universal primary education by 2015 (see graph below). ⓯ Of this total 4 million, it will replace

12. (A) NO CHANGE
    (B) children alive
    (C) children living
    (D) children, and they live

13. (A) NO CHANGE
    (B) cushion
    (C) base
    (D) bolster

14. (A) NO CHANGE
    (B) To help
    (C) When it helps to
    (D) And a help to

15. Which choice most accurately and effectively represents the information in the graph?
    (A) NO CHANGE
    (B) In total 4 million, it
    (C) Of this total 2.6 million, it
    (D) Of this total, 2.6 million will

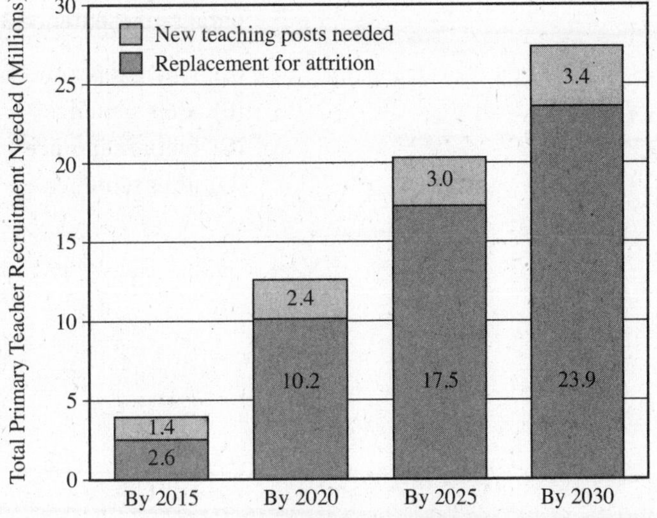

Source: UNESCO Institute for Statistics database

GO ON TO THE NEXT PAGE

teachers who retire, change occupations or leave the workforce due to illness or death. The remaining 1.4 million will be needed to universalize access to primary education and underwrite quality by ensuring that there are not more than 40 students for every teacher.

[1] For this reason, the analysis presented in this paper determines how many teachers would be needed if the goal of achieving UPE was shifted to 16 2020 or 2030. [2] UPE will not be achieved by 2015, however, as 58 million children are still out of school. [3] To achieve UPE by 2020, for example, countries will need to recruit a total of 12.6 million primary teachers. [4] This includes the creation of about 2.4 million new teaching positions and the replacement of 17 17.5 million teachers expected to leave the profession due to attrition. By 2030, the total demand for teachers would rise to 18 27.3 million, with about 23.9 million new posts needed for UPE and the remaining 3.4 million to compensate for attrition. 19

The region facing the greatest challenges by a large margin is sub-Saharan Africa, which makes up more than one-half (63%) of the additional

16. (A) NO CHANGE
(B) 2025 or 2035
(C) 2025 or 2040
(D) 2020 or 2040

17. Which choice most accurately represents the information in the graph?

(A) NO CHANGE
(B) 2.6 million
(C) 23.9 million
(D) 10.2 million

18. Which choice most accurately represents the information in the graph?

(A) NO CHANGE
(B) 27.3 million, with about 3.4 million new posts needed for UPE and the remaining 23.9
(C) 12 million, with about 3.4 million new posts needed for UPE and the remaining 23.9
(D) 20 million, with about 23.9 million new posts needed for UPE and the remaining 3.4

19. For the sake of the cohesion of this paragraph, sentence 2 should be placed

(A) where it is now
(B) after sentence 3
(C) before sentence 1
(D) after sentence 4

GO ON TO THE NEXT PAGE

teachers needed to achieve UPE by 2015 or two-thirds (67%) by **20** 2030 in the region with more than 7 in 10 countries are faced with an acute shortage of teachers. And the situation in many countries may **21** depreciate as governments struggle with overcrowded classrooms and the rising demand for education from growing school-age **22** populations: for every 100 children in 2012, there will be 147 primary school-age children in 2030. Sub-Saharan Africa alone will need to create 2.3 million new teaching positions by 2030, while filling about 3.9 million vacant positions due to attrition.

20. The underlined portion of the sentence should be written as follows:
    (A) NO CHANGE
    (B) 2030, regionally
    (C) 2030. Across the region,
    (D) 2030. Regionally

21. (A) NO CHANGE
    (B) dissolve
    (C) wither
    (D) deteriorate

22. (A) NO CHANGE
    (B) populations, for
    (C) populations; for
    (D) populations for

GO ON TO THE NEXT PAGE

Questions 23–33 are based on the following passage.

The following is an excerpt from President Franklin Delano Roosevelt's Message to Congress on the State of the Union, January 11, 1944.

It is our duty now to begin to lay the plans and determine the strategy for the winning of a lasting peace and the establishment of an American standard of living higher than ever before known. We cannot be content, no matter how high that general standard of living (23) was, if some fraction of our people—whether it be one-third or one-fifth or one-tenth—is ill-fed, ill-clothed, ill housed, and insecure.

This Republic (24) with its beginning, and grew to its present strength, under the protection of certain inalienable political rights—among them the right of free speech, free press, free worship, trial by jury, freedom from unreasonable searches and (25) seizures, these were our rights to life and liberty.

As our Nation has grown in size and stature, (26) however—as our industrial economy expanded—these political rights proved inadequate to assure us equality in the pursuit of happiness.

23. (A) NO CHANGE
    (B) may be
    (C) were
    (D) had been

24. (A) NO CHANGE
    (B) begun,
    (C) begins,
    (D) had its beginning,

25. (A) NO CHANGE
    (B) seizures being
    (C) seizures. They were
    (D) seizures. It was all of them that were

26. (A) NO CHANGE
    (B) moreover
    (C) especially
    (D) specifically

GO ON TO THE NEXT PAGE

(27) "Necessitous men are not free men." People who are hungry and out of a job are the stuff of which dictatorships are made.

In our day these economic truths have become accepted as self-evident. We have accepted, so to speak, a second Bill of Rights under which a new basis of security and prosperity (28) can establish for all regardless of station, race, or creed.

27. At this point the writer is considering adding the following sentence:

We have come to a clear realization of the fact that true individual freedom cannot exist without economic security and independence.

Should the writer make this addition here?

(A) Yes, because this sentence provides support for the main point of the passage, which is that economic equality must be attained in America before people can be allowed "inalienable rights," such as free speech.
(B) Yes, because this sentence is a concise statement of the writer's main idea, which is that economic rights are as important as political rights and go hand-in-hand with them. This is an appropriate place for this statement because in the previous sentence the writer said that political rights alone are not sufficient.
(C) No, because this sentence is not consistent with the view expressed elsewhere in the passage that while the standard of living is important it must always be regarded as secondary in importance to individual political freedom.
(D) No, because such a sweeping contention should be put in the conclusion of the passage, not in the middle of the passage.

28. (A) NO CHANGE
(B) will establish
(C) can be established
(D) established

GO ON TO THE NEXT PAGE

Among these are:

The right to a useful and (29) solvent job in the industries or shops or farms or mines of the Nation;

The right to earn enough to provide adequate food and clothing and recreation;

The right of every farmer to raise and sell his products at a return which will give him and his family a decent living;

The right of every businessman, large and small, to trade in an atmosphere of freedom from unfair competition and (30) dominating by monopolies at home or abroad;

The right of every family to a decent home;

The right to adequate medical care and the opportunity to achieve and enjoy good health;

The right to adequate protection from the economic fears of old age, sickness, accident, and unemployment;

The right to a good education.

(31) All of these rights spell security, after this war is won we must be prepared to move forward, in the implementation of these rights, to new goals of human happiness and well-being.

America's own rightful place in the world depends in large part upon how fully these and similar rights (32) are carrying into practice for our citizens. (33) Nevertheless there is security here at home there cannot be lasting peace in the world.

29. (A) NO CHANGE
    (B) remunerative
    (C) viable
    (D) monetary

30. (A) NO CHANGE
    (B) being dominated
    (C) a dominating by
    (D) domination

31. Rewrite the underlined portion of the sentence for clarity of meaning and expression.
    (A) All of these rights spell security. Since after
    (B) All of these rights spell security. And after
    (C) All of these rights spell security that after
    (D) Being that these rights spell security, after

32. (A) NO CHANGE
    (B) will carry
    (C) have been carried
    (D) had been carried

33. (A) NO CHANGE
    (B) For unless
    (C) In spite of
    (D) However little

GO ON TO THE NEXT PAGE

Questions 34–44 are based on the following passage.

A Letter from Japan

[1] The Doctor took us on Sunday afternoon to his club— (34) which name I think means the perfume of the maple—to see and to listen to some Japanese plays which are given in the club theater (35) building for the purpose. [2] We went there in the afternoon, passing by the Shiba temples, and our carriages were drawn up at one end of the buildings. [3] There everything was Japanese, though I hear stories of the other club and its ultra-European ways—brandies-and-sodas, single eyeglasses, etc. [4] We sat on the steps and had our shoes taken off, according to the Japanese fashion, so as not to injure mats, and we (36) have heard during the operation long wailings, high notes, and the piercing sound of flutes and stringed instruments; the curiously sad rhythm mingled with a background of high, distinct (37) declamation. [5] We walked in with careful attention to make no noise, (38) we forgot that in our stocking-feet we could have made none had we wished, and we found the Doctor's place in a box reserved for him and us, and marked with his name, written large. [6] However that may be, on this side we were in Japan without mistake. [7] Other low boxes, with sides no higher than our elbows as we sat on the mats, divided the sloping floor down to the stage. (39)

The stage was a pretty little (40) building projecting into the great hall from its long side. It had its own roof, and connected with a long gallery or bridge, along which the actors moved, as they came on or disappeared, in a manner new to us, (41) neither did it give a certain natural sequence and made a beginning and an end,—a dramatic introduction and conclusion,—and added greatly to the picture when the

34. (A) NO CHANGE
(B) the
(C) that
(D) whose

35. (A) NO CHANGE
(B) and it had been built
(C) built
(D) having built

36. (A) NO CHANGE
(B) have been hearing
(C) may hear
(D) could hear

37. (A) NO CHANGE
(B) accentuation
(C) pronunciation
(D) remarks

38. (A) NO CHANGE
(B) we had forgot
(C) forgotten
(D) forgetting

39. For the sake of the cohesion of this paragraph, sentence 6 should be placed:

(A) where it is now
(B) after sentence 1
(C) after sentence 3
(D) after sentence 4

40. (A) NO CHANGE
(B) building project
(C) projected building
(D) project building

41. (A) NO CHANGE
(B) not that it gave
(C) despite that it gave
(D) but which gave

GO ON TO THE NEXT PAGE

magnificent dresses of stiff brocade dragged slowly along **42** over the cadence of the music.

43 The boxes were mostly occupied, and by a distinguished-looking audience. And this is because the *N*, as this operatic acting is called, being a refined, classical drama, is looked upon differently from the more or less disreputable theater. Hence the large proportion of ladies, to whom the theater is forbidden. Hence, also, owing to its antiquity and the character of its style, a difficulty of comprehension for the general public that explained the repeated **44** crackle of the books of the opera which most of the women held, whose leaves turned over at the same moment, just as ours used to do at home when we were favored by French tragedy.

42. (A) NO CHANGE
(B) to
(C) beside
(D) below

43. Rewrite these two sentences to make one distinct sentence that makes sense:
(A) The boxes were mostly occupied, and by a distinguished-looking audience, the *N*, as this operatic acting is called, is a refined, classical drama, and looked upon differently from the more or less disreputable theater.
(B) The boxes were mostly occupied, and by a distinguished-looking audience: the *N*, as this operatic acting is called, is a refined, classical drama, and looked upon differently from the more or less disreputable theater.
(C) The boxes were mostly occupied, and by a distinguished-looking audience; the *N*, as this operatic acting is called, is a refined, classical drama, and looked upon differently from the more or less disreputable theater.
(D) The boxes were mostly occupied, and by a distinguished-looking audience that is the *N*, as this operatic acting is called, being a refined, classical drama, and looked upon differently from the more or less disreputable theater.

44. (A) NO CHANGE
(B) rustle
(C) rumple
(D) crimple

STOP

If there is still time remaining, you may review your answers.

3

MATH TEST (NO CALCULATOR)

25 MINUTES, 20 QUESTIONS

Turn to Section 3 of your answer sheet to answer the questions in this section.

Directions: For questions 1–15, solve each problem and choose the best answer from the given options. Fill in the corresponding circle on your answer document. For questions 16–20, solve the problem and fill in the answer on the answer sheet grid. Please use scrap paper to work out your answers.

Notes:

- You **CANNOT** use a calculator on this section.
- All variables and expressions represent real numbers unless indicated otherwise.
- All figures are drawn to scale unless indicated otherwise.
- All figures are in a plane unless indicated otherwise.
- Unless indicated otherwise, the domain of a given function is the set of all real numbers x for which the function has real values.

REFERENCE INFORMATION

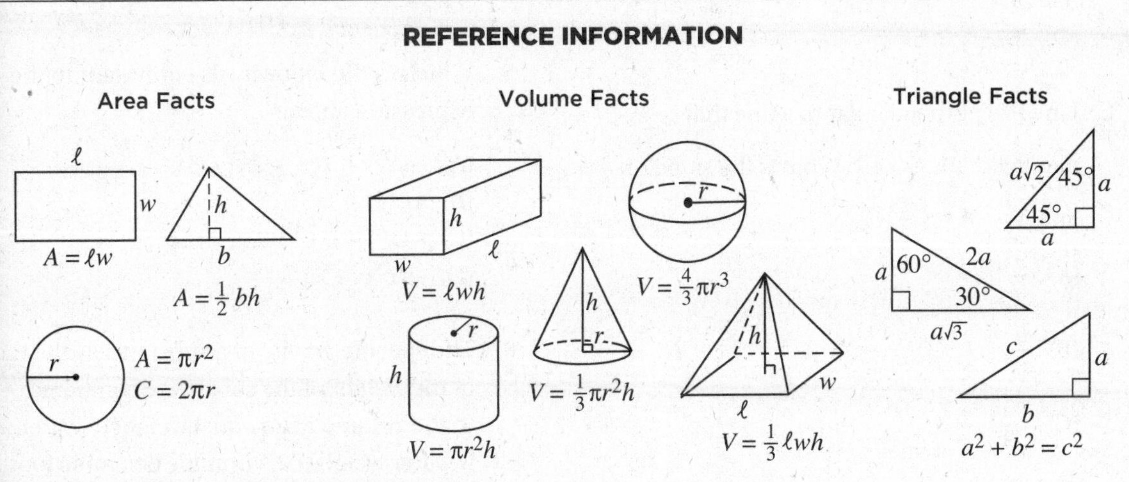

The arc of a circle contains 360°.
The arc of a circle contains 2π radians.
The sum of the measures of the angles in a triangle is 180°.

GO ON TO THE NEXT PAGE

3

1. The Milky Way galaxy contains approximately 250,000,000 stars. Of these stars, about 44% of them have planets and 18% of these stars have planets that are in the habitable zone, i.e., water can remain in a liquid state. What is the best estimate of the number of planets in the Milky Way that are in the habitable zone?

   (A) 20 million
   (B) 35 million
   (C) 55 million
   (D) 100 million

2. If $\frac{2k}{7} = 30$, what is the value of $2k + 7$?

   (A) 105
   (B) 179
   (C) 217
   (D) 287

3. Line A is perpendicular to a line that is parallel to $y = \frac{5}{9}x + 7$. What is the slope of line A?

   (A) $\frac{9}{5}$
   (B) $\frac{5}{9}$
   (C) $-\frac{5}{9}$
   (D) $-\frac{9}{5}$

4. Tina repairs sinks in a large housing development. Each month, the number of sinks she has to repair is represented by the following equation:

   $$B = 360 - 88w$$

   where B is the balance of sinks left to repair and w is the number of weeks she has worked in a certain month. What is the meaning of 360 in the equation $B = 360 - 88w$?

   (A) Tina will repair 360 sinks each week.
   (B) Tina starts each month with 360 sinks to repair.
   (C) Tina repairs 360 sinks a year, almost one per day.
   (D) Tina will repair 360 sinks daily.

$$(-4x^3y - xy^3 + 4x) - (7x - 4xy^3 + 2x^2)$$

5. Which of the following is equivalent to the expression above?

   (A) $-4x^3y + 3xy^3 - 2x^2 - 3x$
   (B) $6x^3y^3 - 3x$
   (C) $-4x^3y + 3xy^3 + 2x^2 - 11x$
   (D) $-9x^3y^3 + 3x$

6. The specific gravity of a substance is the ratio of the weight of the substance compared to the volume of an equal weight of water. If water weighs 62.5 pounds per cubic foot, what is the weight in pounds per cubic foot of a liquid that has a specific gravity of 3?

   (A) .047
   (B) 130
   (C) 187.5
   (D) 260

GO ON TO THE NEXT PAGE

7. If $a^{\frac{3}{2}} = 64$, what is the value of $\sqrt{a}$?

(A) 2
(B) 4
(C) $2\sqrt{2}$
(D) 8

x	$g(x)$
0	6
−2	2
−3	0
−4	−2

8. The function g is defined by a certain polynomial. Some of the values of $g(x)$ are shown in the table above. Which of the following must be a factor of $g(x)$?

(A) $x - 6$
(B) $x - 3$
(C) $x + 3$
(D) $x + 6$

9. If $\frac{m^{x^2}}{m^{y^2}} = m^{36}$, $m > 1$, and $x + y = 9$, what is the value of $x - y$?

(A) 4
(B) 6
(C) 9
(D) 16

10. Sean owed p dollars for a loan he secured for college expenses. He promised to pay off the debt in monthly installments, each installment equal to 20% of the existing debt. After two monthly payments, which expression reflects the balance due on his loan?

(A) $.8p$
(B) $.64p$
(C) $.6p$
(D) $.48p$

11. A commercial pilot is beginning his descent to eventually land at the local airport. His line of sight to the ground is currently at 75.4° and he is currently flying at 7,000 feet. He wants to know what will be the length of his trajectory to the ground. Which of the following equations will help him determine that value?

(A) $\sin 14.6 = \frac{7{,}000}{x}$

(B) $\cos 75.4 = \frac{x}{7{,}000}$

(C) $\tan 14.6 = \frac{7{,}000}{x}$

(D) $\tan 14.6 = \frac{x}{7{,}000}$

12. What is the sum of all values of x that satisfy $4x^2 - 2x - 6 = 0$?

(A) $-\frac{\sqrt{2}}{2}$

(B) $-\frac{1}{2}$

(C) $2\sqrt{2}$

(D) $\frac{1}{2}$

GO ON TO THE NEXT PAGE

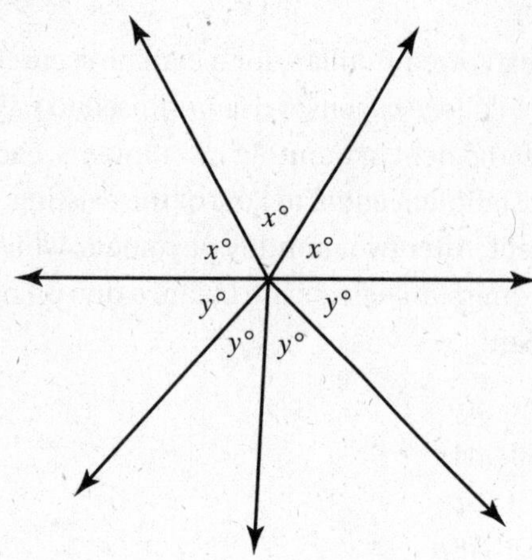

13. In the figure above, what is the value of $(x + y) \div 2(x - y)$?

(A) 3
(B) 3.5
(C) 4
(D) 5.5

$$\frac{6-4i}{2+4i}$$

14. If the expression above is rewritten in the form of $a + bi$, what is the value of $a - 2b$?

(A) $4 + 2i$
(B) $4 - 2i$
(C) $\frac{8}{5}$
(D) 3

15. It costs \$1.85 for x mangoes and \$2.25 for y guavas. Which of the following expressions, expressed in cents, models the cost of purchasing 7 mangoes and 9 guavas?

(A) $\frac{185}{7+x} + \frac{225}{9+y}$
(B) $9\left(\frac{185}{x}\right) + 7\left(\frac{225}{y}\right)$
(C) $7\left(\frac{x}{185}\right) + 9\left(\frac{y}{225}\right)$
(D) $7\left(\frac{185}{x}\right) + 9\left(\frac{225}{y}\right)$

GO ON TO THE NEXT PAGE

3

Grid-in Response Directions

In questions 16–20, first solve the problem, and then enter your answer on the grid provided on the answer sheet. The instructions for entering your answers follow.

- First, write your answer in the boxes at the top of the grid.
- Second, grid your answer in the columns below the boxes.
- Use the fraction bar in the first row or the decimal point in the second row to enter fractions and decimals.

Answer: $\frac{8}{15}$ Answer: 1.75 Answer: 100

Write your answer in the boxes

Grid in your answer

Either position is acceptable

- Grid only one space in each column.
- Entering the answer in the boxes is recommended as an aid in gridding but is not required.
- The machine scoring your exam can read only what you grid, so you **must grid-in your answers correctly to get credit**.
- If a question has more than one correct answer, grid-in only one of them.
- The grid does not have a minus sign; so no answer can be negative.
- A mixed number *must* be converted to an improper fraction or a decimal before it is gridded. Enter $1\frac{1}{4}$ as $\frac{5}{4}$ or 1.25; the machine will interpret 11/4 as $\frac{11}{4}$ and mark it wrong.
- **All decimals must be entered as accurately as possible.** Here are three acceptable ways of gridding

$$\frac{3}{11} = 0.272727\ldots$$

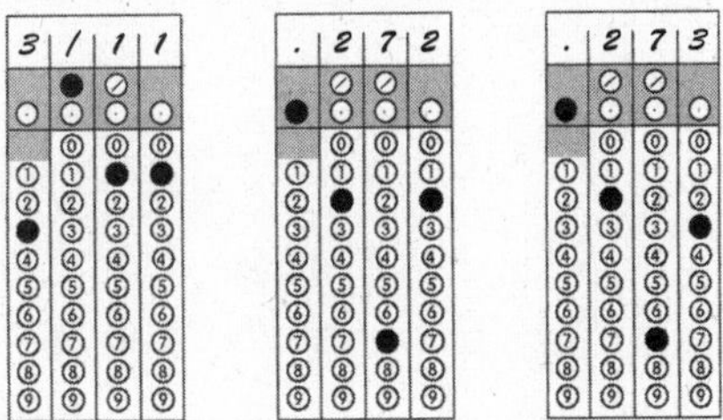

- Note that rounding to .273 is acceptable because you are using the full grid, but you would receive **no credit** for .3 or .27, because they are less accurate.

3

16. Oscar wants to place molding surrounding the floor in his study room that is in the shape of a rectangle. He remembers that the area of the room is 180 square feet and that the width of the room is 12 feet. However, he does not know the measure of the length of the room. His tape measure is out in the car, but Oscar thinks he can solve the problem with simple algebra. Assuming no waste, how much floor molding should Oscar purchase (answers in linear feet)?

$$x^3 - 6x^2 + 2x - 12 = 0$$

17. What real value of x makes the above equation true?

$$mx + ny = 8$$
$$2x + 8y = 64$$

18. In the system of equations above, m and n are constants. If the system of equations has infinitely many solutions, what is the value of $\frac{n}{m}$?

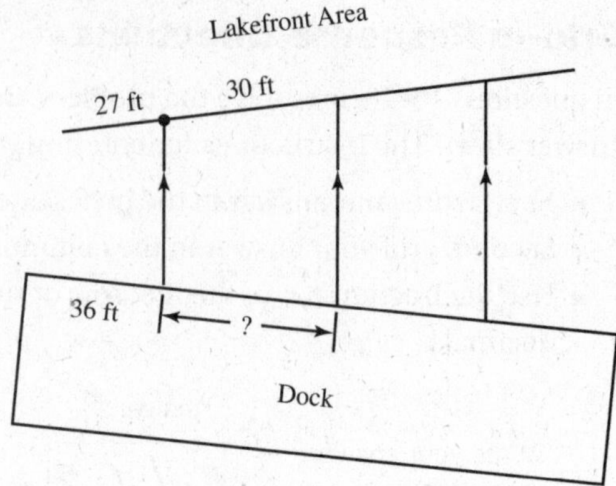

19. The diagram above shows a lakefront area divided into small parcels for boat owners. Each area is marked by a rope to a dock where each owner secures his/her boat. The ropes between the parcels are parallel to one another. What is the length of the docking area in feet for the boat owner who has a 30 foot lakefront border illustrated above?

20. If $f(x) = 2x + 3$ and $f(2x + 3) = 5x$, what is the value of $3x^2$?

STOP

If there is still time remaining, you may review your answers.

4

MATH TEST (CALCULATOR)

55 MINUTES, 38 QUESTIONS

Turn to Section 4 of your answer sheet to answer the questions in this section.

Directions: For questions 1–30, solve each problem and choose the best answer from the given options. Fill in the corresponding circle on your answer document. For questions 31–38, solve the problem and fill in the answer on the answer sheet grid. Please use scrap paper to work out your answers.

Notes:

- The use of a calculator on this section IS permitted.
- All variables and expressions represent real numbers unless indicated otherwise.
- All figures are drawn to scale unless indicated otherwise.
- All figures are in a plane unless indicated otherwise.
- Unless indicated otherwise, the domain of a given function is the set of all real numbers *x* for which the function has real values.

REFERENCE INFORMATION

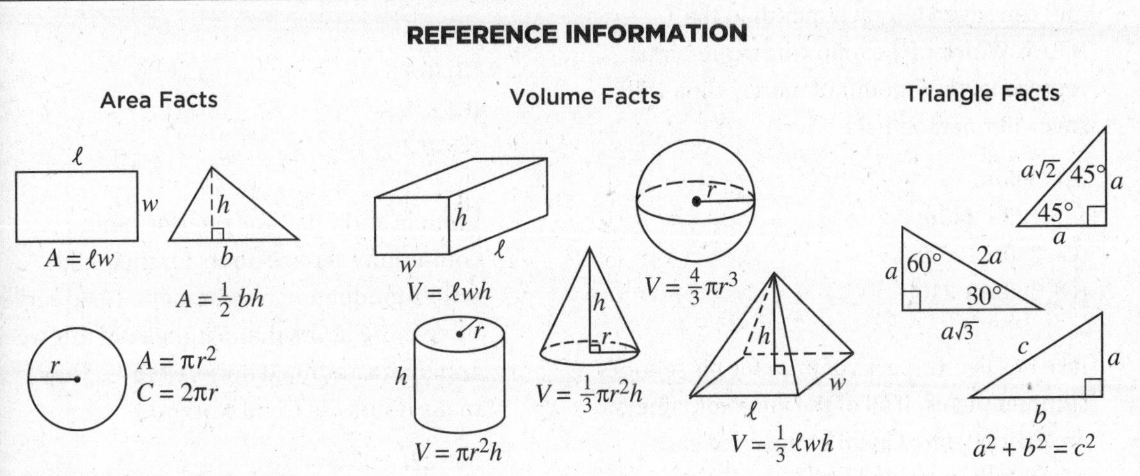

The arc of a circle contains 360°.

The arc of a circle contains 2π radians.

The sum of the measures of the angles in a triangle is 180°.

GO ON TO THE NEXT PAGE

4

1. Andrea has accepted a part-time job as an activities director at a nearby pre-school. She is guaranteed $40 for the one, four-hour shift she works on Wednesday afternoon. If she conducts a group activity, such as a painting class, she is awarded an extra $8 per activity. Which of the following expressions models the amount of money Andrea can make on any Wednesday afternoon?

(A) $40n + 8$
(B) $48n$
(C) 48
(D) $40 + 8n$

2. Gina is saving money for a cross-country road trip with two of her friends. She currently has $240 saved for the excursion and can save $125 each month in the future. Which of the following expressions represents the amount of money Gina will save after m months?

(A) $365m$
(B) $125 + 240m$
(C) $240 + 125m$
(D) $365m + 240$

3. Jake has five 12-packs of juice for his school's summer picnic. If all of the juice containers are divided into 3 main groups and each group is then divided into 5 smaller groups, how many juice containers are in each of these smaller groups?

(A) 2
(B) 4
(C) 5
(D) 10

4. Connor surveyed a random sample of 80 students in his class regarding the need for additional crosswalks at the school. Only 15.6% of the students felt they were necessary. Of the 320 students in his sophomore class, about how many would favor additional crosswalks?

(A) 50
(B) 58
(C) 71
(D) 74

5. The density of an object is found by dividing the object's mass by its volume. If the density of an object is 4 grams per milliliter and its mass is 30 grams, what is the volume in milliliters of the object?

(A) 4.8
(B) 6.1
(C) 7.5
(D) 9.2

6. Virginia and Chad were performing community service hours for their high school graduation requirement. Chad served three more hours than Virginia did this week and their combined hours were 47. How many hours did Chad work?

(A) 22
(B) 25
(C) 27
(D) 31

GO ON TO THE NEXT PAGE

$$y = x^2 - 8x + 15$$

7. The equation above represents a graph of a parabola in the xy-plane. Which of the following equivalent forms of the graph show the parabola's x-intercepts as coefficients or constants?

(A) $y - 15 = x^2 - 8x$
(B) $y + 1 = (x - 4)^2$
(C) $y = x(x - 8) + 15$
(D) $y = (x - 5)(x - 3)$

$$(4 - 3i)(6 + 5i)$$

8. The above expression can be expressed in the form of $a + bi$. What is the value of b in the expression?
(Note: $i = \sqrt{-1}$)

(A) 41
(B) 39
(C) 2
(D) −2

9. The linear function f has values $f(4) = -14$ and $f(-3) = 14$. What would be the value of $f(7)$?

(A) 37.4
(B) 17.28
(C) −26.0
(D) −28.6

Questions 10 and 11 refer to the information below.

The sunrise/sunset was recorded in San Diego during the course of the week of July 21, 2015.

Sun in San Diego—Next 7 days

2015	**Sunrise/Set**		**Day Length**	
Jul	**Sunrise**	**Sunset**	**Length**	**Difference**
Jul 21	5:55 AM	7:55 PM	13:59:21	−1:10
Jul 22	5:56 AM	7:54 PM	13:58:08	−1:13
Jul 23	5:57 AM	7:53 PM	13:56:54	−1:14
Jul 24	5:57 AM	7:53 PM	13:55:37	−1:17
Jul 25	5:58 AM	7:52 PM	13:54:19	−1:18
Jul 26	5:58 AM	7:51 PM	13:53:00	−1:19
Jul 27	5:59 AM	7:51 PM	13:51:38	−1:22

10. Which of the following is **not** true about the data provided above?

(A) To the nearest minute, from 7/21 to 7/27, the length of time the sun was out was reduced by 8 minutes.
(B) There was sunlight for more than 13 hours each day of the week.
(C) To the nearest minute, the sun rose later each day.
(D) The figures in the Difference column represent the decreasing amount of sunlight each day.

11. The category "Difference" decreases during the week because:

(A) As the week progressed, sunrise was generally later and sunset was generally earlier, causing fewer hours of daylight.
(B) Sunrise was generally later; sunset was not a factor in this calculation.
(C) Sunset was generally earlier; sunrise was not a factor in this calculation.
(D) The length of a particular day was shorter than it was in 2014.

GO ON TO THE NEXT PAGE

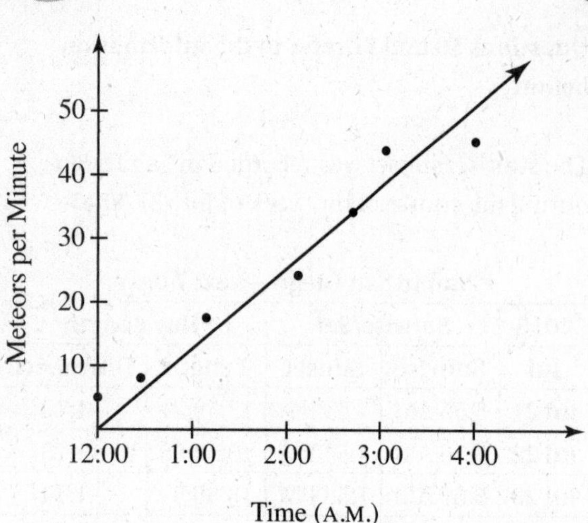

When a comet passes by the sun, it leaves a trail of rocks, ice, and dust. As Earth passes through this trail, some of the particles enter Earth's atmosphere, manifesting as meteorites or "shooting stars." The graph above is the line of best fit of a meteor shower that took place in November 2014.

12. Which of the following can be deduced about the line of best fit and the actual number of meteors seen per minute at 3:00 AM?

    (A) The line of best fit predicted 4 fewer meteors per minute than were actually witnessed.
    (B) The line of best fit predicted 5 more meteors per minute than were actually witnessed.
    (C) There were fewer meteors witnessed at 3:00 AM than there were 2:00 AM.
    (D) The line of best fit and the actual number of meteors witnessed at 3:00 AM were equivalent.

13. Modern television screens are categorized by the lengths of their diagonals. Ethan was watching a show on his 32" screen in which a truck appeared to be 11" long. Had he watched that show on a television that had a 44" inch diagonal, to the nearest inch, how long would the truck appear to be?

    (A) 8"
    (B) 15"
    (C) 27"
    (D) 38"

14. A net deconstructs a geometric solid into two-dimensional plane figures. A net of a cylinder is pictured below.

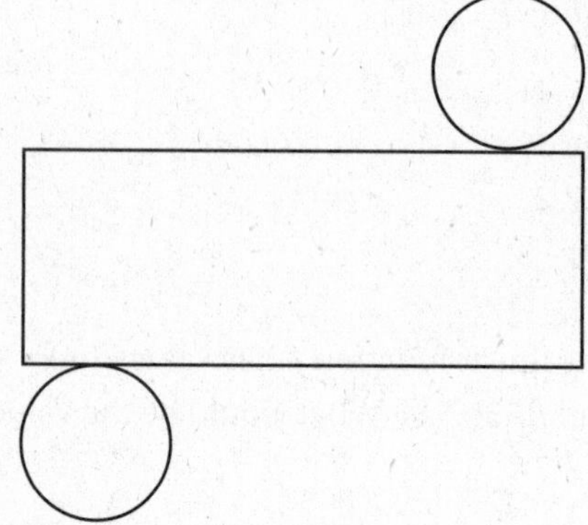

The cylinder above has a volume of 327 cubic inches and a height that measures 6 inches. What is the best estimate of the area, in square inches, of the rectangular portion of the net?

    (A) 121
    (B) 134
    (C) 157
    (D) 208

PRACTICE TEST 6

GO ON TO THE NEXT PAGE

Question 15 refers to the graph below.

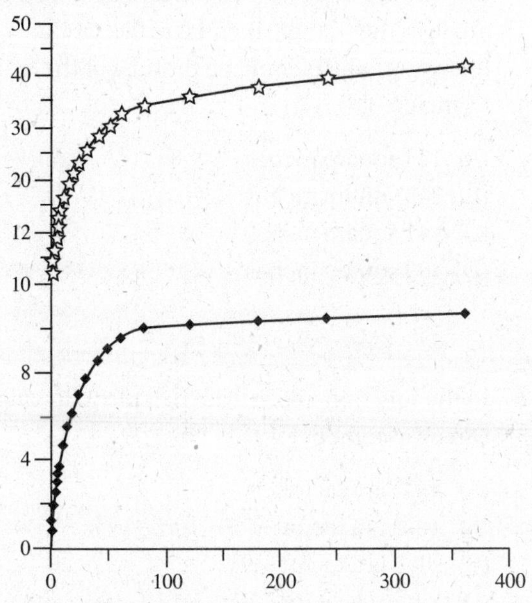

Absorption Rates of Enzyme X and Enzyme Y

15. The graph above represents the absorption rates of two enzymes in the small intestine of a frog. The vertical axis represents the percent of absorption and the horizontal axis represents time measured in seconds. The star symbol represents enzyme X and the diamond-shaped symbol represents enzyme Y. Which of the following **cannot** be concluded about the absorption rates of enzymes X and Y?

    (A) The absorption rates of both enzymes begin to level off at 100 seconds.
    (B) Both enzymes increased at the same percentage rate over the first 100 seconds.
    (C) At 400 seconds, the difference between the absorption rates of enzyme X and Y is about 31%.
    (D) Both enzymes saw their greatest increase in the rate of absorption occurring within the first 20 seconds.

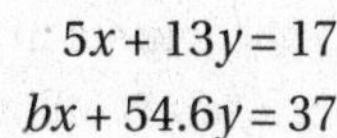

$$5x + 13y = 17$$
$$bx + 54.6y = 37$$

16. In the system of equations above, b is a constant. If there is no solution to the system, what is the value of b?

    (A) 17.4
    (B) 19.6
    (C) 21.0
    (D) 27.3

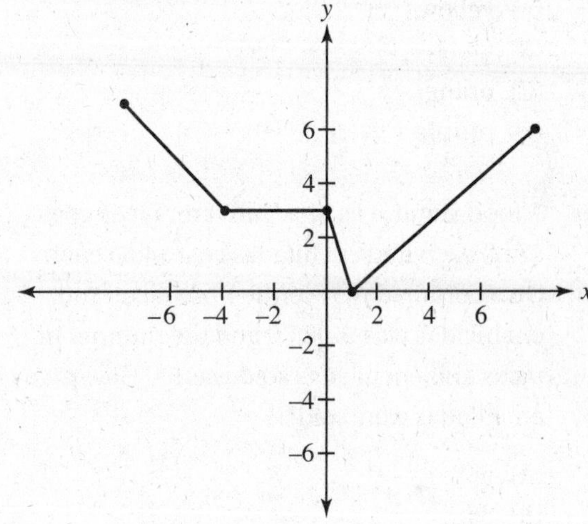

17. The complete graph of the function g is shown in the xy-plane above. What value of x yields the minimum value of $g(x)$?

    (A) 0
    (B) 1
    (C) 2
    (D) 5

GO ON TO THE NEXT PAGE

18. Swimmers who participate in backstroke races depend on a series of banners strung overhead. The banners warn the swimmer that the wall is 5 yards away. A company sells these banners in long cords that repeat a sequence of colors in the following order:

Red Yellow Blue Green Orange Purple

If a high school bought 40 yards of a banner string that contained 75 banners, what was the color of the 59th banner?

(A) yellow
(B) green
(C) orange
(D) purple

19. A food stand sells Mexican fare. Tacos cost \$2.00 each and enchiladas cost \$4.50 each. On a certain day, revenue from tacos and enchiladas was \$198.00 and the number of tacos and enchiladas sold was 54. How many enchiladas were sold?

(A) 54
(B) 36
(C) 27
(D) 18

$$x^2 + y^2 + 6x - 8y = 12$$

20. The equation of a circle in the *xy*-plane is provided above. What is the radius of the circle?

(A) 5
(B) $3\sqrt{3}$
(C) 6
(D) $\sqrt{37}$

21. The lengths of the legs of a particular right triangle are integers. The tangent of an acute angle in the triangle is equal to 0.8. Of the following, which could be the area of the triangle?

(A) 124 square inches
(B) 243 square inches
(C) 441 square inches
(D) 490 square inches

$$C(x) = x^3 + 5x^2 + 5x - 2$$

22. In the function above, which of the following can be assumed?

(A) $x + 3$ is a factor
(B) $x + 2$ is a factor
(C) $x - 5$ is a factor
(D) $x + 4$ is a factor

23. A manufacturer of basketballs charges \$24 for each basketball and sells 1,000 per week. The production control department estimates that for every \$1 discount, the manufacturer will sell an additional 100 basketballs. At what price will the manufacturer maximize revenue?

(A) \$19
(B) \$18
(C) \$17
(D) \$14

GO ON TO THE NEXT PAGE

24. Two types of peaches, classified as A and B, are being cultivated. An estimate of the number of peaches of type A, after a 30-day experiment, is approximately 5,200. If type A peaches grew 30% more quickly than type B, what is the estimated count of the type B peaches at the same 30-day mark?

(A) 3,900
(B) 4,000
(C) 4,200
(D) 4,500

Questions 25 and 26 refer to the following information.

A theater group began with a budget from the city of \$1.5 million. However, the group had seen its annual funding decline by 6.8% per year. By January 1, 2000, its annual budget was \$975,000.

25. What function models the declining balance of annual funding provided by the city?

(A) $f(x) = 1{,}500{,}000(1.068)^t$
(B) $f(x) = 1{,}500{,}000(.932)^t$
(C) $f(x) = 1{,}500{,}000(.068)^t$
(D) $f(x) = 1{,}500{,}000(-.068)^t$

26. Due to decreasing budgets, the city council sought to combine its theater group with another city's group on 1/1/2004. If the 6.8% decline in annual budget funds continued, and the two cities needed to have at least \$1.2 million, how much did the neighboring city have to provide to the budget?

(A) \$684,442
(B) \$521,862
(C) \$484,324
(D) \$464,356

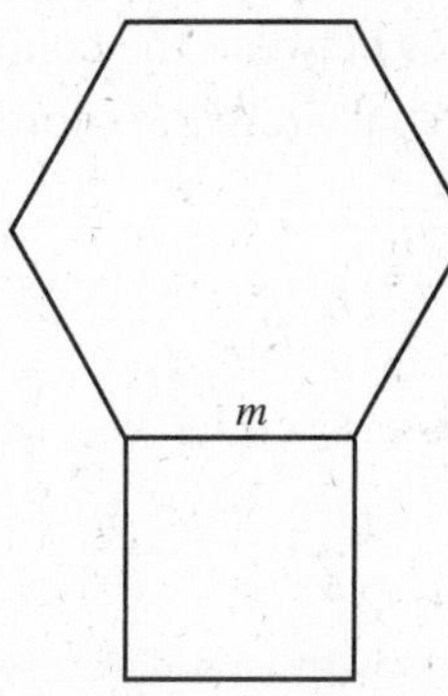

27. The figure above is a regular hexagon with sides of length m and a square with sides of length m as well. If the area of the hexagon is $324\sqrt{3}$ square inches, what is the area of the square in square inches?

(A) 108
(B) 216
(C) 256
(D) 324

$$3x + m = 5x - 6$$
$$3y + n = 5y - 6$$

28. In the equations shown above, m and n are constants. If $m = n + \frac{1}{2}$ which of the following statements is true?

(A) x is y plus $\frac{1}{4}$
(B) x is y minus $\frac{1}{4}$
(C) x is y minus 1
(D) x is y plus 1

GO ON TO THE NEXT PAGE

29. The distance between the points (7, 5) and (x, 4) is 8. What is/are the coordinate(s) of x?

(A) $7+3\sqrt{7}$
(B) $7-3\sqrt{7}$
(C) $3\pm\sqrt{7}$
(D) $7\pm3\sqrt{7}$

30. A scuba diving instructor charges $75 per lesson plus an additional fee for the use of her boat. The charge for the use of her boat varies directly with the square root of the time the boat is used. If a lesson plus 25 minutes of boat time costs $110, what is the total amount charged for a lesson that uses the boat for 36 minutes?

(A) $117
(B) $122
(C) $127
(D) $133

GO ON TO THE NEXT PAGE

Grid-in Response Directions

In questions 31–38, first solve the problem, and then enter your answer on the grid provided on the answer sheet. The instructions for entering your answers follow.

- First, write your answer in the boxes at the top of the grid.
- Second, grid your answer in the columns below the boxes.
- Use the fraction bar in the first row or the decimal point in the second row to enter fractions and decimals.

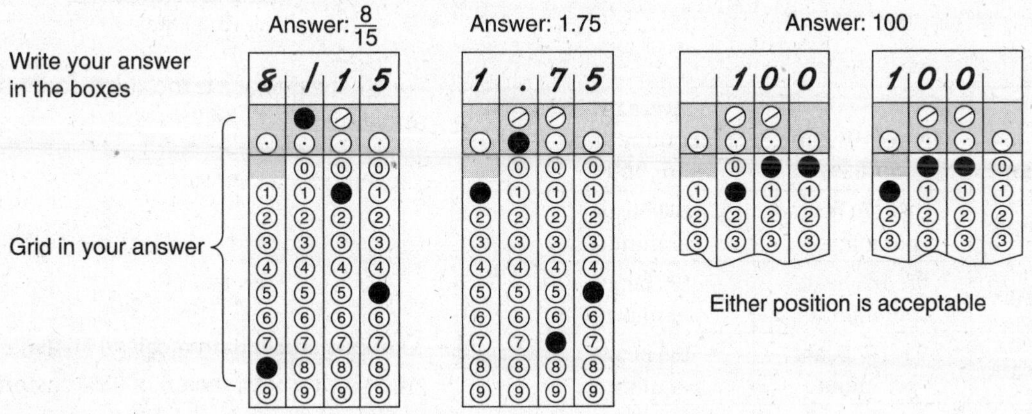

- Grid only one space in each column.
- Entering the answer in the boxes is recommended as an aid in gridding but is not required.
- The machine scoring your exam can read only what you grid, so you **must grid-in your answers correctly to get credit**.
- If a question has more than one correct answer, grid-in only one of them.
- The grid does not have a minus sign; so no answer can be negative.
- A mixed number *must* be converted to an improper fraction or a decimal before it is gridded. Enter $1\frac{1}{4}$ as $\frac{5}{4}$ or 1.25; the machine will interpret 11/4 as $\frac{11}{4}$ and mark it wrong.
- **All decimals must be entered as accurately as possible.** Here are three acceptable ways of gridding

$$\frac{3}{11} = 0.272727\ldots$$

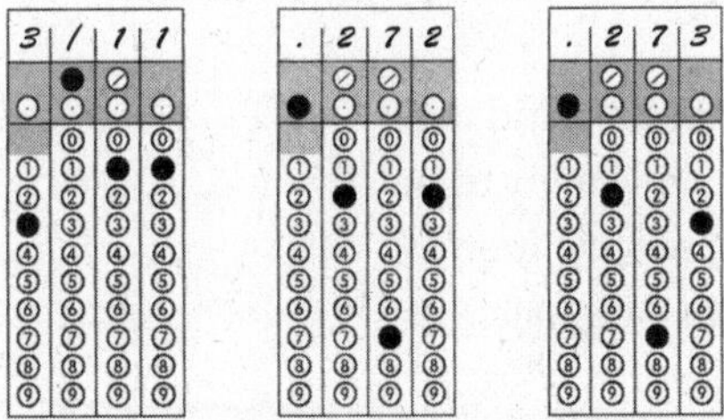

- Note that rounding to .273 is acceptable because you are using the full grid, but you would receive **no credit** for .3 or .27, because they are less accurate.

31. A college uses an auditorium for Psychology 101 lectures due to the class' large enrollment. The auditorium has 6 sections each with no fewer than 100 seats but no more than 150 seats. If every student in the Psychology class is present and the auditorium is filled, what is one possible value of the number of students in the class?

Age	Target HR Zone 50–85%	Average Maximum Heart Rate, 100%
20 years	100–170 beats per minute	200 beats per minute
30 years	95–162 beats per minute	190 beats per minute
35 years	93–157 beats per minute	185 beats per minute
40 years	90–153 beats per minute	180 beats per minute

32. The chart above indicates data relating to heart beat rates for adults between the ages of 20 and 40 as put forth by the American Medical Association. If a woman aged 35 has a heart rate that is the mean of the extremes of the Target HR Zone for her age, what percent of the maximum heart rate is that measure (round to the nearest tenth of a percent)?

33. If the height of a cylinder is doubled and the length of its radius is tripled, how many times greater is the volume of the larger cylinder compared to the volume of the original?

34. In the xy-plane, the point (–4, 8) lies on the graph of the function g. If $g(x) = 2b + x^3$, where b is a constant, what is the value of b?

$$f(x) = \frac{1}{(x-3)^2 + 6(x-3) + 9}$$

35. For what value of x is the above function f undefined?

36. A supermarket chain received an average grade (arithmetic mean) of 65% customer satisfaction from 10 recent customer surveys. The chain manager wants to earn at least an 80% rating from its first 20 customer surveys. What is the lowest score the 17th survey can receive and still achieve the 80% satisfaction rate from its first 20 surveys? (Omit percent sign)

GO ON TO THE NEXT PAGE

Questions 37 and 38 refer to the information below.

Nutritionists recommend daily consumption of 4,700 milligrams of potassium. Men generally consume 3,200 milligrams per day and women consume about 2,300 milligrams per day. Below is a list of potassium-rich foods as recommended by nutritional experts.

Foods with Potassium	Serving Size	Potassium (mg)
Apricots, dried	10 halves	407
Avocados, raw	1 ounce	180
Bananas, raw	1 cup	594
Beets, cooked	1 cup	519
Brussel sprouts, cooked	1 cup	504
Cantaloupe	1 cup	494
Dates, dry	5 dates	271
Figs, dry	2 figs	271
Kiwi fruit, raw	1 medium	252
Lima beans	1 cup	955
Melons, honeydew	1 cup	461
Milk, fat free or skim	1 cup	407
Nectarines	1 nectarine	288
Orange juice	1 cup	496
Oranges	1 orange	237
Pears (fresh)	1 pear	208
Peanuts dry roasted, unsalted	1 ounce	187
Potatoes, baked	1 potato	1081
Prune juice	1 cup	707
Prunes, dried	1 cup	828
Raisins	1 cup	1089
Spinach, cooked	1 cup	839
Tomato products, canned sauce	1 cup	909
Winter squash	1 cup	896
Yogurt, plain, skim milk	8 ounces	579

37. Jake read that the headaches he was enduring after running were caused by potassium depletion. Although he was consuming 3,200 milligrams of potassium daily, he was told he needed at least 10% more potassium than was recommended by nutritionists. To accrue this amount, Jake has decided to consume an extra potato and a cup of lima beans in his daily diet. If he consumes these extra items each day, how much more potassium will he consume than is recommended for his augmented need of this nutrient?

38. Joan consumes 22,400 milligrams of potassium each week. She has decided to add a serving of spinach and a glass of orange juice each day. If she maintains this addition to her daily diet, how many more milligrams of potassium will Joan need to reach the recommended milligrams per week?

If there is still time remaining, you may review your answers.

PRACTICE TEST 6

ESSAY (OPTIONAL)

Directions: This is your opportunity to show that you can read and understand a passage and write an analysis of that passage. Be sure your essay demonstrates a clear and logical analysis of the passage, using precise language.

On the actual test, you will write your essay on the lines provided in your answer booklet; for now, write your essay on lined paper. Remember to write or print legibly so that others can read what you've written.

You have 50 minutes to read the essay and write a response to the prompt provided.

Carefully read the passage below. As you read, think about how Walter T. Stace makes use of

- *reasoning* to develop an argument
- *evidence* to support assertions made
- *language* to persuade the reader

From Walter T. Stace, *The Concept of Morals*, Macmillan Publishers, 1962.

1 According to the ethical absolutists there is but one eternally true and valid moral code. This moral code applies with rigid impartiality to all men. What is a duty for me must likewise be a duty for you. And this will be true whether you are an Englishman, a Chinaman, or a Hottentot. If cannibalism is an abomination in England or America, it is an abomination in central Africa, notwithstanding that the African may think otherwise. The fact that he sees nothing wrong in his cannibal practices does not make them for him morally right. They are as much contrary to morality for him as they are for us. The only difference is that he is an ignorant savage who does not know this. There is not one law for one man or race of men, another for another. There is not one moral standard for Europeans, another for Indians, another for Chinese. There is but one law, one standard, one morality, for all men. And this standard, this law, is absolute and unvarying.

2 Moreover, as the one moral law extends its dominion over all the corners of the Earth, so too it is not limited in its application by any considerations of time or period. That which is right now was right in the centuries of Greece and Rome, nay, in the very ages of the cave man. That which is evil now was evil then. If slavery is morally wicked today, it was morally wicked among the ancient Athenians, notwithstanding that their greatest men accepted it as a necessary condition of human society. Their opinion did not make slavery a moral good for them. It only showed that they were, in spite of their otherwise noble conceptions, ignorant of what is truly right and good in this matter.

3 The ethical absolutist recognizes as a fact that moral customs and moral ideas differ from country to country and from age to age. This indeed seems manifest and not to be disputed. We think slavery morally wrong, the Greeks thought it morally unobjectionable. The inhabitants of New Guinea certainly have very different moral ideas from ours. But the fact that the Greeks or the inhabitants of New Guinea think something right does not make it right, even for them. Nor does the fact that we think the same things wrong make them wrong. They are in themselves either right or wrong. What we have to do is to discover which they are. What anyone thinks makes no difference. It is here just as it is in matters of physical science. We believe the Earth to be a globe. Our ancestors may have thought it flat. This does not show that it was flat, and is now a globe. What it shows is that men having in other ages been ignorant about the shape of the Earth have now learned the truth. So if the Greeks thought slavery morally legitimate, this does not indicate that it was for them and in that age morally legitimate, but rather that they were ignorant of the truth of the matter.

4 The ethical absolutist is not indeed committed to the opinion that his own, or our own, moral code is the true one. Theoretically at least he might hold that slavery is ethically justifiable, that the Greeks knew better than we do about this, that ignorance of the true morality lies with us and not with them. All that he is actually committed to is the opinion that, whatever the true moral code may be, it is always the same for all men in all ages. (His view is not at all inconsistent with the belief that humanity has still much to learn in moral matters.) If anyone were to assert that in five hundred years the moral conceptions of the present day will appear as barbarous to the people of that age as the moral conceptions of the middle ages appear to us now, he need not deny it. If anyone were to assert that the ethics of Christianity are by no means final, and will be superseded in future ages by vastly nobler moral ideals, he need not deny this either. For it is of the essence of his creed to believe that morality is in some sense objective, not man-made, not produced by human opinion; that its principles are real truths about which men have to learn—just as they have to learn about the shape or the world—about which they may have been ignorant in the past, and about which therefore they may well be ignorant now.

Write an essay explaining how Walter Stace constructs an argument to convince the reader that someone who believes in ethical absolutism must also believe that the same morality applies to everyone, everywhere, during all times. Describe and analyze how Stace uses one or more of the elements of persuasive writing listed in the box on page 500 to strengthen his argument. You may also discuss other writing techniques used by the author.

Your essay should not state your opinion on the topic discussed in the passage, but rather analyze how Stace constructs an argument to persuade the reader.

ANSWER KEY
Practice Test 6

Section 1: Reading

1. **B**
2. **A**
3. **D**
4. **A**
5. **B**
6. **D**
7. **D**
8. **C**
9. **B**
10. **B**
11. **D**
12. **B**
13. **C**
14. **C**
15. **C**
16. **D**
17. **C**
18. **D**
19. **D**
20. **C**
21. **D**
22. **D**
23. **A**
24. **C**
25. **B**
26. **C**
27. **D**
28. **A**
29. **C**
30. **B**
31. **C**
32. **C**
33. **D**
34. **A**
35. **C**
36. **A**
37. **D**
38. **C**
39. **D**
40. **D**
41. **A**
42. **C**
43. **C**
44. **A**
45. **C**
46. **B**
47. **C**
48. **A**
49. **D**
50. **A**
51. **D**
52. **B**

Number Correct ______

Number Incorrect ______

Section 2: Writing and Language

1. **C**
2. **A**
3. **D**
4. **C**
5. **B**
6. **C**
7. **D**
8. **B**
9. **C**
10. **A**
11. **A**
12. **C**
13. **D**
14. **B**
15. **D**
16. **A**
17. **D**
18. **B**
19. **C**
20. **C**
21. **D**
22. **A**
23. **B**
24. **D**
25. **C**
26. **A**
27. **B**
28. **C**
29. **B**
30. **D**
31. **B**
32. **C**
33. **B**
34. **D**
35. **C**
36. **D**
37. **A**
38. **D**
39. **C**
40. **A**
41. **D**
42. **B**
43. **C**
44. **B**

Number Correct ______

Number Incorrect ______

ANSWER KEY
Practice Test 6

Section 3: Math (No Calculator)

1. **A**
2. **C**
3. **D**
4. **B**
5. **A**
6. **C**
7. **B**
8. **C**
9. **A**
10. **B**
11. **A**
12. **D**
13. **B**
14. **D**
15. **D**

16. **54**

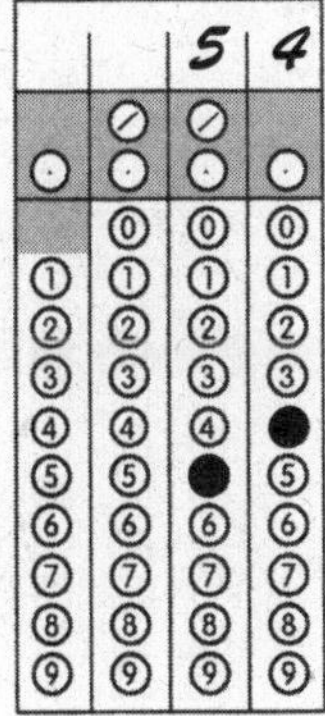

17. **6**

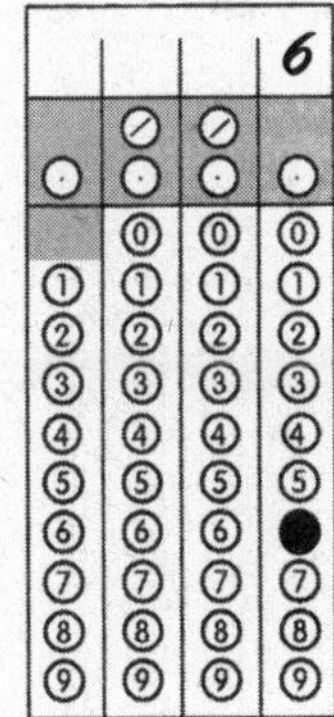

18. **4**

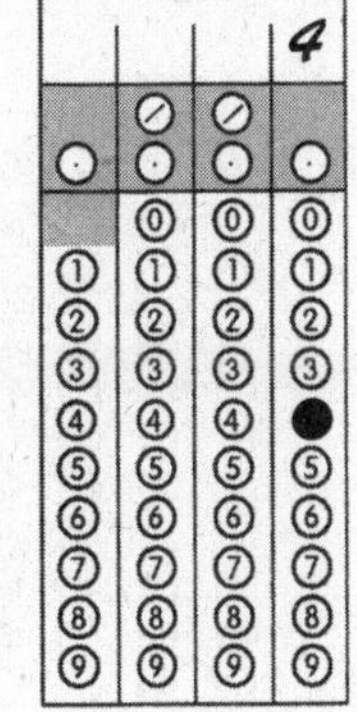

19. **40**

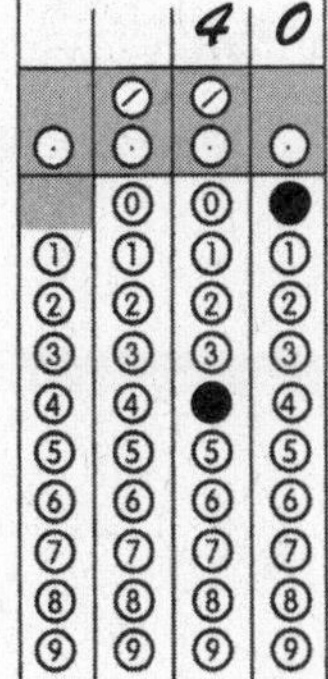

20. **243**

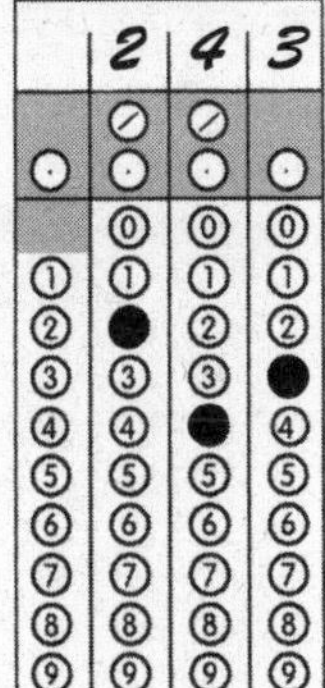

Number Correct ______

Number Incorrect ______

PRACTICE TEST 6

ANSWER KEY
Practice Test 6

Section 4: Math (Calculator)

1. **D**	7. **D**	13. **B**	19. **B**	25. **B**
2. **C**	8. **C**	14. **C**	20. **D**	26. **D**
3. **B**	9. **C**	15. **B**	21. **D**	27. **B**
4. **A**	10. **C**	16. **C**	22. **B**	28. **A**
5. **C**	11. **A**	17. **B**	23. **C**	29. **D**
6. **B**	12. **A**	18. **C**	24. **B**	30. **A**

31. **Answers may vary.** **$600 \leq x \leq 900$**

32. **67.6**

33. **18**

34. **36**

35. **0**

36. **50**

37. **66**

38. **1,155**

Number Correct ______

Number Incorrect ______

PRACTICE TEST 6

SCORE ANALYSIS

Reading and Writing Test

Section 1: Reading ________ = ________ (A)
correct raw score

Section 2: Writing ________ = ________ (B)
correct raw score

To find your Reading and Writing test scores, consult the chart below: find the ranges in which your raw scores lie and read across to find the ranges of your test scores.

________ + ________ = ________ (C)
range of reading test scores | range of writing test scores | range of reading + writing test scores

To find the range of your Reading and Writing Scaled Score, multiply (C) by 10.

Test Scores for the Reading and Writing Sections

Reading Raw Score	Writing Raw Score	Test Score
44-52	39-44	35-40
36-43	33-38	31-34
30-35	28-32	28-30
24-29	22-27	24-27
19-23	17-21	21-23
14-18	13-16	19-20
9-13	9-12	16-18
5-8	5-8	13-15
less than 5	less than 5	10-12

Math Test

Section 3: ________ = ________ (D)
correct raw score

Section 4: ________ = ________ (E)
correct raw score

Total Math raw score: (D) + (E) = ________

To find your Math Scaled Score, consult the chart below: find the range in which your raw score lies and read across to find the range for your scaled score.

Scaled Scores for the Math Test

Raw Score	Scaled Score
50-58	700-800
44-49	650-690
38-43	600-640
32-37	550-590
26-31	500-540

Raw Score	Scaled Score
20-25	450-490
15-19	400-440
11-14	350-390
7-10	300-340
less than 7	200-290

ANSWER EXPLANATIONS

Section 1: Reading Test

1. **(B)** No information about the cause of hotspots is given in Passage 1. The author concentrates on explaining what J. Tuzo Wilson's "hotspot" theory says is caused by hotspots. Information is provided explaining all of the other choices.

2. **(A)** Wilson's theory predicts that a hotspot exists "beneath the present-day position of the Island of Hawaii" (also called the "Big Island") (lines 26–27). The fact that "new volcanic rock is continually being formed" (lines 57–58) suggests that the "Big Island" is located over a hotspot because it is consistent with the hotspot theory.

3. **(D)** The author says, "The vast majority of earthquakes and volcanic eruptions occur near tectonic plate boundaries, but there are some exceptions" (lines 1–3). The passage describes how the "hotspot" theory explains at least some of these exceptions. The "hotspot" theory explains how volcanoes form in the interior of tectonic plates.

4. **(A)** This is the best choice because the passage says that Wilson first "*noted that* in certain locations . . . volcanism has been active for very long periods of time" (lines 13–16). Wilson then "*reasoned* [that] if . . . hotspots existed below the plates that would provide . . . energy . . . to sustain volcanism" (lines 17–21). Finally, he "*hypothesized*" (line 22) about how volcanism occurred in a specific area, creating an island volcano, and about how plate movement affects this process. Note that the process of reasoning Wilson used was *deduction*—reasoning that infers something from a general principle.

5. **(B)** The author describes the "hotspot" theory: "[Wilson suggested that] continuing plate movement eventually carries the island beyond the hotspot, cutting it off from the magma source, and volcanism ceases. As one island volcano becomes extinct, another develops over the hotspot, and the cycle is repeated" (lines 37–42). The final paragraph describes how the structure and age of the Hawaiian Islands support the hotspot theory.

6. **(D)** As mentioned above, theses lines provide the best evidence for the answer to question 5.

7. **(D)** The author says, "They [a team of scientists] deployed a large network of sea-floor seismometers . . . , opening up a window into the Earth" (lines 68–72). The word "window" as it is used here means *a means of observing.*

8. **(C)** It can be inferred that the earthquakes mentioned in line 102 were largely or entirely unrelated to geological activity on or near the Hawaiian Islands because the purpose of recording the seismic waves from the earthquakes was to "determine whether seismic waves travel more slowly through hot rock as they pass beneath Hawaii" (lines 97–100).

9. **(C)** The focus of the passage is on efforts that have been made by scientists to discover the processes that created the Hawaiian Islands. The sentence in which the word *resolve* (lines 113–116) appears is about a difficulty in scientifically establishing the facts about the processes that created the islands' "deep structure."

10. **(B)** Both passages are concerned mainly with what causes volcanic islands to form in the middle of tectonic plates when both the theory of tectonic plates and observation of volcanic activity show that most volcanic activity occurs near places where two tectonic plates meet. Passage 1 describes a theory to explain this, called the "hotspot" theory,

which examines the case of Hawaii as a good example of the phenomenon. Passage 2 describes efforts to confirm this theory, again focusing on the Hawaiian Islands as an example of the phenomenon.

11. **(D)** Much of Passage 1 describes the hotspot theory in considerable detail. The final paragraph describes the geology of the Hawaiian Islands, providing evidence for the theory. Most of Passage 2 is devoted to describing PLUME, an experiment that produced strong evidence for the hotspot theory described in Passage 1.

12. **(B)** In lines 4–21 ("It is in . . . a vast veil."), the author describes how as a child he came to realize that black people are treated differently than white people and are not accepted by them.

13. **(C)** The author says, "The exchange was merry, till one girl . . . refused my card . . . . Then it dawned upon me . . . that I was different from the others; or like, mayhap, in heart and life and longing, but shut out from their world by a vast veil" (lines 14–21).

14. **(C)** The author says, "With other black . . . mine own house?" (lines 36–43).

15. **(C)** These lines provide the best evidence for the answer to the previous question.

16. **(D)** In lines 43–50 ("The shades of . . . of blue above") the author describes how "the prison-house closed round us all." It can be inferred that the prison house symbolizes the prevailing attitudes and limited opportunities available to both whites and blacks. The author says that the prison's walls were "stubborn"—that is, difficult, but not impossible to scale—to the white people but "unscalable" to blacks.

17. **(C)** The author says, "the Negro is . . . gifted with second-sight in this American world . . . a world which . . . only lets him see himself through the revelation of the other world" (lines 52–58).

18. **(D)** We can infer that end means *goal* in this context because the author is stating what he believes should be the goal of the American Negro.

19. **(D)** The author does not appeal to authority. He makes use of all the others.

20. **(C)** This would be the most appropriate title for the passage because this is the author's main concern in the passage—how, as he says in lines 70–72, "The history of this strife,—this longing to attain self-conscious manhood, to merge his double self into a better and truer self."

21. **(D)** The phrase "latent genius" is not symbolic. It refers to intellectual abilities that are not being used. The other choices are used symbolically.

22. **(D)** In context, we can infer that *humoring* means "indulging" because it is stated that Jim is worth a lot to his employers. Thus, they would be likely to indulge him.

23. **(A)** *Fidelity* means *loyalty* and a "fiend" is a *devil.*

24. **(C)** *Drily humorous* is the best choice because the narrator is indirectly and somewhat humorously making the point that not many people are suited by character or temperament for an occupation that calls for qualities such as kindness and patience.

25. **(B)** This can be inferred from information provided in the passage: "Nevertheless . . . he would throw up the job suddenly and depart" (lines 53–55); "His incognito, which . . . go

to another . . . ." (lines 64–70); "He retreated in . . . casually but inevitably" (lines 74–76). We can infer that the "fact" mentioned in line 66 refers to a secret about Jim.

26. **(C)** These lines provide the best evidence for the answer to the previous question. "The fact broke through the incognito" means a fact about him becomes known despite his attempt to conceal it and his true identity.

27. **(D)** The word "incognito" means *false identity*. The phrase "as many holes as a sieve" means that the false identity did not do a good job of keeping Jim's real identity secret.

28. **(A)** This can be inferred from the reason that is given for Jim's leaving seaports: "When the fact . . . go to another" (lines 67–70).

29. **(C)** Jim is described as "powerfully built" (line 2) and "very popular" (line 15).

30. **(B)** These lines provide the best evidence for the answer to the previous question.

31. **(C)** The word "casually" is used to describe the manner in which "the fact" follows Jim. A secret about Jim eventually becomes known in the seaport in which he is working. The word "casually" describes how the secret becomes known after various intervals of time.

32. **(C)** The author is discussing American Indian worship in the past. He says "It [the worship] was silent" (lines 9–10). By "ascended to God" we can infer that he means they did not literally ascend to God but rather that their souls drew close in worship. This is supported by the fact that he says "They believed that He is *nearer to us* in solitude" (lines 13–14).

33. **(D)** Because the author is concerned with the religious beliefs of Indians in the past it is reasonable to infer that he uses the word "original" in line 1 to suggest that these beliefs have changed from what they were in earlier times.

34. **(A)** In lines 26–43 ("There . . . cathedral!") the author describes how God can be perceived in many forms. It is reasonable to infer that the author uses a variety of capitalized names for God to reinforce the idea that God has many forms. Whether God is called "the Unseen" or "Him" does not matter because words can never convey His true nature.

35. **(C)** In the second paragraph (lines 8–25) the author contrasts traditional American Indian religious belief and practice with that of organized religions like Christianity. This comparison portrays Indian religion as superior because it does not have priests, creeds, preaching, proselytizing, or persecution.

36. **(A)** The author is describing the American Indians' experience of God. In lines 28–35 ("He . . . sky!") he describes where Indians believed God could "be met face to face." This "meeting" of man and God is, presumably, spiritual and emotional rather than literal, so the author most likely uses an exclamation mark to help convey to the reader a sense of the religious ecstasy experienced by Indians. The use of an exclamation mark in the next line ("He . . . cathedral!"—lines 35–43) conveys a similar emotion.

37. **(D)** *Rhapsodic* is the most accurate word to describe the language of the third paragraph because *rhapsodic* means "extravagantly enthusiastic; ecstatic." As mentioned in the explanation of the previous question, the author is trying to convey the sense of ecstasy experienced by the Indians. He uses extravagant poetic language to help convey this sense of ecstasy.

38. **(C)** In the fifth paragraph ("The . . . existence"—lines 51–73) the author describes the *bambeday* which would be an important event in the life of a young man. The word *epoch* in context thus means "an important event."

39. **(D)** The author's description of American Indians is very positive, so he would be likely to agree with this statement. There is no evidence for choice (A) and choice (B); choice (C) is rebutted in lines 74–90 ("The . . . men").

40. **(D)** This provides the best evidence for the answer to the previous question.

41. **(A)** A *sage* is a "wise person," and *untutored* means "lacking formal education."

42. **(C)** A "hothouse" in this context is *an environment conducive to vigorous development.* Thus, a "grammatical hothouse" is an environment in which a great effort is made to teach children about grammar.

43. **(C)** It can be inferred from the fact that the author's brother "was raised in the same grammatical hothouse" (lines 10–11) as the author that he would, like the author, be unwilling to consider using substitute words for "his."

44. **(A)** A "neologism" is a *new word.* The author is discussing new words that have been suggested to replace the word "his" used to refer to both males and females.

45. **(C)** The author quotes her father to illustrate the fact that in the past men "viewed the world . . . of artistic creation as a world of males" (lines 56–59). She says she doesn't believe her father was a misogynist (a man who hates women), but that he and other men in the past didn't "really see women" (lines 63–64). In context, therefore, "see women" means *take women seriously.* Clues to the meaning are "blind spot" (line 65) and "invisibility" (line 65).

46. **(B)** In context the word "reactionary" means *extremely conservative.* The author's "reactionary self" would most likely write "his book" because as a conservative she would follow the traditional and accepted practice.

47. **(C)** The author uses the word "slowed" figuratively to mean the sentence would not have been as graceful and effective if E.B. White had used the word "woman" instead of the word "girl."

48. **(A)** In the last paragraph (lines 99–101) the author argues that although "changing our language to make men and women equal has a cost . . . that doesn't mean it shouldn't be done." In the phrase "heedless grace" the word "grace" refers to *elegant writing* and the word "heedless" means *unconcerned.* The author is saying that we should be sad about losing the opportunity to write elegantly, but that we should accept its necessity.

49. **(D)** The author is suggesting that we should accept the necessity of changing our language so that it isn't sexist, but that doing so will undoubtedly be difficult for some people to do graciously. The word "muster" in context means *summon up* and has a connotation of "exerting great effort to summon up." The author is being somewhat jocular in the last sentence of the passage.

50. **(A)** As mentioned in the explanation of question 49, the author is being somewhat humorous in the last sentence of the passage. We can infer that she mainly uses the expression "his'er" to remind us that every writer has to deal with the His'er Problem and

must decide how to do so. The author's use of "his'er," although humorous, suggests that she might even consider using this expression she thinks is "hideous" (line 7) regularly.

51. **(D)** The author would almost certainly agree with this statement because she argues, "Changing our language has a cost . . . That doesn't mean it shouldn't be done" (lines 99–101).

52. **(B)** The author would almost certainly change the sentence so that it doesn't suggest that all writers are all female or all male. Choice (A) does this but would not generally be considered graceful, a quality valued by the author. She probably wouldn't like choice (C) because it uses "his'er," which she believes is "hideous" (line 7). She would probably reject choice (D) as unnecessarily wordy. Choice (B) changes the sentence so that the His'er Problem is avoided.

Section 2: Writing and Language Test

1. **(C)** Choices (B) and (D) create run-on sentences. Choice (B) is grammatical but somewhat awkward. Choice (C) is a better choice because it creates two sentences, each of which clearly expresses an idea.

2. **(A)** Choices (C) and (D) do not create grammatical sentences. Choice (B) does not agree in number with the subject, species. Choice (A) is correct because the verb "cause" (which is the singular form of the verb) agrees in number with the subject, "*P. Falciparum* and *P. Vivax*," which is plural.

3. **(D)** This is the best choice because the part of the sentence after the comma gives contrasting information to that given in the part of the sentence before the comma. The first part of the sentence tells about "the majority" of cases, whereas the second part tells about less common cases (signaled by the word "also"). The subordinating conjunction *although* creates a dependent clause, effectively linking it to the preceding independent clause. Choice (A) and choice (C) make little sense. Choice (B) creates a run-on sentence.

4. **(C)** This choice is correct because it creates a clear and grammatical sentence in which the participial phrase beginning with "concerning" and ending with "States" modifies the preceding noun, "reports." Choice (A) creates a run-on sentence. Choice (B) and choice (D) are awkward and wordy.

5. **(B)** This is correct. The context requires the simple past tense because the sentence is about cases that occurred "in 2010."

6. **(C)** This is the best choice because it is reasonable that it would have been difficult to understand two of the many cases. In context *cryptic* means "puzzling."

7. **(D)** This is the best choice. In context *acquisition* means "the act of acquiring," which makes good sense because the context is a description of information about where people contracted malaria. Choice (A), *procurement*, means "to obtain by effort," and so is not correct.

8. **(B)** This can be seen from the graph. Cases peaked first in January, declined, and rose to a higher peak in July.

9. **(C)** This can be seen from the graph. Cases peaked in August, declined, and then reached a much smaller peak in November.

10. **(A)** This is the best choice. The independent clause after the semicolon provides additional information directly relevant to that provided in the independent clause before the semicolon. Choices (C) and (D) create run-on sentences. Choice (B) is not as good as choice (A) because the colon is not normally used this way.

11. **(A)** This is the correct answer because paragraph 5 provides more information on the main topic discussed in paragraph 4, which is imported cases of malaria in the United States.

12. **(C)** All of the choices are grammatically correct, but choice (C), unlike the others, is both idiomatic and makes good sense in context.

13. **(D)** *Bolster*, meaning "increase" in context, is the best choice. It makes good sense because there are already teachers, but more are needed.

14. **(B)** This is the only choice that is grammatical and makes good sense.

15. **(D)** The correct answer can be determined from the information in the bar graph.

16. **(A)** Choice (A) is correct because the rest of the paragraph only discusses achieving UPE by 2020 or 2030.

17. **(D)** The correct answer can be determined from the information in the bar graph.

18. **(B)** The correct answer can be determined from the information in the bar graph.

19. **(C)** This is the best choice because sentence 2 explains the reason referred to in sentence 1. Also, sentence 2 provides an appropriate transition from the preceding paragraph and a good introduction for the paragraph that it is in.

20. **(C)** Choices (A) and (B) create run-on sentences. Choice (D) does not make good sense. Choice (C) creates a complete sentence that makes good sense. The previous sentence described the situation in sub-Saharan Africa. The phrase "across the region" refers back to the situation there, providing a transition to the next sentence.

21. **(D)** *Deteriorate*, which means "worsen" in context, is the best choice. The answer can be inferred from the context, which describes factors that are predicted to cause the situation to worsen in sub-Saharan Africa.

22. **(A)** This is the correct choice because the information given after the colon gives detailed information about the problem that will be caused by "growing school-age populations" mentioned in the independent clause before the colon.

23. **(B)** This is the correct choice because it creates a sentence that makes good sense and is grammatical. The modal verb may be used here to express a certain measure of likelihood that the "general standard of living" will be high in the future. Choices (A) and (D) are grammatically correct but do not make good sense in context. Choice (C) is not grammatical.

24. **(D)** This is the only choice that is grammatical and makes good sense. "Had," the simple past tense of the verb "have," is used to describe America's past.

25. **(C)** Choice (A) creates a run-on sentence. Choice (C) corrects this error by creating two complete sentences. Choice (D) is grammatical but awkward and wordy.

26. **(A)** This is the correct choice because the context requires a word meaning "in spite of that," which *however* means here. Note that although the punctuation is a bit unusual, it

is nevertheless correct. The author uses dashes to highlight one area (industrial growth) of America's growth.

27. **(B)** This sentence should be added here because in the previous sentence the writer said that political rights, while vital, are not sufficient. This sentence states what else is essential—"economic security and independence"—and provides a transition to the rest of the passage.

28. **(C)** All of the other choices are not grammatical and do not make good sense. In Choice (C) the modal verb "can" is used with the linking verb "be" to indicate possibility.

29. **(B)** The writer is describing "a second Bill of Rights under which a new basis of security and prosperity can be established," so *remunerative* (well-paying) makes good sense. Choice (A) is incorrect because a job cannot be *solvent.* Choice (C) is acceptable, but is not as appropriate in context as choice (B).

30. **(D)** This is the best choice because the word in this blank and "competition" are the objects of a prepositional phrase beginning with "from," so these two words should be the same part of speech (in this case, nouns).

31. **(B)** This is the correct choice because it creates two clear and grammatical sentences. Choice (A) is incorrect because the sentence beginning with "Since" is not a complete sentence. Choices (C) and (D) do not make good sense.

32. **(C)** Choices (A) and (B) do not create grammatical sentences. The present perfect tense is appropriate in context because the sentence describes events in a fairly recent period of American history that are continuing at present.

33. **(B)** This is the correct choice because it creates a grammatical sentence that makes good sense in the context of the paragraph. Note that the preposition *for* is being used here to mean *because.*

34. **(D)** This is the correct choice because it creates a grammatical sentence that makes good sense. *Whose* is a relative pronoun beginning an adjective clause that modifies the noun "club."

35. **(C)** This is the correct choice. It creates a sentence in which the participial phrase "built for the purpose" modifies the noun "theater."

36. **(D)** *Could hear* is the correct choice. In context *could hear* means "were able to hear," which makes good sense.

37. **(A)** All of the words are related to speech. However, choice (A) is correct because *declamation* in context means "forthright projection of words set to music."

38. **(D)** Choices (A) and (B) are incorrect because they create a run-on sentence. Choice (D) is correct because *forgetting* is the present participle of "forget." This creates a participial phrase beginning with "forgetting" and ending with "wished," which is grammatical.

39. **(C)** This is the best choice because sentence 6 is about a contrast with what was said in sentence 3. This contrast is signaled by the word "however."

40. **(A)** This is the correct choice. It creates a clear and grammatical sentence in which the word "projecting" is a present participle and the first word of a participial phrase that modifies the noun "building."

41. **(D)** All of the other choices are not grammatical because they create run-on sentences. This choice creates a clear and grammatical sentence in which the conjunction "but" joins the dependent clause beginning with "which" to the preceding dependent clause. The word "but" is used here to signal a contrast with what was said earlier in the sentence about the actors.

42. **(B)** This is the best choice because it makes sense that the dresses were moved to "the cadence [beat] of the music."

43. **(C)** Choice (A) is a run-on sentence. Choice (D) makes little sense and is not grammatical. Choice (B) is grammatical and makes good sense. However, choice (C) is the better choice because it is more appropriate to use a semicolon than a colon after the word "audience" because the independent clause after the punctuation elaborates on the audience, not on *N* drama.

44. **(B)** Choices (A) and (B) can be used to describe sound, but choices (C) and (D) cannot be so used. A *crackle* is a sharper sound than a *rustle* and is not as appropriate as *rustle* in context because the sound of pages being turned is not sharp. A *rustle* is "a low crisp rubbing sound," which is an appropriate description of the pages being turned by the ladies.

Section 3: Math Test (No Calculator)

1. **(A)** Round 44% to 40% and 18% to 20%. Express both as decimals and multiply them by 250,000,000.

$$(.4)(.2)(250{,}000{,}000) = 20{,}000{,}000$$

Answer choice (A), 20 million, is closest to this figure.

2. **(C)** Solve for $2k$.

$$\frac{2k}{7} = 30$$
$$2k = 210$$
$$2k + 7 = 217$$

You do not have to solve for k in this problem.

3. **(D)** Parallel lines have the same slope. Since the slope of $y = \frac{5}{9}x + 7$ is $\frac{5}{9}$, then a line parallel to it will also have a slope that measures $\frac{5}{9}$. Perpendicular lines have slopes that are the opposite reciprocals of one another. Thus, a line perpendicular to a line with slope $\frac{5}{9}$ will have a slope of $-\frac{9}{5}$.

4. **(B)** Tina starts each month with 360 sinks to repair. As each week passes, Tina will have 88 fewer sinks to repair within the month.

5. **(A)** $(-4x^3y - xy^3 + 4x) - (7x - 4xy^3 + 2x^2)$
Combine like terms.

$$-xy^3 - (-4xy^3) = 3xy^3$$
$$4x - 7x = -3x$$

PRACTICE TEST 6

There are no other like terms so arrange the expression as shown in choice (A).

$$-4x^3y + 3xy^3 - 2x^2 - 3x$$

6. **(C)** Use the ratio $\frac{62.5 \text{ pounds}}{1 \text{ cubic foot}}$ to find the weight of a liquid that has a specific gravity of 3.

$$\frac{62.5}{1} = \frac{x}{3}$$
$$(3)(62.5) = x$$
$$187.5 = x$$

7. **(B)** Raise each side of the equation to the $\frac{2}{3}$ power to isolate *a*.

$$(a^{\frac{3}{2}})^{\frac{2}{3}} = 64^{\frac{2}{3}}$$
$$a = 16$$
$$\sqrt{16} = 4$$

8. **(C)** Note that when $x = -3$, $y = 0$. When a function intersects the *x*-axis in the *xy*-plane then $y = 0$; that *x* value is a root of the function. We therefore conclude that $x = -3$ is a root of the function and adding 3 to both sides yields $x + 3 = 0$.

9. **(A)** $\frac{m^{x^2}}{m^{y^2}} = m^{36}$

When dividing like terms, subtract the exponents.

$$m^{x^2 - y^2} = m^{36}$$

Since the bases are the same, drop m to get $x^2 - y^2 = 36$. Factor by using the difference of squares.

$$(x + y)(x - y) = 36$$

It was given in the question that $x + y = 9$, so $x - y$ must equal 4 because $9 \times 4 = 36$.

10. **(B)** After the first month of paying off 20% of his student loan, Sean's remaining balance looks like this.

$$p - .2p = .8p$$

Sean's loan balance after one month was $.8p$. He now must pay off 20% of the $.8p$ that remains as the loan balance.

$$.8p - (.2)(.8p) = .64p$$

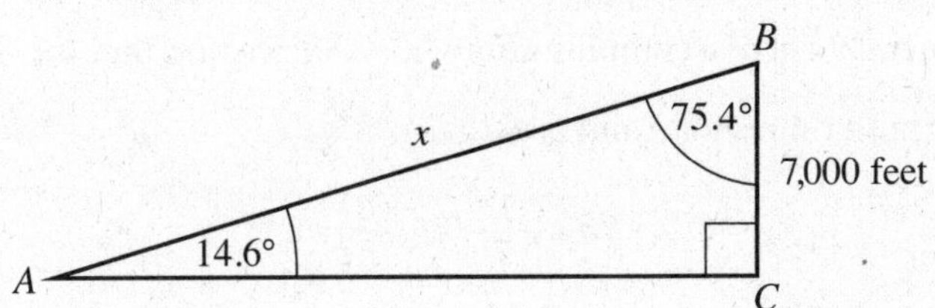

11. **(A)** The descent of the airplane and its eventual landing point can be depicted in the figure above. Although the angle for his line of sight to the ground is 75.4°, none of the other answer choices uses that ratio correctly. Since a triangle measures 180°, we can also use $\angle A$, which measures 14.6°. From that perspective, we know BC is 7,000 feet, $\angle A$ measures 14.6°, and the flight trajectory is unknown. We know the measure of the angle and the opposite side and we want to know the measure of the hypotenuse. The sine is found by using the formula $\frac{\text{opposite side}}{\text{hypotenuse}}$, so we arrive at $\sin 14.6 = \frac{7000}{x}$.

12. **(D)** This problem can be solved by factoring or using the quadratic equation.

$$\frac{-b \pm \sqrt{b^2 - 4ac}}{2a}$$

$$a = 4 \quad b = -2 \quad c = -6$$

$$\frac{-(-2) \pm \sqrt{(-2)^2 - 4(4)(-6)}}{2(4)}$$

$$\frac{2 \pm \sqrt{4 - (-96)}}{8}$$

$$\frac{2 \pm 10}{8}$$

$$\frac{3}{2}, -1$$

The sum of the roots, -1 and $\frac{3}{2}$, is $\frac{1}{2}$.

13. **(B)** The sum of the angles above and below the line are each 180°. Use that information to solve for both x and y.

$$3x = 180$$
$$x = 60$$
$$4y = 180$$
$$y = 45$$

Inputting 60 and 45 for x and y, respectively, yields $105 \div 30 = 3.5$.

14. **(D)** In order to rewrite $\frac{6-4i}{2+4i}$ in the form of $a + bi$, multiply the denominator and numerator by $2 - 4i$, the conjugate of $2 + 4i$.

$$\frac{6-4i}{2+4i} \times \frac{2-4i}{2-4i} = \frac{-4-32i}{20} = -\frac{1}{5} - \frac{8}{5}i$$

PRACTICE TEST 6

Using the general form of a complex number, $a + bi$, we find that $a = -\frac{1}{5}$ and $b = -\frac{8}{5}$. Substituting those values for a and b, we get:

$$a - 2b = -\frac{1}{5} - (2)\left(-\frac{8}{5}\right) = 3$$

15. **(D)** The cost per mango can be found by dividing the cost of the mangoes, 185(in cents), by x, the number of mangoes. Therefore, each mango costs $\frac{185}{x}$. Multiply this value by 7 to find the cost of 7 mangoes.

$$\text{The cost of 7 mangoes is } 7\left(\frac{185}{x}\right)$$

Similarly, the cost of a single guava is found by dividing the cost in cents, 225, by y, the number of guavas. The cost of a single guava is $\frac{225}{y}$. Multiply this value by 9 to find the cost of 9 guavas.

$$\text{The cost of 9 guavas is } 9\left(\frac{225}{y}\right)$$

Add the costs of 7 mangoes and 9 guavas by adding the expressions we have created.

$$7\left(\frac{185}{x}\right) + 9\left(\frac{225}{y}\right)$$

16. **54** The molding, which surrounds the floor, is equal to the rectangle's perimeter. We are missing the length but we know the area and width. The area of a rectangle can be found by using the formula Area = length × width.

Input the known information to solve for "l."

$$180 = l \times 12$$
$$15 = l$$

We now know the rectangular floor has the following dimensions:

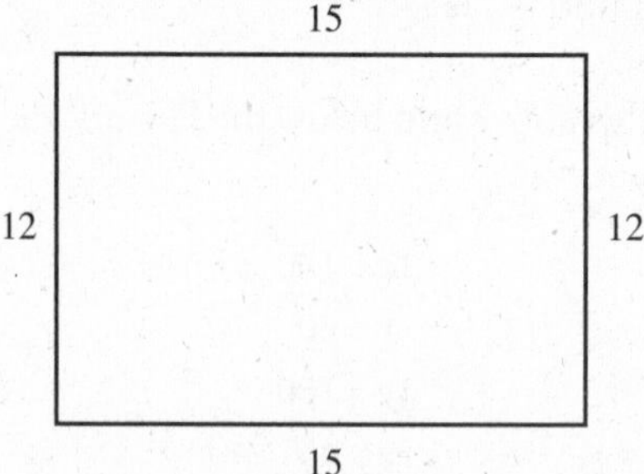

We can use the formula Perimeter = $(2 \times l) + (2 \times w)$ to find the number of feet of molding Oscar needs to surround the floor:

$$(2 \times 15) + (2 \times 12) = 54$$

Oscar needs 54 feet of molding to surround the floor of his study.

17. **6** Factor by grouping.

$$x^3 - 6x^2 + 2x - 12 = 0$$
$$(x^3 - 6x^2) + (2x - 12) = 0$$
$$x^2(x-6) + 2(x-6) = 0$$
$$(x^2+2)(x-6) = 0$$
$$x^2 + 2 = 0 \text{ or } x - 6 = 0$$
$$x = \pm i\sqrt{2} \text{ or } x = 6$$

Of the three solutions, only 6 is a real solution to the equation.

18. **4** In order for a system of equations to have infinitely many solutions, the two equations must be some multiple of one another. Note that 64 = 8 × 8, so 2 must be eight times the value of m and 8 must be eight times the value of n. We conclude that m must equal $\frac{1}{4}$ and n must equal 1. Therefore, $\frac{n}{m} = \frac{1}{\frac{1}{4}} = 4$.

19. **40** If three parallel lines intersect two transversals, they divide the transversals proportionally. The lakefront length that is 27 feet corresponds to a dock length of 36. The lakefront length that is 30 feet should have a docking length that is proportional to the 27:36 ratio. Set up a proportion to find the docking length of the wider dock length. You will find it useful to simplify $\frac{27}{36}$ to $\frac{3}{4}$.

$$\frac{3}{4} = \frac{30}{x}$$
$$3x = 120$$
$$x = 40$$

20. **243** Use $f(x) = 2x + 3$ and $f(2x + 3)$ together to find the value of x. Since $f(x) = 2x + 3$, then $f(2x + 3)$ must equal $2(2x + 3) + 3$. Set that expression equal to $5x$ and solve for x.

$$2(2x+3) + 3 = 5x$$
$$4x + 6 + 3 = 5x$$
$$9 = x$$

Substitute 9 for x in $3x^2$.

$$3(9^2) = 243$$

Section 4: Math Test (Calculator)

1. **(D)** If Andrea worked a four-hour shift and conducted 2 classes, the pay would be 40 + 2(8) = \$56. In other words, she earns her base pay of \$40 and \$8 for each group activity she leads. Therefore, a general expression that represents her pay package is $40 + 8n$, where n represents the number of extra activities performed.

2. **(C)** Gina has \$240 saved so that sum will be part of the answer. Each month, for m months, she will save \$125. Therefore, she will save an additional \$125m after m months. Adding the initial savings and the monthly accumulation of money, we arrive at $240 + 125m$ as the amount saved after m months.

3. **(B)** Find the total number of juice containers by multiplying 5 by 12.

$$5 \times 12 = 60$$

There were 3 main groups of juice containers, so divide 60 by 3 to find how many containers are in each group.

$$60 \div 3 = 20$$

Finally, divide 20 by 5 to find how many containers are in each of the smaller groups.

$$20 \div 5 = 4$$

4. **(A)** The survey size of 80 is sizeable enough to draw conclusions about the class in general. Since 15.6% of the surveyed students felt that additional crosswalks were necessary, that fraction of the entire class will probably feel the same way.

Find 15.6% of 320.

$$320\,(.156) = 49.92$$

Round the answer to 50 students that can be expected to favor additional crosswalks.

5. **(C)** The formula for the density of an object is presented as density $= \frac{\text{mass}}{\text{volume}}$. Input 4 grams per milliliter for the density and 30 grams for mass to find the volume.

$$4 = \frac{30}{V}$$

Multiply both sides of the equation by V.

$$V(4 = \frac{30}{V})V$$
$$4V = 30$$
$$V = 7.5$$

6. **(B)** Since Virginia worked fewer hours than Chad, let her hours be represented by x. Chad worked three more hours than did Virginia, so let his hours be represented by $x + 3$. Their total community service hours were 47, leading to the following equation:

$$x + (x + 3) = 47$$
$$2x + 3 = 47$$
$$2x = 44$$
$$x = 22$$
$$x + 3 = 25$$

Chad provided 25 hours of community service this week for his high school graduation requirement.

7. **(D)** The x-intercepts of the graph of $y = x^2 - 8x + 15$ are the values of x when y equals 0. Replace y with zero and factor $y = x^2 - 8x + 15$.

$$0 = x^2 - 8x + 15$$
$$0 = (x - 5)(x - 3)$$

Note that $y = 0$ when $x = 5$ or $x = 3$. Thus, $y = (x - 5)(x - 3)$ displays the x-intercepts of the parabola as the constants 5 and 3.

None of the other choices, (A), (B), or (C), show the x-intercepts as constants or coefficients.

8. **(C)** Multiply the two parentheses using the FOIL method.

$$(4 - 3i)(6 + 5i) =$$
$$24 + 20i - 18i - 15i^2 =$$
$$24 + 2i - 15i^2 =$$
$$24 + 2i + 15 = 39 + 2i$$

Using the form of a complex number, $a + bi$, 2 is b.

9. **(C)** A linear function can be expressed in the form of $y = mx + b$, where m is the slope of the line and b is the y-intercept. Given that $f(4) = -14$ and $f(-3) = 14$, we know that (4, –14) and (–3, 14) are points on this line. Find the equation of the line connecting (4, –14) and (–3, 14) by first finding the slope.

$$\frac{14-(-14)}{-3-4} = -4$$

The formula for the line is $y = -4x + b$. Find b by substituting either point for x and y.

$$-14 = -4(4) + b$$
$$2 = b$$

The formula for the line connecting (4, –14) and (–3, 14) is $y = -4x + 2$. Substitute 7 for x to find $f(7)$.

$$y = -(4)(7) + 2 = -26$$
$$f(7) = -26$$

10. **(C)** Note the sunrise times on 7/23 and 7/24.

Jul 23	5:57 AM	7:53 PM	13:56:54	-1:14
Jul 24	5:57 AM	7:53 PM	13:55:37	-1:17

The sun rose at the same recorded minute, 5:57, each of these two days. The statement that the sun rose later each day is erroneous. The other statements can be proven to be correct.

11. **(A)** Each day, the sun generally rose later and set earlier, causing a total reduction of the number of hours of daylight during the week of 7/21. The "Difference" category records how much shorter the recorded hours of time there were (in minutes and seconds) when the sun was above the opposite horizons. Both the later sunrise and earlier sunset contributed to this reduction.

12. **(A)** The line of best fit predicted 38 meteors viewed per minute, but the actual number viewed was 42. Therefore the line of best fit predicted 4 fewer meteors than actually were viewed.

13. **(B)** Use the proportion $\frac{\text{length}}{\text{diagonal}} = \frac{\text{length}}{\text{diagonal}}$ to calculate the apparent length of the truck on the television with a 44" diagonal.

$$\frac{11}{32} = \frac{x}{44}$$
$$(11)(44) = 32x$$
$$484 = 32x$$
$$15.13 = x$$

Rounded to the nearest inch, the truck would appear to be 15" long on the television with the 44" diagonal.

14. **(C)** Use the formula for the volume of a cylinder to calculate the radius of the cylinder.

$$\pi r^2 h = 327$$
$$\pi r^2(6) = 327$$
$$r^2 = 17.3$$
$$r = 4.2$$

The circumference of either of the cylinders' bases is also the length of the rectangular portion of the net.

$$C = 2\pi r$$
$$C = (2)(4.2)(\pi) = 26.4$$

Multiply the height of the rectangle by its width.

$$26.4 \times 6 = 158.4$$

Choice (C), 157, is the closest to this answer.

15. **(B)** Although the graphs appear to have the same absorption rate over the first 100 seconds, note the scales on the vertical axis. Enzyme Y begins at about 1% absorption and progresses to approximately 11% at the 100 second mark, a difference of 10%. Although it is not clear what the beginning absorption rate is of enzyme Y, it is less than 10%. By the 100th second, the absorption rate of enzyme Y had increased to approximately 41%, a difference of at least 31%. Thus the two rates of absorption had not been about the same at the 100 second mark as suggested by choice (B). The absorption rates of at least 31% and 10% are not the same.

16. **(C)** Systems of equations have no solution if they are the equations of parallel lines. Although these equations can be graphed, it is much simpler to note the scale factor between the two equations. If the coefficients of x and y are multiples of one another, but the constants are not, the system has no solution.

$$5x + 13y = 17$$
$$bx + 54.6y = 37$$

Divide the coefficients of y.

$$54.6 \div 13 = 4.2$$

The value of b is $4.2 \times 5 = 21$.

Double-check to ensure the constants are not of the same scale factor.

$$37 \div 17 \neq 4.2$$

17. **(B)** The minimum value of $g(x)$ occurs at (1, 0) on the graph. The value of x, then, that yields the minimum value of $g(x)$ is 1.

18. **(C)** The banners are sold in the same sequence of repeating colors:

Red Yellow Blue Green Orange Purple

There are 6 banners in each sequence, so divide 59 by 6 the same way you did in 4th grade.

$$59 \div 6 = 9 \text{ remainder } 5$$

The quotient is not important but the remainder is. The quotient suggests that we have completed 9 full sequences, and we are now 5 deep into the 10th sequence of colors. Count 5 banners into the series to arrive at orange as the 59th banner.

19. **(B)** Although a plug and check strategy is possible for this problem, using a system of equations is easier.

Let x = tacos sold
Let y = enchiladas sold

There were 54 items sold so the first equation is $x + y = 54$. Tacos cost \$2.00 and enchiladas cost \$4.50 and the revenue generated was \$198.00, giving us $2x + 4.5y = 198$.

Use either elimination or substitution to proceed.

$$x + y = 54 \text{ so } y = 54 - x.$$

Substitute $54 - x$ for y in the equation $2x + 4.5y = 198$.

$$2x + 4.5(54 - x) = 198$$
$$2x + 243 - 4.5x = 198$$
$$-2.5x = -45$$
$$x = 18$$

Substitute 18 into $y = 54 - x$ to find the number of enchiladas sold.

$$y = 54 - 18 = 36$$

20. **(D)** The graphing form of a circle is $y = (x - h)^2 + (y - k)^2 = r^2$, where (h, k) is the center of the circle and r is the radius. Convert the equation to graphing form by completing the square.

$$x^2 + y^2 + 6x - 8y = 12$$
$$x^2 + 6x + 9 + y^2 - 8y + 16 = 12 + 9 + 16$$
$$(x + 3)^2 + (y - 4)^2 = 37$$

The radius squared is 37, so find its square root to calculate the length of the radius.

$$r^2 = 37$$
$$r = \sqrt{37}$$

PRACTICE TEST 6

21. **(D)** Since the tangent of the acute angle is 0.8, we could also express that ratio as $\frac{4}{5}$.

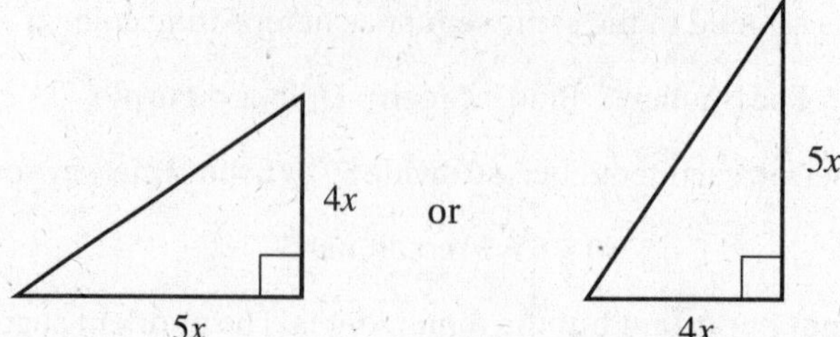

Regardless of which acute angle is used, the calculation of the area will be the same: Either the base is a multiple of 5 and the height is a multiple of 4, or the height is a multiple of 5 and the base is a multiple of 4. If the height, for example, is 28 (4×7), then the base would have to be 35 (5×7). Place 28 and 35 into the area formula for a triangle.

$$A = \frac{1}{2}bh$$

$$A = \frac{1}{2}(28)(35)$$

$$A = 490$$

None of the other answers are the product of heights and bases that are in the ratio of 4 to 5. An alternate way to solve this problem is to experiment solving for area with numbers where heights and bases are in the ratio of 4 to 5 or 5 to 4. Every answer will be a multiple of 10. Only choice (D) is a multiple of 10.

22. **(B)** If $x + 2$ is a factor of $C(x) = x^3 + 5x^2 + 5x - 2$, the remainder, after dividing, is 0.

$$x+2\overline{\smash{)}x^3+5x^2+5x-2}\quad \text{quotient: } x^2+3x-1$$

Since there is no remainder, we know that $x + 2$ is factor of $C(x) = x^3 + 5x^2 + 5x - 2$.

An alternate method to answering this question is to substitute -2 for x and assess the results.

$$(-2)^3 + 5(-2)^2 + 5(-2) - 2 = 0$$

The result is 0, which indicates -2 is a root of the function and $x + 2$ is a factor.

23. **(C)** Let x = the number of \$1 discounts to maximize revenue. $24 - x$ = the reduced price of the basketballs. Revenue equals number sold $\times$ price per item.

$1{,}000 + 100x$ = the number of basketballs sold after x \$1 discounts.

Multiply $(24 - x)$ by $(1{,}000 + 100x)$ to find the equation that predicts maximum revenue.

$$(24 - x)(1{,}000 + 100x) = -100x^2 + 1400x + 24{,}000$$

The number of \$1 discounts is found by using the axis of symmetry formula to find the x-coordinate of the vertex of the function.

$$-\frac{b}{2a} = -\frac{1400}{-200} = 7$$

PRACTICE TEST 6

The manufacturer must make seven, \$1discounts to maximize revenue. Therefore, the cost needed to maximize revenue is \$17.

24. **(B)** Let x = the population of type B peaches at the 30-day mark.

Type A peaches had reached a total of 5,200, which is 30% greater than the total for peach type B. Therefore, the number of type A peaches with respect to type B is $1.3x$. Set $1.3x$ equal to 5,200 to find how many of type B peaches exist at the 30-day mark.

$$1.3x = 5{,}200$$
$$x = 4{,}000$$

25. **(B)** The initial city expenditure was \$1,500,000 yet this amount decreased by 6.8% per year. To calculate the continuous decay of the budgeted amount provided by the city, subtract .068 from 1.0 to see what portion of the last year's budget will be provided this year.

$$1.0 - .068 = .932$$

The exponent t in this case will refer to time in years.

Only choice (B) appears to show moderate decay in the budget. The other answers are too small or too large; choice (D) would offer alternating negative and positive values.

26. **(D)** Although funding for the theater group started out at \$1.5 million, we only know the balance on 1/1/2000, which was \$975,000. The question asks what the balance will be on 1/1/04 so we can assess the financial contribution of the neighboring city. Use the model you derived correctly from question 25, but remember to start with \$975,000.

$$975{,}000(.932)^4 = 735{,}645$$

The city would have \$735,644 in its budget so subtract that figure from \$1.2 million to find the contribution needed from the nearby community.

$$1{,}200{,}000 - 735{,}645 = 464{,}355$$

The nearby community would need to contribute \$464,355 during its first year of the merger.

27. **(B)** A regular hexagon can be divided into six equilateral triangles. Divide $324\sqrt{3}$ by 6 to find the area of one of the equilateral triangles.

$$324\sqrt{3} \div 6 = 54\sqrt{3}$$

An equilateral triangle can be divided into two 30-60-90 triangles.

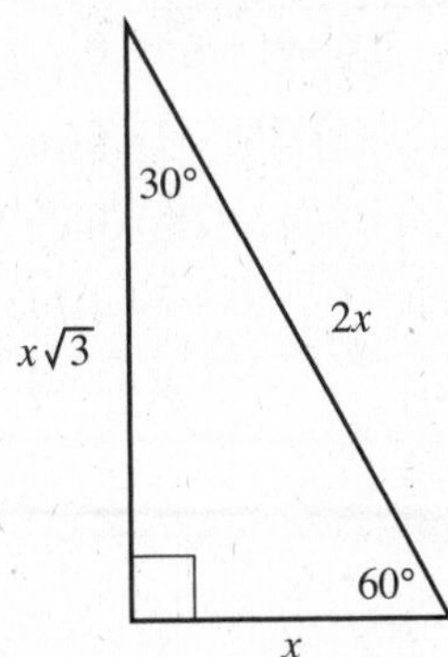

PRACTICE TEST 6

Multiply the base, x, by the height, $x\sqrt{3}$, and $\frac{1}{2}$ and set that product equal to $27\sqrt{3}$, which is one-half of $54\sqrt{3}$.

$$\left(\frac{1}{2}\right)(x)(x\sqrt{3}) = 27\sqrt{3}$$

$$\frac{1}{2}x^2 = 27$$

$$x^2 = 54$$

$$x = 3\sqrt{6}$$

Multiply $3\sqrt{6}$ by 2 to find one side of the hexagon.

$$3\sqrt{6} \times 2 = 6\sqrt{6}$$

The side length of the hexagon is also the side length of the square. Square $6\sqrt{6}$ to calculate the area of the square.

$$(6\sqrt{6})^2 = 216$$

28. **(A)** Combine like terms and solve for m and n.

$$3x + m = 5x - 6 \text{ becomes } m = 2x - 6$$

$$3y + n = 5y - 6 \text{ becomes } n = 2y - 6$$

Substitute $\left(n + \frac{1}{2}\right)$ for m as provided in the problem.

$$n + \frac{1}{2} = 2x - 6, \text{ so } n = 2x - \frac{13}{2}$$

$$n = 2y - 6 \text{ and } n = 2x - \frac{13}{2}, \text{ so } 2y - 6 = 2x - \frac{13}{2}$$

Solve for x because all of the answer choices express x as a function of y.

$$2y - 6 = 2x - \frac{13}{2}$$

$$2y + \frac{1}{2} = 2x$$

$$y + \frac{1}{4} = x$$

29. **(D)** Use the distance formula to find the missing coordinates of x.

$$\sqrt{(x_1 - x_2)^2 + (y_1 - y_2)^2}$$

$$\sqrt{(x_1 - 7)^2 + (4 - 5)^2} = 8$$

$$(x_1 - 7)^2 + 1 = 64$$

$$(x_1 - 7)^2 = 63$$

$$x - 7 = \pm\sqrt{63}$$

$$x = 7 \pm 3\sqrt{7}$$

PRACTICE TEST 6

30. **(A)** The $75 fee for the lesson is a fixed cost. Subtract that amount from the $110.00, the total charged for the lesson and the time on the boat.

$$\$110 - \$75 = \$35$$

Create a proportion based solely on the time paid for the boat. The question indicates the fee varies directly with the square root of the time spent on the boat.

$$\frac{\sqrt{\text{time}}}{\text{fee}} = \frac{\sqrt{\text{time}}}{\text{fee}}$$

$$\frac{\sqrt{25}}{35} = \frac{\sqrt{36}}{x} = \frac{5}{35} = \frac{6}{x}$$

Cross-multiply and solve for x.

$$5x = 210$$
$$x = 42$$

Add $42.00, the fee for the time spent on the boat, to $75.00, the fixed cost of the lesson.

$$\$75 + \$42 = \$117$$

Choices (B), (C), and (D) are incorrect due to erroneous calculation.

31. **Answers may vary. $600 \leq x \leq 900$**
There are a minimum of 100 seats in a section and a maximum of 150. Thus for the six sections in the auditorium we find the following minimum and maximum number of seats.

$$6 \times 100 = 600$$
$$6 \times 150 = 900$$

Thus, the number of students in the class is modeled by $600 \leq x \leq 900$.

32. **67.6** A woman age 35 has a Target HR Zone of 93 to 157 beats per minute. Find the mean of that range by adding 93 + 157 and dividing by 2.

$$93 + 157 = 250$$
$$250 \div 2 = 125$$

Find the percent that 125 is of 185 by dividing 125 by 185.

$$125 \div 185 = .6757$$

Rounded to the nearest tenth of a percent, .6757 is 67.6%.

A heart rate of 125 is 67.6% of the maximum heart rate.

33. **18** The volume of a cylinder is found by using the formula Volume = $\pi r^2 h$, where r is the radius and h is the height. Use simple numbers to verify the ratio.

Let $r = 1$ and $h = 1$ for the measures of the smaller cylinder.

$$\text{Volume} = \pi(1)^2(1) = \pi$$

Doubling the measure of the height gives $h = 2$. Tripling the measure of the radius gives $r = 3$.

$$\text{Volume} = \pi(3)^2(2) = 18\pi$$

The larger cylinder has a volume 18 times greater than the smaller.

34. **36**

$$g(x) = 2b + x^3$$

The point (–4, 8) lies on the graph of the function $g(x) = 2b + x^3$. Therefore, we can say $g(-4) = 8$. Solve for b by substituting –4 for x and 8 for $g(x)$.

$$8 = 2b + (-4)^3$$
$$8 = 2b - 64$$
$$72 = 2b$$
$$36 = b$$

35. **0**

$$f(x) = \frac{1}{(x-3)^2 + 6(x-3) + 9}$$

Division by 0 is undefined so set the denominator of the function f equal to 0.

$$(x-3)^2 + 6(x-3) + 9 = 0$$
$$x^2 - 6x + 9 + 6x - 18 + 9 = 0$$
$$x^2 = 0$$
$$x = 0$$

When $x = 0$, the function f is undefined.

36. **50** The supermarket chain manager wants to earn an 80% customer service rating from its first 20 customer service surveys. Multiply 20 by 80 to get 1,600, the total number of additional percentage points to be amassed. We found that the first 10 reviews yielded an average score of 65% or 10 × 65 = 650 percentage points. Subtracting 650 from 1,600 we get 950, the total number of percentage points to be amassed to earn the overall 80% rating. The question asks what could be the lowest the 17th survey could earn and still achieve the goal of 80% customer satisfaction from the first 20 surveys. Suppose all of the surveys from 11 through 16 and 18 through 20 gave the chain a score of 100%. That would mean those 9 customers added 900 points to the total. Given that we need 950 points from the final 10 customers, the 17th survey could score the chain as low as 50% and the chain would still receive an 80% average from the first 20 surveys.

37. **66** Although the suggested consumption of potassium for men is 4,700 milligrams, Jake's daily running indicates he needs an additional 10% above the norm. Multiply 4,700 by 1.1 to find the potassium requirement for Jake because of his running.

$$4{,}700 \times 1.1 = 5{,}170$$

Jake consumes 3,200 milligrams currently so he needs an additional 1,970 milligrams. By adding an extra potato and a cup of lima beans, he will add 1,081 + 955 = 2,036 milligrams of potassium. Since he needs 1,970 milligrams, the addition of these new foods will provide 66 milligrams more than is necessary.

38. **1,155** Find Joan's daily consumption of potassium by dividing 22,400 by 7.

$$22{,}400 \div 7 = 3{,}200$$

If Joan adds a cup of spinach (839 mg) and a glass of orange juice (496 mg), she will be consuming a total of 4,535 milligrams of potassium per day. Subtracting 4,535 from 4,700 (the recommended amount), we arrive at a daily deficiency of 165 milligrams per day. Multiplying 165 by 7, we find that Joan needs an additional 1,155 milligrams of potassium in her diet each week.

Section 5: Essay (Optional)

SUGGESTED ESSAY TEST 6

Following is an essay written in response to the prompt. It is unlikely that you would be able to write such a full response in the time allowed, so don't worry if your essay is significantly shorter. Use the suggested essay to see how the task might be approached. For practice, you may wish to rewrite your own essay incorporating some of the points discussed in it.

Evidently this passage is a continuation of a discussion in Walter Stace's book The Concept of Morals about whether what is moral is relative—that is, dependent on culture—or absolute—that is, independent of culture and the same for all people at all times. In this passage Walter Stace assumes the premise of the "absolutist" that morality is independent of culture—that "there is but one eternally true and valid moral code"—and then examines the logical consequences and implications if the premise is accepted. Stace himself does not in this passage take a position on whether moral absolutism is correct. His central thesis can be stated thus: If morality is absolute, logic dictates that it applies to all people in all cultures during all times.

Let us examine how Stace develops his argument paragraph by paragraph. In paragraph one he makes the central claim just mentioned, that morality is universal in its application. He uses the extreme example of cannibalism to drive home his point: "The fact that he [the African] sees nothing wrong in his cannibal practices does not make them for him morally right." Cannibalism is an appropriate example to use because all of Stace's readers would, presumably, agree that it is, beyond doubt, morally wrong. Stace uses this example to refute the objection that a moral relativist might make—that cannibalism is moral in a particular culture if it is accepted in that culture—to dramatically demonstrate the falseness of such a belief. Stace's use of language here supports his argument well. His language is colorful, somewhat humorous, and a bit provocative, which helps to hold the reader's interest: "an Englishman, a Chinaman, or a Hottentot," for example, and "ignorant savage." Also effective is the repetition of the word "one" in the final sentence, which emphasizes the idea that there is only one morality: "There is but one law, one standard, one morality for all men."

In paragraph two Stace emphasizes that just as absolute morality is not limited by culture, it is not limited by time. He uses the example of slavery to vividly illustrate this: "If slavery is morally wicked today, it was morally wicked among the ancient Athenians, notwithstanding that their greatest men accepted it as a necessary condition of human society." Like the example of cannibalism used in paragraph one, this is a persuasive example because everyone agrees, presumably, that slavery is, without a doubt, morally wrong. It is also effective because, as Stace points out, the Athenians were "noble" in their other ideas but nevertheless wrong about slavery. This illustrates how even such a people as the Athenians could be wrong about what is moral.

In paragraph three Stace stresses the point that, logically, what any person or any culture thinks is moral has no relevance to what actually is moral. He expresses this clearly and concisely: "But the fact that the Greeks or the inhabitants of New Guinea think something right does not make it right, even for them . . . [Things] are in themselves either right or wrong." He then makes a very convincing comparison between finding the truth about factual, scientific matters and about moral matters to show there is no difference between them in how truth is arrived at. He says that just as people have been wrong about moral matters so also have they been wrong about scientific matters: "We believe the earth to be a globe. Our ancestors may have thought it flat. This does not show that it was flat, and is now a globe."

Stace's language in paragraph three, as in paragraph two, is straightforward, consisting of everyday words and fairly simple sentence structure. This style is suitable because his argument is essentially a series of logical statements. Complex sentence structure and abstract or figurative language would distract the reader from following the carefully constructed sequence of logical statements.

In paragraph four Stace focuses on explaining that belief in absolute morality does not entail belief that any particular morality is the true morality. He uses two examples to clearly illustrate this. First, he gives the example of someone who believes that morality will be far more advanced in five hundred years. Then he gives the example of someone who believes that Christian morality will be replaced by a higher level of moral ideas. In neither case, Stace says, does logic demand that the moral absolutist must disagree based on his belief. In both these cases Stace uses extreme language to emphasize that it does not matter how good or bad any one person or culture judges a particular morality to be. In the first example he uses the word "barbarous" and in the second example he uses the phrase "vastly nobler."

In summary, Walter Stace constructs a convincing argument using careful reasoning and vivid examples to support his main contention that, logically, someone who believes that morality is absolute must also believe that this absolute morality is "but one eternally true and valid moral code."

Refer to the SAT Essay Rubric on page 23 to analyze and score your essay response. For further guidance on this essay and additional practice and evaluation by teacher and author Philip Geer, contact *info@mentaurs.com*.

Acknowledgments

Page 47: from *Indian Country* by Peter Matthiessen, copyright © 1979, 1980, 1981, 1984 by Peter Matthiessen. Used by permission of Viking Penguin, a division of Penguin Group (USA) Inc.

Page 50: from *Flappers and Philosophers* by F. Scott Fitzgerald, 1920.

Page 53: from "Hiroshima: A Soldier's View" by Paul Fussell. Reprinted by permission of *The New Republic*, © 1981.

Page 57: from "The Professionalization of Poetry" in *Heavy Lifting* by David Alpaugh. Copyright © 2007 Alehouse Press. Reprinted by permission of the author.

Page 61: from "Coasts in Crisis, Coastal Change," Jeffress Williams, Kurt Dodd, Kathleen Krafft Gohn, in U.S. Geological Survey Circular 1075, 1990.

Page 64: from "Highlights of Women's Earnings in 2011," U.S. Department of Labor, U.S. Bureau of Labor Statistics, October 2012, Report 1038.

Page 68: from "United States Arctic Science Policy," Alaska Council of Science and Technology, January 1983.

Page 70: from *Museum of Antiquity: A Description of Ancient Life* by L.W. Yaggy M.S. and T.L. Haines A.M., published by J.B. Furman & Co., Western Publishing House, Chicago, IL, 1884.

Page 73: from *History of Woman Suffrage, Volume 1*, by Susan B. Anthony, 1887.

Page 92: from *The Plug-in Drug* by Marie Winn, Penguin Books, 2002, Copyright Marie Winn 2002, Penguin Putnam Inc., 375 Hudson Street, New York, New York.

Page 131: from *Balzac and the Little Chinese Seamstress* by Dai Sijie. Published by Alfred A. Knopf, 2001. English translation Copyright © by Ina Rilke 2001.

Page 134 from *Reflections of a Neoconservative* by Irving Kristol. Copyright © 1983 Irving Kristol. Reprinted by permission of Basic Books, a member of the Perseus Books Group.

Page 137: from "The Clash of Civilizations?" by Samuel P. Huntington. Reprinted by permission of *Foreign Affairs*, Summer 1993. Copyright 1993 by the Council on Foreign Relations, Inc. *www.foreignaffairs.com.*

Page 137: from "Do Civilizations Hold?" by Albert L. Weeks in *The Clash of Civilizations: The Debate* published by the Council on Foreign Relations, 2010. Copyright © 1993 by Albert L. Weeks. Reprinted by permission of the author.

Page 141: from Friend, Milton, 2014, "Why bother about wildlife disease?": U.S. Geological Survey Circular 1401, 76.

Page 145: from Alexis de Tocqueville, *Democracy in America*, originally published in 1835, was translated from French into English by Henry Reeve.

Page 148: from Eagles-Smith, C.A., Willacker, J.J., and Flanagan Pritz, C.M., 2014, "Mercury in fishes from 21 national parks in the Western United States—Inter and intra-park variation in concentrations and ecological risk": U.S. Geological Survey Open-File Report 2014–1051, 54 *p. http://dx.doi.org/10.3133/ofr20141051.*

Page 151: from "You're a What? Ornithologist," Bureau of Labor Statistics, Occupational Outlook Quarterly, Summer 2013.

Page 153: from the Federal Research Division, Library of Congress, *Country Studies: India*, 1996.

Page 155: from *History of Human Society* by Frank W. Blackmar, Charles Scribner's Sons, 1926.

Page 174: from *The Observer:* "Has man sold his soul to the computer?" (circa 1970's, but cannot locate date) by John Davy (Science Correspondent) The Guardian, 536 Broadway, 6th floor, New York, New York 10012.

Page 215: from *The Great Boer War* by Arthur Conan Doyle, 1900.

Page 218: from *Fermat's Enigma* by Simon Singh. Published by Doubleday, a division of Bantam Doubleday Dell Publishing Group, Inc., 1998. Copyright © 1997 by Simon Singh.

Page 220: from "Sustainability and Renewable Resources" by Steven Hayward, Ph.D., Elizabeth Fowler, and Laura Steadman. Copyright © 2000 by the Mackinac Center for Public Policy, Midland, Michigan.

Page 220: from OECD/Nuclear Energy Agency (2000), "Nuclear Energy in a Sustainable Development Perspective," *www.oecd-nea.org/sd.*

Page 225: from "What Poets Can Learn from Songwriters" by David Alpaugh in the October 2011 issue of *Scene4 Magazine.* Copyright © 2011 by David Alpaugh, © 2011 *Scene4 Magazine.* Reprinted by permission of the author.

Page 228: from "Cassini Catches Titan Naked in the Solar Wind," NASA News and Features, January 28, 2015, Preston Dyches *http://www.nasa.gov/jpl/cassini-catches-titan-naked-in-the-solar-wind/#.VNHkMiwpqQ8.*

Page 235: from "You're a What? Acupuncturist," Bureau of Labor Statistics, Occupational Outlook Quarterly, Summer 2002.

Page 237: from *Stained Glass of the Middle Ages in England and France*, Saint Lawrence, B., 1913.

Page 239: from "Adult and Youth Literacy, National, Regional and Global Trends, 1985–2015," UNESCO, 2013.

Page 257: from *Escape from Freedom* by Erich Fromm, Henry Holt, 1941.

Page 295: from *No-No Boy* by John Okada. Published by the University of Washington Press, copyright © 2001. Reprinted by permission of the University of Washington Press.

Page 298: from *Disturbing the Universe* by Freeman Dyson. Published by Basic Books, 1981. Copyright © 1979 by Freeman J. Dyson. Reprinted by permission of Basic Books, a member of the Perseus Books Group.

Page 301: from "Medical Lessons from History," from *The Medusa and the Snail* by Lewis Thomas, copyright © 1974, 1975, 1976, 1977, 1978, 1979 by Lewis Thomas. Used by permission of Viking Penguin, a division of Penguin Group (USA) Inc.

Page 304: from "NASA Finds Friction from Tides Could Help Distant Earths Survive, and Thrive" Elizabeth Zubritsky, NASA's Goddard Space Flight Center *http://www.nasa.gov/content/goddard/friction-from-tides-could-help-distant-earths-survive-and-thrive/#.VNL3bywpqQ8.*

Page 308: from John L. O'Sullivan, "The Great Nation of Futurity." It was originally published in 1839.

Page 311: from "Toxoplasmosis" by Hill, D.E., and Dubey, J.P., 2014, U.S. Geological Survey Circular 1389 *http://dx.doi.org/10.3133/cir1389.*

Page 315: from "Beyond Supply and Demand: Assessing the Ph.D. Job Market," Bureau of Labor Statistics, Occupational Outlook Quarterly, Winter 2002–2003.

Page 318: from *Myths & Legends of Babylonia & Assyria* by Lewis Spence, published by George G. Harrap & Company, Ltd., London, 1916.

Page 320: from "On the Art of Fiction" by Willa Cather, Knopf, The Borzoi, 1920.

Page 338: from the introduction to *Supernature* by Lyall Watson, Coronet Books, 1974.

Page 375: from *The Americanism of Washington* by Henry Van Dyke, 1906.

Page 377: from Suparna Choudhury, "Culturing the adolescent brain: what can neuroscience learn from anthropology?" *Social Cognitive and Affective Neuroscience*, 2010, 5(2–3), 159–167, by permission of Oxford University Press.

Page 380: from *The Art of Teaching* by Gilbert Highet, copyright 1950, copyright renewed 1977 by Gilbert Highet. Used by permission of Alfred A. Knopf, a division of Random House, Inc.

Page 383: from Friend, Milton, 2014, "Why bother about wildlife disease?": U.S. Geological Survey Circular 1401, 76 p., *http://dx.doi.org/10.3133/cir1401.*

Page 387: from *The Autobiography of Charles Darwin* by Charles Darwin, 1887.

Page 390: from "Healthcare: Millions of Jobs," Bureau of Labor Statistics, Occupational Outlook Quarterly, Spring 2014.

Page 393: from *The Indian To-day: The Past and Future of the First American* by Charles A. Eastman (Ohiyesa), published by Doubleday, Page & Company, 1915.

Page 396: from *The History of Cuba,* Volume I, by Willis Fletcher Johnson, 1920.

Page 398: from Hiwasaki, L., Luna, E., Syamsidik, Shaw, R. "Local & indigenous knowledge for community resilience: Hydro-meteorological disaster risk reduction and climate change adaptation in coastal and small island communities." Jakarta, UNESCO, 2014.

Page 417: from *The Underachieving School* by John Holt, Pitman Books Ltd., 1968.

Page 455: from "Hotspots: Mantle Thermal Plumes" in *This Dynamic Earth: The Story of Plate Tectonics* by Jacquelyne Kious and Robert I. Tilling, U.S. Geological Survey, 1996.

Page 455: from "Scientists Locate Deep Origins of Hawaiian Hotspot," press release 09–232, December 3, 2009, National Science Foundation.

Page 459: from *The Souls of Black Folk* by W.E.B. Du Bois, 1903.

Page 461: from *Lord Jim* by Joseph Conrad, 1917.

Page 464: from *The Indian Today: The Past and Future of the First American* by Charles A. Eastman (Ohiyesa), published by Doubleday, Page & Company, 1915.

Page 467: from *Ex Libris: Confessions of a Common Reader* by Anne Fadiman. Copyright © 1998 by Anne Fadiman. Reprinted by permission of Farrar, Straus and Giroux, LLC.

Page 472: from Centers for Disease Control and Prevention, "Malaria Surveillance—United States, 2010," MMWR 2012; 61, pp. 4–6.

Page 475: from "Wanted: Trained teachers to ensure every child's right to primary education 2014," UNESCO, 2014, Policy Paper 15, factsheet 30.

Page 478: from President Franklin Delano Roosevelt's Message to Congress on the State of the Union, January 11, 1944.

Page 481: from *An Artist's Letters from Japan* by John La Farge, published by The Century Company, New York, 1897.

Page 500: from *The Concept of Morals* by Walter T. Stace, Macmillan Publishers, 1962.